The Making of

During the twentieth century Japan was transformed from a poor, primarily rural country into one of the world's largest industrial powers and most highly urbanised countries. While Japanese governments and planners borrowed carefully from the planning ideas and methods of many other countries, however, Japanese urban planning, urban governance and cities developed very differently from those of other developed countries.

Japan's distinctive patterns of urbanisation are partly a product of the highly developed urban system, urban traditions and material culture of the pre-modern period, which remained influential until well after the Pacific War. A second key influence has been the dominance of central government in urban affairs, and its consistent prioritisation of economic growth over the public welfare or urban quality of life. This bias is seen both in the preference for large-scale infrastructure projects over local parks or roads, and in the reluctance to regulate private urban land development activity. André Sorensen examines Japan's urban trajectory from the mid-nineteenth century to the present, paying particular attention to the weak development of Japanese civil society, local governments, and land development and planning regulations. As Japan enters the twenty-first century, it is hard not to conclude that city planning has contributed greatly to the dilemma of "rich Japan, poor Japanese" that is now at the heart of the country's current social, economic and demographic problems.

This is the first book to comprehensively examine the phenomenon of Japanese urbanisation and planning, revealing both the many real successes of Japanese urban management, and many of its resounding failures. Japan's distinctiveness makes it an important case study of urbanisation and its management, and helps to put into perspective the major urban and regional planning issues faced by the other developed countries, as well as sounding a timely warning to the rapidly urbanising countries of Asia. This book includes up-to-date, original material not otherwise available in English.

André Sorensen is Lecturer in the Department of Urban Engineering at the University of Tokyo, teaching Comparative Urban Planning studies and Land Use Planning. Since completing his PhD at the London School of Economics on land development and urban sprawl in the Tokyo metropolitan area in 1998, he has been living and working in Japan, trying to understand why Japanese cities and Japanese urban planning have developed in the way they have.

Nissan Institute/Routledge Japanese Studies Series

For Ito Peng,
Lauren Hikari,
and Raphael Makoto

The Making of Urban Japan

Cities and planning from Edo to the twenty-first century

André Sorensen

London and New York

First published 2002
by Routledge
2 Park Square, Milton Park, Abingdon, Oxon, OX14 4RN

Simultaneously published in the USA and Canada
by Routledge
270 Madison Ave, New York NY 10016

Routledge is an imprint of the Taylor & Francis Group

Transferred to Digital Printing 2006

Typeset in Baskerville by M Rules

British Library Cataloguing in Publication Data
A catalogue record for this book is available from the British Library

Library of Congress Cataloging in Publication Data
Sorensen, André, 1960–
    The making of urban Japan: cities and planning from Edo to the twenty-first
century/André Sorensen.
        p.   cm. – (The Nissan Institute/Routledge Japanese studies series)
Includes bibliographical references and index.
    1. City planning – Japan – History – 20th century. 2. Urbanization –
Japan – History – 20th century. 3. Cities and towns – Japan – History – 20th
century. I. Title. II. Series.

HT169.J3 S67 2002
307.1'216'09520904–dc21   2001058874

ISBN 0–415–22651–1 (hbk)
ISBN 0–415–35422–6 (pbk)

Printed and bound by CPI Antony Rowe, Eastbourne

Contents

Series editor's preface

The terrorist attacks against North American cities on 11 September 2001 have been followed by war in Afghanistan. A remarkable international coalition of governments, centred on the United States, is working by a variety of means to combat terrorism, and at this time of writing the coalition is holding together. Public opinion in several countries participating in the coalition is, however, more ambivalent.

The danger of creating more terrorists by combating terrorism is serious. But the effort to press on with the anti-terrorist campaign – by bombing raids on cities if necessary – is justified in terms of the "defence of the civilised world" against the dark forces of fundamentalism and terror. The notion of "civilisation" has come back into our vocabulary in a big way since 11 September. But it transcends the narrow definitions of that term used by writers such as Toynbee and Huntington; it is seen as embracing, potentially at least, the greater part of mankind. In practice, however, "civilisation" does not fit easily with those hundreds of millions of people who cannot escape from dire poverty, intolerance and exploitation. Unless these problems are tackled with determination and intelligence, it should surprise nobody that terror will be used to horrifying effect against the world deemed "civilised".

In all significant senses Japan today is part of our "civilised world". The average standard of living of the Japanese people is high. The GNP of Japan is second only to that of the United States, and is larger than the combined GNP of all the other countries of Asia. Even the economy of China, though attracting much attention for the rapidity of its growth, is many times smaller than that of Japan. The national interests of Japan, taking a hard-nosed view, lie with the interests of the advanced countries and their broad set of economic, political, social and moral values. Japan in most ways is an open democratic society. Since the early 1990s she has been suffering from severe problems of economic and political mismanagement. In the broadest of terms the problem is one of a painful transition from one form of political economy to another. The process of transition is far from over and mismanagement has cost the economy dear. Japan is also faced by deeper structural problems, including that of a rapidly ageing population. Nevertheless, the key point is that this is a gigantic economy having enormous international weight.

The Japanese, being a proud people and heirs to an ancient civilisation, have long been concerned to map out their own path in the world, and this creates a certain tension with the trends of globalisation so apparent in the world today. Nevertheless, Japan is slowly forging her own set of compromises whereby assimilation to essential global norms of behaviour is tempered by the maintenance of structures and practices based on its own cultural experiences. The next stage, however, in which Japanese expertise and commitment are desperately needed, is in the long and painful task of mitigating and eventually eliminating, not only the common terrorist enemy, but the deepest causes of terrorism, namely global inequality, endemic poverty and squalor, exploitation and rejection.

The Nissan/Routledge Japanese Studies Series was begun in 1986 and has now passed well beyond its fiftieth volume. It seeks to foster an informed and balanced, but not uncritical, understanding of Japan. One aim of the series is to show the depth and variety of Japanese institutions, practices and ideas. Another is, by using comparisons, to see what lessons, positive or negative, can be drawn for other countries. The tendency in commentary on Japan to resort to out-dated, ill-informed or sensational stereotypes still remains, and needs to be combated.

In this book, André Sorensen shows, with great erudition and elegance, the patterns of development of Japanese cities since the castle towns of the Tokugawa period. Many people who have visited the major cities of Japan will have been struck by their vast size and seemingly endless urban sprawl. Anyone concerned to know why the built environment in Japan (apart from the central city areas and nearby suburbs) is so often so numbingly depressing will find convincing explanations here. Sorensen rightly adopts a critical approach to Japanese urban planning (or the lack of it), while carefully probing the historical and institutional reasons for the lack of control over urban and suburban sprawl. He provides an expert guide to Japanese planning processes, and explicates the context of strong land ownership rights and weak land development control regulations. He shows that planning tends to be over-centralised and lacking in control over commercial opportunism in the construction industry.

He ends on a slightly more optimistic note, showing that there has been a significant growth in civil society over the past three decades or so, with some beneficial effect on planning outcomes. But he correctly sees the combination of competitive central bureaucratic management and corrupt interaction between politicians and construction companies as still posing nearly insuperable obstacles to a more enlightened approach to urban development. We need to remember, of course, that most Japanese cities have to accommodate enormous numbers of people on rather small areas of land. But what has been called the "Construction State" is alive and kicking, and has contributed significantly to the economic difficulties of the past ten years.

J. A. A. Stockwin

Acknowledgements

Any substantial research project is bound to result in a wide variety of debts, but those are all the more profound when one is writing about a country and culture not one's own. I have been extremely fortunate to have enjoyed the support and friendship of two mentors who have guided my study of Japanese urbanisation and planning. The first is Professor Michael Hebbert, who first inspired me to study Japan when I was considering a Planning Doctorate at the London School of Economics in 1993. His keen observation and exemplary writings on Japanese planning have continued to provide the compass against which I judge my own efforts.

Far more important to the completion of this volume have been the advice, criticism and support of Professor Okata Junichiro of the Department of Urban Engineering of the University of Tokyo. He has been closely involved in the project since its conception four years ago, and has generously shared his ideas, expertise, research materials and enthusiasms, not least during many enjoyable hours of discussion over excellent Japanese food and drink at our friend Miyamoto's restaurant near the university. From early drafts, and through numerous changes in chapter outline and conceptual approach, Professor Okata has read and commented on virtually every page of the work, and his influences on the final product are too numerous to enumerate. He was also instrumental as the sponsor of my successful application for a Post Doctoral Fellowship from the Japan Society for the Promotion of Science, which provided two years of valuable research funding from 1998 to 2000, and by supporting my application for a two-year contract position as Lecturer in Land Use Planning at the University of Tokyo from 2000 to 2002 when that chance arose. It is no exaggeration, therefore, to say that without Professor Okata's unflagging support, this book would not exist today.

A special thanks is also due to the other members of our research unit, Associate Professor Koizumi Hideki, who was second only to Professor Okata in his cheerful response to requests for obscure documents, second opinions, and references, and Research Assistant Manabe Rikutaro for assistance with computer glitches and incomprehensible administrative obligations. I have also benefited from the help of many of the graduate students in our unit, of whom Akita Noriko, Fujii Sayaka, Murayama Akito, Yasutani Satoru, and Tanaka Masaru deserve special mention. Two years of teaching an Introduction to Japanese Urbanisation and Planning course to graduate students of the Urban Engineering Department have greatly influenced the book, and I would like to thank all my students for their questions and comments, which greatly helped me to clarify my own understanding of the issues addressed here.

Of those who generously consented to read the manuscript, by far the most influential was Professor Ishida Yorifusa, Japan's pre-eminent planning historian, who was kind enough to closely read the entire manuscript, and whose hundreds of detailed comments, corrections and queries have doubtless saved me from many embarrassing errors of fact and interpretation. Deep gratitude is also due to the other readers of the complete draft manuscript, Bruno Peeters, Paul Waley, Jeff Hanes, Watanabe Shun-ichi, and Uta Hohn for their comments, suggestions and encouragement. Many others read one or more draft chapters, including Philippe Baylaucq, Robert Freestone, Carolin Funck, Peter Marcotullio, Brian McVeigh, and Andy Thornley, to all of whom, thank you. A special mention is due my parents, Wilfred and Nathalie Sorensen, who have ever been generous in their encouragement, who read much of the text in various stages of completion, and who finally managed to teach me some of the subtleties of English grammar that had hitherto escaped me. I alone bear responsibility for any errors or misunderstandings that remain.

Many have assisted me in tracking down the illustrations used here, and I have been lucky in the many cheerful and positive replies to my requests to make use of copyright material. I am grateful to the Osaka City Foundation for Urban Technology for permission to reproduce Yamaguchi Hanroku's 1898 expansion plan for Osaka as my Figure 2.5. I would like to thank the librarians at the Hokkaido University Attached Library for permission to use the early map of Sapporo in Figure 2.6, which they hold in their collection, and which was originally published by the Sapporo Education Committee in their Sapporo Historical Maps collection. Ikeda Takayuki kindly permitted me to use a figure from his 1980 PhD thesis for Figure 4.2 of Tokyo Building Line Plans. The Japan General Housing Centre allowed the reproduction of the plans of the Dojunkai housing project of Figure 4.6, and the Tamagawadai portion of Japan's first Garden City in Figure 4.8. Professor Kodama Toru of Osaka City University helped me to locate the plan of the Senriyama housing estate in Figure 4.9, and Mr Hotta Akio, Director of the Osaka City Historical Archives which holds the plan kindly allowed me to copy and photograph it. David Tucker included the plan of Daido, of Figure 4.10 in his PhD thesis, and helpfully instructed me to find the original copy he used in the January 1940 edition of the journal *Modern Architecture* (Gendai Kenchiku). The editors of *Ekistics* were pleased to grant permission to reproduce Doi's 1968 map of the Tokaido megalopolis as Figure 5.8, and the Osaka Prefectural Government Bureau of Public Enterprise, Residential Land office kindly permitted the use of their map of Senri New Town for Figure 5.10. Katsumata Wataru of the Ministry of Construction Building Research Institute allowed me to use his own map of mini-kaihatsu development for Figure 7.4, and Associate Professor Takamizawa Minoru of Yokohama National University loaned me the map of high-risk wooden housing areas in Tokyo from which Figure 9.2 is adapted. I am also grateful to Taylor & Francis Publishers for permission to reproduce in Chapter 3 substantial portions of a paper originally published in the journal *Planning Perspectives* as "Urban Planning and Civil Society in Japan: The role of the 'Taisho Democracy' period (1905–1931) Home Ministry in Japanese urban planning development". Information on *Planning Perspectives* is available at http://www.tandf.co.uk. I am similarly grateful to the editors of the Town Planning Review and Liverpool University Press for permission to reproduce parts of my paper "Building Suburbs in Japan: Continuous unplanned change on the urban fringe" which forms part of Chapter 9.

Last and most importantly, deep gratitude is due to my wife Ito Peng, and our children Lauren Hikari and Raphael Makoto for providing the essential meaning of my life and work during these fascinating and tumultuous years in Japan. While the challenges of balancing two busy academic careers and bringing up two lively children far from home and family have often been stressful, the experience of living and working in Japan during the last seven years has been made immeasurably richer and more rewarding by being able to live it together. We all owe a great debt to all our Japanese friends, neighbours and colleagues who have helped us in ways, large and small, during our stay here.

Figures

Tables

Introduction

During the course of the twentieth century Japan transformed itself from a largely rural country with approximately 15 per cent of its population living in cities, to one of the most urbanised large countries in the world with close to 80 per cent urban population. Superlatives are routinely employed in descriptions of Japanese economic growth and urban development. Of the large developed countries, urbanisation was fastest, and its resulting urban areas biggest. The Tokyo area alone holds over a quarter of the national population, and is now one of the largest urban regions in the world with a population approaching 40 million. Perhaps the most extraordinary manifestation of Japanese urbanisation is the enormous urban industrial belt along the Pacific coastline of the main island of Honshu. Stretching from Tokyo in the east to northern Kyushu in the west, the Tokaido megalopolis, as it is sometimes referred to, houses the overwhelming majority of the Japanese population and productive capacity. Here live some two-thirds of the population, on only 23 per cent of the country's land. Here also, where some 85 per cent of the GDP is produced, are concentrated the bulk of the country's fixed assets, the main research and development labs, international communications facilities and global financial centres.

The world's best and most heavily travelled rail system knits the megalopolis together, allowing fast, safe travel between almost any two points within the area. Even with this efficient rail system, since the late 1960s increasing motorisation has led to increasing road congestion, and the building of vast networks of elevated expressways that snake through the metropolitan areas. Whatever their other demerits, some of which are discussed in Chapter 6, these expressways provide by far the best vantage point from which to experience the Japanese megalopolis. Who can forget arriving in central Tokyo for the first time on the Narita International Airport bus, and after a seemingly interminable drive through the suburbs, winding between gleaming skyscrapers of innumerable strange shapes and sizes on the upper deck of four or five levels of elevated roadway, gazing at busy office workers on the tenth or twelfth floors? Here the sheer scale of megalopolitan urbanisation hits one, not for the last time.

Japanese cities display a fascinating mix of similarities with and differences from cities in other developed countries with similar levels of wealth and urbanisation. At first sight they seem surprisingly similar to Western cities, particularly those of the United States. Larger buildings are almost universally new constructions in steel-frame reinforced concrete and plate glass; there is everywhere the surge of late-model cars and trucks, a proliferation of gas stations, chain convenience stores, shopping malls, category-killer warehouse stores, fast-food restaurants with globally familiar names and logos, and colourful plastic signage and advertising; and the commercial strips along major suburban roads seem like they could be in suburbs almost anywhere. This sort of urban landscape is often somewhat of a surprise and disappointment for first-time travellers from the West, who come so far hoping to find something a little less familiar, a little more exotic. This reaction is perhaps understandable, and has a long history. Seidensticker (1991: 60), for example, notes that even in the nineteenth century there were complaints about the Americanisation of Tokyo. The processes of Westernisation continued and even accelerated through the twentieth century. Little of the historic Japan which features so prominently in coffee-table photo books on the country is immediately evident in modern Japanese cities. A striking feature of Japanese cities is thus their very visible Westernisation, and particularly the American influence on built form.

The observer of Japanese cities, however, gradually becomes aware that behind their surface similarity, in many respects they really are very different from those in other developed countries, and that any superficial similarities serve merely to disguise profound structural differences. Perhaps the most significant of these are two related aspects characteristic of Japanese urbanisation: the intense intermixture of differing land uses, and the extensive areas of unplanned, haphazard urban development. Mixed land use is so prevalent in Japanese cities that it may be hard to believe the government

Figure 0.1 The "busy place" (*sakariba*) of Ueno is one Japan's most enduring central city entertainment and shopping districts, and was already famous in the Tokugawa period for its theatres and nightlife.

Photo A. Sorensen 2001.

implemented urban land use zoning in all major cities in 1919, before such zoning became popular in the US in the 1920s. As explained in Chapters 3 and 6, Japanese zoning systems have consistently been rather inclusive, with most zones allowing a wide range of different uses. Many credit the permissive nature of this zoning with the continuing vitality of Japanese cities, as a great deal of spontaneous urban change is allowed to occur, and a broad intermixture of land uses is the norm. Developments of all sizes routinely include retail, office and residential components, and urban intensification in central city areas has encouraged the creation of crowded, noisy and often flamboyant urban centres. This urban energy is visibly amplified by the lack of controls over outdoor signs, so that the exteriors of buildings are often plastered with all manner of cheerful flashing neon, and the dense overhead wirescape adds to the confusion, as thickets of cables seem to shoot in all directions and at many different levels. The crowds of well-dressed shoppers and businessmen rushing to and from the main stations, the stacks of tiny restaurants in skinny buildings 10 stories high, the enormous congregations of shops and offices all linked together by immaculate subway systems underground and gleaming elevated expressways overhead, all affirm the urban vitality of modern Japan.

High population densities and the intensive mixture of differing land uses in central city neighbourhoods, combined with stable, tight-knit urban communities to form vital, lively city areas that exemplify Jane Jacobs' (1961) conception of healthy city life.

Figure 0.2 Suburban highway retail strips such as this one outside Sanda just north of Kobe are now one of the dominant urban forms in Japan.

Photo A. Sorensen 2001.

Clearly Jacobs' "eyes on the street" approach to urban safety applies just as forcefully in urban Japan today as it did in Greenwich Village in Manhattan 40 years ago. Even in the largest Japanese metropolitan areas such as Tokyo and Osaka, a few steps away from the busy main streets are found quiet residential neighbourhoods with a variety of small shops flanking narrow streets. The human scale of these districts, their efficient use of space, the ubiquitous potted plants on the curb in front of the houses, and the effective restraints on car traffic on the extremely narrow roads all contribute to some of the most positive aspects of Japanese urbanisation: the very widespread existence of healthy and charming urban neighbourhoods, even in the largest cities. As this book shows, the formal urban planning system has played only a minor role in the creation and maintenance of these inner city urban areas. They have instead been shaped by the legacy of the pre-modern street layouts, and by unplanned urbanisation in the modern period, and are a product of enduring social structures and housing preferences. It is thus not sufficient in the Japanese case to equate planned areas with good urban areas, and unplanned areas with urban problems. In fact, some of the best urban environments are those which have seen a minimum of planning intervention, and some of the worst are those which have been comprehensively planned.

This is not, however, meant to suggest that unplanned urbanisation in Japan is without its own problems. Over half the area of Japanese metropolises has developed as unplanned, haphazard sprawl. The extent of unplanned development is most striking on the urban fringe, where the weakness of land development controls and the mixture of land uses that contribute so positively to the urban vitality of central city areas contribute more problematically to this decidedly less attractive aspect of Japanese urbanisation. Here loopholes in the system have continued to allow unplanned, unserviced development. Clusters of tiny houses mix with large and small factories, big-box retail warehouses with large parking lots, high-rise apartment blocks, auto wreckers, noisy scrap metal recyclers and industrial waste incinerators, all interspersed with remnants of rice paddy, fields of cabbages and tree nurseries that continue actively to be cultivated.

Haphazard development on the urban fringe has also meant that local governments in the suburbs have fallen further and further behind in infrastructure provision, and crucial public infrastructure such as roads, sewer systems, parks, and other community facilities remain unbuilt. Vast areas in the suburbs are being built in sporadic fashion and new road systems planned in the 1960s remain fragmentary, with most suburban traffic funnelled into narrow roads which are congested at all hours. Worse, allowing such scattered development along rural lanes means that land prices quickly rise to fully urban levels, making it increasingly difficult to buy land for roads and parks, while private building of lanes and alleyways creates confusing road systems without sidewalks or overall design and many dead ends. Rural areas become gradually built over, and any chance of using natural features such as streams or forested hillsides to create an attractive urban environment is lost. With even sidewalks, sewers or small parks and playlots virtually unattainable, larger-scale urban amenities such as interconnected green networks, bicycle paths, and even decent road networks are out of reach in most cases (Sorensen 2001b).

As Ishida (1991a) has argued, Japanese urban areas have long shown this dual structure of planned and unplanned areas. The planned areas are found primarily in the main commercial centres near main transportation infrastructure, in large-scale industrial developments, large-scale public housing developments and suburban "new towns". Unplanned areas are virtually everywhere else, and include most of the sprawling mixed residential-commercial-industrial districts on the urban fringe. As unplanned growth on the fringe gradually is incorporated into the urban fabric, the characteristic pattern of Japanese cities – bits of planned development surrounded by large areas of incremental, unplanned development – is repeated. This provides quite a contrast with the other developed countries, where a major priority of planning since the end of the nineteenth century has been to create effective systems to control and plan for new development on the urban fringe. In such countries it is left to local governments to regulate new development on the urban fringe in order to ensure adequate public space is gained for roads and parks, that developers pay for their own infrastructure costs so that those costs are not shouldered by local taxpayers, and to prevent undue speculation and land price inflation. Such efforts, it goes without saying, have not always been successful, but at least represent the accepted wisdom, and in many cases this approach has arguably prevented the worst problems.

One consequence is that despite its wealth, Japan has seen real difficulty in translating economic success into a high quality of life for its people, as we are reminded by the frequent complaints about "rich Japan, poor Japanese". Two important reasons are the high cost of land and housing, and the poor urban environments that shape daily life in urban Japan. Urban planning decisions have had far-reaching impacts on the quality of life of the urban residents, who now constitute more than three quarters of the population. The quality and affordability of housing, accessibility to work, schools, and services, and the quality of local environments, have all been greatly affected by past and present planning decisions.

Although during the last 30 years an enormous body of literature on Japanese economic development, business practices, politics, history, literature, and anthropology has accumulated, there is as yet little on Japanese urbanisation, and less on Japanese urban planning. And while as this book will show, Japanese city planning, by commission and by omission, has had profound impacts on Japanese society, and in particular on quality of life in Japanese cities, there has been little research on the development of city planning in Japan and its impact on Japanese urbanisation. This lack of research is unfortunate, although in a sense it is perhaps not so surprising, as Japan is famous for its economic growth, not its city planning.

Yet Japan presents an interesting and important case of rapid urbanisation that should be better understood. During the last quarter century it has been the second largest economy in the world, and one of the most urbanised and densely populated of the large developed countries. At the same time, however, it has quite different traditions of land ownership, historical urban development and governance than the other developed countries. Further, while as in other fields Japanese planners have constantly borrowed from Western ideas and techniques, in implementation these have been transformed, and combined with others of local invention have helped to create a planning system that is different both in conception and in execution than in any of the other developed countries. In a variety of ways the outcomes of urbanisation and urban planning have been very different, and not infrequently, it is precisely these differences that are most interesting. This distinctiveness makes Japan an important case study of urbanisation and its management, as it gives us a useful perspective on some of the assumptions and values implicit in planning approaches in the West which have shared cultural, historical and economic legacies, as well as linked city planning and urban histories. Understanding Japanese urbanisation and planning provides insights into some of the major urban and regional planning issues faced by the other developed countries, because here very different approaches to familiar urban problems have been attempted, and very different outcomes experienced.

The Japanese case is also interesting because it is revealing of some of the planning dilemmas particular to an East Asian country experiencing rapid economic and urban growth. While it is not necessary to suggest that any particular aspect of the Japanese experience will be seen in the other rapidly developing countries in Asia, it seems clear that the Japanese experience will hold many lessons, both positive and negative, about urbanisation and urban planning issues in the Asian context. The fact that Japan has been the first to undergo the transformation from rapid urban industrial growth to a post-industrial information and consumer society suggests that at the very least the case should be carefully examined by policy-makers in the Asian countries where the vast majority of the world's urbanisation is expected to occur during the first half of the twenty-first century.

It is hoped, therefore, that this volume will contribute to bringing the Japanese experience of urbanisation and urban planning into the international discussion of urban studies, urban planning and planning history which has hitherto focused primarily on the European and North American experience, with a largely separate literature devoted to the issues of urbanisation in the developing world. Although no systematic comparison of the Japanese case with other countries is attempted, such comparison is implicit in the work. As a Canadian who studied urban planning thought in London, my understanding of Japanese urbanism can only be that of an outsider who bases his analysis of Japanese urbanisation on a prior study of North American and European urban and planning issues. The position of outsider brings both advantages and disadvantages in the study of cities. The main disadvantage, of course, is that cities are inherently such complex phenomena, influenced by such a great diversity of factors, that it is always possible that the foreign researchers' questions may be irrelevant, their information lacking, or their interpretation wrong. The main advantage is that the experience of foreignness and newness in studying a style of urbanisation different from one's own prompts a different set of questions, and possibly a different set of explanations than those of native researchers for whom their own cities are simply the norm. It can only be hoped that the present work leans more toward the latter than the former.

It is also worth noting that the Japanese experience of modern urban industrial growth and urban planning has itself always been comparative. Ever since the modernising drive to catch up and surpass the West was launched following the Meiji restoration in 1868, Japanese urban planners, government officials, and indeed the Japanese people themselves have conceived of their own experience in relation to Western models, and have implicitly and explicitly modelled their policies on Western examples, especially those of the leading industrial nations of Britain, Germany, France and the US. As in other areas of public and private enterprise Japanese city planning efforts that drew heavily on foreign models produced often dramatically different outcomes, and in studying Japanese urban planning it is often useful to understand both the original version, and the intentions of the borrowers. Where appropriate, therefore, comparisons are made between Western planning policies and their Japanese versions.

In historical studies there is always a tendency to want to line up all the facts into an orderly progression leading towards the present. This is possibly especially the case in city planning, which began the twentieth century with such a strong normative mission: to right the wrongs of the squalid industrial metropolis and to progressively develop a practice that could not only prevent the further decline of urban civilisation, but could also build healthy, beautiful, and equitable cities with good housing for all. Even until the mid-1960s a dominant goal of the planning profession was the gradual improvement of techniques and methods to achieve rational development control and the rational city. Few would argue today that such a future is either possible or even desirable. While the basic goals of healthy, productive and equitable cities may remain, the idea that there might be gradual and steady progress in the development of techniques and methods to achieve them no longer seems tenable. Current practice is characterised by diversity, pluralism and pragmatism, and above all the recognition that planning is inevitably a highly political activity that can never be perfected in the manner of a technical procedure, but must always be negotiated, and will always be contested by a diverse range of interests. There is thus little point in producing a tidy account of an orderly progress towards the present.

Instead it seems useful to pose questions about why urban planning and urban areas have developed in one way here, and differently elsewhere. Why did Japanese cities develop in the ways they did? Why, given the fact that Japan is one of the richest countries in the world, is the quality of life and of the environment in urban areas still so poor? Why is housing still so small and so expensive? Why were more than 35 per cent of all households still not serviced with sewer connections at the turn of the century? Why is so much haphazard unserviced development still allowed when the main goal of the planning system for the last 30 years has been its control? In a country which has had democratically elected local governments since the end of the nineteenth century, why have local electorates not pressed for better local government services? Why has there been so little support or pressure for better urban planning and more effective urban management at the local government level? Why has Japanese urban policy developed the way it has, and where have the key decisions affecting urban change been made?

A variety of explanations have been put forward to explain Japanese urban problems in the post-war period. The most common is that destruction in the Second World War, rapid economic growth and migration to the metropolitan areas created severe housing shortages and difficult city planning problems. There can be no doubt that the war was a major factor inhibiting the development of city planning in Japan. After the war the task of reconstruction was huge, and the shortage of housing amounted to millions of units. Later, rapid economic growth and urbanisation put enormous stress on available resources, making it difficult for governments to provide adequate urban infrastructure. This explanation alone is not adequate to explain the subsequent development of Japanese cities, however. As Calder (1988: 390–3) has pointed out, West Germany was in a similar state at the end of the war with almost all its major cities in ruins, the economy in tatters, and a huge influx of refugees from the east. West Germany (before reunification) also had similar overall population densities to those of Japan, and a major urban industrial agglomeration in the north west. Yet at the same time as experiencing rapid economic growth, albeit not as rapid as Japan, German cities were rebuilt carefully and to a generally high standard. Other factors than post-war destruction and rapid economic growth must be found if we are to fully explain Japan's severe urban problems in the post-war period.

In the course of researching and writing this book it emerged that one of the most distinctive factors influencing the development of urban planning in Japan has been the virtual absence of civil society in the formation of city planning policy and practice, or in creating images of the good city and good urban life. Civil society can be defined as the set of institutions, organisations and behaviours situated between the state, the business world and the family. This includes voluntary and non-profit organisations, philanthropic institutions, professional organisations, social and political movements, and the public sphere (see Hall 1995; Keane 1998; Salamon and Anheier 1997). Although the concept of civil society has recently come into vogue amongst social theorists, the phenomenon is not a new one. The enormously influential international city planning movement that developed at the end of the nineteenth century and during the first decades of the twentieth century is one of the prime examples of civil society actors and institutions creating a radically new policy agenda. Public health and hygiene activists, professional associations of architects, surveyors and engineers, non-profit housing advocates, settlement workers, anti-slum campaigners, friendly societies, labour and cooperative movements and a range of others provided a vocal constituency which backed many of the campaigns for greater government intervention and regulation of what had hitherto been relatively unregulated processes of urban development (see Gorsky 1998; Rodgers 1998; Sutcliffe 1981). Yet in Japan civil society remained, for a number of reasons outlined in this book, extremely weak, to the extent that it has recently been suggested that Japan only saw the birth or rebirth of its civil society during the 1990s (Iokibe 1999; Kawashima 2001; Vosse 1999; Yamamoto 1999b). While other factors, including the urban legacy of Tokugawa Japan, the particularly successful traditional urban patterns, and the persistent prioritisation by policy-makers on the drive to catch up with and overtake the industrial powers of the West over the quality of life of the Japanese people have also played an important role, it is fair to say that one of the most distinctive features of Japanese urbanisation and urban planning in comparison with the other developed countries has been the extremely weak role of civil society in the evolution of city planning policy.

This situation seems to be changing quite rapidly in recent years, and it is significant that local citizen-initiated environmental improvement efforts have been credited with playing a central role in the recent rebirth of Japanese civil society (Amenomori 1997; Iokibe 1999; Yoshida 1999). In the last 5 to 10 years urban environmental issues have begun to play a much greater role in Japanese society, and a range of grassroots movements to work towards better urban planning and local environmental improvement processes has emerged, as shown in Chapters 8 and 9. As Japan moves towards a declining population and an ageing society, the issues of urban amenity and quality of life appear to be taking on a degree of importance that they were not awarded earlier. Major changes are also taking place in Japanese urban areas and the planning system is being reformed and redesigned to accommodate new needs and desires. More than ever, city planning is at the centre of a number of crucial social and political changes, and understanding the city planning system, its development and its impacts on urban growth and urban life is essential to an understanding of Japanese society and its present and future challenges.

In attempting to answer the questions posed above, this book traces the patterns of Japanese urban growth from the mid-nineteenth century to the end of the twentieth century, describing the development of urban planning during that period, and attempting to explain why the planning system developed the way it did and how it has influenced patterns of urban growth. This historical approach was found to be essential because although many of the formal elements of Japanese planning system are similar to and even copied from Western models, they frequently tend to function rather differently in practice. Even to describe the present planning system accurately the historical context of its development is useful. To understand why it developed the way it did, understanding the history is essential.

The approach of the book is essentially chronological, beginning with an outline of the urban legacies of the early modern period. During the Tokugawa period, which lasted from 1600 to 1868 when the Tokugawa regime was overthrown, the urban population grew and a sophisticated national urban system and economy developed. A number of very large cities developed, including Edo (later Tokyo), which was in the eighteenth century probably the largest city in the world with over a million inhabitants, and also Osaka and Kyoto at almost half a million, and several medium sized cities of around 100,000. With rapid modernisation in the second half of the nineteenth century, the first city planning efforts were dominated by the issue of how to modernise the very large urban areas inherited from the previous era. Chapter 1 reviews the forces leading to the development of Japan's sophisticated feudal urban system, the typical urban forms of castle towns, and the main urban legacies of the feudal period.

Three chapters on the pre-Second World War period follow. Chapter 2 describes the major changes of the Meiji period from 1868 to 1912, during which a modern centralised national government, modern industries, railways, and institutions were established. In a surprising range of different policy areas, including city planning, the choices made during the Meiji period have had enduring effects on later Japanese development. Some of these are outlined here. The period between the end of Meiji and the end of the Second World War is covered in two overlapping chapters. Chapter 3 looks at the rapid urban industrial growth of the first decades of the twentieth century, and at the increasing urban and social problems that led to the passage of Japan's first modern planning legislation in 1919. Chapter 4 describes the new planning system in detail, and traces its implementation in the period up to the end of the war.

The post-war occupation and reconstruction years and the period of rapid economic and urban growth of the 1950s and 1960s are the subject of Chapter 5. Here the focus is on the concentration of population in the metropolitan belt between Tokyo and Osaka, and the consequent creation of the great urban industrial sprawl sometimes referred to as the Tokaido megalopolis. This vast linear conurbation is the central fact of post-war Japanese urbanisation, and virtually all subsequent planning efforts have been motivated by attempts to manage the urban challenges posed by the megalopolis. Chapter 6 traces the environmental crisis which was a consequence of rapid and unrestrained economic growth and unregulated urban expansion, the development of significant opposition to the government's "growth at any cost" policies, and the development and passage of a new City Planning Law in 1968 and revision of the Building Standard Law in 1970.

From here the discussion breaks naturally into decades. Chapter 7 discusses the implementation of the new city planning system during the 1970s. Chapter 8 relates the period of conservative resurgence and deregulation from 1980 through to the crash of the bubble economy in early 1990, and Chapter 9 examines the recent development of a renewed energy for improved city planning during the 1990s with the creation of the Master Plan system in 1992, the development of machizukuri practices, and the emergence of historical preservation as a major part of Japanese city planning. Chapter 10 attempts a summary of the major characteristics of Japanese urbanisation and planning, discussing what lessons may be learned from Japan's distinctive patterns of urbanisation and planning practices, and speculating on some major future issues facing Japanese cities.

1 The legacy of the Tokugawa period

Let the reader imagine a space of several miles square covered with yashikis. To walk through the streets inside the castle enceinte was a monotonous and gloomy task. There was nothing to break the dull uniformity of black or white tiles and windows, except here and there a sworded samurai or a procession. Occasional variety was obtained in a very large yashiki by erecting a wall around the entire inclosure, and building the houses inside . . . Within their grounds are groves, shrines, cultivated gardens, fish-ponds, hillocks, and artificial landscapes of unique and surpassing beauty. The lord of the mansion dwelt in a central building, approached from the great gate by a wide stone path and grand portico of keyaki-wood. Long, wide corridors, laid with soft mats, led to the master's chamber. All the wood-work, except certain portions, stood in virgin grain like watered silk, except where relieved here and there by a hard gleam of black lacquer-like enamel.

(Griffis 1883: 397–8)

Although the urbanisation and urban planning of modern Japan, starting with the Meiji period (1868–1912), are the main focus of this book, Japan had a long urban history prior to that time, and pre-modern patterns of urbanisation and urban governance have had enduring influences on Japanese urbanisation and planning. This chapter briefly reviews the development of the national urban system, the urban forms, and the administrative structures during the Tokugawa period (1600–1868). The long period of Tokugawa rule saw the development of a highly integrated urban system and a sophisticated bureaucratic government system to control social change, urban development and economic activity. The period saw enormous growth of urban population and urban areas, and a steady economic integration of the national territory, while at the same time a vibrant urban culture based in the merchant commoner classes developed. As was inevitable, the concepts of the city, and the expectations of city residents of their environment and their leaders also evolved, and many of the assumptions about what cities should and could be like that developed during this period have had long-term effects on Japanese urbanism, and are important for understanding developments during the twentieth century.

In common with many European countries where large cities already existed at the beginning of industrialisation, one of the first tasks of urban planning was the adaptation of these existing urban areas to new demands. In the Japanese case, however, the problem was exaggerated by the suddenness of the change from a closed feudal society during the second half of the nineteenth century to an industrialising and modernising nation which rapidly incorporated Western technologies, industries, and organisational forms. Further complicating matters was the fact that at the outset of modernisation Japan was already one of the most highly urbanised countries in the world, and Tokyo had long been one of the world's largest cities. The urban legacy of the Tokugawa period was rich, and understanding it helps to clarify some aspects of later developments. The aim of this chapter is thus to provide a concise introduction to Japanese urbanisation during the Tokugawa period, and the forces that shaped its development. The first section discusses the formation of the feudal era urban system and the basic features of the social and political structure of the Tokugawa period. The second section outlines the basic structure of urban administration and controls over land use, and describes the urban areas that developed. The third section explores the most important urban legacies of the pre-modern period, and the main problems they posed for the modernising reformers of the Meiji period.

Urbanisation during the Tokugawa period

The Tokugawa period began in 1600 when Tokugawa Ieyasu, the last of three great generals who reunified Japan after a long period of bloody civil wars, won a decisive battle at Sekigahara and established the Pax Tokugawa which was to last for the next two-and-a-half centuries. As an extended period of internal peace after a long period of devastating wars, the Tokugawa period saw an economic revival and improvements in material conditions throughout Japan. The seventeenth century in particular saw a rapid increase in agricultural output, population and economic activity, and rapid urbanisation produced what was probably the most urbanised large pre-modern society outside Europe (Rozman 1973: 6). From the late sixteenth century to the end of the seventeenth, Japan's population grew from about 18 million to more than 30 million (Rozman 1973: 77). At the same time the urban population grew from about 1.4 million (7 or 8 per cent of the total) in the early Tokugawa period to about 5 million (about 16 per cent of the total) by the end of the century (Hall 1968; Kornhauser 1982: 70; Rozman 1973: 272). Population counts during this period are imprecise, as although the commoner population was regularly and carefully enumerated, the numbers of the samurai or warrior class in each domain was considered a military secret and not recorded. Modern estimates of samurai populations are arrived at by extrapolating from the accounting records of their salaries which were paid in rice.

The urban system was dominated by the political and administrative centre of Edo (renamed Tokyo in 1868 at the beginning of the Meiji period), which was in the eighteenth century probably the largest city in the world with over a million inhabitants. Osaka, the main commercial and financial centre, and Kyoto, the ancient imperial capital and centre of the traditional arts and handicrafts industries, were cities of several hundred thousand each. These three main cities were commonly referred to as the *santo* (three metropolises), and were the three main pillars of the urban system. More important in aggregate population were about two hundred castle towns (*Jōkamachi*), distributed throughout the breadth of the archipelago, which ranged in population from one or two thousand to over a hundred thousand (Hall 1968; Rozman 1986). There was also a range of other urban settlements, most of which were smaller than the castle towns, such as the post towns (*shukubamachi*) along the main trunk highways, port towns (*minato*), market towns (*ichibamachi*), and religious centres (*monzenmachi*). At the beginning of the modern period, therefore, Japan had a long tradition of urban settlement and administration, and had already been forced to cope with the problems particular to very large cities before the beginning of industrialisation in the late nineteenth century. The urban areas built during the feudal era, and the urban traditions they represented, have continued to have important effects on Japanese urban development until the present.

The earliest examples of large-scale town building in Japan were the two ancient imperial capitals, *Heijō-kyō* (later Nara) and *Heian-kyō* (Kyoto) which were planned imperial capitals patterned after the Chinese Tang dynasty capital of Changan, and built during a period of strong cultural influence from China. Heijō-kyō, founded in 710, was relatively quickly abandoned with the founding of Heian-kyō in 794, which continued as the imperial capital of Japan and centre of court life (though not always of political or military power) until the Emperor Meiji was moved to Tokyo following the Meiji restoration in 1868. These two cities were the only two in Japanese history that followed the symmetrical planned grid of the Chinese imperial style, and did not have a lasting impact on patterns of Japanese urbanisation, which later reverted to a more indigenous style of asymmetrical and irregular growth. The characteristic form of Japanese urban development prior to the modern period became the castle town, which attained its highest level of development during the Tokugawa period, and among which are counted most of the larger settlements, including Edo, Osaka and Nagoya. The castle town can best be understood in the context of the feudal system that produced it.

Tokugawa rule was founded on a rigid class system based on an idealised Confucian model. There were four main classes, each hereditary: samurai (warriors), peasants, artisans and merchants. In addition there were substantial groups that fell outside those classes, including monks and outcast groups such as the eta and hinin. During the century prior to the establishment of the Tokugawa regime in 1600 by Tokugawa Ieyasu (1542–1616), a gradual process of strengthening of political and economic control over entire domains by the most important feudal lords, or *daimyo*, and the forced removal of land-owning squires from their land to become samurai living in the castle towns had fostered the development of those cities as administrative and military centres. The actual cultivators of the land who had been serfs under the landed squires became *honbyakusho*, or peasants with registered cultivating rights to certain pieces of land and the obligation to pay tax in rice to the lord of their fief. Peasants were not allowed to leave the land and could be brought back by force if they tried to leave. Nor were they allowed to sell the land they cultivated as it was all in principle owned by the emperor (Francks 1992: 102; Sato 1990). Although the peasants were the poorest class, they were regarded as morally superior to the merchants and artisans because they tended the land and produced the staple rice. Artisans were chiefly engaged in producing goods for the samurai in the castle towns, and especially those in the capital Edo. Merchants were regarded as the lowest class because they did not produce anything, although they were increasingly over the course of the period the wealthiest group, and their loans to the perennially indebted daimyo allowed them some role in the feudal political economy. Merchants also performed the essential economic function of buying farm and handicraft goods produced in rural areas and selling them in the towns, providing the vital connection between rural producers and urban markets (Hall 1968: 178–80). While the peasants were tied to the soil and lived in villages, most samurai, artisans and merchants came to live in urban areas, particularly in the castle towns. It should be noted that this class system did not emerge full blown at the beginning of the Tokugawa period, but was a gradual continuation of developments during the sixteenth and seventeenth centuries. By the end of the period, although there had been considerable fraying of this ideal separation of classes, the original scheme still held to a great extent (Rozman 1986).

The economic base of the castle towns was military and administrative. Control over land and the peasants that tilled it was the basis of political power, as the main source of government revenue was the land taxes which were paid in rice. Control became regularised with the conversion of the samurai elite from an essentially military class into an administrative officialdom resident in the castle towns. From these bases their political and bureaucratic authority radiated out over the domains (Hall 1968: 179). This power was increasingly reflected over the course of the period in the development of sophisticated record-keeping techniques to reinforce such control: cadastral maps showing detailed records of plot boundaries and landholdings, administrative and commercial maps of cities and domains, population registers and family registers, and records of taxes and revenues (Sato 1990: 38–41).

This relocation of samurai to the castle towns during the sixteenth century had profound consequences for urban development during the seventeenth and eighteenth centuries. Whereas before they had been largely self-sufficient on their own holdings, in the cities they were forced to sell a portion of their rice stipend to raise money to purchase other necessities. This change encouraged growth in the numbers of merchants and artisans in the cities supplying their needs. Many merchants and artisans moved from older ports, markets and religious centres to supply the growing populations of the castle towns, and these moves were in many cases actively encouraged by the daimyo, who needed both merchants and artisans to supply essential military and other goods and services. As there was significant competition among rival daimyo during the great period of castle-building during the seventeenth century, various incentives such as free land, tax exemptions and promises of orders from the domain were offered. Those recruited in this way became a privileged class among the commoners, and included merchants who could supply arms and gunpowder, and artisans such as skilled carpenters and sword smiths (McClain 1982: 29). Large numbers of commoners also moved spontaneously from rural areas in search of paid labouring work on the numerous construction projects, or to become servants and apprentices in the expanding merchant and artisan sectors, particularly during the seventeenth century when the daimyo were actively encouraging the growth of their nascent castle towns. Urban growth in the seventeenth century was thus primarily generated by the removal of the samurai from their land and their relocation to the castle towns where they were gradually transformed into a salaried administrative class, paid in rice. This prompted a secondary growth of commoner population which later generated its own consumption demands and economic stimulus. As the castle towns reached their full development towards the end of the seventeenth century, about half the population was normally the samurai warrior/administrator class, and the other half was made up of merchants, artisans, labourers and servants (Hall 1968: 179–80). Most of the population lived in rural villages and it is estimated that the samurai population fluctuated between 10 and 20 per cent of the total.

Figure 1.1 Himeji castle, in the city of that name west of Osaka on the Inland Sea, is the most spectacular of Japan's 12 remaining feudal-era fortresses.

Photo A. Sorensen 2001.

The castle towns of the Tokugawa period were largely the product of intense urban-isation in the seventeenth century, as during the eighteenth century populations stabilised. Only some of the castle towns that emerged during this period were based on earlier fortresses built before the establishment of Tokugawa hegemony. As most of those earlier castles had been built in inaccessible locations for easier defence, they had remained primarily military garrisons with little commercial function or civilian popu-lation. When, during the early years of the Tokugawa period Tokugawa Ieyasu was establishing a new system of social and political control over the newly unified nation, one of his most important measures was the Genna Edict of One Castle for One Domain which required that each domain concentrate all its military and administra-tive function in one castle town, and abandon most of the numerous and scattered fortresses of the earlier period. Many of the domains chose entirely new sites, usually centred in the agricultural plains which were their economic base, and along lines of communication such as rivers and highways (Fujioka 1980). Rivers were not only important transport routes, but were also the source of essential irrigation water, and such locations increased the strategic control of the castle town over its hinterland (Hatano 1994: 242–3). They also provided ample space for later development, and as natural routes through mountainous Japan are few, later railroads frequently followed the old highway routes, providing later positive economic benefits. Kornhauser (1982:

76) has argued persuasively that the continued growth and economic success until the present of many of the castle towns established during the early seventeenth century provides strong evidence of the care put into site selection for the new settlements. The castle towns thus formed the administrative and military centres of the feudal domains, which numbered about 260 by the end of the 1600s. The rapid economic growth of the century was then focused on this limited number of locations, as commercial and handicraft activities grew to support the samurai populations of the castle towns, which became great commercial centres and developed their own distinctive urban culture (see McClain 1982; Nishiyama 1997). The seventeenth century in Japan thus saw one of the world's greatest periods of planned new town development, with hundreds of new castle towns forming an urban network that was evenly spread throughout the whole country, as each domain controlled a relatively small territory.

The planned spatial distribution of castle towns, which had become the main urban centres, and within them of social classes, was an essential part of the Tokugawa social and political order. The national settlement system that emerged was a direct consequence of efforts to control the political, economic and military power of the domains, while the inflexible class system was an attempt to prevent social change that might undermine samurai power. Japan was divided into three main areas; those controlled directly by the shogun's government (*Bakufu*) in Edo, those controlled by the inner (*fudai*) daimyo and those controlled by the outer (*tozama*) daimyo. Bakufu-administered areas included most of the Kanto region around Edo, the important commercial city of Osaka, the imperial capital Kyoto and the port of Nagasaki to which Dutch traders (the only contact allowed with the West) were restricted, and several other strategic centres, totalling about a third of the country. The status of each daimyo was determined by the size and location of the domain allotted to him, which in turn was determined primarily by his relationship to the shogun, and in particular by whether he had fought with or against Ieyasu at the decisive battle of Sekigahara in 1600 which established Tokugawa hegemony over all Japan. The closest allies (the fudai daimyo) were granted the domains closest to the core area of Japan between Edo, Osaka and Kyoto. The tozama daimyo, or outside lords, whose ancestors had not been allies of Ieyasu were assigned domains furthest from the core areas. The Bakufu retained, and sometimes exercised, the power to remove daimyo from their domains, or reallocate them as punishment or reward (Oishi 1990: 24). Because the urban population of each castle town was mainly determined by the rice-producing capacity of its domain, and that in turn reflected the feudal hierarchy, the size rankings of the feudal cities came to closely mirror the feudal political order (Kornhauser 1982: 67).

For his own castle and the headquarters of his military government Ieyasu chose a rather unpromising site beside Tokyo Bay, where there was only a little flat land between the low hills of the Musashino plain and the marshy shore of the bay. While the Kanto region in which he located Edo was outside the more economically developed and densely populated region around Osaka and Kyoto, it was the largest alluvial plain in Japan and had enormous potential for growth. This became the site of the de facto capital city and main city of Japan for over two-and-a-half centuries of Tokugawa rule, as even though the imperial capital remained in Kyoto, the emperors were largely powerless and were supported by the shoguns primarily for their symbolic value (Naitoh 1966). Edo grew rapidly around the new castle, and by the beginning of the eighteenth century was probably the largest city in the world with a population of over a million people. The growth of the capital was greatly stimulated by another of the reforms instituted early in the Tokugawa period, the system of alternate residence (*sankin kōtai*). Under this system daimyo were required to spend every second or third year (depending on their status) in residence in Edo, and to leave their families there permanently as hostages. Apart from the immediate value of these hostages for political control, the system also kept the daimyo poor, by forcing them to undertake periodic expeditions to and from Edo and to maintain residences both in the capital and in their domain. McClain (1982: 70) estimates that the expenses of the journeys to Edo and of maintaining over three thousand people who lived in the Edo mansions cost the Maeda daimyo between a third and a half of all domain expenditure by the end of the seventeenth century (see also Yazaki 1968: 210). The travel expenses were particularly heavy for the domains furthest from Edo, as the journeys were long, and the daimyo were accompanied by a large retinue numbering into the thousands for the more important lords, all of whom had to be housed each night in one of the post towns along the route. The regular travel by large daimyo parties also contributed to the growth of the post towns (*shukubamachi*), particularly along the five main national highways, of which the most famous and most heavily travelled was the Tōkaidō from Edo to Osaka (Moriya 1990).

The alternate residence system stimulated the rapid growth of Edo by creating an enormous population of samurai drawn from domains throughout the country. As Hall (1968: 177) notes, in this sense Edo was merely a greatly enlarged version of the system already established by the individual daimyo of forcing their samurai vassals to live in their castle towns. In the case of Edo, the vassals included both the daimyo who brought their own retinue and the samurai from the Tokugawa's own domains, most of whom were required to live in Edo. In total there were 350,000 to 400,000 samurai residents in Edo during the eighteenth and early nineteenth centuries (Rozman 1973: 296). As in the smaller castle towns, the presence of a large number of samurai resulted in the growth of a commoner population of another 500,000 merchants, artisans, servants and labourers to serve them, bringing Edo's population close to the million mark (Rozman 1973: 296). Urban growth, and the emergence of very large cities such as Osaka, Kyoto and in particular Edo, with their vast consumption of goods produced elsewhere, fostered the development of the commercial and economic integration of the nation in integrated supply networks, and the increasing monetarisation of the economy. This encouraged and was made possible by the emergence of merchants and financiers who operated on a large scale, and the development of a rather sophisticated financial system (Hayashi 1994; Sakudo 1990).

Ironically then, even though the Tokugawa ideology was Confucian and agrarianist, extolling the virtue of peasants tilling the soil and the social stability it represented, the Tokugawa policy of centralisation and rationalisation of the settlement system led naturally to increased urbanisation. These contradictory tendencies helped to foster one enduring aspect of Tokugawa era urban thinking: the fear of the city as corrupter of the moral order, and suspicion of the potentially disruptive commoner population (*chōnin*) of the towns (Smith 1978: 50). Urban growth, particularly on the scale seen in the Tokugawa period which created a large urban class of merchants and artisans, inevitably posed a threat to the vision of a stable unchanging order based on the rural peasant tilling his paddies, ruled by a small, elite warrior class. After the initial period of rapid growth and town-building during the seventeenth century, much of the history of Tokugawa cities thus consists of more or less unsuccessful attempts at restricting urban growth by forbidding peasants to leave the land, while at the same time refusing to allow the commoner areas of existing cities to expand. Over the two-and-a-half centuries of Tokugawa rule these factors evolved into a highly developed urban system of integrated spatial, social and political control, which was embodied in the urban administrative structure and in the spatial form of the castle towns, as discussed further below. As noted above, the system of Tokugawa governance did not emerge fully developed at the beginning of the period, but took time to reach its full dimension; and then with economic growth, urban expansion, cultural development, and increasing affluence, it began to depart even further from the ideal during the eighteenth century and into the nineteenth. Neither was the system monolithic, being characterised more by diversity, among the various domains, between the domains and areas administered directly by the Bakufu, and among the Bakufu territories themselves. Osaka, for example, was very different from Edo, which was in turn different from Kyoto or Nagoya, and only some of this variety can be noted here.

Urban administration

One of the most significant characteristics of Tokugawa society was the strict definition of the feudal classes. Great efforts were made to prevent mobility between the classes, and these were largely successful, as only in a very few exceptional cases were inter class transfers allowed. This deeply segmented social structure was, unsurprisingly, reflected in systems of governance. Urban samurai were governed by an entirely different legal and administrative system from urban commoners, who were in turn governed quite separately from the peasants in rural areas. In the case of Edo, each class was administered separately, with a city magistrate (*machi bugyō*) responsible for maintaining order in the commoner areas (*machi-chi*), and a separate temple magistrate (*jisha bugyō*) responsible for the inhabitants of the temple quarters (*jisha-chi*). Similar systems of administration by local magistrates were set up in other cities controlled directly by the Bakufu, including Osaka and Nara, and other castle towns were generally ruled directly by the domain administrations of the different daimyo, again usually through city magistrates. This magistrate system of urban government extended only to the commoner and temple populations, however, as national and provincial administrations had direct control over the samurai areas (*buke-chi*). The spacious residential areas of the daimyo (*yashiki*) in Edo were considered legally a part of each domain, and were governed by their own laws and administration, much as foreign embassies commonly are today. The Bakufu higher officials (*hatamoto*) and the lower samurai were administered directly by the Bakufu as part of the national administration that was organised essentially on hierarchical military lines.

In the commoner areas of Edo were two city magistrates appointed by the shogun to administer law and order, hear appeals and petitions and adjudicate disputes between commoners. These operated in rotation, being on duty for a month at a time, and using the second month to follow up on petitions and resolve such issues as had been brought to them during their on-duty month. The city magistrates were granted a small budget by the Bakufu to maintain a small force of 50 constables and about 200 patrol men.

Kato (1994: 51) suggests it was because there were so few police and administrators serving half a million commoners that the primary strategy for governing the city was the delegation of responsibility for most matters to the merchants and artisans themselves, and encouraging voluntary compliance with administrative dictate. This resulted in the evolution of an elaborate hierarchy of responsibility which served to link the Bakufu officials at the top with individual families at the bottom.

The highest-ranking commoners in Edo were the heads of three families of hereditary city elders (*machidoshiyori*), who were delegated the responsibility of carrying out specific standardised functions of local government, including making sure all laws, proclamations, decrees and regulations were known and followed, maintaining census registers, collecting and submitting taxes to higher authorities, and laying out new commoner districts (Kato 1994: 54). They were not granted a budget or taxation powers to carry out these duties, but were given a number of symbolic and material rewards. The elders were allowed the two distinguishing badges of the samurai class: the wearing of swords and the use of a surname. Each elder also received a large plot of land in Hon-chō, close to the main entrance of Edo castle, which they could lease out to raise money. They also received occasional special grants from the Bakufu. While their position as intermediaries between the Bakufu and the merchants and artisans was no doubt lucrative for the elders, the shortage of revenue with which to run a bureaucratic administration meant that the city elders had to rely on techniques of mutual surveillance for the maintenance of order, mutual responsibility for the payment of taxes, and local self responsibility for the provision of most public goods.

Under the supervision of the city elders were the neighbourhood chiefs (*nanushi*), often also hereditary, who were directly responsible for the various neighbourhoods. According to Kato (1994: 55), by the time the system was fully developed in the early eighteenth century, there were some 250–260 families serving as neighbourhood chiefs for over a thousand commoner neighbourhoods (*chō*), which had an average population of 300. This meant that while some chiefs were responsible for only one neighbourhood, many chiefs were responsible for up to a dozen or more. Their duties were to ensure that all merchant and artisan families within their jurisdiction were aware of and obeyed all laws, ordinances and decrees announced by the city elders, to maintain the census registers for their districts, to investigate causes of fires and supervise firefighting squads, to supervise, witness and record the sale of property, and to collect and administer neighbourhood funds for the guardhouse and gatehouse.

The actual management of the day-to-day activities of each neighbourhood was the responsibility of the local people (*chōnin*) themselves. The neighbourhoods were responsible for collecting funds to pay for firefighting equipment and services, neighbourhood festivals, and maintenance of essential infrastructure such as the roads, fire towers, guardhouses, gates and gatehouses, canals and ditches, and the neighbourhood water supply. Each neighbourhood was subdivided into five family groups (*goningumi*) which were responsible to the neighbourhood chief, and were composed of the landlords and householders (*iemochi*), and landlord's agents (*yamori*) who managed their rental properties. Tenants (*shakuyanin, tanagari*) were not chōnin proper, nor were they members of the goningumi, but were the responsibility of the landlord's agents who represented them in the goningumi and had to guarantee their compliance with directives passed down from above (Yazaki 1968: 218). Compliance with the various rules and regulations was ensured primarily through the fact that all within the group were mutually respon-sible for each other's conduct. Thus if one family failed to pay its share of taxes, the others had to make up the shortfall, and if one member committed a crime, all were responsible to either inform on him, or share in the punishment. As can be imagined, this was an extremely effective system of ensuring the compliance of the population with the minimum of investment in local government, and resembled in its essential fea-tures the social control system established in rural areas, where village self-responsibility was managed through a system of village joint-responsibility for the payment of rice taxes, policing each other's daily behaviour, and maintaining local infrastructure under the paternalistic supervision of the larger landowners (see Sato 1990).

There were significant class differences within the commoner populations particu-larly towards the end of the period. The most privileged were those merchants who had early on been invited to set up in the castle town, and who had often been granted land and/or monopoly privileges. Below them were the leading merchants and most skilled craftsmen who owned establishments on their own land along major streets. Next were established landowners who were wealthy enough to supply labourers and money for public projects (*jinushi*). Below these were tenants who owned their own houses but rented the land they were built on (*jikari*), followed by tenants who were able to rent street-front shops and homes (*omotetanagari*), and at the bottom those tenants who could afford only back-alley accommodation (*uratanagari*) (Yazaki 1968: 216–7). The large majority of the commoner population consisted of landless tenants or servants and apprentices who lived on their master's premises. With the rapid urbanisation of the seventeenth century large numbers of poor migrants moved to the growing cities, par-ticularly when from the mid-1630s wage labour gradually came to replace corvée workers in castle town construction projects (Leupp 1992: 17). The scale of urban construction works was enormous, particularly in the great castle towns. As McClain estimates, during the 1620s the money spent on the rebuilding of Osaka castle alone would have been sufficient to support over 200,000 persons (McClain 1999: 52). As the period progressed the key divide within the commoner population was between a minority who owned land and property and built cheap rental dwellings on portions of their land, and the majority who owned no property and were forced to rent their hous-ing. Leupp contends that in the largest cities "such socially marginal groupings as day laborers, domestics, porters, palanquin bearers, stevedores, manufacturing hands, ped-dlers, beggars and outcastes constituted a vast *population flottante*" which has been estimated to include some 60 per cent of the commoner population by the end of the period (Leupp 1992: 4). It is this large group of people who would have inhabited the rental tenements in the interiors of urban blocks (*urachi*) while the wealthy landowners and merchants lived in handsome shop-houses facing the streets (*omotechi*), as described below.

Although systems of urban governance developed gradually, it seems that by the end of the Tokugawa period most castle towns were governed in a manner similar to Edo, with the domain administrations governing the samurai warrior class directly through a military-style hierarchy, and the commoner population indirectly through pairs of city magistrates who delegated authority to and demanded compliance from a hierarchical chain which stretched through the city elders down to individual families. Perhaps the greatest exception to this model was Osaka, which had emerged by the end of the seventeenth century as the great "merchant's capital" of Tokugawa Japan. While the early shoguns had obliged the daimyo of western Japan to spend a vast fortune rebuilding Osaka castle as their main military stronghold in western Japan in the first half of the seventeenth century, the very impregnability of the fortress and the increasing security of Tokugawa rule meant that eventually they only needed to maintain a relatively small garrison there. In total, all the samurai stationed in Osaka numbered little more than a thousand men, under the command of a castle warden (*jōdai*) (McClain 1999: 50). This in a city that during most of the eighteenth century had a total population of over 400,000. While in most castle towns the samurai comprised about half the population and occupied more than two-thirds of the land, in Osaka the samurai were only a tiny proportion of the population and were restricted primarily to the castle grounds. This unusual population split was in part because Osaka was not the castle town of a domain, with a resident daimyo and his samurai retainers and their families. Instead the shogunate retained direct control over Osaka as their main fortress in the west rather than allocating it to a daimyo. It was also a result of the extraordinary commercial and artisanal success of the city, which supported a population of commoners almost as large as that of Edo without the enormous boost to the local economy of the huge consumption and spending of the samurai stationed there.

In many ways the governance of the city was similar to that in other Tokugawa period cities, with a pair of city magistrates appointed by the shogunate to manage day-to-day affairs. Their duties were also similar to those of magistrates elsewhere, including issuing legal codes, dispensing justice, collecting taxes, plotting new urban areas, maintaining roads, and enforcing commercial regulations, and they were supported by several dozen constables and patrolmen, as well as by commoner city elders and neighbourhood elders (McClain 1999: 53). As Wakita argues, however, the merchant leaders of Osaka enjoyed a greater freedom of self-governance than in other cities. He cites as an example the fact that unlike elsewhere, the neighbourhood elders of Osaka were granted the responsibility of maintaining property registers and verifying property transfers, and so gained a veto power over who could purchase property within their jurisdiction (Wakita 1999: 267). Similarly, Murata argues that Osaka merchants played important supportive roles to the magistrates and other Bakufu and domain officials, for instance as tax contractors and as "merchant delegates" (*yōkiki*) who managed Bakufu and domain affairs in villages in a wide area surrounding Osaka (Murata 1999: 257). Certainly the dominance of commoners in Osaka's population, and the general practice of delegating responsibility for most urban administration such as census keeping, dredging of canals and waterways, and repairing roads, bridges, water supply and drainage systems indicates a relatively high level of organisation amongst the merchant class in the management of their city (Wakita 1999: 268). After all, Osaka was a large and successful commercial and proto-industrial city with a sophisticated port and distribution system, and an enormous production of processed goods for shipment elsewhere in Japan, particularly to Edo (see McClain 1999: 61–3). Still, as Wakita reminds us, even in Osaka – which was in many respects exceptional – self-management should not be confused with autonomy, and the shogunate was careful to ensure that their authority and control over urban centres were unchallenged (Wakita 1999: 267).

In summary, the urban areas of the commoners were administered by representatives of the shogun or daimyo, the city magistrates, who delegated much of the actual responsibility of managing the urban districts to hereditary city elders. To ensure their compliance with official rules and regulations the commoners were subdivided into a large number of individual self-governing neighbourhoods, the chō, which had a certain autonomy based on the enforcement of collective responsibility for taxes, public goods, as well as misdemeanours. As Hall (1968: 181) argues, this self-government was of a very limited sort, however, amounting to little more than the privilege of managing some of their own private affairs. In both village and town, even this small measure of independence carried with it the obligation of being virtually entirely responsible for their own collective needs, such as waste removal, the maintenance of roads, the staffing of the local guardhouses and gates, local poor relief, and the management of local festivals. The public realm was monopolised by the samurai ruling class, while the people were permitted to pursue private gain and their own personal welfare, as long as they paid their taxes and did not intrude into public matters. If any private individual should attempt to transgress the boundaries of his station and intervene in public issues it was considered a form of revolt, and was suppressed without hesitation (see Iokibe 1999). The long period of Tokugawa rule in this way greatly strengthened the tradition of "respect for authority and disdain for the people" (*Kanson Minpi*), an approach to governance which proved enduring.

In much of western Europe independent self-governing cities led the economic and cultural transformation at the end of the feudal period and beginning of the Renaissance, and a tradition of municipal governments with legal corporate status dominated usually by the local bourgeoisie had developed. In Japan, however, there was no such tradition of urban self-government at the time of the transition to industrialisation and modernisation in the Meiji period of the nineteenth century. The idea that cities could or should have self-governing powers, and the legal frameworks that established local governments as corporate bodies which could own property, manage businesses, and keep accounts did not exist in the Tokugawa period, and were slow to develop in the modern period. The limited autonomy of the merchant and artisan classes in the cities has had profound long-term effects on the development of Japanese urban governance and planning.

The spatial structure of castle towns

Over two-and-a-half centuries of Tokugawa rule Japanese cities grew and changed enormously, and urban structure changed along with urban size. These changes were driven partly by military considerations of defensibility, partly by evolving ideas about the spatial segregation of samurai and commoners within the castle towns, and partly by the sheer pressure of enormous population growth and physical expansion. At the beginning of the period when the new castle towns were first laid out military considerations came first, as the country had just emerged from over a century of almost continuous war, and no one knew how long the peace would last. As time went on, however, and the Tokugawa regime became more entrenched, other concerns came to the fore. As McClain puts it, speaking of Kanazawa, "After 1635, the use of urban space became increasingly intertwined with the government's attempt to divide society into status groups. By the middle of the seventeenth century a new ideal had emerged: the distance of a samurai's residence from the castle ought to be proportional to his status within the warrior hierarchy. The daimyo became the sole inhabitant of the castle, and this symbolized his preeminent status. The homes of many important samurai were clustered on the eastern and northern sides of the castle, lesser retainers lived beyond this inner circle, and the lowest-ranking *bushi* tended to live farthest from the castle" (McClain 1982: 77–8). From this attempt to inscribe status relations in the urban structure developed many of the characteristic aspects of castle town structure described below. Despite the persistent attempts of daimyo and the shogunate to shape the growth of castle towns into desired patterns, however, the rapid urban growth of the seventeenth century, and particularly the influx of commoner populations into castle towns resulted in considerable areas of unplanned, organic growth. The ideals of castle town design were somewhat compromised in practice, and particularly toward the end of the period there was considerable blurring of the concept of spatial separation of social classes.

Keeping that qualification in mind, the two dominant ideas of castle town design were the spatial separation of the feudal classes, and the priority placed on defence and control. Castles were designed with a view both to defence from external invaders and from commoner mobs, and in the special case of Edo, from the potentially rebellious daimyo as well (Smith 1979: 64). These various security concerns were the basis of the planning of each castle town with its lord's castle in the centre, his samurai vassals occupying spacious estates surrounding it, the common people – including artisans, merchants and the poor – crowded into their own districts, and another concentrated area of temples near the urban fringe (Fujioka 1980). In contrast to European fortifications which encircled large residential quarters, in Japanese castle towns only the central keep was fortified, and no attempt was made to surround the settlement with walls, the outer perimeter defences being formed by lower samurai residences and temple compounds. The outer commoner, temple and samurai areas were conceived as a part of castle defences, not as something to defend.

The basic structure of a typical castle town is shown in Figure 1.2. The daimyo's castle was the most important feature, and was generally well fortified and surrounded by a moat. The area immediately surrounding the castle was allocated for spacious residential compounds housing the daimyo's highest-ranking vassals, or upper samurai, each in turn housing their own retainers in long barracks on the compound perimeter, which formed an outer wall. The commoner area of the merchants and artisans, or machi, was normally located in front of the main gates to the castle, and along the major roads leading to other parts of the country. Machi districts in virtually all castle towns were laid out in regular grids of square blocks, patterned after the land subdivision system first used in Nara and Kyoto. The machi was very often surrounded by the lower density residential districts of lower samurai, which served the dual purpose of protecting the commoner area and controlling it. Temple districts were similarly placed on the periphery of the town for defensive purposes.

The effectiveness of these various districts in contributing to defence and control arose from the fact that each was routinely surrounded by walls, with guardhouses and gates at entrances and exits. In the case of Edo, the great temples and shrines, the districts of the shogun's direct retainers (hatamoto), and the great daimyo estates each had their own imposing walls and gates. Within the commoner areas, gates and guardhouses separating each residential neighbourhood were closed at night and guarded by the residents on a rotation basis (Kato 1994: 47). In addition to the pervasive internal walls,

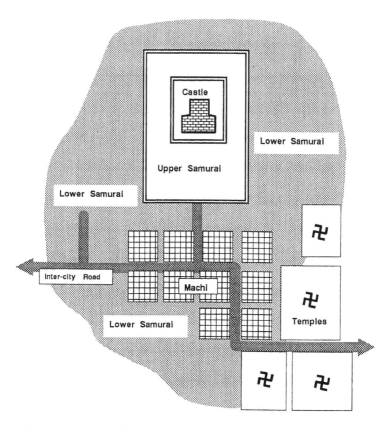

Figure 1.2 The basic elements of the spatial structure of a Tokugawa period castle town (highly simplified diagram).

much use was made of moats and rivers to separate the different districts within the castle towns. Roads were narrow and were laid out with few straight streets, many T intersections, and bridges over moats and rivers were kept narrow to allow greater control over movement (Fujioka 1980: 149).

Land was allocated to samurai based on their rank, and to merchants to encourage them to locate in the castle towns. When necessary, land could be reallocated from one use to another, particularly after fires. McClain gives the example of the forced removal of several commoner wards near Kanazawa castle to make more room for high-ranking samurai who were being moved from within the castle. Although he notes that this case was exceptional in its scale, and that other land equal in quality and value was substituted, it does illustrate the enormous power that daimyo potentially had over land use in their castle towns (McClain 1982: 78). Similarly in cases of expansion at the urban fringe, it was not uncommon for the shogunate or daimyo to relocate agricultural villages to other locations to provide more land for urban use (Wakita 1999: 266). In some aspects, therefore, the degree of spatial control in Tokugawa period cities was much greater than in contemporary European cities or present-day Japan. In particular the spatial separation of classes, and by extension of land uses suggests a clear and effective public power of control over land use at this time. While this interpretation is accurate to some degree, an image of monolithic power would be exaggerated, as there were important limitations to Bakufu power. First, while the overall system of segregation of the different classes remained intact, over the course of the period incremental changes resulted in much blurring of the details. This was particularly true of Edo, which expanded so dramatically during the period that in practice patterns of land use were more complex than in the ideal scheme, as shown in Figure 1.3.

Furthermore, the administrative control of the Tokugawa state was largely restricted to land and population and was never accompanied by effective controls over buildings and infrastructure. In great contrast to European cities of the same period, which had effectively eliminated the scourge of disastrous fires by the simple expedient of requiring the use of fireproof materials, the Tokugawa regime was never able to enforce such a building code, as discussed below. Actual control over specific spaces and land was never absolute: it was normally carried out through a process of negotiation and was constantly subject to incremental slippage.

An excellent example of how spatial control worked in practice is provided by McClain (1994) in his account of the gradual erosion of the firebreak at Edobashi. This was an area near Edobashi bridge just east of Nihonbashi bridge in the central part of Edo, which was expropriated by the Bakufu after the great Meireki fire of 1657 to provide a firebreak and emergency shelter area south of the bridge. The Bakufu confiscated the land and provided the landowners with substitute plots in another location. Although in the following decades the Bakufu steadfastly maintained its claim of ownership, and all involved maintained the increasingly obvious fiction that the area still functioned as a firebreak, over a period of about a century the area became fully built up with merchant housing, commercial stalls, warehouses, stables, archery stalls and tea houses (see also Jinnai 1990: 130). The story is an interesting one and is instructive of the realities of spatial control in Edo. Pressure on space was such that open space was hard to protect, even by the Bakufu, and even with the full powers of ownership and the lofty purpose of fire safety. Bakufu control over space was pervasive but not absolute, and always functioned by negotiation and a certain give and take.

Urban form of the commoner city

The main spatial division of Edo was that between the areas of the commoners (*machi-chi*) and the area of the samurai (*buke-chi*) (see Jinnai 1990; Seidensticker 1991). A third important area was that of the temples (*jisha-chi*). In Edo there was considerable intermixture between these areas on the ground. The three areas each had their own distinctive spatial characteristics, however, and should be examined separately.

Commoner areas were usually laid out in a regular grid pattern of rectangular blocks, following the ancient Chinese model adopted in Kyoto. The city elders were given responsibility for laying out new residential areas for the commoner population whenever the Bakufu allocated new land to the commoner areas. An important characteristic of the commoner areas of Edo was their very high population densities. In late eighteenth century Edo the area where commoners lived totalled about 13 square kilometres, was divided into about 1,700 neighbourhoods (*chō*), and had a total population

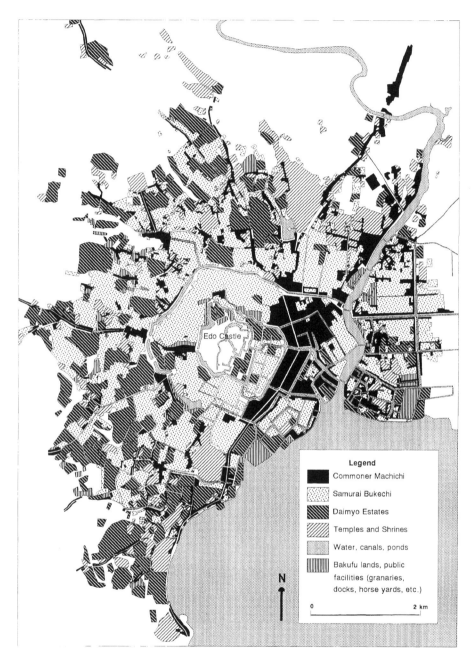

Figure 1.3 The spatial structure of Edo in 1859.

Source: Adapted by the author from an original map drawn by Okata Junichiro in 1981, using the *Bungan Edo Oezu* published by Subaraya Mohei Publishers in Ansei 6 (1859).

Figure 1.4 Imaichō near Nara in central Japan is an almost perfectly preserved town dating from early in the Tokugawa period.

Photo A. Sorensen 2000.

of approximately 500,000 with population densities in the densest areas of up to 58,000 per square kilometre (Rozman 1973: 296). This is an extraordinarily high density if one considers that most dwellings were just one storey high, only a minority having a second storey and virtually never reaching three levels except in the very core of the commoner areas where three-storey shops were not uncommon on corner plots. The average densities in the commoner areas were about four times those of the samurai areas, and close to ten times those of the temple areas. By the end of the Edo period commoner areas had spread east across the Sumida River where a number of new machi areas, including Honjo and Fukagawa were laid out in the eighteenth century, and along several of the main roads leading into the city, as shown in Figure 1.3. Commoner areas had also spread into several lowland areas between the hills of the Yamanote west and south of the castle which had formerly been agricultural villages located among the samurai districts on the hills. Because space was often constricted in these winding valleys, they often did not follow the regular grid pattern typical of commoner areas in the flat lowland areas of the shitamachi (Jinnai 1990: 146).

By far the dominant pattern of the commoner areas of the shitamachi, however, was that of a regular grid of square blocks, each measuring 60 ken by 60 ken, as shown in Figure 1.5. As one ken measured about 1.8 metres, that created a block measuring about 109 metres by 109 metres. Each such block was called a chō, and had an area of

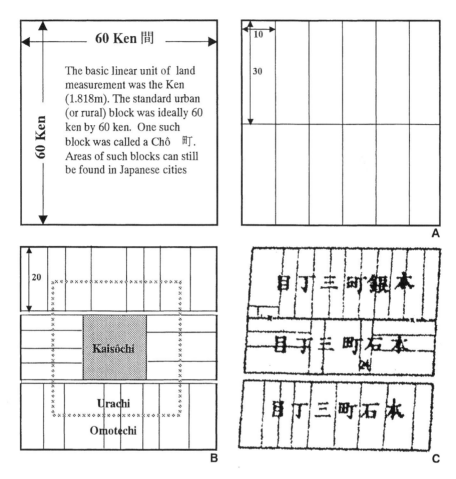

Figure 1.5 The traditional Japanese land measurement system. The traditional system created a grid of blocks measuring about 109 × 109m. In rural areas and in the Hatamoto districts of Edo, each block was commonly divided into 12 sections measuring 10 ken by 30 ken as shown in block "A" above. Block "B" shows the most common subdivision method in the machi areas of Edo where the normal lot depth was 20 ken, thus dividing the standard block into three. Block "C" shows an actual example from the Nihonbashi area of central Edo shown in Figure 1.6.

about 1.2 hectares. The blocks were based on the standard land measurement units borrowed from China at the time of the building of Nara and Kyoto in the eighth century. In the rural context, and in the Hatamoto districts described below, these blocks were further subdivided into 12 sections (*tan*) measuring 10 ken by 30 ken (992 square metres), as shown in block A of Figure 1.5. The tan is still a common size of rice paddy in rural areas today. In the commoner districts of Edo, however, a slightly smaller basic plot size was adopted, and the centre of each block was left as an open space (*kaishōchi*) as shown in block B of Figure 1.5. This allowed some plots to face onto the cross streets, and the open space in the centre of the block was initially used for latrines, a well for the block, a garbage collection area and a neighbourhood shrine. With continued pressure on space and overcrowding in the central areas of Edo during the eighteenth century narrow streets (shinmichi) were built to allow access to the interior of the blocks, and virtually all of these open spaces were eventually built up.

The application of this land measurement system in an actual urban district can be seen in Figure 1.6, which shows the central part of the shitamachi north of Nihonbashi. This area reveals both the regularity of the basic scheme of 60 ken by 60 ken blocks, and the ease with which it was adjusted to take account of irregular features such as canals. Throughout the low city the main irregularities in the grid pattern are introduced by the canals which formed an extensive network. As Jinnai (1990: 128) has shown, water transport dominated goods traffic in the city and virtually all the canals were lined on both sides with wharves and warehouses. Also evident is the fact that while the blocks have generally regular dimensions, the width of roads varies greatly, ranging from 5.4 metres up to 20 metres at Nihonbashi.

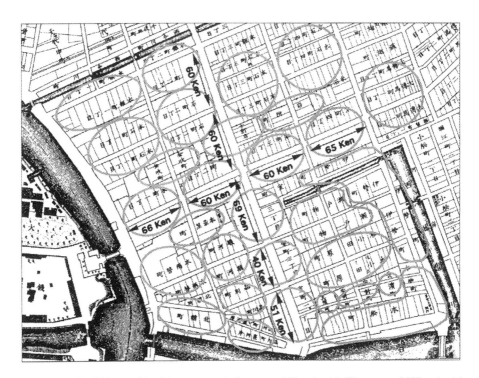

Figure 1.6 The Shitamachi grid system and chō areas, Nihonbashi. The area of Nihonbashi just east of one of the main gates to Edo castle is shown here in a map based on a survey completed 1888. Nihonbashi is the bridge just off the bottom centre. The east west streets align with a vista over the castle grounds towards Mount Fuji in the west. The grid of square blocks measuring 60 ken by 60 ken is clearly visible. Also indicated by the grey circles are the chō neighbourhoods which consist, wherever possible, of both sides of one block-long street.

Source: Detail of the original Tokyo 1/5000 scale Survey Maps produced by the Home Ministry in 1888.

Figure 1.6 also indicates the different residential neighbourhood (chō) in the Nihonbashi area. It is important to distinguish here between the three uses of the term chō. It describes the square block described above, the length of one side of the block (60 ken = 1 chō), and also describes the residential neighbourhood which formed the basic unit of urban administration. The block itself was the original neighbourhood unit that evolved gradually through various stages into the later pattern of the neighbourhood composed of two sides of a block-long street, with gated checkpoints at the main intersections at either end (see Jinnai 1990: 126–39; Mimura, et al. 1998: 45–7; Smith 1979: 78–9). The idea was thus transformed from a discrete block into an extendable row with houses on both sides of the street. As shown in Figure 1.6 however, variations on this pattern were common, and some such neighbourhoods were larger than others. The chō had an average population of around 300 people, and almost always consisted of a diverse cross-section of commoner society, from the wealthy landlords and shopkeepers who owned the handsome machiya shop-houses fronting the street (*omote-chi*), to the tenants of the *nagaya* tenements in the back alleys (*ura-chi*) who were usually either the employees and servants of the merchants, or poor artisans (Rozman 1973: 296). Land use was also typically very mixed, with two-storey shop-houses lining the main streets, and all manner of small-scale handicraft industry in both street-front houses and interior tenements, and high residential densities everywhere. Residents of an individual chō commonly shared the same occupation, as districts tended to specialise in certain trades. It is also clear from Figure 1.6 that almost all plots of land in the commoner areas are deeper than they are wide. This arises in part naturally from the fairly deep blocks, and from the tendency for some lots to be split in half lengthwise. It was also encouraged however, by the fact that annual taxes – originally paid for in labour but later converted to cash – were calculated on the basis of the street frontage of individual properties (Kato 1994: 49). This was a not uncommon device, and a similar tax had profound effects on the development and morphology of Amsterdam, for example.

As shown in Figure 1.3, the machi area included about 30 per cent of Edo and was centred on the Nihonbashi district. This area was virtually all plotted into a grid of square blocks, and was criss-crossed by canals and rivers. It was also tightly hemmed in by samurai areas with little room to expand, except into the marshy areas across the Sumida river and out along the highways to the north, west and south of the city.

Temple areas (jisha-chi)

The second main area was the area of temples, which were granted extensive tracts of land in Edo, amounting to some 15 per cent of the total area of the city by the end of the Tokugawa period (Naitoh 1966). In the eighteenth century there were over a thousand temples in Edo, large and small, with particular concentrations in the north near Asakusa and Ueno, and in the south near Shiba where the present-day Tokyo Tower is located. Although the temple areas were initially administered as one district of the city by their own magistrate, they did not form a contiguous area and were somewhat scattered.

The temples performed a range of functions. Their initial purpose, of course, was religious, and as part of those duties they took care of the dead, an essential function in any large city. Temples and shrines throughout Japan had also long provided the site for periodic markets and fairs and that function continued through the Edo period. Over time many of the temple areas developed into popular entertainment districts, as the temples controlled some of the only publicly accessible open space in Tokugawa era cities where large crowds were allowed to gather. Merchants and entertainers were quick to profit from the fact that the temple festivals and ceremonies often drew large crowds and the areas outside the temple gates (*monzen-machi*, literally "quarter in front of the gate") very often developed into thriving amusement quarters with theatres, tea houses, food stalls, and archery booths whose attendants were attractive young women who also offered more intimate services. In addition, shows and plays were performed on temple grounds and outside the gates. Jinnai (1990: 132–3) suggests that this was because the rules of the temple magistrate were more lenient than those of the city magistrates for the regular commoner areas. At any rate, the districts near temple areas frequently developed into popular entertainment districts (*sakariba*), which were the main centres of the development of commoner popular culture in the Edo era. Seidensticker's fascinating *Low City, High City* (1991) is an extended lament for the decline of these districts and the way of life they represented in the first half of the twentieth century.

The districts fronting on temples usually developed a characteristic urban form, of which present-day Asakusa and Gokokuji in Tokyo, or Zenkoji in Nakano are representative. Whenever possible temples and shrines were approached by a long straight avenue leading through the main gate of the complex to the main temple building, which tended to structure later development, as shown in Figure 1.7. As the numbers of pilgrims, festival-goers, and sightseers swelled, so did clusters of shops catering to the passing trade. These generally formed a long strip development of commercial establishments along the axial avenue. Even within the original temple compounds inside the main gate, temporary stalls selling grilled foods, pounded rice sweets and lucky charms had a pronounced tendency to transform themselves into more permanent enclosures, acquiring over the passage of time customary rights to certain spots that resembled a form of ownership (Yoon 1997). Most of the large and popular temples came in this way to be encrusted with various commercial establishments, and their once large temple precinct was gradually reduced in size.

One last aspect of the temples that must be mentioned here is their role as public space in Japanese cities. Before Japan's opening to the West in the nineteenth century the Western concept of the urban park as a public, green, open space that provided a place to stroll and a taste of the country within the city was unknown. As large green city spaces open to the commoner population, temples and shrines performed many of the functions associated in the West with urban parks. They provided the common people with access to large public spaces that were filled with green plants and tall mature trees, and by providing places for large crowds to congregate and for festivals and performances, they played a tremendously important role in the pre-modern city. There were important differences from Western parks, however. In Japan the green areas with large trees surrounding temples and shrines were symbolic of the sacred places in the mountains and were therefore of primarily religious significance. Western parks were wholly secular, and symbolic of the pastoral man-made landscape (Smith 1979). As the Western park was the responsibility of local governments, early planners took steps to secure park space as towns expanded. In Japan, however, even though

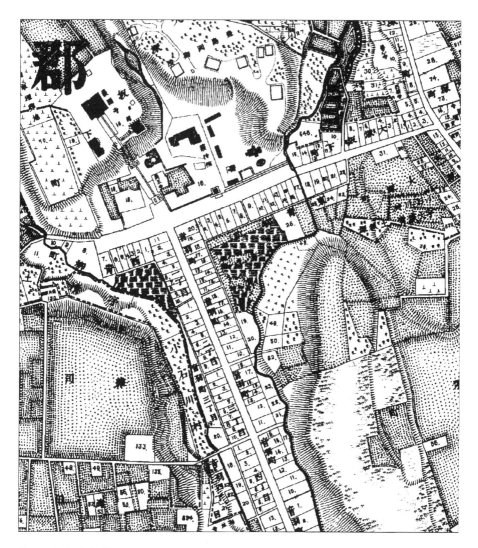

Figure 1.7 Gokokuji Temple and *monzen-machi*, Tokyo. Gokokuji and its approaches in this map from 1888 show the urban form typical of the temple and its *monzen-machi*, or "quarter in front of the gate".

Source: Detail of the original Tokyo 1/5000 scale Survey Maps produced by the Home Ministry in 1888.

temples and shrines fulfilled an essential role as urban open space, they were essentially private and religious spaces, and there was no tradition of public provision and maintenance of open park space in urban areas. While some temple grounds and daimyo estates were transformed into public parks in the Meiji period, as discussed in the next chapter, the idea of the urban park was slow to take hold in Japan and during periods of rapid urban growth in the twentieth century, little space was set aside for parks. Even

Figure 1.8 Asakusa Temple in downtown Tokyo. A typical feature of many temple towns and temple districts is the parallel row of shops lining the main approach axis such as at Asakusa Temple near Ueno in Tokyo.

Photo A. Sorensen 2001.

though temples and shrines continued many of their former roles as public spaces, they did not expand at the same rate as the urban areas they served and the shortage of public open spaces grew increasingly severe with urban growth in the twentieth century.

The samurai city (**buke-chi**)

Samurai occupied the largest area in most castle towns, about two-thirds of the total area of Edo with population densities of up to a quarter of those in the commoner areas (Rozman 1986: 294–6). The size of individual plots, types of land use and over-all configuration was quite different than in the machi areas. In the *buke-chi* land use was virtually entirely residential. That is, neither commercial nor artisanal activities were carried out there, but it should be remembered that the country's governance was conducted by the samurai class, and most of the actual administrative work would have been carried out within the larger compounds of daimyo and higher officials.

The main samurai area extended to about 5 kilometres from Edo castle in a broad arc to the south, west and north of the castle area. Another significant area was found in the east along the Sumida River and its canals. While the main early area of residences of top retainers and daimyo was to the immediate east and south of the castle in the area that is now Marunouchi and Kasumigaseki, by the eighteenth century when Edo was fully developed most daimyo had built a second and third residence further from the centre, and these estates were typically larger and greener than those near the castle. These large blocks of land were scattered throughout the city, where they were interspersed with areas of the residences of high-ranking Bakufu officials and the districts of the lower samurai.

Overall patterns of urban development of the samurai areas in the hilly areas west and south of the castle were structured by three main factors: topography, the basic road network, and the large daimyo estates. Topography clearly came first, as the area was hilly and incised by numerous valleys. The hilly terrain determined the early road system, with the main roads either following the principal ridges or converging on the castle in the center. A secondary set of roads followed the valley floors, and smaller ridge roads interconnected these two systems. As Jinnai (1994: 139–46) shows so convincingly, the ridge and valley roads which remain prominent today were the most important determinant of the area's overall development patterns. Main roads, including the inter-city highways the Nakasendō, the Kōshukaidō and the Atsugikaidō ran along the tops of ridges, and the most important daimyo estates either faced onto these roads, or onto smaller secondary ridge roads that ran at right angles to the main roads. As the daimyo had by far the greatest resources, when they built their second and third residences they selected most of the best sites within a radius of about 5 kilometres from Edo castle. Also, because they were building outside the existing built up areas, estates could be expansive and designed to make the best use of the site topography. In general the daimyo residences were built facing onto the ridge roads so that the ground sloped down towards the rear where ample gardens could be laid out. Whenever possible sites were selected along the south sides of the ridge roads, so that the estate was located on a south-facing slope (Jinnai 1994: 142). Considerable numbers of family members, retainers and servants commonly lived in the daimyo compounds which normally contained a variety of buildings including both formal meeting places and dwellings.

Areas for *hatamoto*, the high-ranking direct vassals of the shogun who administered the Tokugawa lands, tended to follow a different pattern primarily because the plots allocated to them were much smaller, averaging about 2,000 square metres. The main areas in Banchō just west of the castle were laid out soon after Edo was founded, and followed a modified grid pattern similar to that shown in Figure 1.5 (A), and represent a major example of a planned urban area. Hatamoto residences were distinguished by a gated entrance and walled compound with a handsome residence set in a garden. The principal area of hatamoto residences, just to the west of Edo castle, is shown in Figure 1.9.

Areas allocated to the lower samurai followed a similar pattern, although the size of the individual plots was smaller than that of the hatamoto. The residential areas of the lower samurai were the most numerous, covering about 70 per cent of the samurai city. The ideal pattern was a grid of 40 ken blocks with 20 ken deep lots averaging 300 to 600 square metres. The lowest class of samurai were not allocated individual dwellings but lived together in a larger version of the poor commoner's nagaya, the kumiyashiki. Because the lower samurai areas were distributed among the daimyo residences, and constrained by the hilly topography, large areas of systematic grid such as found in the machi areas were not common. Instead, patches of grid were scattered here and there as conditions permitted, as shown in the left side of Figure 1.9. As Jinnai (1990: 145)

Figure 1.9 Urban structure of hatamoto and lower samurai areas of Edo. This detail from a survey map produced in 1888 when the urban structure had changed little from the Edo period shows an area just west of Edo castle. Inside the outer castle moat on the right of the figure are Hatamsto areas, while to the left of the moat are lower samurai and commoner districts.

Source: Detail of the original Tokyo 1/5000 scale Survey Maps produced by the Home Ministry in 1888.

puts it "The result was a mosaic pattern of organic interconnectedness. Clearly, the organisation of the plots was determined by a balance between the planning that was characteristic of castle towns and a more flexible conformance to topography."

Apart from the areas of the hatamoto in Bancho west of the castle, and the area of lower samurai surrounding it, the samurai area was structured by the large daimyo estates established early on as country retreats. The much smaller proportioned residences of the lower samurai were crowded into the intervening spaces, wherever they would fit. As space became tighter toward the end of the period, residences of lower samurai, as well as commoners, were squeezed into every possible leftover space and along the highways leading out of town, and considerable haphazard development occurred. The prevalence of such unplanned development around Edo, which was particularly prominent in the second half of the Tokugawa period, is another indication of the weakening of the tight spatial control that had characterised the first half of the period when the basic structure of the capital was laid out. The samurai area, and to a certain extent Edo as a whole, thus exhibits one of the fundamental patterns still seen in Japanese cities today: patches of planned urban development – usually laid out in grids or modified grids – scattered among much larger areas that are organised only by a main road system which follows the natural topography and patterns of early agricultural development. The interstices between the planned areas are generally filled with unorganised, unplanned growth. For a variety of reasons, this pattern has repeatedly been recreated as cities grew during the twentieth century, as will be shown in later chapters.

The urban legacy of the Tokugawa period

Although the legacy of the Tokugawa era is diverse, it is possible to divide the main influences of urbanism in the period into two aspects. The first relates to urban traditions. Broadly speaking this includes the idea of the city and the understanding of urbanisation and traditions of urban administration, urban life and urban society. Here we are concerned primarily with traditions of neighbourhood self-government, the origins of the Japanese suburban ideal, and the low value traditionally attached to the "planned" urban environment. The second aspect is the built form of existing cities at the beginning of the modern period that provided the context for early planning initiatives, and defined the key problems that modernisers had to confront. These legacies are discussed in turn.

Urban traditions

Defining a particularly Japanese tradition of urbanism is much more difficult than identifying characteristic aspects of urban form, and any thorough analysis of such a tradition is beyond the scope of this book (see e.g. McClain, et al. 1994; McClain and Wakita 1999; Nishiyama 1997; Smith 1978, 1979; Umesao, et al. 1986). A few distinctive features of the pre-modern experience of urban life which are relevant to understanding Japanese urbanisation in the modern period do stand out, however. Perhaps the most important are the distinctive traditions of local administration, the strong tradition of vernacular architecture and town-building, and the pattern of class separation into planned, densely inhabited grids for the commoners and leafy, largely residential areas for the samurai.

Urban governance during the Edo period was extremely weak, and was concerned primarily with law enforcement. Central government retained direct control of the major cities of Edo, Osaka and Kyoto, and also of all other settlements in the core area of central Japan, which comprised about a third of the country. There were no municipal governments as such, with the central Bakufu or domain governments maintaining direct control through the system of magistracies, while most important urban administrative and maintenance functions were delegated to small local neighbourhoods which had to provide for themselves. Very little money was spent on Edo's urban facilities by the Bakufu, with the maintenance of the main bridges and dredging of canals (both important elements of the defence system) representing the only significant outlays. All other requirements were met by local communities themselves, usually at the level of the neighbourhood. Similarly, in the domains the castle towns may have been the seat of the domain government, but that administration was concerned more with the entire domain than the urban area, and normally only about 10 per cent of domain populations lived in the castle town.

The fragmented spatial, social and administrative structure of cities in the Tokugawa period has had deep ramifications. It was first and foremost an extremely effective means of social control, as it divided the commoner population into manageable blocks, each of which was run in the image of a family unit, as were the rural villages on which the system was based. The landlords (*jinushi*) and their agents (*ōya*) took on some of the functions of the rural landlord class towards their tenants (*tanako*) in the back-alley tenements (Kato 1994: 49; Smith 1978: 51–2). This structure was effective in preserving order, and it also contributed to the weak development of any civic consciousness of the city as a political entity, such as developed in Europe and North America. There was little political space between the Bakufu or domain governments as represented by the magistrates, and the local self-managed neighbourhoods in which the concept of the whole city as a political realm could develop. Although to a very great extent each individual neighbourhood was responsible for most urban functions in their area, Smith (1978: 50) emphasises that the autonomy of the chō units was granted on sufferance, and considered a delegated duty rather than a right. He notes that the commoner city was therefore merely an assemblage of independent neighbourhoods with no corporate identity of its own, and its governance closely resembled that of rural villages. One significant result is that the Japanese city was never considered an independent entity, and never developed a distinct civic consciousness as Eisenstadt (1996: 181) has persuasively argued. Whereas in Europe from the end of the Middle Ages through the Renaissance, independent, self-governing cities were able to develop their own traditions of bourgeois government and culture before the advent of eighteenth- and nineteenth-century industrialisation, in Japan that intervening stage was skipped and cities were plunged directly from feudalism into the transition to modernity and industrialisation. This is closely related to a point first raised by Max Weber (1958: 81–3), that although China and Japan each had long urban traditions, neither saw the emergence of a bourgeoisie or landowning urban class which identified its economic interest with the commercial success of its city. Although some degree of self-organisation existed, there was no concept of an urban "citizenry' or larger urban community to which individuals could belong, and the idea of the city as a corporate body did not exist.

Eisenstadt (1996: 182–3) argues that in contrast to Western cities, cities in Japan developed a significant degree of freedom in the commercial and cultural spheres that was not matched by a parallel urban sphere of political freedom. Most tax revenue in the Tokugawa period and the early Meiji period was derived from rural land taxes, which meant urban commercial, handicraft, and cultural activity was allowed to operate relatively freely. At the same time political activity was rigidly controlled, and alternative bases of political power were systematically eliminated, as for example in the case of the persecution of Buddhists and virtual elimination of Christians in the early seventeenth century. Each represented an alternative location of power and authority beyond the existing political structure (Eisenstadt 1996: 187). This resulted in the seemingly paradoxical combination of intensive development in the commercial and cultural arenas, with limited political autonomy or space for local self-determination. From a Western point of view it is hard to conceive of one without the other, as these two aspects were an integrally linked part of the development of cities in pre-industrial Europe. This also serves as a useful reminder of the potential pitfalls of interpreting Japanese urbanisation through the lens of Western assumptions about "the city".

These factors were to have important consequences for urban governance in the Meiji period and later, as there was little political space that might allow the development of either bourgeois or grassroots citizen movements, the consciousness of civic rights and obligations, or the development of the independent bases of political power that are necessary for the emergence of civil society. A space for local mobilisation of local needs has had to be invented in Japanese cities since the end of the Tokugawa period in 1868, and some would argue that it is still in the process of being invented. As shown in later chapters, this weak development of civil society is a distinctive and important characteristic of Japanese urbanisation which has had a great impact on the development of urban governance and urban planning.

Closely related and more positive in impact have been the enduring traditions of community self-provision of basic infrastructure, and self-responsibility for routine maintenance. Both the Bakufu and the domain governments had devolved most responsibility for the provision of basic public goods to the commoners themselves at the neighbourhood level. This was an extension of the ancient practice of encouraging village self-sufficiency to the urban context. The Bakufu also exacted a wide range of labour contributions (corvée) from villages and neighbourhoods which took the form of annual obligations to repair and maintain certain sections of highway, irrigation channel, river embankment, etc. Although the corvée was abolished in 1872 along with the revisions to the tax system, the tradition of community responsibility for local roads and public goods continued. As shown in later chapters successive Japanese governments have until the present made repeated attempts to encourage the continuation of the basic features of self-responsibility for local public goods and welfare services as a way of reducing state responsibility. One enduring result of this system has been the consistently low expectations of local governments on the part of urban residents. The provision of public goods such as sidewalks, street lighting, libraries and parks which are considered a normal responsibility of local government in other developed countries has been kept at the most minimal level, with significant responsibilities still remaining with neighbourhood organisations, as discussed in more detail in later chapters.

A second significant legacy of Edo era urbanisation arises from the institutional separation between the commoner (*machi-chi*) and samurai (*buke-chi*) parts of cities. These two urban worlds lived side by side for over 200 years, yet were enormously different in almost every respect. The commoner city was busy, noisy, crowded and dusty. The samurai city was spacious, leafy, quiet and verdant. The commoner city was planned, in regular grids with straight streets on flat ground. The samurai city was much less planned, with winding roads fitting organically into the hills and valleys. The commoner city was commercially and culturally vital and politically powerless. The samurai city was economically lifeless, followed an austere and disciplined aesthetic and wielded absolute political power. It is very easy to exaggerate the long-term impact of such a divide, but it is hard to believe that there has been none.

Perhaps the most obvious impact is seen in the almost universally held housing ideal of the detached single-family home set in a garden with a perimeter wall and symbolic entrance gate, which is frequently attributed to the desire to emulate the lost ideal of urban living represented by the spacious residential areas of the samurai "high city" (Jinnai 1994: 144; Smith 1979: 92–6). Their green, treed slopes and quiet neighbourhoods provided a powerful vision of an ideal kind of urban residential environment, and in great contrast with the commoner areas, individual houses had the privacy of a garden surrounded by a wall with an entrance gate, and were set in a sea of verdant green. The housing ideal of the emerging middle class which grew notably in size after the First World War was modelled on the spacious detached houses of the samurai elite, and the detached house with a garden became the goal of all those who could afford it. Since the Meiji period, therefore, the enduring residential preference of the Japanese middle class has been for a detached home set in a garden. This preference is thus of primarily domestic origins and is not an import from the Anglo-Saxon countries, although Western suburban housing ideals have doubtless provided it strong support. This preference has had profound consequences for the development of Japanese cities, particularly since the beginnings of suburbanisation in the 1920s. By far the dominant form of owner-occupied housing is the detached single-family home as in Britain and North America, rather than the flatted block as in continental Europe. Terraced apartment houses which became widespread in the great European cities and were built to house all classes during the nineteenth century were virtually unknown before the 1950s. Until as late as the 1970s apartment houses were built mainly as public housing in the suburbs, or as small wooden apartments (*mokuchin*) for the poor in the inner city.

The divided Edo era city provided another enduring contrast between the planned grid of the commoner *machi-chi* and the unplanned organic growth of the samurai *buke-chi*. Planned urban development has seldom been associated in Japan with a high-quality urban environment. On the contrary, the planned environment is more easily associated with the machi – the commercial areas of the inner city – and with enormous monotonous public housing developments for the poor of the post-war period. One of the distinctive features of Japanese suburban development is the rarity of the planned, exclusive, quality residential area. The better residential areas in Japanese cities are often the result of haphazard sprawl into areas of small farms surrounding the city. The comprehensively planned suburban residential development never emerged as a dominant form in Japan as it did in Anglo-American cities.

The legacy of the built city

Reformers of the Meiji era were less concerned with Tokugawa traditions of urbanism than with the physical urban legacies of the feudal period, both positive and negative. Japan at the beginning of the Meiji era was one of the most urbanised countries in the world, and boasted one of the world's largest cities in Tokyo. During most of the period urban planning efforts were directed primarily at existing urban areas and the legacy of the built cities greatly influenced those efforts. Among the positive legacies the most important were probably what Hanley (1997) has described as the high level of material culture and the high physical quality of life that developed during the Tokugawa period. More problematic were the extreme flammability of the cities and the generally poor road systems.

During the Tokugawa period Japan developed a very high level of material culture with cities, urban forms and buildings that were simple and elegant, well adapted to the climate and to economic and transport systems of the time and widely admired by many visitors to Japan (Morse [1886] 1961; Taut [1937] 1958). This legacy of a strong vernacular building tradition is not only a product of the Tokugawa period, as the traditions of samurai and ruling-class housing go back very much further. As Hanley has so convincingly shown, however, their spread throughout Japan and to the commoner population as well as the samurai was a result of the long period of peace and prosperity of the Tokugawa period (Hanley 1997: 48). Peasant and commoner housing developed from crude earth-floored dwellings of one or two rooms at the beginning of the period, to rather sophisticated carpenter-built houses of sawn lumber, with almost universal use of wood and tatami floors, cupboards for bedding, and sliding doors and windows. Hanley argues that these improvements were enjoyed first by the well-to-do, but over time were diffused among the general population to produce a "samurai-sation" of Japanese material culture, so that only the very poor still had earthen floors at the end of the period, and tatami flooring had become the rule rather than the exception. The importance of this successful vernacular building tradition should not be underestimated, as prior to modern building controls and urban planning measures a sophisticated tradition of urban housing and building had evolved. A relatively high level of housing was enjoyed not only by a tiny wealthy elite, but very widely among samurai of all ranks and a significant part of the commoner classes, apart from the poor. The vernacular tradition has continued to provide the image of ideal urban housing long after modernisation had introduced dramatic changes in other aspects of Japanese culture such as clothing.

Hanley also argues that other major factors contributing to the physical well-being of urban residents in the Tokugawa period included their high standards of personal hygiene, good water supplies, and simple but effective measures for dealing with night soil. Certainly the fact that daily bathing was widespread among all classes by the end of the Tokugawa period with public baths almost universally available in urban areas was a major advantage over the European case, where even as late at the mid-nineteenth century bathing was still regarded with suspicion or as downright dangerous by the majority of the population (Hanley 1997: 179).

The issue of water supply is more problematic. Hanley argues that urban water supplies in Japan were very good in the Tokugawa era, particularly in comparison with those of Europe (Hanley 1997: 104–10). As evidence she cites a study presented in Tokyo in 1877 by R.W. Atkinson which concluded that Tokyo's water at its source was exceptionally pure, and that although samples grew increasingly contaminated the further they were collected from the source, it was still probably purer on the whole than that of London at the time (Hanley 1997: 104–5). Considering the size of Edo, it may be surprising that it did not have worse problems, particularly when we consider the very serious contemporary problems encountered by much smaller European and American cities, where polluted water supplies and inadequate disposal of sewage and garbage resulted in filthy cities and regular epidemics of cholera, typhoid and other bacteriological diseases. Hanley is surely correct that the issue must be seen in comparison with other contemporary cities, but it should not be inferred that water supply was not a problem. Early in the Tokugawa period, when Edo was growing rapidly, an elaborate water supply system was created that drew on rivers and ponds in the hinterland to the west. It went first to the samurai areas and the castle which were in any case on higher ground, and then to the commoner areas of the low city. The water was distributed through a complex system of channels and ditches in the overland portion and then underground through a main conduit of stone and secondary lines of wooden planks with bamboo tubes which led to individual shallow wells where people could get buckets of water (Hatano 1994: 245). These waterworks were initially built by the shogunate at its own expense, but later the cost of maintaining the system was almost entirely shifted onto the merchants and artisans who used it, especially after the Bakufu and many daimyo and samurai neighbourhoods developed their own wells and disconnected themselves from the system because of the poor quality of the water towards the end of the seventeenth century (Hatano 1994: 247).

Water supply, however, became a serious public health issue during the nineteenth century. There is some disagreement about the prevalence of major epidemic diseases in early modern Japan. For example, Janetta (1987) suggests that major epidemic diseases such as plague were rare in Japan prior to the mid-nineteenth century, primarily because of its isolation. Hayami, on the other hand, claims typhoid and cholera epidemics were serious problems during the Tokugawa period (Hayami 1986). Both agree that epidemics became much worse in the nineteenth century, with serious cholera outbreaks in the 1860s and two major epidemics in 1879 and 1886 which each killed more than 100,000. As Ishida and Ishizuka note, by the end of the nineteenth century and early part of the twentieth, urban and industrial expansion had resulted in increasing stress in the slums of Tokyo, exacerbated by the poor state of the water-supply systems. The poor who were crowded in the unsanitary wooden tenement houses in the back alleys were particularly threatened by the prevalence of epidemics such as cholera and tuberculosis (Ishizuka and Ishida 1988c: 14).

Greatly mitigating the problems of urban water supply in Japan was the highly effective traditional system of collection of night soil for use by farmers outside the city. Because farmers paid well for this fertiliser, and because landlords' agents had the right to sell their tenants' products, management of human waste was a profitable sideline for slum landlords and there was little motivation to install expensive municipal sewage systems. The night soil collection system gradually declined in the early twentieth century in central Tokyo with the construction of the sewerage system, but it survived until the 1960s in the suburbs and other large cities where sewers were not built until the postwar period (Hanley 1997; Ishida 1994). From the 1960s the decreasing costs and spreading use of chemical fertilisers undermined the market for urban night soil. At any rate, it was partly because these traditional systems were relatively effective that sewerbuilding was given little priority in most Japanese cities before the 1970s.

Certainly the most serious urban problem inherited from the Tokugawa period was the prevalence of devastating fires. The flammability of wooden buildings combined with the high density of dwellings produced a high risk of fire, and indeed throughout the history of Edo in particular, and Tokugawa period cities in general, fires large and small were a constant fact of life. In Edo major conflagrations occurred on average every six years, and many minor ones every year (Kelly 1994: 313). Fires were known as one of the "Flowers of Edo" (*Edo no hana*) and were treated with a surprising degree of resignation considering their frequency and destructive effects. Although intermittent efforts were made throughout the Tokugawa period to introduce fireproof building codes, they were unenforceable due to the higher costs associated with the tile roofs and tiled or mud walls and the consequent stubborn resistance by merchants and artisans, despite their obvious self interest in fire prevention. Heavy tile roofs also posed higher risks in the event of earthquakes, and new regulations imposed in the wake of disastrous fires invariably proved ineffective in preventing the eventual re-emergence of the traditional wooden town forms. Kelly (1994) traces the history of Edo fires and measures to improve fire protection including firebreaks, building control measures and the development of lightweight roof tiles.

The inability to enforce building codes to reduce the risk of fire suggests the relative weakness of Bakufu authority in the face of commoner resistance, as does the gradual erosion of firebreaks such as the one at Edobashi discussed above. It is also possible, as Smith (1978: 50) suggests, that this neglect was related to the fact that the worst problems of fire were in the commoner areas of the city, while the Bakufu and daimyo areas were relatively safer, as they were separated by moats and more spaciously laid out than the crowded commoner districts. Certainly any measures introduced by the Bakufu were primarily designed to prevent fires from spreading to the castle and shogunal properties such as rice granaries and warehouses, and less effort was expended in attempting to prevent fire in commoner areas (Kelly 1994: 323). One area where much effort was expended by Bakufu officials was in organising and reorganising the fire-fighting brigades, and in forcing commoner districts to bear the burden of their staffing and costs. It was these efforts that led to the prominence of commoner fire-fighting squads during the eighteenth century, and the increasing identification of Edo commoners with the bravado and swagger of their squads as the emblem of the commoner city during the early nineteenth century (Kelly 1994: 327–30).

At any rate, the traditions of wooden building (and rebuilding) remained strong, and in the Tokyo of 1879, 97 per cent of all buildings were made of wood; 57 per cent were yakeya (literally a burnable house, or firetrap) with thatch or shingle roofs which easily caught fire from sparks (Ishida 1987: 27). The average life of the yakeya, which comprised a majority of the rental dwellings for commoners, was very short so landlords had no desire to invest in more expensive building methods unless everyone else could be compelled to do so as well. One of the first priorities facing Meiji officials charged with modernising Japanese cities was thus to reduce the risk of fire.

Another serious problem was the state of the roads. The street plans of the feudal era castle towns had been designed exclusively for pedestrian traffic, and had been dictated by strategic concerns. Streets in the town areas around the castle were deliberately kept narrow, as were bridges across the moats which were seldom approached directly by a through street, for easier defence (Fujioka 1980). As a result the sort of grand axial avenue that became popular in baroque Europe was virtually unknown in Japan. Outside of the machi areas roads tended to be both narrow and winding, and even in the machi areas, which had originally been laid out with relatively wider roads, the problem of gradual encroachment of buildings into the roadway was widespread. A recurring pattern was that merchant shop-houses would generally extend their roof eaves (*hisashi*) out over the street to provide a narrow covered walkway and protect from rain the walls of the building and any goods placed outside the shop. In many cases the space under the eaves became a semi-permanent storage place, and then was enclosed and included into the building. Apparently in the early Meiji period several local governments, including those of Osaka (1871), Kyoto (1872) and Tokyo (1874) issued ordinances to regulate the space under the eaves and reclaim space for streets, but only in Osaka were these measures effective (Ishida and Ikeda 1981). While both Tokyo and Kyoto repealed their ordinances in the early 1880s, Osaka carefully mapped the illegal eaves and buildings which protruded into the original street allowance, and after 1917 started a programme of compulsory demolition to reclaim the street area which was completed by 1940.

Another problem was that virtually all roads were unpaved. Even in the Edo period the state of urban roads had been a source of distress, as during the rainy season they turned into quagmires of mud, and in the dry season the wind whipped up choking clouds of dust. Paving of streets was thus a major priority inherited by Meiji city authorities. It is also important that the Bakufu government took little financial responsibility for the maintenance of urban infrastructure apart from the main bridges of national highways and the dredging of canals and moats, each of which were important elements for the defence of the castle. Responsibility was delegated to the leaders of the merchant and artisan quarters themselves, who understandably took a minimalist position towards spending their own resources on public goods (Kato 1994). This sort of street system was viable when most transport was by foot, horse or boat. It posed a serious obstacle to the increase of wheeled traffic which accompanied modernisation and industrialisation. A second major legacy left for urban administrations in the Meiji period was thus the necessity of widening, straightening and paving the streets and bridges.

A related issue that became of concern to modernisers was the shortage of public space such as parks. In the Tokugawa period the Western concept of the urban park as an oasis of countryside within the city was unknown. Instead city people used the streets much more intensely for all manner of outdoor activity (see Ishizuka 1988). Street performing in particular reached a very high level of sophistication with jugglers, storytellers, acrobats, dancers and impersonators all performing either directly on the street, or during festivals and fairs in temporary stalls in public open spaces such as the Shijō in Kyoto, Dōtonbori in Osaka, and Ryōgoku Hirokōji and Ueno Yamashita in Edo (Nishiyama 1997: 230). Temple and shrine precincts with their trees, ponds and gardens also provided green open public spaces. Although the prevailing passion of nineteenth century Western civic improvers for public parks had its influence on early Japanese planners, and public parks were included in some of the earliest town improvement schemes, the provision of public parks with urban growth did not become general practice until after the Second World War. In most cases the traditional pattern of neighbourhood reliance on local shrines and temples as public open space continued. This created serious problems later, as large urban areas were developed in the first half of the century with little public open space.

The urban legacy of the Tokugawa period was thus diverse, ranging from the physical patterns of urban areas to the traditions of city administration, vernacular architecture and the social and cultural understanding of cities, which have proved more enduring than the physical fabric itself. Ironically, Japan's rather effective traditional urban technologies and forms meant there was little pressure to develop effective modern urban planning systems in many cities in the pre-war period. Instead, a few key areas such as improving the water supply, controlling the destructive urban fires, and widening of streets were targeted, while broader issues such as controls over private development and building were slow to develop. Even in the largest cities it was primarily in the central areas that urban planning appeared to be necessary. In suburban residential areas traditional urban technologies and management approaches remained prevalent until the post-war period. Hanley argues that it was precisely the Tokugawa legacy of a rich material culture, good housing and high levels of physical well-being that allowed Japanese modernisers to focus on industrial catch-up and military expansion, while ignoring investment in social infrastructure, because traditional systems were so effective (Hanley 1997: 192). As shown below, this has contributed to some of the most serious urban problems of the post-war period, as investment in social infrastructure continued to lag behind investment in producer infrastructure, even after Japan became a wealthy and primarily urban nation. The legacy of Tokugawa period urbanisation has thus profoundly affected Japanese urbanisation and urban planning during the Meiji period and beyond, as discussed in the next chapters.

2 The Meiji period

Establishing modern traditions

Of all Tōkiyō, the city proper is the most densely populated district, and not the least interesting, as it is thoroughly Japanese, and few traces of foreign influence are to be seen. The Nipponbashi, or Bridge of Japan, is there, the geographical centre of the Empire, from which all distances are measured; the main street and numerous canals run through it, and every part of it is occupied with shops, storehouses, fireproof warehouses, and places of wholesale business, and their deep, heavily tiled roofs almost redeem it from insignificance. The canals are jammed with neatly-roofed boats piled with produce, and on the roadways, loaded pack-horses, coolies, and man-carts with their shouting and struggling teams, leave barely room for the sight-seer. No streets of Liverpool or New York present more commercial activity . . . loading, unloading, packing unpacking and warehousing, are carried on during daylight with much rapidity and noise. One would think that all the rice in Japan had accumulated in the storehouses which line the canals, as well as the energy, bustle, and business of the Empire.

(Bird 1880, 2: 177)

The Meiji period (1868–1912) was a period of enormous change in Japan, which transformed itself from a closed late-feudal society to a modernising state which was increasingly integrated into the world economic and political system. Although it is clear that urban planning was not the top priority of a government concerned primarily with the creation of new national administrative, military and economic institutions, a significant focus of government energy was on efforts to redesign Japanese cities, particularly the capital Tokyo. The story of the development of modern city planning in Japan thus begins in the Meiji period, as state interventions in processes of urban development were prompted both by the changing demands on urban areas arising from modernisation and industrialisation of the economy, and by the government's desire to project a modern and civilised aspect to the outside world in order to persuade the Western powers that Japan was a country to be treated with respect.

Because Japan already had a well-developed urban system and some very large cities at the beginning of the Meiji period, to a great extent city planning was oriented toward resolving the urban problems inherited from the previous era, and adapting Japanese cities to new economic conditions. This problem was similar to that of many European countries where large cities already existed at the beginning of industrialisation, although the problem was exaggerated in the Japanese case by the suddenness of the change in a single generation from a closed feudal society to an industrialising and modernising nation which rapidly incorporated Western technologies, industries and organisational forms. Reforms to government were wide-ranging, and one area of public administration that attracted repeated attention was urban planning.

Meiji leaders became increasingly aware of urban developments abroad towards the end of the century, and eagerly sought to import many of the emerging planning techniques by sending study missions to the West, and by hiring foreign specialists to work and train Japanese practitioners. However, unlike in other spheres such as shipbuilding, railways or armaments manufacture where the Japanese quickly caught up with Western practice, there was as yet no ready-made body of city planning knowledge to access. Even in the most advanced European countries, the concept of city planning was only just being defined during the second half of the nineteenth century, even though states had long intervened in the formation of cities. The new approaches were characterised by the introduction of measures to impose planning constraints and building standards on private landowners, the concern with planning and regulating urban growth to prevent haphazard sprawl on the urban periphery, the development of techniques to allow the differential regulation of different urban districts and the controlling of land uses, efforts to ensure improved housing conditions for the poor, and ultimately attempts to encompass whole cities and city regions with planning frameworks. As Sutcliffe (1981) has shown, although each of these basic elements of the modern urban planning project had been established somewhere before the outbreak of the First World War, no country had yet implemented an effective system to achieve them. The second half of the nineteenth century also saw the emergence of an international planning movement which was instrumental in the rapid dissemination of these new planning ideas through international congresses and organisations.

Although certainly a late developer, Japan's rapid industrialisation from the end of the nineteenth century to the end of the First World War meant that it was not in fact so very far behind other late developers such as Germany, France and Italy. Japanese urbanists were keenly aware of international developments, attending many of the international congresses and bringing back and publicising the latest ideas. Japanese planners quickly attained a high level of technical sophistication in plan-making, although actually implementing their new ideas was more difficult, as in Japan as elsewhere the development of city planning was as much a political process as it was one of technical advances, with plans requiring both political and financial backing to be implemented. As in the West, new planning frameworks were often opposed by political leaders who saw other priorities, and by established property interests who saw only increased costs without compensating benefits.

Understanding the changes of the Meiji period are important because many of the basic characteristics of the planning system that developed then have proved enduring. This is due in no small part to the fact that the urban problems Japanese city reformers and planners were dealing with at the end of the nineteenth century are, to a surprising degree, the same issues planners are dealing with today. These include the need to adapt large, densely built up urban areas developed in earlier periods to current needs, the lack of financial resources for urban planning and improvement, the resistance of landowners and local communities to change which might damage their interests, and the weakness of local governments in the face of strong central government planning and financial and legislative power. As will be shown in later chapters, both the conception of the main urban problems and the approaches to dealing with them which developed during the Meiji period have continued to influence Japanese urban planning throughout the twentieth century.

This chapter begins with a description of the essential features of the political and economic changes of the period, and a brief look at the processes of modernisation and borrowing from other developed countries. The second section examines the main urban planning developments during the period, and the concluding section summarises the most important characteristics of urban planning during the Meiji period.

The Meiji restoration

The beginning of the Meiji period (1868–1912) marks the change from the Bakufu government of the Tokugawa period to imperial rule, and from the late-feudal to the modern periods, or from early modern (*kinsei*) to modern (*kindai*) as Japanese historians put it. The edifice of Tokugawa power, while originally solidly built, was now old and top-heavy – and to continue the metaphor – dry rot had seriously weakened its main pillars. Long years of peace had softened the samurai class who were no longer the warriors who had established the regime, but bureaucrats and administrators. The serious poverty of many samurai, the heavy taxation on the peasantry, the increasing wealth of the merchants, Japan's self-imposed isolation from the world and technological stagnation all produced internal stresses that played their part in bringing down the structure when it was jolted by the external shock of renewed contact with the West in the form of the American "Black Ships" commanded by Commodore Perry in 1853 and 1854. Thus although the immediate cause of the Meiji restoration was the victory of the rebellious south-western provinces of Satsuma, Chōshū and Tosa over the Bakufu forces, the collapse of the Tokugawa social, political and economic structure should be understood in the context of the larger forces at work, as summed up in the Japanese phrase "troubles at home, dangers from abroad" (*naiyū gaikan*) (see Beasley 1995: 21–30; Jansen and Rozman 1986a).

The Meiji restoration brought fundamental changes to all aspects of Japanese society, effecting as it did the rapid elimination of the Tokugawa social and political order that had existed for almost three centuries. The new government abolished the old class system and guaranteed freedom of residence, occupation and religion. The old feudal fiefs were abolished and modern, highly centralised, national administrative organisations were set up in their place. Administrative centralisation took three main forms: rule in the name of the emperor as the central authority, direct administration through a unified central bureaucracy, and equality of the population through universal conscription, the abolition of the old class system, and the stipulation of uniform rights (Jansen and Rozman 1986b: 17). New national institutions of central and local government, primary schools, a national army and navy, a postal system and telegraph offices, police and law courts, banks, factories, newspapers, railways and joint-stock companies all were initiated during this period of rapid organisational change (Westney 1987). The Meiji period, and particularly its first decades, was a time of enormous upheaval.

The single most important motive for the reformers' zeal was national self-protection. Leaders of the period were motivated by the reasonable fear of loss of sovereignty to the Western powers. This was in part a reaction to the increasing presence of the European powers in the region, with the British, Germans and Americans active in China, the Dutch in the East Indies, the British in India, the French in Indochina, and the Russians in the north and encroaching northern China. Fear for national sovereignty was also reinforced by the "unequal treaties" imposed by the Western powers in the 1850s which had eroded Japanese sovereignty by granting foreigners extraterritoriality, open ports, and control over Japanese import tariffs, and which had helped to bring down the Tokugawa government. Exposure to Western military power, industrial technology, and international domination quickly persuaded the Meiji elite of the superiority of Western science and learning and the need to learn from the West. Meiji leaders believed that only by building Japan's military and industrial capacity could they defend themselves against Western colonisation. The main priorities of the Meiji government are summed up in the popular slogans "enrich the country, strengthen the army" (*fukoku-kyōhei*), "civilisation and enlightenment" (*bummei kaika*), and "revise the (unequal) treaties" (*jōyaku kaisei*). The Meiji period was marked by a national consensus on creating national strength in a competitive and predatory external world. As Jansen describes the transition, "With little large-scale violence or class struggle, a consensus was reached on the need for centralisation and on the sacrifices of group interests needed to achieve it. The goals of national prosperity and strength were quickly

Figure 2.1 The main Bank of Japan building, built during the 1890s and seen here from the far side of the Nihonbashi River where homeless men have built shelters on a disused bridge under the elevated metropolitan expressway.

Photo A. Sorensen 2000.

accepted in popular consciousness. Major reforms that established a new social order were adopted and implemented within a short time of their original conception. These are the features that stand out in Japan's rapid transformation from Tokugawa to Meiji" (Jansen and Rozman 1986b: 14). Japan's successful modernisation has been much studied, as the country propelled itself within the space of a few decades into the ranks of the world powers (see Beasley 1995; Eisenstadt 1996; Gluck 1987; Jansen and Rozman 1986a; Westney 1987).

Learning from the West

A central feature of the modernisation programme of the Meiji government was its process of opening to the West and learning from abroad in order to develop a country that could compete on equal terms with the great powers. Although the top priority was unambiguously the development of military and industrial capacity, Western influence was influential in a wide range of other areas as well. As Sukehiro (1998: 65) puts it, Japanese leaders "realized that the basis of Western power was not limited to weaponry; to the extent that such power was based on a civil society that had undergone the economic and social transformations of the Industrial Revolution, Japan's quest for power also entailed the building of political and social institutions based on the Western model." Because many Japanese leaders saw Western forms of industrial growth, socio-political organisation and urbanisation as being closely linked, and because the active borrowing of Western urban theories and planning ideas has played such an important role in the history of Japanese urban planning, it is worth examining the approaches to such cultural and technical borrowing.

The Iwakura mission to the West was without doubt the single greatest such initiative. Headed by Iwakura Tomomi, and including Kido Koin, Ito Hirobumi and Okubo Toshimichi (thus representing almost half of the elite group that controlled the Meiji government), the group was accompanied by almost 50 officials and 59 students who would stay behind at schools and universities throughout the world. Leaving in December 1871, only three years after the overthrow of the Tokugawa order, the mission spent seven months in the US, four in Britain, and then made shorter visits to France, Belgium, Holland and Germany before returning to Japan in 1873. They inspected parliaments, government departments, military facilities, factories, museums, schools, and institutions of every sort, as well as meeting with heads of state and senior ministers in every country (see Nish 1998). While one of the main aims of the trip was to negotiate the revision of the unequal treaties, this was not achieved, and the main impact of the trip was on the attitudes towards the West of those who took part. The huge technological superiority of the West had to be acknowledged, and the participants all came back with a changed sense of Japan's priorities. As Beasley (1995: 87) puts it, "Kido came back a constitutional reformer. Okubo was for the rest of his life an advocate of industrialization. Iwakura, while remaining in most respects a conservative, accepted from that time on that the way forward would have to be in the Western manner." Most importantly, the trip produced a consensus among these three leaders that the top priority for Japan was domestic reform and industrialisation based on Western models, and on returning to Japan they cancelled the plans to invade Korea that had been decided in their absence (Sukehiro 1998: 64). The Iwakura mission, and particularly its impact on the top Meiji leadership was thus instrumental in initiating the period of "civilisation and enlightenment" (*bummei kaika*) during which fascination with and openness to everything Western reached its peak.

The travels of the mission also served to persuade its members of the inadequacy of Japanese cities. Paris in particular impressed the Japanese with its magnificent boulevards and public structures, recently renovated by Napoleon III and Baron Haussmann, and thereafter Paris long represented the urban ideal for many Japanese planners. More generally though, the trip made clear that even in such basics as road paving and widening Japanese cities were far behind even provincial centres in the West, and that great efforts would have to be expended to catch up (Ishida 1991a: 6).

The acquisition of "Western knowledge" took two main forms, trips abroad by Japanese scholars, bureaucrats and students, and the employment of foreign advisers in Japan. Several hundred Japanese students went abroad in the early 1870s, mostly to America, Britain, France and Germany, and studied primarily technology, mining, engineering, law and medicine. The cost of government support for these students was high, however, at about 10 per cent of the total education budget, and numbers dropped towards the end of the decade as Japan's own education systems expanded (Beasley 1995: 89). Foreigners were employed in large numbers to assist in the building of railways, running the new lighthouse service required by the treaties, installing factories, and teaching in schools. They were paid much more than the Japanese, and in large enough numbers to become a major budget item, so they were generally hired on limited contracts with the expectation that they would train Japanese to replace them. As has often been noted the Japanese were not indiscriminate in their borrowings but became increasingly sophisticated, trying consciously to choose the best and most appropriate model for each need. For example, they modelled themselves after Britain for industrial, railway and naval development, Prussia for military organisation, France for its effective and extremely centralised police, legal and education systems, and employed American expertise in frontier agricultural development in their new settlements in Hokkaido (Sukehiro 1998: 64). In the field of city planning, ideas were borrowed from Britain, France and especially Germany, as discussed in more detail below.

Japan was undoubtedly very successful in its adoption of Western technologies and methods in pursuit of industrialisation and military strength. The process was not, however, without problems. In particular the rapid social and economic changes produced stresses in Japanese society, particularly as a result of the increasing disparity between the advanced Westernised elite in the cities and the majority of the population, particularly those in rural areas whose lives had changed little. The rush to adopt Western institutions and technologies during the early Meiji period led many conservative Japanese to think that Japan was mistakenly abandoning its culture and traditions entirely to make a simple copy of modern Western states. They rejected the notion that Japan should uncritically adopt Western ideas as well as technologies and attempted to reassert the importance of Japan's own traditions in opposition to those imported from the West. Pyle (1998) convincingly argues that it was the huge cultural and institutional changes and the seemingly indiscriminate borrowing from the West during the 1870s and 1880s that was responsible for the development of a powerful conservative movement in Japan that remained a dominant force after the 1880s and throughout the twentieth century. Pyle suggests it was primarily those aspects of Western thought that fit well with existing Japanese values that successfully took root in Japan, while others did not survive the transplant: "Those values that emphasized ambition, hard work, the value of education, and the utility of science clearly had the force of history behind them. Other values however, which were drawn from the Western liberal tradition and emphasized the natural rights of humans, the freedom of the individual, the rights of women, and so on, had little basis in Japanese experience and relatively little social support" (Pyle 1998: 105). The beginning of the end of the "civilisation and enlightenment" period is symbolised by the issuance of the Imperial Rescript on Education of 1890 which reasserted traditional Japanese moral values of loyalty, obligation, solidarity and duty to superiors. The 1880s and 1890s saw an increasing volume of criticism of the ideals of the Japanese "Enlightenment". The project of learning from the West and borrowing Western technological, social and political forms became highly politicised, and was eclipsed by the nationalistic and conservative movement to reassert traditional Japanese values.

The new Meiji constitution and national political structure

While the 1870s had been spent consolidating the political power of the new government, it was during the 1880s that steps toward the creation of a new national political structure were begun. A political crisis in 1881 – sparked by the Freedom and Citizens' Rights Movement (*jiyū-minken undō*) which advocated the establishment of constitutional government and an elected parliament – and exacerbated by disagreements amongst the ruling group which had up to that point ruled effectively as a military government, led to the promise to establish a parliament by 1890. In 1885 a cabinet system of rule was introduced, and in 1888 a Privy Council was formed to advise on important issues, including the drafting of a new constitution. The Imperial Japanese Constitution was promulgated in 1889 and came into effect in 1890. The constitution was said to have been bestowed by the Emperor Meiji, and is distinguished by the fact that it was conceived by the ruling elite as a gift to the people from the emperor, and not won by the people through political processes, as had been common in other constitutional states. The emperor became a central figure in legitimising the state, and in theory held the main levers of effective power. In practice, however, he was outside politics, and real power was held by the oligarchs and the bureaucrats who were charged with giving him advice and communicating his wishes.

A two-chamber Diet was established, with the upper house appointed and the lower house elected by an electorate limited to males over 25 years who paid at least 15 yen per year in direct taxes. This resulted in an extremely restricted electorate comprising only 1.1 per cent of the population in the first national elections in 1890, and meant that rural landowners were heavily over-represented, while urban residents of all classes were under-represented (Gluck 1987: 67–8). The cabinet was to be the main executive organ, but cabinets were not necessarily to be drawn from the majority party in the Diet, nor were they necessarily responsible to the Lower House of the Diet, whose main power derived from the ability to reject tax increases. The Privy Council was given significant power to advise the emperor, to whom the military commanders also had independent powers of access. The rather undefined system of decision-making left real power largely in the hands of the ruling elite – the Genrō, or Elder Statesmen – who had carried out the restoration of the 1860s. After initial heated conflicts between the Diet and the ruling elite in the early 1890s, the main power centres in the ministry bureaucracies, the cabinet, the Privy Council, the Diet, and the military eventually found they had to cooperate with each other to some extent to get things done. The undefined structure of decision-making, however, and particularly the ambiguous role of the emperor is widely held to have enabled the bureaucracy and the army to play a central role in the political process (Eisenstadt 1996: 32).

Gluck suggests that the oligarchs had in fact been deeply ambivalent about introducing parliamentary democracy to Japan. Driven in part by the perennial sense of crisis among those who had seen the collapse of the old regime in the face of Western power, the oligarchs were preoccupied by the need to strengthen the country in the face of that challenge. As she puts it, "In 1881 the oligarchs had promised a constitution and a national assembly. They then spent much of the next nine years making the legal and political provisions necessary to insure that the beginning of parliamentary government would not mean the end of their bureaucratic dominance" (Gluck 1987: 21). As she sees it, much of that preparation was tied up in the creation of suitable national myths which would serve to unify the people's energies behind the state, and the parliament was intended more as a means of unifying the people than delegating real governing power to a representative democratic system. The new nationalism that emerged in the 1890s was focused primarily on unifying the nation behind the government, and encouraging the people to bear the hardships imposed by increased spending on the military and burdens of war against China in 1894–5. Gluck (1987: 36–7) contends that it was during the second half of the Meiji period from about 1890 to about 1915 that the key features of Japan's nationalistic ideology were settled. They centred around the emperor who was both a constitutional monarch and a deity, and Japan's distinctive concept of a national spirit or national polity (*kokutai*). This ideology was not formulated as a piece, but emerged gradually as an expression of the nationalistic reaction of the 1890s. Gluck argues that neither was it immediately or wholly accepted by all sectors of the population, but had clearly emerged by the end of the Meiji period as the dominant ideology, with profound consequences particularly during the inter-war period, as discussed in the next chapter.

Centralisation

The Meiji restoration was a top-down revolution of a small number of men drawn from the existing samurai ruling class and the aristocracy, who were acting primarily to further what they saw as the interests of national strength. It was in no sense a revolution of the people seeking a greater share of political power or the benefits of citizenship. This had implications for local government. As Steiner suggests, whereas a local government system that has developed from below may stress the idea that it exists to enable citizens to serve their interests within their own community, and that there should be some limits on the power of the central state to interfere in these matters, a local government system imposed from above by a powerful central state is much more likely to serve primarily as a means of furthering central control, and will stress the duties, rather than the rights, of citizens (Steiner 1965: 35). This was certainly the case in Japan.

One of the most profound changes carried out during the Meiji period was the increased centralisation of government. This was a reaction to the rather decentralised form of government of the Edo period when even though the Bakufu more or less controlled the daimyo, individual domains had a wide degree of independence in their own local administration with the main locus of bureaucratic control being at the local level. In the interest of national strength the reforms of the Meiji government were virtually all oriented towards greater central control, and the weakening of local government independence. Local governments established during the Meiji period were primarily a means of projecting central government power downwards to local areas, rather than an attempt to build independent governments at the local level. Prefectural governments in particular were tightly controlled by the Home Ministry, and prefectural governors were appointees of central government normally drawn from the ranks of the Home Ministry bureaucracy. As Yazaki argues, "Regional and local self-government in this period was not genuine democratic autonomy guaranteed by the national political system. On the contrary, it amounted to a system devised to strengthen central powers, backed ultimately by the authority of the Imperial office. The routine work of public administration was parcelled out to the regional and local bodies without a commensurate division of real authority that would make possible effective sharing in the decision-making processes of government" (Yazaki 1968: 298). Local government was thus conceived primarily as a vehicle for individuals and communities to fulfil their obligations to the state by carrying out the tasks of government that were assigned to them.

A central aspect of the Meiji system was that local governments were responsible for providing a certain range of services for local citizens, while having no authority to exercise governmental authority over them. Activities such as collecting taxes, fees and rents, and building roads, canals and bridges were all considered legitimate areas of local government activity, while functions such as policing, regulating industrial or land use activities, and education were all the exclusive prerogative of central government. This severely limited the range of activities of local governments. As Steiner puts it, "There could be no local police, no local control of nuisances, no enforced zoning, not even a local dogcatcher, unless a national law or ordinance assigned the respective functions to the specific type of local entity in question" (Steiner 1965: 50).

Many such activities, especially policing and education were in fact delegated by central government to local governments. This practice, now called "agency delegated functions" (*kikan inin jimu*) has continued to the present day and encompasses a wide range of local government functions including education, health care provision and urban planning. In the case of urban planning direct central government control of city planning authority through the "agency delegated functions" system continued until a new law was passed in 1999, and thus shaped the operation of the city planning system throughout the twentieth century (see Ishida 2000). The responsibility for carrying out a delegated function is normally assigned to a governor in the case of a prefecture, or a mayor in the case of a city. With regard to the execution of the delegated function the officer is then considered legally the agent of central government, responsible to central government and not to the electors or the prefectural or town assembly. As the range of such delegated functions gradually expanded, and could be delegated by any of the national ministries, the area of independent activity of local governments remained small. There was a continual process of colonisation of local governments by central government ministries which, having delegated a function, then could expand their influence by using local governments throughout the country as proxies. Local governments were thus primarily extensions of the national administration, and there was little local self-government as such.

The weak development of civil society

Although the transformation of Japan into a modern centralised state was impelled by the sense of national crisis, provoked by the fear of loss of sovereignty to the Western powers and therefore explicitly modelled on Western patterns, the very self-consciousness of the policy and the rapidity of the changes led to some key differences from the model. As Eisenstadt (1996: 24) suggests:

> These processes of centralization, economic development, social mobilization, and construction of a new political system with kernels of representative institutions were in their basic outlines similar to the processes of nation building in European nation-states – and in many ways were patterned after them. Yet very quickly there developed some distinctive characteristics of modern Japanese political, economic, and social systems. Among these, the most important was the role of the state in initiating changes and guiding the transformation of society. Such guidance was greatly influenced by the West in an effort to catch up; this resulted in a very high degree of centralization in relation to the level of development, and in the compression into a relatively short period of changes in state building, organizational formulations, and ways of life.

One of the most important consequences of this strong guiding hand of the state in Japan's modernisation was a corresponding weakness in the development of any autonomous public space and civil society which existed outside the state.

The urgent need to catch up to the West meant that the Meiji government imposed strict central control over virtually all aspects of society in the interest of building national strength, showing little tolerance for dissent and actively suppressing opposition movements. The role of government was to strengthen the country while the role of the people was to serve the emperor; his officials were to be respected and obeyed, continuing the tradition of "respect for authority and disdain for the people" (*kanson minpi*) of the Tokugawa period. Little political space was left for the development of independent conceptions of the public good, or for activities that might support them. To cite Eisenstadt again, although "the processes of economic development, urbanisation, and education gave rise of course to kernels of a new modern civil society – various associations, academic institutions, journalistic activities, and the like. But these kernels were not allowed to develop into a fully fledged civil society with a wide ranging autonomous public space and autonomous access to the political center. Public space and discourse were monopolized by the government and the bureaucracy as representatives of the national community legitimized by the emperor" (Eisenstadt 1996: 35). In this way the weak political position of the urban middle class was maintained, and the unusual lack of an urban political sphere – seen as characteristic of the Tokugawa period – was replicated and strengthened in the Meiji period. That was to have important effects on the development of Japanese urban planning, as discussed in more detail in the next chapter. It also had a significant influence on the systems of local government established by the Meiji government.

Local government reform

A new local government system was gradually created during the 1870s to replace the earlier Bakufu and domain bureaucracies. One of its first measures was the abolition in 1871 of the old feudal era domains which had been relatively independently ruled by hereditary daimyo. Whereas in 1870 there had been 274 independent domains (*han*), six major cities (*fu*) and a number of areas controlled directly by the Bakufu, for a total of over 300 administrative units, they were amalgamated in stages until by the end of 1872 there were 72 normal prefectures (*ken*) and three special prefectures (*fu*) (Tokyo, Osaka and Kyoto). Only after the feudal domain system was abolished could the work of creating new forms of local administration begin, although within the old domains a strong self-governing bureaucratic structure had existed which allowed it to emerge relatively unscathed from the turmoil of the period from 1854 when the old system began to crumble to 1871 when a new system was established. This structure remained in place throughout the transition period, collecting taxes, running the local police and maintaining public order and local government functions (Craig 1986: 63; Fraser 1986). The fact that many functions routinely carried out by local governments today were still the responsibility of individual villages and urban neighbourhoods no doubt also contributed to the smooth transition.

In 1875 regulations defining the new system were set forth, placing a central government-appointed governor at the head of each prefecture (*ken* and *fu*). These were responsible for police, maintenance of schools, other public buildings, roads and bridges, local disaster relief, river and harbour infrastructure, census returns and land registration. In 1878 elected assemblies were established in each prefecture to supervise local spending and to advise the governor. Governors had no obligation to take the advice proffered, however, and kept a veto on assembly proposals (Beasley 1995: 74–5; Yazaki 1968: 295–9). The electorate was limited to men over the age of 25 who paid over a certain sum in national taxes, resulting in the restriction of the vote to a rather small proportion of property-owning males. Also in 1878, all prefectures were divided into districts, with wards (*ku*) in the three urban fu and counties (*gun*) in the rest, each of which had an appointed official responsible to the governor.

In practice local authorities had little local autonomy, as virtually all decision-making authority was left with the prefectures, which were in turn firmly under the control of central government-appointed prefectural governors and run as an arm of central government under the Home Ministry (*Naimusho*), which was established in 1873. Steiner notes that in this period the Home Ministry "became an efficient bureaucracy, fulfilling their task with a jealous enthusiasm that prohibited the delegation of power to decide even the smallest details. It has justly been said that the establishment of the Home Ministry helps to account for the peculiarly centralised nature of Japanese government and that local government in Japan cannot be understood without reference to this bureaucracy" (Steiner 1965: 26). This centralisation of political and administrative power in the national government was thus an essential feature of the Meiji restoration. In contrast to the relatively independent domain bureaucracies, the new prefectures were under the direct control of the central government, and their bureaucracies depended on national, not local connections (Beasley 1995: 66; Craig 1986: 57). The enduring pattern of local government dominance by central government was thus first established at the outset of the Meiji period. The centre routinely delegated national responsibilities to localities, "from electing assemblies and collecting taxes to providing police and teachers and building schools. Since the government decreed, but seldom paid for, many of these requisites of state, seventy to eighty per cent of local budgets was devoted to executing national tasks on the local level" (Gluck 1987: 37–8). As Gluck further notes, however, local elites quickly became more politically sophisticated in demanding fiscal trade-offs and bargaining for local interests within the national political scene. Although it is true that there was a sharp increase in centralisation, therefore, processes of national integration were somewhat uneven, and became characterised by the particularism and dependence on political favours from the centre that has continued to the present.

One example of such national government burdens is provided by road spending. Improving the overland transport system was a major priority in the Meiji period, as the Tokugawa system had worked primarily to restrict movement, and the road system – suited primarily for travel on foot – was inadequate for modern industrial and economic development. Bridges over major rivers had been prohibited for strategic reasons, and virtually all road maintenance was paid for by fixed labour contributions from nearby villages (corvée). While road and bridge costs for improving national roads and building bridges was consistently a major budget item during the Meiji period, only a small portion was paid by the national treasury with over 80 per cent of the burden placed on local government taxpayers (Yamamoto 1993: 29).

The 1880s saw the beginnings of major changes to the Japanese economy and cities. In particular, after the mid-1880s railroad construction, increasing factory production, and the granting of increased municipal self-government at the end of the decade all served to speed up the processes of urbanisation (Rozman 1986: 320). The reforms enacted in the early 1870s freed the movement of goods and people and the policies of encouraging modern industry tended naturally to stimulate the growth of urban areas. A location on the emerging rail transportation networks along the Pacific Coast was crucial to urban growth after 1885, particularly after the first national rail links were completed in the 1890s. Further, the former castle towns which retained administrative and military functions via selection as prefectural capitals tended to prosper, while the majority, or those which had lost these functions languished. As administrative rationalisation had drastically reduced the number of prefectures from 302 plus Tokyo, Osaka and Kyoto in mid-1871 to 75 at the end of 1871, and finally to 46 in 1890, the majority of urban growth was focused in about 20 per cent of the former castle towns.

In 1888 local governments were again reorganised and a new, more detailed set of regulations for cities, towns and villages was promulgated and put into effect on April 1, 1889. Thirty-nine cities were incorporated, each with its own mayor (appointed from one of three elected candidates) and an elected city council, again with a tax restriction on the franchise. Local governments were empowered to enact by-laws applicable within their own jurisdiction, although only in areas authorised by central government laws, and substantial administrative control remained with the Home Ministry. The three main cities of Tokyo, Osaka and Kyoto were, however, considered too important to be allowed even such nominal independence, and could not have mayors of their own, but were administered directly by their prefectural governors. This situation lasted until widespread dissatisfaction with this unequal treatment led to a revision in 1898 which set up mayoral offices within the prefectural administrations for the three cities.

One important consequence of Meiji reforms to local government, particularly in the 1890s when the new universal education programs were implemented, was an increase in costs for education, policing and disaster relief, much of the burden of which was placed on local governments (Fraser 1986: 125). Central government was itself short of funds because of its military build up throughout the 1890s, and by 1898 the military accounted for 51.79 per cent of the national budget (Yazaki 1968: 379). The heavy burdens placed on local governments, with increased responsibilities and often less resources provided from the centre meant that they had little inclination or ability to expand their provision of municipal infrastructure. Instead they continued to rely largely on the old community self-responsibility system of the feudal era, which itself was based on a very limited conception of what such infrastructure entailed. Water was generally drawn from wells, waste was either recycled as farm fertiliser or collected by colonies of impoverished rag-pickers, drainage was via open ditches into the nearest watercourse, and the major maintenance obligation was of local roads which were invariably earth-surfaced. The main function of local government, and by far the largest expenditure, was thus for education and the police.

Land reform

One of the most important Meiji era policies was land reform. Restrictions on what crops could be grown were lifted in 1871, and in 1872 land certificates were issued and the feudal ban on the sale and purchase of land was extinguished. The land certificates, which were soon developed into a land registration system, were used as the basis of the new tax system. In 1873 the Land Tax Act was passed which eliminated the old rice taxes and replaced them with a 3 per cent tax on the assessed value of land, payable by the holder of the land certificates. The new revenue was to go to the Meiji state instead of the non-cultivating feudal class. This effectively abolished the taxation rights of the samurai and daimyo class, who were granted government bonds in commutation of their stipends. As part of its tax reform the new government carried out a complete re-survey of all agricultural lands to determine the area, value and ownership of land, and new cadastral registers showing property demarcations and ownership were drawn up. This re-survey took nine years to complete (1873–81) and cost the government almost a full year's revenue (Vlastos 1989; Yamamura 1986).

For the most part the land reform gave land title to the taxpayer, resulting in the creation of a class of small-scale owner-farmers, as well as the institutionalisation of a landlord class as the larger landlords tended to have the upper hand in negotiating with committees set up to carry out the reform. The old pattern whereby individual families farmed a number of tiny plots scattered around their village was now confirmed by the new system of property ownership and families' rights to land were recorded in the new land registers. Land was now a commodity that could be bought and sold, and peasants were no longer constrained to remain on the land – they could sell out and were free to leave.

In practice, however, although urban and industrial employment was starting to appear, there wasn't nearly enough to make a significant impact on the numbers of households dependent on farming. Most therefore stayed on the land, and the increase of the urban population was supplied primarily by surplus agricultural population. In 1873 of a total population of about 35 million, a little over 14 million were engaged in farming and forestry. In 1925 the total population had risen to almost 60 million, yet the number in forestry and farming remained at about 14 million (Beasley 1995: 121). It is significant that this important reform in land ownership was not accompanied by a diminution of rural population, or an increase in the size of landholdings. Most farms were still tiny and composed of numerous scattered plots, and increases in productivity were the result of improved farming techniques, rather than changes in the size of unit farmed. Nothing comparable to the enclosures of Britain, which created vast estates and pushed the landless peasantry into the cities, occurred in Japan.

The land reform of early Meiji created a class of small-scale owner-farmers, and ensured a stable revenue stream for the new government. It also caused a significant extension of the market economy, as farmers no longer paid taxes in rice, but in money, and were thus forced to market their crops to raise the necessary revenue. The change to fixed taxes in money from the old system of a proportion of the crop also created higher risks, especially for the smallest farmers. While rising agricultural production and prices proved beneficial to the farm sector in the first part of the Meiji period, during the 1890s government fiscal retrenchment, recession and deflation created widespread stress in rural areas. While larger farmers and landowners were able to ride out the difficult times, large numbers of smaller farmers fell deeper and deeper into debt and were forced to sell their land bit by bit to larger, more prosperous landowners. Because contemporary agricultural technology favoured labour-intensive production of small areas rather than large-scale farming by hired labour, as land ownership became more concentrated the larger landowners usually leased land out – often to the former owners – rather than operating it themselves (Francks 1984). During the second half of the Meiji period the numbers of farm tenants and smallholders who were partly tenants increased significantly, laying the conditions for the rural poverty and tenant movements of the 1910s and 1920s (Waswo 1977, 1988).

The Meiji land reform's abolition of feudal controls and establishment of a system of private property was important for the establishment of a capitalist economy in Japan, and also had significant impacts on patterns of urban development. As Sutcliffe (1981: 14) has argued, early abolition of feudal controls and development of a free market in land was an essential factor in the industrialisation and urbanisation of Britain, and the delays in land reform in early nineteenth-century Germany proved a significant obstacle to urban expansion in that country. In both Germany and Japan however, the fragmentation of land ownership and irregular patterns of property divisions resulting from land reform created significant obstacles to orderly, planned urban growth, and in both countries contributed to Land Readjustment or replotting, as discussed in the next chapter.

The land reform was equally important in urban areas, as it largely confirmed the ownership of urban land in the hands of the existing owners. The large merchants who owned most of the machi areas of the cities were confirmed as owners of the central business areas. While data on land ownership in urban areas during the Meiji period is scarce, it appears that there was a high concentration of land ownership amongst a relatively small group of merchants (see Okamoto 2000). The majority of urban residents continued to rent space in the nagaya slums or lived in employee quarters, as did the large majority of migrants to urban areas who began to arrive in great numbers after the 1890s. There was an equally great variation among the samurai class. While the ownership of the majority of land in the samurai areas of the cities was confirmed in the hands of the samurai families who lived there, often becoming the major family asset, not all families benefited in this way. Most of the higher-ranking officials of the Edo period had employed numerous samurai retainers who lived within their residential compound. With the ending of their stipends these former officials could no longer afford to keep such a large staff, and most of their former employees had to find new sources of livelihood and a new place to live. The major exception to these arrangements were the daimyo, most of whose lands were confiscated by central government. Their castles and lands in the provincial castle towns were appropriated and later became the sites of prefectural or local government offices, military barracks and other public facilities. In Tokyo the title to their primary residence, which had originally been allocated to them by the Bakufu simply reverted back to the government, and in this way much of the central area of Tokyo fell into public hands. This windfall was used in a variety of ways. Some of the property was sold, the most prominent example being the Marunouchi area directly in front of the palace which was initially used as a military parade ground and was sold to the Mitsubishi company, which still owns it today. Large areas were used for government offices and military bases, while some was turned into parks. The daimyo retained ownership of most of the extensive areas of their second and third residences, however, thus maintaining their status as the owners of most of the residential areas of the high city. These former estates were initially put into use as farmland, and were only gradually subdivided and developed, a process which continued well into the post-war period (Hatano 2000; Kato 1997).

Railway development

A final aspect of Meiji development policy that should be noted here is that the government placed high priority on the development of railways. The transportation system of the earlier Tokugawa period, which restricted overland travel almost entirely to foot with most goods carried in small boats and barges, was recognised as quite inadequate for modern industrial and military development, and the development of a new national transportation system was seen from early in the Meiji period as essential. It is not surprising that railroads were chosen as the mainstay of the new system. By the time of the Meiji restoration in 1868 the great age of railway development was already in full swing throughout the world. Extensive systems were in operation in Europe and the Americas, and the colonial powers were actively building railways in their various colonies. Those Japanese who had visited and studied in the West before the fall of the Tokugawa regime, including several of the Meiji government leaders, were well aware of the revolutionary potential of railway development. This was strongly reinforced by the experience of the participants of the Iwakura mission which had travelled by rail in the US and in Europe. One of the first initiatives of the new Meiji government was to begin railway construction.

The first operating railway line went from the port of Yokohama to Tokyo, and was completed in 1872 as the first section of a planned nationally owned line to extend from Tokyo to Osaka. A second section, from Osaka to Kobe, was completed in 1874 and extended to Kyoto by 1877. Built with British technology and paid for by a bond issue floated on the London market, the lines were much more expensive than originally projected, primarily because everything from rails and bridges to engines and engineers had to be imported. With the various demands on its finances, the government simply did not have the capital to complete the line all the way along the Pacific coast from Osaka to Tokyo (Ericson 1996; Harada 1993: 19).

This shortage of capital proved to be the main constraint on the building of the Japanese rail system. Neither the government nor private sources had funds equal to the enormous capital investment required, so development was initially rather slow. This situation was not helped by the fact that the government was initially keen to control railway development for strategic reasons, and only in the 1880s became more amenable to private sector railway investment when it became clear that it would be necessary to speed development. From the 1880s a boom in private sector railway investment was encouraged and guided by the government's national railway network plan designating which lines should be constructed first and to what standards. By 1902 some 4,843 kilometres of track had been laid by private railway companies compared to only 2,071 kilometres of government-built routes. In 1906 after many years of deliberation the government nationalised all but the local routes, leaving only 717 kilometres in private hands (Ericson 1996: 9; Harada 1993: 57). Private railway development was again allowed after nationalisation, but primarily for local suburban commuter routes which in the metropolitan areas had an enormous influence on patterns of urban growth, as discussed below. The strong priority placed by the Meiji leadership on railway development for military and economic development has had lasting impacts, as Japan continued to intensify its rail system in following years.

The beginnings of modern city planning

The early Meiji period was clearly a time of enormous upheaval and rapid organisational change. Understandably, city planning was not the top priority of the government, which was preoccupied primarily with establishing its own legitimacy, finances, and powers of control, and with national economic growth. The Meiji government did nevertheless put significant effort into city planning initiatives, and some of the enduring characteristics of Japanese urban planning are first apparent in the approaches adopted in this period.

The main town planning interventions during the early Meiji period were closely related to conditions in the urban areas and the institutional framework of local and central administration. As described in the previous chapter, Japanese cities at the beginning of the Meiji period were densely built up and populated, constructed almost entirely of wood, with narrow unpaved streets and inadequate water supply and drainage. While these urban patterns were – apart from the high incidence of fires – well suited to the earlier age, the desire to promote industrial growth, changing transportation technologies and increasing mortality from contagious epidemics required new solutions. The main priorities of urban administration were to reduce the risk of fire, build broad, straight, paved streets, and improve the water supply.

The institutional framework of central and local government had a profound and lasting impact on how these priorities were tackled. As noted, the dominant trend during the Meiji period was towards increased centralisation of the government. Most new institutions and town planning measures were therefore designed with a high degree of central control. In contrast with the development of city planning in most Western countries, where municipal governments frequently led the way in the design of town extension schemes, improved infrastructure and the building of workers' housing, in Japan centralisation of power and finance left very little room for local initiative. The small role of local governments and other local actors in the development of early planning initiatives meant any such efforts tended to reflect central government priorities.

The major urban planning initiatives undertaken by the Meiji government were all in the new capital, Tokyo. To an extent even greater than elsewhere, nineteenth century city planning in Japan was synonymous with planning the capital, and it is in Tokyo that most major new ideas were first tried out, only later being extended to other cities. This emphasis on the capital followed directly from the desire to impress foreigners with Japan's modernisation and civilisation and revise the unequal treaties. Early city planning initiatives such as the Ginza Brick Town, the government quarter at Kasumigaseki and the Tokyo City Improvement Ordinance were all explicitly designed with these motives in mind. Fortunately, to a great degree the requirement for an impressive imperial capital fitted in well with the other obvious priorities of fireproofing and improving traffic arteries and the water supply. The main problem with this Tokyo-centred strategy was that other cities were left largely to their own devices.

The first significant planning project undertaken by the new government was precipitated by a major fire which broke out on 26 February 1872 only four years after the Meiji restoration and while the new government was still consolidating its own control over the country. It destroyed approximately 3,000 buildings which had housed 50,000 people on 95 hectares in the Ginza area of Tokyo. This was an important site bordered by Nihonbashi, the commercial centre of Tokyo to the north, the Marunouchi district – later to become Tokyo's main business centre – to the west, the foreign settlement of Tsukiji to the east, and the newly completed Shinbashi railway station to the south which was the Tokyo terminus of the new railway from the port of Yokohama. Ginza was therefore highly visible to the foreign visitor arriving from Yokohama at Shinbashi station, who would have to cross the area to negotiate treaties at the government ministries, or to go to the foreign settlement and hotel at Tsukiji. Rather than allow the area to be rebuilt in the normal manner along the previous pattern, the government seized the opportunity to redevelop a part of Tokyo into an impressive and fire-resistant district suitable for the imperial capital. Leading figures in the Ministry of Finance – including Ōkuma Shigenobu and Inoue Kaoru – took personal charge of the project and quickly put together a plan to improve the burnt area. Within six days of the fire, a new plan with significant street widenings and a requirement for all buildings to be built in fireproof brick or stone was made public (Fujimori 1982).

The speed of decision-making can be credited to the fact the Meiji government was still new, and the structure of a national government in flux. It was effectively being run by a small group of military leaders who had overthrown the Bakufu. There was no city planning law, and no ministry with formal responsibility for city planning. Leaders of the Finance Ministry were thus able to take the necessary decisions without the need for consultations, or following any set procedure. Even though there was strong opposition to the plan by local residents and property owners, the government proceeded quickly with project implementation (Noguchi 1988: 79). They chose Thomas Waters, an English engineer who had been active in Japan since the 1850s, to prepare the building plans.

The top priorities were road-widening, fireproofing and a "civilised" look, meaning Western style. Roads were widened to four widths of 27 metres, 18 metres, 14.4 metres, and 5.4 metres, paved with brick, and separated vehicles and pedestrians, the first instance of sidewalks in Japan (Ishida 1987: 39). Buildings, either planned or approved by Waters, were mostly terraces and planned in relation to the road width they fronted on. For example, those on 27 metre and 18 metre roads had a 2 metre deep arcade fronting a 6 metre sidewalk, and buildings were 8 metres deep behind the arcade (Fujimori 1982: chapter one). Landowners were required to build in brick or stone, and virtually all of the buildings eventually built were in brick, giving rise to the popular appellation Ginza Brick Town (*Ginza Renga Gai*). The capital's first gas lighting was installed and roadside trees planted, contributing to the intended European flavour and, it was hoped, the revision of the unequal treaties (Noguchi 1988: 76). The Ginza project was begun in 1872 and wound up in 1877, with only about a third of the originally planned 993 buildings actually completed. Financial shortfalls, higher than expected costs, and the unpopularity of the new brick buildings which were considered too damp in Tokyo's humid summers all contributed to the early termination of the project.

There is some disagreement about the success of the Ginza Brick Town. Ishizuka and Ishida (1988b: 8) criticise the heavy-handedness of the government which carried out the project without regard to the opposition of local landowners, and which deliberately displaced the majority of the residents of the area, the poor tenants of the back-alley nagaya who could not afford the expensive new housing that was built. Noguchi (1988: 79) who examined the project from the point of view of its success as a redevelopment notes that many of the properties were vacant for a considerable period of time, that there was a high rate of change in the owners of properties from before the project to after, and suggests that even many property owners could not afford the new style of building. The new Western-style development was also a shock to some foreign visitors who arrived in Tokyo expecting something more exotic. Seidensticker (1991: 60) for example, notes, "Already in the 1870s there were complaints about the Americanisation of the city. Isabella Bird came visiting in 1878 and in 1880 described Tokyo as less like an Oriental city than like the outskirts of Chicago or Melbourne." Noguchi (1988: 77) similarly reports the disappointment of the distinguished Frenchmen Georges Bousquet and Pierre Loti who visited the capital in 1877 and 1885 respectively, and alighted from the train to find a city that appeared to them as ugly as American cities.

On the other hand, Watanabe (1984: 409) is quite certain about the project's success, claiming that it contributed to the formation of Ginza as a place of modern shops dealing in imported goods, and led ultimately to the emergence of Ginza as Tokyo's (and Japan's) prime commercial centre. Fujimori (1982), who is the acknowledged expert on city planning during the Meiji period, and who provides the most complete account of the Ginza development, also describes it as rather successful, and his presentation of the effect of the project on the enduring patterns of land values in central Tokyo is particularly convincing. Whereas in 1878 Tokyo had a single peak of land values at Nihonbashi, by 1933 the area of peak land values had spread along a 2 kilometre stretch of the new Ginza Avenue from Nihonbashi to Ginza Four Chome (see Fujimori 1982: 302–3, Figures 18 and 19). Fujimori also suggests that the Ginza area has dominated Japan's high-end retail market ever since the 1870s, and long remained the area with the highest retail rents. More recent research by Okamoto (2000), who has made a detailed examination of successive projects to redevelop the Ginza area, land ownership and land use change in the area during the century since the project also tends to support the argument that the early Meiji redevelopment project laid a strong foundation for the long-term commercial success of the district.

Of course, these evaluations do not really contradict each other, as the critical view focuses on the project's effects on the displaced population and emphasis on the social impact of planning, while the positive evaluation focuses on the economic benefits. As city planning projects often have a variety of impacts, such judgments depend greatly on one's values.

Tokyo City Improvement Ordinance

While the Ginza Brick Town was a significant project for rebuilding an important section of the central city in the Western style, and provided useful experience in rebuilding with modern infrastructure and road layouts, its larger impact was limited because of the relatively small project area. It became clear that applying such an approach over the whole city would be impossible because of the cost and the limited market for such expensive buildings. The larger problems of the "whole" urban area remained to be tackled. Even before the completion of the Ginza project work was begun to prepare a more comprehensive approach to urban restructuring. These efforts led eventually to the passage of the Tokyo City Improvement Ordinance (*Tokyo Shiku Kaisei Jōrei*) in 1888. This is generally regarded as Japan's first city planning law, and formed the basis of the national City Planning Law of 1919. As it was the main planning legislation during the next 30 years, and established the fundamental approach of later planning laws, it merits close examination.

As noted, the main urban planning problems during the Meiji period and later related to the need to adapt existing urban areas to the changing needs and conditions of a modernising and industrialising nation. In the case of Tokyo these replanning issues were particularly significant because it was already such a large city in the Tokugawa period, and with the termination of the alternative residence system and departure of the daimyo had lost a great deal of its population and much of its economic base. It did not regain its 1850s population until about 1890 and did not expand much beyond its Edo era boundaries for yet another 15 years (Watanabe 1984: 411). Planning for Tokyo's urban expansion was thus not an issue during the Meiji period, and this is reflected in the Tokyo City Improvement Ordinance which was concerned exclusively with the improvement of the existing built up area, not with planning urban growth (Ishida 1987: 51). Also significant is that this first town planning measure applied only to Tokyo. This established an often repeated pattern of dealing with Tokyo's problems first and extending the planning approaches developed there to other areas later.

Work on a new programme for improving the capital began in the Home Ministry in 1876 under the sixth Tokyo prefectural governor, Kusumoto Masataka, who set up a committee to study Tokyo city planning issues. It is notable that planning was begun before the Ginza project was complete, and only three years after the ministry was established in 1873. In 1880 the seventh Tokyo governor, Matsuda Michiyuki, presented to the cabinet and made public the fruits of these efforts in a proposal for the central city of Tokyo entitled *Tokyo Central District Demarcation Issues (Tokyo Chuo Shiku Kakutei no Mondai)*. These proposals were widely debated in the newspapers at the time.

The proposal was developed by the Urban Improvement Committee (*Shiku Kaisei Iinkai*), which included Taguchi Ukichi, an economist, and Shibusawa Eiichi, a prominent entrepreneur. Taguchi (1855–1905) was with the Ministry of Finance from 1875 to 1878 and was one of the most influential of the early advocates of urban modernisation. An economist by training, in 1879 he founded the *Tokyo Journal of Economics (Tokyo keizai zasshi)* which was modelled on the British *Economist* to promote the ideas of liberal free-market capitalism. Taguchi was also an important contributor to the civilisation and enlightenment movement, publishing between 1877 and 1882 his *Short History of the Enlightenment of Japan (Nihon Kaika Shōshi)* and achieving a wide reputation for his ideas. Taguchi was also active in politics in the Tokyo prefectural and municipal assemblies, and from 1894 in the lower house of the national Diet. Although he published frequently on the need for Tokyo port development, fire prevention and a building code, his most famous urban writing was his *Theses on Tokyo (Tokyoron)* published in 1880. Here he argued that full economic development of Tokyo and Japan required improved urban planning for Tokyo, centralisation of government power and economic activity, and an international port to make Tokyo the central marketplace of Japan as well as a great world port. This work, published the same year as the initial draft of Matsuda's Tokyo plan, was in effect simply an argument for its proposals which he had helped to author.

The Matsuda proposal suggested Tokyo's main problem was that it was too spread out, with too much disorderly development and a dangerous concentration of wooden buildings in the centre – particularly the wooden nagaya of the poor – which encouraged fire and the spread of cholera. The main thrust of the plan was to concentrate redevelopment efforts and spending in the central area to encourage the development of high-density multi-storey stone buildings to house well-off merchants and businesses, and so eliminate the poor wooden slums and their residents from the centre of the city. It included details on locations of public buildings, main infrastructure such as roads, canals, bridges, gas and water lines, fire prevention and building-control measures, the development of a port for Tokyo, the demarcation of areas for industry, warehouses and markets, and provision for parks and sewerage (Ishida 1987: 55–6). Paris understandably served as the basic model for the plans, as well as later plans for Tokyo, as it was considered the shining example of mid-nineteenth century urban planning. Also, a central issue in both cities was the cutting of major new boulevards through existing densely built up urban areas. The plan was to be paid for with a tax on goods entering the city modelled on the Parisian *octroi*, which had provided the initial income base Baron Haussmann had leveraged to pay for his massive reconstruction of the city between 1853 and 1870. The Matsuda plan also shows a clear understanding that a central goal of the Parisian reconstruction was to break up concentrations of poor residents in the central city by redevelopment into expensive housing. On the other hand the Tokyo plan's emphasis on the concentration of economic activity and port development in the centre distinguishes it from Haussmann's approach, which focused primarily on grand infrastructure and housing for the upper classes while deliberately pushing factories to the outskirts. Ishida (1987: 58) points out that although the plan was theoretically rather brilliant, including many technical innovations, advanced ideas for public parks and markets, and regulations such as a fire-prevention building code, it was never implemented, reflecting the lack of sufficient political support, administrative machinery to carry it out, or financial resources to pay for it.

One final aspect of these early plans for the new capital that should be noted is that they displayed a revealing lack of concern for the symbolic project of creating a great imperial capital. Instead the focus was on economically oriented issues such as widening main roads, restructuring the central commercial area of the city and building a new port. Most telling is that although the emperor had initially moved into what was left of the Tokugawa palace on arriving in Tokyo in 1868, when that burned in 1873, he and the empress moved to an old daimyo estate which was quickly renamed the Akasaka Temporary Palace, where they were to live for the next 16 years. While plans were soon made to build a new palace, they were not to bear fruit until the late 1880s when a new palace was quickly built in time for the proclamation of the new constitution in 1889. As a result, during the first decades of the new period the symbolic heart of Tokyo within the palace grounds lay quite empty, the den of foxes and badgers. Fujitani (1998: 41–8) argues that the Meiji oligarchy put little priority on remaking Tokyo into a grand ceremonial capital in the early years partly because of uncertainty about the long-term location of the capital, and partly because energy was focused more on the emperor's progresses around the country to show him to the people. In any case, the rebuilding of the palace had to wait, and the building of major ceremonial boulevards although later proposed, was never carried out, as shown below.

One major reform implemented during this period was a fire-prevention measure for the central area of Tokyo under the administration of Governor Matsuda. The immediate motivation for the measure was a series of devastating fires in central Tokyo during the winter of 1881, including one in January in Kanda, Nihonbashi and Fukagawa which destroyed a total of 10,637 buildings, the worst fire of the Meiji period. In February regulations provided for 22 fire-prevention zones arranged in long strips to act as firebreaks as shown in Figure 2.2, and tile roofs throughout the central city area (Fujimori 1982: 62–74; Ishizuka and Ishida 1988b: 39). This regulation was exceptional in the history of Japanese building regulation, as within the fire-protection zones owners were required to rebuild all buildings to the new fireproof standard within seven years. Other building regulations, before and since, have relied primarily on the normal process of obsolescence and have merely required that any new construction conform to the new standard. The 1881 measure was strict, and effective. Watanabe (1984: 408) credits it with the virtual elimination within a decade of the devastating fires that had plagued Tokyo for three centuries. The effectiveness of this regulation, and the strictness with which it was enforced suggests that the weakness of other contemporary attempts to regulate urban building and development sprang not from a lack of state authority, but from a lack of motivation.

In 1884 Tokyo's eighth governor, Yoshikawa Akimasa, presented a revision of the

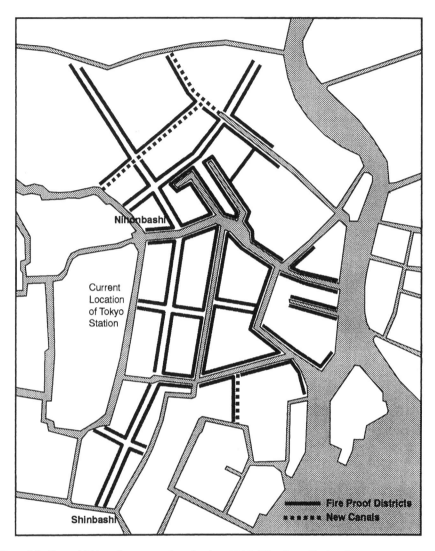

Figure 2.2 Central Tokyo fire-prevention districts, 1881. The first effective fire-prevention strategy in Tokyo's 300 year history was achieved early in the Meiji period by designating 22 fireproof districts in the central area of the city. The designated districts were long and narrow, and virtually all fronted on major streets and canals to reinforce their effect as firebreaks.

Source: Adapted from Fujimori (1982: Figure 25, page 306).

Matsuda plan called the City Replanning Statement which covered virtually the whole 15 wards of Tokyo (not just the central area) and outlined an approach to modernising the transportation system by widening and improving roads, building railroads and canals, and constructing a new harbour off Shinagawa. The harbour was again a central feature, designed to aid the development of Tokyo as a commercial centre, rather than just a government centre. Later that year a Tokyo City Improvement Committee was set up within the Home Ministry with Yoshikawa as chair. Over the next two years the committee further developed the plan and the proposed legislation to carry it out. These deliberations considerably broadened its scope, adding many more major and minor roads, and almost doubled its projected costs (Ishida 1987: 61).

During these years a rival plan for restructuring the capital was being prepared within the Foreign Ministry under Minister Inoue Kaoru. The German architects Wilhelm Böckmann and Herman Ende were commissioned to draft plans for a new government district in Kasumigaseki, the so-called "Project for Concentrating Government Offices in Hibiya" (*Kanchō shūchū keikaku*). This plan focused on the creation of a majestic imperial capital, suitable for impressing foreigners, in aid of treaty revision. It featured the creation of a network of broad ceremonial avenues along which would be aligned major public buildings, a new parliament building, and a new central railway station. As shown in Figure 2.3, the plan projected a baroque vision of the imperial capital which was heavily influenced by contemporary German urban design ideas. Although this plan was dropped when Inoue resigned to accept responsibility for failing to secure treaty revision, it did manage to delay the adoption of the city improvement plan for several years. In the meantime, the budget for harbour construction was diverted to the improvement of harbour facilities in Yokohama, a much cheaper alternative for a government strapped for cash and pursuing a major armaments build up, and the harbour development part of the improvement plan had to be dropped. According to Ishida and Ishizuka cancelling the harbour development plan had far-reaching effects on Tokyo's future development: "In the 1880s there remained various channels of selection, i.e., political city or commercial/economical city, or the city partaking both, but, reaching this stage, the urban improvement project having lost the harbor construction plan broke away from its compromising character, and began to step forwards towards a purely political city, or the Imperial Capital of the State" (Ishizuka and Ishida 1988b: 12). With the abandonment of the Foreign Ministry plan, the extended competition for city planning responsibility between the different ministries was finally concluded in favour of the Home Ministry, where it stayed thereafter.

The draft bill of the Tokyo City Improvement Ordinance (TCIO) (Tokyo shiku kaisei jōrei) was finally submitted to the Privy Council early in 1888, where opposition to its passage was led by Ito Hirobumi, one of the most powerful of the Genrō, and at that time chairman of the Privy Council. After three months of debate in which a wide range of objections to the bill were raised, including that the money should be used for armaments, that national subsidies should not be spent on urban infrastructure to benefit only one area, and that the works should be financed by a special tax paid by residents of Tokyo and not by national funds, the bill was rejected in June. Home Minister Yamagata Aritomo and Finance Minister Matsukata Masayoshi, however, ignored the decision of the Privy Council and approved the ordinance in the Cabinet in August (Ishida 1987: 64). The TCIO was finally passed into law as an imperial edict in August 1888, which proclaimed: "We authorise the government to promulgate the (Tokyo City Improvement Ordinance) for rearrangement of the city streets in view of the permanent advantages to be gained in the municipal administration of commerce, public health, fire prevention, and transportation throughout the entire urban area" (Yazaki 1968: 355). An accompanying provision for the financing of the urban improvement ordinance by a special

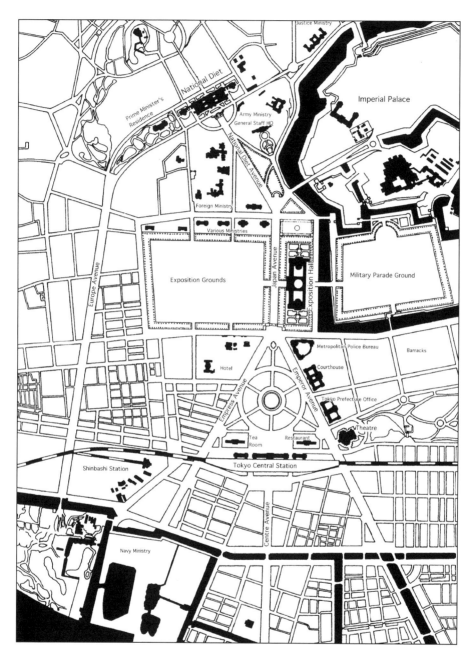

Figure 2.3 The Böckmann plan for the imperial capital government district. Two prominent architect/planners from Germany, Wilhelm Böckmann and Herman Ende, created a scheme of broad boulevards around which the main government ministries could be housed in suitable splendour. The plan is notable for its inclusion of a new central Tokyo station linking lines from north and south through central Tokyo.

Source: Adapted from Fujimori (1982: Figure 50, page 321).

tax on sake imported into Tokyo was also passed in 1888. Although this special tax eventually provided up to a quarter of the revenue for the improvement projects, it did not provide an adequate source of finance, and the project was ultimately sharply curtailed due to lack of funds, as examined further below.

Attempts to pass a building code

The passage of the TCIO was an important step as it was Japan's first modern urban planning law, and included the first overall plans for the restructuring of Tokyo. Before examining the results of that plan, however, it is worth looking at associated attempts to pass a building ordinance for the capital. While originally a bill outlining a building code had accompanied the draft TCIO, it was dropped when the rest of the ordinance was forced into law over the objections of the Privy Council. The failure to enact a building code was tremendously important because without it the TCIO became in effect primarily an infrastructure plan of road-widening and waterworks construction, and contained no measures to regulate private building activity. Thus, although the TCIO designated an overall framework for urban redevelopment, it could not require conformance to its provisions by private actors. Under its first head Nagayo Sensai, the Hygiene Department of the Home Ministry in 1886 developed a model building code to regulate basic minimum standards of road width, etc, in slum nagaya which was adopted by several prefectures including Osaka in the mid-1880s, although not in Tokyo (Ishida 1999). It was not until the 1919 City Planning Law was passed 30 years later that Japan had a national code regulating private building and construction.

The failure to enact even a minimal building code during the Meiji period was an important setback to the development of Japanese urban planning, and is worth understanding. The failure was clearly not because its necessity was unrecognised, nor for lack of active supporters. A code had been a central part of the draft bills and had been much debated. For example, Taguchi had often written of the need for a building code, advocating its necessity to prevent recurring fires (Taguchi 1881, *Kasai Yobō Hō*). Another important advocate of a building code was the novelist, physician and hygienic reformer Mori Ōgai (1862–1922). Mori studied public health for four years in Germany in the late 1880s, when Germany was developing the most advanced urban planning system in Europe. He obtained the report of the 15th assembly of the German Association of Public Health in Strasbourg in September 1889 which adopted a new building act stressing measures to create a more healthy living environment. On his return to Japan he published widely on issues of urban planning and public health including a full translation of the new German building act and recommendations for the preparation of such an ordinance for Tokyo (Ishida 1988: 84; 1991b).

Mori was appointed to an investigative committee set up by the Tokyo Urban Improvement Committee to draft a building ordinance for Tokyo in October 1889, after the failure to pass such an ordinance along with the TCIO. Although early drafts, compiled by an architectural engineer at the Home Ministry included measures for building permissions, fire prevention, building materials and structural safety, Mori objected to the lack of provision for town planning and public health. With the support of the Hygiene Bureau of the Ministry a counter-proposal was drafted which included the bulk of the measures of the German ordinance, along with some measures specific to the

Japanese tradition of wooden housing. Consideration of the draft ordinance continued actively until 1894 when the war with China broke out, but was finally shelved without being enacted. Two further attempts to pass a building ordinance for the capital from 1903 to 1905 and from 1906 to 1913 were again unsuccessful, and it was not until the passage of the City Planning Law and Urban Buildings Law of 1919 that Japan's first building code was enacted. Ishida argues: "the fact that no effective building ordinance existed until then was very unfortunate for the capital city because full-scale urbanisation began there in the 1900s. The suburban districts which evolved with no proper control from the early 1900s to the 1920s are now densely-populated inner urban areas, and posing a serious obstacle to urban planning of the metropolis" (Ishida 1988: 86).

How then to explain the fact that a nationally applicable building code was not passed until 1919? The need for restrictions on building materials and densities was well known and almost annual reminders came in the form of devastating fires. The worsening housing conditions in Japan's larger cities were also increasingly well known, particularly after the publication of the forceful exposés of Yokoyama Gennosuke (1871–1915) (Yokoyama 1899), an investigative reporter for the liberal *Mainichi Shimbun*. Yokoyama was inspired by Charles Booth's monumental *Life and Labour of the People in London* (1889, 1891) and documented the dire conditions of Tokyo slums in the late nineteenth century, which rivalled anything found in either London or New York during the same period. As is well known, increasing awareness of poor housing conditions among the working classes was one of the main driving forces behind the development of planning in those countries (see Hall 1988; Sutcliffe 1981). Efforts to draft an appropriate building by-law were ongoing in the Home Ministry from the early 1880s, and prominent advocates such as Taguchi and Mori had argued both publicly and within government consultative groups for their passage without success. Yet although the need was clear, draft ordinances on hand and debate intense, it was not until 1919 that the first regulatory system governing building by private developers was enacted.

Clearly a range of factors was at work. Political opposition to a building code, at least after the national Diet started sitting in 1890, is not hard to understand. The electorate was limited to those who owned substantial property, precisely the group that expected to be most adversely affected by the imposition of stricter building standards. Landowner opposition to the introduction of a building ordinance is well demonstrated in the Yokohama case where local property owners repeatedly mobilised from the 1870s to the turn of the century to oppose proposed building ordinances because it was expected that the costs of compliance would be high (Hori 1990: 99). Opposition within the Home Ministry was possibly motivated by anticipated difficulties with enforcement, as such a regulatory regime was almost certainly beyond the very limited capacities of the weak local governments of the time, which were still struggling with recent directives to create a universal education system.

The lack of a broader political base supporting such regulation was almost certainly an important factor. Individuals such as Taguchi and Mori were certainly influential, but they were far in advance of the general public in their advocacy of Western planning solutions. In Western countries such as Britain and the US, large reform movements were active in the fight for improved housing regulations. In some cities they or their allies controlled the local governments that were often the leaders in developing new approaches and regulations (Tarn 1980). Active professional associations of architects and engineers were also prominent in pushing for stricter regulations and more sophisticated planning, as is particularly well demonstrated by the case of Germany and Austria (Breitling 1980). In Japan, however, there was little broader political base of support such as the hygiene and housing reform movements or the professional associations of other developed countries. This is certainly related in part to the relative youth of the country's democratic institutions, with political parties still in a very early stage of development and organised lobby groups almost unknown. Political repression of government opponents was also widespread, and almost certainly contributed to the slow development of such groups (Beasley 1995: 75). The severe limitations on local self-government allowed under the Meiji system must also have been important, as there was little political space or powers for local governments to develop new policies independently. The lack of civic consciousness or active bourgeois civic leadership described in the last chapter was also almost certainly a factor. Property-owning groups in the West played such a large part in early planning efforts because as property owners they had potentially the most to gain by becoming involved in local spatial and economic growth. As discussed below, Osaka – which adopted the early building ordinance for slum housing of 1886 – may have been the only exception to this rule with its long-established dominance of merchants in local affairs. Osaka went further in 1909 with the passing of a more detailed local building ordinance that applied to all buildings; although limited local legal authority made it difficult to enforce.

Finally, the key issue of fire prevention was gradually being dealt with, at least in Tokyo. The Matsuda firebreak and roof-tile regulations were reasonably effective in preventing the recurrence of the massive fires of the early Meiji period, and other incremental measures were being implemented. The result was clear however. Meiji urban planning remained at the level of public works projects for building roads and waterworks. Regulation of private activity was only to come later, with the result that to a great extent urban building and urban growth remained outside the regulatory control of government during the Meiji period.

Implementing the Tokyo City Improvement Ordinance

In its final form, the TCIO included plans for the building or widening of 315 streets, improvements to canals, provisions for the extension of the main railway from the terminus at Shinbashi to Ueno and the building of Tokyo Station, many new bridges, 49 parks, 8 markets, 5 crematoria and 6 cemeteries (Watanabe 1984: 411). Top priorities were the road improvements and the creation of a new freshwater supply system. Financial support for urban improvements was approved at much lower levels than intended by those drafting the plan however, which proved an important constraint for those charged with carrying it out (Ishida 1987: 66). Further, with wars against China from 1894 to 1895, and Russia in 1904, state resources were repeatedly diverted to other priorities, particularly to the military and armaments. The main achievement of the TCIO was thus primarily in providing an indication of the future structure of the metropolis. Thus although much of the restructuring of the capital envisaged in the plan remained incomplete when it was wound up in 1918, the plan was essential in co-ordinating such redevelopment that did occur. Before the plan was in place, where fires occurred and areas were redeveloped, they were invariably rebuilt either along the former structure or as an isolated bit of improvement. With the overall structure plan in place, any redevelopment projects such as those by Mitsubishi at Kanda Misakicho and Marunouchi in the 1890s could be slotted into the overall scheme, with the hope that in the long run they would start to attain a more or less complete coverage.

Table 2.1 TCIO project spending 1888–1918 (10,000 yen (%))

	Roads	Bridges	Rivers and canals	Parks	Drainage ditches	Sewers	Water supply	Total
First Stage water supply (1888–1899)	297.93 (30.2)	8.86 (0.9)	1.43 (0.2)	1.97 (0.2)	23.06 (2.3)	–	651.9 (66.2)	985.16 (100.0)
Second Stage tram lines (1900–10)	1568.2 (79.9)	8.25 (0.4)	127.81 (6.5)	3.01 (0.2)	75.12 (3.8)	–	179.6 (9.2)	1962.0 (100.0)
Third Stage sewer projects (1911–18)	730.26 (57.8)	7.70 (0.6)	21.58 (1.7)	1.28 (0.1)	93.41 (7.4)	285.55 (22.6)	123.97 (9.8)	1263.76 (100.0)
Total	2596.4 (61.7)	24.81 (0.6)	150.82 (3.6)	6.26 (0.1)	191.59 (4.5)	285.55 (6.8)	955.47 (22.7)	4210.9 (100.0)

Source: Ishida (1987: 85).

Although the implementation of the TCIO was beset by financial constraints, a number of important redevelopment and city improvement measures were carried during the 30 years that it was in effect. This period is commonly divided into three stages; 1888–99, 1900–10 and 1911–18. The priorities of each stage are clearly evident in the share of funding allocated to the different types of project in each period.

As Table 2.1 shows, the priorities of each period were quite different. While in the first stage of the project two-thirds of available funds were spent on a new water supply system and most of the balance on road improvements, in the second stage priority clearly was given to road improvements, and in the third stage a significant amount was spent on sewerage projects for the first time.

The priority placed on water supply in the early years was a result of the serious problem of repeated cholera epidemics experienced early in the Meiji period. The priority on sewer construction in many European cities had followed from the incorrect theory that disease was spread by bad air, or miasma, and from the generally lower standards of sanitation in most European cities of the time relative to Japan. By the time the Japanese started to confront the problem in the 1890s, however, it had already been discovered that diseases such as cholera and typhus were spread primarily in the water supply, which is why budget priority was placed there. It was also directly a result of the restricted finances available for the plan, as the improvements to the water supply system were financed through a separate budget. The significant expansion in funds in the second phase and their use primarily for road improvements was a result of the scheme to exact contributions for road improvements from the tram companies, described below. This scheme was part of the revised and greatly scaled-down plan approved by the Tokyo City Improvement Committee in 1902, and begun in 1903. Most of the minor road improvements in the original plan were dropped, and energy was focused on building the main arterials that would carry tram routes. In the third stage of the plan, while the bulk of spending continued to be on main avenues, work was begun on a sewer system for the central city area. Drawn up by the English engineer W. K. Burton, it had been part of the initial plan announced in 1888, and had been repeatedly postponed for lack of funds. When the third stage plan was wound up in 1918 only a small portion of the originally planned sewer system in the central city had been completed. As Seidensticker (1991: 83) explains:

> Sewers scarcely existed at the end of Meiji. Kanda had a tile-lined ditch for the disposal of kitchen wastes, but body wastes were left to the *owaiya* with his dippers and buckets and carts and his call of *owai owai* as he made his way through the streets. It was still a seller's market at the end of Meiji; the *owaiya* paid for his commodity. The price was falling rapidly, however, because the growth of the city and the retreat of the farmlands to greater distances made it more and more difficult for the farmer to reach the inner wards. The problem grew to crisis proportions in the Taishō period, as the seller's market changed to a buyer's and in some parts of the city it was not possible to get rid of the stuff. Shinjuku, on the western edge of the city, was known as the great anus of Tokyo. Every evening there would be a rush hour when the great lines of sewage carts formed a traffic jam.

Most of the small amount of funds available for park development were spent on the development of Hibiya Park, the only part of the Foreign Ministry's imperial capital plan to be carried out. This provided a focus for the new government district of ministry offices emerging on the south side of the Imperial Palace on the vacated estates of former daimyo residences. It is worth noting, however, that Hibiya park was not intended primarily as a pleasure park for the use of the people, but as a part of the complex of government buildings, designed both to give a sense of imperial grandeur to the government quarter and act as a firebreak between it and the dense commercial areas of Ginza and Shinbashi (Koshizawa 1991: 5; Maejima 1989).

Other indirect effects of the plan were very important in the changing aspect of Tokyo during this period, however. Perhaps the most important was the sale in 1890 to Mitsubishi of an old military parade ground adjacent to the imperial palace, which it gradually developed as a new central business district, popularly known as the Marunouchi "One Block London" (*Iccho Rondon*) after the Victorian British-style brick and stone buildings built by Mitsubishi. A second key feature included in the plan, but not financed by its budget, was the building of the Tokyo Central Station in front of Marunouchi. Along with the linking of Shinbashi station in the south with Ueno in the north, Tokyo Station is an excellent example of Japanese planning at its best. The planners had clearly learned from the experience of European cities such as London and Paris, where the various rail lines from the provinces each had their own terminus near the edge of the urban core. This created long-term problems in national and metropolitan transportation networks which were only resolved in Paris with the development of the RER network in the 1970s and 1980s, and in London in the 1990s with Thameslink which joins Blackfriars station north of the Thames with London Bridge station to the south, and the much postponed Crossrail, which if built, will connect Liverpool Street Station in the east with Paddington in the west. The new Tokyo

Station neatly solved this problem, and made possible the famous Yamanote loop line which formed the basic element of the capital's commuter rail system, and which has long been one of the busiest rail lines in the world. It was thus during this period that the essential features of Tokyo as a modern imperial capital city started to emerge: the central business district of Marunouchi, the national government centre of Kasumigaseki and the upscale commercial district in Ginza.

Tram development

The tram was an import from the US where, as Jackson (1985) has shown, electric tram lines spread very quickly after basic technical problems were worked out in the late 1880s. By the end of 1903, 98 per cent of America's 30,000 miles of street railway had been electrified (Jackson 1985: 111). The tram was so well adapted to the needs of the time that it quickly spread around the world. Its lower operating costs compared with the old horse-car systems which had high costs in animals, feed and stables allowed reductions in fares, while the improvements in speed to a maximum of 20 miles per hour and averages of 10–15 miles per hour made them more attractive to riders, as well as allowing the extension of lines to a greater distance from the centre.

The first electric tram route in Japan was that of Kyoto which began operations in 1895. In Tokyo the first line was between Shinagawa and Shinbashi, which was opened in August 1903 along the line of a former horse-car route. By November the whole line from Shinagawa to Ueno was in service. In the same year a second electric tram company opened its first route from Yurakuchō to Kanda, and the following year a third company opened a line from Iidamachi to Ochanomizu. From these beginnings electric tram service developed rapidly, and was intimately connected with the completion of the road system envisaged by the TCIO. Because expansion of the tram system was dependent on the widening and straightening of main roads designated by the TCIO, and because the street railways needed local government permission to be able to lay track in the public right of way, the Tokyo government was quick to seize this opportunity to extract financial contributions for completion of main roads from the tram companies. Starting in September 1903, within a month of the opening of the first route, a new scheme was initiated whereby tram companies were required to pay half the construction costs of roads on which their routes ran, and a third of their net profits to the city. In the eight years from 1903 this raised about 3.94 million yen (Ishizuka and Ishida 1988a: 43), and was a major source of finance to complete the TCIO road network. In 1906 the three Tokyo tram companies merged to form the Tokyo Railway Company (*Tōkyō Tetsudō Kaisha*), and in 1911 the city of Tokyo bought the company and thereafter ran the tram system itself. By that point there were 190 kilometres of routes and 1,054 trams in operation (Ishizuka and Ishida 1988a: 44). Passenger volumes rose very quickly. While in 1908 the average number of riders was 446,000, by 1917 that figure had almost doubled to 812,000 (Yazaki 1968: 445).

In the longer run the most important influence of the development of the electric tram system was that it caused important changes in Tokyo's urban structure. These resulted partly from the creation of trunk roads by widening and partly because the trams allowed people to travel much longer distances than they had previously been capable of on foot. It is in this period that significant suburbanisation began in the

Figure 2.4 Trams on Ginza Avenue. Extensive streetcar systems were developed in Tokyo and Osaka during the first decades of the twentieth century in conjunction with major road-widening projects.

Source: Mainichi Shimbun.

fringes around the existing built up area of Tokyo. The trams also meant that many who lived on the edges of the city could travel into the centre to do their shopping, which created a much larger market for big department stores such as Shirokiya and Matsuya, and major shopping districts developed around the places most accessible to trams such as the Ginza, Ueno, and Kanda (Koshizawa 1991: 9).

Developments outside Tokyo

Although Japanese planning efforts were clearly focused on Tokyo during the Meiji period, plans were also being developed for other cities. Notable among these were Osaka and the colonial outpost of Sapporo in Hokkaido.

Planning of Osaka is of particular interest, as some of the most important limitations and strengths of Meiji era planning are clearly visible here. Osaka had occupied an important place in the Japanese urban system during the Edo period as the commercial capital of the country, while Edo was the political capital. Osaka was dominated by its merchant class, which had far outnumbered the small samurai contingent during the Tokugawa period, and had developed a strong tradition of merchant guilds and a degree of self-government. If any city was going to develop a different planning approach from that in Tokyo, surely it would have been Osaka.

The immediate post-restoration years were difficult for Osaka, as in Tokyo, but for different reasons. The restoration caused the collapse of the old Edo mercantile system and Osaka, as the hub of that system, bore the brunt of its collapse. Osaka merchants had developed a sophisticated national financial system based on the city's own silver-based currency, bills of exchange and credit notes issued by the city wholesale brokers. These were all rendered worthless when the central government suspended the Osaka currency in 1868. Further, a major source of the city's trade had been provided by the feudal domain-owned storehouses in the city, from which they supplied national markets for their domain produce. These warehouses were largely closed with the creation of the modern prefectures in 1871, and the debts of the old domains – largely held by Osaka merchant houses – were repudiated in 1875. Whereas Osaka had had a peak Edo era population of 500,000, that had been reduced to 290,000 by 1878 (Yazaki 1968: 317–18).

After the mid-1880s, however, with the establishment of the main Tokaido rail line to Tokyo and the growth of the industrial economy, Osaka became the center of the new textile industry with a wide range of factories established to produce paper, cement, motors and engines, and textile machinery. Osaka quickly became the main centre of commerce, transportation and finance, and its population grew to 340,000 in 1887 and 750,000 in 1897 (Yazaki 1968: 318). This rapid growth brought with it the predictable urban problems, and the Osaka prefectural government established a committee in 1886 to produce a city improvement plan. That plan was ready by 1887 and included a network of roads of different widths and provision for segregating dangerous factories from the existing residential areas (Ishida 1987: 97–8). Unfortunately the local government had neither the financial nor legal capacity to carry it out.

From the beginning of the 1890s Osaka began to outgrow its earlier built up area, and the attention of the prefectural government turned towards the issue of planning its growth. In 1897 the Osaka municipal area was expanded from 150,000 square kilometres to 550,000 square kilometres, an almost fourfold increase, and in 1898 Osaka's first mayor took office. In 1899 the city approved a plan drawn up by the French-trained architect Yamaguchi Hanroku to create a detailed road network for the whole of the new municipal area, which extended the city towards Osaka bay and a new port. As shown in Figure 2.5 the plan proposed a comprehensive network of arterial roads for the new urban area based on a larger grid than that in the existing city. It also proposed a major new port development, and the diversion of the Yodogawa river to the north to prevent flooding. As Ishida (1987: 99) has argued, by concentrating on the planned extension of the urban area this plan represented a major departure from the priorities of contemporary Tokyo planning, which was still largely focused on restructuring the existing urban area. For this reason, Ishida suggests the plan was a pioneering effort in modern Japanese planning, but as with the earlier one, the Osaka government had neither the budget nor the legal authority to carry it out. Little of the Yamaguchi plan was actually completed, the main achievement being a major new road from the main Osaka railway station to the new wharf which carried the city's first tram line, finished in time for the Fifth Industrial Exposition of 1903. Is seems possible that Yamaguchi might have made a major contribution to Japanese city planning, as he was at this time one of only a handful of Western-trained Japanese civil engi-

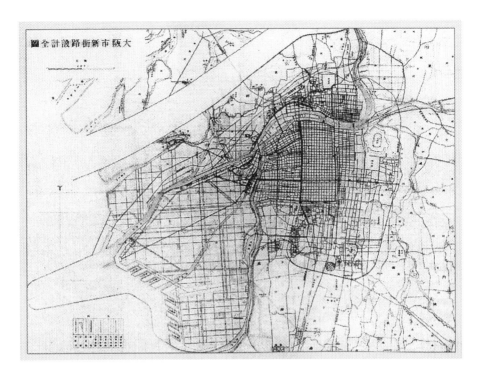

Figure 2.5 Yamaguchi plan for Osaka, 1899. This plan for the expansion of Osaka towards its newly built port is notable as Japan's first large-scale town extension plan. Note the tight grid of the feudal era town, and the larger grid of the new area.

Source: Osaka Municipal Government (2000).

neer/architects, and showed a promising approach to major planning issues. Unfortunately he died in 1900 at the age of 43, shortly after setting up his own architectural consulting firm, and designing the new prefectural government offices for Hyogo in Kobe (Miwa 2000).

The main progress towards improving the urban road network was accomplished by linking road improvements with electric tram development. This was particularly important because while Osaka had a regular grid for most of its central area, the roads were all very narrow, with the main east-west streets just 7.8 metres wide, and north-south streets only 6 metres wide. In contrast with Tokyo, however, in Osaka the tram system was from the start operated as a municipal enterprise. Although private entrepreneurs had proposed a plan for tram construction, Osaka Mayor Tsuruhara Sadakichi argued that all tram development in the city should be municipally owned and operated, a policy that was approved by the municipal council in 1903. The underlying principle was that municipal ownership policy would give greater attention to the needs of the public, while using the profits generated by the tram system to expand the road system and provide other municipal services rather than lining private pockets (Aoki 1993: 80). In fact the Osaka tram system proved highly successful and was rapidly expanded throughout the city, generating substantial profits used in road-widening and bridge construction.

While as noted above Osaka did attempt to enforce a building code, their legal authority was weak and enforcement difficult. More ambitious planning interventions had to wait until the legal provisions of the TCIO were extended to Osaka in 1918, and the City Planning Law was passed in 1919, which is a story for the next chapter. Even though the will to plan was there, along with a significant degree of expertise, central government's monopoly of financial and legal power and its focus on Tokyo, meant other local initiatives foundered for lack of local autonomy.

One city that might contradict this impression that effective planning existed only in

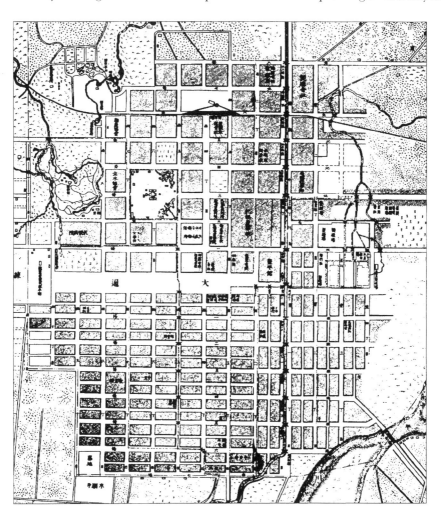

Figure 2.6 Sapporo in 1891. By the end of the Meiji period Sapporo was just beginning to reach the limits of its first plan. Based on the traditional land measurement and urban plotting systems, the city is divided into an administrative quarter at the top of the figure, and a merchant artisan quarter below, separated by Odori Park in the middle.

Source: Sapporo Education Committee (1978: 17).

Tokyo, if there, is Sapporo on the northern frontier island of Hokkaido, which grew during the Meiji period from a tiny settlement of only 624 inhabitants to a city of 95,419 by its end. As shown in Figure 2.6, Sapporo was laid out in an orderly grid with broad streets, a large boulevard leading to the railway station, strategic locations for government offices and military barracks, educational facilities, a hospital, botanical garden, cemetery, Buddhist temple, Shinto shrine, and drainage channels. To a great extent however, this plan must be understood as an exemplar of state-of-the-art city planning at the end of the Tokugawa period. The basic layout of streets seen in the plan had been set by the colonial administration by the sixth year of the Meiji period (1873), and closely follows the traditional grid of 60 ken by 60 ken square blocks.

The colonial administration had the distinct advantage of a clean slate with no pre-existing land ownership, as all land had been confiscated from the indigenous Ainu, whose prior rights to land in Hokkaido have yet to be recognised by any Japanese court. It could therefore impose a tidy grid and reserve generous amounts of land for public use without having to worry about existing owners. The situation in Hokkaido is thus similar to that prevailing in North America and Australia where the surveyor's grid of straight lines could precede any development, and entirely different from the situation in the rest of Japan, where cities invariably grew into densely settled agricultural areas with highly fragmented land ownership and very little public space.

With the exception of the railway and station, however, the plan shown in Figure 2.6 represents what can be understood as a pure expression of the colonial administrator's idea of an ideal urban form at the end of the Tokugawa period. It was characterised by a regular grid of streets, with a commercial area corresponding to the old machi in the south, plotted according to the ancient chō system, and an administrative, educational, and service district in the north near the railway station, which was the counterpart of the old samurai areas, and conforming to the same grid, but plotted more generously with broader streets. These two areas were separated by the broad boulevard now occupied by Ōdori (literally Big Street) Park, now famous for its Sapporo Snow Festival in winter, and its Sapporo Beer Festival in summer. At one end of this boulevard which neatly divided the young city into two-halves was the main military garrison, ready to make sure the two-halves stayed separate.

The grid laid out at the start of the Meiji period easily accommodated the first four decades or so of growth, so Sapporo has perhaps little to say about planning during this time, except that the colonial administration was able to faithfully follow its initial plan. By the end of the Meiji period, however, the grid planned in the early colonial days was largely built up, and problems emerged as Sapporo began to expand into areas originally plotted as farms.

Castle towns during the Meiji period

It is worth summarising the main urban changes experienced by castle towns during the Meiji period, as they comprised the vast majority of urban settlements and a significant majority of the urban population. Figure 2.7 shows the conceptual castle town of Figure 1.1 revised to indicate the main developments of the Meiji years. In most castle towns, the lack of city planning legislation and serious constraints on local government finances meant there was little activity that could be called planning. Urban changes were occurring, however, driven primarily by factors outside the control of local admin-istrations. These were primarily the designation of prefectural capitals in 1879 and the development of the national rail network in the 1880s and 1890s. Castle towns which became prefectural capitals and/or gained rail connections generally prospered, while others languished if they did not have some other special characteristic to drive modern economic growth.

Figure 2.7 shows a castle town which was both a prefectural capital and located on a rail line. As the castle grounds became public property with the abolition of the domains, and were normally the largest block of public land, they almost invariably became the site of the local administrative offices and military garrison of the new national army. Persecution of several Buddhist sects in the years immediately following the restoration further resulted in the seizure of a considerable amount of temple lands, some of which were converted to public parks and the new compulsory public

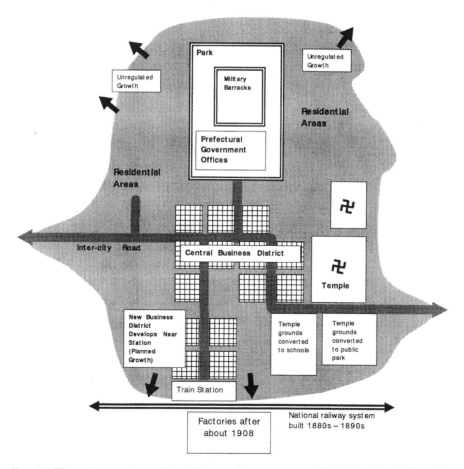

Figure 2.7 The castle town in transition. Many castle towns grew rapidly during the Meiji period, particularly those that became prefectural capitals and were linked to the new national rail net-works.

schools. Former samurai areas also changed their character somewhat, as the samurai lost both their superior class status and their jobs. Some fortunate few entered government service or became teachers. Some became entrepreneurs, using their government bonds as a capital base. Most, however, were forced to eke out a living by setting up small shops or marginal enterprises. The main asset of most samurai was their residence, and many formerly grand samurai residences now sported small shops along the street-front, or were subdivided into smaller plots or simply sold. The former samurai areas thus became progressively more diverse in their land use and occupancy.

All these changes were primarily changes of use which little affected the broader urban form of the castle town. The arrival of the railways, on the other hand, had immediate and drastic impacts on patterns of activity and growth. The main planning efforts were generally directed towards the layout of a new access road to the train station. Such roads were commonly associated with the laying out of a new town area on the traditional grid pattern. These station-front areas gradually developed into a business district which competed directly with the old merchant quarter, in some cases displacing the old central business district, and in other cities simply extending it. As the new railways normally skirted the existing built up area of the towns, the other side of the tracks was generally open country when the line was built. This area not infrequently developed into a mixed industrial/slum housing district, particularly with the expansion of industrial activity after the Russo-Japanese War (1904–5). Other urban growth occurred simply as unplanned sprawl at the urban fringe.

Characteristics of Meiji planning

Perhaps the most significant thing about Japanese urban planning during the Meiji period is the fact that many of its enduring characteristics were first apparent in the approaches adopted at this time. These include some of the great strengths of Japanese planning, and several of its persistent weaknesses. The most important of these are the dominance of central government, the reliance on direct government involvement in building projects, rather than the development of a system for regulating private development and building activity, the consistent lack of financial resources for urban infrastructure, a rapid development of technical sophistication in plan-making, and a high degree of familiarity with current practice in the West.

Certainly the most important feature, and one of the most enduring, is the strong central government control over planning initiatives accompanied by weak controls over private development activities. This derived from the fact that one of the chief goals of the Meiji state was the centralisation of power in the attempt to mobilise national resources and build a strong nation state that could protect itself from the Western colonising powers. Although local governments were established during the Meiji period, they were to a great extent a means of projecting central government power downwards to local areas, rather than an attempt to build independent governments at the local level. Prefectural governments in particular were tightly controlled by the Home Ministry, and prefectural governors were appointees of central government, normally drawn from the ranks of the Home Ministry bureaucracy. This contrasts with several other developed countries where independent and competitive municipal initiative, often led by the local property-owning and entrepreneurial class, was so important in early planning development.

The dominant role of central government had a huge impact on the development of approaches to urban planning. Perhaps the most direct consequence was the focus on Tokyo planning issues and problems as it was at once the largest city and the capital. In the Meiji period Tokyo's urban problems and issues were among the most serious, and the desire of the government to create a suitably civilised imperial capital added to the priority given to planning initiatives there. Through much of the twentieth century, Japanese planning initiatives were grown in Tokyo, often primarily with Tokyo conditions in mind, and then disseminated to the rest of the country, not always appropriately.

During the Meiji period the Japanese government was able to develop a remarkably high degree of technical sophistication in plan-making, often accompanied by impressive familiarity with contemporary developments in Europe and America. Japanese planners were increasingly well informed about contemporary European and American developments towards the end of the period, and were struggling with many of the same issues as planners in countries such as Germany and Britain. The main difference was that in many Western countries the urban planning movement was from its beginnings based in a broad coalition of health and hygiene activists, professional associations of architects, surveyors and engineers, housing advocates, settlement workers, anti-slum campaigners, labour and cooperative movements and a range of others who explicitly put public welfare and urban quality of life forward as the highest values (Hall 1988; Rodgers 1998; Sutcliffe 1981: chapter six). In Japan, however, the development of city planning took place almost exclusively within central government. One consequence was that a central goal of city planning was to be national development through the provision of main infrastructure, and issues of housing and urban amenity occupied a decidedly second place.

Central government control also meant that urban planning repeatedly got caught up in inter-ministry conflicts over jurisdiction and financial control. As shown above, the Home Ministry eventually confirmed its exclusive responsibility for urban planning administration, fending off rival bids by the Finance Ministry which carried out the Ginza project, and the Foreign Ministry which proposed redevelopment plans for the central government district in opposition to the Home Ministry's more comprehensive plans for restructuring the capital as a whole. After this, the Home Ministry formulated planning policy and drafted laws, while the actual planning work was carried out by local governments under close supervision of the ministry, as in the case of the TCIO. Unfortunately, the Home Ministry consistently lost battles with the Finance Ministry over establishing independent sources of funding for urban projects, as seen in the case of the TCIO. Inter-ministerial competition and fragmentation of land use planning responsibilities has been an enduring weakness of Japanese planning, as shown in later chapters.

Watanabe suggests that one of the most lasting results of the TCIO was the establishment of central government responsibility for planning, and local government responsibility for funding public works, aided by central government subsidy (Watanabe 1984: 411; Yamamoto 1993: 29). This pattern has continued until the present, and has consistently meant that ultimate control has rested with the Home Ministry (the Ministry of Construction after the Second World War), which controlled the legal framework and flow of funds. Because the national government always has many other priorities, it has also meant perennial funding shortfalls for essential urban infrastructure.

The weak financial base of urban planning in Japan thus first emerged as a result of conflicts between the Home and Finance Ministries during the Meiji period, and has proven an enduring feature of Japanese planning. To a great extent, it must be conceded that lack of funds for planning was simply and directly the result of the fact that Japan was at this time a poor country, and the government faced wide-ranging demands on scarce resources. In this regard the grudging attitude of Finance Ministry officials toward financing urban infrastructure projects is easily understood, even though planners have often regretted the many lost opportunities in hindsight. In the long run perhaps a more important factor, however, was the reluctance of central government to allow greater powers to local governments to pursue their own planning goals and initiatives. Thus although Osaka was actively drafting ambitious expansion plans, and Kobe and Yokohama were each attempting new planning approaches, such municipal projects were consistently hampered by a lack of local powers and independent sources of finance. In Japan there is little trace of the independent municipal experimentation that was so closely associated with the development of town planning in Germany, Britain and the US (see Sutcliffe 1981).

Planning during the Meiji period also firmly established Japanese government reliance on projects for urban planning and redevelopment rather than the regulation of private development activity. This was to a significant extent a consequence of the basic necessity of building modern infrastructure into a pre-modern urban structure, which lends itself naturally to a project-oriented approach, whereas a regulatory approach is more suited to urban fringe expansion. It was also a result of the high incidence of fires within the densely built up urban area, which during the Meiji period, as throughout the history of Edo, offered opportunities for comprehensive redevelopment of discrete parts of the urban area. These objective conditions were also supported by a reluctance to regulate private urban development. This reluctance is perhaps best reflected in the fact that not until 1881 was an effective regulation to ensure fireproof building construction enforced in Tokyo, even though throughout its 300-year existence the city had been plagued by devastating fires. Even the new regulations passed in 1881 only applied to a small part of the central area of Tokyo, and a more comprehensive building control law was vigorously and successfully opposed. While local governments were active in passing building codes to control nagaya slums in the 1880s, and several cities including Osaka passed somewhat more comprehensive building codes in the early 1900s, the national government did not pass its much discussed building code until 1919, as discussed in the next chapter. In most European countries the very earliest building control laws had been the result of large fires, such as London's Great Fire of 1666, which had prompted the requirement that new building should be in brick or stone. European cities were built in stone and brick, not primarily as the result of a cultural preference for those materials, but because of strict enforcement of building regulations since the seventeenth century.

The development of urban planning practice and planning ideas during the Meiji period was closely associated with the sudden opening to the West, and the rapid and deliberate transformation of the Japanese economy, society and political system along Western lines. As a late developer, Japan had the advantage of being able to learn from earlier experiences in the early industrialising countries, but also suffered from the suddenness of the transition, which allowed little time to build the social and political institutions that were able, in many Western countries, to push for controls on urban land development in the public interest. As shown in the previous chapter the institutional arrangements of the Tokugawa period left a legacy of extremely weak civic self-government, and an underdeveloped bourgeois class which in other developed countries had a deep self-interest in good local government, and in active policies to support the local property market and urban environment. Many of the strongest supporters of better planning in the other industrial countries such as local governments, property owners, and advocates of better housing for the poor, were relatively weaker politically in Meiji Japan. One lasting consequence was the creation of a planning system that was highly centrally controlled, and that had a weak basis of public support.

Also important is that to a very great extent, traditional vernacular patterns of house building and architecture on the one hand, and neighbourhood self-management on the other continued largely unchanged (Hanley 1986). Hanley argues that even though so many aspects of Meiji society were changing dramatically, for most people the continuities in lifestyle, including housing, clothing, and foods were more significant than the changes, and that these continuities probably contributed greatly to social stability and to the success of the larger political and economic changes (Hanley 1997: 175). The persistence of traditional urban material culture and urban technologies well into the twentieth century was possible largely because they were rather successful at creating liveable urban areas. Although with industrialisation and the rapid growth of the largest cities around the turn of the century some severe urban problems began to be generated, particularly for the poor, for much of the population traditional housing and neighbourhoods continued to be comfortable and desirable. For the middle and upper classes, therefore, the need for stronger urban planning was probably not particularly evident, and the poor who were suffering from worsening urban conditions at the end of the Meiji period had neither votes nor political organisations.

At the end of the Meiji period in 1912 Japanese urban policy and urban planning practice were still in their infancy, but were to develop rapidly in the succeeding Taishō period, as discussed in the next chapter.

3 Taishō period urbanisation and the development of the 1919 planning system

I doubt that in those years, the years of prosperity during and immediately after the World War, there was anyone even among the most ardent supporters of Tokyo who thought it a grand metropolis. The newspapers were unanimous in denouncing the chaotic transportation and the inadequate roads of "our Tokyo". I believe it was the *Advertiser* which in an editorial inveighed against the gracelessness of the city. Our politicians are always talking about big things, social policy and labor problems and the like, it said, but these are not what politics should be about. Politicians should be thinking rather of mud, and of laying streets through which an automobile can pass in safety on a rainy day.

Seidensticker (1991) cites Tanizaki's reflections on Taishō period Tokyo.

The next two chapters look at the period from the end of the Meiji era to the end of the Second World War. This chapter examines the social and political context of the passage of Japan's first generally applicable City Planning and Urban Buildings Laws in 1919. Chapter 4 describes the implementation of the 1919 city planning system and the main urban planning projects and changes seen during the 1920s and 1930s.

There are several reasons for the focus of this chapter on the context of the development of the 1919 planning system. First, the early decades of the twentieth century were a period of extraordinary change in Japan, and in a variety of areas ranging from industrialisation and urbanisation to political institutions the pace of development in Japan quickened. The 1919 planning system was clearly a product of its time, and understanding the context of its creation helps to explain the form it took. Second, the 1919 City Planning and Urban Buildings Laws formed the basic planning law and defined the approach to city planning in Japan until they were superseded by new laws in 1968. The 1919 system thus formed the planning framework in Japan for half a century, including during the rapid economic growth period of the 1950s and 1960s. Having a clear understanding of this system is thus essential to understanding twentieth century Japanese planning. Third, while city planning during the Meiji period was limited to a few major redevelopment projects, and was focused on Tokyo, the 1919 system was the first attempt to create a comprehensive planning system that applied to whole urban areas and all major cities, that could structure development activity on the urban fringe, and provided for controls on individual buildings through the Buildings Law. Finally, while many of its features were borrowed freely from examples in other developed countries, the 1919 system is revealing in its differences from planning in these countries, and particularly the differences in outcomes.

While the previous chapter on planning in the Meiji period followed the main planning project, the Tokyo City Improvement Ordinance (TCIO), to its conclusion in 1918, the Meiji period actually ended in 1912 with the death of Emperor Meiji and accession of Emperor Taishō. The "Taishō Democracy" period takes its name from this emperor who ruled from 1912 to 1926, although historians of Japan commonly argue that the period of economic and political development which characterised the Taishō democracy period lasted somewhat longer, from the end of the Russo-Japanese War in 1905 to the end of democratic governments and increasing dominance of the military after the Manchurian Incident of 1931, and it is that longer period which is referred to here (see Gordon 1991). This earlier start is appropriate, particularly as the important urban planning developments of the 1920s are best understood in the context of the social and economic changes that became increasingly apparent after the end of the Russo-Japanese War in 1905. While the Second World War (which for Japan effectively started in 1931 with the deepening involvement in China) was clearly a decisive one in Japanese history, it is discussed only briefly here, as national mobilisation for war gradually put an end to virtually all but military activity during the 1930s. The end of the Second World War in 1945 is the obvious place to stop, as it marks the abrupt change from the pre-war system to the post-war period of occupation and reconstruction and then of rapid economic growth discussed in Chapter 5.

The first section of this chapter outlines the international context of the development of modern city planning. The second section examines the processes of industrialisation and urbanisation of the first decades of the century, and the social and political changes they gave rise to, while the third section describes the development and passage of the 1919 City Planning Law.

The beginnings of modern city planning

The Taishō period was a clear turning point in the development of Japanese urban planning. Whereas during the Meiji period city planning efforts were rudimentary, and largely confined to projects to modernise the capital city Tokyo, during the Taishō period rapid industrial and urban growth created pressure for the development of more activist approaches to shaping urban growth. The new legislation was the first attempt at the design of a comprehensive urban planning system that could achieve planned growth on the urban fringe as well as guide redevelopment in existing city areas. As with city planning innovations during the Meiji period, the 1919 system was strongly influenced by contemporary international planning ideas and practice, and the similarities and differences between new planning approaches in Japan and in Europe and North America are revealing. This section looks first at the main issues addressed by early attempts at urban planning, and then identifies the main factors that served to create a distinctly Japanese trajectory of planning development.

The fundamental conditions that gave rise to modern city planning – industrial development, rapid growth of urban population and area, and widespread environmental degradation in industrial cities – were common to Europe, America and Japan. While Japan was still behind the leading nations in its level of industrialisation at this time, it was not so far behind late developers such as Germany, Italy and France, and even though many rural areas remained little changed from the feudal period, modern industrial growth was concentrated in the main metropolitan areas of Tokyo, Osaka and Nagoya. In many countries concern about urban environmental degradation had similar motivations. For example, concern about unsanitary conditions in the cities was motivated by public health concerns about the spread of disease, and fears about the poor health conditions of the working class in particular were prompted by the requirement for healthy military recruits and workers. Similarly, for many governments the spreading industrial slums were seen as a breeding place of social, moral and political disorder, and the role of planning was to prevent the spread of disease, social conflict, and socialistic ideas by bringing physical order, light and a good environment to the city. It is fair to say that in the early days of planning a strong spatial determinism prevailed, and the belief that improving the physical environment would mitigate social problems was widespread.

In Japan the key actors promoting improved planning measures were the bureaucrats of central government and their representatives in local governments. Japanese policy-makers were keenly aware of economic, social and military developments in the leading industrial nations and had since the early Meiji period been strongly motivated by the need to catch up with Western military and industrial power. The Japanese government and corporations borrowed heavily and deliberately from Western industrial, transport and military technology. At the same time, many government leaders viewed the increasing social and labour conflict and spreading socialist movements of Western nations with alarm, fearing that such problems would inevitably spread to Japan with industrial growth. Here again the Japanese government borrowed, particularly from the social policy of Germany which was seen as a particularly useful model as it was at once a monarchy, a late developing but rapidly growing industrial and military power, and a leader in the development of social insurance, health policy and city planning as strategies to relieve social conflict and encourage national development.

In city planning also, Japanese policy-makers borrowed actively from Western examples of city planning while striving to develop a system that would be relevant to their own particular context. The main issues Western planners were grappling with during the first half of the twentieth century were urban population growth, the supply of affordable housing for the working classes, and the achievement of public controls over land development and redevelopment. Industrialisation had led to rapid increases in urban populations during the nineteenth century, which had in turn led to increasing population densities in central city areas and the spread of the urban squalor and misery aptly described by Hall (1988: 13) as the "City of Dreadful Night". Towards the end of the century new transportation technologies – trains, electric trams, and finally automobiles – allowed the spread of population from the compact early industrial city into the urban fringe, where cheaper land held out the possibility of a solution to the dire housing problems of the inner city. The achievement of that possibility, however, required a number of improvements over existing systems of planning and development control, so that new development would not reproduce on a larger scale the worst failings of the old cities. The difficult issue was how to control urban growth: designing, enacting and implementing legal frameworks that would allow public co-ordination without stifling private building activity; ensuring rational and pleasing urban design while retaining private ownership; and finally the question of requiring developers and landowners to pay a fair share of the costs of the public infrastructure that allowed them to profit from the development of land.

In most of Europe the nineteenth century had seen the gradual development of the legal tools to restrict private land and building development in the public interest. As Cherry (1988) has shown in the British case, while more interventionist planning regimes were consistently opposed in the name of laissez-faire and the sanctity of private property, and by those opposed to local tax rises, proponents of increased environmental control had gradually succeeded in establishing new areas of public activity. As he summarises:

> By the 1880s the practice of public-sector control, and the intervention in private interests concerning land and property by collective, public interests had become a recognized feature of British life. Steps had been hesitant and slow, and attended on occasion by considerable hostility, but they were progressive and seemingly irreversible in the movement towards greater public control of community and environmental affairs. In matters of the regulation of street widths, new highway construction, public health and sanitation, fire control, building construction and space around buildings, important developments had taken place, and an established local government system would jealously preserve hard-won powers.
>
> (Cherry 1988: 49)

As is well known, however, merely regulating road widths and basic minimum building standards may have eliminated some of the worst features of the industrial slum, but did not necessarily lead to well-designed urban areas, creating instead at the end of the century the dreary tracts of "by-law housing" that proliferated in Britain, the spread of the high-density "dumb-bell" tenement blocks in New York City and the overcrowded "Mietskasernen" tenements in Berlin. An important objective of planners at the beginning of the century was thus to create and implement a more positive vision of suburban growth that would allow better design through the more comprehensive treatment of large areas of new development that would permit better road layouts, interesting park systems, and could take advantage of natural site features. This also required the creation of city-wide planning frameworks with differentiation between the treatment of different areas, the creation of effective means to ensure the planned development of new areas on the urban fringe, and the creation of legal, administrative, and financial structures that allowed plan implementation, particularly with regard to the regulation of private land development and building activity.

Another major challenge for planning advocates during the first half of the twentieth century related to the questions of who would pay for public goods, how to ensure that enough of the new housing that would be affordable for working people and not just by the wealthy, how to compensate those whose land was reduced in value by public restrictions on development, and how to recoup for the public purse some of the increase in land value that was the result of public action such as road-building or planning designation. It was essential to resolve these financial issues because, as seen in inter-war Britain, where local authorities were liable to pay compensation for the refusal of development permission, they were unable to effectively control development because of the financial risk. It was further argued that individual developers should not be allowed to pocket the whole of the increase in land values, which were more a result of community action than of developer initiative. These financial issues were at the core of the garden city proposals of Ebenezer Howard ([1902] 1985) who presented a plan whereby quality housing could be provided cheaply because of land purchase at low rural values, and long-term increases in land values would be retained by the community to pay for community social welfare.

Planners in the West grappled with these issues throughout the first half of the twentieth century, with a wide range of outcomes. They also were fundamental to the development of city planning in Japan, where the rapid growth of urban areas was a major factor in the development of the new planning system which would have to resolve the problems of controlling urban growth on the urban fringe, as well as enable the gradual improvement of existing areas which had been the major preoccupation of the TCIO. Better design of transport systems, more integrated planning of large urban areas with multiple local government authorities, protection of land for public facilities such as roads from development, and financing the needed public investment were all priorities in Japan as much as in the West.

While Japanese planners excelled in their ability to borrow, adapt and innovate in the technical aspects of city planning, as is demonstrated by many of the planning regulations and plans discussed below, the planning practices that resulted were quite different from those of the other advanced countries. This is, of course, hardly surprising, as Japan had so recently emerged from its self-imposed isolation from the world, and had quite different urban and governmental traditions. It does, however underline the importance of the Taishō period for understanding Japanese city planning. While the formal Japanese planning system and legal framework grew ever closer to Western models, their outcomes were quite different. The Taishō period was to prove a major watershed in the development of Japanese city planning and of Japanese cities. Two factors were key to the different outcomes in Japan: the highly centralised system of government created during the Meiji period, and the relatively weak development of the middle classes and civil society.

The highly centralised system of government established during the Meiji period was a crucial factor in shaping the development of planning in Japan during the twentieth century. It is notable that although Britain, Germany and the US were important influences they all had relatively strong and independent local governments. In Britain this was the high point of municipal pride and enterprise, and cities such as Liverpool, Manchester and Birmingham had activist and competitive local governments which were leaders in developing new planning ideas and arguing for new planning powers. They demonstrated high levels of competence in managing the complex processes of urban development and change, and since the mid-nineteenth century had steadily augmented their powers and areas of expertise. In newly unified Germany individual state and city governments still had a great deal of freedom to develop their own planning policies, and in America there was a great deal of variation among the different states and a strong tradition of local responsibility for local environmental issues. Sutcliffe (1981: 207) argues that evidence of the importance of such independent local governments is provided by France, where a highly centralised government structure inhibited the development of planning at the end of the nineteenth century.

These traditions of local government independence were particularly important for the development of city planning because as Saunders (1986) has suggested, there are inherent differences between local and central governments. Local governments, being much closer to their electors, are more susceptible to influence by small groups of activists than are central governments and are consequently much more concerned about local environmental issues, while central governments naturally tend to be more concerned with broader national economic and military issues. Such locally influential activists are not limited to those on the left, but in practice often include landowners and developers who have very much to gain or lose through local planning decisions. This can be either a good thing or a bad thing, as such proximity to the local electorate can result in the "capture" of local governments by local actors for purely private ends (Logan and Molotch 1987). In the early days of modern planning, however, such independence seems to have favoured the development of stronger planning systems. Greater independence of local governments can also allow a wider diversity of practices in different places, and a greater likelihood of learning through trial and error.

Japanese local governments had little political, legal or financial autonomy, however, and as the central state grew stronger during the first decades of the twentieth century with greater resources deriving from economic growth and increasing bureaucratic power, the autonomy of local governments grew ever weaker. City planning in particular became an increasingly top-down system under Home Ministry leadership which allowed central government to prioritise economic growth and focus infrastructure spending on railways and main roads, while largely ignoring spending to improve urban quality of life by providing social infrastructure such as parks, sewer systems, and local roads.

A second important factor shaping the evolution of city planning in Japan was that in comparison to many Western countries, in Japan the development of an effective city planning system had a much narrower base of political support. This was critical because in Japan as elsewhere, the development of stronger environmental controls was opposed by vested interests as well as by inertia, and the political obstacles to effective planning were often more substantial than the technical ones. Japan, recently emerged from autocratic feudal rule, had a relatively weak and undeveloped civil society, and the small and politically unorganised middle and professional classes played a much less important role in the development of new urban planning approaches than was common in the West.

In many Western countries a broad range of professional, civic, charitable and special interest organisations provided an important constituency in support of more interventionist approaches to planning. Public health and hygiene activists, professional associations of architects, surveyors and engineers, housing advocates, settlement workers, anti-slum campaigners, and a range of other do-gooders provided a vocal constituency with the political skills, connections and financial resources to back many of the crucial campaigns for greater government intervention and regulation of what had hitherto been relatively unregulated processes of urban development (Rodgers 1998). Also influential were middle class environmental activists and homebuyers who were not shy in insisting on high levels of environmental quality in their own neighbourhoods, as well as state resources, regulation and enforcement to protect their neighbourhoods and housing investments from environmental decline. While some environmental activism was altruistic, and some motivated purely by self-interest, the notion that the state could and should restrict the rights of the private developer and property-owner in the interest of the public good was firmly established through their efforts (see Cherry 1988; Fishman 1987; Sies 1997; Sutcliffe 1981). A key characteristic of this ever-growing group of urban activists was that it operated in the realm of civil society, largely outside the control of governments or private business. As this chapter will show, in inter-war Japan civil society was very weak, and the few organised bases of urban political and planning activism that had begun to develop at the turn of the century had almost disappeared by the start of war in the 1930s. This left a small group of central government bureaucrats far more dominant in the planning system than was common in most Western nations.

Japan's distinctive trajectory of planning evolution and patterns of urban development highlight the point that the development of city planning was necessarily a process of both technical and political development. It only became possible to imagine building cities in different ways with technical advances such as flush-toilets and piped systems for the removal of liquid waste; trams, railways, subways and elevators for transport of people and goods; innovations such as differential land use regulations for different areas of cities; systems for the control of new building activity; and the protection of space for public use on the urban fringe. At the same time planning regulation of private activity is an inherently political act which almost invariably affects the distribution of goods, increasing the value of certain sites and decreasing that of others. The development of stronger planning systems was thus necessarily a process both of technical innovation and political agreement to prioritise planning issues and limit some of the rights of landowners to use their property freely. This and the following chapters explore the particular ways in which these changes played out in the Japanese case.

Inter-war urbanisation, social and political change

The first decades of the twentieth century were a period of enormous change for Japan. By the end of the Meiji period it had established itself as the dominant regional power, having defeated China and Russia in war and having gained a colony in Taiwan, extensive economic interests in Manchuria from Russia, and undisputed control over the Korean peninsula which was annexed in 1910. To a great extent, therefore, the main goals of the Meiji period had been achieved: Japan was an internationally recognised great power, it had achieved revision of the unequal treaties, and had developed modern industries and a strong military. It is important to remember, however, that Japan was still a primarily agricultural nation at the beginning of the Taishō period, and the traditional lifestyles of the majority of the population had been little affected by modernisation and the growth of the industrial economy during the previous 30 years. From the end of the Russo-Japanese War to the outbreak of war in the 1930s the pace of industrialisation and urbanisation quickened, and a much more urban society emerged.

Urban industrial growth and emerging urban problems

Rapid increases in industrialisation and urbanisation were probably the most significant forces propelling social change at this time. In particular the First World War, which Japan entered on the side of Britain, its ally since 1902, speeded the process of industrial economic growth as a result of Allied orders for munitions and other war *matériel*, and also through opportunities for Japanese manufacturers to move into markets abandoned by blockaded European countries such as Germany. At the same time Japanese chemical imports from Germany were cut off, forcing their domestic production. Industrial production almost doubled between 1914 and 1919 and average profit rates for industry increased sharply (Kato 1974: 218). Japan thus emerged as an industrial nation during the Taishō period with a doubling of GNP from 1910 to 1930, and a quadrupling of real output of mining and manufacturing, and of employment in heavy and chemical industries (Yamamura 1974: 301–2).

The period was not one of steady growth, however. In particular the period after 1919 saw a prolonged recession from which Japan would not recover until the early 1930s. That period of economic difficulty affected farmers, light industry and smaller firms disproportionately, and the large financial-industrial combines (*zaibatsu*), emerged at the end of the 1920s in a stronger position as they had both greater financial resources and secure markets in the Japanese military. As Yamamura (1974: 327–8) has argued, the concentration of economic power in the hands of the zaibatsu during the 1920s resulted in greatly increasing disparities in the distribution of wealth and was an important cause of social and political unrest. While rapid industrial growth during the First World War was a crucial factor in transforming Japan into an urban industrial power, nearly doubling the number of factory workers, its effects on the urban working class were mostly negative. Inflation during the war years led to sharply declining real incomes during the years of economic growth which recovered to pre-war levels only by the end of 1919. The working class suffered first from low and declining incomes during the war and then from serious unemployment problems during the slump of the 1920s.

An important product of industrial growth, particularly from 1905 to 1919, was the rapid expansion of urban population. The problems of managing urban growth were particularly serious in the principal metropolitan areas of Tokyo and Osaka. While the population of Tokyo City grew from 1,480,000 in 1905 to 2,070,000 in 1930, the population of the 82 towns and villages surrounding Tokyo grew much more rapidly, from 420,000 to 2,900,000 during the same period (Ishida 1987: 110). Osaka's population, while smaller, showed a similar growth from 470,000 when the city was incorporated and enlarged in 1889 to 1,433,721 in 1924 within the original urban area and an additional 700,158 in the suburban area incorporated into the city in 1925 (Osaka City Association (*Osaka Toshi Kyoukai*) 1992: 78). From 1898 to 1920 the share of Japanese population in settlements of more than 10,000 increased from 18 per cent to 32 per cent, and the total population of the six largest cities (Tokyo, Osaka, Kyoto, Nagoya, Kobe and Yokohama) more than doubled from 3.04 million to 7.63 million between 1897 and 1920 (Yazaki 1968: 391). A combination of factors such as the increased accessibility offered by the expanding system of trams and trains, lack of city planning controls which were non-existent in the rural areas adjacent to the cities, and the rapid increase in urban population led to disorderly sprawl development in suburban areas. Iinuma Issei has called the quarter century from 1900 to 1925 one of Japan's dark periods from the point of view of city planning (cited in Ishida 1987: 112).

Rapid urbanisation caused a range of social problems familiar to students of the industrial revolution in Western countries, of which worsening housing conditions, increasing densities of population in poor areas, and worsening epidemics of cholera and tuberculosis were prominent. These were exacerbated in the Japanese case by the rapidity of the process of economic change, and the very weak infrastructure base of the cities, which was inadequate even before the rapid doubling of urban populations.

Because of widespread poverty among industrial workers housing conditions in urban areas declined, particularly during the First World War. The traditional housing for the urban poor, the back-alley nagaya – essentially long rows of single-storey wooden shacks – became ever more crowded and it was common for a family to live in a single room measuring 3 metres by 3 metres (4.5 tatami mats), and for 15 to 20 families to share an outdoor privy (Yazaki 1968: 450). When the famous British welfare reformer Beatrice Webb visited Japan in 1911 she judged the slums of Osaka to be "as bad as anything in London" with widespread malnutrition, neglected children and inadequate relief efforts (cited in Garon 1997: 45). In a similar vein, Nakahama Toichiro (Nakahama 1889) investigated Osaka's slums and compared them with the worst in Europe. The worsening problems of slum housing were also well reported in the Japanese press at the turn of the century, following on Yokoyama's pioneering research noted in the last chapter. The problems of housing for the urban working classes are closely related to the extreme concentration of land ownership in major cities, with 77 per cent of all housing in Tokyo, and 90 per cent in Osaka rented according to a 1941 survey (Narumi 1986: 65). In addition the larger cities saw the development of large new industrial districts on the urban fringe where workers lived in miserable slums scattered among the factories. Accompanying the expansion of the urban working class there was also the creation of a growing new middle class of civil servants, white-collar workers and professionals who provided a market for suburban housing and were a significant factor behind worsening problems of urban sprawl.

Predictably, worsening living conditions for the poor gave rise to increasing social conflict which was expressed in repeated outbursts of popular protest. The Hibiya Riots of 1905, and the mass protests over the rise of tram fares in the spring of 1906, the movement for constitutional government of 1912–1913, the Tokyo tram strike of early 1912, protests against naval corruption in 1914, all were signs of popular discontent and increasing militancy. The government and ruling elites were particularly shaken by the nationwide Rice Riots of 1918. Although wartime inflation saw general price rises throughout the economy, rice prices rose even faster. While the wholesale price index doubled between 1915 and 1918, the price of rice tripled during the same period. Urban workers were not the only ones to suffer, however, as the mass of poor farmers and fishermen were also caught in the bind of rising prices. Many small farmers were forced to sell their crop when it was harvested to pay rents and taxes, and buy rice back later at inflated prices. Speculation among merchants, landlords and wholesalers was rampant, and tensions finally exploded in July 1918 with several weeks of violent riots and demonstrations spreading throughout the country which were only subdued by the use of the army against the demonstrators (Hunter 1989: 245).

Of equal concern to the ruling elite was the growing membership of labour organisations during the First World War and the dramatic increase in labour disputes and the number of workers involved in them until the summer of 1919 when there were over 2,388 disputes and strikes throughout Japan (Duus 1968: 125). Far from the stereotypical image of docile company unions that has been prominent in depictions of post-war Japan, in the early stage of union development conflict was much more open. Unions were illegal organisations under the provisions of the Peace Police Law of 1900, and labour-organising and work stoppages were brutally repressed. Labour-organising nonetheless continued to spread, and workers became active in the spreading

Figure 3.1 Nagaya in Tokyo. The traditional urban housing for the urban poor, wooden sheds or "longhouses" (*nagaya*) commonly occupied the rear portion of the deep lots. The landowner would often manage and live above a shop fronting the street, while their employees, or poor artisans lived in the rear areas accessed by a narrow covered lane from the street.

Source: *Concentrated Areas of Substandard Housing*, Tokyo Prefectural Education Department, Social Bureau (1928).

movements for universal suffrage, the right to strike and the legal recognition of unions (see Duus and Scheiner 1998; Garon 1987).

As noted in the previous chapter the Meiji government had shown little tolerance for dissent, and wide-ranging suppression of opposition movements, including the banning of mass meetings, the exclusion of leaders from Tokyo, and the censorship of books and newspapers had been authorised under the Peace Regulations of 1887. Those powers to restrict anti-government activity were broadened under the Peace Police Law which banned political activity by women, minors, police and members of the military, outlawed labour-organisation and strikes, and extended Home Ministry administrative controls and supervision over associations, meetings and demonstrations (Hunter 1989: 242). During the Taishō period those powers were increasingly invoked in attempts to prevent the spread of socialism and left-wing activity in general, and the labour movement in particular. Japan's first left-wing political party, the Social Democratic Party (*Shakai Minshutō*) was banned by the government within a day of its founding, and a similar fate met most other such attempts in the following decades (see Beasley 1995; Duus 1999; 1997; Garon 1987; Gluck 1987). Repression of dissent was the ever-present counterpart to the other social policies described in more detail below. Notwithstanding the effective repression of opposition political parties and movements, however, the first decades of the new century also saw significant democratic development, the emergence of greater pluralism and the budding development of civil society.

The budding development of civil society

The Taishō period saw a remarkable development of Japanese civil society with the growth of labour unions, tenants' movements, political parties, and women's organisations. The growth of an industrial economy led simultaneously to the spread of popular protest movements, and to a growing professional and middle class. Each of these in turn led to the development of civil society. Iokibe (1999) argues that compared to the Meiji period, when the government had imposed strict central control over virtually all aspects of society in the interest of building national strength, the Taishō period was one of an "associational revolution" in which a period of sustained peace fostered the development of private activity and a budding civil society between the developmental authoritarianism of the Meiji period and the militarism of the Second World War.

> Looking at the rise and fall of private-sector organizations, we can see that the prewar peak falls roughly in the period centering around the 1920s, between the Taishō Political Crisis (1913) and the Manchurian Incident. In terms of numbers, there was an eruption of private organizations formed before the war, an "associational revolution" in its time; and they were tremendously diverse in purpose and type. Not only were there business-related groups such as the Japan Chamber of Commerce and Industry, but numerous labor unions and welfare societies in every field of industry, the Japan Fabian Society and ideologically inspired organizations such as the National Federation of Levellers, and cultural and academic societies and international exchange groups such as the Pacific Society. The proliferation of nonprofit as well as "value-promotion" organizations was phenomenal.
>
> (Iokibe 1999: 75)

Advocates for improved city planning measures took their place among a wide range of other private interests which worked for the public good at this time. There was a vigorous public debate on urban issues by writers such as the journalist Yokoyama Gennosuke (1899) and Koda Rohan ([1898] 1954), a popular novelist who wrote a visionary treatise on the need to rebuild Tokyo with broad roads, parks, sewers, public markets, and libraries. Even more influential was Mori Ōgai, one of the most prominent writers on urban issues of turn-of-the-century Japan. While his status as a high-ranking military physician means he was a central government officer, Mori was also a widely read novelist and prominent activist on urban issues so can reasonably be claimed as a part of civil society. He wrote a wide range of essays on urban issues, focused primarily on issues of hygiene, public health, sewerage and water supply, and urban planning and building regulation, drawing on his experience studying German military medicine and public health practice for four years until his return to Japan in the early 1890s. On his return he was an advocate of stronger building regulation and urban planning legislation and was a prime mover in failed efforts to pass strengthened building regulations in the 1890s. Mori was also a persistent critic of Japanese urban policy and advocate of a more activist approach to improving housing conditions for the poor (see Ishida 1988, 1991b, 1997, 1999).

More radical were the Christian socialists Abe Isoo and Katayama Sen, both of whom had studied in missionary colleges in the eastern US and had arrived at their advocacy of municipal socialism based on Christian teachings. Katayama, a professional labour organiser, criticised Japanese urban policy of the turn of the century as being simply concerned with economic development, ignoring the plight of poor working people who suffered appalling urban living conditions and excessive rents. While this analysis was hardly new, his solution that the goal of urban policy should be a high-quality living environment for all and that this could be accomplished through a more powerful local government and broader municipal ownership of essential services and housing was radical for the time (see also Duus and Scheiner 1998; Katayama [1903] 1949). A much more mainstream and influential critic was Kuwata Kumazo, a prime mover of the influential Social Policy Association (*Shakai Seisaku Gakkai*) modelled after the German *Verein für Sozialpolitik*, founded by the German historical economists in 1872 to advocate state social welfare legislation to ease class conflict. Kuwata, following the German approach, argued in the paper *Urban Social Policy* that to prevent social unrest urban social facilities should be provided to improve the living conditions of the poor. Local governments should become much more active in modernising urban transport, building parks and providing essential services such as sewers and water supply (Kuwata, 1900: cited in Hanes 2002).

Even more acceptable to the central government leadership in the early years of the century was the well-known journalist Miyake Iwao, who published his book *Urban Studies* (*Toshi no Kenkyū*) in 1908 (Miyake 1908). As Hanes (2002) notes, two of the Meiji oligarchs, Okuma Shigenobu and Inoue Tomoichi even wrote prefaces to the work, giving it the official stamp of approval. Miyake was an advocate of municipal autonomy, and argued that to better deal with emerging urban social problems local governments needed stronger planning powers, and broader sources of local tax revenue such as betterment taxes on increases of land value. Later, in 1916 Kataoka Yasushi, president of the Osaka Architects' Association, and founder of the *Architect and Society Journal*, published a book called *Contemporary City Research* (*Gendai Toshi no Kenkyū*) which introduced the latest ideas from Europe and America and advocated a stronger Japanese planning system. These are just a few examples of the wide range of voices participating in a vigorous debate about the future of urban policy in Japan. They provide one part of the context of the passage of the first modern city planning system in 1919.

The mid-1920s, however, were the high point of this process, after which the areas

Figure 3.2 Nihonbashi, 1928. Proud Nihonbashi (literally "Japan bridge'), Tokyo's main commercial and financial centre in 1928, five years after the 1923 earthquake. Nihonbashi today is shown in Figure 5.14, page 192.

Photo Mainichi Shinbunsha.

of social life that lay beyond the reach of the state grew ever smaller as state power expanded, continuing the processes begun during the Meiji period. By the mid-1930s there was little effective political space for any sort of popular movement directed at influencing government policy. As Eisenstadt (1996: 35) argues, the distrust of open politics as potentially subversive of the development of the "general will" required the conflation of state and civil society. To a very great extent the creation of that "general will" was the job of the Home Ministry, which carried out its task both with police batons and the social mobilisation activities of its local organisers. Both approaches were deleterious to the development of civil society in Japan, which only started to develop once again with the democratic reforms after the Second World War.

Although industrialisation, modernisation and a relatively open political climate during the early Taishō period saw the development of a nascent civil society including a pluralistic discourse about cities, urban problems and urban planning, it was not to last. As Iokibe (1999: 75) put it, Japanese civil society of the 1920s and the Taishō democracy itself were like greenhouse plants which "had not put down the sturdy roots that were needed to endure the cruel assault of ultranationalism and militarism that swept the country following the Manchurian Incident" of 1931. As state power expanded, by the 1930s there was little effective political space for any sort of popular movement directed at influencing urban governments, or improving local environments or housing. This a key feature of Japan's political development, and is an indication of the essential fragility of democratic institutions in the Taishō period.

Taishō democracy

There has been considerable debate about the extent of Taishō democratic develop-ment. The traditional view of many Western scholars has been that it was merely a brief and not very significant detour on the path from Meiji oligarchy to the bureaucratic totalitarianism of the Pacific War years. More recently, however, the argument of Japanese historians that the Taishō democracy period was indeed a time of significant democratic development in Japan has gained increasing acceptance in the West. These debates are reviewed by Gordon (1991) (see also Minichiello 1998; Silberman and Harootunian 1974). One important factor was the waning power of the ageing oli-garchy who had carried out the Meiji restoration and who had effectively controlled the government during the Meiji period. This was paralleled by the gradual increase in the influence of the political parties which led to the first party-controlled cabinet with the appointment of Hara Kei, the leader of the conservative Seiyūkai party, as prime min-ister in 1918. Apart from several brief non-party cabinets immediately after the Great Kanto Earthquake, from then until May of 1932 Japan was governed by party cabinets formed by whichever party held the balance of power in the elected lower house of the Diet, whether the Seiyūkai or its rival the Kenseikai (renamed the Minseitō in 1926) (see Duus 1968; Mitani 1988). During this period the ideal of "normal constitutional gov-ernment", meaning the formation of cabinets and the control of the civil government by the party in control of the elected lower house, attained wide support as the logical development of Japanese democracy.

While in retrospect we may see Taishō democracy as a brief respite on the road towards the totalitarianism of the war, to many Japanese it seemed at the time that the establishment of party cabinets was an important step on the road to greater democ-racy. A number of other important steps were taken in this direction during the 1920s, including the passage in 1925 of changes in the electoral system to allow universal male suffrage. There were important liberal voices in the government such as the "social bureaucrats" described below, and in academia such as the Tokyo University professor Yoshino Sakuzō, a major advocate of liberal thinking through his concept of *minponshugi* (people-as-the-base-ism), which suggested that the welfare of the people was the basic purpose of the state. Yoshino's concept was important because it was successful for a time in maintaining the careful balance between the advocacy of greater democracy through universal suffrage and strengthening of the Diet, while still upholding the absolute sovereignty of the emperor (see Duus and Scheiner 1998; Najita 1974). This was essential because open advocacy of democracy (*minshushugi*) was considered trea-sonous as it implied that sovereignty rested in the people, not the emperor, and treason was punishable by death. Further, the spread of social movements, opposition groups, labour-organising and rural tenant associations all pointed to a more pluralistic politi-cal situation in which competing visions could be aired. The tradition of domination of legitimate activity in the public sphere by government officials thus seemed to be chang-ing in the early Taishō period.

This is only one side of the story, however, for at the same time a powerful counter-current of central state and particularly bureaucratic power was gaining strength. This eventually led to the eclipse of the emerging constitutional democracy of party-controlled cabinets and civil society itself in the early 1930s, and is the other essential background to understanding the planning system that emerged. The weakly democratic political structure created by the Meiji constitution was an important factor in subsequent developments. Japan was still very far from the achievement of a democratic system based on the sovereignty of the people. For example, until the passage of universal suffrage in 1925, the franchise was extremely limited, and had served to restrict effective electoral power at both the national and local levels to a small property-owning elite. The qualification for national elections restricted the electorate to around 10 per cent of males over the age of 25, effectively restricting the vote to wealthy property owners, merchants and industrialists. One unfortunate consequence of this restriction in the size of the electorate was that it made it much easier for politicians to gain election by vote-buying and pork-barrel public spending, which was an important factor in the declining respect for the established political parties and the system they represented during the 1920s (Duus 1968; Najita 1974: 56–7). The restricted electorate also meant, of course, that parties organised to represent the working class had little chance of electoral success even if they were not immediately repressed, and the two established conservative parties based their electoral strategy primarily on appeals to the interests of property owners.

Similar voting restrictions applied at the local level. In Tokyo, for example, only male Japanese citizens over the age of 25 who had lived in the city for over 2 years and paid over 2 yen per year in national or local taxes could vote, again restricting the electorate to less than 10 per cent of adult males. A further significant restriction was the class system of voters based on their share of taxes paid, which was copied from the Prussian system applied in Berlin. Voting power was divided equally between three classes of voters, each of which paid one-third of city taxes. According to a leading contemporary socialist thinker, Abe Isoo, one vote in the top class was worth 1,012 votes in the bottom class (Yazaki 1968: 334).

A second critical factor was the weakness of local government in relation to central government. It is hard to overstate the degree of central government dominance in the period before the Second World War. While municipal and prefectural governments had been the first units of government to be granted an electoral system in 1879, their independent powers were slight, even after the reforms of 1897 which increased the legal powers of prefectures, allowed the direct election of prefectural assemblies which had been indirectly selected by municipal councils, and abolished the special status of Tokyo, Osaka and Kyoto, which had been directly administered by central government. Assemblies were primarily advisory bodies, with no independent powers to legislate or raise taxes. Prefectural governors, appointed by the Home Ministry and responsible primarily to the national government, retained the exclusive power to draft by-laws for central approval and could act on their own authority in many areas, subject only to approval by the Home Ministry (Steiner 1965). Further, heavy government spending during the Russo-Japanese War had prompted sharp declines in local government revenue and spending as central government increased its share of a number of taxes and imposed restrictions on local government spending. These temporary measures were retained after the war's end, however, as central government spending continued at high levels (see Yazaki 1968: 411–13).

The first decades of the twentieth century were thus a period of decreasing local government independence and increasing central government powers. As Yazaki puts it,

"Local administration in this period is not to be equated with self-government. Each administrative unit was regarded as only an inferior level . . . local officials were submissively obedient to national directives. There was no local self-government in the modern sense of the term in these days" (Yazaki 1968: 415). Local governments, even in metropolitan areas, had neither legal authority nor financial independence. It is worth noting that while in comparative perspective local governments in Japan were clearly less independent than those in many of the other advanced nations, this does not mean that local governments in the West were models of democratic practice. They were commonly controlled by local elites, often corrupt, and frequently had less than democratic electoral systems where they were democratic at all, as in the Berlin system mentioned above which effectively reserved control of municipal affairs to a small minority of the old bourgeoisie. In the US, often presented as the polar opposite of Japan with its highly independent local governments, long tradition of universal (male) suffrage, and tradition of seeing municipal politics as the training ground of democratic impulses, its local governments at the turn of the century were nevertheless frequently corrupt, governed by party electoral machines and pork-barrel bosses (Mandlebaum 1965).

The weakness of democratic development in Taishō Japan was not only or even primarily a result of the limited franchise, however, as is suggested by the fact that it was only in the 1930s after the granting of universal male suffrage in 1925 that the formation of party-controlled cabinets ended, and a totalitarian state emerged. Throughout this period the parliamentary parties and their House of Representatives were among a range of power centres within the state. The legal and political structure that developed under the Meiji constitution, with its institutionalised dispersal of power among the *Genrō* (elder statesmen), the Imperial Household Ministry, the Privy Council, and the House of Peers were hardly affected by the shift toward party cabinets that was the most important sign of democratisation. The emperor was the ultimate authority and the organs of state were responsible to him, not the people, and derived much of their power though their interpretation of his will. The prime minister was still not chosen by the parties, but by the *Genrō,* and the Privy Council and the House of Peers could each reject any act of the House of Representatives. Crucially, the army and navy had a great deal of independence from the cabinet, as their supreme commander was the emperor, and they could and did bypass the rest of the government and get direct imperial authorisation for their policies. This structure meant it was relatively easy for the military to gradually seize control of power during the 1930s without the necessity of any sort of coup d'état, or even any constitutional revision.

Silberman (1982: 229) argues that the main beneficiary of the rather undefined relationship between the different power centres was the state bureaucracy, because it gained responsibility for much of the actual policy formation, and argues that by the middle of the Meiji period it had achieved a dominant role in the organisation of interests and the determination of public policy. He further suggests that while there were three main periods in the development of state bureaucratic power from 1868 to 1945, bureaucratic absolutism from 1868 to 1900, limited pluralism from 1900 to 1936 and almost total (civilian and military) bureaucratic control from 1936 to 1945, "The crowning paradox is that despite such pendulum shifts, the bureaucracy continued to enjoy the highest status and the most powerful place in the formation of public policy, a place it continues to enjoy today" (Silberman 1982: 231). Although bureaucratic power was a constant feature of the Japanese state from the Meiji period, however, with the growth of the economy in the early twentieth century, the resources available to it, as well as the scope of its activities expanded enormously. The size of the bureaucracy grew rapidly after the Russo-Japanese War – along with urban/industrial growth – from 52,200 government officers in 1907 to 308,200 in 1920 (Yazaki 1968: 425). Central government spending had tripled in the decade before the war to 289 million yen in 1903, doubled again during the war, then remained at the level of about 600 million yen until 1913 (Pyle 1973: 56). The greatly expanded realm of state activity in developing its new colonies, aiding industrial capital formation, and especially military expansion which consistently consumed about half the budget, required a larger and more activist bureaucracy. Although it is true that the oligarchs had ruled Japan through the bureaucracy during the Meiji period, thus gradually increasing its status, it is fair to say that it was during the Taishō period that the bureaucracy attained its status as an independent and powerful player in the Japanese political economy.

The skewed electoral system, weak local government, and the growth of central government power exercised largely by an elite bureaucracy are all important facets of Japanese political development in the inter-war period. The truly fascinating part of the story however, particularly from the point of view of the development of urban society and urban planning, is the use that the bureaucracy made of its increasing power within Japanese society.

From social mobilisation to social management

During the Meiji period the project of national self-preservation in the face of expanding Western power had served effectively to mobilise popular support, and exhortations to the Japanese people to mobilise their energies and make sacrifices to protect national independence had been very effective. With success in the Russo-Japanese War those goals had been assured, and mass mobilisation of the people became a much more difficult prospect, particularly as the national project shifted from national survival to imperial expansion. The end of the war thus ushered in a new phase of development and modernisation, and as Harootunian (1974) argues the Japanese ruling elite was keenly aware of this ending of the Meiji project and the beginning of a new phase of development during the first decades of the twentieth century. Mobilising the people for the next stage of national development was thus a central concern of Japanese policy-makers. Oka (1982) writes of the distress of the ruling elites over what they saw as the decadence of modern youth, and the loss of consensus over the need to sacrifice individual desires for the national good, describing the Boshin Imperial Rescript of 1908 as an attempt to unify the population behind the new goals of imperial expansion. In this respect the rescript was akin to the sumptuary laws of the Tokugawa period, in that it identified in the people dangerous tendencies towards self-indulgence and luxury which had to be combated as a threat to the strength of the state. Such exhortations to frugality and diligence on the part of the people to aid the state in pursuing national goals is similar to the widespread appeals for national mobilisation, savings and discipline by Western governments during the First and Second World Wars. In the Japanese case, however, such appeals were almost continuous in wartime and peacetime from the early Meiji period to the end of the Second World War, and after.

In a sense, then, Japan was in a state of continuous national mobilisation throughout the pre-war period. Pyle (1973: 57), in his seminal work on Japanese government efforts to use nationalistic social organising to counter the social problems created by industrialism and imperialism, contends that central government bureaucrats saw Japan as embarking on an economic war in which the state had to invest in industrial growth and education in order to develop the resources to support the empire. The people thus had to pay higher taxes, work harder and consume less in order to contribute to national strength. The primary goal of the Japanese state at this time was thus not individual or even collective welfare, but national strength. The problem of course, is that that strategy inevitably had costs, noticeably the increased burdens on the people, as Yazaki argued, "The benefits accruing from public projects have to be weighed against the involuntary commitment to near-poverty on the part of most citizens in support of national policies of industrialisation, expanded overseas trade, colonization and militarization" (Yazaki 1968: 415). A major problem for the state during the Taishō period was that increasing numbers of Japanese questioned this ordering of priorities, as demonstrated by the increasing social conflict and opposition movements generated by the strategy of rapid industrial, military and imperial growth. It was these pressures that generated the period's increasingly active strategies of social management.

During the first decades of the twentieth century the Japanese government stepped up its efforts to mobilise the Japanese people in support of nationalism and imperial expansion. Government officials argued that in order to compete with the wealthier and stronger Western powers Japan would have to rely on the greater unity of its people. Far from relying on some instinctive sense of nationalism, however, as Pyle (1974; 1973) has shown, central government bureaucrats, and particularly those in the Home Ministry, were actively involved in fostering nationalism by "devising techniques to mobilise the material and spiritual resources of the population in order to cope with social problems and to provide support for Japanese imperialism" (Pyle 1973: 53). As Garon (1997) has shown, these efforts were broadened in the 1920s and 1930s into wide-ranging "social management" and "moral suasion" campaigns in support of higher savings, diligence and thrift, better nutrition and hygiene, religious orthodoxy, and "daily life improvement campaigns". These moral suasion campaigns employed existing grassroots organisations such as army reservist groups, agricultural cooperatives, young men's and women's organisations, and neighbourhood organisations to disseminate their messages to the level of individual households, and were able to mobilise considerable public support for and participation in their activities.

One important premise of such bureaucratic social management was the belief that Japan was following universal historical forces in its path to urbanisation and industrialisation. As a late developer, it had the opportunity to observe the mistakes and problems that the more advanced countries had encountered, and could try to avoid or mitigate social problems such as class conflict, labour problems, and the decline of the traditional social mores of peasant villages, etc, that had accompanied urbanisation and industrialisation in the West. This opportunity to learn from the mistakes of others Pyle terms the "advantage of followership" (Pyle 1974). Social policy in Japan was the product of this conception of the close connection between laissez-faire economic liberalism and the emergence of "social problems". It became a basic assumption of many social policy advocates that social policy could mitigate the social problems of industrialisation, and help prevent the emergence of socialism and urban unrest (Pyle 1974: 143). In this the chief model was Bismarckian Germany, another semi-constitutional absolutist state which as a late industrialiser had developed a sophisticated approach to social policy designed to avoid the industrial conflict seen in Britain.

The main instigator behind the development of social management practices was the Home Ministry, which was responsible for the highly centralised local government structure, supervision of national and local police forces, and a wide range of other administrative functions from election management and fire-fighting to city planning. Its chief power base was its control over local administration through appointment of senior staff to prefectural governorships and other key positions in local governments throughout the country (see Steiner 1965: chapter 3). Within the Home Ministry the social developments since the Russo-Japanese War, particularly the spread of socialistic ideas and labour unions were a cause of grave concern. Worsening urban conditions such as increasing poverty and growing disparities of income, documented in the Home Ministry's Bureau of Local Affairs survey of poor households in 1911 and the Tokyo Bureau of Social Affairs survey of 1920, and the evident popular discontent expressed by the Rice Riots of 1918 and other mass demonstrations called for action. The Home Ministry response had two apparently contradictory faces.

On the one hand the Ministry tried to suppress political opposition with its Higher Police and Special Higher Police who were brutally effective in their repression, for example, of socialist and communist organising. On the other hand, the Ministry's social bureaucrats attempted to develop social policies that would alleviate the sources of discontent by instituting social welfare programmes, providing better housing and urban environments through planning, and organising local communities in self-help associations. These divergent strategies shared the goal of reinforcing the strength of the state by ensuring social stability. Where the police attempted to strengthen this stability through systematic elimination of organisations that challenged the status quo, the social bureaucrats sought stability by broadening the franchise to include a broader representation of the population, improving living conditions, and encouraging the development of labour law.

It is important, therefore, to recognise the range of views within the bureaucracy at this time. As Garon argues, while most historians tend to dismiss Japan's inter-war bureaucracy as conservative opponents of the liberal tendencies of Taishō democracy, in fact there was a great deal of diversity within the bureaucracy, and the initiative behind many of the most important progressive reforms came "not so much from the bourgeois parties – and certainly not from the weak social democratic movement – but rather from activist cliques of higher civil servants" (Garon 1987: 73). As he puts it, "Whereas the 'economic bureaucrats' of other ministries worked primarily to further industrial development, the 'social bureaucrats' of the Home Ministry sought to reduce the sources of social unrest that arose from unrestrained economic relations and inadequate living and working conditions" (Garon 1987: 74). These "social bureaucrats" within the Home Ministry argued that the best way to counter emerging social tensions was to improve working and living conditions, and to broaden the franchise in order to prevent the further development of movements that sought to overthrow the state. Among the elite stream of top-level bureaucrats were a considerable number who argued for the power of city planning to improve urban housing and working conditions as shown below, and they should be counted among these progressive social bureaucrats.

Early Home Ministry campaigns such as the Local Improvement Movement (*Chihō Kairyō Undō*) were carried out in rural areas to reinforce traditional community values of mutual support and assistance and prevent the decline of village society. Agricultural cooperatives, community credit societies, youth associations and reservist associations were all enlisted in the job of organising self-help and mutual support groups. Designed in part to further integrate local administration with central government, the movement included efforts to step up the amalgamation of hamlets into larger administrative towns and villages, the mergers of Shinto shrines and their integration into the national administrative machinery, and the promotion of grassroots organisations in support of thrift, diligence and the payment of taxes.

The development of neighbourhood associations

Although the Local Improvement Movement had been primarily directed towards rural areas, both because that was where the majority of the population lived and because the villages were seen as the most stable repositories of traditional values and thus more susceptible to the government's messages, it provided the model for later efforts at social management by the Home Ministry in urban areas. In the 1920s these included a variety of social policy initiatives, including the district commissioner (*hōmen iin*) system, where local "people of virtue" were selected as unpaid intermediaries between the poor and public and private social services. This initiative was consciously modelled on the German *Elberfeld* system of charity organised by local community groups (Ikeda 1986: 251). The district commissioner system was designed to reduce the burdens on public poor relief by organising local volunteers to provide advice and encourage mutual support, and had been disseminated throughout the country by the early 1930s.

One explicit goal of the commissioner system was to revive the neighbourhood responsibility system of Tokugawa Japan, in which rural villages and urban neighbourhoods had shared responsibility for payment of taxes, maintenance of public order and prevention of fires, and the maintenance of local public infrastructure such as roads and wells. To a great extent it was successful in mobilising the urban middle classes in support of the social-policy goals of neighbourhood mutual support and encouraging local charitable support groups to bear a large part of the burden of funding poor relief (Garon 1997: 56). According to Garon (1997: 53–4), "Most urban commissioners appear to have been the owners of small stores or workshops, with a smattering of doctors, priests, and professional social workers. These middle-class elements became further integrated into the state apparatus during the 1920s. Many district commissioners concurrently headed neighborhood sanitation associations and youth associations, served in ward assemblies, or functioned as 'moral suasion commissioners' in the government's ongoing drives to encourage household savings, promote loyalty to the emperor and cultivate good morals." Hastings (1995: 80) also identifies this kind of social stratum among the leaders of neighbourhood organisations in the industrial Honjo ward of east Tokyo in the 1920s. About 80 per cent of chōnaikai leaders were the heads of enterprises located within the ward, including heads of factories, shop owners, doctors and dentists, precisely those most desirous of a clean, safe orderly local environment. The sanitary and youth associations, and others including neighbourhood shopkeepers' associations, shrine parish associations, parent teacher associations, army reserve and veterans groups served as the breeding ground for the emergence during the first decades of the century of a very broadly disseminated network of local neighbourhood associations (*chōkai* or *chōnaikai*) led primarily by the old urban middle class.

There is some disagreement about the degree to which neighbourhood associations were the direct product of government social engineering. Smith (1978) contends they were created from below, resulting primarily from the efforts of local merchants and reflect the enduring tradition of Edo neighbourhood (*chō*) organisations: "Wholly spontaneous organizations at the chō level, the chōnaikai rose in number from a mere 39 in 1897 to 452 on the eve of the Kanto earthquake, by which time about half the city was organised (the other half following quickly in the decade after the earthquake) . . . the chōnaikai were essentially a means of sustaining local community solidarity in the face of rapid population turnover" (1978: 66). Dore, on the other hand, suggests that while the old Edo neighbourhood organisations had virtually disappeared during the upheavals of the Meiji period as new local government organisations took their place, they were increasingly revived after the turn of the century "as local governments saw advantage in having small local organizations to co-operate in public health programmes" (1968: 187). The main activities of the chōnaikai were to organise local garbage collection points and recycling campaigns, sanitation and insecticide campaigns, street-cleaning, installation and maintenance of streetlights, and organising night watches against fire and crime. One thing all agree on is that chōnaikai were dominated by the old urban middle class, landowners and small business proprietors, and that their main function was to carry information and directives down from central and local government to the people, and seldom functioned in the reverse direction, to carry requests or protests towards those in authority. In the pre-war period, and to a lesser degree even today the chōnaikai were in many regards less a part of civil society than they were the lowest-level auxiliary bodies of local administrations.

During the 1930s the chōnaikai were gradually extended throughout the country and transformed into an effective link from central government to virtually every community and home, providing an impressive means of social control. In 1940 the Home Ministry made them compulsory for the whole country and incorporated them into the local government system, giving them responsibility for civil defence, distribution of rations and the promotion of savings associations. They were also used by the ministry's thought police as a way of gathering information on deviant behaviour. As Dore notes, the system was extremely effective in exerting pressure on families and individuals, and their coercive aspects were exploited to the full during wartime. (Dore 1958: 272). With the successful dissemination of the chōnaikai throughout the country the Home Ministry was able to reproduce to a remarkable degree the Tokugawa period system of vertical hierarchical connections reaching from the top levels of the Bakufu and domain administrations into virtually every household in the nation. The chōnaikai were disbanded by the post-war occupation as having been one of the integral elements of the system of totalitarian control that it was attempting to reform, but by the early 1950s they had regrouped, usually under a slightly different name, but with many of the same members, boundaries and functions as the old organisations (see Bestor 1989). While still responsible for a wide range of local duties such as local street and park cleanups, local shrine festivals, recycling programmes, and distribution of local government circulars, however, direct connections to government are largely absent, and few would argue that neighbourhood associations are part of a system of government domination. Japanese neighbourhood organisations have been the subject of considerable study since the 1970s because of the apparent success of Japanese cities in retaining close-knit neighbourhoods and avoiding the Western urban crisis of the 1960s and 1970s of spiralling crime and abandonment of the inner city by the affluent (see e.g. Bestor 1989; Falconeri 1976; White 1976).

In hindsight it is difficult not to see the activities of the Home Ministry in the light of the fact that in the late 1930s the chōnaikai and other community organisations were absorbed into the system of totalitarian control and mobilisation of the country for war. From that perspective the social bureaucrats were little more than advance agents of the totalitarian regime. Without minimising the obvious negative aspects of Japanese social management in the inter-war period, however, another interpretation is possible: that the attempt to organise local community self-responsibility was a reasonable approach to solving the urban social problems that were emerging in the cities. As Hastings (1995) has shown in her detailed study of Home Ministry programmes in poor areas of Tokyo, many of the activities of the social bureaucrats at the local level were clearly of benefit to local communities.

There have also been many positive effects of community mobilisation which have become lasting aspects of Japanese urban life. Japan's close-knit neighbourhood seem to have helped allay many of the urban social problems seen in other developed countries. For example, Dore (1958) describes in detail the close relations of mutual support found in a typical inner city neighbourhood in Tokyo in the early 1950s, and Bestor (1989) was surprised to find that things had changed so little by the time he was doing his fieldwork in the early 1980s. Possibly the most visible manifestation of the maintenance of "traditional" neighbourhood ties are the extraordinary safety and cleanliness of Japanese cities, which are so admired by foreign visitors and residents alike. While the work of the social bureaucrats was clearly one face of the expanding state, therefore, and was unabashedly conducted with the goal of strengthening Japanese economic power and social unity in support of nationalism and imperialism, it is an oversimplification to suggest that all their activities were merely preludes to the totalitarian disaster that followed, or that they may not have had some very positive outcomes in the development of community life and organisation.

The chōnaikai are, however, clearly part of the answer to the question of why the middle class was not more active in municipal politics. The fact is they were very active at the local level, co-opted into government-directed local activities such as providing most of the local social welfare and community services as well as garbage collection and street-cleaning, and providing their own street-lighting. This relieved local governments of the need to provide a range of costly local services, as well as providing a direct conduit for central government information and directives to reach every neighbourhood and ultimately every family in the country. It is possible to interpret this either as a good, or a bad thing, depending on what values are given priority. If social stability is prized, then government social-management campaigns may be considered simply a good thing, as they clearly did lead to greater degrees of neighbourhood mutual self-reliance and self-support. Even without the disaster of the mobilisation of neighbourhood organisations in support of totalitarian government during the war years, however, it is possible to question their real benefit for urban residents. As a means of co-opting urban residents the chōnaikai were extremely effective in preventing the sort of grassroots pressure on local governments that in many Western cities resulted in better municipal services and local environments.

It should neither be assumed that the emerging social management practices were unwelcome, however, nor that the primary goal of the social bureaucrats was the imposition of totalitarian control. In fact, as Garon (1997) has shown, many of the government's efforts at social management, even the most intrusive, relied on a great deal of voluntary participation by Japanese citizens and interest groups, and particularly by the middle class. The chōnaikai were just one example of social management practices in the pre-war period, although one particularly relevant to city planning. Garon details a wide range of programmes aimed at promoting savings, neighbourhood mutual support, encouraging thrift and good household management, promoting a model of the ideal woman as a good wife and wise mother, and the promotion of Shinto as the established state religion while attempting systematically to eliminate the fast spreading "new religions". We cannot know what direction Japanese social management might have taken if Japan had not been simultaneously slipping towards war and the militarism of the 1930s. The important point here is that all of these campaigns served to increase the presence of government in the everyday lives of ordinary people, and served to narrow the space available for independent conceptions of the public good, or independent activities supporting public goals. Civil society had virtually ceased to exist in Japan by the end of the 1930s.

Civil society, social mobilisation and city planning

The weak development of Japanese civil society in this period is important for understanding the development of city planning because in the other developed countries city planning was from the beginning the territory of broad-ranging and shifting alliances of independent groups and associations that argued for city planning as necessary to protect the public welfare, particularly of the urban poor. The development of the international city planning movement was largely generated from within the institutions of civil society, not within the central state, which tended to follow rather than lead. To an extraordinary degree early planning developments in Japan, however, were the work of a small group of elite bureaucrats within the Home Ministry, a fact that continued to shape attitudes towards city planning in the post-war period, long outlasting the particular social and political conditions that gave rise to Japan's heavily centralised system of city planning.

An important legacy of the Taishō era is thus that until the late 1960s or early 1970s there was very little popular support for or expectations of city planning. While it seems likely that in time the developing civil society of the early Taishō period might have generated a broader constituency in support of city planning, that avenue was effectively closed off by the elimination of civil society itself in the inter-war period. This was critical because in Japan, as elsewhere, the development of stronger planning regulations was often vigorously resisted by landowners. In Britain, for example, only a long process of public campaigns was able to overcome the resistance of large landowners to stricter planning regulation and establish the principle that public regulation of urban development was important to protect the public interest. In Japan such an evolution never happened, and the rights associated with land ownership have remained extremely strong. Land ownership rights in Japan are no doubt rooted in the long tradition of control over land and its productive capacity as the basis of political and social power, a feudal socio-political organisation which in Japan lasted until the mid-nineteenth century. This basic conception of land ownership was strongly reinforced by the Meiji Constitution of 1889, which in Article 27 states, "The right to own or to hold property is inviolable" (Tsuru 1993: 164). This reflected the conservative tendencies of the Meiji era when larger landowners cemented their political and social power within the Japanese political economy. The political space and constituency necessary to challenge strong land ownership rights, and advocate a conception of city planning as a project for the pursuit of the public good and the quality of life of urban residents was lacking, and city planning in inter-war Japan remained a central government project, subordinated to national goals of economic and military expansion.

The beginnings of Japanese urban planning

The development of Japan's first modern city planning system was very much a product of the social and political context of the Taishō period: rapid urban and industrial growth, worsening standards of living for the working class, social strife and a spreading labour movement, movements towards greater democratisation and pluralism in political life, and vigorous central government attempts to repress radical political movements on the one hand, while alleviating social conditions through social policy, housing provision, community organising, and improved city planning on the other.

Rapid urban growth caused serious new problems, particularly as Meiji planning efforts had been focused on rebuilding the central area of Tokyo, and had developed few tools for structuring new growth. While in 1900 the population of the then City of Tokyo (approximately the area of the feudal era city) was 1.12 million, that had increased to 2.17 million by 1920. More dramatic was the increase in population of the surrounding 82 towns and villages which were incorporated into Greater Tokyo in 1932 to form what is today the 23-ward area. At the turn of the century those areas were basically rural, and had a population of 380,000, but by 1920 their population had increased by 369 per cent to 1.18 million (Ishida 1987: 110). Virtually all of this urban growth took place as haphazard unplanned sprawl in and around existing farm villages on the urban fringe. Similar processes were at work on a smaller scale in the other main industrial centres of Osaka and Nagoya. The growth of urban population, and in particular the unplanned urban fringe growth outside the old city areas made abundantly clear the need for strengthened planning systems. The first legislative response was the extension in 1918 of the provisions of the TCIO to Osaka, Kyoto, Yokohama, Kobe, and Nagoya, the five largest cities after Tokyo. This was quickly superseded with the passage in 1919 of a new City Planning Law and Urban Buildings Law, which created the first national city planning framework.

The 1919 laws were the first attempt of a Japanese government to create a comprehensive planning system that would regulate whole city areas and allow planned urban growth. The TCIO had been primarily concerned with the improvement of existing areas, and operated mainly through specific development or redevelopment projects. Little attempt had been made to structure the growth of the city as a whole, nor were powers sufficient to regulate private landowners or builders. By introducing land use zoning, building controls, and a system to plan whole city areas the 1919 law was a major turning point and remained in effect for close to 50 years, until it was replaced by the New City Planning Law of 1968. The 1919 law thus provided the planning framework for urban growth in the critical post-war period of rapid economic growth, when Japan's urban population and area expanded so rapidly, so its impacts have been profound.

The development of the new city planning system was closely associated with attempts by reformist bureaucrats within the Taishō Home Ministry to develop social policies to alleviate urban social problems, and the new social welfare and city planning policies developed between the end of the First World War and early 1920s were considered to be complementary by the Home Ministry "social bureaucrats" who designed them (Okata 1986). The development of the new approaches to city planning and social policy were initiated by the reformer Gotō Shimpei, a doctor, bureaucrat and statesman of exceptional administrative talent who had played a key role in reorganising the Japanese colonial administration of Taiwan (Peattie 1988). In 1917 then Home Minister Gotō set up a Relief Section within the Local Affairs Bureau to coordinate efforts to alleviate poverty and unemployment. That small Relief Section was later expanded into a Social Affairs Bureau in 1920 which dealt with unemployment, poor relief, veteran's assistance and children's welfare. It is that bureau which led many of the social management efforts discussed above. Also in 1917 Gotō set up the Urban Study Group (*Toshi Kenkyu Kai*) within the Local Affairs Bureau to study urban planning issues, with Ikeda Hiroshi as director. Ikeda was a graduate of the University of Kyoto law department who had become head of the Home Ministry Roads Bureau at the age of 30 in 1911 (Ishida 1987: 123; Watanabe 1993: 170–2). The study group was chaired by Gotō himself until his death in 1929 (Koshizawa 1991: 14; Okata 1986), and included young bureaucrats from the Home Ministry, several professors from the University of Tokyo, a Diet member, and a newspaper journalist. This was a highly influential group, which apart from researching and lobbying for the improvement of planning legislation, also published the journal *Urban Review* (*Toshi Kōron*) as a forum for enlightened thinking about urban policy.

In May of 1918 Gotō established the City Planning Section (*Toshi Keikaku Ka*) within the Home Ministry, with Ikeda Hiroshi as chief. This was a public confirmation establishing city planning as a function of government, and a means of solidifying the jurisdiction of the Home Ministry. In the same month the City Planning Research Committee (*Toshi Keikaku Chōsakai*) was established to begin drafting a new city planning law. That committee comprised 28 members, including three from the Home Ministry, two each from the academic disciplines of law, medicine, civil engineering and architecture, the mayor of Tokyo, the deputy mayor of Osaka and a Tokyo City Council member (Okata 1986). In the 12 months from July 1918 Ikeda drafted the City Planning Law (*Toshi Keikaku Hō*). At the same time the Urban Buildings Law (*Shigaichi Kenchikubutsu Hō*) was drafted by Tokyo University professors of architecture Sano Toshikata and Uchida Shozō who later became a famous president of the university, and Kasahara Toshiro, a Home Ministry officer and former student of Sano and Uchida. Kasahara later wrote one of the first Japanese textbooks on the new city planning and building regulations that was published in the early 1930s.

The system as envisaged drew from the best practice of several European systems, and if passed in its initial form would possibly have been one of the more advanced planning regimes of the time. The draft city planning law included the main provisions of the earlier TCIO for designating and building public facilities such as roads, a zoning system and building-line system based on German techniques, and an urban version of the Land Readjustment (LR) system (described in more detail in Chapter 4), which had previously only been intended for agricultural land improvement although it had already been used for suburban development outside Kobe and Osaka. It also included several financial measures including a tax on increases in land values (*tochi zōkazei*), a betterment levy (*juekisha futankin*) on landowners who would benefit from city planning projects such as roads and park construction, a system of financial support by central government for designated city planning projects of not less than one-third and not more than two-thirds of the total project costs, and a system of land expropriation modelled on that used so effectively by Haussmann in Paris. Usually literally translated from the Japanese *chōka shūyō* as "excess condemnation", this system allowed expropriation of an area significantly wider than a planned new road so that profits from the sale of the valuable new street-fronting plots could be used to pay the costs of the project. The City Planning Law was complemented by an Urban Buildings Law that detailed the building regulations including permissible building uses, heights and lot coverages of the zoning system. The latter law also included the building-line regulation system modelled after the German *Fluchtlinienplan*. These laws and their implementation are discussed in greater detail in the next chapter.

The proposed laws encountered strong opposition from the Finance Ministry, however, which stubbornly opposed central government financial support for city planning and argued that urban improvement was not an important responsibility of central government compared to education, national defence, transportation and communications (Koshizawa 1991: 17). As a result of Finance Ministry pressure, several key provisions including articles relating to central government financial support for planning projects and the tax on the increase of land values (*tochi zōkazei*) to fund city planning had to be deleted before the law could be passed (Koshizawa 1991: 15). As with the TCIO, therefore, the Finance Ministry was the nemesis of the development of the planning system, and in 1922 the City Planning Bureau of the Home Ministry published a strongly worded complaint against the radical weakening of the law at the hands of the Finance Ministry. As Koshizawa puts it, "The exceptional passion of the document records clearly their agony (*kunō*) that the legislation setting out the beginnings of urban planning in Japan should have had the actual means of carrying out city planning projects torn from it" (Koshizawa 1991: 16). The weakened sources of finance was a major setback for advocates of improved city planning in Japan, and city planners still regret the defeat.

It seems fair to suggest that the dominant view within the government at this time as represented by the powerful Finance Ministry was that city planning – in the sense of planning for the growth and healthy development of a whole urban area, including both its economic development and the quality of life of its citizens – was not a responsibility of government at all. According to this view the only aspects of urbanisation that should be financed or planned by government were major trunk roads, ports, railways, canals and schools, which were already covered by other laws. All of these were infrastructure essential for industrial and military expansion. Public goods such as local roads, sidewalks, parks, street lights, and street cleaning, were discretionary, to be provided neither by central nor local government, but by local residents themselves in a continuation of the self-responsibility system. While the Home Ministry was able to achieve passage of most of its 1919 City Planning system, therefore, the opposition of the Ministry of Finance to the proposed financial measures meant that its achievements would be smaller than hoped, as discussed in the next chapter. Here it is worth looking at one final crucial aspect of the 1919 system; its centralisation of planning power.

Centralisation of planning authority

As the central state grew stronger during the Taishō period, with greater resources deriving from economic growth and increasing bureaucratic control, the autonomy of local governments grew ever weaker to the point where they were operated essentially as local branch offices of the central ministries. The central government bureaucracy held a deep-seated distrust of local government as concerned primarily with the local, not national interest, and as a consequence deliberately kept them weak.

In the area of city planning centralisation of authority was accomplished in two main ways. First, a central aspect of the system of local government established during the Meiji period was that they were responsible to provide a certain range of services for local citizens, but could not exercise governmental authority over them. This restriction of local government activity resulted in the "agency delegated functions" system described in the previous chapter, whereby central government refused to allow any independent police powers to local government. Instead, it would delegate legal power in cases where local governments were required to carry out functions necessitating the use of police power, such as city planning or control of nuisances. Such delegation meant, however, that the local mayor or prefectural governor legally became the agent of central government, rather than being responsible to their own electors. Local governments had almost no legal powers to implement planning policies that differed from those allowed by central government.

Second, under the 1919 law all plans had to be approved by the Home Minister, and each year city planning budgets had to be authorised by the Home Ministry. Although city planning authority was formally vested in local City Planning Commissions (*Toshi Keikaku Iinkai*), these were composed roughly half of local prefectural and municipal assembly members and local mayors, and half of high-ranking prefectural and central government bureaucrats and technical specialists, and were chaired by the prefectural governors who were Home Ministry appointees (Ishida 1987: 114–15). These joint committees were created because it was assumed that large central cities would not absorb smaller suburban fringe municipalities which normally resisted such amalgamation, yet at the same time the necessity of planning the functional urban region was strongly advocated by Home Ministry chief Ikeda (Watanabe 1984: 418). With the passage of the 1919 system central government bureaucrats significantly extended their powers over local city planning efforts. Particularly problematic was that the national legislation admitted no variation in use zones or building regulations between areas with quite different urban patterns and urban problems, and suffered from the attempt to impose a solution to Tokyo's problems on the whole country.

Centralisation of planning power during the Taishō period did facilitate Japan's game of catch-up with the most advanced Western nations. It meant that very quickly a high level of technical expertise in plan-making and legislation drafting was concentrated in the City Planning Department of the Home Ministry. National projects such as the rebuilding of Tokyo-Yokohama after the 1923 Great Kanto Earthquake were pushed forward with great speed. Unfortunately the requirement that all plans and budgets be approved by the central ministry slowed the development of planning expertise at the local level and inhibited the development of alternative or innovative approaches to planning issues. In Japan there was little of the outpouring of small-scale experimentation and local innovation seen in many Western countries. This system stands in great contrast to the spread of zoning in the US during the 1920s for example, where once the legal precedent had been established, local communities across the country voluntarily passed their own zoning by-laws, with wide variations in types of zones designated, reflecting differing local priorities.

Another important outcome of centralisation was a distinct preference for project management over regulatory controls. A small, powerful central bureaucracy found it easier to control a number of specific projects than to manage a complex regulatory system. Until the present the regulation of urban land development and land use in Japan has remained weak in comparative perspective, with no subdivision control or effective means of ensuring that land developers provide even essential services such as sewerage connections or improved local roads (see Sorensen 1999). Instead of regulating urban development, Japanese planners have instead promoted projects for land development and redevelopment, such as LR or urban redevelopment projects. Instead of developing an effective system for managing urban growth and environmental quality, the Japanese government focused on the efficient provision of the infrastructure necessary for economic and military growth. For those purposes a project development style of planning was appropriate.

The centralisation of political power in the Tokyo bureaucracies also tended to inhibit the development of wider public support for city planning, which was seen as a central government imposition rather than a local project. The lack of broader public support for planning left planning advocates in the Home Ministry and local governments weak. Without a broad base of organisational support in local governments or the plethora of citizens' groups and professional organisations that kept pushing environmental issues onto the public agenda in the West, it was easy for the Finance Ministry to block the financial measures that might have given substance to the 1919 city planning system. Even inexpensive measures such as improved regulation of land uses, or stricter requirements for developers to respect planned road networks were difficult to implement because they encountered opposition by vested interests and little support from potential beneficiaries. Whereas the establishment of Western city planning was the result of long campaigns by planning advocates against the established interests of property owners, in Japan such a movement could hardly form.

The lack of a movement in support of planning also meant that there was little public education about the benefits of planning, and little of the popularisation of planning ideas and values which formed such an important foundation for the development of more interventionist planning regimes in Western countries. Instead, effective government campaigns encouraged neighbourhood associations and promoted the idea that local people should be responsible for the cleaning and maintenance of local facilities, waste sorting and removal, local policing and even the support of the poor. The idea that local governments should be responsible for a range of public goods such as the provision of sewerage, sidewalks and local roads, local parks or play-lots, or facilities such as child care centres and libraries was very slow to take root even in post-war Japan.

While it would be incorrect to suggest that the developments during the Taishō period described here can fully explain the subsequent development of urban planning and urbanisation in Japan, they do provide important insights into some of their puzzling features. Certainly, it is hard to understand the twentieth-century development of Japanese urban planning and Japanese cities without first understanding the social and economic context of its beginnings in the Taishō period, the fragile and short-lived development of civil society of pre-war Japan, the extent of government centralisation, and the weak basis of public support for and understanding of urban planning.

4   Japan's first urban planning system

> I imagined the grandeur of the new metropolis, and all the changes that would come in customs and manners as well. An orderly pattern of streets, their bright new pavements gleaming. A flood of automobiles. The geometric beauty of block towering upon block, and elevated lines and subways and trolleys weaving among them, and the stir of a nightless city, and pleasure facilities to rival those of Paris and New York . . . Fragments of the new Tokyo passed before my eyes, numberless, like flashes in a movie.
>
> Seidensticker (1991: 15) cites the reflections of the novelist Tanizaki Junichirō upon hearing of the Great Kanto Earthquake of 1923

The dramatic transformations of Japanese cities accompanying industrialisation and urbanisation signalled for some, who looked back nostalgically to a former golden age, the passing of all that was fine and solid in Japanese society. For others it signalled the beginning of a bright new future of progress and modernity. The passage of a new planning system, and particularly the broad strengthening of powers to control unruly suburban growth held out the hope that cities throughout the country would be able to transform themselves in ways appropriate to the new age. This chapter focuses on the implementation of the new urban planning system passed in 1919, and is divided into four main sections.

The first section outlines the principal features of the new system. The second describes its implementation, and particularly the impacts of the project for rebuilding Tokyo after the Great Kanto Earthquake of 1923, when the new system was just starting. The third section examines several other important cases of planning intervention and planned urban development of the period, including garden city developments, planning in Osaka, planning in the colonies, and early attempts at metropolitan structure planning with green belts and park systems. A final section summarises the main characteristics of city planning in the pre-war period, and describes the main changes in urban areas that occurred during the period.

The 1919 city planning system

The 1919 city planning system had five main parts: a land use zoning system; the Urban Buildings Law which was a building code and provided the detailed regulations for the land use zones of the zoning system; a building-line system to control growth in the urban fringe; a system for designating public facilities which was basically a revision of the earlier Tokyo City Improvement Ordinance (TCIO), and a Land Readjustment (LR) system. These five planning systems are described in turn.

Land use zoning

Japan's first zoning system was a very simple one. It had only three types of land use zones, residential, commercial and industrial, and nothing like the strict separation of uses commonly associated with the term "zoning" in the US was either intended or applied. The zoning system was largely the work of Ikeda Hiroshi, who had become head of the Home Ministry Roads Bureau (*Dobokukyoku Dōroka*) at the age of 30 in 1911. After two years in that post, Ikeda travelled to Europe and America to study planning developments there. He attended an international conference on road planning in London in 1913, then travelled to Germany which had probably the most advanced city planning practice of the time including a variety of zoning systems, and returned to Japan via New York where he learned of the debates about the 1916 New York zoning ordinance (Watanabe 1993: 170). Ikeda subsequently became one of Japan's leading experts on Western zoning systems, and applied his knowledge in the zoning system he devised for Japan.

Ikeda's zoning system was never intended to promote the rigid separation of land uses that is commonly associated with zoning today, but was a sort of inclusive zoning which formalised rights to use land in certain ways. Ikeda explained his zoning concept in a memorandum to the first meeting of the City Planning Research Committee which was in charge of drafting the new planning laws in 1918, when he said the purpose of the use zones was not primarily to enforce a strict regulatory control over land uses in the different zones, but to indicate the future structure of the city in a concrete way by designating the use zones well in advance of urbanisation (Okata 1980: 14). Thus in commercial areas broad boulevards were to be encouraged, in residential areas development projects such as LR should develop narrow residential roads, and in industrial areas large blocks should be created, divided by a few major arterial roads. Indeed, the land uses permitted in the zones of the 1919 City Planning Law were not very restrictive, as shown in Table 4.1.

Put simply, heavy industry was restricted to industrial zones, noisy entertainment uses such as theatres and nightclubs were restricted to commercial zones which also had more permissive bulk allowances, and residential zones had stricter building height restrictions than each of the others. Apart from these restrictions, a broad intermixture of uses continued throughout Japanese cities. Workers' housing continued to proliferate in industrial zones, commercial uses and offices were commonly located in residential zones, and smaller-scale manufacturing plants were located everywhere but in the central business districts where land was too expensive.

The zoning system was used primarily to separate heavy industry districts from residential districts. This was not necessarily to protect homeowners or residents, however, as might be assumed today. Rather it was intended to protect industry from residents' complaints. As the Home Ministry secretary Mizuno suggested to a conference of the Japan Architects Association in 1917, zoning could give a measure of legal protection to large industrial land users. He gave as an example the case of Asano Cement, which when it was first established in Fukagawa in eastern Tokyo was in the midst of open countryside, but gradually became surrounded by workers' housing. The new residents

Table 4.1 Urban Buildings Law zone restrictions, 1919

	Land use restrictions	Permitted coverage	Height limit	Slant plane restrictions
Residential zones	Prohibited uses: Factories with more than 15 employees, or with engines of more than 2 horsepower, or steam boilers; parking garages with more than 5 parking spaces; theatres and cinemas; places of assignation; goods warehouses; crematoria, slaughterhouses and garbage incinerators	Less than 60%	19.7 metres	Building height is restricted to within a slant plane based on the distance from the opposite side of the road to the building front. (Road width × 1.25)
Commercial zones	Prohibited uses: Factories with more than 50 employees or with engines of more than 10 horsepower; crematoria, slaughterhouses and garbage incinerators	Less than 80%	30.3 metres	Same as above, but the slant plane is steeper. (Road width × 1.5)
Industrial zones	No prohibited land uses	Less than 70%	30.3 metres	(Road width × 1.5)
Undesignated area	Apart from factories of large scale, or that may present public health hazards or that are dangerous, no prohibited land uses	Less than 70%	30.3 metres	(Road width × 1.5)

Source: Ishida (1987: 134).

were bothered by the heavy pollution of the cement factory, and became increasingly vocal in their protests. Eventually the company relocated to an area of reclaimed land in Tokyo Bay off Kawasaki, apparently in part to escape the constant complaints (Okata 1980: 18). Although the City Planning Research Committee had engaged in considerable debate about the issue of allowing housing in industrial areas, such housing was still allowed after 1919.

There were three other kinds of special zones that could be overlaid onto the three basic land use zones: Scenic Areas (*Fūchichiku*), Beautiful City Areas (*Bikanchiku*), and Fire Prevention Areas (*Bōkachiku*). The first was used primarily to protect natural areas of special significance such as those near important Shinto shrines and major parks. The second was intended primarily to help create dignified urban areas primarily in city centre areas such as the Marunouchi district. Its goal was thus to create modern new civic centres along the lines of those advocated by the American City Beautiful movement. These zones each allowed planning authorities substantial discretion to approve or deny planning permission based on an approved plan which set standards for the area; in other zones any conforming development was as-of-right. The Fire Prevention Areas were a legacy of the TCIO, and were applied primarily in densely built up city centres and along major roads to act as firebreaks. There were

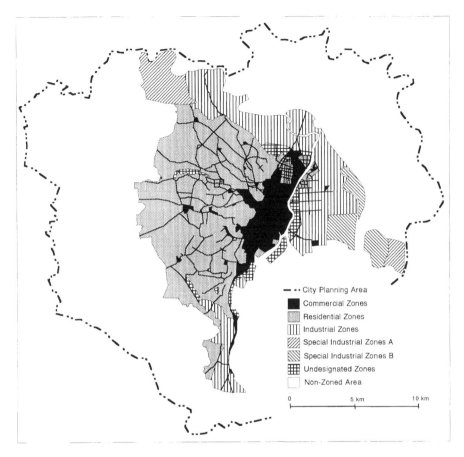

Figure 4.1 Tokyo's first zoning plan, 1925. Virtually all of the "low city" areas west of the Sumida River (corresponding roughly to the old commoner areas) are zoned commercial, the area east of the Sumida is zoned industrial, and the old "high city" in the hilly Yamanote district is zoned residential, with commercial strips following the main roads. Also notable is the considerable area which was left "undesignated", particularly along the Tokyo Bay coast and along the Sumida east bank.

Source: Adapted from Ishida (1987: 136).

two types of Fire Prevention Areas. Type One allowed only brick, stone and reinforced concrete buildings to be built, while Type Two zones also allowed wooden buildings that had been fireproofed with tile roofing and stone or stucco and tile cladding over the wooden frame. Brick and stone structures were still not terribly common apart from government buildings and major private buildings such as banks and department stores because of the expense and engineering requirements of earthquake-proofing.

Zoning plans were quickly designed and approved in the six largest cities, but only rather slowly adopted elsewhere. Of the 97 cities and towns to which the City Planning

Law applied in 1930, only 27 had adopted zoning plans (Ishida 1987: 135). Although the coverage of the planning law was broadened in 1933 to cover all cities and selected towns and villages, even as late as the 1960s many urban areas had enacted no zoning at all. This was due in part to the high degree of central government control, and the resulting administrative complexities involved in designating zoning plans. For example, the process of zoning designation before 1968 was: 1) a municipal (or prefectural) government submits the draft zoning plan to the prefectural governor; 2) the governor submits the draft zoning plan to the Home Ministry; 3) the Ministry consults the regional planning committee (*Toshi Keikaku Chihō Shingikai*) which was set up by the Home Ministry in each prefecture; 4) the Ministry finalises the zoning plan; 5) the Home Minister approves the zoning plan; 6) the zoning is announced in the official gazette (*Kanpō*), upon which it was legally enforceable. In practice the main responsibility for drafting zoning plans rested with the Departments of City Planning at the prefectural government level, as all but the largest municipalities lacked staff with adequate expertise. These prefectural planners worked closely with their counterparts at the Ministry of Construction (MoC), and in fact many of the officers and engineers at the prefectural offices would have been national ministry staff on loan to the prefecture. It is also worth remembering that until the occupation reforms of local government after the Second World War, prefectural governments were essentially branch offices of the national administration, governors being appointees of the Home Minister. The Home Ministry thus kept a close control not only of the legal framework of the planning system, but also was closely involved in the design and approval of individual municipal plans throughout the country.

This cumbersome, top-down system was almost certainly a factor in limiting the use of zoning. Possibly a more important factor at this time was the fact that apart from the growing industrial and port cities such as Osaka, Yokohama and Kobe, there was little perceived need for a zoning system at all. As noted, the main impact of the zoning system in terms of restricting land uses was to segregate large-scale heavy industry, and few regional towns had seen much of that yet. It also seems likely that the attempt to apply a one-size-fits-all zoning system to the whole country greatly limited its usefulness, as no local government was allowed to modify the zone criteria to adapt them to their specific local circumstances. This was unfortunate because conditions were quite different even among the main metropolitan areas. Osaka had very different patterns of land use than Tokyo for example, or Kyoto, Yokohama or Kobe. Also, as there was only one standard for residential areas, one for commercial and one for industrial, there was no way of designing specialised regulations for already built up areas, partially built up areas, or areas of future development. This limited the usefulness of the zoning system as a tool for structuring subsequent urban growth, as it was simply modelled on existing use patterns of metropolitan areas as a way of limiting the number of non-conforming uses. This precluded the possibility of using zoning to create different patterns in new urban areas.

The Urban Buildings Law

The second part of the 1919 system was the Urban Buildings Law. Apart from a couple of earlier prefectural building codes such as that of Osaka, this was Japan's first building code and was an important step forward, as before its passage planners had been little able to control inappropriate or dangerous building. As with the zoning ordinance, it was quite simple. It provided the detailed descriptions of allowable land uses, building coverage and heights, for each of the three land use zones as shown in Table 4.1, as well as details of permitted building materials and minimum window area for air circulation, etc, for each zone.

It is notable that even today, the City Planning Law defines only the names of the different zones, and the procedure for designating and approving them, while the Urban Buildings Law provides the more detailed description of allowable land uses, lot coverage ratios and height limits. This reflects the focus of the laws on controlling building types and volumes rather than land use. If we consider the relatively weak restrictions on permitted land uses, and the fact that the main restrictions were on building size, coverage and materials, it seems fair to suggest that the early Japanese zoning system was more about building control than city planning, which would be dealt with primarily by other measures. As shown in Chapters 6 and 9, the Japanese zoning system has remained quite consistent until the present, although more zones have been added.

The building-line system

The building-line system was the second important part of the Urban Buildings Law and was modelled after the German *Fluchtlinienplan* system which provided legal controls over the growth of urban areas. In essence, the system was based on three articles of the Urban Buildings Law. One defined roads as any public right of way, 2.7 metres (9 feet) wide or greater. This followed the precedent of the much earlier Tokyo Metropolitan Police regulation for the minimum width of the interior lane servicing Tokyo's slum nagaya districts. A second designated the edges of all such roads as building lines, while a third article declared building could only take place on lots with frontage on a building line.

In the German case the building-line system created a highly effective restriction on building in rural areas surrounding existing towns, and was the legal basis for the much envied German "town extension plan" system. In Germany, however, the law on street lines (*Fluchtliniengesetz*) made it the duty of municipalities to draw up extension plans for areas outside their boundaries, made the compulsory purchase of land for the new streets automatic, and allowed the cost of building, draining and lighting them to be charged to the owners of land fronting on them (Sutcliffe 1981: 19). The practice of charging adjacent landowners for the building of roads was widespread in Europe in the nineteenth century, and commonly adopted in the US, as for example in the case of the building of the Manhattan grid (Span 1988: 25). In many of the German states the law on street lines also allowed towns to refuse permission for any new building that was not sited on a municipally planned street. The German system was therefore much stricter than the Japanese version as in Germany the building line permitting new construction was created by municipal planning action through the creation of an extension plan. In the Japanese case, all existing roads of over 2.7 metres automatically became building lines. This caused serious problems of implementation, as in many Japanese rural areas land ownership was highly fragmented and there were far too many existing rural lanes which automatically qualified as building lines. Further, the process of compulsory purchase of road allowances was much more restrictive in Japan, reflecting strong constitutional guarantees of land rights. Even where building-line plans were designated, they were much more difficult to implement than in Germany. While the Japanese version was not as comprehensive as in Germany, considerable use was made of the betterment provisions of the 1919 City Planning Law which permitted municipalities to recoup a portion of the costs of road, canal and park building through special assessments (*juekisha futankin*) on nearby landowners of up to a third of the costs. As the system was not spelled out in great detail in the law different cities adopted varying approaches to the assessments. In Kyoto, for example, of the one-third of costs assessed to landowners, half was allocated to adjacent landowners and half to all landowners within a certain distance of the new facility based on the area of land they owned (see Ishida 1990). One prominent case where significant use of special assessments on adjacent landowners was used to finance the building of roads occurred in Osaka during the 1920s and 1930s, under Seki Hajime, Osaka's activist mayor, as described below.

Still, the building-line system was a considerable advance on earlier practice. In particular the fact that building-line plans could be designated for undeveloped urban fringe areas (the "positively designated building line"), and that new building was prohibited within the designated roadway provided a powerful new tool for preventing haphazard sprawl on the urban fringe. As shown in Figure 4.2, building-line plans could be used to designate a basic road network in undeveloped areas. The fact that the building

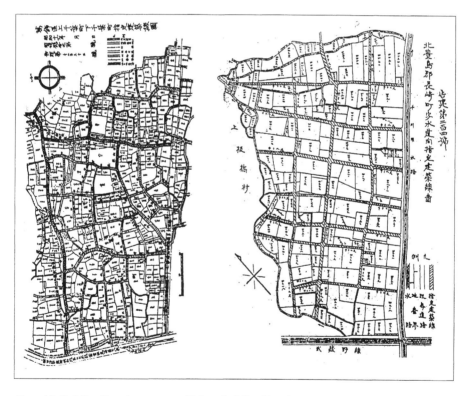

Figure 4.2 Building-line plans, western Tokyo. Building-line plans were prepared and approved for much of the new suburban area of western Tokyo during the 1930s.

Source: Ikeda (1980: 255).

prohibition within designated road allowances did not require compensation meant that a plan could be effectively enforced until such time as money could be found to actually carry out planned road construction. If landowners along a designated building line wished to build, they were also obliged to construct the road in front of the building, although the road standards were not as high as those in Germany. The planning and designation of building-line based extension plans were actively carried out in the pre-war period, amounting to over 300 areas between 1923 and 1941 in the Tokyo area alone (Ishizuka and Ishida 1988c: 23). The system was also widely used in the other main metropolitan areas including Yokohama, Nagoya and Osaka although with significant variations in practice (Ikeda 1983). In other research Ishida and Ikeda found that about two-thirds of the length of positively designated building lines in the Tokyo suburbs had been effective in regulating the development of road systems on private land (Ishida and Ikeda 1979). This conclusion must be understood in the context of a system that was very weak in its control over private development, and which was being used to regulate urban development in a context of fragmented land ownership and limited public investment in local public goods. The great achievement of the building-line system was in preventing the very worst sorts of unserviced sprawl by ensuring a certain minimum of road access where it was implemented, but even at its best it still tended to provide urban areas with the very minimum degree of public space in the form of roads.

Facilities designation

The city planning facilities (*toshi keikaku shisetsu* or just *shisetsu*) designation system was the main legacy of the TCIO to the Japanese planning system, and the relevant articles of the 1919 City Planning Law were copied almost directly from the earlier ordinance. The Japanese word *shisetsu* does not translate easily into English. It is usually translated either as "facilities" or as "institutions". When translated as "facilities" the term refers to public infrastructure such as roads, parks, sewerage, etc. The meaning of the term in the TCIO was "hard infrastructure". In the 1919 City Planning Act, however, the term *shisetsu* began to be used more broadly to refer to zoning districts and LR projects as well, which are not hard infrastructure but are plans, regulations, or "institutions".

The designation and building of public facilities was in many regards the main planning activity undertaken under the 1919 planning system. While as noted above many local governments had still not implemented land use zoning by the outbreak of the Pacific war in 1941, virtually all provincial towns had designated their city planning area and roads or other such public facilities (Nonaka 1995: 33). As shown above the TCIO had been designed primarily to improve roads, water and sewer systems in Tokyo's existing built up area, and such improvements have remained a pressing concern in towns throughout the country. At first the main concern was to widen the main roads in existing areas to accommodate the increasing volume of wheeled vehicles in lanes that had earlier carried exclusively foot traffic.

Other public facilities projects included parks, scenic areas designation, LR projects, sewerage facilities, playing fields, and public markets and squares. In common with the approach of the TCIO, in the 1919 system public facilities designation did not necessarily mean that a budget for actually building the facility existed. Rather, it was primarily a declaration of intent to indicate where a road, park, etc, would be built if funds should be secured in future. Designating public facilities was thus essentially a matter of drawing lines on a scale map and getting it approved by the central office of the Home Ministry. This was intended to provide a guide for private activity which took place between designation and actual building of the facility. Such designation was not compensable, but neither did it carry any strong regulatory restriction. Landowners could, for example, build within the limits of a designated city planning road as long as the building was not more than two stories and was easily removed (i.e., not reinforced concrete). This was not a great restriction at a time when the vast majority of buildings were wooden and of one or two stories. If and when the road was built, the land and any buildings had to be purchased at fair market value. This was thus a much weaker system than the building-line system described above. Nonetheless, such public facilities designation was arguably the main planning activity in the pre-war period, with virtually all cities, towns and villages using the system to designate plans for public facilities, especially city planning roads.

In the long run probably the most important contribution of the public facilities designation system is that it effected a drastic centralisation of city planning power in the Home Ministry. Prior to 1919 local governments had considerable freedom in city planning matters because there was no national law that regulated planning matters. After 1919 if local governments wished to receive central government subsidies, or if they wanted to buy land for public facilities by compulsory purchase, they had to submit all public facilities plans to be approved by the Home Ministry through its local planning committees. This requirement included all the city planning facilities mentioned above including city planning roads, zoning plans, LR projects, etc. The legal process for city planning designation (*Toshi Keikaku Kettei*) that had been developed to allow direct Home Ministry control over the implementation (by the Tokyo municipal government) of the TCIO by its inclusion in the 1919 City Planning Law at one stroke gave central government sweeping powers of detailed planning control over the whole country. Local governments were also persuaded with the promise of partial central government funding for approved facilities that they could ill afford to build by themselves. There can be no doubt that this was a decisive turning point in the evolution of Japanese city planning, and partial decentralisation of power has only been allowed in 1968 with the passage of the New City Planning Law, and again with the major revisions to the law in 1999 and 2000 described in Chapter 9.

Land readjustment

The last important planning system introduced in 1919 was LR. Organised either by local governments or private associations of landowners, its most common use has been to develop land on the urban fringe for urban uses. In essence, LR is a method of pooling ownership of all land within a project area, building urban facilities such as roads and parks and dividing the land into urban plots. There are two key aspects of the use of the method in Japan. First is that all landowners involved must contribute a portion of their land – usually about 30 per cent – for public uses such as roads and parks, and some to be sold as urban plots at the end of the project to help pay for project design, management and construction. Second is that in the case of Association projects, which are the most common type, if at least two-thirds the landowners owning at least two-thirds of the land in the designated project area agree, all landowners can be forced to participate in the project and contribute their share of land area. This prevents projects being blocked by a single uncooperative landowner, or by free riders who want to gain project benefits without contributing to project costs.

Land Readjustment had been used for agricultural land consolidation in Japan since the Tokugawa period and had been widespread since the 1860s. In 1899 the Agricultural Land Consolidation Law (*Kōchi Seiri Hō*) was passed to facilitate agricultural land improvement through grouping of scattered landholdings into larger plots and building irrigation systems (see Latz 1989: 38). The law followed the German model of LR in its legal form. During the last decade of the nineteenth century the practice of LR was greatly improved and promoted in Germany by Franz Adickes, the *Oberburgermeister* of Frankfurt-am-Main from 1891 to 1912 and one of the leaders in the German urban planning movement, responsible for a range of municipal improvement projects in Frankfurt and the creation of Germany's first set of differential building regulations or area zoning (Sutcliffe 1981: 32). He is credited with the development of the German Land Readjustment Law (the *Lex Adickes*) which was first presented to the German parliament in 1892 and finally passed in an amended form in 1902 (Sutcliffe 1981: 37). Nishiyama argues that earlier Japanese practices of land consolidation and replotment were incorporated into the early legislation and the German contribution was one of legal form more than of fundamental practice. He suggests that the German law "provided the opportunity of refining traditional Japanese agrarian land rearrangement practices into a modern statutory land management device" (Nishiyama 1986: 331).

In the agricultural context, after revisions to the law in 1909, the emphasis shifted from farmland replotment to irrigation and drainage projects (Latz 1989: 39). The new technique was also quickly put to use in urban fringe settings for the consolidation of plots and provision of urban infrastructure. Hayashi notes that there were already eight LR projects totalling 1,480 hectares started in the Nagoya area before the passage of the 1919 City Planning Law, which included the first provisions specific to urban LR projects. These projects were all on the urban fringe and aimed at new urban development, even though they were carried out using the Agricultural Consolidation Law (Hayashi 1982: 107). Ishida notes that a major obstacle to using this law for urban projects was that it prohibited including lots with buildings within the LR project area unless *all* such owners consented. This obstacle persisted in the 1919 law and was only eliminated in 1931, after which urbanisation-type LR projects increased greatly (Ishida 1986: 80). A number of cities, especially Nagoya and Osaka (see Figure 4.7) used LR projects with considerable success to develop urban fringe areas in the pre-war period.

The most important change to the LR practice in the 1919 law was that public authorities were empowered to become LR implementing bodies, whereas before this time only individuals and associations could initiate projects. This contrasts with the German case where municipal action was most important. Land Readjustment has played a very important role in Japanese city planning both for urban fringe land development and for urban redevelopment, and LR projects account for about 30 per cent of the Japanese urban area. Apart from urban fringe development projects, the large-scale urban rebuilding projects after the Kanto earthquake of 1923, after the Second World War, and most recently after the Great Hanshin Earthquake of 1995 are the most prominent cases. LR was also used extensively to build large-scale public housing and new town developments and since 1969 a variation of the method, the Urban Redevelopment Law (*Toshi Saikaihatsu Hō*), has been used to redevelop the busy commercial districts fronting on train stations. As is commonly asserted in Japan, "Land Readjustment is the mother of town planning."

Land Readjustment became of even greater importance for urban development after the 1960s, and is examined in greater detail in Chapters 6 and 8. Here it is worth noting simply that while the method was useful as a means of promoting planned development in suburban areas, and was commonly used in conjunction with the building-line system, the urban areas so developed were of generally rather low standard. As projects were financed by the sale of reserve land provided by participating landowners, they put constant pressure on project organisers to minimise the land contribution, and projects tended to produce areas with the lowest standards of design, road provision and urban services. Projects developed before the passage of the Land Readjustment Law in 1954 (which replaced the LR provisions of the 1919 City Planning Law) were not required to set aside space for parks or to provide sewerage, and road provision was of the most basic sort. Such projects did however, provide a basic road grid and rationalise land ownership patterns, thereby preventing the worst sorts of disorderly sprawl development. Land Readjustment has been highly popular with local governments because it provides a low-cost means of achieving orderly urban growth. In particular, land contributions by participating landowners reduce or eliminate the need to purchase land for public uses such as roads and parks, an essential feature after rapid inflation of land prices in the post-war period.

Implementing the 1919 system

For a number of reasons the 1919 laws failed to enable the kind of positive environment for city planning that had been hoped. In part this was because several of the key financial aspects of the laws were deleted before passage as noted above. Also, the zoning measures as enacted were relatively weak as each zone allowed a wide mixture of different uses. For example, almost all commercial and office uses and a wide range of smaller factories could still be built in residential areas. Only large factories and entertainment uses such as theatres were prohibited. In industrial zones the construction of housing was still permitted, so areas of intermixed heavy industry and housing continued to spread.

One of the main arguments for the passage of the 1919 law had been the absence of regulations over suburban development. In the Tokyo area most suburban growth occurred as disorderly unplanned sprawl, and from 1905 to 1920 the suburban population had increased from 420,000 to 1,180,000. Further, while the 1919 law did extend city planning powers to these suburban areas, it took some time to prepare the first plans. The law came into effect in January of 1920, and the City Planning Area (CPA) for Tokyo, which was set at approximately the current 23-ward area, was approved in 1921 and announced in April of 1922. From this time the plans and consultations for initiating LR projects, designating public facilities such as main road networks, and drafting the building-line plans in the suburban areas were started. This work was largely completed in August of 1923, as was the first zoning plan for the city of Tokyo which was to go into effect in September. Unfortunately, on 1 September 1923 the Great Kanto Earthquake struck, and along with much else, the plans burned in the ensuing fires. Further, one of the significant impacts of the disaster was a huge relocation of population from the burned-out central areas to new suburban areas. Between 1922 and 1930 the population in these areas doubled from 1,430,000 to 2,900,000 due primarily to hasty relocation of those displaced by the disaster. This unfortunate timing meant that there was little chance to carry out an orderly, planned urbanisation in the area, which today is the part of central Tokyo with has the worst urban problems, including very little public space, poor roads and many dense wooden apartment buildings (Ishizuka and Ishida 1988b: 211). Further, the focus of money and planning expertise on rebuilding central Tokyo undoubtedly drew attention away from the problems of other cities and the larger project of establishing an effective system for planned urban expansion.

The 1923 Great Kanto Earthquake and reconstruction projects

Almost certainly the most important factor behind the disappointing results of the new system was the occurrence of the earthquake just as it was being established. The earthquake caused extensive damage in Tokyo and Yokohama, with roughly 140,000 killed or missing, over 44 per cent of the urban area of Tokyo destroyed by fire and some 73.8 per cent of all households affected (Ishizuka and Ishida 1988b: 19; Watanabe 1993: 219). Almost all the old, densely populated central areas of Tokyo that had been commoner areas during the Edo period were destroyed by fire. Of the old "low city" of Tokyo, almost nothing remained, while in the former samurai areas in the foothills to the west, the "high city", few large fires were seen. As Seidensticker

Figure 4.3 Ginza Avenue after the Great Kanto Earthquake of 1923, the shocked survivors surveying the wreckage of Tokyo's formerly glittering commercial core.

Source: Tokyo Reconstruction Survey Commission (*Fukkō Chōsa Kyōkai*) (1930).

(1990) argues, Edo finally disappeared in the earthquake as it was the old "low city" that was Edo's heart, and which had retained many of its basic urban features during the first half-century since the Meiji restoration.

The day after the earthquake while fires were still burning, Gotō Shinpei was reappointed Home Minister as part of the cabinet of Yamamoto Gonnohyōe, a non-party prime minister appointed by the Genrō after the earthquake to establish a national unity government to deal with the crisis. Gotō was a logical choice as he already had experience as Home Minister, and had subsequently been mayor of Tokyo from 1920 to 1922 when the first round of planning under the new city planning laws was drafted. At that time he had been the sponsor of an ambitious long-term plan for modernising the capital popularly known as the "800 million yen plan" because of its extravagant budget. Gotō saw the earthquake as a golden opportunity to carry out the restructuring of Tokyo into a modern city and proposed the creation of a national government agency that could carry out the project under the direct supervision of the Home Ministry. The Imperial Capital Reconstruction Board *(Teitō Fukkō-in)* was established on September 19 by cabinet order with Gotō as president. Gotō proclaimed his goals as:

1   refusing the relocation of the capital;
2   an ambitious reconstruction programme with a budget of 3 billion yen;
3   use of advanced Western planning techniques;
4   strong controls over the independent rebuilding activities of landowners so as to be able to achieve the rational road network that had been so frequently planned and frustrated during the previous 50 years (Watanabe 1984: 420).

Of several spending plans considered, ranging up to 4 billion yen, the board settled on a one billion yen plan in October. The Finance Ministry opposed this high figure, and the budget was cut to 600 million yen. When the plan was presented to the Diet, the leading party, the Seiyūkai, further reduced it to 470 million yen. Finally, the Yamamoto cabinet fell in early January 1924, Gotō lost the Home Ministry portfolio, and in February the board was downgraded to a Reconstruction Bureau *(Fukkōkyoku)* and placed outside the control of the Home Ministry (Tucker 1999: 131).

Although political opposition to Gotō's plan succeeded in forcing drastic cuts in the projected budget for reconstruction, several basic elements of his approach survived. In particular, the Ad Hoc Town Planning Act which he drafted was enacted in December of 1923 and came into effect in March of 1924, setting out the approach to reconstruction which was followed over the next seven-and-a-half years. The central aspect of this Act was a redesign of the LR procedure to allow its use in the redevelopment of existing built up areas. The main changes were that the new Act empowered the Reconstruction Board to design and carry out its own projects with no requirement to gain the consent of the landowners concerned. The use of LR in this way allowed the board to sidestep the legal requirement that all land expropriated for building roads and public facilities had to be compensated at fair market value. The Act authorised compensation only for any decrease in lot size of over 10 per cent. Proponents of the LR approach argued that this was not expropriation without compensation, but simply the application of the normal LR principle that landowners make contributions of land for

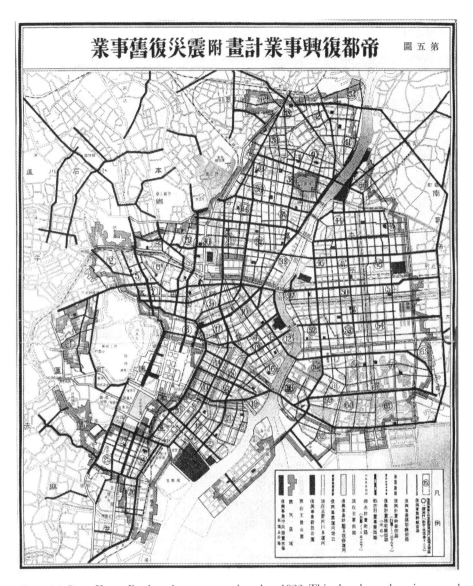

Figure 4.4 Great Kanto Earthquake reconstruction plan, 1923. This plan shows the primary and secondary trunk roads network built as part of the Tokyo Earthquake Reconstruction Project.

Source: Imperial Capital Reconstruction Project Maps Book (*Teitō Fukkō Jigyō Zuhyō*) (1930).

public facilities and to finance the project, while benefiting from increases in the value of their land as a result of the project. The essence of the reconstruction project was thus a very large-scale use of the LR method. Of the 3,636 hectares of destroyed area in Tokyo, 3,041 hectares were divided into 65 project areas and redesigned and rebuilt in stages (Tokyo Municipal Office 1930: 73).

Opposition movements

The large-scale use of LR without gaining prior consent from landowners, and particularly the provision withholding compensation for the first 10 per cent of land contribution had the unsurprising effect of giving rise to large and well-organised landowner opposition movements. They protested the 10 per cent land reduction as unconstitutional, and their main goals were to achieve postponement of the projects so that the system of land assessment and compensation could be revised. The movements had considerable initial success, and in February of 1925 the Tokyo City Assembly passed a motion opposing the forced use of LR. In March the Lower House of the Diet unanimously passed a similar motion and proposed fundamental changes to the Ad Hoc Act. In October of the same year the League to Promote Improvement of Land Readjustment Projects presented its suggestions for changes to the LR programme, but the Reconstruction Bureau offered only minor changes to the compensation and proceeded with the projects as planned. Faced with its inability to stop the projects, opposition gradually died out (Ishida 1987: 158; Koshizawa 1991).

While from a town planning point of view the use of LR in this way was logical, it is also easy to understand the landowner opposition. Tokyo was clearly in need of a more modern street structure and more public space than it had inherited from the feudal era. The TCIO projects had only succeeded in widening a limited number of the main roads and at great cost. What better time to carry out a thorough redesign than after the earthquake when almost half the urban area – and virtually all the old crowded commoner districts – had been reduced to ashes. Requiring a 10 per cent land contribution from all landowners through LR was also a fair answer to the need for more road space, and was clearly more equitable than fully expropriating the few owners whose land was located in the path of new roads. It would also allow a critical cost saving compared to the purchase of land on the scale required, especially as enormous outlays were in any case required to rebuild essential bridges and other public facilities.

On the other hand, the landowners had a legitimate point. A basic principle of LR, and the reason why so many projects have been voluntarily accepted by the landowners involved, is that the increase in land values resulting from the provision of roads and services almost always means that landowners end up with more valuable land holdings even when the remaining area is smaller than they started out with. This had been shown to work well in suburban fringe areas, but such a result is much less certain in the redevelopment of already fully urban areas. First, it is unlikely that simple road-widening can achieve any dramatic increase in land values, at least not compared to those common with initial conversion from rural to urban land. Second, many of the landowners were the owners of small plots in central city areas where they both lived and worked, and could only benefit from increases in land value if they were to sell their land. Much more likely was that they would simply be forced to make do with slightly smaller business premises, and hope that increased traffic would compensate.

The mass opposition to the compulsory 10 per cent land contribution, the well-organised opposition movement, and its failure in the end to influence government policy are typical of attempts by local people to influence planning policy in Japan. Such cases are numerous, and several more recent examples are described in later chapters. The case illustrates the significant advantages and risks of a planning system dominated by central government. Because the reconstruction project was directly carried out by the central government, planners could ignore public opposition that would almost certainly have stopped a local government from proceeding. The Reconstruction Board pushed ahead with the plan essentially unchanged, and offered the opposition movement only some minor concessions on the rate of compensation for land expropriated over the 10 per cent limit. In a case where the public interest is so strong such an approach may be justified. The process can hardly have served to increase public support for planning among those affected, however, and seems more likely to have reinforced the conception of city planning as merely another government activity that had to be accepted when it could not be effectively opposed.

Although it can have been of little consolation to those who lost land through the reconstruction projects, it may be that the top-down approach in this case did in fact serve the public interest in the long term. Carried out over the seven years from 1924 to 1930, the reconstruction project successfully modernised the central areas of Tokyo and provided much of the basic infrastructure that has supported Tokyo's growth until the present. The project established a rational network of primary, secondary and tertiary roads throughout the central city area of Tokyo totalling 253 kilometres in length. These included Showa Avenue with a width of 44 metres running from Shinbashi to Ueno through the centre of the old town, and in all 52 major new arteries were built in the old city of over 22 metres in width and totalling 114 kilometres in length. Some 121 public schools were rebuilt in fireproof materials, many of which are still in use today and were designated shelter areas in case of earthquakes or fires. Some 55 parks were built totalling about 42 hectares in area including many in areas of the old city that had virtually no open space, and others built as playgrounds adjacent to schools. An interesting innovation given the tight constraints on space was to create mini pocket-parks at each end of almost all the rebuilt bridges as sitting places with trees and planters for the use of local residents. The project also reconstructed over 400 bridges in steel, and generalised the provision of sidewalks which had previously been virtually unknown in Japanese cities. In March of 1930 ceremonies were held to celebrate the completion of the Imperial Capital Reconstruction Project. Leaders of the project were tremendously proud of their achievement, and published that year a two volume, 1,874-page set of documents commemorating the project (Tokyo Reconstruction Investigation Commission (*Fukkō Chōsa Kyōkai*) 1930) as well as a small volume in English (Tokyo Municipal Office 1930) in order to show the world their achievement.

Examination of the plans and many of the still-existing products of the reconstruction project suggests the project leaders pride in their accomplishment was well-justified. The plans themselves are quite sophisticated and balance nicely the constraints of working within the existing urban structure, yet at the same time cutting major new boulevards and creating a new roads structure in the central area. A five-layered hierarchy of roads from the widest boulevards down to the smallest lanes was colour coded on the main reconstruction plan, and provides a nice example of a well-designed road hierarchy.

While the various public facilities described above were without doubt a major contribution of the reconstruction project, a look at the detailed plans reveals a major part of the work must have been the changes to the road system and the associated changes to property divisions and relocations of remaining buildings. As shown in Figure 4.5 the LR projects involved major dislocations of existing property owners. Not only was a network

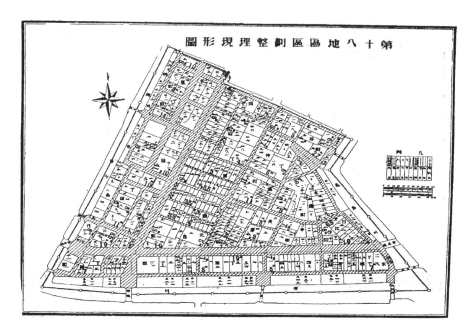

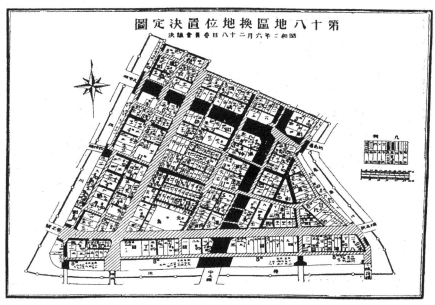

Figure 4.5 Tokyo earthquake reconstruction – LR project. The area destroyed by fire in the Great Kanto Earthquake was divided up into districts to be rebuilt and reconfigured with Land Readjustment projects. These two maps show Land Readjustment District #18 in downtown Tokyo east of Tokyo station and bounded on three sides by canals. The upper shows land ownership and road patterns before the project, and the black areas of the lower map show new areas of road space created by the project.

Source: Tokyo Reconstruction Survey Commission (*Fukkō Chōsa Kyōkai*) (1930: 848a).

of broad avenues created, but also many of the smaller streets were aligned into through roads, straightened, and regularised from narrow winding lanes suitable mainly for foot traffic to roads suitable for vehicles. To accomplish this in LR projects over an area of 3,041 hectares in the centre of a densely built up area was a monumental task.

Long-term impacts

The project also had a number of important long-term impacts on the practice of city planning in Japan. Apart from the fact that for most of a decade the bulk of the nation's city planning resources were poured into the reconstruction effort, with the result that other cities were left as before the 1919 law pretty much to their own resources, three effects are worth noting here. The use of the LR technique in fully built up urban areas was established; a large cadre of professional city planners was trained; and an organisation to build public housing on a large scale was created.

As noted above, prior to the Tokyo earthquake reconstruction project, LR had been used almost exclusively for agricultural land reorganisation and urban fringe land development projects. While the LR method had been applied to rebuild two Tokyo areas destroyed by fire in Waseda and Shinjuku in 1920 and 1921 respectively, those projects had been carried out under the provisions of the 1919 law with the consent of the landowners involved. The ad hoc city planning law passed at the end of 1923 created a new administrative structure and procedure for LR. Not only could LR projects be carried out directly by central and local governments, but there was no requirement to achieve the consent of the landowners first, an important aspect of the normal system. The direct design and management of LR projects by public bodies has since been used in various ways, for example in the building of military facilities during the 1930s and 1940s, in the reconstruction of major cities after the war, in the building of large-scale housing projects and new towns in the 1960s and 1970s, and in the numerous local government-sponsored urban fringe projects designed to prevent urban sprawl. By developing a procedure that allowed central and local governments to use LR projects proactively instead of waiting for local landowners to start projects, a powerful tool for the positive planning and development of urban areas was created. Several such uses of LR are examined in later chapters.

It is widely felt among Japanese planners that in the longer run the most significant impact of the reconstruction project was its effects on the practice of planning itself. The very high visibility and prestige of the project, and its evident success in transforming and rebuilding a vast area of central Tokyo were a tremendous boost both to the public image of city planning in Japan and to the self-image of its practitioners. Because of the enormous scale of the project and its long duration, the project served as the training ground for a whole generation of young planners who went on to form the core of the Japanese planning profession until well into the post-war period. In all some 6,000 people worked for the Reconstruction Bureau, many of whom were young engineering and architecture graduates who later dispersed to take up planning jobs in prefectural and municipal offices throughout Japan, on the local City Planning Commissions (*Toshi Keikaku Iinkai*) set up throughout the country by the Home Ministry, and in the Japanese colonies of Taiwan, Korea and Manchuria. A further benefit was that officers within the bureau created a range of instructional materials explaining the new city planning systems and laws to project workers, and these were subsequently published and became the standard reference works for the fledgling planning profession (Ishida 1987: 151; Koshizawa 1991: 84–5).

A closely related development was the creation of the Dōjunkai Foundation. The name cannot be translated literally into English, but means roughly "Mutual Prosperity Association". The foundation, formed in May of 1924 with the aim of supplying both housing and work for earthquake victims, was established with 10 million of the 59 million yen in donations given to aid victims of the earthquake. The foundation first focused on building large-scale temporary wooden housing facilities (*barraku* or "barracks" in Japanese) immediately after the disaster, but after building a small amount of such housing, they quickly turned to a variety of projects to research, design and introduce new housing styles. They eventually built a total of 5,653 units, including temporary dwellings immediately after the earthquake. The long-term influence of Dōjunkai arises from its model housing schemes, particularly because it involved many young architects in projects to adapt European-style housing types to Japan. Dōjunkai

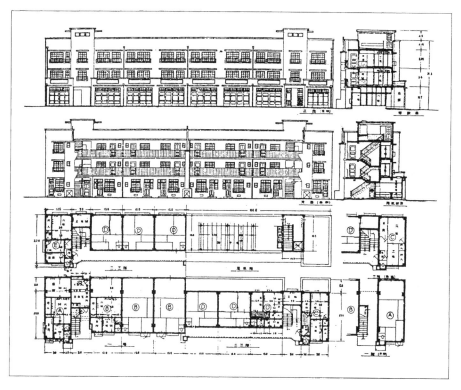

Figure 4.6 Dōjunkai housing development. Dōjunkai, established with donations for the victims of the Great Kanto Earthquake of 1923, after completing the building of emergency shelters, conducted a wide range of experiments in slum housing upgrading and pioneered the building of multi-storey ferro-concrete housing complexes in Japan. The apartment block shown here is a part of the Sarue project to upgrade a notorious slum in what is now Koto Ku in eastern Tokyo, completed in 1930.

Source: Japan General Housing Centre (*Nihon Jutaku Sōgō Centaa*) (1974: 41).

built the first mid-rise housing for the middle class, and experimented with reinforced concrete apartment buildings such as those built at Daikanyama and Aoyama, and also with projects for the improvement of slum housing areas into mid-rise concrete apartments such as the large project at Sarue-chō in Fukagawa ward shown in Figure 4.6 (Ishizuka and Ishida 1988b: 21). A significant number of the talented young city planners and architects who received their first practical experience in this earthquake reconstruction project went on to play important roles in the post-war period, as did many of those who were involved in Dōjunkai.

Two further long-term impacts of the earthquake should be mentioned. First, in response to the pressing need to provide shelter after the quake, the building code was relaxed, with the proviso that any buildings that did not conform were only temporary and would have to be replaced within five years. Because of public pressure this obligation was delayed and then dropped for almost all buildings, with the result that much of the central area was rebuilt with flammable wooden buildings, even within the areas that had long been designated as fireproof districts. These districts went up in flames again during the American firebombings at the end of the Second World War. Second, as mentioned above, the earthquake gave a huge boost to suburban population growth, and most of that rapid growth occurred as haphazard sprawl in farming areas adjacent to the city. Yet another belt of unplanned growth on the fringe of Tokyo was created, and the new building-line plans and LR projects of the 1930s were mostly outside that belt.

Osaka, garden cities, colonial capitals, and metropolitan structure plans

Although the Tokyo reconstruction project clearly dominated city planning activity and budgets until it was completed in 1930, there were other important city planning efforts both during and after the reconstruction that should be noted. Four examples stand out: municipal enterprise in Osaka, garden suburb developments, colonial city planning and metropolitan structure planning. Each of these are examined briefly.

Municipal enterprise in Osaka

An indication of just how limiting was the central government vision of planning is provided by the Osaka case. As the nation's second largest city and main industrial and commercial centre Osaka was relatively wealthy, with a substantial and rapidly expanding textile manufacturing and heavy industry base in the first decades of the century. It also benefited from a substantial measure of local pride and wore its nicknames the "Manchester of the Orient" (*Tōyō no Manchesutaa*) and the "City of Smoke" proudly. Osaka also had the good fortune of successfully recruiting Seki Hajime, one of Japan's leading political economists and urban thinkers from the Tokyo Commercial College (later Hitotsubashi University), as deputy mayor in 1914. Seki had studied in Belgium and Germany, had written on urban social and planning issues and was well aware of contemporary developments in Europe. Seki became mayor in 1923, and made city planning and municipal reform a central part of his agenda throughout his career in Osaka. If any city could have established an alternative vision and practice of city planning in the inter-war years, it would surely have been Osaka.

In his early years in the job as deputy mayor Seki outlined a broad programme of urban social reform and a vision of the role of municipal government and city planning that was very different from the approach being pursued by the national government at the time. The top priority of national government urban policy was unambiguously the promotion of economic development through the building of roads, bridges, railways, and ports. Seki advocated what was in this context a radical vision of urban management and planning which stressed that the main goal of municipal government was to serve the public welfare by expanding municipal enterprise and city planning as a social enterprise. Seki was also a consistent advocate of municipal political autonomy, the municipal ownership of city utilities, and was deeply concerned with the housing conditions of the urban working class. He argued that local governments should take the lead in expanding the provision of social services, and that the goal of city planning should be the creation of cities that are comfortable to live in with high levels of amenity for the majority of residents. Seki condemned the urban real-estate speculators who constructed flimsy slum housing for workers and were able to charge exorbitant rents because of the housing shortage in growing Osaka. One key issue that had stymied efforts to implement earlier urban expansion plans such as that of Yamaguchi discussed in Chapter 2 was that powers of eminent domain to expropriate land for roads were very weak. This effectively left the city government at the mercy of local landowners who could charge extortionate prices for small strips of land to build roads, even though a primary effect of those new roads would be to increase the value of their remaining land. Seki therefore advocated municipal control of the processes of urbanisation on the fringe so as to provide inexpensive housing for the working classes in a high-quality residential environment.

Seki's administration saw the construction of broad new boulevards, a harbour, an extensive network of city-owned tram lines, a subway system, electricity, and freshwater and sewerage systems. Apart from these traditional urban infrastructure concerns, under Seki the city also established a wide range of new social programmes and facilities through the Social Bureau established in 1918. These included "municipally-run retail markets, a central wholesale market, employment offices, pawnshops, lunch counters, public baths, technical schools, maternity hospitals, nurseries, day care centres, hospitals, and municipal housing" (Hanes 2002: 203). Seki also founded the Osaka City University, which had the first Urban Administration Faculty in Japan (Miyamoto 1993: 54).

Under Seki's leadership Osaka set up a city planning committee in 1917, and prepared a draft city planning law designed to allow the city to improve existing built up areas and adequately plan and develop land on the urban fringe. The committee also started to prepare a comprehensive urban plan to include areas outside Osaka's existing urban area, and began a campaign to gain central government passage of the draft planning law and comprehensive plan as national law. While this plan was being prepared the national City Planning Research Committee (*Toshi Keikaku Chosakai*) was established to begin drafting a new city planning law under the leadership of Ikeda Hiroshi, as described in Chapter 3, and Seki was invited to become a member. Instead of gaining central government approval and passage of the draft Osaka law, Seki participated in drafting a national law that applied to all major Japanese cities. According to Watanabe (1993: 151–60) the Osaka draft made an important contribution to the development of the national law. That may be so, but as argued above, one of the key outcomes of that law was a radical centralisation of planning authority in the central government Home Ministry. Ishida suggests, however, that a major reason Seki was persuaded to accept the national law was that it included provisions for national financial support for city planning projects (Ishida 2000: 4).

Unfortunately, as we have seen, the Ministry of Finance strongly opposed the national treasury funding for city planning projects advocated by the Home Ministry. While national funds were spent on local projects throughout the pre-war period, the share tended to be rather small. For example, in Osaka's "First Urban Plan" carried out under the new City Planning Law from 1921 to 1942, national subsidies accounted for only 2 per cent of the total project cost of 160 million yen, with the bulk of the expense covered by municipal taxes, profits from the municipally owned streetcars, and local bonds. A full 18 per cent of the total cost was collected from landowners who benefited from the newly widened roads as special assessments (Matsuzawa 2000: 70). The Osaka special assessment system had been strongly advocated by Seki, and was somewhat different than that of the 1919 City Planning Law, as it was based on a system of assessments of the land values adjacent to roads before and after the road building project (Okayama 2000: 77). This version of a betterment levy was allowed by a special decree of the Home Ministry in 1922 for Osaka only (Ishida 2000: 5), and other cities used the simpler system of dividing a third of the costs among nearby landowners. In the end, therefore, with the 1919 City Planning Law Osaka lost municipal control of city planning, yet in return received precious little in financial support from the national treasury.

Hanes also argues that the loss of municipal autonomy in planning was to play a key role in frustrating Seki's vision of urban planning as a vehicle for social reform and the improvement of urban housing for the working poor. The key to his strategy was that the city would build a large-scale system of new roads with tramways extending outside the existing urban area. These areas would be developed with LR projects as garden suburbs, and the city would build large amounts of new housing for rent and for sale at reasonable rates to working people, as discussed further below. The Home Ministry, however, blocked the ambitious approach of the Osaka Urban Improvement Committee's draft comprehensive plan: "Osaka's First Urban Plan (*Dai Ichiji Toshi Keikaku*), which Prime Minister Hara Kei signed into law in 1921, was but a ghost of the proposal advanced by the city three years earlier. Seki's grand vision of a Greater Osaka (*Dai Osaka*) was ultimately whittled down to little more than a network of modern roads and bridges at the city's core" (Hanes 2002: 236). The Osaka First Urban Plan and its successor the Osaka Comprehensive Plan (*Sōgō Osaka Toshi Keikaku*) of 1928 were essentially programmes of road, canal and bridge building, which however necessary, did not do much to make the city more liveable for the poor. It seems clear that the new process whereby central government officers wielded broad powers to approve, deny and alter all local government plans enabled the central government to ensure that city planning would henceforth conform to its own rather limited programme of main infrastructure building, even in cities such as Osaka where leaders had different and broader ideas of what urban planning could accomplish.

Because Osaka received so little support from central government, it was necessary to use the least expensive measures. Osaka copied the approach of the TCIO projects by using streetcar revenues to pay for an extensive programme of arterial road-widening. With the major expansion of Osaka city in 1925, the city administration

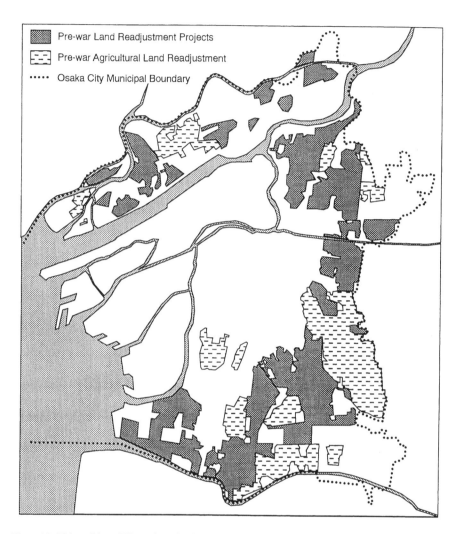

Figure 4.7 Urban fringe LR projects in Osaka. Osaka under Mayor Seki Hajime was a leader in planning for urban expansion in the pre-war period.

Source: Adapted from Osaka Municipal Government (2000: 98).

made it a top priority to develop the new urban area as LR, and was actively involved in planning and encouraging the projects. By 1940 over 64 Association-type LR projects had been completed, totalling some 3,500 hectares (Osaka City Association (*Osaka Toshi Kyoukai*) 1992: 80). Figure 4.7 shows the extent of Association-initiated LR projects on the urban fringe of Osaka from 1924 to 1940. As the figure shows, the area developed with these projects was very substantial, covering much of the area urbanised during the period. The projects helped to establish a basic road grid and regularised plot divisions at little cost to the government. They did little, however, to further Seki's vision of salubrious city-built garden suburbs affordable by the working class.

Garden cities and suburban railway development

An important example of the effect of Western planning ideas on Japanese practice is provided by the development of interest in garden cities. In the Japanese case, the first comprehensively planned suburban developments were a direct product of the garden cities movement in Britain. Only a few years after the publication in Britain of Ebenezer Howard's ([1902] 1985) proposal for urban reform through the building of new towns in the countryside, the Local Government Bureau of the Home Ministry published *Den'en Toshi* (literally "Garden City") in 1907 (Watanabe 1993: 41). Not, as some have supposed, a translation of Howard's book, the volume was rather an introduction to Howard's concept based largely on A. R. Sennet's *Garden Cities in Theory and Practice* (1905). The Japanese publication prompted wide-ranging debate amongst those interested in urban planning, and in 1918 the Den'en Toshi Company was launched to develop two garden cities in Senzoku (18 hectares) and Tamagawadai (10 hectares). Included in the group of promoters was Shibusawa Eiichi, the most prominent entrepreneur of the Meiji period and an advocate of city planning since his involvement in the early TCIO proposals. This company became the largest suburban developer of the Taishō period, and eventually evolved into the Tokyū Corporation which developed an enormous area of suburban Tokyo and Yokohama with its strategy of railway building linked to suburban LR projects after the war (Matsubara 1982). Tokyū is now one of the larger of the many suburban railway/land development/department store operators in Japan.

One of the first actions of the company was to build a new railway line which started service in March of 1923. Sales of lots in the Senzoku area closest to Tokyo were begun in 1922, and in Tamagawadai in August of 1923. The developments proved a huge success, aided no doubt by the fortuitous timing of the Kanto Earthquake disaster which destroyed much of central Tokyo and spurred rapid suburban development just at the time that lots were going on sale. These were essentially upper middle class housing developments, and the land company attempted to protect the character of the area through covenants which specified much stronger building and land use controls than those in the current planning law. Watanabe (1984) argues that although these agreements were legally unenforceable, they were respected by the wealthy residents as a protection of lifestyle and property values. This early precedent for such an approach to protecting residential areas did not become widespread, however, and the lack of such protections for residential areas became one of the most distinctive characteristics of Japanese suburban development in the post-war period.

Den'en Chofu is still famous as a high-class residential area, but it was never a garden city along the lines envisaged by Howard, and as practised in Britain in the post-war period. The basic idea of the Garden city – that it be independent of the metropolis and self-sufficient in jobs, and that community ownership of land and a protective greenbelt would allow affordable housing and improvements in social welfare – were not a part of the Den'en Toshi idea. What remained was the vision of spacious suburban living which was successfully marketed to the emerging Japanese middle class. These developments were therefore garden suburbs, and remained dependent for jobs and services on the central city, although it should perhaps be noted that the original vision of a self-contained garden city was never attained anywhere, even in post-war Britain, which possibly came closest (Thomas 1969; Hall and Ward 1998).

多摩川台住宅地平面図

Figure 4.8 Tamagawadai plot layout and street plan. Tamagawadai was part of the first garden suburb built in Japan.

Source: Japan General Housing Centre (*Nihon Jūtaku Sōgō Centaa*) (1984: 38).

The Japanese garden cities were basically speculative land developments that returned a high rate of profit for their initial investors (Watanabe 1980: 139). That fact notwithstanding, the provision of quality residential sites in a comprehensive development was a first in Japan, and the project of providing a residential environment in a bucolic leafy setting away from the city was an important precedent.

Although the Den'en Toshi Company is by far the best known Japanese example of a garden city builder, another attempt established in Osaka by Seki Hajime followed Howard's social housing vision more closely. As noted above, one of Seki's main concerns was the dire housing situation in industrialising Osaka, and his preferred solution was the large-scale development of land on the urban fringe for low-cost workers' housing linked to the city by new mass transit facilities. One element of Seki's strategy was the establishment in 1920 of a limited dividend land development company as a partnership of the City of Osaka and a number of the city's wealthy financiers. The company was incorporated with the stipulation that it would return no more than 6 per cent of its profits to shareholders, and would retain the surplus "to expand its business for the public good" (Kodama 1993: 37). While considerably higher than contemporary limited divided companies in Britain, 6 per cent was quite modest in the Japanese context of the time. The Den'en Toshi company, for example, issued annual dividends of 10 per cent after 1923 when land sales began (Kodama 1993: 34).

The Osaka Housing Management Corporation (*Osaka Jūtaku Keiei Kabushikigaisha*) started operations in 1920 with a paid-up capital of 2.5 million yen plus 1.5 million yen in the form of a low-interest loan from the city of Osaka, which in turn had borrowed the money from the Home Ministry Social Bureau. The company then proceeded to buy land in rural areas outside Osaka and develop it as housing land. The money from the loan was used primarily to build houses for rent and sale, and a total of 438 rental houses were built with the loan money and rented out by 1923. A second loan to allow the continued expansion of the subsidised rental housing programme was expected to receive approval from the Home Ministry in October of 1923, but after the Kanto earthquake virtually all such spending came to an abrupt halt, and the loan was never issued. After 1923 the company shifted its business strategy to more land subdivision and sales, gradually increased its dividends, and eventually was merged with the New Keihan Railway Company Ltd. in 1928, ending this brief experiment with social housing land development (Kodama 1993: 39; see also Terauchi 2000). Possibly as a result of this change in management, all the open space indicated on the plan in Figure 4.9 was eventually built up, including the planned park. Only the roundabout in the road leading to the station remains, housing a fountain, some benches, and a stone marker to memorialise the work of the Osaka Housing Management Corporation.

During the 1920s many other suburban railways developed on the garden suburb model, using a combination of railway building and land development (Arisue and Aoki 1970; Ericson 1996). A particularly popular method was to link the development of a

Figure 4.9 Senriyama housing estate promotional plan. This 1923 promotional map of the newly laid out housing estate at Senriyama, north of Osaka, shows a plan typical of many from this period. It is composed of simple modified grids, orientation to the train station that provides access to the metropolitan centre, a small park, and an overall layout that is structured primarily by the land that the developer was able or unable to purchase, and the hills surrounding the site.

Copy of original plan, held by the Osaka Municipal Central Library, Osaka Historical Archives.

school with a new railway station and land development scheme. This "college town" (*gakuen-toshi*) method provided an initial base of demand for both land and rail service, and can be found throughout the western suburbs of Tokyo, including Oizumi-Gakuen, Seijo-Gakuen and Tamagawa Gakuen. Such developments were also popular in the Osaka region, with dozens of small housing developments scattered throughout the suburban areas surrounding Osaka, Kobe and Kyoto. The leading private railways greatly expanded their networks during the 1910s and 1920s, and the Hankyu, Hanshin and Kinki Nihon railways were leaders in establishing new suburban land development/housing schemes, many of which bore names with variations on the garden city theme (see Katagi, et al. 2000).

There were several factors that contributed to the boom in suburban housing at this time. First, as mentioned above, the rapid growth of the economy during the first two decades of the century had led to a swelling of the ranks of the working class crowded into existing urban areas and new industrial districts adjacent to them. This caused both upward pressure on rents and a declining quality of life in the large cities. Second was the rapid expansion of white collar middle class salaried workers who filled management positions in the emerging industrial sector and staffed the growing government bureaucracy. This new class could afford a daily train fare which the working classes could not, and provided a growing market for suburban homes beyond the urban fringe industrial belts out in the open countryside where land was cheaper and the environment better. While the old urban middle class tended to hold on to their city centre shop-houses, these were frequently devoted primarily to the business, and the primary residence shifted to the new suburbs as in the case of Tanizaki's Makioka family ([1946] 1993). Third was technological development in the railway industry where electrification was proceeding rapidly, especially in the suburban lines in the metropolitan areas, allowing a much more flexible approach to the development of new lines and stations than was the case with steam engines, which were slower to accelerate and more suited to inter-city trunk lines where the stations were spaced further apart (Aoki 1993: 94).

A fourth factor was also crucial: government regulation of the rail industry. As discussed in Chapter 2, in 1906 the state had bought out virtually the whole private railway sector (at that time with almost twice the length of track in service as the government-built railway system) to create a national inter-city rail system, leaving only a few lines in private hands, primarily those in the larger metropolitan areas where there had been considerable duplication. The only avenue for further private railway investment was in these local lines, and much of the capital released by nationalisation was used in this way. Naturally the key to suburban rail development was the simultaneous development of suburban housing estates, both to develop a daily commuting population who would use the train line, and because the profits from land development were commonly greater than ticket sales. In this the Japanese railway entrepreneurs were following the established practice of the other developed countries, especially the US, where streetcar and railway suburbs for the middle and upper middle classes had formed the dominant pattern from the second half of the nineteenth century (see Jackson 1985; Warner [1962] 1978). It is in this period from about 1910 to the mid-1930s that most of the suburban rail lines which have become such an important feature of metropolitan Japan became established, often initially as tramways or as light electric railways. The typical pattern was to build a terminal station as close to the city centre as possible, preferably near a main station of the national railways or in the case of Tokyo and Osaka on the central loop line. The line would then extend out into the countryside serving existing villages and often anchored at the far end by a spa, amusement park or zoo developed by the rail company. The line thus carried commuters to the city during the week, and day-trippers in the opposite direction on weekends.

There is another particularly Japanese twist to this story that greatly influenced the railway boom of the period. Throughout the pre-war period railway development had been tightly controlled by the government as essential to the national interest. Thus while private railways had been encouraged during the Meiji period, their routing and technical standards had been closely regulated, allowing a relatively easy integration of the system on nationalisation. The control over railway investment and construction continued during the Taishō period, however, and the building of new national rail lines and the granting of permits for private lines became highly politicised. The two main conservative political parties of the period had sharply differing approaches to railway policy. The Seiyūkai, which formed the first "party cabinet" under Prime Minister Hara Kei in 1918, and which is often thought of as the more conservative of the two parties, made expansion of railway systems to local areas throughout the country one of its main policy planks. In 1922 the Seiyūkai passed a revised Railway Construction Law which authorised the building of over 10,000 kilometres of new national rail lines in local areas throughout the country. Unlike the previous law which had specified the schedule for building of new lines, the new law left timing unspecified. Combined with the fact that far more lines were authorised than could be built in the foreseeable future, this left the actual decision on the timing of local line construction in the politicians' hands. Unsurprisingly the lines in districts that had elected Seiyūkai members to the Diet were approved first, and as such rail lines could have an enormous impact on the local economy and land values, opened lucrative opportunities for graft. Hara, a brilliant politician who founded what was in effect Japan's first modern political party, is also remembered as the father of Japanese money politics. Similar opportunities presented themselves in the approvals process for permits for new private suburban lines, and often the main factor in the building of new lines was a government permit, or lack thereof.

Many of the suburban land development companies seem to have made real attempts at developing sophisticated urban designs, although the emphasis was clearly on profitability. Provision of parks and other public open space was generally limited. The market for quality suburban residential areas was growing during the inter-war period, although restricted at this time to the upper middle class, which was still quite small. These early beginnings of large-scale suburban housing development were interrupted by the increasing militarisation after the early 1930s, the devastation of wartime bombing, and the serious housing shortages and poverty after the war. These put a break of some 30 years between these early experiments in quality suburban housing estates and the resumption of widespread suburban development in the late 1950s. This break appears to have been decisive in preventing the development of a stronger trend towards the development of large planned suburban communities in Japan, particularly as conditions were so different after the war, as discussed in the next chapter.

Perhaps the greatest long-term impact of these garden city projects was the creation of a strong link between suburban land development and private railway building. Land development along the rail line, usually linked to the building of new stations, provided the core revenue of these companies rather than passenger ridership. In large part because of the high profitability of their land development measures, the private rail companies were able to build dense networks of private commuter lines outside metro areas in the pre-war period. These commuter rail lines had huge impacts on urban form, promoting dispersed patterns of metropolitan growth and encouraging the creation of the rail transit-based metropolitan areas that were typical of Japan in the second half of the century. In particular, two features of Japanese urbanisation that were fostered by the strong role of private commuter lines in suburban growth were the characteristic urban pattern of dense clusters of shops around the outlying commuter stations, and the important nodes that developed at the downtown terminal stations or where they joined with national rail lines. Already in the pre-war period several of these, such as Shibuya and Shinjuku in Tokyo and Namba in Osaka had formed into significant commercial and entertainment subcentres (Sorensen 2001a).

In the Japanese case then, the main contribution of the garden city idea was neither the social ownership message of Letchworth, nor the development of salubrious upper middle class suburbs such as Hampstead Garden Suburb north of London or Radburn in New Jersey, but land speculation connected to transit development as in pre-war Los Angeles. In Japan, however, the rail companies only started seeing serious competition from private automobiles in the late 1970s, whereas in the US the average working family commonly owned a car in the 1930s. Instead of being gradually eliminated by rising car use, then, in Japan the suburban railway systems continued to dominate patterns of urban growth for much of the rest of the century.

Planning in the colonies and occupied territories

Hein (2001) argues that some of Japan's most visionary urban planning was undertaken in the colonies, where the city planners' strong technical abilities were unconstrained by the political and social constraints of the home country. Planners were able to design bold experiments in urban planning, and were even able to carry many of them out because they did not need to take any account of existing property owners or local sentiment. As Hein puts it, they were able to plan as though for a "void territory", avoiding the perennial problems of local landowners, existing urban areas, and the political and financial constraints that blocked planning efforts in Japan. As Peattie argues, Japanese colonial administrators, operating with enormous administrative and legislative powers and broad freedom from constraint either from Tokyo or from indigenous feelings were very effective urban planners and created "a number of handsome colonial capitals . . . which rivalled Western colonial cities in Asia and were better planned, more ordered, and more attractive than many cities in the home islands" (Peattie 1988: 264). Hein suggests that the technocratic vision of planned metropolitan development was able to flourish in the colonial environment, resulting in some of the most outstanding work of Japanese planning such as the plans for Daidō in Inner Mongolia (now Shangxi province) shown in Figure 4.10. The remarkable success of Japanese planners in the colonies in both the development and implementation of visionary plans supports the idea that one of the primary obstacles to comprehensive planning in the home islands was not any lack of technical ability, but rather the political weakness of the planning movement. In the 1930s many of Japan's most prominent planners went to the colonies and occupied territories and attempted to implement ambitious urban plans. As Tucker (1999: 236) puts it, "The army's seizure of the Northeast unloosed this ambition by giving planners the means and the conquered space to build their ideal city. On what they often called the 'blank page', or 'white paper', of China, they believed they could build the 'New Capital' just as they wished."

It seems hardly necessary to point out that the indigenous Chinese inhabitants of Manchuria were unlikely to have been very enthusiastic about any plans for their cities that regarded them as non-existent and their land as a void territory. This episode in Japanese planning does serve to highlight one of the central contradictions of twentieth-century planning, that between those who saw it primarily as a means of improving quality of life and living environments in urban areas, and those whose primary goal was the creation and implementation of visionary plans for urban areas. An important contemporary example of the latter is Le Corbusier's "*Plan Voisin*" which proposed the flattening of most of central Paris and the creation instead of a vast open space studded with high-rise towers, expressways and a park-like open space. Le Corbusier's plans are also useful in reminding us that colonial planners were not the only ones who dreamed of blank pages devoid of existing residents or histories. Such daydreams were

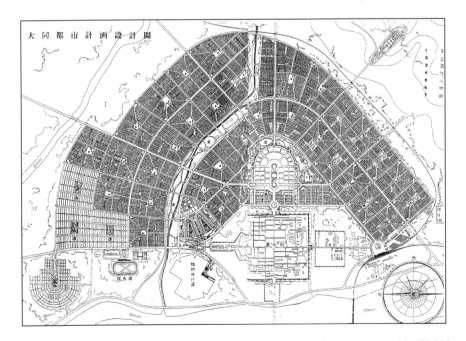

Figure 4.10 Daidō in Inner Mongolia. Comprehensive Plan for Daidō, prepared by Uchida Yoshikazu in 1938. To be developed by using the profit from city control of the land development process, the plan included plans for airports, cemeteries, athletic facilities, shrines and temples. Most of the area is composed of residential neighbourhood units based on an elementary school area, with commercial facilities in the centre, and an industrial area on the outside.

Source: *Modern Architecture (Gendai Kenchiku)*, vol. 8, January 1940: 47 reproduced in Tucker (1999).

in fact rather common, being shared by the designers of new capitals such as Brasilia, by the various schemes to fill in Tokyo Bay during the 1950s and 1960s discussed below, and by North American city planners in the 1950s and 1960s who bulldozed poor neighbourhoods in order to create public housing estates and new business centres. Although planning approaches that put priority on the people living in the planned areas are vastly more difficult to implement, and harder to draw nice axonometric drawings of, by the end of the century blank slate planning for existing urban areas had been largely abandoned, and in Japan a style of planning that is focused primarily on negotiating with local residents the incremental improvement of existing built up areas has become the dominant form of urban planning. But that is a story for later chapters.

Metropolitan greenbelt structure plans

One final aspect of pre-war planning efforts must be mentioned. Since the early 1920s attempts to create rational plans for the overall growth of the larger metropolitan areas were an important part of Japanese city planning thought. A variety of efforts to structure the growth of the larger urban areas were considered, which were important precedents for post-war metropolitan plans. Early metropolitan structure planning was strongly influenced by European ideas. Several Japanese planners including some from the Home Ministry's City Planning Department had attended the influential 1924 Amsterdam International City Planning Conference, where a central topic of debate was the issue of planning the metropolis, and a highly influential model was that of the core city ringed

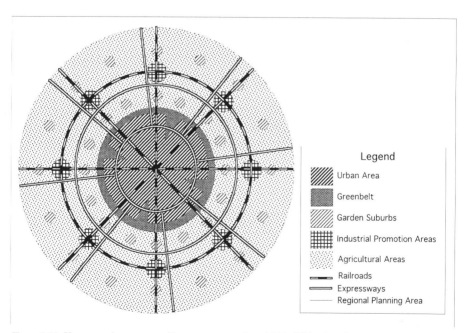

Figure 4.11 Kanto region metropolitan structure plan, 1940. This plan for the Tokyo region of 1940 shows significant influences from European planning thought.

Source: Adapted from Tokyo Metropolitan Government (1989: 39).

by greenbelt and surrounded by satellites linked by a radial and loop rail system. The Kanto Region Metropolitan Structure Plan proposed by the Tokyo Area City Planning Committee of the Home Ministry in 1940, shown in Figure 4.11, is widely considered to have been influenced by the metropolitan planning ideas of the 1924 conference.

This model of metropolitan structure is also very similar to Howard's earlier "social city" scheme (Howard [1902] 1985 frontispiece), which was familiar to Japanese planners. The model has been adapted to the Japanese context in several significant aspects, however. The "garden suburbs" in the Kanto plan are the numerous small settlements scattered throughout the agricultural hinterland of the metropolis. These correspond, it seems safe to assume, to the garden suburbs already being built by the private railway companies. The key locations at the intersections of the radial rail lines with the circumferential line outside the greenbelt are reserved in the Kanto plan for industrial promotion areas (the word used is *kōgyō*, a term which refers to manufacturing industry rather than business in general), and not the garden cities of Howard's plan. The priority given to industrial development reflects the timing of the release of the plan in 1940, when Japan was already mobilised for total war and the development of munitions industries was the top national priority. Several such industrial promotion areas and military cities (*gunto*) were actually built during the war as a way of dispersing munitions plants from central Tokyo (Ishizuka and Ishida 1988c: 25).

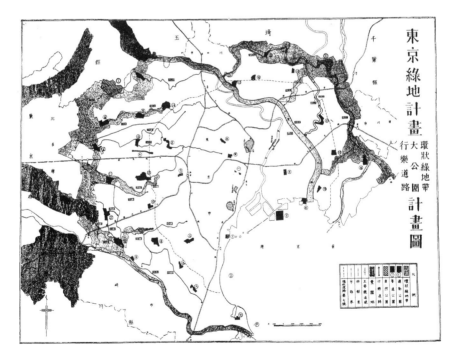

Figure 4.12 Tokyo green space system plan, 1939. This plan for a green space network for Tokyo originated in the debates about metropolitan structure of the 1920s. In 1932 a Tokyo Regional Green Space Council was established, and this is their final proposal of 1939.

Source: Tokyo Green Space Planning Council (*Tokyo Ryokuchi Keikaku Kyōgikai*) (1939).

Preparations for war aided the implementation of a greenbelt plan which had been in preparation since the formation of the Tokyo Regional Green Space Council in 1932. This group started to develop a plan for a regional green space system, following the basic ideas for metropolitan planning advanced at the Amsterdam conference of 1924. According to Ishikawa (2001: 244–59), the thinking of the council was also strongly influenced by the American metropolitan parks movement of the nineteenth century in its attempt to create a park system. While at the outset, however, the concern was with recreational green space for Tokyo citizens, as Japan slid deeper into war in the 1930s the need for air defence measures was used to promote the idea. Their proposals were made public in 1939, and included an extensive greenbelt of 13,730 hectares, 40 large parks totalling 1,695 hectares, and 591 small parks totalling 674 hectares (Ishizuka and Ishida 1988c: 52). The plan, reproduced as Figure 4.12, cleverly integrates existing unbuilt land on the urban fringe with the main river valleys and topographical features of the metropolitan area. There was neither budget nor land acquisition mechanism adequate to carry out the plan, however, until the 1940 revision of the City Planning Law which included air defence as a goal of city planning, and defined green spaces as public facilities, thus making expropriation of land for the greenbelts and parks legally permissible. In this way a considerable area of land for greenbelts was bought, totalling some 646 hectares, while much of the remainder of the planned greenbelt area was simply designated as Air Defence Open Space and used for anti-aircraft batteries and fighter interceptor bases. After the war the areas which had been purchased were eventually turned into some of Tokyo's larger metropolitan parks, while the rest of the open spaces were gradually built over (Ishizuka and Ishida 1988c: 23). Ishikawa details the process by which the areas designated as green space in the 1939 plan were gradually reduced in 29 stages between 1949 and 1969 (Ishikawa 2001: 265).

Major urban changes during the inter-war period

Summarising urban developments of the Taishō period is much more difficult than for the preceding Meiji period, as they were both more extensive and more diverse. Figure 4.13 attempts such a simplified summary using the model castle town introduced in previous chapters. The three most important features of urban change were extensive unplanned growth on the urban fringe; the development of new intra-urban transport facilities such as electric trams and private suburban railway lines; and the tentative beginnings of planned suburban growth, with the planning and designation of suburban arterial road networks which remained largely unbuilt, and the development, largely through private initiative, of suburban LR projects. As noted above, in most provincial cities city planning was synonymous with public facilities designation and construction – an improved trunk road here, a park there, or the laying out of some new streets near a rail station. All of this was essential public works, but few provincial towns attempted any large-scale planning interventions. The focus of most population growth pressure was in the larger centres such as Osaka, Nagoya, Yokohama and Kobe, and it was in these centres that more active planning efforts were carried out.

The characteristic feature of Japanese urban growth – small islands of planned development set against a background of haphazard sprawl and structured by large-scale transportation systems – is thus seen clearly for the first time in this period. Several other

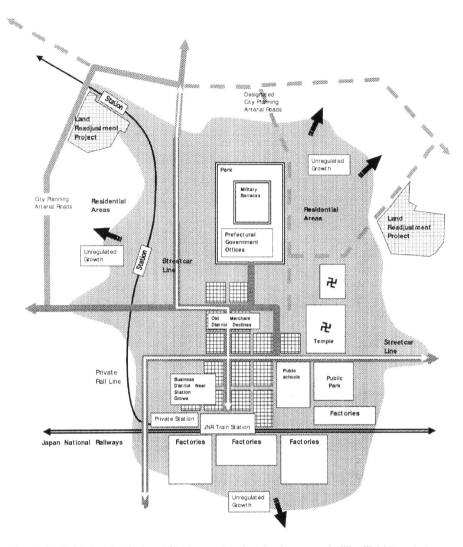

Figure 4.13 Taishō period industrialisation and early suburban growth. The Taishō period saw further rapid growth of the main provincial towns. The new planning system began to have an impact during the 1920s, with the designation and building of city planning arterial roads, and the spread of LR projects to develop land on the urban fringe. Most growth, however, was still unplanned, unserviced building on the urban fringe.

features are worth noting. Large-scale factory growth occurred primarily near the railway lines, but smaller-scale enterprises continued to be distributed throughout the urban area, with little separation of land uses. Although the 1919 City Planning Law introduced a three-part land use zoning system to separate residential, commercial and industrial areas, in practice patterns of development were little affected partly because many castle towns did not bother to pass zoning plans at all, and in those that did the new zoning plans had only just been prepared and approved before the beginning of war diverted most energies away from urban planning and development. Further, the zoning system was not very restrictive in any case, as became more clear in the post-war period discussed in the next chapter. Finally, in 1943 exceptions to the Urban Building Law had the effect of suspending the zoning system apart from the fire-prevention zone and the open space areas (Ishizuka and Ishida 1988a: 54).

Characteristics of inter-war planning

The inter-war period played a pivotal role in the development of the planning system. Japan had developed an urban industrial society which quickly reproduced many of the serious urban problems that had prompted the development of modern urban planning in the West during the nineteenth and early twentieth centuries. The combination of a broad recognition of worsening social problems in the cities with a process of democratic development through the emergence of party cabinets and the broadening of the franchise led to a real shift in government priorities away from the almost single-issue focus of building national military and industrial strength, which had characterised the Meiji period, to a broader range of policy approaches including policies aimed at alleviating emerging social conflicts. One aspect of the reform measures was the creation of a more sophisticated urban planning system, as embodied in the 1919 City Planning Act.

At the same time the highly centralised structure of government created during the Meiji period, and the central policymaking role of the bureaucracy had decisive effects on the planning system that emerged. Of all the industrial countries at this time, Japan created what was probably the most centralised structure of urban planning with virtually every city plan and budget throughout the country subject to the approval of Home Ministry officers. A positive result of this structure was the rapid development of a high level of technical expertise by an elite group of planners in the Home Ministry, and in affiliated bodies such as the Tokyo Reconstruction Bureau and Dōjunkai. These planners had built up considerable experience on the Tokyo reconstruction project and through study of Western systems. As shown by some of the city plans produced during this period, the technical sophistication of Japanese planning was considerable at this time.

Unfortunately, despite the increasing sophistication of planners and the planning system, most new urban growth continued as unplanned sprawl. Throughout the period there was little control over suburban development at the same time that there was increasing private sector speculative land development. This was no doubt in part a result of the Kanto earthquake, the continuing poverty of much of the country, and the increasing mobilisation for war. But this explains neither the lack of effective regulatory enforcement mechanisms to control suburban growth, nor the failure to effectively enforce those that existed.

It seems clear that the creation of an effective planning system was hindered by the high degree of government centralisation and the weak political support for urban planning. The conventional explanation is that opposition by the Finance Ministry and the unfortunate timing of the Kanto earthquake made implementation of the new system difficult. Then in the 1930s war put an end to most urban development and planning apart from that necessary for military bases. While those are certainly important parts of the picture, they neglect to mention the crucial lack of political support for urban planning at this time. Without the broad base of organisational support in local governments, citizens' groups or professional organisations that kept pushing environmental issues onto the public agenda in many Western countries, it was extremely difficult for advocates of planning whether inside or outside the Home Ministry to overcome opposition to increased regulation of urban development and increased spending on urban planning projects. This, however, raises the question: why was there so little political support for city planning? Charles Beard, the renowned American historian, former director of the New York Bureau of Municipal Research, leading figure in the American municipal reform movement, and consultant to Gotō Shinpei on the reconstruction of Tokyo after the earthquake posed the same question, and his thoughts on the topic are worth examining.

Beard succinctly analysed in 1923 the main reasons why, in his view, Japanese urban planning was not developing in similar ways to Western countries in his book *Administration and Politics of Tokyo*: "It is evident from the foregoing facts that Tokyo has possessed a certain degree of self-government for more than thirty years, and that there is an increasing interest in civic affairs among the people. One is moved to ask, therefore, why it is that the city is so backward in many things like sewers, paved streets, and transportation. Thousands of citizens have long enjoyed the right to vote. Why have they not used that right to compel a transformation of material aspects of the city?" (Beard 1923: 145). Beard identified a number of reasons:

1   the elected mayor's powers were weak, and policy was controlled by the city council and by prefectural and imperial officers;
2   the people of Tokyo had recently emerged from a feudal order, were used to obedience, and not to self-assertion and self-government;
3   Tokyo was mainly a collection of villages with a metropolitan centre, and the great mass of the population was composed of small shopkeepers and villagers who were politically unorganised;
4   in the West organised labour had a profound impact on municipal politics, even developing complete municipal programmes, "In Tokyo, however, the working classes, broadly speaking, cannot vote, are not organised, and have no municipal interest or programme" (Beard 1923: 147);
5   imperial bureaucrats were "often ardent advocates of enlightened policies, but they are not as a rule zealous to promote the rapid growth of a public sentiment which might endanger their prerogatives" (Beard 1923: 147);
6   the women's movement was weak, and women still had no vote;
7   "The system of suffrage, nominations, and elections does not encourage the public interest on any of the main issues such as roads, sewers, sanitation, transportation, congestion, or public health" (Beard 1923: 148).

Thus in a few pages Beard neatly summarised the political economy of urban planning in pre-war Japan. To his admirable summary only a few small points might be added. Beard describes several factors prominent in the development of planning in the US that he found lacking in Japan. He failed to note two important positive factors that worked against the development of stronger public support for better city planning practice in Japan in the inter-war period. First is the fact that traditional Japanese urban development and management strategies were still widely practised and quite effective. Apart from the crowded and miserable industrial districts of the urban working class, which as Beard noted still had not been enfranchised, Japanese urban areas were still reasonably successful as living environments at this time. Pre-modern systems of waste management still functioned efficiently, and the addition of modern water supply and rail transport systems enabled much of the growing middle class to enjoy reasonable residential standards without the need for much planning intervention. Good housing in excellent environments could easily be found in suburban areas where there was little need for modern city planning measures as they were still of very low density in a semi-rural environment as the emerging middle class was still quite small at this time. The continuing effectiveness of pre-modern urban technologies seems likely to have greatly slowed the development of public pressure for a stronger modern city planning system.

A second significant factor was the active and highly successful social mobilisation efforts of Home Ministry bureaucrats described in the last chapter. Those campaigns drew on strong traditions of neighbourhood mutual support and patriotic feeling to promote neighbourhood organisations that were responsible for a wide range of local urban services including sanitation and immunisation campaigns, poor relief, street lighting, cleaning, maintenance, and neighbourhood festival organisation. The urban middle class, who provided the leadership of neighbourhood organisations, were increasingly drawn into government campaigns for greater neighbourhood self-reliance during the inter-war period. These arrangements significantly improved urban living conditions and reduced the need for modern urban infrastructure and planning, even as industrialisation and urban growth increased it. Despite the unfortunate abuse of neighbourhood organisations during the war, it seems clear that they were not only successful in contributing to the quality of urban life, but also in creating a stronger sense of community in the cities. By promoting such urban organisations the government managed both to reduce the need for modern urban planning measures and divert the energies of those who might have desired better urban governance into state-organised forms of social mobilisation.

War and destruction

Japan's deepening involvement in the China war after 1931 and the gradual descent into total war meant that increasingly little time, energy, or resources were devoted to urban planning after the mid-1930s. After the American capture of Saipan island in 1944 regular bombing raids were commenced against Japanese cities. The use of incendiary bombs against cities densely built of wood and paper was devastating, and most Japanese urban areas were consumed in the resulting fires. Japan's population in cities of over one million (at that time only Tokyo and Osaka qualified) dropped from 12.4 million in 1940 to 3.9 million in 1945 as a result of the destruction of the housing stock and mass civilian evacuations. Surrender was finally announced after the almost complete obliteration of two cities in the southwest, Hiroshima and Nagasaki by atomic bombs in August of 1945. Defeat in war marked the end of an era, and the occupation and post-war reconstruction described in the next chapter began a new one.

5 Post-war reconstruction and rapid economic growth

> "The Era of High Speed Growth" is the mantra used to characterise the two decades after 1955. It has been repeated so often that it may seem trite, but there is no other way to understand this period. Growth overshadowed everything. It also consumed everyone's energies and attention. And its consequences reached into every nook and cranny of Japanese society.
>
> (Allinson 1997: 83)

Japan's war ended with the announcement of unconditional surrender in a radio address to the Japanese people by Emperor Hirohito on August 15, 1945. The war had been extraordinarily destructive, and had cost Japan dearly. Quite apart from the enormous human and material costs in the Asian countries Japan had invaded, still an ever-present source of tension in relations with its neighbours over 50 years later, Japan itself had been devastated by its pursuit of Asian domination through military conquest. Some three million Japanese had perished in the war, and 15 years of steadily increasing expenditure of the nation's human, material and spiritual resources had left the country physically shattered, demoralised and on the brink of starvation. Incendiary bombing by American B-29 bombers in the last two years of the war, and particularly after February of 1945 had reduced most of Japan's larger cities to ashes, while Hiroshima and Nagasaki had been completely obliterated by nuclear bombs. The majority of buildings in Japanese urban areas had been lightly built of wood, tile and paper, and incendiary bombs had proven highly effective in setting them ablaze. Almost ten million people had lost their homes to fire. Little was left standing in most of the bombed cities apart from a few modern concrete buildings in commercial centres and the occasional stone or mud *kura*, or family storehouse of a rich merchant or landlord which stood bleakly above the blackened wastes. The task of reconstruction had to start literally from the ground up on the conclusion of hostilities.

This chapter reviews the period from the end of the war to the rapid economic growth of the 1950s and 1960s. The chapter has three main parts. The first covers the period of post-war reconstruction, looking particularly at the impacts of the occupation reforms and urban reconstruction projects of the early post-war period. The second looks at the transformation of Japan from a tottering and devastated shell at the end of the war to an economic superpower and the world's second largest economy during the period of rapid economic growth. The main focus is on the concentration of population and industry in the main metropolitan areas and the formation of the vast urban industrial sprawl sometimes referred to as the Tokaido megalopolis, which stretches from Tokyo in the east to Fukuoka in the south west. The third section reviews the main urban planning initiatives during the rapid economic growth period, and describes briefly the megalopolitan problems that were one of the most prominent products of the rapid growth period, and which became the main issue for urban planners and policy-makers after rapid growth had ended.

Post-war occupation reforms and reconstruction

Japan faced an enormous task of rebuilding shattered cities, providing housing, and rebuilding an economy that in the previous 15 years had been organised primarily around support of military adventure. Such was the state of post-war devastation that many occupation observers believed there was a serious possibility that Japan would continue to be an economic basket-case for the long term. Mass starvation was prevented in part by substantial shipments of American food grains, and partly by the fact that many urban residents had left for rural areas and family homes, where food and shelter were more available.

The American-led occupation saw the reconstruction of the nation's political and

Figure 5.1 Tokyo in ruins, again. Tokyo was left a charred ruin by incendiary bombing during the last two years of war. This photo, taken 16 August 1945, looks east across the Sumida River to Honjo ward, one of the main working class industrial districts.

Photo Mainichi Shinbunsha.

social institutions as of primary importance. The main goals of the occupation were to demilitarise and democratise Japan. The occupation authorities were idealists who tried to create a new democratic Japan that would not be a danger to its neighbours, and so sought to eliminate the social and political structures that had led to totalitarian control and military aggression. The principal political reforms were the establishment of a new constitution which based sovereignty in the people, the creation of a new electoral system based on universal suffrage and equality for all, the creation of an independent judiciary, reform of the local administrative system to allow greater independence for local governments, and the elimination of the power of the military and Imperial Court, although the emperor was allowed to retain status as a constitutional monarch without effective political power.

The reforms to the Diet kept the bicameral legislature but abolished the peerage and ensured that both houses were elected, with the prime minister elected by the lower house, and cabinets responsible to the Diet, rather than the emperor as in the past. This eliminated the ambiguities of power inherent in the old constitution which had allowed gradual shifts in actual political control from the Genrō during the Meiji period to the political parties and bureaucracy in the Taishō period, and finally to the bureaucracy and the military during the war. Equally significantly, the new constitution vested sovereignty in the people instead of in the emperor for the first time in Japanese history.

Reforms to the education, economic, local government, and police systems were considered particularly important in order to promote a political and social environment more amenable to democratic government, and eliminate the repressive features of pre-war Japanese state control. The education system, which was accused of inculcating nationalist doctrine, was reformed and decentralised with the creation of elected local boards of education. The *zaibatsu*, or major family-controlled corporate groups, were seen as having been too deeply involved in the military industrial complex of pre-war Japan and as continuing to hold too great an economic power, and were consequently broken up. A new Labour Union Law was passed which guaranteed the right to organise and engage in collective bargaining and strikes. A new system of local government was established, in which prefectural governors and city mayors were directly elected instead of appointed by the Home Ministry as in the past, and prefectural and city assemblies were given expanded powers. The national police system was also abolished with control over police being transferred to local Public Safety Commissions on the American model. When the Home Ministry showed reluctance to implement these two key challenges to its main pre-war power bases, it was abolished in December 1947 and replaced by the ministries of Labour, Health and Welfare, Construction and the Local Autonomy Agency (which supervised the local government system). The Ministry of Construction (MoC) inherited the city and regional planning functions of the Home Ministry, including responsibility for river management.

There is no doubt that the occupation reforms contributed greatly to the democratisation of Japanese society by eliminating many of the institutions that had allowed the state to dominate the people. Although the reforms were handed down from above by what was in effect a military dictatorship of the occupation authorities, the utter catastrophe that had resulted from earlier policies had fostered wide support for change, both among those who had opposed the previous regime and those who had supported it. At the same time, many of the occupation reforms did not work in entirely the ways that the occupation intended, some failing completely while others were reversed after the occupation ended, as discussed below. Further, no society can change completely in a few short years and recent historians have been at pains to stress the continuities between pre-war and post-war Japanese society (Allinson 1997; Johnson 1982). Of these perhaps the most important continuity was provided by the central government bureaucracy. The occupation used the Japanese bureaucracy as an intermediary instead of attempting to govern the country directly. This greatly enhanced its prestige as one of the few pre-war institutions that were effectively exonerated from blame for the wartime debacle. Also the disbanding of the military, the elimination of the political role of the imperial household and the weakening of the old conservative political parties through purges of much of their leadership meant that the bureaucracy emerged as an even more powerful institution than it had been before the war.

As shown below, city planners were a part of that bureaucracy, and although the Home Ministry was divided into several parts, with city planning, civil engineering and river engineering departments forming the core of the new MoC, bureaucrats were still able to block occupation reforms intended to decentralise planning powers to local governments. City planning was largely a story of continuity before and after the war in terms of legislative framework, administrative structure and key actors. The generation of planners who had found work opportunities in the colonies and occupied territories played an important role in the post-war reconstruction projects.

It is also important to note that the elimination of police repression, the granting of greater local government independence, the reforms to the education system, the legalisation of labour-organising, and the stress on individual citizens' rights all contributed to the growth and development of civil society, or areas of citizen activity that are outside the control of the state. That also was a necessarily slow process, as social changes do not occur overnight, but the post-war period has seen the gradual increase in independent citizens' organisations and movements which have ultimately had profound effects on city development and on the urban planning system, as shown in Chapters 6, 8 and 9.

While the occupation reforms clearly did help to create the necessary conditions for the growth of a democratic, peaceful and capitalist Japan in the post-war period, many of the specific reforms did not work out entirely the way their authors had intended, tending rather to be transformed in their implementation. The particular ways in which individual reforms worked out were structured by the interactions between American and Japanese actors, by the fact that the occupation chose to work through the existing Japanese government bureaucracy, and by the ways in which the various sectors of Japanese society responded to the post-war challenges (see Dower 1999). Reforms with significant bases of support in the bureaucracy or among the people tended to have more lasting effects than others which did not. In particular, land reform and the new constitution were widely supported and had long-term impacts. The changes to labour law, education reform and local government restructuring produced more mixed results, while the attempt to dissolve the huge financial/industrial conglomerates (*zaibatsu*) had very little impact at all as very quickly new organisational structures emerged which fulfilled many of their functions (Allinson 1997: 63). Of the various occupation reforms, the land reform and reforms to local government structure had the most important long-term impacts on urban planning and urban growth.

Land reform

A sweeping land reform was carried out under the occupation, motivated by the belief that rural unrest and tenant poverty had provided a significant base of support for some of the more extreme nationalist and imperialist policies of the pre-war period. Land reform had important long-term impacts on later urbanisation by breaking up most of the larger landholdings. Under the reform one-third of the national total of farmland was redistributed from landlords to owner-cultivators. All the land of absentee landlords, and all the leased-out land of cultivating landlords above 1 hectare (4 hectares in Hokkaido) was bought by the government and resold to tenants. Further, all owner-cultivated land above 3 hectares (12 hectares in Hokkaido) was bought and redistributed, thus setting an upper limit on the amount of land any one farmer could hold (Dore 1959: 138). The effects of reform in rural areas were enormous. The final reports of the land committees who had carried out the reform at the village level showed that a total of 1,128,000 hectares of rice land and 790,000 hectares of dryfield land had been bought from 2,341,000 landlords, and resold to 4,748,000 tenants. The amount of rice land cultivated by tenants dropped from 53.1 per cent of the total in 1941 to 10.9 per cent in 1950. At the same time, owner-cultivated rice land rose from 46.9 per cent to 88.9 per cent. A further direct effect of land reform was a decrease in the average size of cultivated holdings as large holdings were broken up. There was a reduction in the number of operated holdings above 2 hectares, and a significant increase in operated holdings of less than 0.5 hectares, from 33 to 41 per cent of all farms. Therefore, over 2.5 million farms – 40 per cent of the total – were less than 5,000 square metres in size, or smaller than a large suburban residential plot in the US. At the same time there was an increase in the total number of farms from 5.4 million in 1940 to 6.2 million in 1950 (Dore 1959: 175).

The really important change was that these were no longer tenant farmers, operating a landlord's land from year to year with little security of tenure and a living level at or below the subsistence level. Dore pointed out in 1959 that a peasant family which owned its land, however small, was much less likely to move away to the city in search of work than a tenant (Dore 1959: 263). This observation proved prophetic. The tenacious refusal of Japanese farmers to sell their land has been a central problem both for agricultural policy and for urban planning in the post-war years. The small size of farms hindered efforts to create a more efficient and competitive farm sector, and throughout the 1950s the farm population stayed at the high level of over 6 million farm households and 16–16.5 million farm workers. The speed of the land reform was also directly responsible for the scattered landholdings of the post-war period because they were not consolidated as part of the process (Teruoka 1989). Land reform was limited in theory to agricultural land as commercial, industrial, residential and forest lands were outside the process (Hanayama 1986: 186; Teruoka 1989). As may be imagined in such an enormous project, however, there were many complications in practice. For example, special rules had to be developed for suburban areas where there was an intermixture of rural and urban land uses. In general, however, patterns of urban landholding were not strongly affected by the land reform process, although rural land ownership patterns did have significant impacts on patterns of later urbanisation as cities grew. Put simply, fragmentation of land ownership has been an important contributor to suburban sprawl, as examined in greater detail in Chapters 7 and 8.

Greatly reinforcing the impacts of fragmented land ownership on post-war land development patterns has been the constitutional protection of land ownership rights. The strong rights accorded to Japanese landowners under the post-war constitution have gained some fame and even notoriety as a result of cases such as the Narita Airport debacle which reached its peak during the 1970s and 1980s (see Apter and Sawa 1984), but which is still not entirely resolved at the time of writing. It is widely believed that one of the root causes of these problems was the American-imposed constitution, which guarantees such strong constitutional rights to land ownership. As Tsuru (1993) carefully explains, however, the American draft of the article on land rights was strongly resisted by the Japanese side, and was eventually replaced by wording suggested by the Japanese government. The original Article 28 in MacArthur's draft read, "The ultimate fee to the land and to all natural resources reposes in the State as the collective representative of the people. Land and other natural resources are subject to the right of the State to take them upon just compensation therefore, for the purpose of securing and promoting the conservation, development, utilization and control thereof", and the next article went on to state that "the ownership of land imposes obligations" (cited in Tsuru 1993: 27). This wording indicates a strong recognition of the public interest in land ownership and use, and the mention of the associated obligations is similar to the well-known West German approach which stressed the obligations of land ownership, and upon which has been based a much more interventionist approach to land planning and regulation. This approach of the MacArthur draft was eventually replaced by the following wording suggested by the Japanese side which is now Article 29 of the Japanese constitution: "The right to own or to hold property is inviolable. Property rights shall be defined by law, in conformity with the public welfare. Private property may be taken for public use upon just compensation therefore." Tsuru (1993: 27) suggests that this wording is basically identical to the old Article 27 of the Meiji constitution, and is much more conservative in its protection of the rights of landowners and its weak conception of the public interest than the initial American draft. Later attempts to devise effective strategies to regulate and control land development have frequently run afoul of this constitutional roadblock to effective land regulation, as shown below. This episode is a useful reminder that the post-war constitution was not simply imposed on Japan as written by the occupation forces, but was a much more contested document, on which the Japanese side had significant influence. The common assertion that the strong rights of land ownership in Japan are a legacy of the American occupation, and reflect American constitutional thinking, is clearly incorrect.

Local government reform

Another focus of occupation reform efforts was the local government system, which was understood to have been essentially an extension of the administrative power of the central government in the pre-war period. In order to encourage greater democracy in Japan, to give local people more say over local affairs, and particularly in order to develop local governments as the training grounds for democratic thought and behaviour that they were idealistically seen to be in the US, a new Local Autonomy Law was passed at the same time as the new constitution in May of 1947. The main change was the institution of direct elections for prefectural governors who had until this point been appointees of the Home Ministry, and an expansion of the powers of prefectural and municipal assemblies. Prefectural governments were also given more tax authority, and control over the newly decentralised education system and police forces.

The new electoral system in the prefectures and municipalities has remained in effect; however, local governments did not gain the degree of independence that the occupation authorities had intended. In fact, central government officials worked hard to maintain their old dominance over local affairs. Allinson (1997: 72) sets out the problem clearly:

> Allied reformers underestimated the determination of former officials from the old Home Ministry who staffed the new (Local Autonomy) agency – men who never abandoned their desire to preserve every ounce of control over local affairs. Central officials sought control through three avenues: finance, duties, and personnel. They tried to keep local governments dependent by forcing them to rely on central government grants, rather than local resources, for their operating revenues. They subordinated local governments by requiring them to carry out a wide range of duties mandated by the national government, and they tried to subvert local autonomy by appointing incumbent and retired central government officials to the best administrative positions in cities and prefectures.

Each of these three avenues allowed central government to keep a tight rein on local government activity during the post-war period, and central government control over finances and appointments to key positions have been keenly resented by local governments as sharp limits on their autonomy.

It can be argued, however, that it has been central government control over "duties" which has played the main role in maintaining the power of central ministries. This was a product of the "agency delegated functions" (*Kikan Inin Jimu*) system which was first established during the Meiji period, as described in Chapter 2. With regard to the execution of the delegated function the officer is considered the agent of the central government, responsible to the central government and not to his or her electors or the prefectural or town assembly. According to the MoC in *City Planning in Japan*, "Although the prefectural governor is elected by universal suffrage, he is legally required to act as an agent of the national government as far as city planning is concerned" (Japan Ministry of Construction 1991b: 13). This meant that important decisions such as approving a zoning plan had to be approved by a higher authority, and could effectively be controlled by the central ministry. It also meant that lower levels of government had no authority to set their own independent planning rules or by-laws but could only work within the national legislation. This was probably not a big issue in the reconstruction period, but it certainly became an issue as Japan became wealthier in the 1960s and after, as shown below.

Although a tax reform commission headed by Dr. Carl Shoup of Columbia University had recommended in 1949 that local governments be allowed a stable revenue source of their own, and specifically suggested that town planning be fully decentralised to local control, few of its recommendations were adopted because of intense opposition in the Diet and central government ministries (Beasley 1995: 221; Ishida 1982; Steiner 1965: 108). According to Ishida, the Japanese government's own commission set up after receipt of the Shoup Report to investigate local administrative reform recommended that town planning be decentralised: "The report clearly stated

'Town Planning and town planning projects shall be the responsibility of municipalities. Laws shall be changed to give municipalities autonomous power to decide and implement matters related to town planning.' The report even asserted that the legal structure of the 1919 Town Planning Act hampered autonomy of local public entities" (Ishida 2000: 8). In response to this pressure the MoC examined the possibility of revisions to the City Planning Law based on the Shoup Report, and issued a draft revision in 1952 which included provisions for decentralisation and citizen participation. This draft revision was never implemented, however, as ultimately the MoC resisted changing the centrally controlled system. Ishida notes that among the MoC's stated reasons for not being willing to transfer power to local governments were that they did not have the planning resources to do effective planning, that city planning often required coordination between several municipalities, and that planning could be "distorted" by local politicians (Ishida 2000).

The idea that local politicians could "distort" planning decisions has been a long-standing rationale used by central government bureaucrats to deny local governments the legal authority to make planning decisions. Given the enormous profits to be gained by changing land designation or public spending plans, the potential for corruption affecting local planning decisions is certainly real, and such corruption has not been uncommon in other countries. Japan was in a desperate situation during the immediate post-war period with widespread food shortages, industrial production at a small fraction of pre-war output, and its larger cities mostly blackened and in smouldering ruins. If we consider this from the perspective of central government bureaucrats who had been trained to perceive of issues of national development and national strength as their exclusive responsibility, then it is easier to understand their reluctance to relinquish their monopoly of authority over city planning decision-making. From this perspective Japan was at a crucial turning point; the job of reconstruction had to be carried out in the most efficient manner possible, and only the central bureaucracy had the expertise, breadth of vision, and moral and legal authority to direct the rebuilding of the economy and the country. Be that as it may, there can be no doubt that an important opportunity to decentralise city planning authority was lost during the occupation because of the determined efforts by central government bureaucrats to retain their powers. City planning continued as before the war, a central government-dominated activity. In some ways the degree of central control was even increased. For example, because of the severe financial crisis during the occupation a clause was included in the law regulating local government finances that as a temporary measure municipalities would be required to gain central government permission to issue bonds. This "temporary" measure is still in effect today, and has been used effectively by the central government to control local government spending. This may very well have been an advantage during the post-war reconstruction period, but it caused increasing problems later.

Post-war urban reconstruction projects, 1945–55

As noted above, most Japanese cities were smouldering ruins at the end of the war and housing shortages were severe. In the 115 cities that were included in the reconstruction planning, burned areas totalled 63,153 hectares, 2,316,000 dwellings were destroyed, 9,699,000 people lost their homes to fire, and 331,000 were killed. In Tokyo alone most of the built up area had burned and some 750,000 houses destroyed. The repatriation of some six million Japanese soldiers and civilians from overseas in the early post-war period aggravated the serious housing shortage, calculated by the MoC at 4,200,000 dwellings (Ishida 1987: 210). Urban economies had been shattered both by bombing and by 15 years of ever-increasing focus on military adventure. There were severe shortages of building materials, as much of Japanese industrial capacity had either been destroyed or converted to military use. In 1945 the industrial capacity was approximately 10 per cent of what it had been in 1930, and basic construction materials such as steel, wood, glass, tile, and cement were all in short supply.

Nevertheless, ambitious plans for reconstruction were prepared, based on the experience of the Tokyo Earthquake Reconstruction Project. In December of 1945 a Basic Policy for War-damaged Areas Reconstruction (*Sensaichi Fukkō Keikaku Kihon Hōshin*) was passed which set ambitious targets for rebuilding, including detailed and strengthened land use planning controls, building standards and controls on building coverage. The policy established a target of 10 per cent of all urban areas to be allocated to park and playground use, and the designation of broad greenbelts to prevent sprawl. To create grand avenues, establish firebreaks and to accommodate future motorisation, large boulevards of over 35 metres in width were to be built in medium sized towns, and over 50 metres in width in large sized cities (Koshizawa 1991: 200–1; Nakamura 1986: 20).

In September of 1946 the Special City Planning Act (*Tokubetsu Toshi Keikaku Hō*) was passed. It followed closely the approach of the 1923 Kanto Earthquake Reconstruction Law, relying primarily on the use of Land Readjustment (LR) projects to achieve urban restructuring, and establishing a War Damage Reconstruction Board (*Sensai Fukkō In*) similar to that set up for the Tokyo Earthquake Rebuilding Project (Ishida 1987: 227; Koshizawa 1991: 200). The law allowed local governments to carry out LR projects unilaterally without the need to gain the consent of landowners. The main differences with the 1923 law were that the area of land to be contributed to the projects without compensation was increased from the 10 per cent of the earthquake reconstruction to 15 per cent, and generous greenbelts were to be designated around the built up areas.

The post-war reconstruction was seen as an opportunity to restructure Japanese urban areas with more modern layouts. While Tokyo had seen extensive restructuring during the previous decades, most small and middle sized Japanese cities had retained their old narrow and congested street patterns. A primary goal of the projects was thus to ensure that substantial improvements were made to urban road systems. An examination of the plans for reconstruction which were all published in a 10-volume report on the reconstruction project (see Japan Ministry of Construction 1957–63), reveals an ambitious reconstruction effort aimed at taking advantage of the wartime destruction to modernise Japanese urban areas. Planners attempted to achieve longstanding goals of road-widening and park provision in cities throughout the country. It seems safe to suggest that these plans represent the full vision of how the 1919 city planning system was to work, particularly outside the metropolitan areas. Broad arterial roads were laid out, parks areas were designated, extensive areas were planned for existing and future commercial, industrial and residential development, and future rail stations, port districts, and main infrastructure such as bridges were mapped out. In larger towns one or two 100 metre roads were cut into the existing central area as combination traffic artery, open space, grand boulevard, and firebreak. In small and medium sized cities they were 36 metres and up. Reflecting the ideas of the Tokyo Green Space Plan of 1939 and contemporary thinking in Britain, extensive green areas were established in the outskirts of all the larger cities although in most cases these took the form of large blocks of green space, usually in hilly or mountainous areas, and only in a few cases took the form of greenbelt.

On the other hand, the post-war reconstruction plans also reveal the real limitations of the 1919 system. The plans were primarily concerned with the use of LR to build a few major arterial roads, mostly by widening existing routes. Large areas of land on the fringe were zoned residential or industrial, but without any powers to guide urban design or development standards, and future patterns of development were largely at the discretion of landowners. In the existing areas the main activity was the building of a few wide roads, straightening others, and perhaps creation of a station plaza.

Many of Japan's most prominent architects, including Takayama Eika (Nagaoka), Tange Kenzo (Hiroshima and Maebashi), and Take Motō (Nagasaki and Kure) participated in the reconstruction planning work, helping in preparing plans for towns throughout the country (Ishida 1987: 222). Special attention was paid to Hiroshima, and progress on the reconstruction gathered pace with the designation in 1949 of the Hiroshima Peace Memorial City to commemorate the victims of the nuclear bombing. Also in 1949 a competition was held for the design of a peace memorial park in the Nakajima district in the centre of Hiroshima, and close to the hypocentre of the bomb blast. A group led by Tange Kenzo, then an assistant professor at the University of Tokyo won the competition, and the memorial park as built closely followed that original design (see Sugimoto 2000: 20).

It is also interesting to note that for the first time in Japanese planning history budget priority was given to reconstructing peripheral areas ahead of Tokyo. Shortfalls in central government financial support because of the post-war economic crisis and widespread opposition to the contribution-without-compensation of up to 15 per cent of landholdings hindered progress, and the programme was only completed in 1959. Still, it is probably better to stress the real achievements of the project, undertaken under severe economic conditions in the immediate post-war period. While the reconstruction scheme was originally planned to undertake a comprehensive LR of over 65,000 hectares, in the event it covered 28,000 hectares in 102 cities. That is still a very substantial achievement, particularly as much of the shortfall in area completed was in Tokyo, as discussed below. Outside Tokyo, over 60 per cent of the planned area was carried out, resulting in some major improvements in many small and medium sized cities that had previously experienced difficulty in financing and carrying out significant urban projects in the past.

The post-war reconstruction project of Nagoya is one of the most famous, and one of the best documented. The Nagoya project covered virtually the whole of the central city area as shown in Figure 5.2, and was instrumental in creating the axis of two 100 metre wide boulevards that structure the central area. About 23 per cent of the area of Nagoya was destroyed by bombing at the end of the war, and LR projects were planned for 4,400 hectares to rebuild the city. Financial cutbacks eventually reduced that area to 3,450 hectares which were finally completed in the early 1990s after over 40 years of effort. In this respect Nagoya was rather a special case, as few of the post-war reconstruction projects lasted so long or attempted such a comprehensive restructuring. It does highlight one important aspect of the LR method, however, that it can be used effectively to redevelop fully built up urban areas. Thus in the Nagoya case it was not necessary to prevent

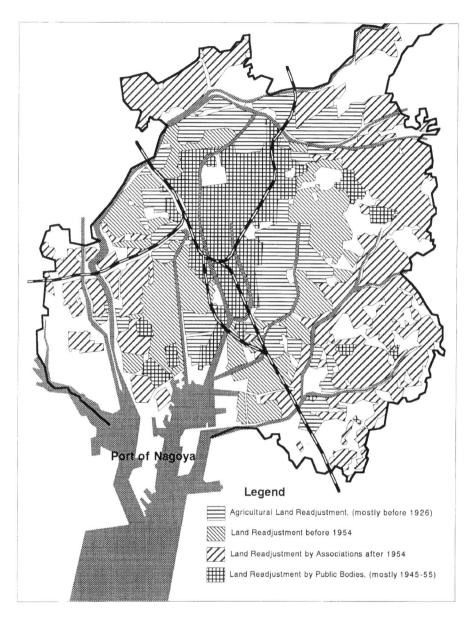

Figure 5.2 Nagoya LR projects. Nagoya is famous in Japan as one of the few cities that achieved comprehensive development and redevelopment by Land Readjustment. In the pre-war period the municipal government had strongly encouraged LR on the urban fringe by actively supporting LR Associations. Virtually the whole central city area was rebuilt through public LR projects as part of the post-war reconstruction project, and was restructured with a grid of broad new avenues, including two of 100 metres in width.

Source: Adapted from Nagoya City Planning Bureau (1992: 51).

the erection of buildings on urban sites pending their reconfiguration during the reconstruction project. Instead, urban landowners were allowed to rebuild, and projects were carried out on a piecemeal basis over many years.

Nagoya is thus one of the few major Japanese cities to have comprehensively restructured its road network into a planned system of major arterials, secondary arterials and local streets. This is certainly convenient for drivers, and Nagoya is noticeably less congested than Tokyo or Osaka. Another positive result has been the systematic provision of large numbers of parks, large and small. Still, when in Nagoya one cannot help wondering whether it was necessary to get rid of so much of the old pattern, and whether the city might not have been better off with a less thorough redesign. As Seidensticker puts it, "In Nagoya the wide streets took away the past. The bombings, it might be argued, had already taken it away; but one has no sense, along the broad avenues of central Nagoya, of all the people who lived there over the centuries. Not much is old in Tokyo, but the street pattern is, and it makes Tokyo seem warmer and cosier than Nagoya, a much smaller city" (Seidensticker 1990: 147).

One further aspect of the post-war reconstruction projects outside of Tokyo should be mentioned. While the projects were used successfully to build a number of major avenues in central areas, and to reconfigure and widen many of the narrow central city streets, the provisions for park space and greenbelts were not as successful. Some parks were built, but not nearly on the scale that had been planned, and not even close to the 10 per cent that had been called for in the 1946 law. Among the reasons for this failure were the severe financial situation after the war which limited the budget available to purchase such land, and the resumption of rapid urban growth after the 1950s which caused strong pressure to develop these lands. Also important was the fact that the Japanese planning system had only very weak powers to restrict development in designated green areas, short of actually purchasing the land. In the 1930s and during the war the designation of green space had carried considerable weight both because of wartime urgency and the considerable moral and administrative power of the Home Ministry, which also controlled all levels of police forces. In the post-war period with the disbanding of the Home Ministry and the greatly weakened moral authority of the national government and especially the police forces, a simple administrative order to block development of land on the urban fringe held little force. Further, in the 1930s and during the war there had been little urban development pressure in any case. After the mid-1950s, with rapid economic growth development pressure on the fringe became much stronger, and planning departments had little success in trying to prevent development in the greenbelts.

Post-war reconstruction of Tokyo

If the local plans were ambitious, the plan for the reconstruction of Tokyo was a dream. It envisioned a radical transformation of the capital into an entirely new urban form with clusters of dense urban uses nestled against a background of green space, green corridors and broad tree-lined boulevards. Tokyo was far the worst hit of Japanese cities, and of the 60,000 hectares planned to be rebuilt through the reconstruction projects, 20,000 were in Tokyo. That this area was actually larger than the area destroyed during the war, which totalled slightly more than 16,000 hectares is one indication of its ambition. The plan, reproduced in Figure 5.3, was designed primarily by Ishikawa Hideaki, head of the planning division of the Tokyo Metropolitan Government, and proposed a radical restructuring of the Tokyo area.

Ishikawa's post-war Tokyo reconstruction plan closely followed the Metropolitan Green Space and Air Defence Open Space plans of 1939 that Ishikawa had also been involved in preparing. The post-war plan, however, took the opportunity of wartime destruction to push the greenbelts and green corridors deep into the central city area. Tokyo would thus be radically restructured and subdivided into specialised sub-cities with populations of 200,000 to 300,000 by an extensive network of ring and radial parkways, greenbelts and corridors, which were to total some 43 per cent of the city area. In the inner areas the green corridors were planned to be parks and broad boulevards, and in the outer area the greenbelt would remain as farmland, permitting only farmers' dwellings and other existing uses. The extensive green areas would in this way break the giant city up into a number of smaller units. Strict controls were to be placed on the outer green areas, which would remain as farmland to help guarantee a degree of food self-sufficiency. A major theme of the plan was to keep the population of the

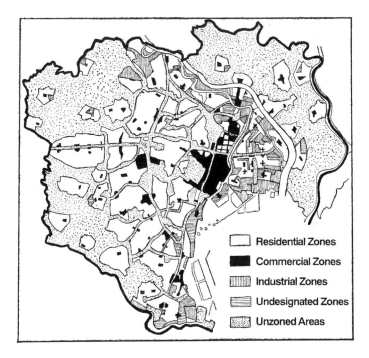

Figure 5.3 Ishikawa plan for Tokyo. The post-war reconstruction plan for Tokyo was both the most ambitious, and the least realised of all the reconstruction projects. The plan, designed by Ishikawa Hideaki, head of the Tokyo Metropolitan Government Planning Division, sought to cut a generous network of green open spaces within the old densely built up city area. Shown as "unzoned areas" on the plan above, these would serve as parkways, public open space, and firebreaks, and would divide the city into many self-contained units of between 200,000 and 300,000 population. On the outskirts the unzoned areas would continue in cultivation, and would form a permanent greenbelt where building would be restricted.

Source: Hoshino (1946: 6).

ward area of Tokyo at the 3.5 million that remained in 1945, compared to the more than 6.5 million in 1940. Instead of allowing the rebuilding of Tokyo at its former high population densities, reconstruction would be strictly controlled, and most of the population would be resettled in satellite towns scattered throughout the Kanto plain. Although the enormous amount of green space was reduced from the original concept, the plan as passed by the government in 1946 retained 18,933 hectares of green space, or almost 34 per cent of the city area (Ishida 1987: 226).

It is important to recognise that this plan falls squarely in the Japanese metropolitan planning tradition established during the 1920s and 1930s, discussed in Chapter 4. Post-war Japanese planners saw the destruction of their cities as an opportunity to start again, freed of the constraints of the existing urban fabric which had been conveniently burned away by American bombs. Nor was this reaction unique to Japan. Not a few British planners regretted that German bombers had not quite finished the job of destroying the existing, squalid urban areas of the industrial revolution so that a fresh start could be made with a clean slate. In Tokyo the bombs, aided by cities built of kindling and paper, had obliterated virtually everything, allowing planners the luxury of starting from first principles. As Ishida describes Ishikawa's plan, "It was like drawing an ideal city on a piece of white paper" (Ishida 1987: 223). It is no coincidence that this is reminiscent of the "blank page planning" style of Manchuria, where a generation of Japanese urban planners had found employment for the previous 15 years. It was in Manchuria that Japanese planners had developed their visionary metropolitan planning skills (Hein 2001), and the Tokyo plan of 1946 reflects that experience, particularly as several hundred of these experienced planners were among those repatriated in 1945–6, and many were given jobs in the reconstruction projects.

The fear of overgrown metropolitan areas was not just a Japanese concern. In Europe and North America concern over the growth of larger and larger urban areas continued to escalate during the 1930s and 1940s. It seemed to many that such growth was creating enormous, costly and possibly irreversible dysfunctions. The main evils arising from overgrown cities were seen as congested transport systems, particularly roads; rising land costs; longer travel-to-work times which, quite apart from the time costs to individuals would result in productivity losses because of worker fatigue; decreased access to open space and the countryside; increased need for costly investments in new infrastructure; increasing pollution of air and water; worsening health problems; and even increasing moral degeneracy and crime (Mumford 1940; Saarinen 1943). The expanding metropolis was also seen as creating problems beyond its borders, by draining productive investment and population from declining areas, and swallowing up valuable nearby farmland in endless suburban housing development. With the timing of this emerging analysis before and after the Second World War the issue of metropolitan growth also took on strategic dimensions. Concentration of productive capacity in one location made it more vulnerable to attack from the air, while the loss of farmland made the goal of food self-sufficiency harder to attain (Barlow Report 1940). A variety of solutions to the perceived problems of metropolitan over-growth were proposed. Prominent among these were Howard's garden city proposal, the regional plan of New York and its environs (1927–31), Saarinen's (1943) plan for the gradual and progressive dissolving of the city into its hinterland, and Abercrombie's Greater London Plan of 1944.

Needless to say Ishikawa's Tokyo plan was not implemented. As always, there were many reasons, but three seem to have been critical. The first problem was the shortage of funds. Despite the fact that the plan was to be implemented by LR – a relatively inexpensive means of restructuring existing urban areas, especially with the 15 per cent compulsory uncompensated land contribution – the plan would have been very expensive to implement. The amount of land that would have had to be purchased to create the green networks in the existing built up area was staggering.

This in itself might not have been decisive, but for the fact that the country as a whole was devastated, many other cities needed rebuilding and the economy was in a state of near collapse. Scarce funds had to be spread to a wide range of demands, and those allocated to urban rebuilding had to be divided into many slices. At the time of the Great Kanto Earthquake, the economy had been relatively robust, help had poured in from cities around the country, and yet the reconstruction costs had still been a major strain on national finances. Further, a combination of factors weakened Tokyo's financial position. The complexity of the Tokyo situation with its vast size and high density of property ownership, and the ambitious scope of its reconstruction plan meant that Tokyo got a slow start on its reconstruction projects. In the meantime, the funds went elsewhere. While in 1945–6 Tokyo had received a share of the national reconstruction budget roughly equal to its share of the bomb damaged areas (26.6 per cent), that subsequently dropped steadily, and by 1949 Tokyo was only receiving 10.9 per cent of the national reconstruction budget (Ishida 1987: 230). In 1949 a financial crisis of runaway inflation caused by the government spending far more than it was earning in taxes sparked intervention by the occupation authorities. The ensuing stringent controls on spending became known as the "Dodge Line" after the Chicago banker Henry Dodge, who had been brought over to advise the occupation and the Japanese government on how to stop the inflationary spiral. Some of the spending cuts were applied to the reconstruction projects, which the General Headquarters of Allied Powers (GHQ) recommended be entirely suspended apart from road construction – the Americans thought Japanese roads deplorable.

One outcome was that in June 1949 the urban reconstruction projects were reviewed and saw drastic cutbacks. Where LR projects had already begun the process of land replotting and moving of buildings, it was considered too late to cancel them as commitments had been made to the landowners involved. Projects which had not yet been started could be cancelled much more easily. Most cancelled projects were in the three main metropolitan areas, especially in Tokyo where LR projects were most difficult to carry out because of complex land ownership, tenancy and sub-tenancy patterns. Of the 20,000 hectares originally planned for Tokyo, only 1,380 (6.8 per cent) were completed, and Tokyo accounted for 61.2 per cent of all cancelled projects. While the planned area for parks in Tokyo was only reduced by 41.4 per cent, those that remained did not necessarily get built but survived primarily as a planning designation in the hope that they could be built later (Ishida 1987: 231) As shown in Figure 5.4, the LR projects in Tokyo which were implemented were primarily those in station-front areas along the Yamanote line such as those at Shibuya, Shinjuku and Ikebukuro which allowed the completion of the plans of the 1930s to rationalise transport connections and station areas in those important suburban subcentres. The vast majority of Tokyo was rebuilt in an ad hoc fashion along the former pattern.

The second reason for the failure to rebuild to plan was that, as after the Kanto earthquake, opposition movements quickly organised to oppose the LR projects. The

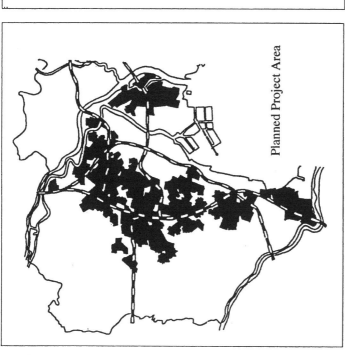

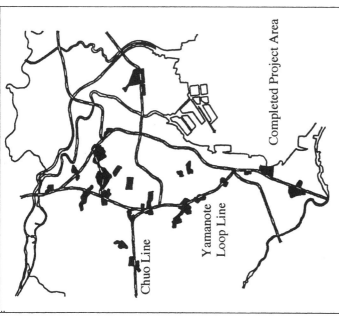

Figure 5.4 Planned and completed LR projects, Tokyo post-war reconstruction. An ambitious programme of LR was planned to rebuild almost all of the existing built up area outside of the areas reconfigured after the 1923 earthquake. In the end, only a small proportion of the planned area of Tokyo reconstruction projects was carried out. Most that were completed were centred on major rail stations along the JR Yamanote loop and the Chuo line.

Source: Adapted from Tokyo Metropolitan Construction Department (1987: 21, 34).

proposal to increase the uncompensated land expropriation from 10 to 15 per cent, and the scale of the clearances that would have been required to accomplish the expansive open space plans would have provoked such a response almost anywhere. As it happens the occupation GHQ also opposed uncompensated expropriation and required that it be changed to a system of compensation at reduced rates in 1949 (Ishida 1987: 228). This was probably of little consolation to landowners who lost their land, as galloping inflation would have quickly reduced the value of any financial compensation. The fact that the planning system had at that time no means of prior public consultation also could not have helped. For such a radical plan to appear, as it were, out of the blue would have been a shock to many of the landowners who were scheduled to lose their land. Although the concept of "public participation" was not yet current anywhere at that time, other mechanisms such as public competitions for plans and advance publication of proposals served similar purposes. In the US in the pre-war period most large-scale planning proposals had to be put to local electorates for approval of the right to issue bonds to finance them. The fact that the government was broadly discredited for having lost the war and driving the country to ruin would not have helped the case for a continuation of past autocratic planning approaches.

Third, the fact that it was a highly unrealistic plan cannot be avoided. As Koshizawa (1991: 203) observes, the Tokyo plan was the most idealistic and least achieved of all the reconstruction plans. While it is true that common sense suggests that the moment to achieve a radical restructuring of towns is precisely when most of the buildings have been destroyed, in practice it is not an easy time to do so. Destroyed along with all of the buildings and goods was the urban economy, jobs, capital and tax revenues. Pressure to rebuild quickly was high, yet even relatively minor road-widening or straightening takes considerable time to negotiate. To rebuild a city from first principles, "as though drawing on a white sheet" is that much harder. It may be that the experience of such planning in Manchuria, where existing property ownership patterns could be disregarded, had been simply too exciting for the planners to give up. But while the built fabric of Tokyo had been virtually obliterated, what remained were property ownership patterns, including public property in the form of streets, parks, canals, and other infrastructure. Property ownership patterns could not be erased by a few bombs, and these proved decisive in structuring the rebuilding of Tokyo. While LR could be an effective tool for realigning urban property boundaries and for marginally increasing the share that belonged to the state, it by no means offered a clean slate, being rather a guarantee of equitable treatment of property rights. It seems fair to conclude that the idealism of the 1946 Tokyo plan and its proposal to radically restructure the city as part of post-war reconstruction, contributed significantly to its failure in implementation. Unlike the period following the earthquake, after the war Tokyo was largely rebuilt in an ad hoc manner, with only small areas reconfigured according to the master plan.

Both the occupation reforms of Japanese political and social institutions and the post-war urban reconstruction efforts can be considered qualified successes. While each programme remained incomplete and produced some unintended results, in each case substantial achievements were recorded, and the basis was laid for future recovery and growth. The establishment of a democratic constitutional government with sovereignty based in the people, and the widely supported land reform which radically restructured rural land ownership patterns were significant achievements. At the same time, attempts to decentralise government power and create a more independent and financially stable local government system were thwarted by central government bureaucrats who equated their own continuing power with the national interest. In city planning, post-war reconstruction projects achieved basic modernisation of a large number of small and medium sized cities, while achieving less in the great metropolitan areas, and very little in Tokyo, the hardest hit. More importantly, the old pattern of central government control over city planning was confirmed and even reinforced, particularly by increased financial controls over local government. The reconstruction efforts were therefore successful in preparing Japan for the extraordinary period of rapid economic growth that was to come, while at the same time leaving important areas of unfinished business that were to generate increasing problems later.

Rapid growth and metropolitan concentration

As Allinson argues, rapid economic growth was the defining characteristic of the early post-war decades (Allinson 1997: 83). During the 1950s and 1960s economic growth was the unquestioned top priority of the central government. Although this focus on increasing GDP to the virtual exclusion of any other priorities ran into increasing opposition during the 1960s, as discussed in Chapter 6, it was, at the outset at least, widely supported by an impoverished nation. In the present context the most important consequence was rapid urbanisation, the concentration of population and productive capacity in the great metropolitan regions of the Pacific coast, and the corresponding depopulation of peripheral areas.

The vast interlocking set of metropolitan regions created during this period is usually referred to as the Pacific Belt, or Tokaido megalopolis after the old feudal era highway that had linked Osaka with Tokyo through Nagoya along the Pacific coast. It was here that the highest rates of industrial expansion occurred, and where the urban and environmental problems created by industrialisation were most severe, and it was here that the first broad-based citizens' movements in favour of stricter environmental controls and better urban planning arose, which ultimately led to thorough revisions of the planning system in 1968, as described in the next chapter. The concept of megalopolis, and the urban problems associated with it in the Japanese case are discussed at the end of this chapter. This section is devoted to an examination of the processes of economic growth and urbanisation that created the Tokaido megalopolis. In order to put the changes of this period into perspective, wherever possible the data cited cover the period from the beginnings of industrialisation before the First World War to the 1980s. Many accounts of Japan's rapid economic and urban growth make the mistake of starting with the post-war period, which obscures the fact that to an important degree the processes of the rapid growth period are in fact a continuation of those begun in the pre-war period.

Economic growth

Most accounts of Japan's post-war industrial growth abound with superlatives. From 1953 to 1971 Japan's average real annual increase in GNP was 9.17 per cent, with increases in the 1960s regularly topping 10 per cent. Glickman (1979: 3) cites 1976 OECD figures showing comparative growth rates for selected countries: from 1960 to 1975 Japan had an average growth rate of 8.9 per cent, while the US averaged 3.2 per cent, the UK averaged 2.4 per cent, and France averaged 5.2 per cent. Although post-war growth was initially a result of the need to rebuild industry destroyed by war, mining and manufacturing production being only 17 per cent in 1946 of what it had been in 1941, pre-war levels of production had been regained by 1953. In fact, most of the subsequent growth in Japanese industrial production was in new fields which had been of only minor importance before the war. In the rapid growth period Japan became a world leader in a wide range of industries including steel production, cars, ships, televisions, and electronic equipment.

The spatial distribution of industrial production, on the other hand, largely followed pre-war patterns. Yamaguchi (1984: 264) argues that the four major industrial zones of Tokyo-Yokohama, Nagoya, Osaka-Kobe and Northern Kyushu were well established before the Second World War, as were the six metropolises of Tokyo, Osaka, Kyoto, Nagoya, Kobe and Yokohama. Murata has shown convincingly how significant was the

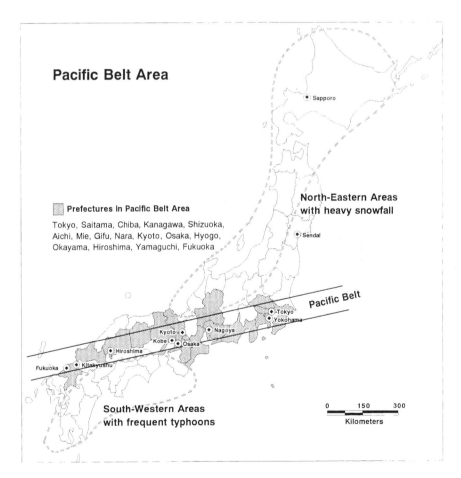

Figure 5.5 The Pacific Belt. The Pacific Belt area was the scene of Japan's "miraculous" post-war period of rapid economic growth and the formation of the Tokaido megalopolis.

Source: Adapted from Honjo (1978: 15).

concentration of post-war industrial growth in the Pacific Belt, shown in Figure 5.6, with over 77 per cent of industrial production located there, while the rest of Japan stagnated in terms of industrial development and even tended to lose what advantages it had to the more competitive areas nearer the Pacific Belt (Murata 1980: 248). Miyakawa (1980) argues that the main reason for increased concentration in the post-war period was the strong advantages of existing industrial areas in terms of port and rail infrastructure, and particularly the agglomeration economies offered by proximity of firms to other firms.

Table 5.1 Share of manufacturing output, Japanese regions and Pacific Belt, 1909–80 (% of national output)

	Area (% of Japan)	1909	1920	1930	1940	1950	1960	1970	1980
Hokkaido	22	1	3	3	3	4	3	2	2
Tohoku	21	4	4	4	4	6	5	5	6
Hokuriku	3	4	3	3	3	4	2	2	2
Chugoku	8	5	5	5	5	7	7	7	8
Shikoku	5	3	3	3	2	4	2	3	3
Kyushu	11	6	8	8	11	9	7	5	6
Tokyo MA[a]	4	18	20	21	29	22	28	30	27
Nagoya MA[b]	6	11	10	11	10	11	12	13	13
Osaka MA[c]	5	35	33	31	25	23	23	20	17
Three MAs	14	64	62	62	63	56	64	63	56
Pacific Belt[d]	23	73	74	74	78	72	78	76	71
Kanto, Kinki, and Chubu, outside the MAs[e]	14	14	12	12	9	11	11	13	16

Source: Compiled from *Historical Statistics of Japan*, 2: 414–18.

Notes: The definitions of regions follow those of the 4th Comprehensive Development Plan, National Land Agency, 1987: 167 see Figure 5.1.
a   Tokyo Metropolitan Area (TMA) includes Tokyo, Kanagawa, Saitama and Chiba prefectures.
b   Nagoya Metropolitan Area (NMA) includes Aichi, Gifu and Mie prefectures.
c   Osaka Metropolitan Area (OMA) includes Osaka, Kyoto, Hyogo and Nara prefectures.
d   The Pacific Belt includes the TMA, NMA, and OMA plus Fukuoka, Yamaguchi, Hiroshima, Okayama and Shizuoka prefectures.
e   This is the rest of Kanto, Kinki and Chubu which is outside the MAs, including Ibaragi, Tochigi, Gunma, Yamanashi, Nagano, Shizuoka, Shiga and Wakayama.

The dominance of the Pacific Belt region throughout the twentieth century is clear from Table 5.1 which shows the changing relative share of total manufacturing output of the different Japanese regions from 1909 to 1980. It is perhaps unnecessary to note that as the table shows only relative shares, it conceals a vast increase in actual output, from a national total of 792 million yen in 1909 to 214,699,797 million yen in 1980 (current prices). For our purposes, however, it is the relative share that is most revealing. The Pacific Belt area, which includes some 23 per cent of the Japanese land area, has consistently been responsible for about three quarters of Japanese manufacturing output. Particularly notable is the fact that far from being a post-war phenomenon, this concentration in the Pacific Belt has been the dominant pattern from the beginnings of Japanese industrialisation.

Several other patterns are worth noting. First, in the period before 1940 there is a considerable stability in the relative share of the different regions with the exception of the Tokyo Metropolitan Area and Osaka Metropolitan Area. From 1909 to 1940

Tokyo's share increases from 18 per cent to 29 per cent, while Osaka's share decreases from 35 per cent to 25 per cent. To a great extent that shift can be attributed to the increasing importance of military procurement in manufacturing output, much of which was concentrated in the Tokyo area. At the same time, Osaka's important textile industry was greatly hurt by wartime blockades of raw materials and markets and conversions of plant to war use. Second, between 1940 and 1950 the share of the metropolitan areas and particularly that of Tokyo decreased sharply, while all other regions gained share. That shift can be attributed largely to the fact that the destruction of industry by wartime bombing was greatest in the metropolitan areas. Third, the period from 1950 to 1960 sees a sharp reconcentration in the Pacific Belt area during the first phase of the rapid economic growth period. After 1960, however, the share of the Pacific Belt decreases, particularly because of the declining share of Osaka, while peripheral regions such as Tohoku, Chugoku and Kyushu see an increase in share. Finally, while in 1909 the share of output of the prefectures close to the three metropolitan areas (i.e., the balance of Kanto, Kinki and Chubu regions) corresponded exactly to their 14 per cent share of national area, they lost share steadily up to 1940, when they collectively were responsible for 9 per cent of national manufacturing output. During the rapid growth period their share increased from 11 per cent in 1950 to 13 per cent in 1970, and between 1970 and 1980 they saw a rapid increase to 16 per cent of the total. This increase in share reflects the expansion of manufacturing industry into areas adjacent to the metropolitan areas, close to their important markets.

Glickman (1979), whose classic study *The Growth and Management of the Japanese Urban System* is still one of the best examinations of the processes of urbanisation during the rapid growth period, documents the growth of employment in the Tokaido region during the 1950s and 1960s. He notes that it grew faster in employment and in population than the rest of the country in both decades, and that the Tokaido area was especially dominant in the creation of manufacturing jobs. In the first decade, the population of the Tokaido region grew by 32 per cent, while the rest of the country grew by only 12.3 per cent, and in the second decade the Tokaido population grew by 31 per cent, the rest of the country by 10.4 per cent. Total employment in Tokaido grew by 39 per cent to 24.4 million jobs in the 1960s, while in the rest of the country it grew by only 21 per cent to 10.5 million jobs. All these measures show the Tokaido region increasing its dominance as the primary centre of population and employment.

The essential feature of rapid economic growth in the post-war period is thus that industrial growth was concentrated in the Pacific Belt area. That concentration was a dominant factor in the enormous shifts in the distribution of population which created the metropolitan regions.

Growth of urban population

The transformation of Japan from a primarily rural and agricultural nation to an overwhelmingly urban and industrial one has taken place almost entirely within the last 100 years. Although the most dramatic phase of Japanese urbanisation occurred in the post-war period, significant foundations for Japan's later urbanisation were laid in the pre-war period. By 1940 the urban population had already risen to almost 38 per cent of total population, the shift from agriculture to industry was well started, and the basic pattern of industrial and population concentration in the Pacific Belt had already been established. Pre-war urbanisation is dwarfed, however, by the scale of post-war urban and industrial growth, as shown in Table 5.2

Table 5.2 Japanese urban population (1,000s,%)

Year	National population	City population[1] (%)[2]	DID population (%)[2]
1920	55,963	10,097 (18.0)	–
1930	64,450	15,444 (23.9)	–
1940	73,114	27,577 (37.7)	–
1950	84,115	31,366 (37.3)	–
1960	93,419	60,895 (65.2)[3]	40,830 (43.7)
1970	104,665	75,429 (72.1)	55,997 (53.3)
1980	117,060	89,187 (76.2)	69,935 (59.7)
1990	123,611	95,643 (77.4)	78,152 (63.2)
1995	125,570	98,009 (78.0)	81,254 (64.7)

Source: Japan Population Census 1995.

Notes:
1 Population in officially recognised cities.
2 As a percentage of the national population.
3 During the 1950s amalgamations of local governments significantly increased the number of local governments officially recognised as cities.

Whereas in 1920 only 18 per cent of the population lived in cities, by 1995 that proportion had risen to 78 per cent. Because national population was also growing, the total urban population increased by 95 million over the 70-year period, a truly vast number of new urban residents. As Harris (1982: 56) puts it, "Among major countries, Japan has had the highest, sustained, long-range average rate of urban increase. Japan had an average increase of 3.7 per cent per year compounded annually during the sixty-year period 1920–1980." There is no question that the scale and duration of Japanese urbanisation has been enormous, but it is important to qualify this picture somewhat. The sharp increase in the urban population during the 1950s seen in Table 5.2 is due in part to amalgamations of villages into larger administrative units to achieve economies of scale in service provision. This resulted in the incorporation of many rural villages into nearby cities, inflating the urban population artificially. On the other hand, there were also no doubt cases where amalgamations simply reflected the fact that existing village administrative boundaries had been rendered obsolete by rapid urban expansion.

Because of the weakness of the "city" definition in measuring actual urban population in Japan, the Population Census of Japan devised a new definition of urban population within Densely Inhabited Districts (DID) which was first used in the 1960 census. The DID is intended to correspond to the urban built up area and is defined as groups of contiguous enumeration districts with a population density of 4,000 or more inhabitants per square kilometre, and a total population of 5,000 or more. By this measure, in 1960 when DID areas were first designated 44 per cent of the population lived in them, and by 1990 that proportion had risen to 63 per cent.

Some of the problems associated with definitions of urban area are avoided in one tabulation of the population census which divides the population into those living in

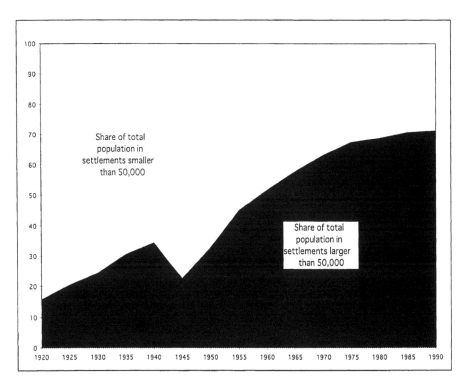

Figure 5.6 Shift from rural to urban population.

Source: Japan Census 1990.

settlements of over and under 50,000 regardless of whether the settlement is labelled a "city", as shown in Figure 5.6. If the interruption of the war years is ignored, the shift of Japanese population from rural to urban settlements occurred at a relatively steady rate between 1920 and 1975, after which the rate decreased. By 1990 the share of population in settlements of over 50,000 had stabilised at just over 70 per cent. The war was a very significant interruption, however, even if the long-range transition appears to have been little affected. Figure 5.6 shows two main effects of the war. Between 1940 and 1945 there was a drastic drop in the share of population living in cities from 35 per cent to 23 per cent. That decrease was most pronounced in the largest metropolitan areas, which saw well over half their population evacuated to rural areas. The second effect was, of course, a correspondingly much faster increase in urban population after the war, as refugees returned and new migrants arrived. During the 10 years from 1945 to 1955 the share of urban population increased from 23 per cent to 45 per cent, a near doubling. It is important to remember that accounts of Japanese urbanisation which start from a base of 1945 are therefore exaggerated, as that population increase includes many long established urban residents who were returning from evacuation. It is clear, however, that Japan has seen a transformation from a primarily rural to an over-whelmingly urban country in the short period of 70 years.

Rural to urban migration

Much of the growth of urban population of Japan was a result of a large-scale migration from rural prefectures to the metropolitan regions of Tokyo, Osaka and Nagoya. From 1920 to 1965 all prefectures that were not in these three regions consistently had net out-migration, with the exception of Fukuoka in northern Kyushu Island which gained in the period 1925 to 1935 because of the development of the iron and steel industry there, but subsequently lost population, particularly with the decline of the coal mines between 1955 and 1970. The migration towards the three metropolitan regions has been the dominant feature of urbanisation throughout the century in Japan, and corresponds to the shift from agricultural employment to industrial and service employment which was concentrated in the three metropolitan areas. However, as Hama (1976) has argued, the crucial difference between pre-war and post-war urbanisation is that in the pre-war period, it was caused mainly by excess rural population being pushed into urban areas, and was not accompanied by decreases in agricultural population. In the post-war period, migration levels were so great that most rural areas experienced absolute decreases in population during the 1950s and 1960s.

During the 25 years from 1950 to 1975 the Tokyo metropolitan region, including Tokyo, Kanagawa prefecture immediately south of Tokyo, Saitama to the north, and Chiba to the east had an average annual net in-migration of 285.7 thousand people. During the same period, the Osaka metropolitan area including Osaka, Hyogo, immediately west of Osaka, Kyoto to the north-east, and Nara to the east had an average annual net in-migration of 115.4 thousand, and Aichi prefecture including Nagoya had an annual net in-migration of 39.7 thousand (Harris 1982: 70). These are large numbers of migrants, with a net total of about 11 million migrants from rural to metropolitan prefectures over the 25 year period.

Net migration to the three metropolitan areas is thus the most significant aspect of the urbanisation process in Japan. The enormous scale of migration in the rapid growth period is shown in Figure 5.7. Total migration to the three metropolitan regions rose quickly in the 1950s, passing the million persons-per-year mark in 1960, and remaining above that level for the next 13 years until the first oil-price shock in 1973. However, out-migration from the metropolitan regions continued to rise steadily until the same year, when it roughly equalled in-migration, resulting in sharply decreasing net migration rates between 1963 and 1966, and after 1970. During the second half of the 1970s there was actually a slight net out-migration from the metropolitan regions. However in the 1980s, out-migration continued to decline, while in-migration continued steadily, resulting in a resumption of net in-migration, particularly to the Tokyo region.

Tsuya and Kuroda (1989) attribute this slowing of migration to the slowing of economic growth caused by the oil-price shocks of the 1970s, combined with possible effects of a government regional policy of dispersing economic growth away from the metropolitan areas, as discussed further below. With a rise in the rate of migration from metropolitan regions to non-metropolitan regions, the result was a small net migration to non-metropolitan regions between 1975 and 1980, the only 5-year inter-censual period with such a result since the war. Because of the decrease in out-migration, and substantial rates of natural increase which were higher in the metropolitan regions because many of the in-migrants were young adults, the population of the non-metropolitan

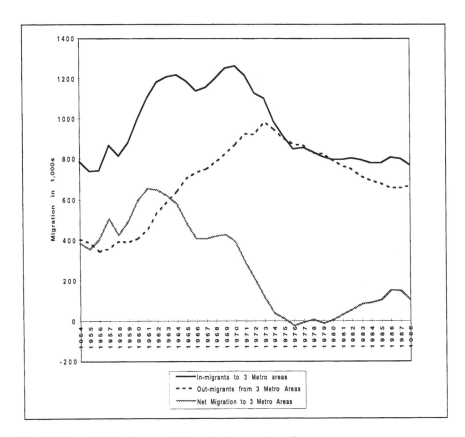

Figure 5.7 Annual migration to and from the three metropolitan areas.

Source: Kuroda (1990: 120).

regions grew by over two million in 1970–75 and in 1975–80. After 1980, the balance of migration shifted again slightly in favour of the metropolitan areas, with rates of migration from metropolitan regions decreasing and rates from non-metropolitan regions increasing, resulting in a resumption of net migration to metropolitan regions, particularly that centred on Tokyo (Tsuya and Kuroda 1989: 215). Even with a resumption of net migration to the metropolitan areas, since the 1980s the main factor in metropolitan population increase has been natural increase due to their relatively young population profile.

Figure 5.7 also shows a very large-scale migration stream out of the three metropolitan areas to non-metropolitan regions. For example, Tsuya and Kuroda (1989) showed that rapid population growth of the metropolitan regions was caused primarily by massive in-migration of young people, particularly males aged 15–24 from the non-metropolitan regions. This migration was strongest during the 1950s and 1960s, but continued into the 1980s at a lower rate. These migrants mainly moved to start university or find jobs. After the 1970s many of those aged 25–34 moved back to non-metropolitan regions, and many adults older than 24 moved from metropolitan core regions to metropolitan suburbs (Tsuya and Kuroda 1989: 220). The move from the metropolitan regions to non-metropolitan regions is referred to as "U-turn" migration, while the move from metropolitan cores to metropolitan suburbs is referred to as "J-turn" migration. These types of return migration became much more important after the 1970s.

Urban growth in Japan is best understood as a process of concentration of population into the Pacific Belt region, and particularly its three principal metropolitan regions of Tokyo, Osaka and Nagoya, from all other parts of the country. Although the Pacific Belt was the setting of the main pre-war urban centres, after the war its dominance increased, with most new productive capacity during the rapid growth period of the 1950s and 1960s being located there. Economic growth in Japan resulted in increasing disparities between the core industrial area of the Pacific Belt and other peripheral areas which remained poorer and less developed. These regional disparities become an increasing focus of government policy from the 1960s, as discussed below.

The Tokaido megalopolis

The scale of urbanisation during the rapid growth period was so vast that new concepts of metropolitan organisation had to be invented to describe it. The most influential of these was the idea of megalopolis coined by Jean Gottmann, a French regional geographer whose seminal study of the original megalopolis of the northeast seaboard of the US initiated the field. In the megalopolis stretching from Boston to Washington Gottmann believed that he had identified a wholly new type of urban area which would become characteristic of future urbanisation (Gottmann 1961: 9). Megalopolis was not distinguished merely by its size, but by the expansion of the megalopolitan space economy to the point where it included vast areas between and around the old metropolitan centres:

> The old distinctions between rural and urban do not apply here any more. Even a quick look at the vast area of Megalopolis reveals a revolution in land use. Most of the people living in the so-called rural areas, and still classified as "rural population" by recent censuses, have very little, if anything, to do with agriculture. In terms of their interests and work they are what used to be classified as "city folks", but their way of life and the landscapes around their residences do not fit the old meaning of urban. In this area, then, we must abandon the idea of the city as a tightly settled and organized unit in which people, activities, and riches are crowded into a very small area clearly separated from its nonurban surroundings. Every city in this region spreads out far and wide around its original nucleus; it grows amidst an irregularly colloidal mixture of rural and suburban landscapes.
>
> (Gottmann 1961: 5)

This characterisation of patterns of urbanisation in the northeastern US so aptly described patterns of development in the Tokaido region that the concept was quickly imported to Japan, and a substantial literature on the Tokaido megalopolis followed, not least by Gottmann himself (see Doi 1968; Gottmann 1976; Gottmann 1980; Miyakawa 1990; Murao 1991; Nagashima 1968, 1981). Figure 5.8 shows Doi's calculation of the extent of the megalopolis in which he argues that the extension from Kobe to

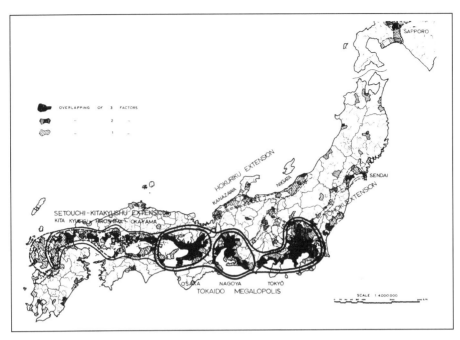

Figure 5.8 The Tokaido megalopolis. Urban geographers worked hard in the 1960s to determine the extent and characteristics of Japan's megalopolis. Doi was one of the first to suggest that the area from Okayama to Nagasaki, which he called the Setouchi-Kitakyushi Extension, should be considered as part of the megalopolitan area.

Source: Doi (1968: 99).

Kitakyushu be included as part of the expanding core region. Doi shows Shichoson (cities, towns and villages) which have an overlapping of one to three of his selected indicators: population density of over 300 per hectare, population increase higher than 5 per cent in the period 1960–5, and "production of yearly additional value of more than 10 trillion yen in industry" (Doi 1968: 96).

Particularly attractive to the Japanese urbanists who so eagerly embraced Gottmann's analysis was his emphasis on the positive aspects of megalopolitan growth. Gottmann was careful to guard against the alarmist view often associated with urbanisation on a massive scale. He notes, "What is happening in Megalopolis today has been described as a pathological phenomenon, a sickness, a cancer . . . Urban growth in general has been discussed and condemned on moral grounds for a long time. Such debate is expectable and desirable, but on the whole history has shown the condemnation to be unjust." While there are problems in Megalopolis, he continues, "the population is on the average healthier, the consumption of goods higher, and the opportunity for advancement greater than in any other region of comparable extent" (Gottmann 1961: 13–16).

Hanes (1993) provides a detailed review of the development of Japanese discourse about their emerging Tokaido megalopolis, which was decidedly ambivalent. The mainstream view was consistently one of pride in Japan's economic growth and metropolitan expansion. Japanese planners and politicians eagerly embraced the new idea of megalopolitan growth as a good thing, and were proud that their very own mega-lopolis was one of the biggest of all. Others were less certain, pointing instead to the emerging problems that unbroken urbanisation from Tokyo to Osaka was causing. To a certain extent the old anti-urban tradition of the Tokugawa period, which located the core values of Japan in rural traditions of solidarity, wholesome hard work and deference to authority, had a part in the anti-megalopolitan sentiments. Probably more important, however, were more modern and practical concerns about deepening inequalities between the economically dominant metropolitan regions and the declining periphery, and emerging worries about the environmental and economic consequences of over-concentration in the Pacific Belt region. These concerns became increasingly important planning issues towards the end of the rapid growth period, as discussed below.

Planning and rapid economic growth, 1955–68

During the rapid growth period the overwhelming top priority of the Japanese government was to promote economic growth, and the state put all its resources behind its strategy of heavy and chemical industry-led economic expansion. Because there was such a clear necessity to recover from the destruction of war, the alliance of central government bureaucrats, the ruling Liberal Democratic Party (LDP), and big business were given a very free hand to pursue their development strategy. Samuels (1983: 168) has called the period from the end of the war to the middle of the 1960s a "conserva-tive's paradise" in which there was an "unassailable consensus" on economic reconstruction and rapid growth. Many of the consequences of economic growth were desired, and broadly supported. Economic growth and expansion of manufacturing industry allowed increasing incomes and greater availability of jobs, rising wages and an increasing supply of food and consumer goods. Local governments competed with each other to attract major industrial projects. In many regards this was the period in which central government had the most power and autonomy ever. The ruling conser-vative parties had healthy majorities after the formation of the LDP in 1955, and an expanding economy raised everyone's standard of living, muting criticism by the opposition. The power and prestige of the bureaucracy had been greatly enhanced during the occupation, and the new constitution had eliminated the complex division of power that had prevailed during the pre-war period.

Although the Local Autonomy Law imposed by the occupation had resulted in inde-pendently elected prefectural and local governments, because during the first two post-war decades the conservatives controlled central government, virtually all prefec-tural governorships and most municipal governments, it was relatively easy for them to set the agenda for all levels of government. Central government also provided incentives such as grants-in-aid and bond permits to local governments which cooperated by helping the expansion of new industries in their area through gifts of land, temporary property tax exemptions and local infrastructure (Steiner 1980: 5). The perennially financially hard-pressed local governments were used to following central government guidance, and they were easily convinced that new industries would broaden the tax base in the future. Central government also used its dominance over prefectural and local governments to ensure that they actively worked to convince local landowners to assemble large blocks of land when industries wanted to expand their premises or establish new facilities. National, prefectural and local officials were extremely effective at twisting arms when necessary to overcome local opposition to industrial development (see Allinson 1975; Broadbent 1989, 1998).

The development of competitive export industries was seen as the basis of national economic survival. Komiya (1990) reports that the common slogan, "Export or die", reflects the attitude of Japanese policy-makers of this period. To achieve higher exports, the government encouraged the concentration of industry in the Pacific Belt region to help foster agglomeration efficiencies. The New Long-Run Economic Plan (*Shin Keizai Keikaku*, 1958–62) stressed "strengthening the foundation of industry", "sophistication of the industrial structure", and "heavy and chemical industrialisation" as the top priority policy objectives. While Japan maintained a relatively free market economy with firms free to locate where they wished, the Japanese government also actively worked to persuade firms to follow its direction. Such persuasion is often called "administrative guidance" (*gyōsei shidō*) in Japan, and consisted largely of informal directions, suggestions and advice to individual firms. Firms often found it advantageous to follow government administrative guidance, both because close cooperation with ministry bureaucrats could yield real advantages, and because the bureaucrats could make things difficult for those firms that did not. To aid the growth of targeted industries the government used subsidies to foster their growth, preferential tax treatment for depreciation and income from exports, and low-interest loans (Komiya 1990: 8).

For the sake of efficiency, and to be able to take advantage of agglomeration economies, most public investment such as that in roads, ports, land reclamation, and railways was concentrated in the Pacific Belt region. Economic development was thus encouraged there, especially in heavy industrial sectors such as steel, petrochemicals and shipbuilding. The state was particularly important in the development of the integrated industrial complexes build on extensive landfills in tidal bays throughout the Pacific Belt region. Generally referred to as "*kombinato*" after their Soviet model, these complexes served to boost efficiency by combining several aspects of a given industry on one large site with its own port facilities (Kornhauser 1982; Murata and Ota 1980). This odd mix of communist planning and capitalist ownership is characteristic of Japanese development policy in the rapid growth period. These projects aided industrial growth by providing large sites at low cost for expanding industries, and the central and prefectural governments played essential roles by persuading local governments and buying out local fishing rights in the offshore areas as well as coordinating transportation and industrial water supply infrastructures (Tsuru 1993: 102). Glickman shows that as a result of the focus of government policy on the development of the heavy and chemical industrial sector in the Pacific Belt region from 1955 to 1960, most public funds were invested there with little going to the poorer and more remote regions. He interprets this as a clear indication that economic efficiency goals dominated those of interregional equity (Glickman 1979: 255).

This pattern continued into the 1960s. The main priority of the important Income Doubling Plan of 1960 was rapid economic growth. Government proposed large increases in investment in social overhead capital for roads, water supply and port installations in the Pacific Belt region. Saburo Okita, who worked on the plan, concurs that most government investment was still in the core area during the early 1960s and that this contributed to increasing levels of concentration of industry and jobs. He also documents one important unintended outcome of the Income Doubling Plan. Before it had even been passed, it had created a decisive political problem for the LDP government, which had a very important base of support in the peripheral districts which were beginning to push for a greater share of public investment. The plan was delayed in the cabinet for two months after being submitted to the prime minister, primarily because of objections that adequate consideration was not given to improving conditions in the underdeveloped areas. The plan was passed only after a statement was attached that promised to draft a national plan to promote development in backward areas through public spending, tax measures, etc, and to "materialize desired geographical distribution of industries" and so "eliminate the backwardness of the respective areas" (Okita 1965: 622). This political pressure from within the LDP was combined with increasing awareness of the diseconomies associated with over-concentration. From this point, future economic development plans came increasingly to call for decentralisation, restrictions on industry in the metropolitan areas and development of the backward areas. This was the origin of the Comprehensive National Development Plans (CNDP).

The basis of the national/regional planning system had been established by the Comprehensive National Land Development Act of 1950 and subsequent Comprehensive National Development Plans of which the first was passed in 1962. That plan focused on the reduction of regional disparities by promoting the dispersal of industries which was primarily achieved by the designation of the New Industrial Cities. These were intended to be growth centres in peripheral regions which would encourage the slowing of migration towards the metropolitan areas by providing jobs closer to home. Central government was to increase spending on infrastructure in these areas to encourage industrialisation. Fifteen new industrial cities were designated in the plan, many of which were outside the main growth region of the Pacific Belt, as shown in Figure 5.9. Before the New Industrial Cities had a chance to become established, however, business pressure induced the government to reverse course and return to its original bias towards industrial efficiency and concentration in the core region. In 1964 six "Special Areas for Industrial Concentration" were designated, all of which were within the core Pacific Belt region (see Calder 1988: 285; Honjo 1978; Murata and Ota 1980: 178). These new industrial areas subsequently attracted the bulk of new investment and hampered the development of the earlier designated New Industrial Cities.

Glickman describes the shift in the 1960s from a concentration policy to one of more overall development as primarily a change in what the government was saying, rather than in what it was doing. As he puts it, "Despite rhetoric to the contrary, the government has never had a very strong decentralization policy. Public investment remained heavily concentrated in regions central to the economy until the late 1960s and was not destined to be distributed to the more backward regions until later" (Glickman 1979: 248). He shows that government spending on productive infrastructure consistently favoured the Pacific Belt region. In fact, while central government economic plans were calling for decentralisation of both private investment and public spending during the 1960s to counter the perceived over-concentration in the Pacific Belt, government spending in the core regions actually increased as a percentage of the total, and remained higher on a per capita basis than the lagging peripheral regions.

There is considerable disagreement about the role of government industrial policy in Japanese economic growth. On the one side is Johnson's (1982) classic and persuasive argument that the economic planning bureaucrats in the Ministry of International

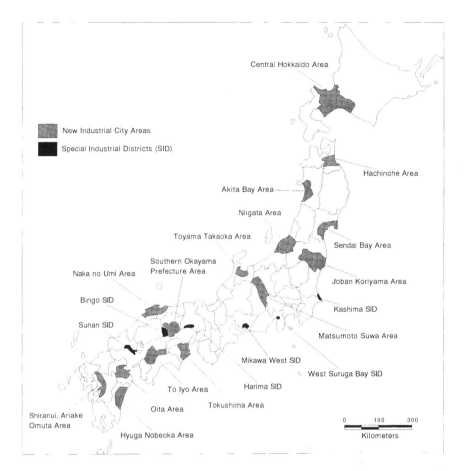

Figure 5.9 New Industrial Cities and Special Industrial Districts, 1962. In response to a strong lobbying effort by politicians from peripheral areas, economic development policy was shifted in 1962 from the focus on building industrial agglomerations in the Pacific Belt, to dispersing industries to all parts of Japan. The impact of the New Industrial Cities was greatly reduced, however, by the subsequent designation in 1964 of six Special Industrial Districts within the Pacific Belt in response to business counter-lobbying.

Trade and Industry (MITI) had played an important, if not decisive role by ensuring on the one hand that available capital, foreign exchange and new technologies went to those firms most able benefit from them, and on the other hand by organising cartels to ensure that the chronic over-investment and hyper-competition of the major corporations did not result in widespread bankruptcies in periods of retrenchment. Others question the importance of MITI, suggesting that other factors were more significant such as the international economic environment, a huge and well-educated reserve workforce in rural areas that was able to move to cities and prevent wage price inflation, cheap energy and raw material supplies, and a large stock of available technology that could be imported cheaply from abroad. Okimoto, for example suggests that the economic bureaucrats had neither the degree of responsibility for events that they later claimed, nor any particular prescience in picking winning industries to promote (Okimoto 1989).

There is little doubt, however, that the government approach to city planning and urban and regional infrastructure investment was an important contributor to economic growth. The vast expansion of economic activity required better roads, ports and railways, and a huge supply of new industrial land. The government focused its planning efforts and budgets on the provision of that industrial infrastructure, as shown by Yamamura (1992: 48), who notes that while 41 per cent of the public works budget was allocated to roads, harbours and airports in 1960, and 49.9 per cent in 1970, the percentage devoted to housing and sewer systems was 5.7 per cent in 1960 and 11.2 per cent in 1970. The focus of resources on producer infrastructure is enthusiastically reviewed in a recent book by Mosk (2001), who concentrates on the positive benefits to economic growth while ignoring the various human costs of the strategy.

Morimura (1994: 8) has characterised this stage of planning intervention as the "demand-response pattern of urban planning", in which the main priority was "primarily flow countermeasures focusing on the development of key facilities and industrial facilities". This characterisation usefully summarises the planning style of the period which was based on large-scale projects to expand electricity supply, water supply, industrial land supply, trunk roads, worker housing, railway and distribution facilities, and port development. Huge investments were made in coastal landfills and the land was given to major corporations for industrial sites at a fraction of its worth. There was correspondingly little priority given to other considerations such as long-term patterns of growth, residential quality of life, social capital formation in the form of parks, libraries and recreation facilities, or the broader environmental consequences of urban industrial expansion.

Central government also effectively used its monopoly over political and planning power to ensure that other investment in infrastructure went to producer infrastructure by actively opposing spending by local government on social infrastructure and residential areas. Local investment in social overhead capital was restricted in two main ways. First, central government strictly controlled local government spending on infrastructure such as local roads and sewerage at the same time as it strongly encouraged local government investment in serviced industrial sites and arterial roads. Administrative controls over approvals of city planning projects gave the MoC wide powers to control local planning policies. Financial control was effected partly by keeping local governments poor and dependent on central government grants, and partly by prohibiting local government borrowing without the permission of central government, as noted above. This system contrasts strongly with that in the US, for example, where major city borrowing is often dependent on approval through popular ballot by the local taxpayers who will have to pay back the loans (see e.g. Wilson 1988: 130). Second, the government used its regulatory control over the banking system to prevent the use of bank loans for home mortgages so there would be no competition for capital from consumers. Availability of housing mortgage finance was restricted to public sources before 1965 to ensure that available capital went into industrial expansion. Specialist private sector housing finance institutions similar to the Savings and Loans in the US and Building Societies in Britain have not yet developed in Japan (Seko 1994a: 52).

While the city planning contribution to Japanese rapid economic growth has been largely neglected, there is no doubt that the concentration of available resources on industrial infrastructure – at the expense of urban social infrastructure – contributed to economic growth. It also contributed to long-term quality of life problems in cities and the growing environmental crisis discussed in the next chapter.

Land readjustment, the all-purpose planning method

In 1954 a new LR Act (*Tochi Kukaku Seiri Hō*) was passed to replace the LR regulations of the 1919 City Planning Law. The 1954 law made a number of important changes to the practice, as well as consolidating the existing regulations. Leaseholders of land were included formally for the first time in the project implementing body, local public corporations were allowed wider scope to implement LR projects and increased processes for review of "action and replotting" plans and participation by those affected by projects were included. This act remains in force to the present day as the basic LR law. The law has been widely used and in an extraordinary variety of circumstances, primarily for urban expansion into agricultural areas, but also for downtown redevelopment, new town building, public housing projects, railway and mass transit development, and others. One important feature of the new law was that it empowered the national government to subsidise local government initiated projects. The money was drawn from the Road Improvement Special Account which collected the revenues of the gasoline tax (Ishida 1986: 83). The reasoning was that where arterial roads (i.e., city planning roads – *Toshi Keikaku Dōro*) were constructed by LR projects it was unfair to force local landowners to bear the whole burden, as the roads would primarily benefit others outside the project area. Therefore road funds could be used to subsidise road construction at the same rate as though the land had been purchased. This quickly became the major source of funds for local government-led LR projects and allowed a significant expansion in the total area of new projects during the second half of the 1950s from less than 1,000 hectares per year of new projects nationally in 1955, to over 3,000 hectares per year by 1960 (Kishii 1993: 13). Ishida argues that it also resulted in a significant shifting of emphasis of LR projects towards the building of arterial roads (Ishida 1986: 83).

The continued focus of government spending on industrial growth and producer infrastructure also contributed to an increased reliance on LR projects for the planning and improvement of residential areas. As noted above, they were particularly useful because land contributions from the participating landowners both eliminated the need to purchase land for roads and parks, and also made substantial contributions towards the construction costs of roads and sewers because some contributed land was sold as urban plots. The possibility of self-financing urban development projects was particularly attractive to local governments which bore the brunt of costs for basic infrastructure in the rapidly expanding urban areas, at the same time as their revenues were strictly limited by central government controls on allowable local taxes.

The literature on LR often stresses the importance of the method during the rapid growth period. For example, Nagamine argues that the Japanese state spent little on social overhead capital, instead devoting all available resources to enabling rapid industrial growth. Land readjustment thus played a crucial role in Japan's economic success. As he puts it: "One of the major factors in accounting for the prosperity of the Japanese economy is that her people have opted to tolerate, rightly or wrongly, a meagre resource allocation for their living conditions, thereby leaving the maximum amount of resources for industrial development . . . Japan has been able to afford only such a living environment as LR could offer. Indeed LR has been the most vital tool for Japan to muddle through, coping with heavy demands for urban land and resource constraints, particularly during the high economic growth period" (Nagamine 1986b: 52). The argument is thus that LR was crucial in the Japanese case because the state invested little in social overhead capital instead putting all available resources into aiding industrial growth, while letting the private sector, through LR, take care of discretionary spending on housing, sewerage and local roads. Honjo makes a similar point: "The conditions under which Japan developed were so severe that it was impossible to do more than the bare minimum. The accumulated capital was always mobilised for investment in productive sectors, and an urban development policy focused on infrastructure was promoted. Urban land development was carried out with the support of landowners by skilfully sharing with them the development benefits. The housing supply was left to the private sector, and only during emergencies such as natural disasters were public measures initiated or expanded" (Honjo 1984: 28).

Not everyone would agree that the Japanese people actually *chose* to tolerate a meagre allocation for their living conditions. It might be more accurate to say that the government chose that resource allocation, and effective opposition to those policies was only slow to mobilise. Nor did people always accept LR projects. In fact, as discussed above, widespread opposition to LR occurred during the implementation of the post-war War Damage Reconstruction Plan. Organised opposition by landowners was a major factor in the failure of the reconstruction plans, particularly in the case of Tokyo, although financial shortfalls also contributed to the failure to complete them (Ishida 1987: 229–30; Calder 1988: 395). Ishida also notes that the opposition movements established to fight against the War Damage Reconstruction projects were an important base for the later formation in 1968 of the All-Japan Land Readjustment Opposition League (*Kukaku Seiri Taisaku Zenkoku Renraku Kaigi*) which was formed to share information, resources and opposition strategies among the proliferating local anti-LR movements, and which remains active to the present day.

Local opposition to LR projects appears to have grown in tandem with the increase in the area of new LR projects begun after the passage of the 1954 Land Readjustment Law. As noted above that law gave expanded powers and central government road funds for local governments to plan and execute their own LR projects, which thus became the main vehicle for local governments to carry out ambitious land development and arterial road construction projects necessitated by rapid economic growth. During the late 1950s and early 1960s there was a rapid increase in the area of local government-initiated projects, which could be carried out without the consent of affected landowners (Sorensen 2000a).

LR projects also provided the only means of detailed planning control over layout of local roads, as the building-line system of the 1919 City Planning Law was abolished with revisions to the Building Standards Law in 1950. For a number of reasons – including landowner opposition, and the fact that LR projects are an inherently slow way of carrying out urban land development because of the number of people directly involved – local governments were unable to start projects in much of the rapidly growing urban area, resulting in continued expansion of urban sprawl.

The beginning of large-scale public housing construction

It was also in this period that the state first became involved in the large-scale building of public housing in the metropolitan areas. The huge influx of migrants prolonged and exacerbated the post-war housing shortage, and led to a housing policy that resembled more an emergency shelter programme for refugees than a careful city planning programme. Such housing was in one sense also infrastructure to support industrial development, as metropolitan areas needed enormous quantities of cheap housing for workers to ensure an adequate supply of labour to growing industries. It is also true, however, that this marked a significant shift in government policy, which apart from a few very small-scale projects such as those by Dōjunkai before the war had previously left housing supply almost entirely to the private market. In 1955 the earlier Housing Corporation was reformed and expanded into a new Japan Housing Corporation (JHC), whose mandate was to supply large volumes of housing in metropolitan areas with housing shortages. The JHC was the first to build multi-storey housing blocks on a large scale in Japan, which had previously seen almost exclusively low-rise housing of two and occasionally three stories. In addition, after the New Residential Area Development Act (sometimes referred to as the New Towns Act) was passed in 1963, the JHC became an important vehicle for building "new towns". The first generation of Japanese new towns included Tama New Town Near Tokyo, Kozoji New Town near Nagoya, and Senri New Town near Osaka. Although these included small commercial centres for

Figure 5.10 Senri New Town housing. These five-storey walk-up apartment blocks in Senri New Town north of Osaka are typical of the economical public housing of the 1960s and 70s. This area in Senri is adjacent to the main rail station, allowing easy access to central Osaka. Single-family houses are located further from the station on the hills in the background.

Photo A. Sorensen 2000.

local residents, they were unlike the British new towns in that they never attempted to create a balance between local jobs and residences, but remained primarily dormitory suburbs of the metropolitan core areas where most of their residents worked.

In the development of what were essentially very large-scale housing estates (*danchi*), the JHC used a version of LR which Nakamura calls "pre-emption-cum-Land Readjustment"

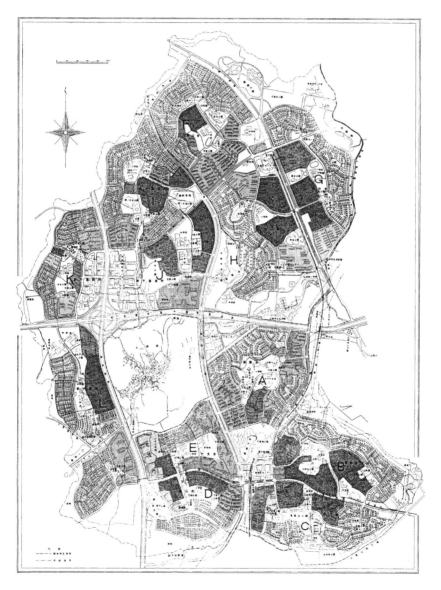

Figure 5.11 Senri New Town Master Plan. Senri, north of Osaka, is typical of the "New Towns" which started to appear in the mid-1960s. While still primarily designed to supply large volumes of new housing, Senri also included a town centre, expressway grid, rail stations, and recreation facilities.

Source: Osaka Prefecture (1970: 56).

(*Sakigai Kukaku Seiri*) (Nakamura 1986: 22). The JHC was required to gain ownership of 40 per cent or more of the land within a project area before it could initiate a project. It could do this in either of two ways; by purchasing 40 per cent of the land area on the open market, or by using its power of pre-emption, which gave it the first option of purchase when a parcel came on the market. Once it attained the 40 per cent ownership level the JHC was empowered to initiate a LR project. The JHC used LR primarily to develop large-scale housing estates, but also used it to create many industrial estates (Miyakawa 1980: 275).

The JHC public housing programmes created a variety of problems, of which possibly the most serious was a product of the JHC policy of building high-rise housing estates on greenfield sites far from existing settlements. This was justified by the fact that as such land was much cheaper, greater numbers of units could be built for the same budget, and the primary responsibility of the JHC was to produce housing in large volume. Unfortunately, this caused serious hardships for the new residents of the projects, who found themselves far from shops and other services and from the main commuter rail lines leading into the metropolitan centres where many of them worked. Such housing projects were also a major contributor to urban sprawl and eventually generated heated opposition from local governments which found that they had to bear the burden of providing schools, water supply, sewers and other municipal services for thousands of new residents (Ishida 1987: 296). On the other hand, it is well known that one of the central difficulties of urban planning in an advanced industrial society is the coordination of various policy instruments such as land use planning, taxation, capital spending on infrastructure, and transportation planning, so that they reinforce each other instead of working against each other. That was the optimistic goal, for instance, of the American "Model Cities" programme of the 1960s that failed so utterly to achieve its goals (Cullingworth 1997). It may therefore be unfair to criticise Japanese planners for having been unable to do all that much better.

The case of JHC housing usefully illustrates one of the central problems of the Japanese city planning system of the 1960s. The development project approach and dominance of central government meant different policies were not well coordinated and little attention was devoted to possible adverse consequences. Central government agencies were able to press ahead with projects even when local governments opposed them or lobbied to have them modified. On the other hand, it is important to note that Japan has never experienced the serious social problems that have become associated with public housing estates in other countries (Newman 1973; Power 1997). Although early Japanese housing estates from the 1950s and 1960s exhibit many of the worst practice design features that have been blamed in the West for crime and juvenile delinquency in these areas, they do not appear to have had the same impact in Japan, where vandalism and personal safety in public estates are non-issues.

The political and community organisation of danchi are discussed further in the next chapter; but one final point should be made about Japanese public housing: it did get better over time. The earliest public housing of the 1950s was particularly ugly, consisting of uniform rows of dull blocks, and provided only a very low standard of housing, usually two rooms, a tiny dining-kitchen area and a toilet. Bathing facilities were commonly provided in a separate public bathhouse (*sentō*) in the traditional manner. It should be remembered, though, that Japan was quite poor at this time and these estates were more or less crisis management efforts, housing for the economic refugees that were pouring into the cities. Redevelopment of these estates began during the 1990s as this standard of housing was no longer in demand. The estates of the 1960s were much more advanced, both in terms of design and provision of amenities such as playlots, schools and retail facilities and in terms of the quality of the housing provided. The new towns in particular were concerted efforts to achieve comprehensive development with park and pedestrian networks, neighbourhood units, and concentrated areas of high-density housing and commercial uses near the commuter rail station. Both Senri New Town near Osaka, shown in Figures 5.10 and 5.11, and Tama New Town west of Tokyo are good examples of towns planned during this period.

National Capital Region plans

Planning for the future structure of the capital region began again in the 1950s with the beginnings of economic revival and renewed growth of urban population. In 1950 the National Capital Construction Law (*Shuto Kensetsu Hō*) established the National Capital Construction Committee to prepare long-term plans for Tokyo prefecture. This law was a result primarily of efforts by the Tokyo government to obtain special status as the capital and a higher level of central government support for planning and rebuilding projects (Ishida 1987: 249). A second law, the National Capital Region Development Law (*Shutoken Seibi Hō*), and the National Capital Region Development Committee were established in 1956. This body was charged with the development of a regional strategy for the whole Kanto region up to a radius of 100 kilometres from Tokyo Station, including seven prefectures surrounding the capital as well as Tokyo prefecture. The committee drafted the National Capital Region Development Plan (NCRDP) which was approved in 1958 (Ishida 1987: 273).

The first National Capital Region Development Plan of 1958, shown in Figure 5.12, designated a broad greenbelt around the existing built up area of Tokyo, in emulation of Abercrombie's Greater London Plan (Hanayama 1986: 26). Controls were placed on the location or expansion of industries and universities within the existing built up area, with development to be channelled to satellite towns beyond the greenbelt. The greenbelt was to act as a *cordon sanitaire* around the existing built up area and maintain a clear separation between Tokyo and its suburban satellites (Alden 1984: 72). The greenbelt was, however, overwhelmed by a combination of greater than expected economic and metropolitan growth, and active local opposition to its implementation. A recent study of the failure of the first Capital Region Improvement Plan to control actual patterns of growth suggests that the lack of concrete legal measures to enforce provisions of the plans, and the fact that the local governments affected were pursuing contrary pro-growth policies were the key factors in undermining its effectiveness (Kurosawa, et al. 1996; see also Ishida 1992). Through a combination of political lobbying and landowner strategies of actively subdividing and selling farmland in the proposed greenbelt area forces opposed to the plan were able to ensure that its greenbelt provision would be unenforceable. In response the second National Capital Region Development Plan (NCRDP) of 1968 eliminated the greenbelt and designated the whole area outside the existing built up area and within a 50 kilometre radius of Tokyo Station a Suburban Development Area, while retaining the satellite cities in the northern part of the region.

An excellent example of the dominant planning style of the rapid growth period is the Neo-Tokyo Plan for Tokyo Bay proposed in 1959 by the Industrial Planning Conference,

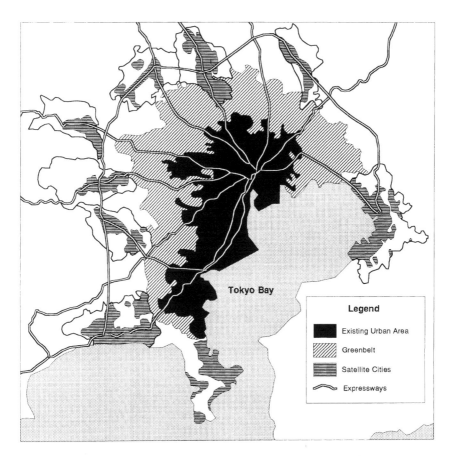

Figure 5.12 The first National Capital Region Development Plan of 1958 was in significant respects a reaffirmation of the basic principles for the planning of Tokyo outlined by Ishikawa in his reconstruction plan of 1946. While the network of open spaces in the central city area has been deleted, the plan still called for strict limits on the population growth of the existing urban area. A greenbelt would provide a clear boundary to the urban area, and new development would be encouraged in a series of industrial satellite towns ringing the urban area.

Source: Adapted from Tokyo Metropolitan Government (1989: 58).

a private sector think-tank and lobby group established by the Electric Power Central Research Institute, a semi-private body funded by a 0.3 per cent levy on the profits of private electric companies, and charged with the development of the nation's electric power and energy resources. In fact, as Samuels (1983: 171) has argued, the body was more a lobby group for big business than a research organisation, and used its huge financial resources to generate support for its proposals among LDP Diet members.

Unconstrained by budgetary considerations, the Industrial Planning Conference proposed an ambitious plan to transform Tokyo Bay into a vast new urban industrial area to link Tokyo, Kanagawa and Chiba, and create a new regional transport hub to replace Tokyo Station. As Samuels describes it:

In July 1959, the Industrial Planning Conference set forth its "Neo-Tokyo Plan". This was by far the most important and most comprehensive regional plan to appear during the high-growth era in post-war Japan. In an era of ambitious plans this was the most ambitious; in an era of private-sector leadership, this was a prototype. The plan called for 400 million square meters of landfill along the Tokyo Bay coasts, and in addition the creation of an enormous 200–million-square-meter landfill island directly in the middle of the bay. In all it proposed that fully two-thirds of Tokyo Bay be filled in. The landfill island in the midst of the Bay was the proposed site of a new central rail and motor transport facility which would connect Tokyo to both the Tohoku and Chubu regions.

(Samuels 1983: 171)

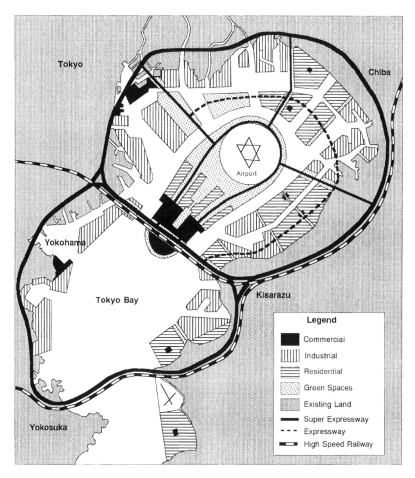

Figure 5.13 The Neo-Tokyo Plan of 1959 proposed the filling in of the bay and the creation of a new city. This plan was never built, but it was highly influential, inspiring a number of famous proposals for building in the bay, and elements such as the expressway from Kisarazu to Tokyo, and the bay shore loop expressway have recently been completed.

Source: Samuels (1983: Fig. 5.4).

The Neo-Tokyo Plan spawned a large number of similar projects by other public and private organisations. For example, soon after the plan was published, the MoC adopted its main elements as official policy, and started survey work on the Tokyo Bay circular highway, major new landfills and engineering studies for two major new bridges from Chiba to Kanagawa. The architect Kenzo Tange later contributed his own version of the plan which essentially borrowed all of the main ideas, and which by contributing a better design subsequently became much more famous than the original.

The plan had strong support from the large industrial concerns of the Chiba Konbinato which would benefit from better access to the Tokyo/Yokohama industrial belt and which were its main backers. The plan ran into significant opposition within the LDP, however, which was largely composed of members from outside the Tokyo region who saw little reason to support more spending in Tokyo. The MoC never fully gave up on the idea, even though it was relegated to the back burner several times. The plan for the cross-bay tunnel and bridge was pushed forward again during the 1980s as part of the wave of large-scale projects of the time, and was actually completed in 1997, as described in Chapter 9.

The Tokyo Olympics

The premier city planning project of the early 1960s was undoubtedly the preparation for the Tokyo Olympics. Tokyo was selected in 1959 to be the host city for the summer Olympics of 1964, and being chosen was a source of great national pride, coming as it did relatively shortly after the end of the occupation, and symbolising Japan's re-entry into the community of nations as a sovereign state. The occasion was used by the Tokyo government as an opportunity to leverage in national government funds to build some much needed urban infrastructure, and most Japanese accounts of the city planning impact only briefly mention the sports facilities built, focusing instead on the roads, expressways, subways, monorail, sewers and water supply improvements that were rushed to completion in time for the games. These all had an enormous impact on the city because rapid economic growth of the 1950s had resulted in terrible congestion problems in central Tokyo, where few of the main arterial roads planned in the post-war reconstruction plan had actually been built, and the traffic system was still largely based on that created during the earthquake reconstruction project of the 1920s when there had been far fewer automobiles.

Major road improvements were undertaken for the Olympics, and several important portions of the planned system of radial and orbital routes were completed in time for the games. Thirty routes totalling 138 kilometres in length were built, including Aoyama Dori (radial road number 4) which linked the main Olympic facilities in Yoyogi Park and the Komazawa Olympic Park, and a long stretch of Kannana Dori (orbital road number 7), an important north-south route in western Tokyo running near Komazawa. Preparations for the games also gave a great boost to the construction of subway lines in Tokyo, and in 1962 eight lines were approved with a total length of 177.5 kilometres. This was a major expansion to the existing system which still had only three lines then operating, the Ginza line which had been completed before the war, the Marunouchi line which was partially in operation in 1954, and was completed in 1959, and the Asakusa line, which was partially in operation from 1960 and was completed in 1968. One other line, the Hibiya line was completed in 1964 and was in operation in time for the games. Another addition to the city's public transit system completed just in time for the Olympics was the Tokyo Monorail linking Hamamatsucho Station on the Yamanote line with Haneda Airport, which was at completion the longest in the world. And finally, the first Bullet Train (*Shinkansen*) was completed in time for the opening of the games in order to show off Japanese operational and technological advances. The building of a new, broad-gauge trunk line from Tokyo to Osaka to replace the narrow-gauge Tokaido main line had been debated and planned by transport planners since the 1920s, starting interestingly with the omnipresent Gotō Shinpei, who was the first director of the Railway Agency in 1909 (Aoki 1993: 84); however, the Olympics provided the excuse to finally build it, and economic growth provided the funds. The building of the Shinkansen, which has for long remained the fastest and safest rail system in the world was a huge boost to national pride and played an important role in cementing the Tokyo-Nagoya-Osaka axis as the core area of Japanese economic development.

In the long run probably the greatest impact of the Olympics on Tokyo was the building of the inner-city elevated expressway system. The Metropolitan Expressway Corporation was established in June of 1959, and the central network of five expressway routes totalling 31.7 kilometres were completed just in time for the opening of the games in 1964 (Kudamatsu 1988: 40). The expressway system so dominates the central area of Tokyo that it is impossible not to notice it. Some regret that it destroyed many of Tokyo's downtown canals, and forever changed Tokyo's relationship to its roots in water transport (Jinnai 2000: 45; Seidensticker 1990: 229). Large parts of the old canal network were filled in, others became expressway tunnels, and much of the

Figure 5.14 Nihonbashi and the metropolitan expressway. Tokyo's noble Nihonbashi, a beautiful historic structure and the symbolic heart of Japan from which all distances throughout the archipelago are measured, buried beneath the elevated metropolitan expressway is expressive of the values of the rapid growth period (see Figure 3.2, page 97).

Photo A. Sorensen 2000.

remainder were covered by elevated expressways. This saved greatly on the cost of buying expensive downtown land, but unfortunately transformed what might have been one of Tokyo's great urban assets into dank, shaded and noisy bits of water. Even the noble Nihonbashi, traditional centre of Tokyo and the point from which all distance markers in the nation are measured was sacrificed to the needs of expressway construction and now sits in the shadow of the giant steel structure overhead. Jinnai (2000: 46) argues that this cavalier treatment of the city's historic waterfront spaces, which had been central to Edo culture and commerce, was part and parcel of the larger drive toward the modern economy and technology of the rapid growth years, represented in Tokyo by expressways and high-rises. High dikes and barbed-wire fences were built along the rivers, and factories and refineries replaced the old river-front restaurants and pleasure spots nostalgically celebrated by Seidensticker (1991).

On the other hand, the expressways, now totalling 263.4 kilometres in length, are undoubtedly among the best vantage points to see the city. The upper decks of the elevated expressways provide a perspective of the city that is quite different from that of the thronging streets below. The expressway has even found approval from avant-garde architectural critics:

> The Tokyo Metropolitan Expressway is without doubt the most outstanding and important structure in the fabric of the city. Massive concrete and steel beams support a vast network of roadways that weaves its way through the entire capital, its tentacles stretching as far as the outlying districts of Yokohama, Saitama and Chiba. This traffic roller-coaster flies through and over the cityscape, skimming low-lying rooftops, snaking between towering office blocks and diving into underground tunnels. It adds a further dynamic dimension to the hilly Tokyo landscape, drawing attention to the constantly changing levels and differences between areas, whether industrial, residential or commercial. This three-dimensional, sequential space has no comparison worldwide.
>
> (Tajima 1995: 16).

Clearly, how one evaluates the expressway system is a matter of taste, but there is no doubt that without it Tokyo would be a quite different place. Similar systems have been built in Osaka and Nagoya since the 1970s, with rather similar results. In Nagoya the expressway plans met with significant and well-organised (albeit unsuccessful) public opposition as they were to be built overtop several of the major boulevards which had been constructed at great expense as an embellishment to the downtown area during the post-war reconstruction projects. There is little doubt that the original intent of the boulevards of providing major linear park and open spaces in the congested inner areas has been compromised by the elevated expressways, as the boulevards are no longer open space.

Accelerating urban change with rapid economic growth

Rapid population growth in the metropolitan areas combined with rapid economic growth to propel an acceleration in the rate of change in Japanese urban areas. While the most explosive population growth occurred in the main metropolitan areas, considerable population growth also occurred in the largest towns, even in the declining peripheral areas as young people moved from smaller villages to urban centres. This was particularly true of prefectural capitals, especially those on the main rail lines or near the Pacific Belt region. Some of the main changes are summarised in Figure 5.15.

The main planning activity and expenditure was usually seen in the core area near the rail station and main commercial districts. This was particularly true of the post-war reconstruction projects which were used primarily to build a few wide boulevards in the central area, often from the train station to the old castle grounds as in Himeji, for example. The reconstruction LR projects were also primarily carried out in central

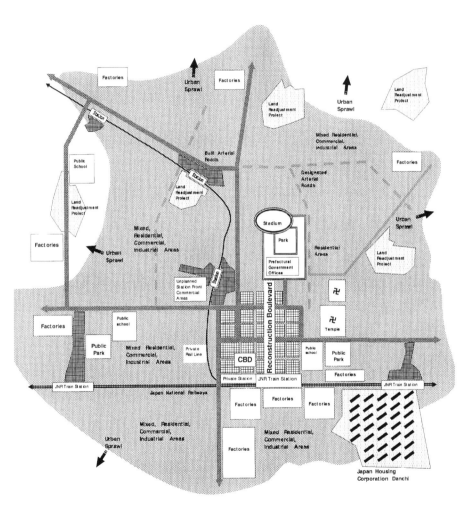

Figure 5.15 Urban change and rapid economic growth. Urban growth in the post-war period was much faster, and patterns of development grew more complex as the economy developed. Most urban areas contained a wide range of land uses, and haphazard unserviced development dominated on the urban fringe. The main focus of post-war reconstruction projects was the widening and straightening of main roads in city centre areas, often including a major boulevard of 50 to 100 metres width. Streetcar systems were also increasingly eliminated to provide more space for cars and buses.

areas to widen and rationalise the city centre road network. Apart from the main cities such as Tokyo, Osaka, Kobe and Yokohama widening of roads in existing areas had been simply too expensive, and apart from one or two main highways the road network in central areas had been inherited from the feudal era. The priority in reconstruction was thus often to improve these central areas with a main boulevard or two and basic network of main roads that would allow for increasing automobile traffic. Economic growth also led to growing private investment in office buildings and department stores in the central business districts, although these seldom exceeded five or six stories in height due to the restrictive building code.

Many prefectures also rebuilt their prefectural offices during this period to accommodate growing prefectural staffs arising from the expanded responsibilities gained under the occupation reforms. Until the bubble economy years of the late 1980s, virtually all prefectural government offices dated from this period of the 1950s, and were characterised by the dull modernist reinforced concrete brutalesque that was popular throughout the world in the 1950s and 1960s. With increasing prosperity in the 1960s, many of the larger cities built or rebuilt sports complexes, often featuring a baseball stadium on or near the old castle grounds.

In existing built up areas there was also considerable unplanned development with the expansion of the station-front shopping districts (*shōtengai*) near national and private rail lines. This unplanned growth sprang spontaneously from the growing commuter traffic served by the stations, with the number of shops and size of the district closely related to the number of passengers using the station. In the more successful and well-organised districts the local shop owners' association (*shōtenkai*) arranged for the building of covered walkways or even the roofing over of entire streets to create the Japanese equivalent of the shopping mall. These improvements and the provision of emblematic street lighting, special paving and seasonal decorations were normally funded by contributions from all the member businesses, with some municipal government support for major expenses such as arcades. These shopping districts were similar to the American version in that they provided a wide variety of stores and restaurants in one place, very often with a pedestrian-only street, all protected from the weather by a roof. They also emerged as local community centres where people could meet, go to the bank or do their shopping. The differences from the American model, however, are even more significant. The Japanese shōtengai is very often attached to a rail station, particularly in the metropolitan areas, and grows organically into the existing built up area, in contrast with the US model which is normally on the urban fringe near major road intersections, and surrounded by acres of parking. In Japan there is seldom any parking, and the ownership of the shops tends to be highly dispersed, instead of in a single corporate ownership. The internal streets are also still public property, as opposed to being private property as in the US. The shōtengai provided an efficient and attractive form of shopping district that fit well with the needs of a largely rail-based transportation system and became a characteristic part of Japanese urban areas.

On the urban fringe there were an increasing number of LR projects carried out particularly where arterial roads had been designated. The post-war reconstruction projects had designated comprehensive networks of arterial roads in urban fringe areas, but there were often neither budgets to build them nor means of preventing development within the road allowance. Land Readjustment projects were thus an essential means of

Figure 5.16 This covered shopping street in Kurashiki, Okayama prefecture, which winds its way from the main train station to the famous historical preservation district (see Figure 9.4, page 322) is a typical example of a Japanese Shōtengai.

Photo A. Sorensen 2000.

gaining land for public use and for leveraging in national funds for road construction. New schools tended to be located beyond the existing built up area as land was cheaper there, even though they usually served populations that lived closer to the centre.

Factory sites also tended to be scattered throughout the urban fringe, even though large areas of unbuilt land there had been zoned either residential, industrial or green space as part of the post-war reconstruction projects. This was partly because the zoning system was in any case rather permissive with residential areas excluding only the largest factories, and partly because the zoning system had been suspended entirely during the war with factories dispersed to areas outside the cities for strategic reasons. Although these large sites often did not conform with zoning plans, they were normally allowed to continue and even grow as exceptions. Large-scale public housing developments by local and national governments also tended to be built on the urban fringe, or well beyond the fringe where land was cheaper.

Apart from these many planned interventions in the growth of the city, large areas of land continued to be developed piecemeal as haphazard sprawl. Many factors contributed to sprawl. First, the housing shortage and speed of urban growth was such that the government deliberately kept development standards low so as to encourage private housing development at low prices. Even if local planning authorities had wished, there was no legal means of requiring private developers either to conform to a planned road network or to provide essential public goods such as sewers, parks or sidewalks. The old building-line system had been abolished in 1950 when the old Urban Buildings Law was replaced with the Building Standards Law (*Kensetsu Kijun Hō*), so even that means of creating some sort of coherence in local road development had been lost. The building-line system was replaced with a new regulation, the Road Location Designation System (*Dōro Ichi Shitei Seido*), which lacked the previous system's key feature of allowing detailed design and designation of road layouts in advance of urbanisation, which Ishida and Ikeda refer to as "positively designated building lines" (Ishida 1979). The new system worked primarily to ensure a certain minimum road width where new development occurred. In existing built up areas or mostly built up areas developers were required to leave 2 metres from the centre line of the road to the front edge of the land developed or redeveloped. The basic standard was thus that roads in residential areas should be a minimum of 4 metres in width. In many areas even that standard was not achieved, as the centre line of many narrow roads had not been precisely surveyed, making the provisions of the law difficult to enforce (Takamizawa, et al. 1980). Finally, as land ownership was highly fragmented and capital scarce, land development often proceeded in small stages, often of less than 10 houses or wooden rental units at a time. The result was the incremental building of extensive new urban areas, confusing and substandard local road networks with the bare minimum of road space, no sidewalks, and no parks.

The traditional pattern of Japanese urban development, with large areas of unplanned development interspersed with pockets of planned development structured by transportation networks therefore continued during the rapid growth period.

Deepening urban and regional problems

Rapid economic growth, and the enormous shift of population from peripheral regions to the Pacific Belt/Tokaido megalopolis region created growing urban and regional problems, and led to increasing debate about how to counter them. These debates focused on two linked aspects of the problem. On the one hand was the issue of inter-regional equity. In peripheral regions which were losing population and stagnating economically, concern was growing that most young adults were leaving for the metropolitan regions and school enrolments were dropping. These regions were faced with the prospect of long-term decline and a preponderance of older residents placing an increasing burden on social services with a declining pool of taxpayers. This situation created a major political problem for the LDP, with its strong electoral base in rural and peripheral regions. Quick and ineffectual action had been taken with the passage of the first CNDP in 1962, as described above. By the end of the 1960s, with concentration in the metropolitan regions still accelerating, backed by the uninterrupted focus of the bulk of public infrastructure spending in the core areas, the issues of place equity began to attract growing public attention.

The second aspect of the new thinking about the impacts of rapid economic growth was a growing understanding of the significant urban problems being created in the metropolitan areas. Harris in his review of Japan's post-war urban geography describes the emerging problems in the Pacific Belt thus:

> Diseconomies in the metropolitan concentrations became increasingly apparent. Traffic congestion worsened with the rise in the number of private automobiles. Industrial sites proved more difficult to find. Land reclamation in the shallow bays

became more expensive. Demand for industrial water grew rapidly, but at the same time restrictions were placed on the pumping of ground water, because the pumping led to serious problems of land subsidence in the low lying areas in the three major industrial regions. Problems of air pollution became acute because of the heavy concentration of industries and the high sulphur content in much of the petroleum used by them. Public opposition to pollution and more stringent governmental regulations became important considerations. Concerns for amenities and environmental protection increased.

(Harris 1982: 75–6)

It is hardly an exaggeration to say that the problems associated with the Pacific Belt concentration have dominated the discourse of urban and regional planning in Japan since the 1960s.

Tanaka Kakuei, prime minister of Japan from 1972 to 1974, nicely summarised what had become the conventional wisdom in Japan regarding these twin problems of congestion in the metropolitan regions and decline on the periphery in his book *Building a New Japan*:

The rapid economic growth of postwar Japan, particularly since the mid-1950s, has spurred industrialization and urbanization throughout the nation. The result has been the excessive concentration of both population and industry in the Tokyo-Nagoya-Osaka belt along the Pacific coast, forming a hyper-dense community the likes of which is not to be found elsewhere in the world. All of the major industrial nations of the world are today faced with the common agonies of inflation, urban deterioration, environmental pollution, stagnant agriculture, and spiritual frustration amidst material affluence. This is especially so in Japan. Smaller than the single state of California, Japan has nearly one-third of the people concentrated on a mere one percent of the land, making the tempo of social and economic change so much the greater.

(Tanaka 1972: i–ii)

Tanaka's view that over-concentration in the metropolitan areas was the ultimate source of their urban environmental problems, and decline in the periphery was widely shared when his book was published in the early 1970s, and his plan to restructure the Japanese space-economy by encouraging development in the regions was highly appealing. The outcomes of Tanaka's proposals are explored further in Chapters 7 and 9.

It is hard to avoid the conclusion that the approach to city planning during the rapid growth period played an important role in the emergence of these environmental problems. Explanations such as that in Tanaka's book, which describe them as a regrettable but unavoidable result of rapid economic growth in a geographically limited area are very common in descriptions of Japanese urbanisation. The further point is often made that because of the extremely difficult conditions after the war with widespread destruction and terrible housing shortages, the country was starting from such a low base that little was to be expected, and some urban problems were unavoidable. There is no doubt that all of these factors contributed to Japanese urban problems. They are not sufficient explanations, however. Similar conditions of rapid economic growth in small geographic areas, terrible wartime destruction and severe post-war housing shortages prevailed in West Germany in the post-war period, yet its cities were carefully rebuilt in a planned manner, with few of the urban problems that were endemic in Japan in the rapid growth period (Calder 1988: 390–3). It seems fair to say that Japanese urban problems were not simply a matter of rapid urbanisation and over-concentration, but rather that the value put on economic expansion to the virtual exclusion of other priorities also played an important role. This bias remained fundamentally unchanged before the passage of the New City Planning Law of 1968, and helped to create serious urban environmental problems during the period of rapid growth.

The Japanese urban planning system before 1968 was characterised by an orientation towards project planning and implementation, rather than towards an attempt at an effective regulatory system, and was paradoxically highly centrally controlled at the same time that it was extremely laissez-faire. It was centrally controlled in the sense that the central government retained a tight grip on power and the purse strings, and was largely able to prevent local governments from developing their own planning strategies. It was laissez-faire in that regulation was kept to an absolute minimum in order to allow the greatest freedom for profitable development. Unfortunately, these strategies, while contributing to economic growth, also led to the severe environmental crisis described in the next chapter.

Solving the major urban and environmental problems created by the rapid urban and industrial growth of the 1950s and 1960s became a major public policy issue in Japan during the 1960s, and a renewed focus was placed on the role of city planning in managing urban growth, preventing environmental problems and providing for increased urban quality of life, as discussed in the next chapter.

6 Environmental crisis and the new city planning system of 1968

Some of the readers may remember seeing that classical Japanese film *Ikiru* which was the story of an ailing ward official who, with the support of local citizens, finally succeeded in overcoming all the hurdles and resistance in creating a small park for citizens, and died smiling alone on the swing in the park. Contrast this with the smooth, matter-of-fact way in which hectares and hectares of new land have been created for industries by filling up the shore-line sea. This latter project, once conceived in the minds of some government officials, goes through steps which are well grooved for eventual fulfilment. The contrast is like the one between a large number of people, women and children included, trying to push a heavy cart over an uncharted wild terrain without a road, and a team of trained staff driving a stream-lined train over a polished rail.

(Tsuru 1993: 137–8)

In the early post-war years the necessity for prioritising reconstruction and economic development had been clear. After 15 long years of war during which virtually all Japanese national resources had been poured into military adventure, most Japanese were poor, standards of living had steadily declined, and malnutrition was widespread. Rapid economic growth and the rebuilding of the country during the 1950s and 1960s was thus widely supported, and the benefits of economic growth were widely shared and appreciated. It was not long, however, before serious problems began to emerge. Of these the most serious was the environmental destruction and pollution caused by very rapid growth, concentration of productive capacity into a small geographic area, and virtually non-existent government pollution standards or enforcement.

This chapter looks at some of the problems that arose from rapid industrialisation, including pollution and urban sprawl, and one of the responses of the government, the passage of a new city planning system in 1968.

Environmental crisis

Rapid economic and population growth in the Pacific Belt area resulted in deteriorating living conditions in many growth areas. The strategy of concentrating industrial development in the Pacific Belt corridor, and focusing new industrial and infrastructure investment in clusters of interrelated industries in close proximity to each other on planned sites facilitated the acceleration of economic growth, but it also resulted in the concentration of the negative effects of industrial and population growth into very small areas. McKean argues that although by the late 1960s Japanese consumption of energy per capita was still only about 25 per cent of that in the US, because of the high concentrations of population and industrial activity, Japan was twenty to thirty times more likely to have serious pollution problems in certain areas (McKean 1981: 18). By the early 1960s, the enormous scale of industrial investment and lack of controls on pollution emissions resulted in some of the worst concentrations of air pollution in the world, and high levels of waste emissions into rivers and streams. In addition, the weak zoning regulations meant that many of the worst polluters were situated in close proximity to high-density residential areas.

The result was a severe environmental crisis. Large numbers of people died from water and air pollution, and from eating poisoned food. The first cases of all the major pollution-related diseases appeared in Japan, with hundreds of deaths recorded. Large numbers of people suffered intensely painful and debilitating diseases, children were born deformed and/or mentally disabled, and where family breadwinners were crippled serious repercussions were felt by their entire families, particularly as most victims were among the working poor (Iijima 1992). Far greater numbers suffered chronic environment-related illness and received official government recognition as pollution victims, which entitled them to relief and medical aid. This was extended to over 73,000 people by 1979 (McKean 1981: 20). There is also no doubt that many more were harmed, many seriously, than were officially compensated. Air pollution was caused directly by industrial expansion and increased car and truck use, with total emissions of sulphur dioxide and nitrogen oxides tripling during the 1960s. Water pollution was exacerbated by the increase in population and caused by untreated industrial discharges directly into watercourses; increasing use of agricultural chemicals such as BHC and DDT – introduced in 1945 and widely used until they were banned in 1972 – which eventually leached into both ground and surface water supplies; and significant increases in municipal sewage wastes. Before the 1960s most municipal wastewater systems only transported wastewater without treating it, discharging it directly into rivers. It is worth noting that outside the major metropolitan areas and even in the metropolitan suburbs, most nightsoil was still used as fertiliser in the traditional manner, so little was actually flushed into the wastewater stream. This situation began to change quickly after the 1960s with the decreasing cost and increasing use of chemical fertilisers, and the rapid decrease in demand for nightsoil. Although construction of sewerage systems and treatment plants has been a major Ministry of Construction (MoC) priority since the 1960s, by 1970 only 16 per cent of the population were connected to sewage systems, and even by 1988 the rate was still less than 40 per cent (Barret and Therivel 1991: 35). By 1998 that had increased to 64.7 per cent connected to public sewer services, leaving more than a third of houses still unconnected.

Although the story of Japanese environmental pollution, its effects on affected communities and their suffering and uphill battles for recognition and compensation is gripping and often heartrending, it has been extensively discussed in other works and need not be repeated here (see e.g. Barret and Therivel 1991; Broadbent 1998; Hoshino 1992; Huddle and Reich 1975; Iijima 1992; McKean 1981; Reich 1983a; Ui 1992b). In the present context the pollution disaster is important first because growing environmental conflict was a major factor behind the development of the 1968 City Planning

Law, and second because the reaction to environmental problems is revealing of two important features of Japanese society which help to explain the development of the city planning system; the approach of government to resolving the pollution problems and the patterns of citizen protest and mobilisation in reaction to environmental crisis.

It is clear that rapid economic growth produced huge social costs while allowing dramatic increases in general standards of living. As Taira (1993: 173) argues, during the rapid economic growth period Japanese corporations vigorously resisted "internalising" the social and environmental "external" costs of production by installing pollution control equipment or by cleaning up environmental hazards that they had already caused. The corporations responsible also denied their responsibility when pollution victims protested, and lied, concealed evidence, and did everything possible to prevent outside investigators from determining their true responsibility. Although this sort of behaviour is reprehensible, it is hardly exceptional amongst private corporations in capitalist economies, which have often seen their sole responsibility as making profits

Figure 6.1 Osaka in the 1950s. Osaka enjoyed its status as Japan's leading industrial city, and was proud of its nicknames "the Capital of Smoke" and "the Manchester of the Orient". During the rapid growth period Osaka could rightly boast of its status as workshop to the world, and many of Japan's premier heavy industrial conglomerates which led the economic expansion of the rapid growth period were based in the Kansai region centred on Osaka.

Photo Mainichi Shinbunsha.

Figure 6.2 Mixed land use in the 1960s. The results of rapid economic growth, a narrow government focus on industrial expansion, indiscriminate location of new factories, weak land use and development controls, and almost non-existent pollution regulations were predictable: a severe environmental and health crisis emerged during the 1960s.

Photo A. Sorensen 2001.

in whatever ways they can get away with. More surprising is the reaction of the national government agencies whose responsibility is often seen to include the protection of citizens from the ill effects of uncontrolled corporate behaviour. In Japan during the 1950s and 1960s, however, the government ministries were still focused entirely on promoting economic growth and colluded in industry efforts to evade responsibility (Reich 1983a; Ui 1992a; Upham 1987). The priority given by national ministries to protecting industry from complaints was particularly tragic, as it not only prolonged the suffering of those afflicted by debilitating and painful disabilities, but intensified their shame as they were effectively told that their affliction was their own fault. If any further evidence were required that a highly distinctive conception of the state interest and responsibility towards its citizens still prevailed in Japan, the pollution disaster provides it. The self-appointed role of the government was to promote national strength through economic growth, and the people were expected to do their best to further that growth. The purpose of economic growth was not to improve the welfare of the people, who were expected to save money by living frugally and working long hours, but to increase the strength of the state. The old feudal and Meiji period idea that the people were there to serve the state, and not vice versa, had clearly not lost much of its potency.

The second aspect of the pollution disaster that is important here is its effects on patterns of citizen protest and the development of civil society. The environmental crisis was an important factor promoting the development of civil society in Japan, by greatly increasing the legitimacy of citizen activism and protest. In the early stages of the environmental crisis a traditional form of citizen activism was common, with victims using protests and negotiations to beg for compensation from the companies responsible (Koschmann 1978; Walthall 1991). The companies and government in response granted a minimum of sympathy money while extracting promises of future good behaviour by the victims so as to prevent any real challenge to the status quo (Hoshino 1992). As exemplified by the cases of organic mercury poisoning at Minamata and Niigata, the response of the companies was to deny their responsibility for the pollution. To this end, and with the active complicity of the government which shut down several university research projects into the causes of pollution diseases, the companies obstructed efforts to determine the causes and nature of the pollution problems. During the 1960s, with increasing public recognition of the responsibility of the polluting companies for the spread of disease and death, and their own increasing desperation, the victims were less willing to be bought off with small sympathy payments. Traditional prohibitions against unilateral action were cast aside, and several of the victims groups launched into more aggressive tactics including direct action such as sit-ins, damage to company facilities, and ultimately suing the offending companies in court for compensation. When the "Big Four" anti-pollution court cases were decided in 1972 in favour of the victims, and stiff penalties were levied against the polluting companies – a vindication of the justice of the victims' cases – it sent a strong message that citizen protest was a legitimate part of modern society, and a wave of public support emerged for pollution victims who had earlier been treated with little sympathy.

After the late 1960s and particularly during the first half of the 1970s, there was an enormous increase in the number of citizen movements against pollution and environmental degradation. These groups were a powerful indication that a new type of citizen consciousness had arisen in Japan, and that people were no longer willing to leave important issues that affected their health, their families, and their communities entirely up to the politicians and corporations. The anti-pollution citizen movements indicate that a much stronger civil society was emerging in Japan that could define its own goals even in opposition to those of the government if necessary. As Iijima puts it, "Pollution, occupational hazards, and consumer health problems caused by flawed or poisonous products have been more effective in inducing citizen-based mass movements than any other type of social disaster since the beginning of Japan's period of modernization" (Iijima 1992: 154). Those citizens' movements and their impacts on national politics and policies are discussed further in the second section of this chapter. Here it is worth looking more closely at one key aspect of environmental degradation that resulted from rapid urbanisation – urban sprawl.

Suburbanisation and urban sprawl

The environmental crisis was not just a question of air and water pollution. A further issue was the poor and worsening living conditions in expanding metropolitan areas. McKean (1981: 19) points out that complaints about noise, vibrations, blocking of sunlight, proximity to electrical transmission wires, and foul smells have consistently outranked air and water pollution in the numbers of formal complaints lodged. These kinds of problems are all directly related to the rapid and haphazard growth of urban areas and the intense intermingling of different uses that the inclusive zoning system allowed. That is, these sorts of environmental problems were the direct result of poor land use planning as much as they were the result of pollution itself. In particular the continued building of housing in and adjacent to heavy industrial areas created serious problems. While it is clear that the weakness in pollution controls greatly exacerbated the problem, and that with stricter regulation the worst pollution problems receded after the 1970s, other problems of noise, heavy traffic and toxic contamination of groundwater continue to plague the mixed residential/industrial areas that were formed during the rapid growth period.

One feature of Japanese post-war urbanisation which began during the early 1960s and has since become its dominant characteristic is the mass suburbanisation of the population. Suburbanisation has occurred throughout the country, but has been particularly important in the metropolitan areas because of the much higher rates of population growth there. While the 1950s saw ever-increasing concentration of population in the metropolitan core areas, from 1960 to 1965 Tokyo prefecture had a net loss of migrants for the first time. In fact, while the Tokyo region as a whole continued to grow strongly, the central 23-ward area of Tokyo was losing population absolutely after 1960, beginning the process of suburbanisation that was to dominate the following period (Glickman 1979: 19). While metropolitan areas including the central cities were still attracting strong migration from rural prefectures, even greater numbers of people were leaving the central areas for adjacent suburbs.

Table 6.1 Population increases by distance bands within MMAs

Area	Distance (km)	Increase rate (%)							
		'55–60	'60–65	'65–70	'70–75	'75–80	'80–85	'85–90	'90–95
Tokyo	0–10	13.4	−1.4	−6.5	−6.5	−6.3	−1.7	−6.9	−5.4
	10–20	**29.8**	25.3	11.9	6.2	2.1	3.1	4.1	0.8
	20–30	22.7	**40.4**	31.6	22.5	9.2	8.3	11.7	**9.3**
	30–40	15.4	37.0	**43.6**	29.7	14.2	8.5	12.8	−1.7
	40–50	3.1	14.9	19.6	22.1	**16.1**	10.2	18.6	7.4
	50–60	na	na	na	na	na	9.2	**22.3**	7.5
	60–70	na	na	na	na	na	4.4	15.6	3.6
	Total	18.5	19.7	15.9	12.7	6.4	5.8	8.0	2.7
Osaka	0–10	**20.7**	12.3	2.2	−3.4	−3.7	−0.4	−0.7	−1.0
	10–20	19.5	**41.3**	**32.5**	19.5	7.2	3.7	2.5	−0.4
	20–30	13.3	20.7	25.0	**22.3**	8.4	5.6	6.7	0.3
	30–40	7.8	12.9	15.5	13.2	**8.6**	**6.2**	**7.1**	2.6
	40–50	7.4	4.5	5.2	6.7	3.1	2.4	5.4	**4.8**
	Total	13.8	16.7	13.0	9.0	3.7	3.0	3.2	0.9
Nagoya	0–10	**19.1**	13.8	6.3	2.5	−0.3	0.9	2.4	−0.4
	10–20	12.4	**24.3**	**23.4**	**19.6**	9.3	4.8	15.3	**5.1**
	20–30	7.8	14.0	19.6	15.7	**11.1**	**8.1**	**20.2**	4.2
	30–40	7.4	8.7	6.5	7.5	4.7	3.8	12.2	2.8
	40–50	−1.0	1.0	3.3	6.7	5.4	3.4	12.6	1.6
	Total	10.9	13.0	11.1	9.7	5.4	4.0	10.0	2.7

Note: Bold figures show the band with the highest growth rate.

Source: Population Census of Japan, various years.

This pattern is clearly shown in Table 6.1 which shows the rates of population increase in the three metropolitan areas by distance band from the centre. While the innermost area of Tokyo loses population after 1960, the band with the highest growth rates (bold figures) moves steadily out from the central areas over time. For example, in Tokyo in 1960–65 the 20–30 kilometre band had the fastest growth rate, but in 1965–75 this passed to the 30–40 kilometre band, and in 1975–80 to the 40–50 kilometre band (Hebbert and Nakai 1988b). By 1985–90 the 50–60 kilometre band was fastest growing. This pattern was broadly repeated in Osaka and Nagoya, though later, and in less extreme fashion, reflecting their smaller size and slower rates of growth. Thus although the central metropolitan prefectures experienced very large out-migration after the mid-1960s, most of those migrants moved to adjacent prefectures, pushed by expanding central area businesses and rising land values, and pulled by lower housing costs. This follows the familiar pattern of metropolitan deconcentration seen in many other developed countries.

Even in wealthier countries with stronger urban planning systems the scale and speed of suburbanisation that took place in Japan would have presented serious planning challenges, and urban sprawl is by no means only a Japanese phenomenon. In fact, in many ways the extent of metropolitan dispersal and the long-term problems created by sprawl are even greater in the US than in Japan (Garreau 1991; Kunstler 1993). There are important differences between sprawl in Japan and in the other developed countries, however. The term is commonly used to describe situations where urbanisation proceeds in low-density patterns, leaving many undeveloped spaces, spreading over a far larger area than necessary and leading to a range of problems such as higher costs for public infrastructure and services, longer travel times and the inefficient use of land. These are all problems in Japan as much as anywhere. Japanese-style sprawl has the additional feature that a large proportion of new development in the metropolitan suburbs occurred as very small developments of one to ten houses on existing rural lanes, with no improvements to road networks or sewer systems (Sorensen 1999). This type of haphazard scatter of new development in suburban areas is strongly resisted in the other developed countries. Even the US, which has much more serious problems of urban sprawl than any of the European countries, has effective subdivision-control regulations that ensure new suburban development is generally permitted only if developers provide local roads, parks, sewers, water supply, and even contributions to new schools and highway networks that are required by the new population. In Japan the weak planning system was unable to prevent haphazard, unserviced development as before the major revisions of 1968, laws restricting the right of landowners to divide their land into smaller pieces, and requirements for certain minimum levels of services to be provided when new houses were built were extremely weak and had little effect.

Several other factors tended to encourage scattered development in Japan. First, because there were no development or subdivision controls, all land within commuting distance of the major employment centres could be developed for residential use. The city planning system established in 1919 had put little priority on the development of suburban areas, and had included no minimum standards for development, or powers for planning authorities to make development permission contingent on building local infrastructure. According to the MoC (1991a: 25) in their description of the shortcomings of the planning system during the period of rapid growth, "The 1919 Act did not provide strong enough legal effects to control disorderly urbanisation in the peripheries of cities." Second, in the three metropolitan areas there were at the beginning of the rapid growth period already well-developed rail systems which allowed non car-based commuting to a very large area. Many of these railways were private commuter lines which had a great incentive to help increase the commuter population along their lines by promoting land development. The private railways also earned higher fares' income from longer trips, another incentive to develop ever further from core employment areas. Further, most employers directly subsidise their employees' transit fares as the government allows this to be excluded from employees' taxable income, which has been described as a major support for a more extensive urban form in Japan (Hatta and Ohkawara 1994). Third, small farmers who held the bulk of the land on the metropolitan fringe were often unwilling to sell, or if they did, would sell a small piece and retain the rest. Prospective homeowners had to search further and further from the urban core to find affordable land. Even though within a radius of 20 kilometres from Tokyo Station there were still tens of thousands of hectares of undeveloped farmland as late as 1990, the spread of suburban development had already reached as far as 50 kilometres from Tokyo Station by 1960 (Hanayama 1986). The physical area of Tokyo is thus much greater than it might otherwise have been.

Urban sprawl created two main problems. On the one hand, the half-rural, half-urban areas created real hardships for their residents with inadequate roads, lack of sewerage, lack of public facilities such as parks, sidewalks, community centres and libraries, and close intermingling of residential areas with obnoxious neighbours such as car-wrecking yards and polluting factories. On the other hand, these huge areas of sprawl development along rural lanes were creating great obstacles for the future urbanisation of the region, as once rural areas are even partially built up it becomes vastly more expensive and disruptive to build proper roads and sewers afterwards. And acquiring land for other more discretionary types of public open space such as parks is virtually impossible after land has reached fully urban values.

Rapid and unplanned urban growth thus contributed greatly to environmental degradation in Japan. The spread of factories and housing was responsible for a highly visible loss of environmental amenities, as beaches and coastal areas disappeared beneath landfills for industrial complexes, hills and forests were razed and paddies filled in for new housing. The adverse impacts of all these processes were exaggerated by the weak land use planning system, as much development proceeded haphazardly, spreading over far larger areas than necessary, and the issue of urban sprawl (*supurōru*) became widely discussed as a critical problem facing Japanese cities during the 1960s. A growing body of research on urban problems associated with sprawl was already putting the issue firmly on the government's agenda during the early 1960s, which resulted in a raft of study groups, commissions and committees (Ishida 1987: 297–8). These debates were central to discussions about revisions of the city planning system, but concrete measures to address problems of urban sprawl were not introduced until late in 1968, when political pressure to do so became overwhelming, as discussed below.

The political economy of growth

There are a wide range of competing explanations for the long rule of the Liberal Democratic Party (LDP) over Japanese politics in the post-war period. From its founding in 1955 with the merger of the two main conservative parties, until 1992 the LDP enjoyed uninterrupted rule over Japan, and again since 1994, in coalition with several minority parties has managed to stay in power and control the government. Many observers accept that the relationship between the ruling LDP, the bureaucracy and the business community have formed the key to understanding Japanese government and policy. Johnson's theory of the "developmental state" was a particularly useful exposition of this model. His description of the "triangle" of LDP, bureaucracy and business is classic and worth citing:

> The central institutions – that is, the bureaucracy, the LDP and the larger Japanese business concerns – in turn maintained a kind of skewed triangular relationship with each other. The LDP's role is to legitimate the work of the bureaucracy while also making sure that the bureaucracy's policies do not stray too far from what the public will tolerate. Some of this serves its own interests, as well; the LDP always insures that the Diet and the bureaucracy are responsive to the farmers' demands because it depends significantly on the overrepresented rural vote. The bureaucracy, meanwhile, staffs the LDP with its own cadres to insure that the party does what the bureaucracy thinks is good for the country as a whole, and guides the business community towards developmental goals. The business community in turn, supplies massive amounts of funds to keep the LDP in office, although it does not thereby achieve control of the party, which is normally oriented upward, toward the bureaucracy, rather than downward, toward its main patrons.
>
> (Johnson 1982: 50)

This description presents what was for some time the dominant model of the Japanese political economy, and just such "iron triangles" of bureaucracy, LDP and big business are still widely referred to. In Johnson's conception the bureaucracy is the dominant player, with the LDP functioning primarily as a shield to protect the bureaucrats from particularistic interests that would hinder their pursuit of the technocratically optimal economic growth policy. Business interests supply the money required to keep the party electoral machine running, but gain little leverage over policy through their party connections. Instead, they benefit by maintaining close ties with the bureaucracy, which supplies valuable information and protection from foreign competition. Johnson therefore describes the Japanese state as strong, bureaucracy dominated, effective at policy formulation and implementation, and relatively insulated from competing political pressures generated by citizens' wants and aspirations. It was thus able to pursue long-term policies without the political necessity of short-term benefits common in other democracies. This conception of the state works particularly well in explaining Japanese politics during the rapid growth years of the 1950s and 1960s. The widespread acceptance of the need to rebuild the economy and the very real material benefits that resulted from economic growth helped to maintain public support for this strategy.

While few would disagree that the "iron triangle" of LDP–bureaucracy–big business is central to understanding post-war Japanese politics, however, after the mid-1980s this conception of the Japanese state as strong, technocratically oriented and bureaucratically controlled was increasingly challenged. The main problem with this elite view of power in the Japanese case is that it does not adequately explain the state's responsiveness to interest group pressure and support for small business and other groups. Muramatsu and Krauss (1987) argued, for example, that Johnson's analysis gave far too much weight to the bureaucracy and notions of a national pro-development consensus in formulation of policy, and ignored the role of political strategy, political leadership and political coalitions and competition in determining the goals of development and the particular form it took. They argued that the Japanese state was better understood as a system of "patterned pluralism". In this conception, they suggested that in the 1970s and especially in the 1980s new patterns of policymaking emerged which resulted from increasing penetration of the policymaking process by interest groups. Thus "Japanese policymaking is characterised by a strong state with its own autonomous interests and an institutionalised accommodation among elites, interacting with pluralist elements" (Muramatsu and Krauss 1987: 537). The bureaucracy thus has much less autonomy than in Johnson's conception and autonomous bureaucratic power is compromised by the need to accommodate political actors and elites as well as organised pressure groups.

Another of the works which made an important contribution to this revised analysis of the state was Calder's (1988) examination of the LDP's strategies for remaining in power. Calder's analysis is particularly useful for understanding policymaking for city planning. He argues that the LDP maintained power by tending to the needs and demands of its core clientele of supporters, particularly in times of crisis. He shows how, aided by the ever increasing resources available to the state as a result of the booming economy, the LDP was able to expand its base by incorporating new groups into its "circles of compensation". He also makes the important distinction between policymaking for the traded international sector and for the largely non-traded domestic sector. With his model of a "bifurcated political economy" Calder is able to explain the coexistence of a highly efficient and competitive international sector with the proliferation of inefficient sectors such as agriculture, distribution and small-scale labour-intensive industries. The basic argument is that in the traded international sector, a technocratic approach is pursued which is relatively insulated from domestic political interference. This he attributes primarily to the fact that in this sector there were relatively few opportunities for redistributive, clientelistic relations to develop. On the other hand, policymaking for the non-traded sectors such as public works construction, agriculture and the distribution system, where there was a large and well-organised political constituency and thus significant scope for redistributive pork-barrel style politics, has been consistently compromised by political actors. This has resulted in inefficient, highly protected and patronage-ridden sectors of the economy, with substantial government intervention in the form of rice price supports, aid to small business and a perverse regional policy with extensive programmes of public works in remote parts of the country.

By documenting the patterns of LDP policymaking in response to its perceptions of its own crisis of survival as the ruling party from its formation in 1955 to the mid-1980s, Calder was able to show that rather than being simply a strong technocratic state largely insulated from democratic political pressures, in fact the Japanese state is better understood as having been responsive to particular constituencies because of the electoral weakness of the ruling party. Further he shows that the LDP successfully used the increasing resources of the state to progressively broaden the "circles of compensation" which benefited from its redistributive policies. The greatest beneficiaries were those able to supply secure electoral support to the party, of whom the most important were consistently the farmers. By dividing the activities of the state into two realms – the traded international sector, characterised by bureaucratic independence and a technocratic policy apparatus, and the non-traded domestic sectors, characterised by political intervention and a redistributive, pork-barrel approach to policy formation – Calder was able to explain much of Japanese state activity that did not fit with a purely technocratic, bureaucracy dominant model.

Certainly the key city planning developments at the end of the 1960s and early 1970s, including the creation of the new city planning system in 1968, passage of strict pollution control legislation in 1972, and creation of the National Land Agency and new National Land Planning Law in 1974, all suggest a government that was more responsive to public pressure and electoral challenge than is suggested by Johnson's "iron triangle" hypothesis. It also seems clear that the growth of citizen movements in opposition to government policy and the steadily increasing strength of opposition parties in national elections – particularly in local elections during the 1960s and early 1970s – appears to have been crucial in pressuring the government to reform the city planning system in 1968, and bring in strict anti-pollution measures in the early 1970s.

The growth of citizens' movements

Although the peak of the membership and political influence of citizen's movements came in the early 1970s, they had started to protest against industrial pollution as the cause of disease from as early as the beginning of the 1960s. For example, three of the "Big Four" pollution cases settled in the early 1970s in favour of the plaintiffs first came to public prominence in the early 1960s: Itai Itai disease in Toyama in 1961, Minamata disease in the late 1950s and Yokkaichi asthma in 1960 (McKean 1981: 45–63). Even more significantly in terms of urban planning, in 1963–64 in the Mishima-Numazu area residents organised the first successful anti-*kombinato* citizens' movement. News reports of severe pollution problems caused by the Yokkaichi City oil and petrochemical complex near Nagoya helped local residents mobilise opposition when a similar complex was planned for their area. The success of that movement gained national media coverage and provided proof that it was possible to oppose industrial development and protect the local environment (Huddle, Reich and Stiskin 1975; Lewis 1980). Throughout the 1960s there was a rising level of concern about environmental problems, and the development of citizens' movements in response to environmental pollution was an important factor in mobilising Japanese people to be more active in challenging government priorities (McKean 1981).

While the Big Four were tragic cases of industrial irresponsibility, and a case such as Mishima-Numazu was a dramatic and well-publicised success of local opposition, the really significant fact was that these were not isolated cases. In fact, throughout the 1960s and well into the 1970s citizens' movements became more and more numerous. According to Krauss and Simcock (1980), for example, in 1971 alone local governments received 75,000 pollution-related complaints, and there were as many as 10,000 local disputes in 1973. While most individual groups focused on local issues and tended to have a short life span, either collapsing after defeat or folding up after victory, their very numbers assured their importance. The growth of citizens' movements had a particular impact on land development activities. Whereas previously developers were able to rely on the ability of local governmental and business elites to assemble land for their projects (see Allinson 1975; Broadbent 1989, 1998), after the 1960s they often encountered organised resistance by residents and farmers who opposed development (Krauss and Simcock 1980: 196). Even the old neighbourhood associations became more independent, and many associations, especially newly organised ones in new housing areas became active channels for citizen mobilisation. Whereas until this point local neighbourhood organisations served primarily as a means of communicating information and demands downwards from local government to the people, during the 1960s newly formed *chonaikai* and *jichikai* started to mobilise to make demands on local government (Ben-Ari 1991; Nakamura 1968).

In his description of the impacts of rapid urban growth Ishida (1987: 300) notes the wide variety of these local movements to oppose the development plans of national and local governments, such as "Land Readjustment opposition movements, road pollution opposition movements, movements to protect sunshine rights, and movements to protect natural and cultural resources from development". At the same time, there were also movements formed to "demand road paving, gutters, emergency facilities, children's playgrounds, public parks, educational facilities, libraries, and other local public facilities". He also suggests that whereas in the beginning the citizens' movements tended to be highly fragmented into each local issue, with simple and restricted goals, soon quite a few of the movements became much more sophisticated. Along with doing research and educating others about urban planning procedures and issues, they also started to make links with other groups that were concerned with similar issues around the country and formed national alliances.

As an example, Ishida (1987: 301) describes the evolution of a group that organised to oppose LR projects. Although the movement was small at the beginning, by establishing national links it quickly spread, and was able to play an important role in helping to organise the 1963 Toyoda LR Project Opposition League in suburban Nagoya, and in the setting up of an environmental protection group to oppose LR in Fujisawa City in Kanagawa prefecture in 1966. By 1968 a national organisation of citizens' groups opposing LR projects had been formed. The National Land Readjustment Countermeasures League was active in publishing practical materials to instruct local groups in how to organise to oppose LR projects. This group is still active, and continues to publish under the imprint of the Local Government Research Institute (*Jichitai Kenkyusha*). Ishida (1987: 303) suggests that one of the major causes of opposition to LR projects at this time was that residents in areas where projects were being started by local governments would find out that long before any of the local residents and landowners were informed, the decision to carry out the project had been taken as part of plans to build trunk road networks. He argues that it was this kind of "not informing" that created the citizens' movements.

Unfortunately, even though there is no doubt that the growth of citizens' movements was tremendously important for the development of civil society and the evolution of the city planning system, in practice their concrete successes have been few. The vast majority of such movements ended without having attained their goals. As Tsuru explains, "As we study each one of the cases of such movements, we cannot but be impressed with one feature that is common to practically all of them. That is the tremendous amount of energy and time that is voluntarily put into a campaign without any monetary remuneration on the one hand, and the quiet stone-wall character of the opposition which has all the paraphernalia of the establishment on its side including 'the law's delay and the insolence of office' on the other" (Tsuru 1993: 137–8).

In the longer run, even though so many citizens' movements achieved little for their efforts, the cumulative impact of their very numbers proved great, as this huge wave of local opposition movements transformed Japanese politics, especially at the local level, and led to an electoral crisis for the ruling LDP government in the late 1960s and early 1970s.

Electoral crisis of the LDP

While the increasing awareness of environmental and congestion problems had not produced significant changes in the planning strategies of the government, what seems to have prompted action was a rising sense of political crisis for the ruling LDP. The breakdown in the growth consensus and the rise of citizens' movements translated into electoral challenges to LDP dominance. During the two-and-a-half decades from 1952 to 1976, the LDP share of the popular vote in House of Representatives elections decreased unilinearly, while the total progressive vote (JSP and JCP) steadily increased. Significantly for questions of urban planning, while local government had been until the mid-1960s the almost exclusive territory of conservative politicians, by the late 1960s conservative dominance was clearly on the wane. Although opposition parties had focused their energies on national politics after the war and during the 1950s, from the early 1960s they more actively fielded candidates and pushed reform agendas at the local level. This was translated into a steady growth of reformist city councillors, mayors, and governors during the 1960s and early 1970s (Allinson 1979: 138–40; MacDougall 1980: 65–9).

While nationally the conservatives were still in control of 71 per cent of city assembly seats as late as 1975, their continued strength was largely in rural areas and smaller cities. In the largest cities they suffered dramatic decreases in their share of the popular vote after 1959, with the result that by the early 1970s the executive office of all of the largest cities in Japan was controlled by progressive candidates. In 1975 there were only seven "designated cities" in Japan; Tokyo, Yokohama, Nagoya, Kyoto, Osaka, Kobe, and Kitakyushu. Of these only economically declining Kitakyushu was governed by a conservative mayor in 1975 (MacDougall 1980: 84).

For example, in the local government elections of 1963 both Yokohama and Kyoto elected reform city governments, and in 1964 a National Conference of Progressive Mayors was formed. In the 1967 local government elections many progressive mayors were elected, both in the central areas of major cities and in rural areas. Perhaps even more threatening for the LDP was the fact that progressive candidates won the governorships of key prefectures as well, most notably of Tokyo by Minobe Ryokichi in 1967. In the Tokyo Metropolitan Area (TMA) at the peak of progressive political power in 1975, of the four prefectures only Chiba, the most rural, still had a conservative administration. Tokyo, Kanagawa and Saitama were all run by progressives. One of the key reasons for progressive electoral success was that the reform governments put the concerns of citizens' movements about city planning and control of development high on their agenda (Ishida 1987: 305). As Samuels (1983: 190) puts it, "The left came to power by convincing enough of the electorate that the conservative central government and their allies in the localities were responsible for the pollution, the lack of social programs, and the support of business interests at the expense of residents."

Krauss and Simcock (1980: 196) argue that even more significant than the development of citizens' movements in semi-rural areas to oppose industrial developments such as Mishima-Numazu was the "veritable explosion of protest in urban and suburban areas" against industrial plants and highway interchanges, and for governments to provide essential services such as sewers, parks and sidewalks. The consensus on growth had truly ended and a new, more complex period began in which sharply differing ideas of the future of urban areas and of the country were in competition. The progressive candidates for local government office made improving the urban environment through better urban planning, more sensitivity to local people's needs and investment in social overhead capital a central part of their programme.

It is widely agreed that it was in response to these pressures that the LDP passed new city planning legislation in 1968. For example, Calder (1988: 405) notes that it was just before the July 1968 Upper House elections that the LDP announced an Urban Policy Outline and passed the new City Planning Law. He argues that although the law had been in preparation for many years, it was finally passed as a result of the fear by LDP legislators that the increasing political opposition represented by the citizens' movements would have electoral impacts at the national level. Ishida (1987: 303) also, in his authoritative history of Japanese planning attributes the development of the new planning legislation of 1968 to two main factors: first, the intensification of city problems and chaotic land use caused by the high economic growth policy, and second, the upsurge of citizens' movements and progressive local governments.

The New City Planning Law of 1968 generated high hopes that local governments would finally have the tools to control land development and improve the environmental and amenity standards of residential areas. The environmental catastrophes of the 1960s and the reluctance of those in power to acknowledge the severity of the problems until forced to do so had mobilised local groups to fight for local interests. Local mobilisation was particularly intense over environmental issues, and the conception of these was broad enough to include local urban amenity and planning issues.

The 1968 planning system

This section outlines the main elements of the new planning system that was created as a result of the 1968 New City Planning Law (*Shin Toshi Keikaku Hō*). It is worth describing the system in some detail, as this was the first full-scale revision of the law since it was first passed in 1919, and although various changes and additions have been made since, the 1968 law continues to form the basic city planning system. It was primarily directed at controlling the rampant urban sprawl that had been identified as the key urban problem during the 1960s. The main target was therefore the urban fringe areas that were experiencing rapid population growth as a result of the interlinked processes of metropolitanisation and suburbanisation. The two key measures of the new system, *Senbiki* and Development Control, were both designed to control the process of conversion of land from agricultural to urban uses. It was understood that the critical requirement for the development of the urban fringe was to control new development so as to ensure that roads and sewers, parks and schools were built in advance of, or in tandem with development of land from rural to urban use. Other laws, such as the Urban Redevelopment Law (*Toshi Saikaihatsu Hō*) passed in 1969 were designed to allow the improvement of already built up areas. One further important change was the major revision to the Building Standards Law in 1970 which introduced the detailed regulations backing the new zoning system of the 1968 law.

There were five main changes introduced in the legislation. First was the delegation of responsibility for urban planning to prefectural and municipal governments. The second was the plan to divide City Planning Areas (CPAs) into two zones, the Urbanisation Promotion Area (UPA) where planned urbanisation was to be promoted, and the Urbanisation Control Area (UCA) where urbanisation was to be restricted. This system quickly became known as "*Senbiki*", literally "drawing the line" between the two areas. The third new element introduced in the 1968 law was the "development permission" system. This was based on the earlier Subdivision Project Control Law (*Takuchi Zōsei Jigyō Hō*) of 1964, which gave planners stronger authority to set standards for public facilities that would be a requirement for approval of development projects. It also was designed to regulate development in UCAs. The fourth change was the introduction of measures to allow public participation in urban planning, and the fifth was the introduction of a more sophisticated zoning system with an increase from four to eight zones. Each of these five aspects are discussed in greater detail below.

There were understandably high hopes that the new system would allow a measure of control over the development of new urban areas. At the same time that reformist local governments were being elected in many areas of the country, the central government had conceded them powers to carry out urban planning and development control to shape patterns of growth. For the first time there was a prospect of effective urban planning through control over development. It was expected that the new system would allow local governments and planners to catch up with infrastructure backlogs, control the location and quality of new development, and provide the better quality urban environment that everyone agreed was needed. As Ishida (1987: 297) argued, the experience of the 1960s had resulted in the development of a general consensus in support of the need for increased planning and stricter controls over development.

Delegation of planning powers

Under the 1919 Act, the MoC had held all city planning powers for the entire country. Under the 1968 Act, the responsibility to prepare, approve and implement plans was delegated to prefectural and municipal governments. It is perhaps surprising that the central government was willing to give up such powers, especially during a period when local governments were increasingly controlled by progressive parties. If we recall, however, that local planning and environment issues were becoming highly controversial, generating widespread and intense protest and local opposition, handing these problems to the newly elected progressive local governments seems perfectly rational. It is also important to note that although from this point local governments would take the heat for planning problems and conflicts, their freedom to develop independent policies was rather limited in practice. There are a number of reasons why this was so, which can only be touched on briefly here. The key means for central government's continued dominance were through legal controls, financial controls and personnel transfers.

The first aspect of legal control was the fact that even though planning activities were delegated to local governments, the "agency delegated functions" (*Kikan-Inin-Jimu*) system continued in force. Even after the 1968 law was implemented, therefore, central government not only had the power to legislate the rules and goals which local governments had to follow, but could also exercise direct top-down control when desired. Further, local governments still had no legal power to enforce stronger codes than established by central government ministries. This restriction came to seem more onerous in the 1970s, when many local governments that had come to power promising to be more proactive about local urban and environmental issues and found their options severely constrained. Various creative ways around these restrictions have been developed, particularly since the 1980s, as described in Chapters 8 and 9, but there is little doubt that they have seriously limited the policy options of local governments.

Central government also has considerable power over local government policy and programmes through financial controls. The most important element of financial control is due to the fact that 70 per cent of local government income consists of transfers from central government, most of which are for the non-discretionary programmes local governments must deliver. Local governments have long complained about the underfunding of central government mandated programmes, which is commonly referred to as the problem of "excess burdens" without adequate compensation. Shindo (1984: 119) suggests that "the financial situation of local government is deeply integrated with the financial and monetary policies of the national government. The prefectural governments are under the control of the national government, while they in turn act as controlling organs, with respect to local allocation tax grants, national treasury disbursements, and local bonds, to the municipal governments." Only some 30 per cent of local government revenue comes from locally raised taxes, giving rise to the common description of local governments as being "30 per cent autonomous". While this is higher, for example, than in Britain, where locally raised taxes account for less than 20 per cent of local revenue, the lack of autonomy is nonetheless keenly felt.

Another important means of central government control over city planning, is through personnel transfers from central ministries to local government departments. Samuels (1983: 47–55) has provided a useful description of the various forms these personnel "loans" (*shukko*) take. In the area of city planning this has meant that often key staff, particularly at higher ranks, of prefectural government city planning departments are on loan from the MoC. According to Woodall (1996: 63), MoC bureaucrats typically spend between two and four years attached to prefectural or municipal governments as departmental or section chiefs. This is thought especially important when new policies are being put in place. So for example, when the initial Senbiki was carried out in Saitama, many of those involved were the same MoC officials who had participated in drafting the law (Capital Region Comprehensive Planning Institute 1987: 6–7). Of course, as these MoC officials are highly skilled, and have strong connections to the centre, they are welcomed by local governments. Thus the MoC is able to exercise substantial control over local planning at several stages of the planning process.

Apart from these usually temporary personnel transfers, however, other means of transfer of personnel from central to local governments are pervasive and effective in solidifying the influence of central government ministries over local governments. For example, Chalmers Johnson (1995: 221) has recently noted that well over 50 per cent of prefectural governors are former central government officials, and virtually all deputy governors, heads of general affairs bureaux and financial section chiefs in provincial administrations come from the Ministry of Home Affairs (*Jichisho*).

Thus, while the delegation of planning powers was real, and certainly a crucial step in the development of a more effective city planning system, it should not be thought that suddenly local governments had the freedom or finances to follow their own course in planning matters. Rather, while they had been given duties and responsibilities, power over overall strategy and policy as well as implementation continued to reside in central government.

Senbiki: "drawing the line" between town and country

The Senbiki system was the centrepiece of the 1968 planning system and was designed to be the primary planning tool for controlling patterns of urban growth. The intention was to halt the scatter of new residential development outside urban areas by dividing urban fringe areas into two zones, the UPA (*Shigaikakuiki*), where new development would be encouraged, and the UCA (*Shigaikachōseikuiki*), where it would be restricted. It was hoped that by thus concentrating new development in the UPA, a more efficient provision of municipal infrastructure such as roads and sewers could be achieved, at the same time as protecting farming and green areas in the UCA and preventing the disorderly sprawl development that had been identified as one of the chief urban problems during the 1960s.

The UPA was to include existing urban areas, and areas where planned urbanisation would be carried out within the next ten years. Because the UPA was intended to be fully built up within a decade, a mechanism was established to allow for reviews every five years to allow expansion of the zone thus creating a rolling supply of new development land. The UCA therefore consisted both of areas which should not be developed at all, and areas which would be held in reserve for future development when appropriate. The UCA is thus not like greenbelts in the UK which are intended to remain permanently undeveloped.

It is worth noting that the original draft bill of the Consulting Committee on Urban Land presented in March 1967 included four designated zones instead of two. They were 1) existing built up areas and areas immediately adjacent; 2) those areas where planned urbanisation is to be carried out within 10 years; 3) areas where there might be a possibility of development in future but where development should be restricted for the time being; and 4) long-term preservation areas for agriculture, forest, areas of natural beauty, etc. In the process of turning the draft into the 1968 law, however, the first and second areas were amalgamated as UPA and the third and fourth areas became UCA, apparently both because of anticipated difficulties in carrying out the zoning, and because of political bargaining within the government by relevant ministries (Hebbert and Nakai 1988b: 44). It is widely agreed that this ambiguous character of the UCAs, including both long-term preservation areas and a reserve of development land, was one of the most important causes of the serious practical problems of implementation of the system (Hebbert and Nakai 1988b: 44; Ishida 1987: 309).

It should be noted that Senbiki is only applied to CPAs, not to the whole country, and that not all CPAs have yet been divided. Although it was intended that they would eventually be divided into UPA and UCA, the priority in establishing the system was the three metropolitan areas, cities with a population of more than 100,000, and areas targeted for growth such as New Industrial Cities. Senbiki has been applied primarily in the fast-growing metropolitan areas and larger cities.

Because Senbiki was intended as a strategic planning tool, it had to be carried out at a scale larger than the individual municipality. Therefore prefectural governments were given the responsibility for designating the two areas, drawing the line between them, monitoring development and carrying out reviews each five years. While the initial Senbiki was carried out directly by prefectural governments, since then most of the work has commonly been delegated to municipal governments, while prefectural governments retained ultimate responsibility.

The focus of the Senbiki system on the urban fringe is clear as it is primarily a tool to divide areas designated for development from areas in which development would be restricted. Because land within the UCA could be rezoned in future reviews to provide more UPA development land as the existing UPA became fully built up, the intended effect on the process of urban growth was to allow staged development in manageable tranches, rather than allow the continuation of scattered development over the whole of the urban hinterland. In this way local governments could focus their development and planning efforts on the undeveloped part of the UPA, where, in the words of the MoC (Japan Ministry of Construction 1991b: 39), "Urbanisation must be systematically and preferentially made within ten years."

Local governments were to actively promote planned development in the unbuilt part of the UPA through LR projects and by requiring private developers to provide their share of infrastructure through the development permission system. LR was thus the main positive planning tool, while development permission would provide the primary regulatory tool within the UPA. According to the MoC (Japan Ministry of Construction 1991b: 40): "UPA should not expand over a large area. It should be made in a compact manner, with the area undergoing or scheduled for the Land Readjustment projects, urban development projects and other planned development of large-scale [sic] as the core in the case of new urban area; thereby ensuring efficient public investment, and the achievement of systematic urban development."

Development permission

The development permission system was an important counterpart to the Senbiki system in that it was the main regulatory tool to ensure that private development in the UPA was carried out in a planned and orderly manner. For the first time city planners had the legal authority to withhold permission for land development projects unless certain conditions were met. Before this local governments had no legal authority to refuse developments that complied with zoning and building standards regulations, no matter how large they were. The new system allowed planners to require that infrastructure facilities be provided as a condition of granting permission to develop land. In this context, the two key elements were land for roads and contributions to sewer systems. Previously landowners could subdivide, sell, or build on land with no requirement to contribute to these network services, an important and hard to remedy cause of substandard development. This was a big step; as the MoC (Japan Ministry of

Construction 1991b: 16) claims, "Of all the systems in the history of Japanese city planning, it is the development permission system that was epoch-making."

Land development was curiously defined as "changes in land demarcation and configuration mainly for the construction of buildings or for the construction of golf courses, concrete plants and other specific structures" (Japan Ministry of Construction 1991b: 32). Those intending to develop land within the UPA had to obtain permission from the prefectural governor (or from the mayor in designated cities). The development permit system thus controls land development activities, especially changes of use from agricultural to urban uses, in cases where buildings are to be built. Unfortunately, this left out a broad range of land development activities and land uses, which local governments were unable to control with the development permit system. For example, parking lots, scrap metal yards, gravel and building materials processing facilities and industrial waste-processing facilities all escaped regulation in this way. As no building was needed, they were not "changes in land demarcation and configuration for the construction of buildings or other specific structures" and did not require a development permit. The consequences of this loophole are discussed further in Chapters 8 and 9.

In theory, this system could have allowed planners to make land development conditional on the developer providing infrastructure or compensating the local government for additional burdens on local services, similar to subdivision control in the US. And in fact, municipal governments were able to some degree to achieve this through development permissions, and through local "development manuals" (*kaihatsu shidō yōkō*). These manuals were local non-statutory codes indicating how much developers would have to contribute to local roads, parks and school facilities, etc, in order to gain a development permit, and were thus similar to the "Supplementary Planning Guidance" notes published by some British local governments. Municipalities were able to use their bargaining power (primarily their control over water supply and sewer connections) to gain local benefits from development, and their effectiveness is witnessed by the efforts of the central government during the deregulations of the Nakasone era in the 1980s to restrict their use (Hebbert and Nakai 1988a).

From the beginning, however, there were significant exemptions to the development permission system, limiting its effectiveness. Development permission applies to both UPA and UCA, though with considerable differences. In the UPA the main exemption relates to the size of development, with any development of less than 0.1 hectares (1,000 square metres) being exempt, while in CPA areas which have not been divided into UPA and UCA the threshold is 0.3 hectares. As discussed in Chapter 7, this exemption was significant because it encouraged large numbers of small developments which resulted in continued sprawl development.

In both the UPA and UCA all developments by central and local governments and by public developers such as the Japan Housing and Urban Development Corporation (JHUDC) are exempt from the requirement to obtain development permission, because state-sponsored projects are likely to both conform to official plans and provide their share of infrastructure. Therefore this exemption is not very significant in the UPA, where public projects help to ensure systematic development. However, the exemption has been significant in the UCA, which, as Hebbert (1994: 83) has shown, has served as a reserve of relatively cheaper land for public projects such as roads, schools, public housing and industrial parks. He argues that of all the loopholes to development in the UCA, such public projects probably do most to undermine its non-urban character.

It was originally intended that almost all development would be prohibited in the UCA, with permission only granted in "exceptional" cases. However, exceptions originally included large developments of more than 20 hectares which would not interfere with planned urbanisation in the CPA (including LR projects), housing for relatives of farmers, and other developments not expected to encourage urbanisation in the area such as churches and petrol stations. The complete, and long, list of the original exceptions and those resulting from deregulation are given in Hebbert and Nakai (1988b: 390).

Hebbert and Nakai (1988b: 31) have also shown that the development permission system strongly encourages smaller developments, both because of the exemption for developments under 1 hectare, and because of the progressively higher standard of infrastructure for larger developments. The larger the development, the greater the proportion of land that must be devoted to public use, and therefore the smaller the proportion that can be sold and the less profitable the development.

The main problem with the development permission system in the UPA, however, was that only a relatively small part of the total area was developed in this way. While a considerable area was developed with development permits within the UPA in Saitama, it only amounted to 7.5 per cent of the new Densely Inhabited District (DID) area in Saitama between 1965 and 1985. A much larger area was developed as LR projects, amounting to 23.02 per cent of the new DID area. If we include public housing projects, a total of 34.06 per cent of the new DID was developed "systematically" during the two decades (Sorensen 2000b: 282; Saitama ken 1992: Table E-1). The rest either remained undeveloped, or developed as unplanned sprawl.

Public participation

Although the provisions for public participation were supposed to be an important part of the new planning legislation, they seem to have been quite limited in practice and were more a statutory requirement to *inform* than inviting real public participation in planning decisions. For example, Ishida notes that while the citizens' movements mobilised around self-government slogans such as "the real leaders of community building are the local people" ("*Machizukuri no shuninkō wa jumin da*"), a MoC spokesman described the reason for implementing the citizens' participation regulations as, "We don't want them to complain they didn't know about it" (Ishida 1987: 303) indicating that there were differences of opinion as to what "public participation" should mean in practice. In fact, the statutory public participation measures were little more than a requirement to display plans in a public manner, and hold public hearings for local people to express their opinion. There was no requirement for such opinions to be listened to. Public participation in city planning decision-making is not simple, and many such attempts throughout the world have been criticised as failing to provide any meaningful degree of participation in the process. In practice, public participation often allows for little influence by the public on planning decisions, and attempts merely to provide information, or the registering of complaints. In this regard the Japanese system of 1968 was not much better or worse than most other contemporary participation efforts.

At the same time it should be noted that the degree of public participation has been highly variable between different municipalities and administrations. For example, public participation and consultation was avowed as an important principle of some progressive governments, perhaps best exemplified by former Tokyo governor Minobe's famous "bridge philosophy" that he would never build a bridge if a single resident were opposed, stressing that "democracy was a time consuming, but necessary process" (Samuels, 1983: 213, also see McKean 1981: 102–8). Ishida (1987: 318) also mentions several positive examples of citizen participation in the local plan-making process in Tokyo wards. Not all local governments were this committed to the principle, however, and it seems that there was a significant degree of variation in practice, depending on the priorities of the local government and the degree of mobilisation of citizens' groups.

It is also important to distinguish between formal and informal participation in planning. For example, Shida reviews the American and Japanese provisions for citizen participation and notes that in comparison to the US, "the level of citizen participation in city planning in Japan is very limited indeed" (Shida 1990: 17) because final decision-making authority rests with prefectural governors or the Minister of Construction. Hebbert and Nakai (1988b) come to a broadly similar conclusion in their description of public participation in the Senbiki process. They show that the structure of participation, restricted to residents directly affected, and with no obligation for their opinions to be taken into consideration results in little interest in public hearings, with many cancelled because nobody attended. They also note however, that an important reason for this lack of interest may be that there are more effective ways of participating in the prior consultations and negotiation that take place before the formal proposal is put forward. Thus the really significant arena for "public participation" in Japan is the process of consultations, persuasion and recruitment of supporters before plans are formally submitted.

In this process however, not all local residents are equal. In practice, the definition of stakeholders is quite restrictive. The real consultations and *nemawashi* (literally "root binding" meaning preparing the ground through extensive discussion with those concerned) takes place with those who own land or property, with whom a degree of public participation takes places that is probably equalled in few other systems. In LR and redevelopment (*Saikaihatsu*) projects the formal agreement of all or a two-thirds majority of landowners is required by law. In practice, unanimous consent is the aim, as even lone objectors can cause real difficulties during project implementation. Therefore authorities involved in trying to initiate such projects are forced to discuss and negotiate with landowners in order to convince them to consent to the project. Landowners, and especially the larger landowners, then have a high level of participation backed by what is almost a veto power, but this level of direct involvement is not common among other residents (Sorensen 1998).

Zoning and building standards control

As noted above, before 1968 Japan's zoning system allowed differentiation between only four land use zones; industrial, light industrial, commercial and residential. The introduction of a new zoning system with eight different use zones and numerous discretionary special zones allowed much more detailed planning. Apart from specifying land uses, the use zones detail permitted building heights, floor area ratios (FAR), and coverage ratios of individual sites. With the possible exception of Category I

Table 6.2 Japanese land use zoning system of 1968

---

1. *Category I Exclusive Residential zone*: restricted to low-rise dwellings only (including detached houses, multiple unit dwellings, dormitories, and boarding houses), almost all other uses are prohibited. However, combined uses, such as residences with an office or shop included, are allowed if under a certain scale, and uses not seen to conflict with a residential area, such as nursery schools, primary schools, and junior and senior high schools, libraries and museums, shrines temples and churches, homes for the aged, and police boxes, etc, are permitted.

2. *Category II Exclusive Residential zone*: same as the above, except that it is designated for medium- and high-rise residential development. Additional permitted uses include universities and colleges, hospitals, retail outlets (including department stores) and restaurants, office buildings and combined uses larger than the "certain size" mentioned in #1 above.

3. *Residential areas*: allow all of the above and include further permitted uses such as hotels and motels, bowling alleys and swimming pools, pachinko parlours and shooting galleries, driving schools, bakeries, tofu makers and other small food plants, non-noxious industrial plants with a floor area less than $50\,m^2$, and facilities for storing or processing hazardous materials such as explosives, oils and gases in very small amounts.

4. *Neighbourhood Commercial districts*: allow all the above, plus warehouses with a floor area over $50\,m^2$, and non-noxious industrial plants with a floor area less than $150\,m^2$.

5. *Commercial districts*: allow all of the above, plus theatres, movie theatres, variety halls and game houses, restaurants, bars, cabarets, dance halls and massage parlours.

6. *Light Industrial districts*: allow all uses except noxious and hazardous industries, and slaughterhouses, sewage plants, etc.

7. *Industrial districts*: allow all uses except schools, universities, hospitals, hotels and motels, and theatres, restaurants, bars, etc.

8. *Exclusive Industrial districts*: exclude all but industrial uses, and shrines, temples and churches, old peoples homes, and police boxes, etc.

Source: MoC (1991: I–45, 46 and II–15, 16).

Exclusive Residential zones, and Exclusive Industrial zones, the new use zones were structured to allow a broad mixture of uses, as shown in Table 6.2.

It is clear from the zones outlined in Table 6.2 that a wide variety of uses are allowed in all but zones 1 and 8. In fact only those two zones have much effect in restricting land uses. In all the others a high degree of intermixture of different uses is common, and it is virtually impossible to distinguish between the different zones on the ground. Zoning in Japan is thus quite unlike that common in North America, where zones are commonly used in a highly restrictive way to separate different types of land use.

The total national area of each use zone as of 31 March 1975, after the first round of zoning had been completed, is given in Table 6.3 which shows that the three residential zones account for almost 70 per cent of the zoned area, and less than a third of this residential area is Category I residential. The rest of the residential zone permits a much higher mixture of uses than is common in, for example, most US residential areas.

Another important point that is not evident from the written description of zoning policies is that in many Japanese urban areas, especially older ones, the zones are often small, and it is not unusual for residential zones to be physically intermixed with commercial and industrial districts. Also, as the new zoning was only implemented in 1971, many existing uses in already built up areas were "grandfathered", or allowed to continue as exceptional

Table 6.3 Status of land use zoning, 31 March 1975

	Area (hectares)	*% of zoned area*
Total zoned area	1,481,454.0	100
Category I Exclusive Residential	304,334.5	20.5
Category II Exclusive Residential	272,500.3	18.4
Residential	453,795.0	30.6
Neighbourhood Commercial	44,135.5	3.0
Commercial	61,342.0	4.1
Light Industrial	150,068.7	10.2
Industrial	84,272.6	5.7
Exclusive Industrial	111,005.4	7.5

Source: Japan Ministry of Construction (1975: 2).

cases. The result has been high degrees of intermixture of different uses, to the extent that it is quite difficult to perceive that any zoning regime has been in effect.

Several Japanese commentators have pointed out the positive consequences of the high degrees of mixed use in Japanese cities. The economic and cultural vitality of Japanese cities and particularly the safety and continuing liveliness of central city areas, for example, has been favourably contrasted with American cities (Jinnai 1994; Watanabe 1985: 272–6). Japanese urban areas have also avoided the high degree of residential segregation that is prevalent in the US, with most residential areas including residents with a wide range of incomes (Fujita and Hill 1997). Criticism of the rigid separation of uses in North America is also common, particularly with the emergence of the "new urbanism" of the 1990s which advocates neighbourhood design that permits walking or bicycling to shops and most services and promotes lively urban areas (Calthorpe 1993; Downs 1994; Jacobs 1961). For those who enjoy the vitality and urbanity of Japanese cities, including the present author, it is precisely these aspects of Japanese urbanism that are most valued, and it is hard to escape the conclusion that a more rigid, exclusionary zoning system such as that practised in many North American cities would have undermined these qualities. In fact, Japanese central city areas, with their high levels of mixed use, high residential densities, and high levels of public transport usage may be considered something of a model of sustainable urbanisation, as suggested by Shelton (1999). It thus seems reasonable to argue that there have been some very positive consequences of Japan's radically inclusive approach to land use zoning, as does Hohn (2000: 548): "The fragmentation of urban space in Japan has thus primarily positive connotations, for this guarantees variety, liveliness, colour, variability and contrast with simultaneous integration in a common network which makes for cohesion. The key to success lies in the inclusive philosophy of flexible direction, in the general openness of town planning to new ideas and stimuli."

This is only one side of the picture, however. The positive aspects of the inclusive zoning regime are found primarily in the central city areas where the mixture of commercial, employment and residential uses positively reinforce each other. It is also these same central city areas that have received repeated planning interventions since the Meiji period, with incremental improvements to road systems, the provision of sidewalks, building of subways, installation of sewer and water supply systems, etc. A much more problematic aspect of the weak zoning system has been the consistent willingness to allow the building of housing in heavy industrial areas. While this may have permitted some workers a convenient walk to work, it also greatly contributed to the serious health problems associated with industrial pollution that became widespread during the 1960s. Similarly, on the urban fringe lax controls over land use have created many serious problems. In particular, many of the worst bad neighbours such as industrial waste-processors and incinerators, car-wrecking yards, and dusty gravel crushers locate on the urban fringe where land is cheaper. While it is true that "clean" high-tech employment may be compatible with residential and commercial uses in the central city, many of the rather low-tech, space-intensive functions that are drawn to the urban fringe are still highly problematic when intermixed with residential uses.

Further, with the spectacular inflation of land prices of the later 1980s, others have noted that the openness of the zoning system encouraged the spread of price inflation from commercial areas to residential areas. It was argued that the price rises caused by the speculative boom of office building was able to spread to residential areas because developers could realistically expect that residential sites could be rezoned and redeveloped to office use. It was also argued that a stronger zoning system could have substantially prevented the spread of price inflation beyond commercial areas (Hayakawa and Hirayama 1991: 151–64).

In summary, the new planning system introduced in 1969 provided a much expanded range of tools for planners to tackle the urban planning problems that had emerged as a by-product of the period of rapid economic growth. The main focus of the new system was the rapidly growing suburban fringes of the metropolitan areas where urban and industrial growth was concentrated, although several of the new measures were important more generally such as the new zoning system, and the devolution of planning powers. At the same time there were clear limitations to the new system, and significant powers were retained by the central government. The real test was to come with the implementation of the system in the 1970s.

7 Implementing the new city planning system

> The rapid growth that began in the last half of the 1950s brought about an excessive concentration of population and industry along the Pacific coast, transforming Japan into a unique society of high population density. While the big cities suffer from the pains and irritations of overcrowding, rural areas suffer from the exodus of youth and the resultant loss of vital energy for growth. Rapid urbanisation has bred increasing numbers of people who have never known the joys of rural life, chasing rabbits in mountains, fishing for crucians in streams, whose only home is a tiny apartment in some huge city. With such a situation, how can we pass on to future generations the qualities and traditions of the Japanese people?
>
> (Tanaka 1972: iii)

The beginning of the 1970s was a time of great optimism about urban planning in Japan. A new city planning system had just been initiated, local governments had apparently finally been given both the tools and the legal authority and responsibility for urban planning, and the first plans were being developed and adopted. The implementation of the new system was accompanied by great expectations on the part of local governments and planners that they would now be able to catch up with infrastructure lags, control the location and quality of new development, and generally provide the better quality urban environment that everyone agreed was needed. Further, in the early 1970s the progressive local governments, which had placed the improvement of the urban environment and respect for citizen needs at the top of their political agenda, were still growing in strength and electoral success. In April 1971 Minobe Ryokichi, the progressive governor of Tokyo, was re-elected with two-thirds of the vote, while the LDP incumbent governor of Osaka lost to progressive challenger Kuroda Ryoichi. This meant that the political, economic and cultural "capitals" of Japan, Tokyo, Osaka, and Kyoto prefectures were all governed by socialist/communist-supported governors. Progressive governors were also elected in Okinawa, Saitama and Okayama prefectures in 1972. As well, most of the other large cities in Japan had progressive mayors by 1975, including Nagoya, Yokohama, Kyoto, and Kobe (MacDougall 1980). In the areas of urban planning and social welfare services local governments were significantly expanding their expenditures, and expectations were high that a new era of urban planning for improved local quality of life had begun.

The passage and implementation of the 1968 City Planning Law, 1969 Urban Redevelopment Law, and the 1970 Building Standards Law were only one part of the extensive programme of new legislative initiatives for environmental management of the early 1970s. Other important measures were initiated during the "Pollution Diet" of 1970 in which no less than 14 laws related to controlling environmental pollution were passed or revised, including one that established a new ministry, the Environment Agency, to monitor and implement the new environmental laws. In 1974 the new National Land Agency (NLA) was established and legislation passed to create a new national land planning system and to unify and coordinate the various existing agencies and plans for metropolitan areas and the regions.

By the end of the 1970s, however, it was clear that there were serious problems with the new planning system. Critically, it had failed to halt the worst problems of urban sprawl, and had been weakened both as a result of the initial implementation and by subsequent policy revisions. Sprawl was continuing and even accelerating in the metropolitan regions and a major revision to both the City Planning Law and Building Standards Laws was being prepared to introduce the new District Planning system, designed to allow more detailed planning control over urban areas.

This chapter reviews this tumultuous period of new planning initiatives of the 1970s. The first section briefly reviews the changing economic context of the early 1970s and the major "shocks" – as they are invariably termed – of changing exchange rates and soaring oil prices that led to the end of rapid growth, and describes the introduction of new measures for pollution control passed in 1970. The second section looks at the implementation of the new city planning system during the early 1970s, and the main problems encountered. The third section describes the major new initiatives in national land planning passed in 1974, and the creation of the NLA. A final section reviews the main elements of urban change of the 1970s.

The changing context of the early 1970s

As discussed in the previous chapter, one of the most important products of the decades of rapid economic growth was environmental crisis and a rising tide of citizen activism to fight the adverse effects of pollution and uncontrolled urban industrial growth. The opposition parties took advantage of these widespread concerns and gained the leadership of most of the major cities in the country by blaming the crisis on the alliance of big business and the LDP, and promising to shift priorities from industrial development to social services, environmental improvement and better urban planning. Even at the level of national politics, the LDP had seen its share of the vote decline steadily throughout the 1960s, and was in real danger of losing its majority by the end of the decade.

In the last chapter it was argued that the new city planning system of 1968 was passed in response to these changing political conditions; but the crisis did not stop there. Public concern over worsening pollution problems continued to mount, and the peak of citizen mobilisation actually came in the early 1970s, when hundreds of groups were active (McKean 1981). A turning point in policy approaches to pollution seems to have come in July of 1970 when serious photochemical smog incidents in Tokyo sickened over 8,000 (McKean 1981: 117). In one of the best examples of the responsiveness of the LDP to electoral pressure, and the effectiveness of the Japanese bureaucracy in drafting legislation, in late 1970 the so-called Pollution Diet passed or amended no less than 14 laws to control environmental pollution, and the next year another bill was passed establishing the Environment Agency under the Prime Minister's Office to monitor and co-ordinate environmental improvement efforts. The new pollution control regime created what were at the time the strictest environmental pollution standards in the world. One law set up a system whereby polluters were forced to pay for the costs of pollution control measures, and another enacted strict penalties for human health injuries caused by pollution emissions, and allowed the use of epidemiological evidence to establish responsibility for health damage (Barret and Therivel 1991: 39).

Another important factor in the changing attitudes of government and business towards pollution issues in the early 1970s was the victory by the plaintiffs in all four major pollution damage lawsuits. These were the mercury-poisoning disease case of Minamata in Kyushu, the "*itai itai*" (literally "it hurts it hurts") disease of cadmium poisoning, the Yokkaichi case of respiratory diseases caused by air pollution, and the Niigata Minamata disease case. These cases all awarded significant damages to the victims of pollution, but more importantly they established clear legal precedents about the responsibility of polluting companies for any health damage, and about the standards of proof required to prove health damage was due to pollution. The new legal framework for pollution control was highly successful, initiating a period of enormous private investment in pollution control and prevention measures, with the share of investment in these measures as a proportion of total investment in plant and equipment increasing from 3 per cent in 1965 to 18.6 per cent in 1975 (Tsuru 1993: 137), a rate far higher than in any of the other developed countries. Combined with the effects of the hike in oil prices discussed below and the resulting efforts at energy conservation, as well as slower rates of economic growth, over the next decade pollution emissions fell dramatically. Japan gained a well-deserved reputation for having successfully dealt with its industrial pollution problems at the same time as maintaining a level of economic growth that was significantly higher than the other developed countries.

The "shocks" of the early 1970s

The other major change of the early 1970s was a result of a series of "shocks" (*shokku*) which jolted Japanese society, forcing a major reconsideration of Japan's place in the world and of its future economic outlook. There were two "Nixon shocks". The first was his sudden opening of diplomatic relations with China in July 1971 without advance warning to Japan, which significantly altered the political and strategic landscape in East Asia, leaving Japan feeling isolated and having to scramble to catch up to the changing situation. The second came in August 1971 with the abrupt and unilateral decision by the US to abandon the post-war system of fixed exchange rates between the US dollar and other currencies, as well as the dollar's fixed exchange rate with gold. This change applied to other currencies as well as the yen, but it is generally agreed that it was designed primarily to address what was felt to be the unrealistically low value of the yen. During the occupation the yen had been pegged at 360 to the dollar in order to help encourage the rebuilding of the Japanese economy, in what Tsuru (1993: 120) suggests was akin to giving a favourable handicap to a convalescent golfer. By the early 1970s the Americans believed such treatment was no longer warranted, and that the low yen was an important factor behind the growing Japanese trade surplus with the US. The third major "shock" was the sudden rise in oil prices engineered by the

Organisation of Petroleum Exporting Countries (OPEC) in 1973. Japan, almost wholly dependent on imported oil for its energy supplies, was hard hit, particularly as a major engine of growth had been the chemical industries whose basic raw material was oil. The combination of these shocks not only contributed to the ending of rapid growth, but also strongly reinforced the traditional Japanese sense of insecurity about its dependence on imported raw materials and foreign markets for its economic health.

While there is no doubt that the rise in the yen against the dollar and particularly the dramatic rise in oil prices played a large part in bringing rapid growth to an end, it is unlikely that growth of over 10 per cent per year could have continued much longer. Quite apart from the increasing environmental problems, and increasing opposition of the Japanese people to the government's single-minded focus on industrial promotion policies, many of the factors contributing to rapid economic growth in the previous decades were unlikely to contribute greatly to further growth. Most of the reserve of workers who could migrate to the metropolitan areas had already done so, the Japanese economy had already largely incorporated the available new technologies and benefited from their productivity gains, and the most convenient shorelines near the metropolitan areas had largely been filled in and replaced with industrial complexes. Finally, the continuation of rapid growth along the lines of that of the 1960s would also have required unbelievable increases in raw materials and energy consumption. The position was after all much different from that in 1960, when Japan had just begun the process of rapid growth and was still a relatively small economy. By 1970 Japan was one of the largest economies in the capitalist world, behind only the US after surpassing West Germany in 1969, making it the second largest economy in the world if we exclude the Soviet Union, which formally at least had a GDP larger than Japan (Calder 1988: 103). To continue rates of economic growth of between 8.5 and 10 per cent per year, Japanese economic planners confidently projected a tripling in primary energy requirements by 1985, including a major commitment to the building of nuclear power plants. It was also predicted that growth on this scale would require a corresponding increase in new factory sites, of which some 45 per cent was to be provided by land reclamation of coastal waters. Thus, while in the whole period up until 1969 a total of 27,184 hectares had been reclaimed, economic planners confidently published a target of 43,200 hectares of new landfill during the period 1971–75 (Tsuru 1993: 103). In a similar vein Prime Minister Tanaka's national plan, discussed below, which was premised on spreading the fruits of growth around the country by building new transport links, confidently predicted that 20 per cent of the level land in Japan would be needed to accommodate new expressways. The fact that prior plans had been consistently outperformed made it seem perfectly reasonable to project continuing economic growth at these rates.

In any case, the near tripling of oil prices in 1973 quickly translated into recession in 1974, when Japan saw a drop in GDP for the first time since the beginning of the 1950s. The very high dependence on imported oil, most of it from the Middle East, meant that the Japanese economy was more strongly affected than most by the price rise. In the slightly longer run, however, energy conservation efforts, rationalisation of production processes, and the still strong international competitiveness of Japanese industry meant that the Japanese economy was able to recover from the crisis faster than most, albeit at a lower growth rate than before, averaging about 5 per cent growth in GDP over the next period.

The "Building a New Japan" boom

A notable casualty of the oil crisis-induced inflation and recession was Prime Minister Tanaka's plan to "Build a New Japan". Tanaka had become prime minister in 1972 promising to implement ambitious plans to restructure the patterns of industrial distribution in Japan, aiding the dispersal of industry throughout the country by pouring vast sums into building new national networks of Shinkansen lines, expressways and bridges linking the major islands. This plan was designed to solve at one stroke the twin problems of

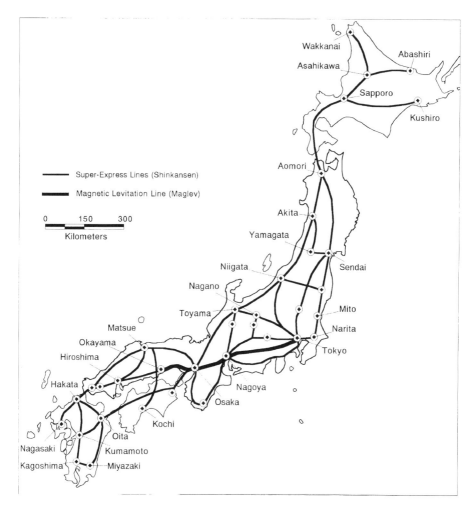

Figure 7.1 Tanaka's plans for new Shinkansen and expressways. An important stimulus for Japan's second bout of national land price inflation of 1972–3 was the publication of Prime Minister Tanaka's "Building a New Japan" plans. The main policy was to be the building of a comprehensive network of Shinkansen lines, and 6,000 kilometres of new expressways.

Source: Adapted from Tanaka (1972: 123).

overcrowding in metropolitan areas and depopulation in rural areas. Based on optimistic projections of continued 10 per cent per annum growth, the plan projected the need for thousands of kilometres of new expressways to carry the billions of tons of freight that would be generated by the dispersal of industry. Tanaka's plan was largely borrowed from earlier plans developed by the Ministry of International Trade and Industry (MITI) while he was its minister, and followed closely within the Comprehensive National Development Plan (CNDP) tradition of national planning discussed in Chapter 5.

The plan was also politically expedient, as it promised major public spending in the predominantly LDP-controlled rural and peripheral areas that had long been arguing for increased public expenditure on infrastructure improvement, which had remained concentrated in the Pacific Belt area. The new Shinkansen line to Niigata, the first of those projected in the plan to be built, and completed in the early 1980s, is widely considered to have been influenced by the fact that Tanaka represented a Niigata district in the legislature, an inference supported by the fact that three Shinkansen stations were built in his relatively remote electoral district (Calder 1988: 281). While by the end of the century a large number of the projects proposed in Tanaka's plan had been completed, with the slowing of economic growth in 1974 the plan was quietly dropped from active consideration. Tanaka himself was forced to resign as prime minister in 1974 because of his implication in a major bribery scandal, although he retained his Diet seat and remained one of the most powerful figures in the government until a major heart attack took him out of public life in February 1985.

One of the plan's major impacts was to spark a frenzy of land speculation in places to be made accessible by the new rail, road and bridge links. Land speculation in the places to be favoured with new Shinkansen stations and expressways resulted in the second major post-war bout of inflation in land prices, with increases of over 30 per cent nationwide during each of 1972 and 1973. The sudden land price inflation was accompanied by a panic inflation in basic consumer goods, and the widespread hoarding and shortages of toilet paper, laundry detergent and cooking oil give an indication of the degree of nervousness that the hard times of before rapid growth could return.

There were two longer-term impacts of the land price inflation of the early 1970s. The first of these was that people seeking to buy residential land in the metropolitan areas were forced to look further and further from the metropolitan core areas to find land that they could afford. The early 1970s were the peak of gross migration to these areas, and the influx of people created a huge demand for new housing land. The rise in land prices created further pressure towards sprawl development at the very time that the new planning system – established primarily to control urban sprawl – was being established. The various manifestations of this conflict are reviewed in more detail in the next section. The second product of the land price inflation of 1972–3 was the establishment of a new National Land Planning system and NLA in 1974. This new system had actually been in the planning stages for some years, and would have been necessary for the enactment of Tanaka's rebuilding Japan plan, so some sort of National Land Planning system might have developed in any case. Pushed through the legislature in response to the land crisis in 1974, the NLA took over the staff and planning functions of the CNDP and the three metropolitan planning agencies for the capital area, Osaka and Nagoya. The agency was also given responsibility for land price monitoring and countermeasures, and an elaborate system was set up to monitor land prices and allow government intervention if prices were deemed to be too high (Alden 1984; Kirwan 1987). The timing of the NLA's establishment just after a major bout of land price inflation helped to shift the priorities of the agency from a simple focus on large-scale national development planning to a more regulatory stance. The new national land planning system and its implementation are described in more detail in the section on national land planning (see page 243).

Implementing the new city planning system of 1968

As noted above, the new city planning system ran into serious problems during its implementation during the 1970s, and by the end of the decade it was understood that sprawl had not been stopped, haphazard development was continuing apace, and new revisions to the planning system were being drafted. The almost complete failure of the new city planning and national land planning systems to fulfil their stated goals stands in striking contrast with the remarkable success of Japanese government and industry in the areas of pollution control, energy conservation and avoiding the stagflation of the 1970s and the serious recession of the early 1980s that afflicted virtually all the other developed countries. It is worth asking why were there such different outcomes in these different policy areas.

As described in Chapter 6, the main goal of the New City Planning Law of 1968 was the prevention of urban sprawl. Rapid urbanisation during the 1950s and 1960s in the context of extremely weak controls over new development on the urban fringe had resulted in extensive areas of partially urbanised, unplanned and unserviced development outside existing urban areas. The problem was most severe outside Tokyo and Osaka, which were experiencing the greatest population increases, but many other large and medium sized cities were experiencing similar problems on a smaller scale. As discussed in Chapter 5, the revisions to the Building Standards Law in 1950 had abolished the building-line system. That meant that there were virtually no planning controls on urban fringe development. While the post-war reconstruction projects had designated a basic network of arterial roads (*Toshi Keikaku Dōro*) and zoned large areas of new development land outside the existing built up areas, these did not provide an adequate framework for managing rapid growth. First, as noted in Chapter 4, the zoning system was rather inclusive, with the main restriction being that the largest factories were allowed only in industrial areas, and noisy commercial uses like cabarets and theatres were allowed only in commercial areas. In residential areas virtually all uses from small factories to department stores were allowed, and housing continued to be built in heavy industrial areas. The main differentiation between the zones was that residential zones allowed the least bulk and lot coverage ratios, and commercial zones the highest.

Second, there was no effective system for securing land for public uses such as roads and parks on the urban fringe, and it was extremely difficult to achieve planned development of new roads or to control the building of private roads in those areas. Land Readjustment (LR) projects continued to contribute a significant area of planned serviced development, but elsewhere there was little alternative to municipal purchase of the required land for local roads and parks or other community facilities. Because of the extent of new development, and particularly after the rapid rise in land prices in the early 1970s, such land purchase became prohibitively expensive. And in any case, the focus of most municipal and prefectural spending was on the development of the arterial road system, and on land assembly and servicing for industrial sites to create jobs and raise taxes.

The result was that the vast majority of urban development occurred as unplanned, unserviced sprawl with tiny developments of a few houses along existing farm lanes and on short dead-end lanes extending from them. The term "sprawl" (*supurōru*) has a slightly different meaning in Japan than in the other developed countries. In Japan the term refers to haphazard, unserviced development along existing rural lanes. That was a common usage of the term in the West before the Second World War, but such development has been mostly eliminated in the years since, and the term "sprawl" is now more commonly used to refer to patterns of metropolitan growth that spread over larger areas than necessary because of low densities, leapfrog development that leaves large tracts undeveloped, or patterns of development that tend to reduce accessibility and increase road use and congestion (Cervero 1989; Ewing 1997).

There are three main arguments against allowing unregulated or expansive urbanisation, all of which were employed in support of the new planning system passed in 1968. First, such patterns of development greatly increase the costs of the provision of infrastructure. Many public services such as sewers, gas supply, roads, and even mail delivery have certain basic costs per linear foot regardless of how many users there are, and where houses are very spread out the fixed costs have to be shared among fewer households. In Japan ultimate densities are normally relatively high, but it can take 30 to 50 years to reach full build out (Sorensen 2000b). As a result, in many areas of sprawl development in Japan basic services have only been installed when the area is mostly built up, and it is very expensive to retrofit partly built up areas with roads and sewers (Kurokawa, et al. 1995). Second, if unregulated sprawl is permitted without setting aside land for roads and public facilities such as parks, such land must be purchased later at fully urban prices, instead of at either the pre-urbanisation rural land price or acquired for free as a condition of land development. The high cost of land, and the need to demolish or move many buildings to achieve basic road networks or parks is a fundamental reason for the continuing shortage of such basic infrastructure in Japan. The third common argument against allowing unplanned development on the urban fringe is that such development eliminates the possibility of a design that might create pleasant urban environments through interesting road layouts or pedestrian routes, or make best use of existing natural features and preserve valued amenities such as hills or streams (Hough 1995; Unwin [1909] 1994).

Unfortunately, therefore, although haphazard, unserviced development creates few problems at first, and can even allow a very high quality of living environment for the first new arrivals who enjoy what remains essentially a rural environment, after a certain threshold of population density increasingly severe problems begin to emerge: increasing density leads to road congestion which requires costly road upgrading, water supply and sewers need to be built, and schools and other public services need to be expanded. Many local governments which were struggling to catch up by building basic infrastructure such as sewers and improved road networks in their existing built up areas saw themselves falling further and further behind as enormous new areas of haphazard sprawl spread into nearby rural areas. The deepening infrastructure deficits and rising financial obligations of metropolitan fringe municipalities were a cause of alarm and a major motivation for the passage of the new planning system in 1968.

As explained in Chapter 6, two of the main new provisions introduced in the 1968 law were intended to address the problem of unserviced development. Development permission was intended to allow local governments to require that land developers provide contributions to road systems, sewer facilities and open space, while Senbiki was intended to provide a growth boundary within which urban development would be contained. That growth boundary could be expanded at 5-yearly intervals, so it was not intended to create a permanently protected rural area in the Urbanisation Control Area (UCA), but merely to concentrate new building activity in a smaller area near the existing built up area, and prevent the spread of new development over too large an area. It was hoped that a combination of public developments, such as for schools and housing, private developments under the development permit system which would conform to planned road networks and contribute their fair share to network infrastructure, and LR projects, would ensure that most of the new Urbanisation Promotion Area (UPA) area would see fully serviced development instead of continuing unserviced sprawl. As planned development proceeded the growth boundary could be moved further out, thus allowing staged development in manageable tranches.

The question is, given that the new planning system had been explicitly designed to prevent further sprawl, why did such patterns of development continue in the 1970s? There were four key ways in which the city planning system was compromised: 1) the over-designation of UPA; 2) the failure of the proposed land tax reform; 3) the creation of significant loopholes that allowed sprawl development in both the UPA (*minikaihatsu*) and UCA (*kisontakuchi*); and 4) very loose planning regulations in non-Senbiki areas.

Over-designation of UPA

It is possible that the over-designation of the UPA was the single most important cause of the ensuing problems. That the UPA was too large at the initial designation is widely agreed. As shown in Table 7.1, in each of the metropolitan areas the area of UPA was much larger than the existing built up area as represented by Densely Inhabited Districts (DID). This was particularly true in the suburban areas such as Saitama, Chiba, Kobe, and in Nagoya, while less true of Tokyo and Osaka because virtually the whole prefecture was already built up. It seems very unlikely that an area equal in size to all existing built up areas would be developed within 10 years. The actual patterns of development described below only confirm this supposition.

Table 7.1 Ratio of UPA to existing built up area in 1975

	DID (ha)	*UPA (ha)*	*Ratio of UPA/DID (%)*
Saitama	40,810	65,290	160
Chiba	32,710	60,765	186
Tokyo	91,460	104,124	114
Kanagawa	67,650	90,788	134
Tokyo MMA	232,630	320,967	138
Aichi	52,140	104,490	200
Mie	11,120	20,867	188
Nagoya MMA	63,260	125,357	198
Kyoto	18,100	24,873	137
Osaka	72,540	87,589	121
Kobe	38,680	64,481	167
Osaka MMA	129,320	176,943	137

Source: Compiled from MoC Toshikeikaku Nenpo (1979: 10–11).

Figure 7.2 shows the actual patterns of building in an area of newly designated UPA in Omiya, north of Tokyo, during the period 1968–91. Because the area so designated was much larger than necessary for land development requirements, the total area built up increased from 24.4 per cent of all buildable land in 1968 to 51.2 per cent in 1991. The rate of build up from 1979 to 1991 was only 1 per cent per year, suggesting that it may take another 50 years to reach full build out. Worse, the area was much larger than the local government was able to organise into LR projects, so more than half the area was developed as haphazard sprawl along existing lanes. The hopes that the new UPA would be developed and serviced comprehensively by LR, public development projects for housing and schools, etc, and by development permit have been dashed (see Sorensen 2000b: 307).

It seems that the main reason the UPA was so broadly over-designated was the pressure from farmers and farm organisations to include as much land as possible within it, and from the Ministry of Construction (MoC) to ensure that an adequate supply of raw land was available. For example, Hanayama (1986: 101–3) documents the process of the initial Senbiki in Hachioji, a city in the western suburbs of Tokyo. The First Basic

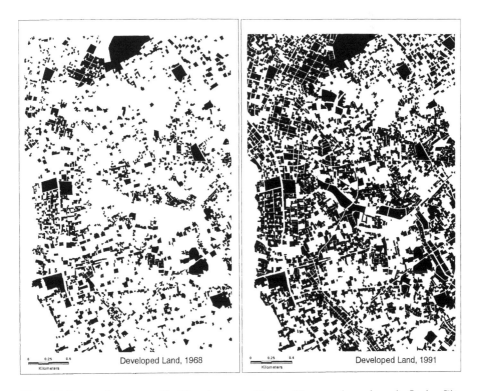

Developed Land, 1968   Developed Land, 1991

Figure 7.2 Scattered patterns of build up in eastern Omiya. The area shown here, in Omiya City in the suburbs north of Tokyo, was primarily farm and forest land in 1968, and was designated as UPA to be comprehensively developed into urban areas within 10 years in 1970. Although much development took place over the next two decades, by 1991 less than half the buildable land had been built up, little of the area was serviced by sewers, and the road system remained woefully inadequate for the increased population (see Sorensen 2000b, 2001a).

Draft Plan made public by the Tokyo Metropolitan Government (TMG) in April 1970 designated 5,748 hectares of Hachioji as UPA (31 per cent of the total area of the city), but virtually all landowners in the affected areas wanted their land to be zoned as UPA. They therefore organised petitions and direct lobbying of local government officials in Hachioji and the TMG. These efforts resulted in a further 1,525 hectares being designated UPA for an ultimate increase of 26.5 per cent in the area of UPA (to 7,273 hectares or 39 per cent of the city area). Hanayama notes that virtually the whole area of the initially proposed UCA that was not steep mountain slopes was subject to such petitions. In the second draft, most of the gently sloping land was zoned UPA.

Hebbert (1994: 77) also describes the over-designation of the UPA as the unsurprising outcome of a policy conflict between those who wanted as much area designated UPA as possible, and those who wanted to keep it as compact as possible. On the first side were lined up the property development industry including the Real Estate Association, Urban Development Association and National Federation of Land and Building Agents, the prefectural governments who were keen to sustain strong growth in suburban areas in order to relieve the pressure on housing markets, and landowners such as farmers and their organisations who had a clear interest in ensuring their holdings were zoned UPA. On the other side were local governments which argued for smaller, more compact areas to be designated UPA. According to Hebbert, Japanese municipal authorities recognised clearly the additional costs imposed by scattered development. As the additional tax revenue brought in by residential expansion was not enough to cover expenditures and all municipalities had large infrastructure backlogs, municipalities tended to prefer compact, efficient patterns of urban development instead of the sprawl which was encouraged by over-designation of UPA. Local governments were by far the weakest player in this contest, however, and in the end a much larger area of UPA was designated than was really necessary, as became clear in the following decades.

UPA agricultural land tax reform

One of the key factors affecting the implementation of the Senbiki system in the 1970s was the failure to implement planned reforms of the land tax system. Although it was intended that as part of the new planning system introduced in 1968 all land in the new UPAs would be taxed based on market value assessments, with revisions to the tax law passed by the National Diet in March 1971 aimed at achieving that end, skilful lobbying of LDP Diet members by the farm lobby was successful in attaining broad loopholes in the new tax which allowed virtually all farm land in UPAs to retain preferential tax treatment – meaning they commonly paid 1–2 per cent of the tax paid on nearby residential land (Yamamura 1992: 44).

This failure to reform taxes on agricultural land within the UPA was important because Japanese farmers have tended to hold on to their land as long as possible, often maintaining it in active agricultural use long after it is ripe for development. Because they have tended to retain ownership of urban fringe farmland, farmers have played a much more important role in urbanisation in Japan than in other developed countries. The reasons for this landholding behaviour are complex and have been examined thoroughly elsewhere (see e.g. Hanayama 1986; Noguchi 1992b; Sorensen 1998; Yamamura 1992). Explanations have included cultural factors such as the traditional

Japanese family system which discourages the sale of family land assets (Fukutake 1967), legal and administrative barriers to the sale of agricultural land (Hayami 1988: 61), market factors such as the high and rising price of land which created an incentive to speculate in land (Yamamura 1992), tax incentives which made farmland assets an extremely favourable tax shelter (Noguchi 1994; Noguchi 1990; Noguchi 1992b), and weak land development regulations which allowed farmers to subdivide and sell land on a plot by plot basis at fully urban prices with no requirement to provide urban services (Hanayama 1986; Mori 1998). The last two factors are arguably the most important, and are directly related to the almost legendary political power of farmers in Japan.

This power is well known and is demonstrated by the fact that they have received increasingly favourable treatment from the Japanese state in the post-war period (Calder 1988; Donnelly 1984; Yamamura 1992: 44). For example, by the late 1980s Japan's rice prices were more than eight times world levels, while Japan incurred increasing inter-national trade friction by continuing to enforce strict controls on imports of foreign rice. Farm support programmes have long taken a large part of Japanese budgets, despite the opposition of the Ministry of Finance and Federation of Economic Organisations (*Keidanren*) (Calder 1988: 231). Farmers have also benefited from the fact that they pay tax on a much lower proportion of their income through the expansion of various deductions (20–30 per cent) than is the case for others such as non-farm self-employed (60–70 per cent), or the unfortunate urban worker whose taxes are deducted at source (90–100 per cent) (Hayami 1988: 61).

The success of farmland owners in preserving tax reductions for farmland in urban areas is one of the best demonstrations of the influence of the farm lobby over the LDP and national government policy, and one of the clearest cases of the LDP rewarding one of its core client groups at the expense of the public interest. While since the mid-1960s repeated attempts have been made to eliminate the special tax exemptions on farmland within urban areas, these efforts were consistently defeated by the farm lobby (see e.g. Hanayama 1986; Noguchi 1992b; Otake 1993; Yamamura 1992). Finally in 1992 a tax reform was passed which allowed owners of farmland to choose between continuing to pay the reduced tax level and forgoing the right to develop their land within 30 years, or to start paying a higher rate of tax equivalent to that on other UPA land and keep their full rights to develop. The land designated as continuing farmland with lower tax rates is called Productive Green Land (*Seisan Ryokuchi*). Of those in Tokyo, just less than half chose to keep their low tax status and designate their land as Productive Green Land, forgoing the right to develop for 30 years. In the suburban prefectures a much lower percentage of land was designated as Productive Green Land, (24 per cent in Saitama, 23 per cent in Kanagawa and 19.3 per cent in Chiba). Similarly in the other metropolitan areas, the central city areas saw a higher percentage of farmland designated as Productive Green Land, in Osaka 40.8 per cent, Kyoto 49.7 per cent Hyogo 36 per cent, Nara 28.2 per cent, and Aichi 17.4 per cent. It seems that farmland owners in suburban areas gave a much higher priority to the possibility of developing their land to urban use in the future, whereas a higher proportion of those who still owned land in the metropolitan core prefectures were content to forgo the possibility of development in the foreseeable future in order to retain their tax break.

The fact that farmland owners in urban areas were able to delay tax reform for almost 25 years was crucial because as Hanayama argues, differential taxation for

UPAs, and UCAs was a central feature of the 1968 City Planning Law. If the land tax within the UPA had been fairly high, based on market value, and accompanied by lower rates in the UCA with strong restrictions on the right to develop land, then the distinction between UPA and UCA would have been real, and the rationale for the land tax as a special purpose tax for providing planning and infrastructure in urban areas would have been clear. As he puts it, "The discussion that separated the two policy instruments, though these were the integral components of land policy, can be registered as one of the gross errors in the post-war history of internal administration" (Hanayama 1986: 132). When farmland within the UPA was exempted from market value taxation, all farmers wanted to have their land zoned UPA, and were largely successful in lobbying for a much larger UPA than was actually necessary (Hebbert and Nakai 1988b: 40; Ishida 1987: 310). These several factors combined to produce a situation that was unusually favourable for the owners of farmland on the urban fringe, and this in turn was a major factor in the shortage of land supply which contributed greatly to rising land prices in metropolitan areas.

For municipalities struggling to provide services to large UPAs, the persistence of extensive areas of cultivated land within the UPA was a serious problem because it promoted the leapfrogging of new development. This made systematic provision of new infrastructure impossibly expensive, and large-scale tax exemptions for farmland also resulted in a weakened local tax base. It is hard to say whether the persistence of farmland within the UPA, the loss of tax revenue, or the contribution to rising land prices was the most damaging effect of the failure to reform the land tax system on the efforts of local governments to achieve planned urbanisation within their new UPAs. Certainly, however, the combination of these was disastrous and further reinforced the reliance of local governments on LR for land development within the UPA, as described below.

Problems with the development permission system

While the development permission system did greatly increase the ability of local planning authorities to manage development by allowing them for the first time to make permission for land development conditional on developer provision of infrastructure, numerous loopholes in the system allowed increasing volumes of development to slip through without the need for development permits. The two most important of these loopholes were *minikaihatsu* and *kisontakuchi*. In a sense, these are both aspects of a similar phenomenon, the former being found primarily in the UPA, while the latter is found exclusively in the UCA. However, each in their respective areas formed the main avenue for the continuation of scattered disorderly development, and thus served to negate efforts to promote planned development.

Mini-kaihatsu (literally mini-developments) had always formed a part of Japanese residential development, however after 1968 they gained rapidly in importance because of the loophole that exempted developments of 1,000 square metres or less within the UPA from the need to gain development permission (see Katsumata 1993, 1995). While in the 1968 law prefectures were given the option to reduce this limit to 500 square metres, only a few did so, including Kanagawa prefecture south of Tokyo which as one of the earliest prefectures to experience significant suburban development has a long experience with trying to control sprawl. In the Japanese context of small houses on

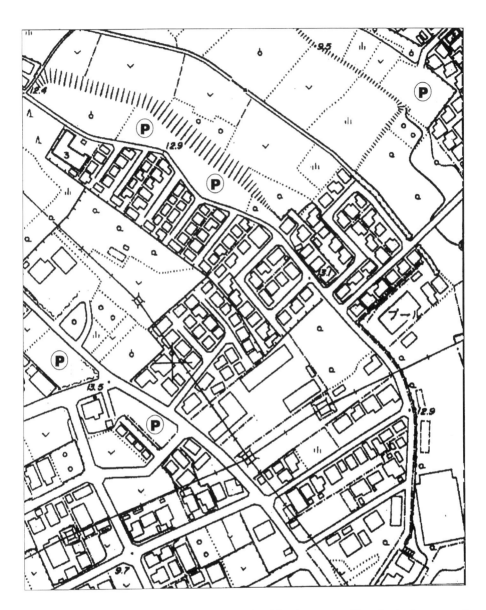

Figure 7.3 Mini-kaihatsu development in Urawa City. The dense area of housing in the centre of the map is a good example of mini-kaihatsu style development. Houses are built fronting on dead-end lanes built at right angles to an existing rural road. These houses are serviced neither with sewers nor piped gas, but rely on septic tanks which must be regularly pumped out, and bottled gas. The internal roads are privately owned, and are very often unpaved. Note the narrowness of the main access road, the lack of through connections, the parking areas provided off site, and the houses built under a high-voltage electric power line. The bottom left is part of an area developed with LR.

Source: Adapted from Urawa City Planning Survey 1: 2,500 Map.

small plots, however, this was a very considerable loophole indeed, particularly as before the 1992 revisions to the city planning law, local governments were not legally allowed to impose or enforce minimum plot sizes. As Mori has recently shown, in 1990 the average plot size of agricultural land converted to housing sites (including detached housing developments and multiple unit developments) was only 423 square metres (Mori 1998). A typical mini-kaihatsu development consists of 12 houses fronting on a narrow 4 metre lane running at right angles from an existing road. If each house occupies about 60 square metres and the road occupies 176 square metres, then the total area of the development will be only 896 square metres, and thus will be exempt from the need to apply for a development permit. It is also worth noting that the traditional land unit described in Chapter 1, the tan, which is a very common size for rice paddies after land improvement projects, measures exactly 300 tsubo, or 991.7 square metres, conveniently sized to be exempt from the requirement for development permission. It is hard to imagine that no one realised that most development would be able to slip through this loophole, and raises the question: Why was the system designed so that the majority of development could avoid its provisions?

Of course, many other developments consisted merely of one or two or three houses built on plots severed from a field, or as infill in partly built up areas. During the 1980s, many small developments resulted from the redevelopment of a generous sized plot first severed in the 1960s, on which two to four houses could profitably be built. In the absence of legislated minimum lot sizes, the only limit to such subdivision of plots is the ability to build a house that can be sold.

Kisontakuchi, which translates literally as "existing building plots" was the result of a loophole in the regulations controlling development in UCAs created in 1975, to maintain an earlier exception to UCA building controls that had been included in the 1968 City Planning Law. One Article defined "existing rights" (*kitokuken*) within the UCA where building plots were considered to have existed prior to UCA designation. This seems a reasonable measure, and was directed particularly at cases where, for example, a building had existed earlier but had not yet been rebuilt when the law came into effect. Landowners were simply required to register the existence of the plot within five years of the law coming into effect in 1969. Many did not do so, and farmers and their representative organisations lobbied hard to regain their right to build based on "existing rights". In response the kisontakuchi loophole was created. Unfortunately it was singularly badly designed, and allowed many more "existing building plots" to be created than initially imagined.

Although the precise definition of kisontakuchi varies from one prefecture to another, in Saitama, for example, a plot qualifies if: "a) it is located *either*: i) inside a settlement, part or all of which lies within 500 metres from the edge of an Urbanisation Promotion Area, and which consists of more than 50 dwellings built at less than 50-metre intervals; *or* ii) outside but within 50 metres from the edge of such a settlement; *and* b) the land register or other evidence proves that the site had urban use at the time of the UCA designation" (Hebbert and Nakai 1988a: 389). Because of the high density of population and the history of scattered development in farming areas on the urban fringe in Japan, this loophole immediately served to allow a considerable amount of development in the UCA.

Unfortunately, as shown by Morio, Sakamoto and Saito (1993: 253–8), the real problem is that such building plots have tended to multiply in the years since 1975. The

Figure 7.4 Mini-kaihatsu development in Kasukabe City. While the mini-kaihatsu areas shown in Figure 7.3 are not necessarily a bad living environment, surrounded as they are by fields and forests, real problems emerge when extensive areas develop in this way. This area in Kasukabe City, northeast of Tokyo was formerly rice paddy, and the regular grid of plots and access roads is the legacy of an agricultural land improvement project. Development of 8–12 houses fronting on a dead-end lane from the main road slips neatly under the 1,000 square metres threshold for development control, in what is often referred to as "*ittan kaihatsu*" or "one tan development".

Source: Courtesy of Wataru Katsumata (2001).

reason is that the regulation did not set any time limit for the registration of "existing building plots". Therefore as some "existing building plots" were developed in the 1970s, these new buildings helped to make new sites eligible, for instance by bridging the gap between two settlements of 50 dwellings, thus making the entire second settlement a part of a settlement within 500 metres of a UPA. In this way large numbers of new plots became eligible for "existing building plot" status. Similarly, any expansion in the total UPA, or creation of a new area in the UPA can set off a domino effect by creating large new areas which then became eligible for "existing building plot" status. By way of illustration, during the five years from 1986 to 1990, there were 147,148 building permits issued in the UPA in Saitama, and 50,606 in the UCA. During the same period, there were 14,625 permits issued for kisontakuchi, or about 29 per cent of the total within the UCA area (Saitama ken 1992).

The consequence of the large volumes of development that occurred in these ways was the continuation of scattered, unserviced development throughout the urban fringe area, both UPA and UCA. Figure 7.5 shows an example of the pattern of development in the UCA of Inage-ku, Chiba City. The new planning system was clearly able neither to ensure planned, serviced development in the UPA, nor to prevent continued sprawl in the UCA.

Planning problems in undivided city planning areas

One further problem with the 1968 city planning system is that although city planning areas (CPA) cover a very large area, much larger than the actual built up area, only about half the CPA was divided with Senbiki into UPA and UCA. In 1999 the undivided CPA areas totalled 43,420 square kilometres, or 11.6 per cent of the national land area, representing just under half of the CPA. The undivided CPA includes many urban areas, even though they include none of the largest metropolitan areas. At the time the 1968 City Planning Law was passed growth of population and jobs was heavily concentrated in the core metropolitan areas of Tokyo, Osaka and Nagoya, and in many other areas that were experiencing stable or declining populations, stricter planning laws were not considered necessary, so the CPA was not divided into UPA and UCA. After the mid-1970s, migration to the metropolitan areas declined greatly, and many smaller cities started to see serious growth pressures. These have occurred both as a result of population growth and because increasing affluence, motorisation, smaller household sizes, and changing retail patterns have caused significant demand for land on the urban fringe. These factors have resulted in increased development pressure in the undivided CPA of regional cities, and in serious problems of urban sprawl. Figure 7.6 illustrates this problem clearly.

While the national area of development permits issued within the UPA has remained stable at around 4,000 hectares annually, development permits issued increased dramatically in both the UCA and in undivided CPA during the 1980s. It should be remembered that much development occurred in all three areas without the need for development permits, especially in the UPA, so these figures do not indicate the total area of development within each area, only that which received a development permit (Japan Ministry of Construction, 1992: 250).

Existing urban areas in the undivided CPA were zoned with the same zoning code as the UPA of metropolitan areas. Although this system is not perfect, it served as a basic regulatory framework for those areas. The problem is that the great majority of land lies

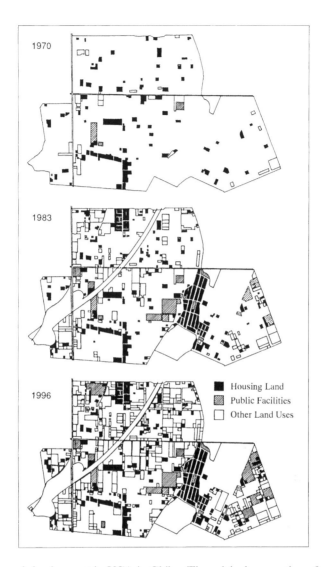

Figure 7.5 Sprawl development in UCA in Chiba. The original conception of Urbanisation Control Areas was that they would strongly restrict land development to urban uses and control urban sprawl. As this area of UCA in Chiba prefecture so clearly shows, however, a wide variety of loopholes allowed development to continue in a relatively unrestricted manner.

Source: Mikuni (1999: 187).

outside those zoned areas, including the outskirts of many substantial cities, and is very lightly regulated indeed. These areas, called "white" or "blank" areas, are subject to development permits, but these are much weaker in undivided CPA than in the divided areas, applying only to developments of over 3,000 square metres, compared to 1,000 square metres in the UPA.

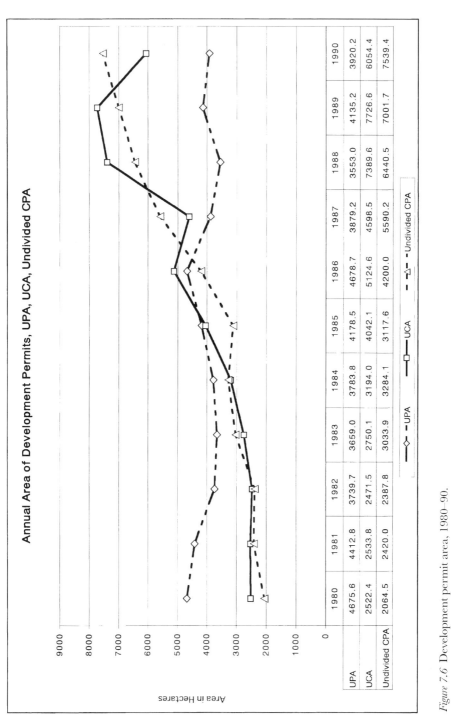

	1980	1981	1982	1983	1984	1985	1986	1987	1988	1989	1990
UPA	4675.6	4412.8	3739.7	3659.0	3783.8	4178.5	4678.7	3879.2	3553.0	4135.2	3920.2
UCA	2522.4	2533.8	2471.5	2750.1	3194.0	4042.1	5124.6	4598.5	7389.6	7726.6	6054.4
Undivided CPA	2064.5	2420.0	2387.8	3033.9	3284.1	3117.6	4200.0	5590.2	6440.5	7001.7	7539.4

Annual Area of Development Permits, UPA, UCA, Undivided CPA

Area in Hectares

UPA — UCA — Undivided CPA

Figure 7.6 Development permit area, 1980–90.

Source: MoC Construction White Paper (1992: 50).

Building controls are also applied uniformly over all the "white areas". These consist of a site coverage ratio of 0.7 and a floor area ratio (FAR) of 4. The building code, which is applied uniformly throughout Japan, also applies in these areas, but has no impact on the location of development. In part because of these weak regulations, and in part because land is less expensive than in metropolitan areas, many of these areas have experienced serious problems of scattered development of resorts, mini housing developments, pachinko gambling parlours and big-box retail stores especially since the late 1980s. The weak development regulations in the undivided areas mean that many provincial cities and many towns in undivided CPA areas have experienced serious problems in controlling urbanisation (Uchida and Nakade 1997). How to provide better regulatory frameworks in these areas is currently a major Japanese planning issue.

Unfortunately, even though stopping sprawl development and achieving planned, serviced development of newly built up areas on the urban fringe was the top priority for the new planning system, only a relatively small portion of the new urban area was developed in a planned manner. Most newly developed urban areas continued the old pattern of scattered, unserviced development, avoiding the obligation for development control.

National land planning

The final important plank in the raft of environmental legislation passed in the early 1970s was the National Land Use Planning Law (NLUPL) and the establishment of the NLA in 1974 as the keystone of a comprehensive system to administer and regulate land resources throughout the country. The NLA was intended to provide an overall coordinating function over the various environmental management and planning laws that had been revised and created during the late 1960s and early 1970s.

The immediate motivation for the passage of the NLUPL in 1974 was as a response to the problems of rapid land price inflation, which spread throughout the country in 1972 and 1973 with the "Building a New Japan" boom sparked by Prime Minister Tanaka's proposal to build a vast network of new Shinkansen lines, expressways and bridges linking the four main islands. The publication of detailed proposals for the location of these new facilities, and their promise to drastically reduce travel times to Tokyo prompted a frenzy of speculative land investment in areas expected to have much improved access to the metropolitan core areas.

The need for the NLUPL arose because unlike Britain, for example, where the Town and Country Planning Law applied to both urban and rural areas, in Japan the City Planning Law applied only to urban areas and their immediate hinterlands within the CPA. Other planning laws and agencies were responsible for agricultural areas forest areas, and national parks. Rapid urbanisation had made it clear that some sort of coordination between the different plans was necessary. In addition, the increasingly ambitious CNDPs which were proposed to correct the linked problems of over-concentration in the metropolitan areas and depopulation in rural areas, as well as Tanaka's "Building a New Japan" proposals had highlighted the need for a coordinating land planning agency that had a national perspective.

The new NLA had three main functions. First, it was to take over several existing government planning functions such as the responsibility for the CNDPs and their preparation from the Economic Planning Agency. It also absorbed the staff and functions of the National Capital Region Development Agency, the Kinki Region Development Agency (Osaka, Kyoto and Kobe), and the Chubu Region Development Agency (Nagoya), which had each hitherto had their own regional headquarters.

The second function of the NLA was to establish long-term programmes for land use at the national, prefectural and municipal levels. A National Land Use Plan would coordinate the execution of the five main land planning laws: the City Planning Law, the Agricultural Promotion Areas Law, the Forest Law, the Nature Park Law and the Nature Conservation Law. While the City Planning Law of 1968 introduced the development permission system in city planning areas which had been divided into UPA and UCA, in 1974 the system was enhanced to apply the development permission system in all CPAs including those not yet so divided. Also in 1974 amendments were made to the Forest Law and the Nature Park Law to regularise the development permit systems in their planning areas. Similar amendments were made to the Agricultural Promotion Areas Law in 1975.

A third major initial task of the NLA was to monitor land sales and curb land price inflation through land transactions controls. Land transactions controls included the requirement that notification must be given of all land transactions above a certain size (over 2,000 square metres in the UPA, over 5,000 square metres in the rest of the CPA outside the UPA, and over 10,000 square metres in non-CPA). Prefectural governors were also given the power to apply "Control District" status on any area where land prices were increasing sharply, and in control districts recommendations could be made that the agreed price on any particular land sale was too high. Although prefectural governors were in theory given the power to cancel land transactions where the land price was deemed too high, in fact that power has never been exercised, as it was felt by the authors of the system that it should only be used in emergencies (Fukuoka, 1997: 166). Negotiation and "administrative guidance" is used instead.

The national land planning system enacted in the early 1970s is comprehensive, systematic and rational, and provoked both admiring and critical comments from land use planners from around the world after it was introduced (see e.g. Alden 1984; Dawson 1985; Hebbert 1989; OECD 1986). Five interlocking plans covering urban areas, agricultural areas, forest areas, park areas and nature conservation areas were initiated under the umbrella National Land Use Guideline and a General Land Use Plan administered by prefectures. These plans were authorised by a National Land Use Planning Law to be managed by a National Land Use Planning Agency which was responsible directly to the Prime Minister's Office. The cascading series of interlocking plans from the national to the local levels was impressive in its breadth and complexity. Seldom had so all-embracing and thorough an attempt at planning a national territory been made. Alas, the Japanese system is also an excellent illustration of the principle that such systems are only as effective as their implementation – the proof of the pudding is in the eating.

There have been two major problems in implementing the system. The first is a consequence of the complex structure of a system which is enacted in five basic laws drafted, administered and enforced by three different national ministries. A product of Japan's long history of bureaucratic sectionalism and competition, the compromise where each ministry contributed a law relating to the land area under its jurisdiction meant that none of the ministries had to relinquish any administrative territory. In addition to the development permit system for urban land already operated by local governments under the 1968 City Planning Law, each national ministry established its own notification/development permit system for the land under its jurisdiction and supervised the local committees set up to operate it. This means that within any given municipal area there are five competing planning and regulatory frameworks applying to different areas administered by different national ministries, a problem which continues until the present. The purpose and administrative methodology of these areas differ, and there is no higher level system to knit each separate plan for individual areas together at the level of the municipality. Such a higher level plan would have required either granting substantial administrative power to municipalities to coordinate and administer the plans, or the establishment of a powerful national agency that could have enforced their coordination. Either way the existing ministries would have lost direct control over changes of land use in the areas under their jurisdiction. In part because of the failure to allow municipal governments the power to create their own binding general plans to control land development within their municipal area, municipalities have independently developed their own Municipal Development Plan and development control systems. These local efforts make no attempt to coordinate the five national planning systems, nor to establish a long-term master plan, but attempt merely to effectively control development and major land use change in their whole territory. These systems are unrelated to the national level land planning system, and are sometimes in conflict with it. In many cases the national planning frameworks acted more as a hindrance to rational development planning at the local level than as a help. One interesting exception was the village of Tsukuicho in Kanagawa prefecture, which used its authority granted under Article 8 of the National Land Use Planning Law, which allows municipal land use plans, to create its own land use Master Plan which it then backed with a local municipal ordinance. Such local ordinances are discussed in more detail in Chapter 9.

The second major system-wide problem is that the coverage of the five different systems is not comprehensive: the failure to coordinate the various plans has left numerous "white areas" that are not covered by any of the systems. There are also significant areas within each system which are very loosely regulated, and where development is hard to prevent. Further, it is very difficult to regulate development issues such as built form and design in any of the areas. These various weaknesses have combined to allow a great deal of inappropriate development. These issues are explored in greater detail below.

The five basic national land use planning laws

As noted, the function of the National Land Use Planning Law (NLUPL), is to coordinate the land planning functions of the five subsidiary laws. To accomplish this it sets targets for the amount of land in each category at the national, prefectural and municipal levels as the National Land Use Plan (*Kokudo Ryo Keikaku*). Although the Japanese term translates literally as National Land Use Plan, at the national level there is no mapping of the different areas involved, only numerical targets for land areas and guidelines for prefectural planning efforts. The NLUPL also mandates the designation of Prefectural General Land Use Plans, which are in theory superordinate plans which coordinate the operation of the five separate laws. In practice they are merely an assembly and record of the areas which are designated under each of the five categories by the relevant ministry staff. Prefectural planners have no powers to actually change the areas which are designated by individual ministries.

Table 7.2 Official planned area under each of five laws

	Area (km²)	% of national land	Date
1 City Planning Area	96,930	26	1996
of which UCA	38,920	10.4	
of which UPA	14,590	3.9	
of which undivided CPA	42,420	11.7	
2 Agricultural Promotion Area	172,200	46.2	1998
of which Designated Agricultural Use Land (blue areas)	51,250	13.7	
3 Forest Area	251,460	67.4	1996
of which National Forest and Protected Forest	123,350	33.1	
4 Nature Park Area	53,350	14.3	1998
of which Nature Park Special Areas	33,870	9.1	
5 Nature Conservation Areas	1,008	0.3	1998
Area not covered by any plan	2,390	0.6	
Total 1,2,3,4,5	574,948	154	
National land area	372,780	100	

Source: National Land Agency White Paper (1998).

While the National Land Use Guidelines and the Prefectural General Land Use Plans seem to suggest a strong policy to control land use in different areas, in practice they are not intended to designate such land, but are merely a record of designations made under each ministerial planning system, collated at an area level. Each ministry thus retained autonomy within its own jurisdiction.

Several points can be made by reference to Table 7.2 which shows the area administered by each of the five national land planning laws. The first point is that there is considerable overlap between the different plans. The total area covered by the five plans amounts to 154 per cent of the national land area, even though 2,390 square kilometres are not covered by any plan. Many areas are covered by two laws, and some by three. Second, only about half of the CPA has been divided into UPA and UCA, which are relatively strictly regulated. The other half of the CPA is undivided and is relatively unregulated. Similarly, only a third of the Agricultural Promotion Areas, half of the Forest Areas, and three-fifths of the Nature Park Areas are relatively strictly regulated. The balance of the areas are very weakly regulated, and it is rather easy to carry out development activities in them. This has been a major weakness of the system, as discussed in more detail below.

In response to the passage of the City Planning Law of 1968 the Ministry of Agriculture, Forests and Fishing (MAFF) drafted the Agriculture Promotion Areas Law (APAL), which was passed in 1969. The APAL was explicitly an effort to defend MAFF turf against the inroads of the MoC, and was understood as such when it was passed. The problem was that the MoC's new system to divide the CPA into UPA and UCA established urban planning development control over a much larger area than the existing built up or zoned areas in its attempt to prevent urban sprawl. Naturally, in the Japanese geographical context where the urban and agricultural areas are crowded together in narrow alluvial plains, urban fringe areas were almost all actively farmed. The MAFF considered the UCA their own territory even though the UCA was within the CPA. Ceding control over land development activity in these predominantly agricultural areas to the MoC was not to be countenanced. MAFF therefore developed the APAL as a way of establishing its own regulatory control system over the conversion of land from agricultural to urban use in order to strengthen its hold over farmland in the UCA.

The Agricultural Promotion Areas Law achieved this by allowing the designation of Agricultural Promotion Areas and Agricultural Improvement Plans. These improvement plans are not just land use plans, but also function as a Master Plan for the development of the farm industry in each area. One part of each Agriculture Improvement Plan is a land use plan which divides all farmland into two categories, designated "Agricultural Use Land" (usually referred to as "blue areas" as they are coloured blue on maps) and other agricultural land. Blue areas are in principle the best agricultural land and are not to be converted to residential land and will not receive land development permits. The total area of Agricultural Promotion Areas is 172,200 square kilometres representing 46.2 per cent of the national land area, and blue areas are 51,250 square kilometres, or somewhat less than a third of the Agricultural Promotion Areas. Agricultural land not designated as blue areas can be developed. Development simply requires a development permit from the prefectural governments which is generally not difficult to obtain.

The other three national land planning laws work in a similar fashion. The Forest Law (also administered by MAFF) includes measures for designating Forest Planning Areas in regional Forest Plans. As with the Agricultural Promotion Law, the Forest Law divides forest areas into two types, designated Protected Forests and others. Within designated Protected Forests development activities are basically prohibited, and in other forest areas any development of over 1 hectare requires a development permit from the prefectural government. This means that developments of less than 1 hectare can easily be carried out, and even developments of over 1 hectare will normally receive a development permit if a certain ratio of the forest area is preserved. Conversion of most forest land is thus relatively easy, and the only forests that are well protected from development are those which are nationally owned, and those which are designated Protected Forest. Similarly, the Nature Park Law (administered by the Environment Agency) allows the ministry to designate Nature Park areas, and prepare park plans. There are two types of Nature Parks: National Parks and Quasi-National Parks. National Parks are designated and directly managed by the national government, while Quasi-National Parks are proposed by prefectures and approved by the national government, and are managed by the prefectures under supervision of the national government. Within parks it is possible to designate Special Districts, Special Conservation Districts, or Marine Districts within which any development requires a development permit, and it is possible to strictly limit the scale and location of development. Outside of special districts it is not very difficult to gain permission for land development. Also administered by the Environment Agency, the Nature Conservation Law carries probably the strictest restrictions on development and changes to the environment. It is also by far the smallest by area, at 1,008 square kilometres, only 0.3 per cent of the national land area, less than half the area that is covered by none of the laws. The act provides for the protection of wilderness areas and nature conservation areas and mandates the drafting of conservation plans. There are three types of areas that can be designated under the act: Wilderness Areas, Natural Environment Protection Areas, and Prefectural Nature Conservation Areas. Within Special Districts designated under the act the regulatory power is quite strong, while within Regular Districts some development is permitted by development permit. Under each of the five main land planning laws therefore, there are some areas which are quite strictly regulated, and others which are rather weakly regulated.

Local responses

The weak relationship between the various national land planning frameworks and municipal government planning needs has meant that local governments had to develop their own systems for land use planning and management. Naturally within the UPA, and to some degree within the UCA they had a range of tools to guide development. The problem was greatest outside these areas; in the undivided CPA, in undesignated "white" areas, and in the weakly regulated parts of forest, agricultural and nature conservation areas. Although not all local governments were active in developing more comprehensive planning methods, to a certain degree all local governments were under pressure to discover more effective ways of controlling haphazard development. The weakness of existing development control systems, and particularly the significant loopholes that allowed large numbers of small developments to slip beneath development permit thresholds have resulted in steadily increasing infrastructure backlogs. The huge financial burdens for the retroactive provision of such services has been an important factor in the poor financial health of many local governments in growth areas, and local governments have therefore sought methods and legal powers to prevent further haphazard development on the urban fringe lest they never catch up.

   The main issues from the local government point of view are: first, the development permit standards within both the UPA and UCA areas are too weak, particularly since the various deregulations of the mid-1980s, and the number of developments that escape the need for a development permit at all (and hence the requirement for infrastructure contributions) is too large. Second, the non-divided "white" areas where there is no land use designation have invited much haphazard development, particularly with increasing motorisation during the 1980s. In the Japanese geographic context of crowded urban and agricultural areas mixed together on narrow alluvial plains, the problems of the national land planning system have become deeply interconnected with city planning and urban growth management problems. As discussed in Chapter 9 a major new focus of planning activity during the 1990s has been the creation of local ordinances to regulate development in the urban fringe areas outside the UPA areas and even outside the CPA.

The third comprehensive national development plan

One of the most original products of the newly established NLA was the third CNDP (*Sanzenso*) of 1977. In the early 1970s a serious review of the unlimited economic growth assumptions of the second CNDP (*Shinzenso*) was begun, and with the escalation of metropolitan problems in the early 1970s pressure for significant changes in approach began to build. In particular, a number of incidents in 1973 in the Tokyo area were emblematic of increasing urban stress and conflict. First, the simmering "garbage war" (*gomi sensō*) in Tokyo burst into national attention when Koto ward in the working class industrial area of Tokyo's port – and which included the main garbage disposal landfills in Tokyo Bay – decided to block garbage trucks from Suginami ward in the affluent western suburbs where local residents had blocked the construction of a garbage incinerator that would have burned their garbage locally (McKean 1981: 102–8). Second, in March of the same year a riot broke out at the Ageo city rail station north of Tokyo among commuters frustrated with long commutes in overcrowded trains. Third, in residential areas throughout the capital local citizens' groups were bitterly opposed to the building of high-rise apartment buildings which blocked the sunlight for surrounding houses (Ishizuka and Ishida 1988b: 30). These protests eventually resulted in the sunlight protection ordinances discussed below. On the larger stage, the confluence of economic, pollution and political crises had discredited the old approaches to economic growth and the building of massive infrastructure for industrial expansion and created pressure for a new approach to urban and regional policy. Tanaka, who for a time had been Japan's most popular prime minister ever on the basis of his broad and optimistic future vision, had been skewered by the oil crisis and by his own corruption. His popularity fell from a high of 62 per cent when he took office in 1972 to a mere 27 per cent only eight months later (Pempel 1998: 182–3). The LDP, in the face of its declining popularity and mounting urban problems, needed to adopt new approaches to urban and regional issues to solve its electoral crisis of the early 1970s (Calder 1988: 105).

The third CNDP (*Sanzenso*) of 1977 thus took a very different approach to national land planning, proposing that instead of large-scale transportation systems to link the country together with shorter travel times, the development of the social and service infrastructure of local areas should be emphasised in order to allow residents a high level of quality of life without the necessity of moving to the metropolitan areas. This proposal clearly followed on many earlier suggestions for the promotion of decentralisation, but the oil shock appears to have changed the political climate, and the idea of decentralisation appears to have been taken much more seriously. As the MoC later explained, the plan "aimed to enhance historical, traditional and cultural characteristics of regions, and focused on improving living environment rather than on infrastructure or industrial project implementation" (Japan Ministry of Construction 1996: 30).

This was quite a significant shift in direction. The political and economic tumult had evidently given the more visionary planners at the NLA the opening they needed, and as with the Ishikawa plan for the post-war reconstruction of Tokyo, a startlingly utopian vision of Japan's future development course became official government policy. Shimokobe Atsushi, a senior planner at the NLA, proposed that development be based on the drainage region to encourage social sustainability and quality of life, and balance between water resources and water demand for agriculture and industry. Christened the Settlement Zone (*Teijūken*) concept, the plan mixed the famous American New Deal Tennessee Valley Authority approach to regional development planning with a Fourierist utopian vision of integrated and sustainable communities and proposed that Japan be divided into 300 planning regions where nature and human settlement could be in balance. The idea even had a resonance with Japan's feudal past, when the approximately 300 feudal domains had been very much based on the river basins, and control over water supply had been the source both of sustainable rice agriculture and of political power. Whether utopian or not, the plan was quite probably doomed to irrelevance from the start, as the NLA had remarkably little budget or powers to persuade other government bodies to follow their lead. Other ministries had their own projects and the money to fund them, and the local governments in depopulated areas which might have been interested in the plan's message were too dependent on central government construction projects to have much of a say in the matter. As with the Ishikawa scheme for Tokyo's post-war reconstruction, events ran away with this plan, and as the Japanese economy powered ahead into the 1980s, shifting further and faster into high technology, precision manufacturing and the financial services industries needed to manage the spread of Japanese corporate investment around the world, the vision of sustainable river valley settlements was displaced by the need to plan for World City Tokyo. A new CNDP was on the drawing boards by 1983, but that is a story for the next chapter.

The non-binding characteristic of the CNDP, and the planning autonomy of the different ministries is illustrated by the fact that ground was being broken on another, radically different national project at about the same time: the major bridges linking the main island of Honshu with the southern island of Shikoku. Shikoku had been suffering from economic decline and loss of population throughout the post-war period, and from 1955 the Japan National Railways had been studying routes for a bridge to link the island to the economic growth areas of Honshu. In 1968 the Ministries of Construction and Transportation had decided to build three bridges to the island, apparently as a result of political pressure from high-ranking LDP politicians including former prime ministers Miki, Ohira, and Miyazawa whose constituencies would benefit from the links, even though significant opposition to the plans existed, and serious questions about the necessity for and economic viability of three sets of bridges had been raised (Barret and Therivel 1991: 171). The Honshu-Shikoku Bridge Authority was set up in 1970, and detailed plans for the three bridges finalised in 1972. Details of the bridges were also included in Tanaka's "Building a New Japan" proposals (Tanaka 1972: 134). Although the scheme was temporarily shelved in 1973 following the oil crisis, the bridges were soon back on the agenda, and construction on the easternmost bridge near Osaka over Awaji Island began in 1976, while the westernmost bridge closest to Hiroshima began in 1977, and the middle set of bridges was begun in 1978. It is significant that even though these new transportation networks proposed in the second CNDP and Tanaka's plan were dropped from the third CNDP, their construction nevertheless proceeded.

It seems hardly necessary to point out that these two approaches to national spatial development were moving in opposite directions. The MITI/Tanaka approach was to disperse industrial development throughout the archipelago by building a vast national transportation system of expressways and high-speed rail links to every corner of the country. The third CNDP, on the other hand, was promoting river basin-based "settlement zones" in which the focus would be sustainability and quality of life. The two approaches share the uncontroversial goal of encouraging job growth in peripheral areas, but the means of achieving that growth were very different. Most telling is the fact that the transport network was still being built out at the end of the century, albeit at a much slower pace than originally projected, while the "settlement zone" concept was designated for the dustbin in the early 1980s.

Patterns of urban change in the 1970s

With economic growth, the increasing wealth of the country, and the completion of the most urgent tasks of post-war rebuilding, it becomes more difficult to briefly summarise the main patterns of urban change during the 1970s, and any such summary will necessarily be a great simplification of more complex patterns of change. That said, probably the most important change was the acceleration of the shift of population from central city areas to the suburbs. This section looks at three aspects of that process, the key role of railway networks, the continuing pattern of large areas of unplanned sprawl interspersed with areas of planned development, and the beginnings of high-rise redevelopment in existing urban areas, and conflicts over how to control the impacts on nearby residences.

The importance of railways in suburbanisation

While economic growth slowed after 1974 and net migration to metropolitan areas stopped entirely during the second half of the decade, growth of urban areas continued and even accelerated during the 1970s. This was possible both because the huge concentrations of people who had located in the metropolitan core areas during the rapid growth era were now moving to the suburbs in search of better housing, and because of high rates of natural increase in the metropolitan areas. Provincial cities also saw significant population growth and expansion in area because of a combination of reduced net out-migration to metropolitan areas, and rapid suburbanisation. This process of suburbanisation of population followed similar such processes in many other developed countries (Champion 1989).

One big difference between suburbanisation in Japan and in most of the other developed countries is that in the Japanese case suburban development was almost entirely structured by rail commuting. The powerful role of suburban commuter railways in suburbanisation is primarily a result of three factors. First, ownership of private automobiles was very low until the 1970s, with really widespread car ownership only seen in the second half of the 1980s. This was in part a result of a government policy to restrict private car ownership to ensure that greater financial resources were available for capital investment by industry. Japan had car ownership rates of only 16 per thousand in 1960, a much lower rate than either Singapore or Kuala Lumpur which were much poorer cities at that date (Barter 1999: 275). Second, employment has continued to be located predominantly in city centre areas which are very well served by railway and subway transit systems. The massive decentralisation of employment seen in the US has not occurred. As has often been argued, it is the decentralisation of both jobs and residents that is most closely associated with increasing dependence on private cars (Cervero 1989, 1995). Third, road networks were poor, and central city areas are both highly congested and have few parking spaces, making travel to employment in the centre by private car both more expensive and more time consuming for most commuters. Suburbanisation has thus been based primarily on rail travel via the extensive networks of the national railways and in the metropolitan areas also on private commuter railways. Services in each of these have been steadily upgraded throughout the post-war period, particularly through electrification and double tracking, but such was the speed of suburban population growth that chronic overcrowding has been the norm since the early 1960s.

Rail-based suburbanisation has had profound consequences on patterns of urbanisation. First, development tended to proceed along the length of the radial rail lines from the centre to the periphery. The typical pattern of development of the private commuter lines was for the rail operator to build a large department store at the city centre terminal, and a large amusement park at the rural end of the line. Communities along the rail line tended to identify themselves with the railway, and the term *"ensen"* development (meaning communities along the line) evolved to describe it. Second, the dominance of railways for metropolitan travel created the typical pattern of dense commercial areas which crowd around each rail station to serve the passing trade, with residential areas spread out within walking distance of each station. Third, rail networks probably helped to spread out the area over which new residential development occurred, as travel was relatively easy compared to private cars and companies were given tax incentives to subsidise the commuting costs of their employees. The fact that few commuters pay the full financial costs of their commute is widely regarded as a factor contributing to extensive patterns of urban development.

Planned and unplanned suburban development

As discussed above, one of the main priorities of the 1968 planning system was to ensure planned development on the urban fringe. Unfortunately, as a result of the many factors discussed in the second section of this chapter, urban sprawl continued and even accelerated during the 1970s. The old pattern of large areas of unplanned urban fringe development interspersed with areas of planned development continued to spread. It seems clear that the new development permit system for large-scale private developments initiated by the 1968 City Planning Law did greatly improve the ability of local governments to ensure adequate development standards in such developments. Minimum provisions for parks, sewer systems, road widths and other public facilities were stipulated, and local governments were given the authority to withhold development permits where proposed developments did not conform. The development permit system also was employed by many local governments to create their own development manuals (*kaihatsu shidō yōkō*) which specified even higher standards than the national law. While these were legally unenforceable, local governments could and did use them effectively in their negotiations with developers. These development manuals are discussed in more detail in Chapter 8.

That the new system had not eliminated all of the serious problems seen in large-scale planned residential developments, however, is shown clearly by Ben-Ari's (1991) case study of a suburban housing area developed in the 1970s near Kyoto. The suburban estate he studied, developed from the late 1960s to the mid-1970s and housing a total of just under 2,000 households, shows that many of the former problems of substandard development continued under the new system. Not only had bribes (*uragane*) to high-ranking prefectural government officers enabled the developer to gain approval for greatly weakened development standards for the area, but in many cases even these lower standards had not been followed in actual construction. Roads were built narrower than normally permissible, and with such a thin layer of paving that they cracked and filled with potholes within a few years. The sewer system was built with pipes that were too narrow, causing frequent blockages, and the purification plant was insufficient to handle the volume of waste by the time the development was fully built out. No land was initially allocated for parks, playgrounds or schools, and these were achieved only after long negotiations between an active residents' movement, the developer and the local government in the mid-1970s (Ben-Ari 1991: 79). Ben-Ari argues that such corruption was endemic throughout the construction industry and arose primarily because of the rather flexible regulations of the development permit system combined with the pork-barrel approach to public infrastructure building of the long-ruling LDP. In the prefecture in question a subsequent investigation found that the prefectural governor, leading construction companies and others were all involved in large-scale systemic corruption, and one man was convicted and spent time in jail. These sorts of problems were a major factor in the spread of citizens' movements and progressive local administrations during the 1970s.

One of the most interesting aspects of Ben-Ari's study was his examination of the processes of politicisation of the local residents, and the role of the neighbourhood organisation (*jichikai*) in lobbying with the developer and local government for redress, including the building of parks, schools and a community centre. It seems that finally, with the success of the anti-pollution citizens' movements, and the growing assertiveness of residents' movements, the legitimacy of local residential environmental activism was becoming established. The growth of civil society-based movements that could fight for and win concessions in the form of improved living conditions was beginning to change the context of city planning.

It seems clear that the passage of the 1968 planning system was a necessary but not sufficient condition for the defence and improvement of urban quality of life. While the stricter standards for large-scale development specified in the development permit regulations were the fulcrum against which residents' movements could push, without their organised pressure it seems that much urban development continued as before. There was also considerable diversity among local governments, with some administrations taking the lead in using the new planning powers in positive ways, and others needing outside pressure before changing their approach. As shown in the case of sunshine rights rules, there were even cases where entirely new regulations for the protection of residential quality of life were the product of citizens' movements.

High-rise development and sunshine rights

Two changes to building regulations during the 1970s have had significant long-term impacts on Japanese cities. The first was a change to building height limits during the major revisions of the Building Standards Law of 1970 required by the 1968 City Planning Law revisions. Improved building technology had made it technically possible to build earthquake-proof high-rise buildings. Until 1968 there had been a strictly enforced height limit of 30 metres throughout Japanese urban areas, with a limit of 10 metres in residential areas, but in 1970 the absolute height limit was abolished entirely in commercial and industrial areas. Only in Exclusive Residential #1 areas was the limit of 10 metres retained. Allowable building heights were still limited by slant plane restrictions, the width of adjacent road, and the FAR, but the revision allowed much greater building heights, particularly in commercial areas, but also in Residential and

Exclusive Residential #2 areas which included most of the pre-war city area. This change had a significant impact because commercial areas were scattered throughout Japanese urban areas, and were often zoned in long strips on both sides of major roads. High-rise building in commercial zones could therefore affect many residences.

The second major change, legal protection for sunshine rights, followed from the first, and was a result of protests over high-rise buildings that blocked sunlight to neighbouring buildings. The impact was therefore not on the patterns of urban growth on the urban fringe that have concerned us most in this chapter, but on patterns of built form in existing built up areas. The conflict over "sunshine rights" is also characteristic of citizen protest and mobilisation over urban redevelopment, and of patterns of government response to such protest during the 1970s.

The root of the problem was that local governments had no legal way of opposing any development that conformed to zoning and building standards laws, meaning that unpredictable changes in old neighbourhoods were common. As the land use zones allowed such a wide range of uses in most districts, and FARs were quite generous, it became very common for developers to buy land in existing neighbourhoods and build large high-rise apartments, resulting in a boom of condominium development (the so-called *Manshon* boom) in the early 1970s. This created intense conflicts between the existing residents of neighbourhoods and the developers who were building high-rise apartment blocks. Various negative impacts of such redevelopment projects were complained of, including increased congestion, blocking of views, etc, but none were so bitterly resented as the blocking of sunlight by high-rise buildings. Japanese houses are almost invariably oriented to face the south, and a daily ritual of housewives is to air out bedding and washing in the sun. Where direct sunlight is blocked the quality of life in the shaded location is permanently worsened.

In Musashino City in western Tokyo prefecture, groups of homeowners who were protesting against high-rise development persuaded the mayor, a reformist politician who had been backed by the JSP and JCP parties of the left, to support new city guidelines requiring anyone planning a building of over 10 metres in height to first obtain the consent of surrounding residents. This was backed by the threat that the city would refuse to allow the building to be connected to the city water supply and sewerage networks. In addition, a Tokyo-wide liaison organisation of sunshine rights groups was formed which won a number of court cases against builders who had blocked the sunlight to other neighbouring buildings, and a variety of damages were awarded to complainants. In 1972 the Supreme Court determined that Article 25 of the constitution which guarantees "minimum standards of wholesome and cultural living" protected the right to sunshine, and that infringements of sunshine rights were liable for damages (McKean 1981: 113). In 1973 the citizens' movement drafted and presented their own proposal for a sunlight protection ordinance (*Hiatari Jōrei*) to the Tokyo Metropolitan Government. As Ishida and Ishizuka suggest, "This was an epochal development in the citizens' movement in that it progressed from simply opposing things to actively proposing policies" (Ishizuka and Ishida 1988b: 30). Through the 1970s a large number of sunshine rights cases were won against offending builders and even against the government in the case of an elevated expressway.

In such a context it is hardly surprising that the government worked quickly to revise the building regulations. The level of uncertainty about what was permissible and what would incur liability to pay damages was high enough that builders ran an unacceptably high risk of losing court battles with neighbours, even where they had complied with existing regulations. The MoC drafted a revision to the Building Standards Law that included many of the proposals of the citizens' movement, and those revisions came into effect in 1976. The revision required all local governments to draft their own sunshine standards that specified the minimum hours of unimpeded sunlight cast to the north of new buildings at the winter solstice when the sun is at its lowest.

It took not only citizen mobilisation, but also political backing by supportive politicians, and perhaps even more important, a threat to the viability of land development projects to change the Building Standards Law in favour of sunlight protection. In this case the Supreme Court decision had sharply raised the level of risk by making it very uncertain which developments would be subject to orders to compensate neighbours, and by how much. The legislative response was quick, as it would surely have been in any of the other developed countries in such a situation.

The sunshine rights movements were significant partly simply because they were one of the first cases of successful citizen mobilisation to change planning law. Perhaps more important in the longer run is that since the 1970s such grassroots organising around local environmental and quality of life issues has gradually taken a more and more prominent role in shaping Japanese urban areas. The local citizens' environmental movements of the 1970s, and particularly the sunshine rights movements, marked the beginning of the more active involvement of civil society actors in processes of urban change in Japan.

8 From planning deregulation to the bubble economy

Tokyo has become something of a monster city. It seems to have set itself the task of outstripping all other cities on earth without really having worked out what that entails – like the nation in microcosm, if that is the right term for the world's biggest conurbation . . . Tokyo has become so large, such a devourer of resources, that it pushed its most intractable problems beyond the metropolitan borders and, more importantly, beyond national borders. In other words, Tokyo Mondai, the "Tokyo issue", is rapidly becoming the concern of people outside Japan. The problem takes shape from the serious distortions that exist in Tokyo. These manifest themselves, I would suggest, in a deterioration in living standards at the very time when the nation as a whole is becoming richer and more powerful than ever before. In the vacuum caused by the lack of serious public debate on what sort of city Tokyo should become, the commercial and administrative manipulators can chart out their own strategy, which rests on the premise that whatever pronouncements are made in public, property prices must never be allowed to fall, and on a refusal to tamper with the complicated regulatory environment, claiming that to do so would be to infringe personal rights. Pious comments from manipulators on high and a general exasperated wringing of hands among the public seem to be leading to acceptance of what should be an unacceptable situation.

(Waley 1991: viii–ix)

The onset of the 1980s brought a very different political and economic climate which had profound effects on urban planning in Japan. This chapter reviews the period from the elections of 1980 in which the LDP regained both a majority (50.9 per cent) of the votes cast in a lower house election for the first time since 1963 as well as a strong majority of seats (57.9 per cent), until the burst of the bubble in the first months of 1990. This period saw a very different approach to urban planning, environmental and public welfare issues than that seen in the 1970s. While the 1970s were characterised by a pattern of increasing regulation of land development and environmental pollution and rapidly expanding social welfare spending, the 1980s saw attempts to reverse all of these trends, some of which were more successful than others.

As discussed above, in response to its steadily declining electoral fortunes during the 1960s, the LDP had started actively to court urban voters in the late 1960s, and the passage of the new City Planning Law of 1968 was only the first of a long series of legislative initiatives designed to re-position the party as the champion of positive environmental and social welfare policies, as well as the party of business and rural areas.

When confronted with massive citizens' movements protesting worsening urban environments and inadequate social infrastructure in the late 1960s and early 1970s, the LDP worked actively and largely successfully to co-opt the issues which had proved popular for progressive politicians who had gained office by blaming worsening environmental problems, weak urban planning systems and inadequate social welfare and health care spending on the LDP. The LDP responded with a vast array of new legislative initiatives, from the new city planning system of 1968 to the pollution legislation of the early 1970s, and the creation of the national land planning system in 1974. 1973 was even declared the "First Year of the Welfare State" (*fukushi gannen*) as the national government expanded national welfare programmes and spending. Several of the new policies were simply borrowed from those of reformist city and prefectural governments, while others were generated within the bureaucracy and within the ruling party. Calder (1988) has argued that it is this responsiveness in the face of electoral pressure and its ability to include new groups and issues in its orbit that was the key to LDP dominance of post-war Japanese government. Other political scientists argue that this period saw the emergence of a form of pluralistic policymaking under the umbrella of LDP rule (Muramatsu and Krauss 1987). It is clear, however, that the LDP succeeded in restoring its electoral fortunes primarily by adopting policies more favourable to the environment and to the needs of urban residents.

The new policy direction of the 1970s created two important problems for the ruling party, however. First was the question of how to finance the growing government spending on welfare programmes. Welfare spending of all sorts expanded greatly during the 1970s, but the ruling party was reluctant to increase taxes, particularly when they were so close to losing their overall government majority, so most of the new spending was simply covered by the easy political choice of deficit financing. By the late 1970s overall government debt levels had increased dramatically, and conservatives within the LDP were starting to push for fiscal discipline. As Pempel describes the shift in party thinking:

> Deficit financing had the obvious advantage of being far less visible to the general public than major hikes in taxes. But as public deficits mounted, the idea of emulating Western-style welfare programs came under withering attack, particularly from the business sector and the MOF. Furthermore, policy changes had pre-empted the opposition's ability to exploit pollution or welfare as issues to attack the conservatives. Indeed, in the 1979 lower house election the LDP finally stemmed its twenty year decline in vote share. Then in the famous "double election" of 1980 its proportion of seats jumped from 49.3 to 57.9 percent and the opposition parties were effectively brushed to the sidelines. The electoral turnaround for the conservatives allowed a return from "lifestyle politics" to "fiscal restraint".
>
> (Pempel 1998: 188)

Electoral success, the disarray of the opposition parties, and the decline of the citizens' movements allowed the LDP to bring the short period of welfare expansion to a close in the early 1980s with Nakasone's "administrative reform" policies. Administrative reform was intended primarily to reduce government deficits by reducing welfare programmes that took the form of automatic entitlements. Instead of becoming a "welfare state" Japan would try to become a "welfare society" in which the main burden of welfare services for the elderly, the sick and others unable to work would be placed on the family rather than the state (Goodman and Peng 1996). In this the LDP was responding to the demands of its main sponsors in the business community for reductions in government spending and a return to a relatively strict fiscal policy (Pempel 1998: 190). The 1980s became a decade of unchallenged LDP dominance, while the main opposition parties remained divided, and unable to offer a credible alternative to the governing party.

The second political problem arose from LDP attempts to court urban voters during the early 1970s through better planning policies and stricter urban development laws. The problem was that any serious attempt to improve city planning laws and particularly to manage growth on the urban fringe required policies that limited the development rights of landowners and the profitability of land speculation and development. Such changes could only come at the expense of core LDP support groups in the farm and land development industries. That the LDP was not really seriously trying to solve problems of urban growth is suggested by the critical loopholes initially left in the development control system, by the introduction of new loopholes through the 1970s, and by the failure of land tax reform as described in the last chapter. More telling, however, is that when LDP political fortunes had improved in the late 1970s and early 1980s, one of the first priorities of the party was to weaken the planning system established during the previous decade.

This chapter examines several aspects of this tumultuous period of the 1980s. The first section looks at the broader context of economic change accompanying globalisation and the internationalisation of the Japanese economy, and the rise of Tokyo as its ever more dominant centre. The second section looks at the new District Planning system introduced in 1980 which was in many ways a continuation of the growth of city planning power of the 1970s, and which was to have profound effects on Japanese city planning during the 1980s and 1990s. The third section describes the deregulation policies attempted by the Nakasone government in its efforts to stimulate private sector activity. The fourth section outlines some of the main changes to Japanese urban areas during the 1980s, and a brief concluding section describes the disaster of the bubble economy period.

Unipolar concentration in Tokyo

Throughout the period up to the bursting of the bubble economy in the early 1990s, Japan posted significantly higher rates of economic growth than any of its major competitors in the industrialised world. In the 1970s after a sharp and brief decline following the 1973 oil crisis, economic growth resumed and Japan avoided most of the decade of "stagflation" that dogged the other developed countries in the 1970s, as well as the damaging round of high interest rates that finally brought inflation to an end in the early 1980s at the cost of a deep recession. As a result Japanese economic growth during the period from 1970 to 1990 was greater than any of its major competitors, and by 1988, Japanese GDP per capita stood at $19,905 (having increased by 10 times since 1970) higher than that of the US at $18,570 (3.75 times increase) and of West Germany at $18,373 (6 times increase) (Tsuru 1993: 182).

At the same time the Japanese economy changed greatly during the late 1970s and early 1980s, shifting from the old growth sectors of heavy and chemical industries to the new growth sectors of precision machinery, electronics, automobiles, and finance. The decline of the once dominant heavy industries such as shipbuilding in the 1970s was due in part to the oil crisis, which sharply reduced orders for new supertankers, and in part to the increasingly strict pollution regulations in Japan, which made further investment in Japan in the heavily polluting chemical and aluminium industries unattractive. In the longer run, however, the rise of the yen was the main factor in the structural shift of the Japanese economy away from heavy industry, as it made emerging competitors such as South Korea relatively cheaper production locations for heavy engineering. At the same time, the rising yen encouraged increasing flows of Japanese foreign direct investment (FDI) to Korea, Taiwan, Southeast Asia, the US and Europe. Whereas during the rapid growth period most Japanese FDI had been to develop sources of important raw materials, during the 1980s the bulk of FDI was for development of overseas manufacturing and assembly operations. These investments took advantage of the stronger yen, lower wages and pollution standards abroad, and enabled major Japanese manufacturers to avoid increasing protectionism in some of their major markets.

The spread of Japanese corporate investment around the world was an important factor in the emergence of Tokyo as one of the financial capitals of the world, as an increasingly sophisticated financial services industry emerged to service the far-flung web of overseas corporate investment. The second pillar of Tokyo's financial strength arose from steadily increasing Japanese trade surpluses which were recycled primarily into American government treasury bonds, thus indirectly financing the increasing American trade deficits, and directly financing the growing federal fiscal deficits resulting from the Reagan tax cuts and military build up. Japan's shift in role during the 1980s from a country whose economy and financial system was largely internally focused, albeit with an important export surplus, to one that was increasingly linked into the global capital and financial markets is illustrated by its changing investment profile. In the late 1970s, "Japanese investors accounted for only 6 per cent of direct investment outflows from the major industrial nations, 2 per cent of equities outflows, 15 per cent of bond outflows, and 12 per cent of short-term bank outflows. By the late 1980s, these figures had swollen to 20 per cent of international foreign direct investment, 25 per cent of equities, 55 per cent of bonds, and 50 per cent of short-term bank loans" (Pempel 1998: 147). The majority of Japanese international financial and management activity was carried out from Tokyo, directly resulting in the emergence of Tokyo as one of the command and control centres of the world economy, one of the top three "global cities" along with New York and London (Sassen 1991).

During the 1980s a substantial literature developed on the impacts on the "world cities" of increasing globalisation following the research agenda first proposed by Friedmann and Wolff (1982). In the case of Tokyo, work by Fujita (1992) and Machimura (1994) sought to comprehend the changes wrought by the increasing role of global capital in the restructuring of Tokyo. Although it has proved quite difficult to pinpoint particular changes that should be credited to globalisation rather than other factors, there is wide agreement that the key factor propelling Japanese urban change during the 1980s was the concentration of business functions in Tokyo. Often referred to as "unipolar concentration in Tokyo" this phenomenon is blamed for a range of ills, including worsening congestion and air pollution, rising land prices, and their associated ills of urban restructuring and increasing wealth inequalities (Fujita 1992; Hatta and Tabuchi 1995: 86; Rimmer 1986).

The emergence of Tokyo as the dominant engine of economic growth in Japan during the 1980s had profound impacts on Japanese urbanisation and planning. From 1980 to 1985 more than 80 per cent of new jobs were in service industries including the financial sector, and about half of all new service sector jobs were created in the Tokyo area (Miyao 1991: 132). Tokyo greatly increased its dominance as the premier location for Japanese corporate head offices during the 1980s. By 1990 half of all companies had head offices or main branches in Tokyo, 80 per cent of all clearings by value were based there, and 85 per cent of all foreign corporate offices (Iwata 1994: 41). Tokyo increased its economic lead over Osaka, and even attracted the head offices of many prominent Osaka-based firms during the 1980s (Miyamoto 1993).

Many have argued the importance of the concentration of central government functions in Tokyo as an important factor in its economic dominance, as corporations needed to locate close to the central ministries to be able to gain access to crucial contracts and information (Miyakawa and Wada 1987). Similarly, an increasingly important job for local governments has been to attract central government spending in their area. Hatta and Tabuchi (1995: 86) even suggest that the 1980s saw a re-emergence of the "alternate attendance" system of the Tokugawa period, with top local government officers forced to spend much of their working time visiting Tokyo in order to solicit central government spending in their region. In the 1990s these practices came under increasing criticism as many local citizens' groups took their own local governments to court for spending millions on "wining and dining" central government bureaucrats, and each other, in exclusive clubs in Tokyo.

Within Japan the ever growing dominance of Tokyo has had profound consequences. During the rapid growth period Japan had three major industrial areas, with relatively equal shares held by Osaka and Tokyo, and a slightly smaller concentration between them in Nagoya. From the 1980s this structure began to change as the Osaka economy stagnated and Tokyo surged ahead (Miyamoto 1993). While the economy of the Osaka region was based significantly on the traditional large-scale heavy engineering and chemical industries, the Tokyo region was made up predominantly of thousands of small firms, many of which were changing to high-tech and flexible production methods in the 1980s. The Tokyo region emerged as the centre of rapidly growing high-technology industries in the 1980s, especially in the prefecture of Kanagawa immediately south of the capital (Obayashi 1993). Further propelling the emergence of Tokyo as the dominant economic hub was the concentration of international financial and management functions in the region mentioned above, and the continued growth in the dominance of Tokyo in education, culture and media production (Cybriwsky 1998).

A direct consequence of Tokyo's economic dominance was the resumption of net migration to the capital region in the 1980s after a period of greatly reduced interregional migration in the late 1970s, resulting from the economic slowdown and decreasing regional disparities (Mera 1989). Thus throughout the 1980s Tokyo was the only region with significant net gains from migration. Ishikawa and Fielding (1998) argue that patterns of Japanese migration changed fundamentally during the 1980s, suggesting that while the enormous net migration towards the three metropolitan areas during the rapid growth period was driven by expansion of the economy and the creation of millions of new jobs, significant net migration during the 1980s was seen only towards the Tokyo region, and was caused primarily by structural changes resulting from the transformation of Tokyo into a world city, including industrial restructuring and changing residential land prices. Net in-migration to the Tokyo region (Tokyo, Kanagawa, Saitama, and Chiba) increased steadily through the 1980s and reached a peak of just over 160,000 per year in 1987 before declining again to a net outflow in 1994.

All these processes contributed to the phenomenon referred to in Japan as "unipolar concentration in Tokyo" (Hatta and Tabuchi 1995), in which Tokyo cemented its dominance of all areas of national life from government to corporate decision-making, finance capital, international trade, education, and media production. In the 1980s more than ever, to be successful meant to live and work in the Tokyo region, even though that often meant higher living costs, longer commuting times, and a lower quality of housing.

Regional planning and technopolis building

One product of the "unipolar concentration" phenomenon was a revision to the Comprehensive National Development Plan (CNPD). The fourth CNPD, approved in 1987, was designed primarily to address the renewed concentration of jobs and people in the Tokyo region and its corollary of population decline and job shortages in local regions, and applied from 1986 to 2000. Interestingly, the first draft of the plan published in 1986 stressed the importance of Tokyo as a world city and financial centre, proposing to strengthen its international functions. That emphasis created such a strong backlash of opposition from the regions that little mention of strengthening Tokyo's functions remained in the plan as finally approved. Instead, Tokyo's dominance was identified as a major problem it would address.

In its final version the basic goals of the plan were:

1   "to vitalize each area through local settlement and interaction among areas;"
2   "International Integration and Reorganization of the Global City Functions;"
3   "to provide the country with a safe environment of high qualities" (Japan National Land Agency 1987: 4–5).

The main levers for revitalising peripheral areas was the improvement of transportation networks and the fostering of regional science and technology and tourism centres, of which the Ministry of International Trade and Industry's technopolis plans were to play an important role. The phrase "reorganisation of global city functions" referred to the policy of dispersal of international functions from Tokyo to Nagoya and Osaka. Instead of attempting to limit the role of Tokyo as a global city, however, global functions would be supported in all three of the main metropolitan areas. It was hoped that the CNDP would help to create "a country where, on the basis of securing a safe and pleasant national land, a number of polar areas with their own characteristic functions coexist without an excessive concentration of population and economic, administrative and other functions in particular areas and where each area interacts with others and foreign countries to mutually complementary and stimulating [sic]"

(Japan National Land Agency 1987: 6). Many commentators dismissed this as simple window dressing, arguing that in reality the main thrust of the plan was to encourage the growth and restructuring of Tokyo into a centre for international, informational and financial activities (see e.g. Machimura 1992; Watanabe 1992).

One of the more concrete of the wide range of national and regional development plans of the 1980s was the Ministry of International Trade and Industry's (MITI) technopolis scheme. Motivated again by the perceived over-concentration of population in the main metropolitan regions, the technopolis programme was designed to create a number of high-tech communities, modelled in part on Silicon Valley in California. Of the many such attempts to create an innovative milieu for technology development around the world, the Japanese project was one of the most carefully watched and widely written about (see Castells and Hall 1994; Edgington 1994; Masser 1990; Stohr and Pönighaus 1992). The idea was that each technopolis would become a high-tech industrial city of about 50,000 population outside but near a "mother city" of at least 150,000 people, with high-speed transport facilities allowing a one-day return trip to either Tokyo, Osaka or Nagoya. Candidate sites also had to have large land areas available for development, and an existing nearby university with high-tech education or research. Technopolises were to create a high amenity residential environment to attract and keep the creative high-tech talent, as well as providing public infrastructure such as testing and training facilities, and encouraging links between academic and private researchers. It was also hoped that the creation of such high-tech cities would encourage Japanese corporations to relocate to the peripheral regions of Japan, instead of moving offshore to Taiwan, Korea and Southeast Asia.

The technopolis concept was thus an interesting mix of three of the key strands of Japanese developmental planning: the garden city concepts of high-amenity suburban residential environments of the 1920s and 1930s would be linked to the indicative economic planning of the high-growth period through the provision of main infrastructure, and to the regional development ideas of the 1970s by promoting indigenous technological development in settlement regions throughout the country. Eventually 26 sites were designated in almost every prefecture outside the main metropolitan regions, drawing much criticism that too many sites would spread the programme too thinly, and that MITI had caved in to political pressure in allowing sites that did not fit the original criteria. The eagerness of local politicians to gain a technopolis in their area is understandable, as they were to create abundant and high-paying jobs, as well as luring in considerable national government spending. Although the original intent was that local and prefectural governments were to provide the bulk of the finance, the national government was responsible for much of the hard infrastructure, and the Ministry of Construction (MoC) reported that it had spent an average of $200 million each for 11 of the technopolises by 1990 when the programme was only partly finished (Castells and Hall 1994: 117).

An evaluation of the impact of technopolis development on regional disparities in the formation of high-tech plants by the respected European regional scientists Walter Stöhr and Richard Pönighaus suggested that the technopolis programme had indeed had positive initial effects in broadening high-tech development in peripheral prefectures. The strongest such effects were seen in prefectures with technopolises located along high-speed shinkansen rail lines, and that had easy access to Tokyo (Stöhr and Pönighaus 1992: 618). The initial success of the programme was in part related to the enormous wave of

Figure 8.1 Technopolis locations throughout Japan. Although the original concept suggested that only a small number of sites be designated, as a result of intense lobbying by prefectural governments, some 26 technopolis areas were designated throughout the country in the mid-1980s.

investment in new plant and equipment during the "bubble economy" period of the second half of the 1980s. MITI's first review of the programme showed that over 2,500 plants had located in the first 14 technopolises between 1984 and 1989, allowing the programme to be declared a success (Edgington 1994: 137). After the collapse of the bubble in 1991, however, such new plant formation quickly dropped off, making it harder to discern clear positive impacts, and some evaluations are quite pessimistic about the long-term impacts of the policy. Castells and Hall (1994: 141–2), for example, suggest that two main conclusions emerge from a range of studies of the programme. First, they argue that it does not seem likely a majority of the technopolises will be successful in the long run. Instead, they predict that only the eight technopolises within 300 kilometres of Tokyo are likely to generate much new activity. Second, they suggest that as the dispersed locations have encouraged the location primarily of branch plants without significant research and development capacity, the concept of creating many small Silicon Valleys is flawed and the main innovative region will continue to be Tokyo.

In the present context the technopolis programme is of great interest whether or not it succeeds in promoting a high-tech boom in the peripheral regions of the country. It represents the first attempt by the national government to encourage high-quality integrated new town development that provided not only mass housing, but also places of work, high-amenity residential areas and educational and recreational facilities. Previous new towns had been primarily large-scale dormitory developments to serve burgeoning metropolitan areas, and were often drearily functional in their design. Even Tsukuba, the academic new town north east of Tokyo that was in many ways a model for the technopolis programme is not really a nice place to live, with lots of cheap prefabricated apartment blocks for the government research officers transferred there. Many of the new technopolises were very well designed with high standards of public and private facilities, providing a high quality of urban environment. This was of course in part a product of the greatly increased wealth of the country and the bulging treasury of the bubble period, and it is worth remembering that the programme was at bottom justified as economic development. The fact remains, however, that national government ministries had finally acknowledged that high-quality residential environments were worth investing in, even if only for the key high-tech workers who would lead the country in its competition with Silicon Valley.

District planning

The introduction of the District Plan system in 1980 was probably the most important addition to the Japanese city planning system since its introduction in 1968. District planning, modelled on the German *Bebauungs Plan* system (B-Plan), was developed in response to the realisation during the second half of the 1970s that in fundamental ways the high hopes that the 1968 system would allow the improvement of urban environments and the prevention of further haphazard unserviced sprawl were not being achieved. In this sense, the District Plan system was a continuation of the movement of the late 1960s and early 1970s towards greater environmental consciousness, stronger pollution control and more effective city planning. Specifically, the new District Planning system was designed to counter a fundamental weakness of the 1968 city planning system that had resulted in continuing problems during the 1970s: there was no legal basis for detailed controls over urban development or redevelopment. Planning authorities had great difficulties in controlling the layout or design of new local roads, apart from the requirement that they be a minimum of 4 metres in width. Nor could they control the size, form, orientation, or design of buildings if the proposed development was within the relatively generous limits imposed by the zoning and building standards systems. Neither was there any legal basis for preventing the subdivision and redevelopment of existing urban plots. These shortcomings created quite different planning problems on the urban fringe and in existing urban areas.

On the urban fringe the main problem was that the 1968 system provided no way of imposing an overall design on private roads built in newly developing areas. This weakness was in part a result of the replacement in 1950 of the building-line system with a much simpler regulation of minimum road widths (as described in Chapter 5). While the building-line system had allowed a relatively detailed planning of new road systems during the 1930s and 1940s by the simple preparation and approval of a plan, after 1950, apart from city planning road designation which was only used for the largest arterial roads, local planners had few controls over local road layouts or plot sizes. This combined with the various loopholes in the development permission system to allow the proliferation of unplanned sprawl development and mini-kaihatsu shown in the previous chapter. Even in larger, better serviced developments, however, there was no way of requiring that separate projects conform to a larger plan for a whole district. As a result, many newly developing areas ended up with patchy, fragmented local road systems that failed to provide minimum levels of accessibility, and the achievement of good urban designs that made effective use of natural features, preserved green areas, or produced attractive districts was almost impossible (Sorensen 2001b). It was hoped that district plans would solve these problems by allowing the drafting of legally binding plans to control future road layouts in as yet undeveloped areas. In this sense the District Plan system was intended as a belated replacement for the building-line system provided in the 1919 Urban Buildings Law.

The problem in existing built up areas was quite different. There the main issue was that local governments had no legal way of opposing any development that conformed to zoning and building standards laws, meaning that unpredictable changes in old neighbourhoods were common. As the land use zones allowed such a wide range of uses in most districts, and floor area ratios (FAR) were quite generous, it became very common for developers to buy land in existing neighbourhoods and build large high-rise apartments, resulting in the boom of high-rise condominium development (the *Manshon* boom). This created intense conflicts between the existing residents of neighbourhoods and developers who built high-rise apartment blocks as described in the previous chapter. Because there were also effectively no restrictions on the subdivision of existing building plots, redevelopment of existing sites was also quite common. Many large older houses were demolished and replaced with three or four smaller ones. Such micro redevelopment could not be prevented by the planning system, which meant that it was impossible to protect existing neighbourhoods from gradual environmental decline by overcrowding. These weaknesses placed real limits on the possibilities for the improvement and protection of existing urban areas from inappropriate or damaging redevelopment. This was particularly a problem in historic areas, where the specific provisions for building restrictions were very weak, amounting primarily to height restrictions slightly stronger than in normal areas. While specific individual buildings could be designated as nationally protected, there were no legal means to regulate the building style or form of new buildings constructed nearby. This meant that it was in practice impossible to protect historic urban areas from being destroyed. District Plans would greatly enhance the legal framework for such historic preservation efforts, which are examined in more detail in Chapter 9.

A final hoped-for effect of District Plans was that as they allowed the selective strengthening of zoning laws in specified districts, it would be possible to modify the zoning system of the national City Planning Law to suit individual conditions in individual cities. Until District Planning, local governments could only use the predetermined set of land use zones set in the national legislation. As noted in previous chapters, these had functioned as a sort of lowest common denominator, and were suited primarily to the main metropolitan areas. District Plans held out the promise that finally a more detailed, individualised planning for individual districts would be legally permitted, including the drafting of zoning regulations specific to particular areas.

Basic features of the District Plan system

Inspired by the German *Bebauungs Plan* system, the District Plan system was proposed by the MoC City Planning and Building Committees in 1979, and was passed into law as major amendments to both the City Planning and Building Standards Laws in 1980. As the MoC describes it, District Planning "aims to enhance the characteristics of the defined district by presenting policy directions of improvement and detailed control; of building construction including design components; site planning; architectural design and location of open spaces within the district" (Japan Ministry of Construction 1996: 41). Within the District Plan area, a range of new planning restrictions were made possible, including controls over new road layouts, lot sizes, building design, building setbacks, and construction materials. Apart from the use of private building covenants, these sorts of restrictions were new for Japan, which had hitherto been very reluctant to restrict the freedom of developers in this way. District Plans were to be the responsibility of municipal governments, as they were to provide detailed planning of relatively small areas of several hectares. While the Japanese District Plans look like and function very similarly to the German B-plans on which they are modelled, the main difference is that in Germany B-plans are much more widely used, and in Germany you cannot build anything outside of B-planned areas without special building permission. In Japan District Planned areas are still rather the exception than the rule, and such a strong restriction on land rights, while effective in the German case, would probably be politically impossible.

District Plans have two parts, a statement of policy intent, and a District Improvement Plan. The policy statement is akin to a master plan for an area, and outlines both the objectives for the district, and a vision of its future state. This can include a visual element such as a rendering of the desired future aspect of the area. The policy statement can include "future images; land use; facility improvement including access roads, small parks and other public open spaces; setbacks and building design; and landscaping" (Japan Ministry of Construction 1996: 42). There have been many cases where only the policy statement has been passed, without being followed by a District Improvement Plan because the policy statement carries no legal power to restrict private building activity, and it is relatively easier for a municipal government to approve such a statement, even in cases where the local residents do not agree with it.

The District Improvement Plan document includes specific regulations that will be used to enforce the provisions of the plan. It consists of two parts: one relating to public facilities, and another with detailed regulations on private development within the plan area. The district facilities plan can include elements such as a detailed road plan, other public space such as parks and other facilities which are to be used by the residents within the district. The focus is on small-scale district facilities that will further the achievement of the vision of the future district outlined in the policy statement. Larger infrastructure such as main roads, even if included within the district, are still governed by the normal City Planning Law.

The really original aspect of the District Plan system is that local governments for the first time had the legal power to impose more detailed restrictions on private development activity than allowed by the zoning and building standards systems. Regulations on private building activity may include land use; maximum and minimum lot coverage, building height and FAR; setbacks from property lines; shape and design of buildings; building materials, colours and styles; and landscaping details such as design of fences and preservation of existing trees.

Because the regulatory power of these plans can be so strong, the legislation also required significant public participation in plan formulation and approval. In particular, a very high level of agreement among residents and landowners is necessary, in practice meaning that a minimum of over 90 per cent must agree to the plan before it can be approved. Local governments will therefore go to considerable effort to gain support for the plan among local people before attempting to pass such a plan. As can be imagined, this requirement made it quite difficult to apply District Plans over large areas, and greatly restricted their use in practice. It is interesting to note that this requirement for exceptionally high levels of acceptance of District Plans before their official passage is almost universally followed, even though it is not actually specified in the City Planning Law.

Also affecting the implementation of the new system was the timing of its introduction in 1980. As noted above, the 1970s had been a decade of increasing government regulation of urban development and greatly increased spending on social welfare. By the beginning of the 1980s the climate had changed dramatically, and the focus was on cutting government spending and deregulation, as described below. This could not fail to affect the way the new system was implemented, and it was not long before revisions were made to the system. While as originally drafted the District Plan system could only be used to make existing zoning regulations stricter, in 1988 the law was amended to allow more flexibility in the use of District Plans by relaxing limits on allowable FAR or lot coverage, for example.

Although this was at one level simply a part of the ideologically inspired deregulation drive of the early 1980s, in some ways the revisions strengthened and improved the District Plan system and broadened its possibilities. In particular, the "Special District Plan for Redevelopment" system has since been widely used in cases of redevelopment of the abandoned factory sites which became increasingly more common during the 1980s with the move of many manufacturing industries offshore. This is examined in more detail in the section on deregulation, below. Similarly, in older, densely built up neighbourhoods with inadequate roads, a FAR bonus and extra height allowance can be granted to landowners who donate a certain amount of their land to allow road-widening. Another important amendment was to allow the passage of District Plans in the Urbanisation Control Area (UCA) instead of only the Urbanisation Prevention Area (UPA) as was originally allowed. Where deregulation allows a trade-off between some relaxation of existing standards in return for needed public goods, and helps to persuade landowners and developers to accept design controls, the result can be a net gain for the public.

Four main uses of District Plans have emerged: first, in new suburban developments District Plans have been very widely used as a way of preventing future changes to the character of the district. Because existing planning regulations included no regulation of subdivision, and regulation of land use was very weak, even in the best urban areas redevelopment of house plots to apartments or shops was common. The passage of a District Plan allows detailed regulations over future redevelopment, land use and built form, and can give a measure of security for homeowners that unwanted urban redevelopment will not occur in their neighbourhood. They are also easy to implement, as they are applied when the area is first developed, before significant population exists.

Surprisingly, apart from private deed restrictions which were very difficult to enforce, this system provided the first such planning protection for residential areas in Japan. Second, District Plans for Historical Preservation and development control in districts neighbouring historic areas have also been important and are discussed in the next chapter. Third, redevelopment projects of specific sites such as the disused factory sites discussed above, and fourth, incremental improvement of existing built up areas.

From one point of view the District Plan system has been somewhat disappointing as the total area covered by such plans is rather small. In many cities they govern only one or two small areas, because it has been very difficult to attain the high levels of agreement that they require. On the other hand the fact that local governments gained significant new powers of detailed planning has in practice had profound long-term consequences for city planning practice. Local governments could now make detailed plans specific to their own local circumstances, could create enforceable design guidelines, and could prevent unwanted redevelopment in existing neighbourhoods where District Plans had been approved. These new powers enabled some local governments to develop new methods of community-based planning and public participation during the early 1980s. These methods, while diverse, are generally referred to as *"machizukuri"*, and developed during the 1980s and 1990s as the most important broad-based movement in support of strengthened local planning in the history of Japanese city planning. While the Japanese term translates literally as "city making" it has a strong implication of "community building", or "community development". As the Japanese idea of machizukuri is much richer and more complex than any of these English translations suggest, we will use the Japanese term here.

It would be wrong to suggest that the District Plan system created machizukuri. Rather, it provided a legal framework which enabled a wide variety of planning activities to be carried out more effectively. In many cases, local governments built on the "development manuals" approach of using the development permit system as the basis for negotiating for local benefits from developers (Uchiumi 1999). They were in effect using a statutory process of permit approval in combination with non-statutory procedures of negotiation and consultation to achieve greater levels of public benefits than legally required under the City Planning Law. The District Plan system provided a much stronger legal basis for these negotiations, because the potential regulatory power was much stronger.

The other defining characteristic of machizukuri has been the development of systems of local resident participation in detailed local planning and development control. In part this is a product of the law. The 1980 revision of the City Planning Law that created the District Planning system required municipal governments which use the system to pass two local ordinances. One ordinance was to establish citizen participation procedures in the planning process, and the second was to create special building regulations within the District Plan area that could be legally enforced under the Building Standards Law. As is well known, however, such legal requirements for participation are easily fulfilled without giving any meaningful role to local residents, and there have certainly been many District Plans passed with only perfunctory public participation. The importance of the Taishido and Mano cases in the development of machizukuri is that these were two highly successful early examples of District Plans in which genuine public participation really was central to the process.

The Taishido and Mano machizukuri ordinances

The two most influential early machizukuri ordinances were created in the Taishido district in Tokyo's Setagaya ward, and the Mano district in Kobe. The significance of the ordinances lies in their comprehensiveness in addressing the serious challenges of upgrading inner city problem areas, the degree of involvement of local residents in the formulation and enforcement of plans, and the widely shared perception that they were highly successful in fulfilling their goals.

Setagaya ward is the largest and most populous of the 23 special wards of central Tokyo, and is located to the south west of the CBD. Setagaya has traditionally been seen as one of the high-class residential areas of Tokyo, and includes Den'en Chōfu, the early garden suburb developed in the 1920s as discussed in Chapter 4. The population of Setagaya ward increased rapidly during the rapid economic growth period, and while much undeveloped farmland remains in the ward today, the older areas nearest the CBD were experiencing serious problems of overcrowding, and formed part of the notorious "wooden apartment belt" of substandard rental housing that hugs both sides of the Yamanote loop line (see Figure 9.2). In 1975 local government in the "special wards" was reformed and the previously appointed mayors were replaced with directly elected mayors. The first mayor of Setagaya under the new system was a populist named Oba for whom local environmental improvement was a top priority, and who has remained in office until the present, winning repeated re-election. Elected to office at the height of the sunshine rights battles described in the previous chapter, one of his early initiatives was the passage of a local ordinance in 1978 designed to control the development of large-scale condominiums by requiring that developers negotiate directly with the local people affected by their plans. Such local ordinances lack the legal power of compulsion, but are backed by the moral authority of the local government and its power to make life difficult for developers who do not cooperate.

The other key factor that led to the development of the Setagaya Machizukuri Ordinance was an urban renewal initiative led by the Tokyo Metropolitan Government (TMG). In the mid-1970s the TMG had begun a new project aiming at the subsidised urban renewal of the wooden apartment belt areas, and two areas in Setagaya ward qualified based on their population densities, number of dangerous wooden dwellings, and percentage of substandard narrow roads. The main issue in these renewal plans was to make the districts safer in the event of earthquake, as a major earthquake on the scale of the 1923 disaster was expected to occur in Tokyo during the 1990s. In 1979 the Kitazawa and Taishido areas of Setagaya ward were designated Disaster Prevention Urban Renewal Areas (*Bōsai Toshi Zukuri Chiku*), and renewal plans were begun. Then in 1980 the District Plan was introduced, and it was decided to carry out the urban renewal project using the new system.

The Setagaya local government immediately began work on a local ordinance that would link the new District Plan system with their own earlier efforts at community participation in plan-making and negotiation with developers. The result was the Setagaya Machizukuri Ordinance passed in 1982. This ordinance is deceptively simple, and includes only five articles, but has been a highly influential model on which much later planning activity has been based. In essence the ordinance allows the mayor to designate Machizukuri Promotion Areas in consultation with local residents. The designation of the area must be formally approved by the local council, which must then publicise the designation. A Machizukuri Council (*Machizukuri Kyōgikai*) is then formed to represent the local residents. Members of the council should serve voluntarily, must have close knowledge of local needs and conditions, and must be supported by a majority of the residents in the designated area. While some Machizukuri Councils have been democratically elected, many others have been more informally selected or self-selected. Such informal methods follow the long-established practice of local community organisations such as the Chōnaikai, where "consensus" decision-making is the rule. Once selected, the Machizukuri Council is approved (*Kyōgikai no Nintei*) by the mayor, and achieves a formal legal status as the representative of the local residents.

The substance of the method is contained in Article 2 which states that in order to achieve a safe and high-quality living environment, the mayor and Machizukuri Council can make an agreement that requires developers to give notice and consult with the local government on any land purchases or sales, building projects or other development activity within the designated area. This allows a process of review of such activity by the local government in consultation with the council. Until and unless a District Plan is approved for such an area – and in many later machizukuri projects formal District Plans have not been approved – there is no legal compulsion for developers to follow the requirements for notification and consultation. As noted above, however, it is not so easy for developers to simply ignore local government wishes, particularly in designated machizukuri promotion areas. In the case of the Taishido area a District Plan was also passed, and that gives a much stronger legal basis to the notification and consultation process, as it gives the local government the legal power to refuse permission to developments that do not conform to the plan. Article 3 of the Setagaya Machizukuri Ordinance outlines procedures for public participation before passage of the District Plan, and Article 4 authorises the local government to hire private planning consultants to work with local Machizukuri Councils and to provide subsidies for their activities. Such subsidies, while generally very small, make it much easier for the councils to carry out their work (Setagaya Ward Branch Office Machizukuri Section 1993).

An essential feature of the Setagaya ordinance is the establishment of a role for local citizens in formulating and carrying out machizukuri projects using the framework of the District Plan system. It seems that the local residents' priorities have largely been followed in the prioritisation of projects such as the creation of more pocket parks and playlots, whereas the original priority of the TMG was for road-widening and large-scale redevelopment. Another key factor was the formal role given to the Machizukuri Council, and the creation of the notification/consultation system of negotiation with prospective developers, which has allowed some substantial community input into development control in the area. The two-tier system of machizukuri plan based on persuasion, and legally enforceable District Plan has been widely copied. Even more common has been the simple machizukuri model in which no District Plan is ever legally passed, and enforcement is based only on persuasion.

In the Taishido case, significant progress in carrying out the plan has been achieved, aided by the fact that significant subsidies have been available from the TMG for land purchase for pocket parks, renovation of wooden apartments, and road-widening, as shown in Figure 8.2. The importance of the Setagaya approach to citizen participation and formal recognition of a Machizukuri Council should not be underestimated, as in

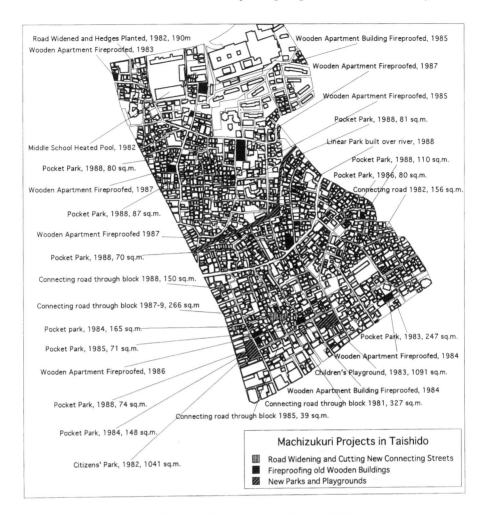

Road Widened and Hedges Planted, 1982, 190m
Wooden Apartment Fireproofed, 1983
Wooden Apartment Building Fireproofed, 1985
Wooden Apartment Fireproofed, 1987
Wooden Apartment Fireproofed, 1985
Pocket Park, 1988, 81 sq.m.
Linear Park built over river, 1988
Middle School Heated Pool, 1982
Pocket Park, 1988, 80 sq.m.
Pocket Park, 1988, 110 sq.m.
Pocket Park, 1986, 80 sq.m.
Wooden Apartment Fireproofed, 1987
Connecting road 1982, 156 sq.m.
Pocket Park, 1988, 87 sq.m.
Wooden Apartment Fireproofed 1987
Pocket Park, 1988, 70 sq.m.
Connecting road through block 1988, 150 sq.m.
Connecting road through block 1987-9, 266 sq.m
Pocket park, 1984, 165 sq.m.
Pocket Park, 1985, 71 sq.m.
Pocket Park, 1983, 247 sq.m.
Wooden Apartment Fireproofed, 1984
Wooden Apartment Fireproofed, 1986
Children's Playground, 1983, 1091 sq.m.
Wooden Apartment Building Fireproofed, 1984
Pocket Park, 1988, 74 sq.m.
Connecting road through block 1981, 327 sq.m.
Connecting road through block 1985, 39 sq.m.
Pocket Park, 1984, 148 sq.m.
Citizens' Park, 1982, 1041 sq.m.

Machizukuri Projects in Taishido
Road Widening and Cutting New Connecting Streets
Fireproofing old Wooden Buildings
New Parks and Playgrounds

Figure 8.2 Taishido area machizukuri. Forming one small part of Tokyo's notorious wooden apartment belt, the Taishido area was typical in its concentration of tightly packed wooden houses and apartments, many dwellings built on narrow, privately owned dead-end lanes, and utter lack of park space. The Taishido area is now famous as a successful case of citizen participatory machizukuri of incremental improvement through park building, road improvement, and the fireproofing of dangerous buildings.

Source: Adapted from Setagaya Ward Branch Office Machizukuri Section (1993).

a number of other districts where Earthquake Prevention Renewal Areas were designated in central Tokyo, the heavy-handed approach of the local government and stubborn local opposition have produced 20 years of stalemate (Cibla 2000).

The Mano area Machizukuri Ordinance, passed in 1981, was quite different in its origins, but in the end takes a very similar approach to the incremental improvement of an inner city area through citizen participation. The Mano district is a mixed industrial residential area of about 40 hectares and with a population of about 9,000, located in the inner-city area of Kobe, near Osaka. Residents began to mobilise to oppose the increasingly severe pollution problems of the district in the early to mid-1960s. From the early 1970s these groups focused increasingly on local quality-of-life issues, including neighbourhood greening, and gaining local community facilities such as parks and community centres for the elderly. The first machizukuri organisation formed in 1971 was born of these efforts, and continued on this basis as an essentially local community organisation until 1978. Then, with the assistance of a sympathetic city council and advice from academics from Kyoto University, a more ambitious approach was started and organising begun to create a long-term vision for improving the physical and social quality of the district, and a strategy for achieving it. A machizukuri study group (*machizukuri kentō kaigi*) was established in 1978 that included 27 members from the local community (15 from neighbourhood organisations, 8 from shopkeepers and industry organisations, and 4 from other local organisations). Assisting the group were four academics and four Kobe city government officers (Kodama 2000; Nakamura 1997: 29). The machizukuri movement in Mano thus grew endogenously out of earlier community organisations, not as the creation of government (Evans 2001; Takamizawa 1999). Takamizawa (1999) argues that this constitutes a major difference between Taishido and Mano. In Mano there was an existing citizens' movement for urban improvement efforts which the ordinance was attempting to support, whereas in Setagaya the local government defined the area based on the disaster prevention programme of the TMG and effectively created the citizen organisation. The fact that Mano was a bottom-up process and Taishido top-down helps to underline the point that the defining feature of machizukuri is intensive public participation, not the issue of top-down or bottom-up. Further, while Mano is widely hailed in the Japanese planning literature as a real model of bottom-up city planning, Evans (2001) notes that such true bottom-up planning is extremely rare, and that Mano's uniqueness may be a big reason for its popularity among Japanese planning academics.

In any case, the Mano group embarked on an ambitious programme to examine the main issues of their area and create a long-range community improvement plan. Three main goals were to stabilise the population of the district, which had been declining, establish a better local environment and improve coexistence with the industrial employers nearby. The main proposals were greater separation of residential and industrial land uses by encouraging relocation of industries to the southern part of the district, street-widening of major roads to allow easier access for emergency vehicles and safer passage for children going to school, and a range of other physical improvements such as redevelopment of the worst rental housing units into public housing and building of a community centre (Kodama 2000: 44). As with Taishido, the creation of the District Planning system created the opportunity to actually achieve some of these goals, and the machizukuri district planning process in the Mano area produced considerable results, as discussed in more detail in Chapter 9.

Deregulation

While these efforts to craft a more effective system for detailed local planning and local environmental improvement were being pursued, another major wave of change to the city planning system was building. Starting in the early 1980s, and peaking during the five years that Nakasone Yasuhiro was prime minister (1982–87), deregulation and "administrative reform" (meaning smaller government) had significant impacts on the planning system that were broadly contrary to the efforts of those involved in District Planning. Whereas the District Planning system was designed to increase the degree of regulation over development and redevelopment of urban areas, advocates of deregulation were promoting greater freedom for urban development projects. While in the long run District Planning appears to have been more influential, deregulation had important impacts on the planning system during the 1980s.

Political support for deregulation

There is no doubt that the conservative revival and the push for deregulation and smaller government in Japan was influenced by the rise to power of free market champions such as Margaret Thatcher in Britain and Ronald Reagan in the US. Domestic political changes were also important, however, particularly the growing central government fiscal deficits of the 1970s, and the much strengthened majority of the LDP after 1980, described above. The Japanese deregulation efforts of the mid-1980s were not simple imitations of their Anglo-American counterparts, however, but were rather the product of complex domestic political and economic pressures. It is worth looking more closely at the three main influences that contributed to the particular forms that deregulation of urban land-use planning took. First was the conservative anti-regulation/pro-business ideology of the era. Second was the increasing friction generated by Japan's huge and constantly growing external trade surpluses and international pressure for Japan to increase domestic demand to reduce them. The third factor was the domestic political and economic pressure to expand spending on pork-barrel public works projects.

It is important not to underestimate the impact of the shift in the global ideological climate of the late 1970s and early 1980s. While the neo-conservative revolution was possibly most influential under the Thatcher and Reagan regimes in Britain and the US, its impact was felt much more widely. The decade of stagflation of the 1970s with its declining economic growth and damaging inflation had deeply shocked many in the developed countries, and had greatly undermined confidence in the Keynesian welfare state model of increasing government intervention in the economy and increasing state spending to provide a social safety net and reduce social inequalities. Many were persuaded that while that model had seemed to work well during the booming post-war decades, those approaches were no longer viable, and smaller governments and greater reliance on free markets were the solution to the economic troubles of the past decade.

In Japan, even though economic growth had continued at a higher level than the other industrial countries and inflation had been tamed more quickly, there was a real fear among conservatives that if Japan continued on the path of increasing welfare spending then future economic decline and moral decay was inevitable. This scary future was neatly packaged in the public debate as the "English disease" of fading economic prospects, spiralling social conflict and inner city decline attributable to big government and over-generous welfare spending, as well as visible minority immigration. The implication clearly was that drastic measures had to be adopted to prevent this sort of contagion infecting Japan. While it is no doubt true that this spectre was advanced partly for simple partisan political reasons and to advance staple conservative policy approaches, it is also clear that many sincerely believed the old model of increasing government spending was no longer viable, and the changing economic climate of the 1970s appeared to give strong support to these views. The project of building a welfare state, which had been begun in 1973 with a flourish, was ended in the early 1980s. Japanese government was to remain small.

The attitude towards deregulation was more ambivalent, as while Japan was undoubtedly among the most highly regulated of the advanced industrial countries, and many argued that over-regulation was stifling economic growth, others still believed in the positive role the government had played in facilitating rapid economic growth and economic prosperity. In particular, while many LDP politicians and business leaders were pushing for deregulation, the bureaucracy was much less committed to reducing its own powers, and worked but slowly to dismantle its own control apparatus, while other sectors such as agriculture and small businesses which benefited from government intervention were not slow to defend the status quo. In the arena of city planning the main conflict was between reformers in the central government backed by the land development and construction industries, and local governments which were attempting to defend their planning powers, as described below.

The second major element of the debate was supplied by increasing international criticism of Japan's huge external trade surpluses. At first glance the connection between urban land use planning deregulation and external trade issues is not obvious. The link is that one of the remedies repeatedly prescribed by Japan's trading partners was the stimulation of domestic demand to reduce the dependence of Japan's economy on export-led growth, and the increase of imports from other nations. Japan was repeatedly urged to shift from export-led growth to domestic demand-led growth. The problem was that a key constraint on domestic demand in Japan has consistently been the high cost and small size of housing. The focus on urban development and deregulation as a means of stimulating domestic demand is succinctly explained by Hebbert and Nakai:

> Besides its immediate multiplier benefits, urban redevelopment is seen to hold the key to the distinctively Japanese problem of market saturation within the domestic economy. Household ownership rates of most standard consumer durables (except cars) already approach 100 percent. Further consumption growth can only come either through refining and updating the product, which is constrained by the rate of technological innovation, or by enlarging the physical capacity of dwellings – essentially containers for consumer durables – which in the Japanese case are of course notably smaller than those of any other country of comparable living standards. Housing, in other words, is the key strategic variable in the stimulation of domestic demand.
>
> (Hebbert and Nakai 1988a: 385)

This linkage allowed Nakasone and his supporters to make the highly appealing argument that trade friction with Japan's key trading partners, particularly the US, could be reduced, economic growth increased, and quality of life improved, all by the simple and inherently popular expedient of improving the quality of the people's housing. Who could disagree?

The actual means of achieving these goals were, unsurprisingly, more controversial. The Nakasone administration proposed that the main culprits preventing improved housing conditions were over-strict land use and zoning regulations. One of the first actions of the Nakasone government on taking office in 1982 was to direct the MoC to review the zoning of all the areas in central Tokyo that were zoned Exclusive Residential #1 so that they could be rezoned to Exclusive Residential #2, in which high-rise buildings could be built, and Tokyo could begin to look more like New York (Hebbert and Nakai 1988a: 386; Miyao 1991: 132). This was a highly public and controversial challenge to the planning powers of local governments, as zoning was one of the few areas they could fully control. This was particularly controversial as many of the wards in central Tokyo had prepared their zoning revisions of the 1970s with extensive public participation, and the designation and location of Exclusive Residential #1 districts had been one of the most contested aspects of the new zoning.

Before discussing the various urban planning deregulations in more detail, it is worth mentioning the third important factor that shaped the Nakasone urban policies in the mid-1980s; the programme of expanding domestic demand through increased spending on public works. While the "administrative reform" efforts of the Nakasone government achieved significant reductions in total public spending during the mid-1980s, primarily through major reductions in welfare spending, it simultaneously carried out a major increase in spending on public works. One important source of finance for this burst of public works spending was the windfall profits generated by privatisation of major public corporations such as JNR and NTT. The main strategy was the sleight-of-hand of relying heavily on public works spending through the Fiscal Investment and Loan Programme (FILP) known as *zaito* in Japan. The FILP lends savings deposits in the postal savings system to local governments and central government administrative bodies such as the Japan Housing Corporation (JHC) for investment in public infrastructure projects including sewers, harbours, bridges, and public housing. The scale of spending on infrastructure under this programme is so enormous that it is often referred to as Japan's "second budget". While this scheme provided an effective means for redressing critical infrastructure shortfalls during the rapid growth phase, many are now critical of its lack of effective controls on spending. In particular the fact that such enormous spending effectively sidestepped the legislative process and was controlled directly by the bureaucracy, and the fact that the accounting of the funds spent and decision-making process lacked transparency have led to current moves to reform the system (Yoshida and Naito 2001).

Such public works spending, it was argued, could efficiently boost the domestic economy because of its high multiplier effects through spending on domestically produced building materials, machinery, relatively high labour costs and through its stimulus of private investment in land and building. Even more important, such spending promised to help remedy Japan's notoriously poor infrastructure base which, as documented by the OECD (1986), was a major constraint on both the quality of life in Japanese cities and on the possibility of more intensive urban development. For example, as became clear later, a much more important practical limit on new building in central Tokyo than zoning regulations was and is the shortage of roads, sewers and water supply (Onishi 1994).

Increased spending on public works was also directly a response to international political pressure, particularly from the US. The US–Japan Economic Cooperation Agreement of October 1986 specifically called for increased Japanese government spending on infrastructure, and supplementary budgets were passed in 1986 and 1987 to allocate some 8.6 billion yen in extra public works spending to appease US negotiators

(Hebbert and Nakai 1988a: 385). Similarly enormous spending commitments were made during the Strategic Impediment Initiative (SII) talks of the late 1980s and early 1990s.

Increased spending on public works had the added benefit for the ruling party of greatly expanded opportunities for pork-barrel style spending in electoral districts throughout the country. While such politically motivated public works spending had long been a prominent feature of Japanese politics, as in many other countries, the scale of such spending increased greatly during the 1980s and 1990s. Central government spending became an important measure of the local Diet member's "pipeline" to the big spending ministries, and LDP politicians were always quick to take credit for spending in their district (see McGill 1998; Woodall 1996). It is also significant that while up until the mid-1970s central government infrastructure spending had been strongly concentrated in the metropolitan Pacific Belt region (Glickman 1979), from the mid-1970s, and particularly during the 1980s, spending was predominantly in peripheral areas (Calder 1988).

A major proponent of increased spending on public works was the Japan Project Industry Council (JAPIC), founded in 1979 as a lobbying consortium of over 160 major Japanese corporations including the large-scale general contracting companies, as well as major industrial groups such as steel producers and the main trading corporations. JAPIC became so large and influential during the mid-1980s that people started calling it the "second Keidanren" (Otake 1993: 249). JAPIC lobbied for many of the large-scale development projects envisioned in Tanaka's "Building a New Japan" proposals described in Chapter 7, including the series of bridges linking Shikoku (the smallest of the four main Japanese islands) with Honshu (the largest), the Kansai International Airport on a man-made island near Osaka, the cross-Tokyo Bay bridge and tunnel project now called the "Aqualine", as well as numerous new expressway and shinkansen projects (see Barret and Therivel 1991; Oizumi 1994; Otake 1993; Samuels 1983). A more detailed discussion of spending on large-scale infrastructure projects is undertaken in Chapter 9, as it is during the 1990s that many of these projects were completed, and also that such spending reached its climax as a part of attempts to revive the stagnant economy. Here it is merely worth noting that during the 1990s many of these projects have proven of dubious benefit relative to their costs, and the public corporations set up to build and manage them have required massive infusions of new public funds to reduce their debt burdens because of dramatically lower rates of usage (and toll revenue) than projected.

It is also significant that while spending on public works increased dramatically during the 1980s, the serious infrastructure deficits of Japanese cities remained. This was partly because new areas of unserviced sprawl continued to be developed, thus contributing to infrastructure shortfalls, as described below. Perhaps more important, however, is the fact that most of the new money was spent on large-scale construction projects such as the bridges to Shikoku and the Tokyo Bay tunnel, while local governments continued to be left to their own devices in dealing with local infrastructure such as sewers, local roads, and other community facilities including child care centres, libraries and recreation facilities. It is no coincidence that the focus on large-scale projects followed the agenda of JAPIC and created significant revenues for its members. The priority placed on large-scale projects such as bridges and tunnels also reflects the fact that these sorts of projects are the easiest to design and implement under the direct control of the central government and its agencies. They also avoid much of the messy and time-consuming negotiations over land purchase and the reliance on local governments for implementation. The programme of public works spending also contributed unfortunately to ramping up investment in land development, which culminated in the disastrous period of the "bubble economy" described below.

City planning deregulation

Deregulation of city planning was carried out throughout the 1980s in a range of initiatives. The first attempted to loosen zoning regulations in central Tokyo to allow more intensive development. A central and early part of Nakasone's deregulation campaign was the order in March of 1983 from the MoC to local governments to encourage development by relaxing regulations. Specifically, they were to increase the ratio of building volume to lot size, rezone residential zones to commercial, and weaken various restrictions on development in the UCA (Hayakawa and Hirayama 1991: 153; Otake 1993: 243). The central government also strongly pressured local governments to weaken or abolish their non-statutory "development manuals" (*Kaihatsu Shidō Yōkō*) which specified required levels of contribution to public space and sewer facilities required to get a development permit.

City planning deregulation during Nakasone's term in office was highly controversial, with a range of actors supporting deregulation, and another group opposing the weakening of the city planning system which was only just starting to achieve a measure of control over urban development, such as through the newly implemented District Planning system. Of those supporting deregulation, one group included those such as Nakasone and his political advisors, who were avowedly motivated primarily by an ideological commitment to free markets and small government. Possibly more important were their political supporters in the land development and construction industries, who sought relaxation of land planning regulations that would allow increased profits from land development. In particular the Real Estates Association (large developers), the Urban Development Association (developers owned by private railway companies), and the National Federation of Land and Building Agents (small and medium sized developers) argued strongly for planning deregulation (Hebbert and Nakai 1988a). Many of the members of these organisations had large landholdings and anticipated higher profits from relaxation of specific regulations on building in the UCA, for example, or of height limits in central Tokyo.

Deregulation has also been supported by a number of urban economists who argued that city planning regulations were responsible for inefficient urban development patterns. As ever, the focus of these arguments was on the Tokyo region, even though changes to planning laws would affect urban areas throughout the country. In particular the relatively low intensity of land use in central Tokyo compared to that in other major cities in the developed countries was seen to be a problem. For example, the Tsukuba National University economist Miyao Takahiro argued that a key urban problem in Tokyo was that planning restrictions limited the height of buildings in central Tokyo, and land transaction controls made it difficult to redevelop central city areas to more intensive uses such as high-rise condominiums. He thus argued for increased deregulation, suggesting that the vigour of private sector needed to be freed from excessive planning regulations in order to "take full advantage of the vitality in the metropolitan regions" (Miyao 1987: 58–9). Specifically, deregulation should ensure that "excessive restrictions of the residential area development guidelines by local municipalities would be corrected" (Miyao 1987: 59). In a later paper he argued that "to solve Japan's land problems, it is essential that excessive regulations over land transactions and land use be removed. Now is the time to make bold deregulatory moves, which are long overdue" (Miyao 1991).

Otake (1993) suggests that in the deregulation debates the MoC was internally deeply divided, with one group strongly supporting deregulation to enable high-rise building in central Tokyo, and another group of urban planners who opposed deregulation, arguing that not only would it create serious problems, but it would also be unlikely to lead to the desired result of increased high-rise building, as other factors than planning regulations were probably more significant in preventing high-rise redevelopment. He argues that it was probably Nakasone's direct and specific deregulation instructions that were decisive in tipping the balance in favour of the deregulators.

The main opponents of planning deregulation were local governments, supported by the citizens and residents of central city areas who were lobbying for greater protection from unwanted high-rise developments, and advocates of better city planning rules and stronger housing policies. The opposition of local governments to deregulation seems to have been motivated primarily by concerns over infrastructure provision, particularly in areas on the urban fringe. There local governments have worked hard to increase their abilities to limit urban sprawl, and force land developers to pay a fair share of the costs of essential urban infrastructure. The development permit (*kaihatsu kyoka*) system initiated in 1968 had been designed primarily with this linkage in mind, as described in Chapter 6. Many local governments had reinforced this system with their own non-statutory development manuals which specified in detail the sorts of infrastructure contributions (or equivalent "development charges') expected for different types and sizes of development. These manuals virtually all specified higher levels of infrastructure provision than the City Planning Law, and while not legally binding, were supported by local government control over the permit process, water supply and sewer connections. Most developers found it easier to cooperate and negotiate than to try to challenge local government guidance directly. The exceptions that proved the rule were provided by a few famous cases of developer intransigence that also served to underline the weak legal position of local governments when developers refused to comply (Ruoff 1993).

Development manuals started to become the object of central government scrutiny in 1980 when the MoC and the Ministry of Home Affairs (*Jichishō*) conducted a survey of all 1,007 existing manuals. The Nakasone government subsequently targeted the manuals with a series of ministerial circulars requesting specific changes which included suggestions "to reduce the scale of 'development charges' imposed on the private sector; to clarify the purpose of such charges; to limit requirements upon developers for infrastructure provision; to shorten the consultation period between local government and developers; to lessen the period required for an archaeological survey; and to remove requirements for formal third-party agreements between developers and neighbours of proposed developments" (Hebbert and Nakai 1988a: 389). It is worth noting that these sorts of requirements are precisely what the Setagaya local government and others were establishing and strengthening as part of their machizukuri ordinances established as part of the District Planning system described above. Efforts to weaken the development manuals, while successful in some cases, were strongly resisted by local governments, many of which continue to operate versions of the system today. While such planning approaches were under pressure from central government during the 1980s, they have continued to proliferate and formed one of the main areas of planning activity during the 1990s, as described in the next chapter.

Other efforts at deregulation were more effective. Land development controls on the urban fringe were particularly strongly targeted. There were three main efforts to deregulate the Senbiki system of zoning the City Planning Areas (CPA) into UPA and UCA. First, in 1980 the MoC issued a circular that detailed for the first time specific conditions for allowing changes of designation from UCA to UPA and vice versa during the quinquennial Senbiki reviews specified in the 1968 City Planning Act. The main criterion was that conversion of UCA to UPA would be allowed primarily in cases where large-scale planned developments that provided their own infrastructure, such as Land Readjustment (LR) Projects, were to be carried out. A second intervention that similarly targeted changes to UCA/UPA designation introduced the idea of the "reserved population" which could be designated to any control area and allowed greater flexibility in the calculation of housing need and land requirements. In practice this allowed the rezoning from UCA to UPA at any time, not only during the Senbiki reviews carried out every five years. These changes allowed the development of the "flexible Senbiki" system described below. A final and even more drastic deregulation was carried out in 1987 which allowed provincial cities with declining populations to abandon Senbiki altogether, although to date only one city, Miyakonojo in Kyushu, has done so (Wada 1998). The revision also reduced the minimum gross population density required for the UPA to 40 persons per hectare from 60, to allow easier rezoning from UCA to UPA (Hebbert and Nakai 1988a: 388).

The actual impacts of these deregulations were mixed. While some deregulation is credited with serious later urban problems, especially the various loopholes that allowed continued sprawl development in the UCA, other changes were used creatively by local planners and turned to their advantage, such as with "flexible Senbiki". Other changes were actively supported by planners as improvements to the planning system which offered greater latitude for active management of urban change, such as the "Special District Plan for Redevelopment" (*Saikaihatsu Chiku Keikaku*) system for major urban redevelopment projects. The system was allowed by a revision to the City Planning Law passed in 1988 that permits significantly higher FAR allowances than specified in the zoning code in return for private investment in compensating public facilities. It is generally considered a part of the deregulation process because it allows a breaching of the formerly strict limits of the zoning system. Many planners, on the other hand, have supported the system as a creative and useful development that facilitates the achievement of public goals.

The most common use of the Special District Plan for Redevelopment system has been to redevelop large inner-city factory sites. Developers have a real incentive to promise substantial public benefits from redevelopment because under the industrial zoning the maximum FAR is 200, 300 or 400 per cent, while approval of the district plan can allow the higher FAR applicable in commercial districts (600 per cent or higher). Plans have included privately paid-for public benefits such as public plazas and open space, generous road systems and street furniture in return for approval. The granting of private land for public road systems is particularly important in the case of Japan, where urban land is so costly that local authorities find it almost impossible to buy land. Significantly, because the system applied only to specific large-scale sites that were to be redeveloped, the normal zoning system remained intact in other areas, even though some of the more radical proponents of deregulation had proposed that zoning be weakened more generally. On the other hand, for some observers one of the most problematic aspects of the redevelopment District Plan system is the fact that within the District Plan area zoning restrictions are eliminated entirely, so the outcome is highly dependent on the negotiating powers of the planning authority. The possibility of public benefits come at some risk of public losses.

Many local government planners welcomed the opportunity to use zoning more flexibly in specific districts, as it allowed them more room to negotiate for local planning benefits in return for specific increases in allowable floor space, etc. At this stage of deregulation the basic zoning system remained intact, and deregulation only applied to specific districts where comprehensive redevelopment was being undertaken. It was only with the economic decline of the 1990s that more radical attempts were made to weaken further the basic restrictions provided by the zoning system, but that is a topic for the next chapter.

There is widespread agreement that some serious problems were exacerbated by deregulation. Many have argued it was an important contributor to the excesses of the bubble economy that had such profoundly damaging effects on the Japanese economy (see Hayakawa and Hirayama 1991; Hebbert and Nakai 1988a: 394; Oizumi 1994). While it is probably true that the various attempts to stimulate land development activity were important contributors to land price inflation, it is clear that deregulation was only one of a number of factors that contributed to the bubble phenomenon. For example, the privatisation of government-owned corporations and sale of government-owned land has also been widely criticised as a key factor in the land price inflation of the bubble economy period (Hayakawa and Hirayama 1991: 161). Where deregulation may have been more important is in its worsening of the impact of the bubble on particular communities and on the poor. For example, Hayakawa (1991) details a number of the adverse impacts inner-city communities of land development practices during the second half of the 1980s. While the numerous instances of aggressive real estate developers employing gangsters and thugs to beat up tenants and force them to move out of their buildings are shocking, the more pervasive problem was that land prices increased so rapidly that most new housing within the metropolitan areas became unaffordable for the average working family, and already poor housing conditions became notably worse (see also Noguchi 1994; Seko 1994a). Deregulation policies have also been criticised for worsening housing problems for the poor and elderly (Hayakawa and Hirayama 1991: 160).

These conditions also contributed to a significant increase in inequality in Japan as those who already owned land assets profited greatly, while those who owned no real estate faced ever greater obstacles to the purchase of a house (Tachibanaki 1992, 1994). Prospective homebuyers were forced ever further from metropolitan central areas, thus increasing the tendency to urban sprawl, and were forced to borrow ever larger amounts of money, leading to the development of two-generation mortgages as paying off such a large sum was impossible in one working lifetime. Worse, with the collapse of the bubble in the 1990s many of these home loans were guaranteed by property that was worth less than the loan. It is worth looking in more detail at some of the effects of deregulation on the urban fringe. The example of flexible Senbiki provides a useful glimpse of the urban development issues on the urban fringe, and is also another case where what was originally intended as deregulation was turned to advantage by prefectural and municipal planners.

Flexible Senbiki

After the first Senbiki reviews were completed at the end of the 1970s it became clear that the new system was not operating in the way intended. While the primary goal of Senbiki was to prevent sprawl and promote planned development, the first decade of the new system had seen an *increase* in the tendency to mini-kaihatsu in the UPA and continued disorderly development in the UCA. Local governments were still struggling with the enormous costs of trying to catch up with substantial infrastructure backlogs, and in many cases were falling further behind. It is in this context that the flexible Senbiki system emerged. As it was clear that local government was not likely to gain greater regulatory power or increased financial support in the context of ongoing deregulation, existing powers had to be used more creatively. The powers of Senbiki zoning could be used as a bribe to induce landowners to join an LR project, the land development method that could be relied on to achieve some measure of planned and serviced urbanisation at low cost.

As mentioned above, one of the early moves towards deregulation was the MoC circular that detailed for the first time specific conditions for allowing changes of designation from UCA to UPA and vice versa during Senbiki reviews. The main criteria was that conversion of UCA to UPA would be allowed primarily in cases where large-scale planned developments that provided their own infrastructure, such as LR projects, were to be carried out. With the support and encouragement of the MoC each of the three suburban prefectures surrounding Tokyo (Kanagawa, Saitama and Chiba), started to use the Senbiki system as a way of encouraging large-scale planned development, although as no new national laws were passed the details of each prefecture's approach varied (Capital Region Comprehensive Planning Institute 1987; Narai, et al. 1991).

In the case of Saitama, the prefecture reviewed its long-term strategy through the Saitama Basic City Planning Policy Review (*Saitama-ken Toshi Kihon Keikaku Sakutei Chōsa*) of 1983. In order to encourage more planned developments and achieve infrastructure targets, the prefecture developed two new techniques for modifying the operation of the Senbiki system, the Pre-arranged Senbiki Planned Development method (*Yotei Senbiki Keikaku Kaihatsu Hōshiki*) hereafter referred to as the Pre-arranged Senbiki method, and the Temporary Reverse Senbiki method (*Zantei Gyaku Senbiki Hōshiki*) henceforth the Reverse Senbiki method. They were ready for use starting in 1984. The Pre-arranged Senbiki method was applied to the UCA, and the Reverse Senbiki method to the UPA. If the Pre-arranged Senbiki method can be described as the "carrot", the Reverse Senbiki method was the "stick".

Put simply, the Pre-arranged Senbiki method was a way of encouraging planned large-scale development projects through the granting of a zoning bonus. Developments

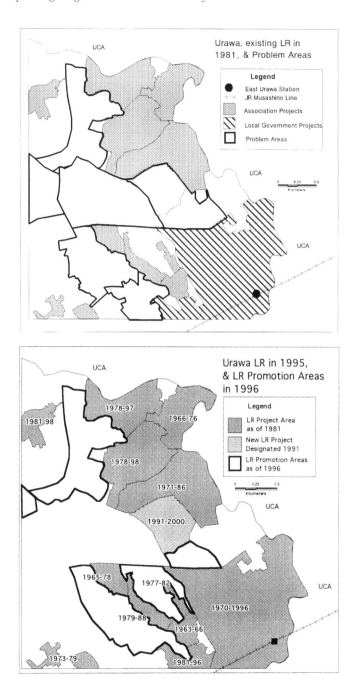

Figure 8.3 Designated problem areas in Urawa. In the Urawa City area shown above, the local government worked hard to persuade local landowners to consent to LR projects, but by 1996 only one small new project had been started, and many planned projects had been abandoned or scaled down in size.

in the UCA which would provide their own roads, sewers and other public facilities such as parks received a rezoning to UPA upon their legal initiation. This zoning incentive was primarily directed at encouraging the initiation of LR projects, although a significant number of large-scale private developments were also granted rezoning to UPA. In Saitama, for example, during the seven years from 1984 to 1990 (inclusive), there were a total of 2,104 hectares of land transferred to the UPA as a result of this method, of which 485 hectares were private developments, and the remaining 1,619 hectares were LR projects. Thus, LR projects accounted for 77 per cent of the total. During the same seven-year period, a total of 3,297 hectares of new LR projects were initiated in Saitama, so slightly under half of all new LR projects initiated in the period were a result of the Pre-arranged Senbiki method (Narai, et al. 1991: 701; Saitama ken 1994).

The Reverse Senbiki half of the method is somewhat more complicated, but follows the same logic of using Senbiki as a tool to persuade landowners to consent to LR projects. The essence of the policy was that designated problem areas would be downzoned to UCA from UPA if agreement could not be reached on initiating a LR project. The impact of such a downzoning was potentially substantial, as land values were significantly lower in UCA areas, and allowable development more limited than in UPAs.

Following the first Senbiki review of 1977–79 the prefectural planning department designated some 10,000 hectares of existing UPA zoned land as "Designated Problem Areas" (*Mondai Shiteki Chiku*) representing some 27 per cent of that part of the UPA that was not Densely Inhabited District (DID) in 1970. These were areas within the UPA which had remained predominantly in farm uses, and where there was neither a planned comprehensive development such as LR nor a minimum of residential development. The "problem areas" were thus areas where sprawl-type development could be expected in future if they were not developed comprehensively. Areas which were already substantially developed, even in a haphazard, unserviced manner, could not be downzoned to UCA, and would in any case have been difficult to develop as LR. These areas, often quite extensive, were left to other future remedial measures.

In practice, the required "agreement on comprehensive development" to prevent downzoning was defined as the consent of a group of the larger landowners within each area to form a LR Organising Committee (*Hokininkai*). It is important to note that the requirement was to start a committee to initiate LR, not to actually legally initiate a project, as it was felt this would take some time. This was to have important consequences later. The job of negotiating landowner consent fell to the municipal planning departments, as they are the ones with city planning responsibility and existing relationships with individual landowners in the areas in question (Narai, et al. 1991: 701). In practice it has proven difficult to gain consent from landowners to proceed with many of these planned LR projects, and less than a third of all those planned had been begun by 1995. An example of a target area in Urawa City is shown in Figure 8.3, where only one new project covering part of one problem area had been begun by 1995, while many projects had been abandoned and a number of others were still in the organising stages.

Of the 10,000 hectares initially designated problem areas, local governments were able to establish LR organising committees for a total of 7,500 hectares, or 75 per cent of the area. Another 1,550 hectares were acknowledged to have enough development to escape downzoning as "Existing Urban Areas" (*Kisei Shigai Chiku*), and the remaining

950 hectares were in fact downzoned to UCA. Importantly, however, as of 1995, a full 10 years after the LR organising committees were established, LR projects had been legally initiated in less than 40 per cent (2,800 hectares) of the areas which had escaped downzoning by agreeing to do so (unpublished data provided by Saitama Prefecture City Planning Department). Further, despite the best efforts of the local governments involved, it seems increasingly likely that much of the remaining area will never be converted to LR projects, as many small developments have been built in the meantime and the easiest areas to organise were initiated first, leaving a remnant of those which have for one reason or another been more difficult.

The LR projects started as a result of the flexible Senbiki policies are a significant proportion of the total new LR during the period the policy was in place. Of 6,758 hectares of new LR projects initiated between 1980 and 1995, some 4,600 hectares, or close to 70 per cent, were directly a result of the two policies. It thus seems that the policies have been very successful as a means of promoting greater use of LR projects for land development. However, by definition all Pre-arranged Senbiki projects result in the conversion of UCA land to UPA, and this makes significant contributions to increasing the spread of sprawl development in metropolitan areas (Sorensen 2000b).

It appears that the threat to downzone was credible enough for most "problem areas" to establish organising committees. However, in a majority of the original problem areas which were able to avoid Reverse Senbiki downzoning it proved impossible to gain consent to start LR projects. According to prefectural officials, Reverse Senbiki will no longer be used because "it aroused too much opposition, doing it again would be really like beating up the landowners with a stick, and would not be effective again" (Interview Saitama Prefecture City Planning Department 15 July 1995). On the other hand it is expected that Pre-arranged Senbiki will be increasingly used in future to encourage the use of LR (Sorensen 2000b, 1999).

While the intent of the central government was clearly to allow the easier conversion of UCA to UPA, the policy as practised by Saitama prefecture can hardly be called deregulation. In fact, while the conversion of UCA to UPA in the case of LR projects and other planned developments has clearly increased urban development in previously undeveloped areas, this is at least urbanisation that is well serviced with basic infrastructure. The possible negative impacts of such expansion of the UPA appear to have been more than compensated by the aggressive use of the threat of Reverse Senbiki downzoning to persuade landowners to join LR projects, even though not all the planned projects have been successfully started.

The bubble economy

The strength of the Japanese economy during the 1980s, and particularly the gravity-defying climb of land and stock prices from 1986 to 1990 combined to inspire a sense of confidence in the economy's invincibility that was far from the traditional sense of insecurity over Japan's lack of basic resources and dependence on world markets. As Pempel so aptly describes the situation:

> The oil shocks and the labor shortages had been dealt with far more successfully than in other countries. Major manufacturing firms had emerged far stronger.

The rapid rise in the yen had encouraged many of them to shift their focus from "exporter" to "investor." Consequently numerous Japanese firms prospered despite the oil shocks, the stunning escalation in the yen, and the rise in overseas protectionism. Asset holders were particular beneficiaries. Between 1986 and 1990, land prices and Tokyo stock exchange values soared. Japanese tourists, toting wads of the ever more valuable yen, roamed the world filling Louis Vitton [sic] suitcases with foreign goods. Glitzy Ginza tea shops catered to the nouveaux riches by offering chocolates sprinkled with real gold. Japanese journalists delighted in noting that the book value of the five-kilometer circle of land that housed the Japanese Imperial Palace had a value greater than the entire state of California. A wave of worldwide trophy purchases came under Japanese ownership. Real growth rates averaged 4.5 percent per year from 1985 to 1989, a full percentage point or more ahead of any other industrialized democracy. Trade boomed, current accounts ballooned, foreign reserves expanded geometrically. Nine of the world's ten largest banks were Japanese. Flush with capital, Japan became the world's largest creditor nation. The economy seemed to defy comparative economic experiences and business cycles. Triumphalism swept the nation.

(Pempel 1998: 196)

The visionary side of Japanese planning also resurfaced with a vengeance during the 1980s, spurred by the growth of Japan's giant integrated general construction companies, whose profits and technological capabilities expanded enormously. In the context of fabulous increases in land prices, the engineering and design staffs of the major general contractors developed a number of visionary new projects for restructuring and reengineering Japanese cities, and particularly Tokyo, that rivalled the Neo-Tokyo Plan of the 1950s in scale and audacity. A number of these projects are showcased in Golany, Hanaki and Koide's (1998) volume *Japanese Urban Environment*. Notable is Ojima's proposal for a network of deep underground service tunnels carrying remote-controlled goods distribution and garbage disposal vehicles, oil, gasoline and kerosine pipelines, water and sewer mains, as well as electric, optical and other cables in a dense lattice under Tokyo totalling 312 kilometres in length (Ojima 1998). Even more fantastic are the Laputa Plan proposals by Obayashi Corporation for a series of 1 kilometre square platform cities to relieve crowding and the lack of park space in Tokyo. A new ground level would be created some six to eight stories (31 metres) above existing ground level on which ample open space would be landscaped. Residences for 40,000 and workplaces for 53,000 workers would be provided in high-rises and on the edges of the structure where natural light was available. Transportation facilities, parking, infrastructure, cinemas, factories, warehouses, and indoor athletic centres would be housed in the enormous dark spaces under the platform (Obitsu and Nagase 1998: 325–7). Similar is the plan for an 800 metre high (150 floors plus radio antenna) tower in Tokyo Bay that would provide a total interior floor area of 1,000,000 square metres, and would be on the scale of a large central city unto itself (Obitsu and Nagase 1998: 328–31). The most extravagant is the plan to move most of the manufacturing plants of central Tokyo into a vast series of 30 metres tall by 20 metres wide tunnels dug into the continental shelf under the ocean where no land rights exist. The plan calls for robot manufacturing facilities to fill 505 tunnels each of 15 kilometres in length for a total tunnel length of 8,475 kilometres with a floor area of about 170 million square metres (Obitsu and Nagase 1998: 330–5). These proposals make the Neo-Tokyo Plan seem pretty tame, but follow the same general philosophy. Unlimited urban industrial growth coupled with unlimited supplies of energy, raw materials and high-tech engineering expertise fuelled the fantasies of brilliant engineering minds.

Two unifying characteristics of all these projects are an assumption of ever-rising land prices, which would make even extraordinary costs justifiable, and an engineering approach to solving urban problems that quite ignores their social implications. Apart from certain problems of costs and benefits, it seems fair to say that in most Western countries these proposals would run into immediate and determined political opposition by those who still remember or are still dealing with the various problems associated with the Corbusian modernist project, which replaced existing urban areas with towers set in a park. The Laputa proposal, for example, closely resembles Le Corbusier's own *Plan Voisin* for central Paris of 1925, which few would seriously propose today.

Unfortunately, or perhaps fortunately, the hubris and grand visions of the bubble era were to be short lived. Stock prices crashed in 1990, and shortly after came the inevitable drop in land values with a gradual but persistent decline in prices ever since. As of 2001 the Japanese economy had not yet recovered, and the 1990s were being referred to as Japan's "lost decade" of almost non-existent economic growth and widespread business failure under the weight of crushing debt burdens resulting from bubble-era excesses. The causes and problems of the bubble economy have been thoroughly examined elsewhere (Noguchi 1992a; Oizumi 1994: 204; Wood 1992). It is widely agreed that among the causes of the bubble were the lowering of interest rates to counter the rise of the yen after the Plaza Accord in 1985, lax regulations on bank lending using land as collateral, and the weakening of land regulations through deregulation. These factors combined to allow many businesses to borrow money to make speculative purchases of land, while putting the land itself up as the main loan collateral (Noguchi 1994: 18). The impacts of the bubble on the Japanese economy have been profound. The nation's financial system is still near collapse, even after the infusion of tens of trillions of yen in the late 1990s to help banks recover from the bad debts left by the collapse of the real estate bubble. The once mighty Japanese insurance industry, holding the largest asset base of any in the world in the late 1980s now has a negative net worth, and only a few firms are expected to survive. Many others have been bought out at fire-sale prices by foreign firms, primarily from the US. The weakness of the financial sector was a major drag on the economy throughout the 1990s, as most banks virtually stopped lending, hitting hard the small and medium sized enterprises which depended on bank loans for their operating capital.

The boom and bust in property prices also had a range of damaging effects on urban areas. As in earlier periods of land price inflation, the steep rise of land prices in the late 1980s led to land development ever further from urban core areas, even though much land remained undeveloped closer in. Land prices were so high that most families simply could not afford to buy a house, and this was seen as an increasing source of inequality among Japanese people as those with land assets saw their net wealth increase enormously (Seko 1994b; Tachibanaki 1992). Watanabe reported that during the first half of 1989 the average price of residential condominiums within 10 kilometres of Tokyo station was 15.6 times the average income of white-collar workers, while in the

10–20 kilometre range it was 10.7 times annual earnings (Watanabe 1992: 31). In the other developed countries a range of three to four times annual earnings is considered affordable for the average family. Housing poverty began to be more and more actively debated as a pressing public issue. Local governments similarly found it more and more difficult to buy needed land for public facilities, and ever larger shares of infrastructure budgets were devoted to buying land even while infrastructure completion rates declined.

One important consequence for the development of urban planning is that as land price inflation problems became more serious and more widespread, the moves towards deregulation launched by the Nakasone government were increasingly widely criticised. Many concluded that rather than deregulation, a stronger land law and land controls were necessary to control land speculation and stop the rise of land prices. One of the products of these debates was the passage of the Basic Land Law in December of 1989, which declared among other things that the public welfare is paramount in the use of land, that land use must be planned, and that land ownership is accompanied by the responsibility of land use (see Otake 1993; Ishi 1991; Fukuoka 1997; Anchordoguy 1992). While many have argued that the land policy measures enacted in the late 1980s and early 1990s were too little, too late, by the end of the 1980s the pendulum had clearly swung back full circle from deregulation towards renewed support for stronger land development and planning controls.

9   The era of local rights

Master plans, machizukuri and historical preservation

It is said that of Japan's thirty thousand rivers and streams, only three remain undammed, and even these have had their streambeds and banks encased in concrete. Concrete blocks now account for over thirty percent of the several thousand kilometers of the country's coastline . . . And then the electric wires! Japan is the only advanced nation in the world that does not bury electric lines in its towns and cities, and this is a prime factor in the squalid visual impression of its urban areas. Out in the suburbs, the use of electric lines is even worse. I was once taken to see the new Yokohama residential district Kohoku New Town, and was amazed at the multitudes of enormous steel pylons and smaller utility poles clustered everywhere – a hellish web of power lines darkening the sky above one's head. This in a site which is considered a model of urban development.

(Kerr 1996: 49–50)

The 1990s saw dramatic changes in the economic, political and urban context in which Japanese planning and urban development functioned. In large part these changes were initiated by the bursting of the bubble economy, starting with the collapse of stock prices which began on the first trading day of 1990, and accelerated with the beginning of land price declines in 1992. The bursting of the bubble was only the beginning of the trouble, however, as when the tide of overinflated asset prices receded it revealed a sorry mess of bad debts and wasteful spending that the froth of the economic bubble had helped to conceal. These contributed greatly to the decline of Japanese economic growth during the 1990s, which has been lower than any other developed country.

The bursting of the bubble thus gave birth to a decade of serious challenges for Japan. Stagnant economic growth, revelations of massive corruption in public works contracts, the perception of incompetence in the bureaucracy, the collapse of LDP majority rule and the failure to find a new political balance all led to the frequent description of the 1990s as a "lost decade" for Japan. These problems have had enormous and diverse impacts on the practice of city planning during the decade. One impact arose from massive central government spending on large-scale infrastructure projects in attempts to restart economic growth. A second has been a marked deterioration of both central and local government finances due in part to declining tax revenues, and also significantly to increased spending on economic pump-priming efforts. The dire financial situation of many local governments in particular has made it extremely difficult to expand city planning spending. In addition, the discrediting of central government has led to widespread calls for a more radical decentralisation of planning authority, which finally resulted in significant changes to planning law in 1999. At the same time there has been increasing pressure for better quality of life in urban areas and more effective urban planning measures. The enormous growth of voluntary activity, non-profit and non-governmental organisations and citizens' movements directed at environmental improvement has been a major contributor to the growth of civil society in the 1990s. The first part of this chapter outlines the major contours of this changing context.

The major part of this chapter describes three important new planning practices. Master Planning, machizukuri, and historical preservation are described in pages 300–25. These new planning approaches have become increasingly widespread and popular and represent a major shift in Japanese urban planning practice. They are all municipal government-based and involve significant public participation in plan formation. They also all represent a much broader conception of the public good and the legitimate public interest than did the old top-down central government dominant style of planning. While many of these new approaches are still in the formative stages, in the realm of city planning and civil society the 1990s have been anything but a lost decade. Whether these new city planning methods and energies will be overwhelmed by the deep troubles of the economy and the political system remains to be seen, but they form at least one bright spot in an otherwise gloomy picture. The final part of the chapter summarises some of the major urban changes during the last decade of the twentieth century.

Economic and political crisis – the "lost decade"

The asset inflation crisis of the bubble economy period was finally punctured in 1990 when the Ministry of Finance stepped in to decrease financial liquidity and imposed sharp new restrictions on lending for property purchase and development. Apart from in the equities markets, there was no real "burst' of the bubble, but rather a prolonged process of asset value deflation after 1992. Ironically, although the land price monitoring and control system established in the 1970s under the National Land Agency (NLA) had been ineffective in preventing the damaging land inflation from 1985 to 1989, the system as strengthened in 1987 was quite effective in presenting at least the appearance of an orderly decline of land prices after 1992. While all had agreed that land inflation had to stop, a drastic decline of land prices was even more feared in 1992, as such an enormous volume of loans had fuelled the bubble that serious declines of land values threatened the financial system itself, as almost all loans were backed by land as collateral. With the collapse of the stock market Japanese banks were already suffering erosion of their capital base, and significant write downs of bad loans would threaten their viability. After 1992 a key goal of land policy, therefore, became to prevent a sudden crash of land prices in order to protect the financial system. The 1974 system of land price monitoring and reporting established to control rapid rises in price was put into reverse and helped encourage a gradual decline in land values. In fact, it is probably more accurate to say that the appearance of gradual decline was achieved because, as Wood (1992: 51) has argued, the published land prices were largely fictitious since the land market had become highly illiquid as a result of a serious shortage of land buyers. Where no land transactions were made in a monitoring area, no change of land prices was recorded, and many recorded purchases were merely insider deals where major corporations were offloading real estate to subsidiaries at official prices (which were much higher than real market prices) for accounting reasons. Significant land purchases were also made by local governments in the early 1990s. As these purchases were usually made at "official" prices far higher than they are today, and far higher than real market prices at the time, such purchases have left local governments open to the accusation that they were merely helping favoured companies rather than pursuing a rational land banking strategy.

Unfortunately, the gradual decline of land prices appears to have allowed many financial institutions to simply put off the painful measures required to fix the damage done by the bubble. Bad debts were concealed and financial reconstruction delayed, greatly increasing the ultimate damage to the financial system and capital markets. Whereas in the US a similar crisis hit the Savings and Loan industry after the collapse of the late 1980s property boom there, after initial dithering and inaction an effective rescue plan was put in place, and the worst was over by 1995. By the end of the 1990s the Japanese financial system was deeply in crisis, and the government was forced to bail it out with some 30 trillion yen in financial support, of which 7.5 trillion yen was used to strengthen the capital base of the main city banks. The Japanese insurance industry, which had boasted the largest asset base in the world in the 1980s, had a negative net worth by the end of the 1990s, and bankruptcies became increasingly frequent. Even by 2001 the financial sector was still teetering on the brink of collapse, and at the time of writing the government is considering a second infusion of more trillions of yen. Pempel also notes that the super-low interest rate policy of the Bank of Japan is effectively a means of transferring huge sums from Japanese savers to the bailout of financial systems, as during much of the last decade interest on Japanese savings accounts has been at record lows (Pempel 1998: 143).

The end of the bubble and the damage to the financial system had major impacts on the Japanese economy, and left a legacy of anaemic economic growth in the 1990s. The first half of the decade averaged a sluggish 1.9 per cent per year, and growth averaged less than 1 per cent for the second five years. The overhang of bad debts greatly impeded economic recovery as banks became reluctant to lend at all, and small and medium sized businesses which provided the bulk of employment and output and which were highly dependent on bank loans for operating capital found that they could no longer borrow. For a Japanese economy and society that had been used to much higher level of growth, this has had serious repercussions with many predicting the end of the "lifetime employment system", record rates of unemployment and homelessness, and a deteriorating financial picture for both central and local governments. The slowdown in economic growth has affected government finances in two main ways; by a sharp reduction in tax revenues and a dramatic increase in expenditures, most of which were spent in Keynesian efforts to get the economy rolling again. Between 1992 and 1999 the government spent more than 120 trillion yen on pump-priming measures, of which about 70 trillion yen was spent on public works projects. At 100 yen to the US dollar, which may be taken as a convenient rate for a period during which the dollar-yen rate actually fluctuated wildly between 80 to 145 to the dollar, that would be some $US 700 billion in public works.

Even before this latest binge of public works spending Japan was often referred to as the "construction state" (*doken kokka*) in the Japanese media because of the vast size and political power of the Japanese construction industry, which at about 20 per cent of GDP is approximately double that of the other developed countries (see McCormack 1996). Much of the construction industry is dependent on public works spending. In 1997 public fixed investment equalled 7.8 per cent of Japanese GDP, well more than double the share in the US and France which were each 2.8 per cent, and more than triple the share in Germany at 1.9 per cent or Britain at 1.6 per cent (Kase 1999: 19; Pempel 1998: 183). In Japan some 6.8 million construction workers and their families represent about 20 per cent of the electorate (McGill 1998: 45). Even with the recession during the 1990s construction has remained a huge industry, partly because of the enormous investments in public works designed to get the economy going again. While there was a total of 82.4 trillion yen in construction by both private and public sectors at the peak of the boom in 1990, that had declined somewhat to 70.4 trillion in 1997. At the same time, however, the share of public construction rose from 29.4 per cent to 43.3 per cent, indicating that the sharp increase in public spending helped to prevent a larger drop (Kase 1999: 19).

Sadly, only some of this spending can genuinely be credited with conferring benefits on the Japanese economy or the Japanese public. Apart from the inflated costs resulting from systemic corruption described below, the fact that much of the money was spent on massive projects such as those promoted by the Japan Project Industry Council (JAPIC) – including the Tokyo Bay tunnel, the bridges to Shikoku, and the Kansai Airport – has tended to limit the real benefit to the average taxpayer. While many projects during the rapid growth period had high multiplier effects by generating other economic activity, and fulfilled real needs, many recent projects are almost entirely useless and are determined primarily by the need to spend increasing volumes of public works finance. It was simply much easier to spend the vast amounts of money that were available on large projects.

This has led to some serious mistakes in projecting demand and revenues of major projects. One striking case is that of the cross-Tokyo Bay bridge and tunnel, now called the Aqualine, the origins of which were described in Chapter 5. The project was revived in the 1980s, and the 9.5 kilometre tunnel and 4.4 kilometre series of bridges was completed by the Japan Highway Public Corporation (JHPC) at a cost of 1.44 trillion yen in 1997 (McGill 1998: 47). After total demand during its first year of operation of just over half of that originally projected, total trips have declined in each year since then, making it virtually impossible for the Aqualine to pay off its costs with its own revenues. The persistent and gross errors in demand projections suggest that future traffic demand is not actually an important factor in project planning in Japan. As Ogasawara Tsunesuke, executive director of the JHPC and one of the planners of the Aqualine explained to the Asahi Shimbun, "You have to understand that the goal of the project is not to satisfy demand" (quoted in McGill 1998: 48). A disarmingly frank statement that fits well with Samuels' (1983) account of the political origins of the project.

Another example of useless or harmful spending is on coastal defences against erosion. It is often noted with dismay that vast stretches of the Japanese coastline have been covered in concrete tetrapods (four-pointed concrete blocks that can weigh up to several tons). While it is true that Japan experiences frequent typhoons, and certainly needs sturdy harbours, lining the coasts which are mostly rocky in any case has been widely criticised as redundant, ecologically destructive and simply ugly. It turns out that a major reason for such spending is that while large-scale construction projects in urban areas are often opposed by local residents, causing delays, and land improvement projects in rural areas require intensive consultation with farmers to gain their agreement, there is little opposition to coastal "improvement" and budgets can be spent promptly, resulting in a much higher completion rate than with other types of projects (Kase 1999: 17). Similar reasons are responsible for the popularity of massive bridge and tunnel projects. The only land needed is that for approaches, while the main costs are incurred in throwing spans of steel over water, or boring tunnels under mountains, neither of which require expensive and time-consuming land purchases.

The dire financial straits of central and local governments

The spending binge of the 1990s left a damaging legacy, however, as Japanese government debt ballooned to unprecedented proportions. As of the end of March 2001 outstanding long-term debts held by central and local government are expected to total 642 trillion yen, or about 125 per cent of GDP (Yoshida and Naito 2001). That is an alarming figure, and by far the highest among the OECD, as Japan has now outpaced even Italy, long considered the developed economy most threatened by government deficits and massive long-term debts. While the fact that most of the debt is held by Japanese savers and financial institutions means that the danger of foreign threats to Japanese financial stability is small, the low rates of interest on Japanese financial instruments also mean that Japanese investors are earning only very small returns on their capital.

Even these figures conceal much larger total debts because much of the infrastructure spending of the last 20 years is off government accounts. Thus organisations such as the Honshu-Shikoku Bridge Authority which built the vastly expensive bridges connecting Shikoku with Honshu is a special public corporation whose accounts and debts are not included in the above calculation of government indebtedness. Yet the bridge authority is in serious financial trouble, and it is expected that its debts will have to be assumed by the JHPC because it will never be able to pay ballooning interest charges out of its own revenues. The bridge authority now has 4.37 trillion yen in debts, but only 3.53 trillion yen in largely non-marketable assets, and generates only 100 yen of revenue for every 200 yen in expenditures, most of which is for interest payments (Yoshida and Naito 2001). This financial debacle is partly a result of wildly over-optimistic traffic predictions, partly because construction was more expensive than it should have been, and partly because there was probably little need for three bridges to Shikoku in the first place. The bridges were instead motivated by the political needs of three high-ranking LDP politicians, who each secured a bridge for their district, as discussed in Chapter 7. Astoundingly, two more bridges to Shikoku are still actively being considered, even though traffic on the existing three has been far lower than predicted. A lobby group of influential politicians has vowed to ensure that the bridges – over the Hōyo channel between Kyushu and Shikoku, from Awaji island to Osaka, and over Ise bay near Nagoya – will be built. As recently affirmed by the 72-member group's secretary-general, Etō Seishirō, a former Defence Agency chief who represents Saeki in Ōita prefecture at one end of the proposed Kyushu-Shikoku bridge, "Building these bridges will save the Japanese economy. We will see to it that they are built, even if we have to resort to legislation" (quoted in McGill 1998: 44).

While moving the debts of the failing Honshu-Shikoku Bridge Authority to the JHPC will clearly solve the bridge authority's financial problem, the highway corporation has its own difficulties. As of 1998 its debts stood at 23.67 trillion yen. The JHPC is unlikely to default on its loans, though, as it receives significant revenue from toll highways throughout Japan and massive revenues from the gasoline tax, which have been dedicated exclusively to the building of new highways since its initiation in the 1950s. Huge debts have also been accumulated by other public corporations such as the JNR Settlement Corporation which assumed the debts of the national railways upon their privatisation, and the Hokkaido-Tohoku Development Finance Corporation which developed the disastrously failed industrial land developments in Tomakomai in Hokkaido and Mutsu-Ogawara in Aomori, each of which were originally designated in Tanaka's "Building a New Japan" plan.

Particularly problematic are local government finances which have deteriorated dramatically during the 1990s. This has been a result of declining tax revenues and increased demands for spending by central government. The latter have been partly generated by the major new public works spending, where as part of its pump-priming efforts the central government urged local governments to greatly increase their own infrastructure spending. Local government project spending subsequently increased at a higher rate than central government spending, urged on by a boost in central government permits for local government bond issues (Jinno 1999: 7). The result has been a serious increase in local government indebtedness. Whereas in 1990 total local government debt amounted to 15 per cent of GDP, that figure had increased to 37 per cent by 2000 (Schebath 2000: 3). This has had predictable impacts on local government debt service costs, which have increased from an average of 11.2 per cent of local revenues (local taxes plus the global grant from central government) to 16.4 per cent (Schebath 2000: 3). The central government has traditionally held that debt service costs going over 15 per cent presents a danger signal. Similarly, the flexibility of local budgets has steadily diminished as debt service charges increase. The ratio of mandatory expenditures (personnel expenses, social welfare costs and debt service charges) as a proportion of local revenues (local taxes plus the global grant) has risen from 70.2 per cent in 1990 to 89.4 per cent in 1998 (Schebath 2000: 4). Most Japanese local governments were over the recognised danger limit of 75 per cent in 1998, including 46 of 47 prefectures, and 85 per cent of all municipalities. The metropolitan areas are particularly hard pressed, and Osaka and Kanagawa in particular were forced to spend 112 and 106 per cent of their local revenue for mandatory expenditures in 1997 (Schebath 2000: 5). That is, they had to borrow just to meet basic operating costs, let alone all the other varied other costs to which 30 per cent of spending had been devoted just 10 years earlier.

Public works corruption and the dangō system

The vast spending on projects of questionable value could at least be defended on the grounds that it was creating employment and was preparing the ground for a revival of economic growth. Less defensible have been revelations of systemic and pervasive corruption in public works spending that has greatly inflated its costs. The scale of the corruption revealed was enormous. A particularly damaging round of scandals was touched off when in March of 1993, LDP Deputy Prime Minister Kanemaru Shin was arrested for receiving a 500 million yen pay-off from Sagawa Kyūbin, a parcel delivery company, and resigned his party post. Public prosecutors subsequently found 100 kilograms of gold bullion, tens of millions of yen in cash, and some 3 billion yen in anonymous bond certificates in Kanemaru's offices and homes (Pempel 1998: 140; Woodall 1996: 12). Evidence gathered in the ensuing investigation revealed massive and systematised corruption in public works contracts throughout the country and led to an even bigger scandal involving many of the major general contracting companies that dominated the construction industry. Dubbed the "Zenecon" (*general contractor*) scandal, in the spring and summer of 1993 it revealed pervasive bid rigging of public works contracts, and a massive flow of bribes from the contractors to politicians. Eventually high-level officials of eight major construction companies, the mayors of Sendai city and Sanwa town, the governors of Ibaraki and Miyagi prefectures and a Diet member were arrested on corruption charges (Woodall 1996: 13; McCormack 1996: 36).

In fact later revelations showed that actual arrests in the case only touched the surface of the problem, as it seems that virtually all public works contracts during this period were the subject of collusive bid-rigging practices (*dangō*). The dangō system is a product of the fact that almost all public works contracts in Japan were conducted under the "designated bidder" system, in which a limited number of designated contractors were allowed to bid for contracts. These contractors then took turns to submit the winning bid and thus eliminated competitive bidding. In the vast majority of cases, winning bids were just under the designated maximum allowable amount, because public works bureaucrats routinely leaked such information to the bidders. In return they often received lucrative employment in major corporations after early retirement from government service in what is called "descent from heaven" (*amakudari*). A percentage of these inflated profits was then channelled to the LDP to ensure the continued flow of such projects, often targeted to particular districts. The vast spending on public works projects for roads, tunnels, rail lines, landfills, sewers, airports and ports turned out to be central to the LDP-dominated government system (McCormack 1996: 35). As Woodall put it, "the dangō system is entwined in the mechanisms of political power in Japan's economy. Construction contractors reap inflated profits, government officials glean administrative power and postretirement security, and legislators harvest political contributions and campaign support. The losers of course are the taxpayers: by various estimates, bid rigging and political pay-offs inflate the cost of public construction in Japan by 30 to 50 per cent" (Woodall 1996: 48). That was 30 to 50 per cent of an enormous total in public works spending, representing a colossal waste of taxpayers' money.

Corruption was also found to include national and local bureaucrats as well as politicians. In the mid-1990s new public information disclosure laws were used by citizens' groups to force disclosure of prefectural and local government accounts. By 1996 corruption and falsification of accounts had been exposed in 25 of the 47 prefectures, and it was revealed that some 7.8 billion yen had been spent by local officials on wining and dining central government bureaucrats and each other in Tokyo (Yoshida 1999: 41). As Pempel notes, "Fabricated and padded expense accounts, bogus trips, and nonexistent staff were exposed as deeply entrenched 'norms.' At least three governors quit and some thirteen thousand officials were disciplined" (Pempel 1998: 143). During the last several years a large number of court cases have been launched by disgruntled local tax-payers who want to force their local government officials to pay back the money wasted, and to create transparent accounting standards for local governments so that such excess will not be allowed again. It is also worth noting that the very fact that citizens' groups mobilised to force the release of the data, and were able to publicise it and publicly humiliate prefectural and local government officials represents an enormous change in Japanese attitudes. Such a spectacle would have been hardly imaginable a generation earlier, when respect for and deference to officialdom were still virtually seamless.

One of the most surprising aspects of all these revelations of systemic corruption is that accounting systems, both public and private, had been so loose as to allow such huge sums to disappear unnoticed for so long. One means is a catch-all item in tax filings called "unaccounted-for expenditures", which Japanese corporations are allowed to use to avoid detailed accounting of expenses as long as they pay a higher rate of tax. The construction industry regularly accounts for 60 to 75 per cent of these unaccounted-for expenditures, and in 1990–91 three major general contractors, Shimizu, Taisei and Kajima reported 150 billion yen in such expenditures (Woodall 1996: 47). While this does not mean that all of that amount necessarily went to bribes, it is an indication of how easy it is to conceal large amounts of under-the-table payments. The public corporations are by all reports even less transparent in their accounts, and startlingly simple methods have been used to conceal worsening problems. For example, even though the Hokkaido-Tohoku Development Finance Corporation spent enormous amounts to develop industrial land at eastern Tomakomai in Hokkaido, there turned out to be little demand for the land and sales were negligible. As cash ran out and interest payments increased, the development corporation resorted to the simple expedient of arbitrarily re-evaluating the value of their landholdings upwards to allow new borrowing against their increased land assets. Those new loans were then used to pay interest on existing loans. Ironically as the book value of the land was pushed up it became ever harder to sell. Amazingly, it was only the collapse of the Hokkaido Takushoku Bank in 1998 that eventually brought this blind alley to public attention and not routine government oversight.

The Kobe earthquake

A further blow to the confidence of the Japanese people in their government came with the catastrophic Kobe earthquake, which struck on 17 January 1995 and killed over 6,400 people, destroyed or damaged 250,000 homes, and left hundreds of thousands homeless and without water, electricity and other essential services. The central government, which lacked a clear emergency response system, took half a day to even realise how serious the problem was, and more days to effectively mobilise help, later explaining that the army was not called in because the prefectural governments affected did not make the request. Worse, bureaucratic agencies showed their arrogance and incompetence by insisting that the body-searching dogs of foreign emergency rescue crews be quarantined for six months before being allowed to enter the country, even as hundreds lay still buried alive beneath the rubble, and rejected an offer of free mobile phones for use in rescue work because the phones were not certified for use in the Kobe region (Pempel 1998: 141). As Sassa (1995: 23) argued, "The worst part of the administration's failure in crisis management was that it 'struck out' without even swinging at the ball. Nothing could be more shameful than the inaction, indecision, and inertia that characterised the initial response to the disaster." This inaction and confusion is all the more surprising if we consider that big earthquakes are so frequent in Japan that disaster preparedness might be assumed to be a routine part of government competence.

Apart from the human and material damage in Kobe the two main results of the Kobe earthquake were the greatly undermined respect for the central government bureaucracy, and a greatly bolstered sense of the importance of voluntary self-help activity. Sassa (1995: 25) suggests that "the Kobe earthquake not only destroyed a major city; it also wrecked the nation's confidence in the central government's ability to cope with crises". The earthquake also greatly reinforced the status of volunteers and of voluntary activities, as it was private assistance and local neighbourhood solidarity that made the greatest impact on restoring order in the devastated region in the wake of the disaster, not the government. The immense outpouring of assistance from the rest of the country, and from around the world, and the concern and desire to help shown by hundreds of thousands of volunteers cheered the earthquake victims at the same time that it impressed the rest of the country and the rest of the world.

The new sense of respect for voluntary activities, and the growing feeling that the central government could not be relied on gave a major boost to advocates of a strengthened role for civil society in Japan. One example has been the recent success of a campaign to ease restrictions on the registration of non-profit organisations (Kawashima 2001). As Yamamoto has argued, the Kobe earthquake "galvanised the forces already at work attempting to build a stronger civil society. The sudden attention given to civil society, thanks, in large part, to the outpouring of support by over 1.3 million volunteers and a large number of non-governmental organisations, paved the way for legislative proposals to facilitate the incorporation process and provide incentives for tax-deductible contributions" (Yamamoto 1999b: 8). The new emphasis during the 1990s on civil society, voluntarism and decentralisation is discussed further below.

Political instability and change

Needless to say, the revelations of corruption, incompetence, and bureaucratic indifference have deeply undermined public trust in the government and the bureaucracy, and have had significant impacts on the political system. In one sense corruption scandals were nothing new, as a more or less uninterrupted stream of such revelations about politicians had been seen throughout the post-war period, and they had been accepted with a certain degree of resignation as an inevitable aspect of politics during the rapid growth period. The repeated revelations of corruption in the bureaucracy have come as more of a shock, as the bureaucracy had long been seen as a safeguard against the particularism and pork-barrel approach of the politicians. With the economic collapse at the beginning of the 1990s Japanese voters seem to have become less forgiving. With the breaking of the Sagawa Kyūbin and Zenecon scandals just before the elections of July 1993, the LDP fared poorly and lost its legislative dominance for the first time since its formation in 1955. Ironically the loss of power was only partly a result of voting changes as the conservative vote remained little changed, and it was actually the socialists who suffered most, losing nearly half their seats. More damaging to the LDP was the internal fragmentation of the party and its desertion by conservative splinter factions who worried that the party had made itself unelectable.

The fragmentation of the LDP led to a confusing period of ever-changing coalitions and short-lived cabinets from 1993 to 1996. The first of these was formed by a coalition of eight anti-LDP parties including the socialists, the Komeito and the former LDP splinter groups under a cabinet headed by Prime Minister Hosokawa. Although in power less than a year, the Hosokawa government managed to pass a reform of the electoral system which replaced the former multi-member electoral districts with 300 new single-member districts and 200 seats to be filled by proportional representation from party lists. It was hoped that this new system would help undermine the dominance of the LDP and reduce the need for huge spending during elections, which was believed to have been a major factor behind the perpetuation of money politics.

In the end the LDP was only out of power briefly, as in the summer of 1994 the party formed a coalition with their long-time arch-enemy the socialists, with a socialist prime minister, Murayama Tomiichi at the helm. In January of 1996 Murayama was replaced by Hashimoto Ryūtarō, and in the 1996 elections the LDP won a plurality of the votes and came within a hair of an outright majority of seats. The socialists paid heavily for their brief moment in power, losing many seats in the election and many more as socialist Diet members switched to other parties, and the legislature became increasingly dominated by a range of conservative parties and factions. A number of opposition parties joined forces in 1996 to form the Democratic Party of Japan (DPJ). By 1996 the three main conservative parties, the LDP (239 seats), the New Frontier Party (156) and the Democratic Party (52) dominated the Diet compared to the old parties of the left, including the JSP (15) and the JCP (26), which had been reduced to a small minority. Competition was thus primarily among conservative factions. Since 1996 the LDP has maintained its control of the government albeit in coalition with a shifting cast of junior coalition partners. Although the New Frontier Party fragmented in 1998 with most of the departing members joining the DPJ, which has since become the main opposition party, the opposition has remained fragmented and unable to present a credible alternative to the long-ruling government party, and the left in particular has been marginalised. Through all these changes, the main policy continuity during the 1990s was ever increasing deficit spending in efforts to stimulate the economy, which led to the present debt crisis.

The era of local rights

One final and much more hopeful aspect of the changing political context of the 1990s must be mentioned, the growing pressure for more decentralisation, greater legislative and financial independence for local governments, and greater freedom for non-profit organisations (NPOs). One important element of this wide-ranging movement has been the pressure of citizens' organisations for greater city planning authority at the local government level. Advocates for a strengthened role for civil society in Japanese governance have declared this the "era of local rights" (*chihōbunken no jidai*) (Kobayashi 1999; Local Rights Promotion Committee (*Chihō Bunken Suishin Iinkai*) 1997). The main argument is that while it may have been the case that during the postwar reconstruction and rapid growth period a strongly centralised government was efficient, now that Japan has developed into an advanced nation the centralisation of power in the central government bureaucracy acts primarily as a drag on the social, political and economic development of the country. As Iokibe recently argued:

> Respect for the private was fully recognised in principle in Japanese society after the end of Second World War, but that did not mean that the tradition of authoritarian rule led by the bureaucracy had disappeared. The power of the bureaucracy to issue permissions and certifications, handle matters at its own discretion, and exercise broad monopolies on information continues to prevail. The bureaucracy still holds many of the privileges of a semi-independent kingdom that are beyond the reach of democratic controls. Many officials in the bureaucracy are convinced that their institutions represent the sole legitimate agencies that possess the qualifications and the ability to formulate state policy for the public good. Today, however, this mentality of bureaucratic superiority has been profoundly shaken. Development-oriented policies planned by the bureaucracy and the immense powers needed to implement them have all but become things of the past . . . as society becomes more advanced more weight will have to shift from the public to the private. Now that the state has become too big to look after the needs of individuals and too small to deal with the larger, globally related issues, citizens and private organisations endowed with a spirit of self-help and a sense of responsibility for the public good should play a much larger role in its stead.
>
> (Iokibe 1999: 91–2)

In this movement one of the key areas where local governments have been pushing for greater independent authority free of central government control is city planning. This is hardly surprising as frustration with the limited scope of planning powers allowed by central government legislation has been growing for a long time. The struggle for greater local rights to create and implement independent planning policies is in large part a continuation of efforts during the 1980s to use local development manuals and machizukuri ordinances to achieve local planning and urban improvement priorities. These systems were rather weak, however, and the nationally controlled planning system limited the options available to local planners. Debates over local independence became ever more prominent during the 1990s. One of the first significant developments came with the 1992 amendment to the City Planning Act. The main changes introduced by that act are discussed in the section on the Master Plan system (p. 300), here it is interesting to note that for the first time ever the opposition parties submitted their own full draft of proposed changes to the national City Planning Act. Prepared largely by volunteers who were active in city planning affairs as lawyers, urban planners, private sector planning consultants, local government officers, academics, and citizens who had been active in city planning issues, among a number of other changes the opposition draft law proposed that local assemblies should have the power to approve town plans (Ishida 2000: 11). Hitherto town plans and ordinances had been approved simply by municipal mayors under the permission of prefectural governments, while elected assemblies had no say in such decisions. The opposition draft was largely ignored by the LDP, but an important precedent had been set and some of the proposed decentralisations were finally enacted in the amendments to the law passed in 1999 and 2000, discussed below.

One of the main changes to the act in 1992 was the introduction of new zoning categories. New zoning powers had been demanded by the Tokyo Metropolitan Government (TMG), which was attempting to respond to the declining population in its central business areas as residents moved to the suburbs or were pushed out by the redevelopment of residential areas to office uses. The TMG had insisted that local governments should have the legal power to draft and approve their own special local zones to meet local conditions. As Ishida notes, the Ministry of Construction (MoC) continued its steadfast opposition to such independence for local governments, arguing that "regulations on land use for urban planning purposes should be set by national act based on the spirit of the Constitution which stipulates in Article 29 that 'Property rights shall be defined by law'" (Ishida 2000: 11). This legalistic argument that all legislation affecting property rights can only be passed as national legislation has long been the MoC's main defence of its denial of local autonomy in planning issues, and actually derives from the Meiji era centralisation of legal authority, long before the current constitution was enacted during the post-war occupation.

While independent powers to create special types of zones was denied in the 1992 revisions, however, the campaigns for decentralisation during the 1990s eventually bore fruit with the passage of important amendments to the City Planning Law in 1999 and in 2000. The fundamental change in 1999 was the abolition of the old agency delegated functions (*kikan inin jimu*) system that sharply restricted the freedom of local governments by making them the "agents" of central government in the carrying out of planning functions. As mentioned in previous chapters, this rule had the pernicious effect of making local mayors legally responsible to central government in the performance of city planning duties, and denied local governments any independent legal authority to regulate the activities of citizens apart from that delegated by central government. This limitation was the front-line defence of the central government against local planning ambitions, as any local ordinance, however duly passed by a municipal or prefectural assembly, could be enforced neither by the police nor in the courts. After the amendment of 1999, planning became a local government function (*jichi jimu*) instead of a delegated function, and "functions delegated to prefectural governors' became "functions initiated by prefectural governors" (Ishida 2000: 12). Although there is no doubt that these changes will allow real change to local planning practice, it is too soon to know how those changes will manifest themselves. Also, Ishida points to two reasons for caution in assessing the prospects for fundamental change. First, he explains that the amended act requires "lower-tier governments to 'consult with the upper-tier government and obtain its agreement.' Although the term 'consult' implies that all governments are on an equal basis, 'agreement' implies that the former top-down relationship would be preserved" (Ishida 2000: 13). Second, and possibly more importantly, he notes that central government still controls the purse-strings, and local governments have been given no more financial autonomy than they had before. They will still be deeply dependent on central government subsidies, particularly given the deep fiscal holes most local governments have buried themselves in during the last ten years. Still, not all city planning activity requires spending, and given the creativity with which a number of local governments were able to extend the limited legal powers available to them under the previous system, perhaps he is being too pessimistic. On the other hand, the central government bureaucrats have also been creative and tenacious in maintaining their authority. It is too soon to tell.

The next round of amendments to the City Planning Act passed in June of 2000 attempted to further decentralise the operation of the planning system, granting further powers for local governments to adopt local approaches to planning issues. The two main changes are a system to allow bottom-up input into the formation of planning law itself, with a formal "suggestion system" (*mōshide seido*) under which citizens, organisations or local governments can make suggestions on planning issues to higher levels of government. There is no requirement that such suggestions be acted on or responded to, so it is still unclear what impacts this will have. The second important change is that the amended act allows the "flexible operation" of town planning systems by local government. Among other things, this allows local governments outside the metropolitan areas to abandon the use of Senbiki if they want. The amended act also specifically authorises local governments to pass their own ordinances on a wide range of issues, including land use control, development permission and citizen participation (Ishida 2000: 14). The various activities and planning initiatives which local governments have undertaken as non-legally-binding machizukuri ordinances can therefore now be undertaken and enforced under the legal authority of the City Planning Law. That this was an enormous step towards decentralisation is certain, as will be shown in the section on machizukuri ordinances which makes clear the sharp limits on the legal authority of local government planning powers before this recent change.

Master Plans

The municipal Master Plan system was indirectly a product of the bubble economy period. After the peak years of land price inflation in 1986 and 1987 weaknesses in the land use planning system were increasingly criticised in the media and in public debate more generally. Particularly widespread was the accusation that weak zoning controls in residential areas had allowed shortages of office space in central Tokyo and speculation in commercial properties to cause rapid land inflation in nearby residential areas because developers could reasonably expect to convert land in areas zoned residential to office use (Hayakawa and Hirayama 1991). Along with the general move towards support for a new basic land law and stronger controls over land speculation were calls for better land use planning laws. Also, as noted above, Tokyo had been pushing strongly for the power to create its own special zones in the central ward area to counteract depopulation there. In response the relevant MoC committee proposed that the zoning system be revised from the 8 categories allowed under the 1968 law to a 12 category system as shown in Table 9.1. The four new categories added were all variations on residential areas, and were intended to allow further differentiation between different types of residential areas. In particular the old Residential zone was divided into three categories. Residential zones under the 1968 law, it will be remembered, allowed almost any use, although with a lower permitted floor area ratio (FAR) and plot coverage than in commercial districts. The majority of the existing built up area of most Japanese cities in 1968 had been zoned Residential, with the CBD zoned Commercial, large industrial areas zoned Industrial, and future residential areas on the fringe zoned Exclusive Residential.

Table 9.1 Evolution of Japanese land use zoning categories

1919	1950	1968	1992	Purpose
Residential district	Residential district	Category 1 Exclusively Residential district	Category 1 Exclusively Low-storey Residential district	To protect living environment for low-rise housing (maximum height: 10m, small store of offices up to 50m^2 permitted)
			Category 2 Exclusively Low-storey Residential district	To protect living environment for low-rise housing (maximum height: 10m, certain types of stores and offices up to 150m^2 permitted)
		Category 2 Exclusively Residential district	Category 1 Exclusively Medium-high Residential district	To protect living environment for medium-high-rise condominiums (certain types of stores and offices up to 500m^2 permitted)
			Category 2 Exclusively Medium-high Residential district	To protect living environment for medium-high-rise condominiums (certain types of stores and offices up to 1500m^2 permitted)
		Residential district	Category 1 Residential district	To protect a residential environment (certain types of stores and offices up to 3000m^2 permitted)
			Category 2 Residential district	To protect a mainly residential environment
			Quasi-Residential district	To ensure harmony with housing and motor vehicle-related facilities, etc, by a roadside
Commercial district	Commercial district	Commercial district	Commercial district	To facilitate commercial and other business activities
		Neighbourhood Commercial district	Neighbourhood Commercial district	To situate stores for the residents in the neighbourhood (theatres and dance halls are prohibited)
Industrial district	Industrial district	Industrial district	Industrial district	To facilitate the industrial function
	Quasi-Industrial district	Quasi-Industrial district	Quasi-Industrial district	On the premise of intermingling with housing, small-scale factories that do not cause serious hazards are permitted
		Exclusively Industrial district	Exclusively Industrial district	To formulate large-scale industrial area (housing is prohibited)

Source: Japan Ministry of Construction City Bureau (1996: 18).

Districts zoned Residential had thus included a majority of the older urban areas which were characterised by high levels of mixed use, and generally the lowest provision of basic infrastructure such as roads and parks. The parts of these areas that were adjacent to the CBD came under increasing speculative pressure during the late 1980s, and the subdivision of the Residential category into three new land use districts seen in Table 9.1, was intended to allow local governments to protect some parts of these old Residential districts for long-term use as housing, while explicitly zoning the rest for mixed commercial/residential development. Instead of granting Tokyo the right to draft its own zoning regulations, the MoC responded by adding four new zones that applied nationally, continuing the well-established tradition of applying solutions to Tokyo problems to all cities throughout the country while denying individual cities the right to unique solutions.

The municipal Master Plan system was created as part of the same revisions to the planning law because several members of the committee argued that the increasingly detailed land use planning allowed by the City Planning Law made little sense without an overall comprehensive plan to guide such decisions. In fact such a Master Plan system had been a long-term goal of many planning advocates who had been frustrated with the limitations of zoning for planning longer-term structural change in urban areas. The 1992 revisions to the City Planning Law provided the opportunity to have such a system included in the law.

Unfortunately, there was little agreement about what such a system should mean, how it should operate, or what a plan should look like. As a result the legislation that created the new Master Plan system was rather vague. The system was established by Article 18-2 of the City Planning Law (*Toshi Keikaku Hō*) which consists of four clauses: first, local governments in City Planning Areas must formulate a fundamental city planning policy (*Toshi Keikaku Kihon Hōshin*) for their whole jurisdiction. Second, local governments must ensure that local public opinion is reflected in that policy by taking concrete measures such as public hearings or other public participation measures. Third, local governments must publicise the policy and notify their prefectural government about it. Fourth, future city planning decisions must conform to that fundamental policy. All local governments within CPAs are *required* to prepare such plans. Inaction is not an option. It is also significant that future planning policies and plans *must* conform to the basic policy contained in the Master Plan. This suggests that they could have significant impacts on future activity if they specify detailed goals and policies.

It is clear that such instructions could be interpreted in a number of different ways. For example, a "fundamental city planning policy" could conceivably be expressed in several lines of text, without recourse to maps or diagrams – and in fact no mention is made in the law of plans or diagrams. Interestingly, the system immediately became known as the Master Plan system (*Masutaa Puran seido*) and is almost invariably interpreted as requiring a map of the municipal area with the fundamental policies marked on it, accompanied by a written statement of those policies. Most prefectures quickly published guidelines to aid municipalities in the preparation of the new plans. Further, in 1993 the MoC distributed to municipal governments a very idealistic circular on the new Master Plan system, emphasising the duty to ensure public participation and an easily understandable basic policy. It is widely agreed that the Master Plan and participatory process of Setagaya ward in central Tokyo were seen as a model case by the MoC (Morimura 1998). The Setagaya Master Plan approach was developed from the Setagaya machizukuri process in Taishido and Kitazawa described in Chapter 8.

As might be expected, there has been much variety in the plans produced, with some local governments – such as that of Kamakura discussed below – taking the new system to heart and doing extensive public consultation in the formulation of detailed long-term goals, and others producing a simple document that merely fulfils the statutory requirement with the vaguest and least controversial of "fundamental policies". Local governments were also slower than expected in their preparation of the first round of plans. This is partly because all local governments were required by the 1992 legislation to prepare a complete rezoning of their municipal area with a deadline of 1995, and that work was given priority. As of December 1999 some 608 local governments, or 30.1 per cent of those with CPAs, had completed their Master Plans (Ishida 2000: 12).

It is not at all surprising that there should be considerable variety in practice, but some proponents of a stronger planning system have been publicly disappointed in the quality of the plans that resulted. One prominent advocate of Master Plans, Morimura (1998: 299–300), suggests that there is a large gap between the ideals of Master Planning and the actual practice of most municipalities. He identifies three main problems with the Master Plan system in practice: first, most municipalities have little experience or in-house expertise available to assist in preparing such plans. This is partly because many local governments outside the metropolitan areas are quite small in population, and have very small planning departments. Their lack of planning experience is also, of course, a result of the fact that central ministries kept such a tight leash on power leaving few important decisions to the local level. Master Plans are also quite a radical new departure for Japanese city planning, including both a requirement for a long-term vision of urban change and fundamental policies to accommodate it, and a statutory requirement for public input into formulating such policies. This contrasts greatly with the rather rigid, top-down city planning tradition that was primarily concerned with public facilities designation and zoning plans. Many local governments thus experienced a steep learning curve in the preparation of their first round of Master Plans. Second is the lack of budgets to prepare the new plans. For many local governments this is simply one more unfunded obligation imposed from above by central government, and already tight local government budgets allowed few new funds to be allocated for plan preparation, public participation or publication. Third is the whole vexed question of what public participation should really consist of and how it is possible to really reflect public wishes in a planning process or document. Morimura (1998: 300) suggests that the system as proposed was probably too idealistic, and suffered from a lack of existing models or experience in such plan preparation.

A further problem is that while local governments are responsible for Master Plans, they have very few effective powers to carry them out. The main local government responsibilities are for zoning, District Plans, Land Readjustment (LR) and urban redevelopment. These sorts of projects are all useful primarily for improvement of relatively small areas. Zoning has been the main structure planning tool in the past, but it is relatively inflexible as only minor changes can generally be made, and is in any case rather porous. All of the main planning decisions that can strongly affect long-term urban changes are controlled by other levels of government. These include Senbiki, which is the division between Urbanisation Promotion Areas (UPAs) and Urbanisation Control Areas (UCAs), large-scale infrastructure projects, and major new transportation systems. All of these decisions can have major impacts on long-term changes to the patterns of urbanisation that Master Plans are meant to shape, yet are not controlled by local government, nor need take the Master Plan into account. On the other hand, the system is still new and it should be expected to have a few teething problems at first. Many are still optimistic that in the long run the new system will contribute greatly to city planning in Japan. The basic concept that local governments should formulate such basic policy statements and involve local people in their preparation is widely supported. As Ishida suggests, the Master Plan system may ultimately function as "a school of decentralization and citizens' participation in urban planning" (Ishida 2000: 12). It remains to be seen what their impact on future urban change will be.

Kamakura Master Plan

The Master Plan developed in Kamakura during the early 1990s is in many ways typical of a successful Master Plan process, although Kamakura itself is hardly a typical Japanese town, having both a rich historical legacy, and above average financial resources. Kamakura is located in Kanazawa prefecture to the immediate south of Tokyo, and in the post-war period has become one of the Tokyo-Yokohama region's metropolitan suburbs, with a significant proportion of its population travelling to work each day in the metropolitan central areas. Kamakura was the Japanese capital from 1192 to 1333 and is a major tourist destination for Japanese and overseas tourists who come to visit the many old Buddhist temples and Shinto shrines for which the city is famous. Kamakura also has a long tradition of citizen environmental activism dating back to 1963 when the local government's plans to develop an area of woods behind the famous Tsurugaoka Hachimangu shrine into housing became public. Local citizens formed the Kamakura Landscape Preservation Society, along the lines of the British National Trust, which managed to buy a portion of the planned development site and block the larger development. This successful intervention is credited with the spread of such movements and the Kamakura group was involved in the later formation of the Japanese Association of National Trust Movements (Hohn 1997: 218). This history of effective citizen activism and local pride in the historical legacy of the area means that Kamakura is hardly typical of Japanese towns, particularly in the widely shared desire to protect the city from inappropriate development. The case should thus be understood as representing one of the more successful of the first round Master Plans as a participatory planning process. It is still, of course, too soon to tell how successful it will be in structuring longer-term patterns of urban development.

The public participation process followed in making the plan is worth reviewing, as it is being copied elsewhere. The formal process of creating the plan began in 1994 and lasted four years with final approval in 1998. Apart from the fact that a new mandatory planning responsibility had just been handed to the local government, two main factors prompted the plan-making process. First, in early 1993 the local government city planning department had begun a review of its development manual (*kaihatsu shidō yōkō*), with the purpose of revising it to promote the development of the Ōfuna district in the north west of the city. Second, in the fall of that year, Takeuchi Ken, a civil engineer by training, was elected as Kamakura's new mayor. One of Takeuchi's main planning priorities was to create a machizukuri ordinance in conjunction with the revisions to the local development manual, in order to protect green areas within the UPA and guide the redevelopment of districts such as Ōfuna. A notable aspect of the Kamakura case is that the master plan was prepared in conjunction with the passage of a machizukuri ordinance. Citizen participation was central to the plan-making process, involving citizen input at several stages, as described below.

In 1994 a small steering committee was established to manage the process. Consisting of 5 academic planners, 3 prefectural planning staff, and 14 staff from the Kamakura city planning department, the committee was responsible for managing the process of public participation as well as gathering necessary materials and preparing draft proposals. In 1994 the steering committee held an initial series of meetings with civic organisations, conducted a survey of citizen opinions, and drafted an initial policy statement outlining the basic approach of the planning process and its goals. The plan was to be able to have a first draft for discussion by the end of two years, and then use another two years to have more detailed discussions and prepare and approve a final document.

During the second year of activity from the fall of 1995, the main activity was the holding of a series of four citizens' workshops in which a total of 290 citizens participated. Workshop news bulletins were released after each workshop, and the steering committee published its first draft set of proposals for discussion. In one workshop participants from 11 different districts in Kamakura were divided into area groups to discuss issues specific to their local areas. Another workshop consisted of a walking tour of the city followed by a discussion.

From December of 1996, at the beginning of the third year of activity, preparations began to prepare a draft Master Plan. A new, larger and more citizen-based Kamakura City Master Plan Drafting Committee was formed. It included 15 local residents, 5 delegates from civic organisations, including the local Chamber of Commerce and the Farmers Cooperative, and 6 planning academics, including an architect, traffic planner, parks planner, civil engineer, environment specialist, and retail specialist. This group had nine meetings to prepare the draft plan, all of which were open to a public audience, and a committee newsletter was published after each meeting. During 1997 seven subcommittees were formed, one for each district of the city to consider issues specific to each area. Those subcommittees held a total of 32 meetings, each of which lasted about four hours. A range of methods were used to publicise the activities and discussions of the Master Plan Drafting Committee. Discussion materials generated by the committee were published and distributed to almost all households in the city as an insert in newspapers (most households take newspapers in Japan). A reply card for comments was included in this package, and several hundred were returned to the committee. An internet web page was also created to publish the discussion materials and accept e-mail comments. Five public meetings attended by a total of 164 participants were held in different parts of the city to discuss the proposals.

In October of 1997 Mayor Takeuchi was re-elected, and in November the final draft Master Plan was published and distributed to all households as a special issue of the city newsletter. At the end of November a further five meetings were held to discuss the final draft plan, and a public display of the plans was installed near the main railway station. In January of 1998 the Drafting Committee held its final meeting and presented its final report and draft plan to the City Council. In March the plan was approved by the City Council and authorised by the mayor. It seems fair to say that good faith efforts were made to inform local residents about the plan process and contents, reflect citizen opinion in the plan, and provide opportunities for people to participate and comment in a variety of ways. The exercise seems to have been rather successful.

The main goals adopted by the plan were the protection of the green hilly areas surrounding the old capital area, the restriction of further automobile traffic increases in the area, the creation of a park-and-ride system to help reduce car traffic, and the

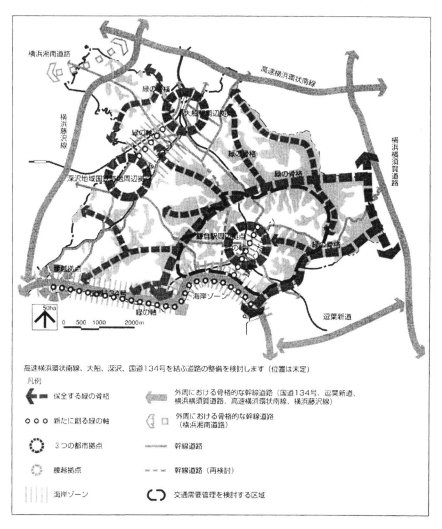

Figure 9.1 The Kamakura Master Plan identifies the major areas of wooded hills (shaded light grey in the background) as the major structural feature of the city, and identifies the major ridges and minor ridges extending from them (indicated by dark dashed lines) as a green framework to be preserved. Three main urban centres are identified, with a major growth axis between the two in the northwest, Ōfuna and Fukazawa, while the growth of Kamakura, the third centre, is to be restrained. The traffic exclusion zone is indicated by the black lung-shaped line around the old city of Kamakura, in the south east corner of the area.

Source: Kamakura City (1998).

establishment of a major development axis near Ōfuna, away from the historic capital area. Interestingly, the first two goals, protecting the green hills and the park-and-ride system were proposed in an earlier plan of the 1970s which was also prepared with public participation. Also, the main ring of wooded hills surrounding the capital has been protected since the Ancient Capitals Law was passed in 1966, partly as a result of the activities of the citizens' movement mentioned above and two similar movements in Kyoto and Nara in the early 1960s. Unfortunately, that law protected less than half the woodlands in the municipal area, leaving a very large area at risk of development. One of the main priorities of the Master Plan is the designation of a much larger area for preservation. The strategy adopted is to designate a green backbone along the major ring of mountains surrounding the historic capital, with numerous secondary ridges extending from it. While the main ring is already protected by the 1966 law, the secondary ridges forming attractive wooded areas which extend into and structure the main residential areas in the city were not protected. The goal is to create a new and much larger area of protected woodland along these secondary ridges, which are mostly privately owned. Simple designation in the Master Plan provides no legal sanction against development, but carries considerable moral authority as the policy of the local government and will of the citizens. It is not clear how successful the city will be in protecting these larger areas from development, as strong restrictions on landowners' development rights are still quite difficult in Japan, and are almost certain to run into stiff opposition, even in cities such as Kamakura where historical and environmental consciousness is high.

The second major policy is to attempt to reduce traffic congestion in the old central capital area, a major tourist destination with a very limited road capacity which becomes severely congested on weekends and holidays. This congestion is a serious inconvenience and health problem for local residents, and a major detractor from the beauty of the city. The main solution proposed by the Master Plan was to establish a park-and ride system allowing visitors to park their cars outside the central city area and ride shuttle buses in to the centre. This is a reasonable idea, but luring car-borne visitors out of their cars and into buses is never easy, and the effectiveness of this policy remains to be seen. The park-and-ride policy does usefully illustrate one of the major problems for Master Plans mentioned above, that few of the relevant planning powers are actually controlled at the municipal level. For example, in the 1960s the prefecture approved a major new arterial road from Ōfuna in the north through the old capital area to the seaside as a bypass to the heavily congested existing routes. Although the road has been bitterly opposed by local residents since it was first designated, the local government had no choice but to include it in the official Master Plan because it is a legally designated "city planning road". All they could do was to mark it "under review" and draw it with a dashed line in the plan, even though it seems likely that the building of a major new arterial road through the centre of the old capital could only undermine the goal of reducing automobile traffic in the centre.

The third major policy direction is to promote significant new urban development along a north-south axis from the major rail station at Ōfuna to the nearby secondary centre of Fukuzawa. Encouraging growth in this axis also seems likely to help protect the historic capital area and wooded hillsides from development. Again, however, the difficulty is that there are few powers to actually restrict development in other locations.

Simply designating a growth axis will not reduce the expectations of landowners elsewhere that they should be able to profit from land development. The fact that the powers of local governments to achieve the goals set out in Master Plans are still quite limited may prove disillusioning for those who set high hopes in the system.

On the other hand, there are many very positive aspects of the Kamakura process, and the degree of citizen participation was admirable. It is even possible to say that the Master Plan produced is appropriate and sets a high standard. While Kamakura is certainly a special case, given its rich historical legacy and tradition of citizen activism, it seems that here at least the new Master Plan policy may have functioned not only as "a school of decentralisation and citizens' participation in urban planning", but actually may produce some positive effects on the ground. Certainly the fact that all municipalities throughout the country have been required to prepare Master Plans and carry out public participation exercises seems likely to have been a great boost for participatory planning in Japan, even if not all the plans so prepared are very substantial, and not all local governments subsequently followed through with ongoing participatory approaches.

Machizukuri

It is widely believed among planners in Japan that the recent spread of citizen participation in local environmental improvement efforts and in planning processes represents the most hopeful development in Japanese planning in many years. A wide variety of such practices are grouped together under the umbrella designation "machizukuri". Unfortunately, the term machizukuri has been used to describe an extremely wide variety of activities during the last twenty years or so in Japan. Indeed the variety is so great that it is arguable that the term has become a rather vague catch-all that serves more to confuse than clarify. Formed by combining the noun *"machi"* which means town, neighbourhood, quarter, or community, with the verb *"tsukuru"* which means to make or build, machizukuri is generally translated as "community building" or "town-making", but can also be rendered as "community development" with all the more political and social implications of that phrase. Confusingly, the term is used to describe a wide range of quite varied city planning techniques in Japan, from LR to downtown redevelopment to historical preservation to small-scale local improvement efforts. Even farther afield the term machizukuri has also been widely used in its purely "community development" sense to refer to attempts since the early 1980s to create a Japanese-style welfare system which relies on families, volunteers and neighbourhood organisations to provide basic social welfare services in an ageing society (Sakano 1995). In an echo of pre-war social management practices, the main thrust of these policies was the reinforcement of neighbourhood organisations (*chōnaikai*), and volunteer community welfare guidance officers (*minsei'iin*), and encouragement of volunteer self-help organisations to help bear some of the growing burden of social welfare services for the elderly, and in 1994 the Ministry of Health issued a circular to local governments encouraging the establishment and support of volunteer organisations and citizen participation in "welfare activities" that describes them as "machizukuri" (Sakano 1995: 249–60). Even local community economic development and place marketing efforts have been referred to as machizukuri, and in their more nostalgic and touristic incarnations are sometimes referred to as *furusatozukuri,* or hometown-making (Robertson

1991). An enormous Japanese literature has accumulated on the development of machizukuri in recent years (see e.g. Kobayashi 1999; Nakai 1998; Nakamura 1997; Okata 1994; Takamizawa 1999; Watanabe 1999).

Even if we define machizukuri much more restrictively as meaning small-scale urban planning projects which involve local people, there are still a tremendous variety of such projects. For example, many local governments describe LR as machizukuri, even though LR projects are a traditional part of the Japanese city planning system, and are rarely initiated by local people, but are usually the result of intensive organising efforts on the part of local government LR departments (Sorensen 2000a). Just as importantly, participation in LR projects is not open to all local residents, but only to landowners and land tenants, so the model of participation is much more restrictive than the more recent wave of participatory approaches. To distinguish such traditional city planning projects from more recent participatory planning efforts, the term "citizen participation-based machizukuri" (*shimin sanka no machizukuri*) has recently become popular (see e.g. Watanabe 1999). This is a useful distinction, as the defining feature of the major changes to Japanese planning practice during the 1990s has been the shift towards greater citizen participation in city planning. While for convenience the term machizukuri is used in the rest of this chapter, it refers only to citizen participation-based machizukuri projects and processes for local urban environmental improvement, not to LR, community economic development projects, or traditional top-down city planning approaches.

Understanding recent attempts to develop effective city planning measures based on the involvement of local people is useful for four main reasons. First, for many involved directly in city planning efforts in Japan, machizukuri is the main hope for the development of an effective city planning practice. Although it is still a developing practice therefore, it is widely expected to be central to the future development of city planning in Japan. Second, in its emphasis on local control and citizen involvement, machizukuri is essentially a rejection of the last 80 years of city planning in Japan, which was characterised by top-down central government bureaucratic control. Understanding machizukuri, and the reasons why it is seen as important, thus helps to put Japan's city planning history into perspective. Third, the development of machizukuri represents a major expansion of the goals of Japanese city planning, from its traditional narrow role as the facilitator of economic growth through the provision of producer infrastructure, to a new set of people-focused goals including improved urban quality of life and quality of urban residential environments. Finally, as shown in earlier chapters, an important characteristic of Japanese urban planning has long been that it has had a very weak basis of public support. It has been argued that in large part this has been because city planning has been imposed from above to further national developmental goals rather than in response to people's needs, and subject to local control. A consequence has been that city planning efforts have frequently been met with resistance and organised opposition, even when they are presented as being in the public interest. It seems possible that, with the rapid spread of machizukuri processes to cities and towns throughout the country, involving citizens and neighbours defining their goals and hopes for the improvement and protection of their communities, finally a broad base of support for city planning for the public good and local environmental improvement may be becoming established. If that does occur then it will represent one of the biggest changes in Japanese city planning since it first began in the Meiji period.

From development manuals to machizukuri

It is fair to say that the development of machizukuri begins with the passage of the 1968 City Planning Law, with its partial decentralisation of planning authority to local governments, and its introduction of the development permit system (Uchiumi 1999). Based on their power to issue development permits for large-scale developments, during the 1970s many local governments passed their own development manuals (*kaihatsu shidō yōkō*) (as discussed in Chapters 7 and 8), which codified and made explicit local government standards for developer contributions to local infrastructure in compensation for the extra burdens the proposed development would impose. Common requirements were minimum standards for local roads internal to the development, and contributions towards the improvement of external access roads, nearby schools, and sewerage systems. Directed at land developers, these manuals specified higher standards for development permission than the City Planning Law and Building Standards Law required. They were thus not legally enforceable, but were based on a system of "advice" and "persuasion", a variation of the famous Japanese practice of "administrative guidance" or extra-legal bureaucratic arm-twisting and back-scratching.

Local governments were caught between the increasing pressure from local voters to strengthen local planning controls on, for example, industrial pollution, high-rise apartment redevelopments and undesirable urban fringe developments, and the denial of adequate legal powers or financial resources by central government to be able to satisfy such demands. One of the main responses of local governments was the development of a range of persuasion techniques originally based on development permit powers. The persuasive powers of local government were not inconsiderable, even under the 1968 system. In particular, as local governments controlled both the building permit and development permit processes, as well as water supply and sewer connections, developers usually found it easier and faster to cooperate with local governments than to fight against them. Even so, there were many weaknesses with this system. One important problem was that as no development permits were required outside the CPA, local government persuasion was much less effective in non-CPAs. Further, because of the peculiar definition of land development used in the 1968 law, "changes in land demarcation and configuration mainly for the construction of buildings or for the construction of golf courses, concrete plants and other specific structures" (see Chapter 6) many types of changes to land use do not fall under the provisions of the development permit system. For example, the conversion of farmland to uses such as parking lots, gravel extraction pits, waste processing facilities, used car junkyards, etc, does not necessarily involve the construction of a building, and thus does not require a development permit. Also, most small-scale local governments didn't have responsibility for development permit approvals as prefectures usually operated the development control and building permit process directly in municipalities of less than about 200,000 population, so many small local governments that passed development manuals had few powers to enforce them. One final problem with the system is that it applied a single standard uniformly to the whole CPA in each municipal area. It was difficult to apply individual standards that fit the particular characteristics of individual districts. For all these reasons it was found necessary to pass regulations and notification/guidance systems in the form of local government machizukuri ordinances in order to strengthen the development control system, close numerous loopholes in its application, and impart a certain amount of flexibility in its operation.

A second major reason for the widespread adoption of machizukuri ordinances to strengthen development control systems was as a means of mobilising local support for city planning and development control. It was found that in order to make local detailed planning work, it was essential to gain the cooperation and participation of local people. In large part this is precisely because the local governments involved were attempting to operate stricter standards for development permission than actually permitted in national law. By organising local residents who were pushing for better local environmental amenities and development controls, local governments were able to gain the moral high ground against developers and landowners who wished for weaker development standards. Establishing public participation procedures also helped because where developers were forced to negotiate directly with local residents, they found it harder to refuse to cooperate. In particular, in municipalities on the urban fringe, the problem is not only to implement higher development and design standards than is possible with development manuals, but also to inhibit certain kinds of development in specific areas. As preventing development is a much stronger level of control than simply requiring higher development and design standards, the local governments needed to gain the strong backing of local citizens. The creation of development control ordinances with the participation of affected residents became a major tool for mobilising public support.

While in the 1970s the development manuals were largely based on the development permit system established in the 1968 City Planning Law, the passage of the District Plan system in 1980 gave a much stronger legal basis for stricter local development control approaches. The two precedent-setting cases were that of the Mano district in Kobe, and the Taishido area in Tokyo's Setagaya ward. As discussed in Chapter 8, in each of these cases, a local machizukuri ordinance was passed in conjunction with a District Plan for the same area. The machizukuri ordinance provided a mechanism for citizen participation in both the development of goals and the carrying out of the plan including enforcement of development control, while the District Plan could provide substantial legal authority as it was based on national city planning law. Over the course of the 1980s and 1990s the variety and sophistication of machizukuri ordinances gradually increased, and in the second half of the 1990s there was a veritable explosion of such activities.

In the early 1990s a further motivation for local governments to formally pass their planning policies in the form of ordinances resulted from central government "administrative reform". In response to the legal precedents established by a large number of lawsuits that had been brought against the government's "administrative guidance" system, the Government Procedure Law made clear for the first time that administrative guidance was only a request by the government, and not legally binding. Because the power of developers to refuse to cooperate with local government administrative guidance was made much stronger, it became imperative that the notification/guidance procedure become legally formalised in an ordinance (Okata 2001). Still, until the legal reforms of 1999–2000, the weak land development control system, and the lack of legal powers to enforce stronger standards than those provided in national law were the key factors affecting the development of machizukuri techniques.

Three types of machizukuri ordinances

In Japan there are two types of local planning ordinance. The first are ordinances passed under the authority of national laws such as the sunshine protection ordinances (*hiatari jōrei*) described in Chapter 7. As these are authorised by the Building Standards Law they can be enforced by the police and defended in court. The second are those passed only under the authority of local municipal by-laws. Most machizukuri ordinances are of this latter type. Until the important amendments to the City Planning Law of 1999 and 2000 described above, which finally granted independent legal authority for city planning to local governments, machizukuri ordinances passed under the authority of local municipal by-laws were not backed by the police power, and were very difficult to defend in court. Since the early 1980s three main types of machizukuri ordinance have developed: District Plan, Land Use Control and Historical Protection.

District Plan machizukuri ordinances

District Plan-type machizukuri ordinances are linked to the 1980 district plan system, which allows local governments to pass ordinances under the authority of the City Planning Law and Building Standards Law. The precedent-setting ordinances of Kobe's Mano district and Tokyo's Setagaya ward Taishido district were each passed in 1982 by expanding on the original intent of the District Plan system as described in Chapter 8. Although this type of machizukuri ordinance is fundamentally similar to a District Plan in the setting of detailed standards for new development and redevelopment in the target area, they also go beyond district planning by establishing an ongoing statutory role for a citizen's Machizukuri Council in monitoring and approving development in the area. The ordinance is based on an area machizukuri plan that has been discussed and approved by a Machizukuri Council of local residents, and then passed as an ordinance by the local government. Within the plan area there is a measure of control over land development activity, although this control is not particularly strong, as any provisions that go beyond the fairly restrictive measures allowed in the City Planning Law can only be enforced by persuasion. Where an actual District Plan has been passed as well, the legal basis of development control is much stronger, but in many cases only a machizukuri ordinance has been passed.

Following the precedents established in Kobe and Setagaya, the common procedure for passing a District Plan-type machizukuri ordinance is as follows. The mayor designates a target area and the local Machizukuri Residents' Council is established with a membership of local residents and leaders. Once the local council has been established, the mayor officially recognises it. Such recognition gives the council a legal identity and allows it to receive small amounts of funding support for incidental expenses. There follows a procedure for officially designating the machizukuri promotion area, upon which the residents' council can submit a Machizukuri Proposal to the local government. The mayor (and sometimes also the local assembly) examines the proposal and approves it. Once such a plan is approved, anyone who wants to develop within the area designated by the plan is required to "notify" (*todokede*), "consult" (*kyōgi*) and take "advice" (*kankoku*) from the local government before proceeding with development. The local government is required to respond to the notification and may or may not respond with advice.

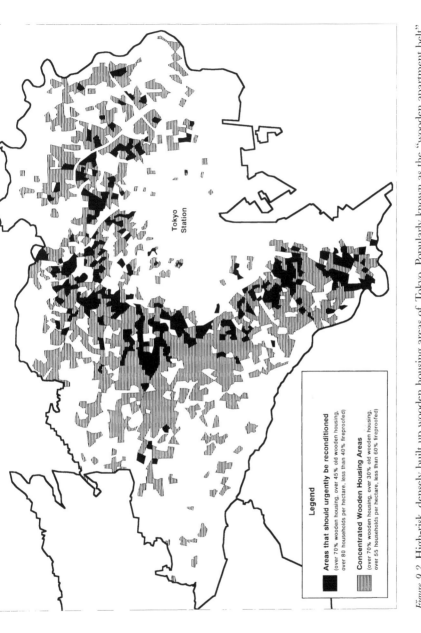

Figure 9.2 High-risk, densely built up wooden housing areas of Tokyo. Popularly known as the "wooden apartment belt" (*mokuzai apaato chitai*) these areas have been among the main targets of Tokyo government efforts at disaster prevention and are recently the focus of many machizukuri and redevelopment efforts.

Source: Adapted from Tokyo Metropolitan Government (1997: 19).

Legend

Areas that should urgently be reconditioned
(over 70% wooden housing, over 45% old wooden housing, over 80 households per hectare, less than 40% fireproofed)

Concentrated Wooden Housing Areas
(over 70% wooden housing, over 30% old wooden housing, over 55 households per hectare, less than 60% fireproofed)

Tokyo Station

There are also cases where the residents' council must also by notified and consulted before starting. The sanctions against developers that do not cooperate or do not follow the advice are rather weak. Basically, in such cases the local government can only publish the names of the developers to embarrass them.

In the 1990s one of the most widespread applications of District Plan-type machizukuri ordinances has been for the incremental improvement of densely built up inner city areas such as Mano in Kobe and Taishido in Setagaya. Many such inner areas originally developed during the pre-war period with almost no planning controls on their growth. The results were extremely narrow streets, few parks or other public open spaces, and an extraordinarily high density of population. These areas were largely rebuilt with cheap wooden housing after the war along the existing pattern, especially in Tokyo and Osaka, which still retain the largest such problem areas. As shown in Figure 9.2, an enormous area of Tokyo is considered at high risk in the event of the large earthquake which is now overdue. The problem of narrow streets in such older built up areas is one of the most serious issues facing Japanese cities. While the Urban Buildings Law specified in 1939 that the basic minimum standard for housing plots is that they must front on a road of 4 metres or wider with road frontage of at least 2 metres, in fact about 40 per cent of housing plots nationwide front onto narrow roads of less than 4 metres in width (Kato 1988: 448). Quite apart from quality of life issues such as crowding, lack of sidewalks for the elderly and children, traffic congestion problems and shortage of parking spaces and space for street trees in such areas, the Kobe earthquake of 1995 served as a reminder that such areas are the most dangerous in times of disaster. In areas where streets were narrow damage was much greater because fires spread easily, and many fires could not be put out at all because emergency vehicles could not gain access. Over 90 per cent of the 6,000-plus victims of the Kobe earthquake were in those old, densely built up areas.

The extreme difficulty of improving these problem areas is not hard to imagine. Lack of public space, tiny plots, high population densities, high land prices, and their very extent makes the simple approach of purchase and clearance virtually impossible. Add to that the fact that these are long-established and tight-knit communities that fiercely resist plans to uproot and rebuild their neighbourhoods, and the endurance of these problems becomes more understandable. The project for Disaster Prevention Urban Renewal Areas (*Bōsai Toshi Zukuri Chiku*) started by the TMG in the mid-1970s to completely rebuild many of these areas into high-rises largely ground to a halt in the face of community opposition (Cibla 2000). The success of the citizen participation machizukuri projects in Taishido and Mano pointed to a way out of the impasse, and the incremental improvement approach of projects controlled by local residents gradually became the accepted best practice for improving such areas during the 1990s. Such incremental approaches, while extremely labour intensive, bring the advantage that they can invigorate local community activity without eliminating the existing urban fabric, and can address some of the more serious shortcomings of unplanned urban areas such as narrow roads, lack of sidewalks, and lack of local parks and open spaces.

A recent example of the use of a District Plan in conjunction with a machizukuri ordinance to gradually improve an area of narrow streets is found in the Sanshi Shikenjō Atochi area in the Suginami ward of Tokyo. There a District Plan was passed which increases allowable building height, FAR and plot coverage ratio where landowners rebuild their buildings leaving a setback of a metre or more along roads designated for widening to six metres. As noted in Chapter 8, one of the deregulations of the mid-1980s was to allow District Plans to weaken as well as strengthen statutory limits for building coverage, heights and FARs. The use of such bonuses as a way of persuading landowners to voluntarily give up a slice of their valuable land for road-widening avoids the need for extensive land purchases which would make such projects impossibly expensive. The main problem with the machizukuri approach is that it tends to be very slow, and such gradual improvement runs the risk of leaving crucial improvements incomplete when disaster strikes. Still, lacking a better alternative, these District Plan-type machizukuri projects were among the most widely used during the 1990s.

Land use control machizukuri ordinances

A second very common type of machizukuri ordinance has been that for land use control, particularly in urban fringe and exurban areas. Land use control type machizukuri ordinances developed because of two fundamental weaknesses of the 1968 City Planning Law. First, as described in Chapter 7, the law provides little legal control over development in "city planning white areas", which are areas within the CPA, but outside the UPA and UCA and outside settlements that have been zoned with land use zones. In these city planning white areas development permits are required only for developments of over 3,000 square metres. Another kind of "white area" is the area outside the CPA where there are only extremely weak legal powers to control land development, no FAR or building coverage limits, and a development permit requirement only for developments of over 20 hectares. This allowed relatively unrestricted development in exurban areas. Second, as noted above, because of the peculiar definition of "land development" in the City Planning Law, much land conversion to parking lots, waste disposal sites, car-wreckers, gravel processing yards, etc, could not be controlled under the development control system, even within UCAs that were in principle subject to strong controls on land development. As a result, shortly after the passage of the 1968 law many local governments outside the CPAs began to create their own "development standards ordinances" to control land development in areas where the development permit system could not be applied. Such ordinances are fundamentally similar to the development manuals within CPAs. The main difference is that they are not backed by the legal power of the development permit system. There are cases where development permit-type systems have been established, and also cases where "notification, consultation and advice" systems have been set up. The primary targets of many of the early ordinances were gravel extraction facilities and industrial waste disposal facilities. Gravel quarries have become an increasingly common disfigurement of the Japanese countryside because of the vast quantities of concrete being poured (McGill 1998). Most land use control ordinances require that developers wishing to develop areas larger than the specified limit notify and consult with the local government. Many ordinances also oblige developers to hold explanation meetings with local residents at the same time that they hold their consultations with local government, and some also require the consent of the residents' council before development can proceed. Municipalities have the discretionary power to give developers "advice" and again, if the advice is not followed, usually all the local government can do is publish the names of offenders to embarrass them (Matsumoto 1999).

One of the precedent-setting cases of land use control-type machizukuri ordinances is that of Okayama prefecture. In the early 1970s Okayama, located midway between Osaka and Hiroshima on the Seto inland sea, was experiencing a burst of growth resulting from the building of the Sanyo Shinkansen and Chugoku Expressway. Investment capital poured in from the Osaka region, particularly into the area around the Mizushima New Industrial City, resulting in the rapid spread of sprawl development. Conditions were particularly bad in the northern part of the prefecture which was outside the CPA (Okata 1999: 125). In 1973 the prefectural government passed an ordinance which imposed a two-level development control system throughout the prefecture. Developments of over 10 hectares were required to consult with the prefectural government before the purchase of the land, whereas developments of over 1 hectare were subject to a development permit system designed primarily to ensure adequate public services and fire prevention facilities were available. At the same time the prefectural government passed a model "development control" ordinance for municipalities to copy, on which many municipalities based their own development control ordinance (Okata 1999: 127). One example was the town of Akasaka which was located outside the CPA and experiencing extensive disorderly development, particularly of gravel extraction pits because of the high-quality gravel produced there. The town passed a land use control ordinance which required that virtually all developments meet certain development standards of roads, parks, parking spaces, etc, and that developments of over 1,000 square metres (0.1 hectares) would be subject to a process of consultation with the local government to ensure that they conformed with the municipal land use plan. Developers who did not notify (or made a false statement) could be assessed a fine of up to 30,000 yen, but there was no penalty on developers who did not follow municipal advice. The ordinance has generally been difficult to enforce, many scattered developments have occurred, and some developers have simply ignored the requirement to notify the local government (Wada 1999: 153).

The number of land use control ordinances increased greatly during the second half of the 1980s when a resort development boom (*rezōto kaihatsu bumu*) started, and there was a rapid increase in the development of resort condominiums (*rezōto manshon*) and resort, hotel, golf course, and cottage developments in non-Senbiki and non-CPA local areas far from the main urban areas. These problems were exacerbated in the 1990s as the spread of motorisation encouraged the growth of mini-developments and road-side shopping strips further and further from the main urban areas. Local governments in many scenic areas that relied primarily on tourism as their economic base began to see the danger that unrestricted development posed to their economic future.

Faced with their inability to prevent damaging development, the small-scale local governments in many resort areas (such as hot springs, skiing areas, seashore, and high mountain meadow areas) started to pass land development control ordinances to gain some control over these new patterns of development. In the period from the mid-1980s to the mid-1990s these development control ordinances were commonly established with a community consultation procedure and local machizukuri plans, with a designation procedure similar to District Plan-type ordinances (Okata 1999: 134). In whole local government areas, notification/consultation systems were put in place to control large-scale buildings such as condominiums, office towers and factories, and to control building form and design, especially building height, colour and materials. Such ordinances allowed local governments to designate Landscape Protection Areas and prepare a Landscape Protection Plan and Landscape Protection Standards. The ordinances commonly create a duty for developers to notify the local government prior to all new construction and any changes to the exteriors of buildings within these areas. Developments which do not conform with the standards are subject to advice by the local government, but if the advice is not followed, all the local government can do is publish the name of the developer.

A prominent example of the most recent wave of landscape protection machizukuri ordinances is in Hotaka, a rural town that has been grappling with methods to control development and protect a beautiful natural environment. Located in the northern Japan Alps area of Nagano prefecture, Hotaka is a short distance from the growing regional centre of Matsumoto to which it is connected by a convenient rail line. During the late 1980s and early 1990s the town was subject to the full range of exurban development pressures, including ski resorts, suburban commuter housing and second homes for the wealthy, and roadside retail developments. From 1985 to 1999 the population increased from about 20,000 to 30,000, and a large share of new development was along rural roads in mini-developments that fell just under the limit for development control. These often took the form of "one tan development" (*ittan kaihatsu)* in areas where rice paddies were laid out in one tan plots of 991.7 square metres, conveniently under the 1000 square metres threshold required for development permits, as described in Chapters 1 and 7. In this case it is possible to see how far landscape protection machizukuri processes have progressed from the early land use control ordinances, which sought merely to limit the worst sorts of gravel extraction and waste disposal facilities. In Hotaka a comprehensive approach drawing on the experiences of earlier machizukuri processes and on the Master Plan system has been attempted. The goal of the ordinance is not merely to prevent adverse development, but to work towards positive patterns of development that will enhance the "rich green environment and quality of life of the town" (*midori yutakana sumiyoi machi*) (Hotaka Town 1999).

The project to draft a machizukuri ordinance began in 1995 with a survey of local residents to determine their opinions about the necessity of some sort of improved land use planning control. Many responded that they were concerned about recent land development activity and that some sort of control was necessary. In 1996 the town received funding from the NLA and Nagano prefecture to carry out a thorough land use framework survey in the whole municipal area. The survey involved explanation meetings with local residents, a survey of each household, and the drawing up of a land use plan, and is credited with beginning the process of forming local resident agreement on a development control system. In 1997 Hotaka was selected by the NLA section charged with developing a new planning policy for the lightly regulated city planning "white land" as a test case, and was given significant funding support to develop a municipal land use control basic plan and district land use control plans. Such funding is important because most small local governments simply do not have the funds to take on ambitious new projects, as they are struggling just to manage their current responsibilities.

In accordance with the conditions of the funding, a council made up of municipal and prefectural officers, academic practitioners, and citizen representatives was formed to develop the policy. The mayor and deputy mayor held an intensive series of discussions in each of the town's 23 districts. A land use control general plan was prepared by the council, published and put on display. In 1998 another council, including a number of citizen representatives was formed to draft a machizukuri ordinance to promote the basic land use control plan. The draft ordinance was completed and made public, and towards the end of the year the mayor was re-elected. In early 1999 the ordinance was approved and put into effect by October of that year (Okata 1999: 141–2).

The main issues addressed by the ordinance were the fact that in the city planning "white land" which covered most of the municipal area there were few controls or policies for land use, and haphazard development of farmland to residential uses was allowed just about anywhere. A top priority was the control of the small residential developments that were popping up throughout the agricultural areas surrounding the town. Second, given the recent rapid population increases, the fact that the town had an existing water supply and disposal capacity for about 40,000 people provided a strong incentive to introduce an overall control policy for limiting future population growth to 10,000. Finally, it was hoped to protect existing large blocks of farmland and create a basis for high-quality residential areas by guiding development into clusters. As the extensive areas of "white land" were within a CPA, all developments of over 3,000 square metres were automatically subject to development permission controls. The existing development manual imposed a further obligation of consultations with the local government on all developments of over 1,000 square metres. Unfortunately there had continued to be many developments of less than 1,000 square metres which were essentially impossible to control. Such mini-developments were a problem because they tended to be developed as tiny plots, which made it impossible to retain large-scale trees on them or to landscape in keeping with the idea of a green city. In response the ordinance lowered the bar to place development controls on all developments of over 500 square metres throughout the municipal area, and imposed minimum plot sizes and stricter building coverage ratios (Okata 1999: 143).

The key feature of the land use basic plan established by the machizukuri ordinance was the division of the whole urban area into small districts. In each district a public meeting is held, and local groups are encouraged to form a Machizukuri Council. The councils are approved by the mayor and charged with developing a District Machizukuri Plan, created through a series of public participation and consultation workshops. Two-thirds of local residents must approve the plan to make it an official District Machizukuri Plan (Hotaka Town 1999: 5). Where such plans are in place, they must be taken into account when proposals for new development or redevelopment are made for the district. Developers must also gain the approval of local government before they can proceed. Although the consent of local residents is not always necessary, the local government will not normally give approval without it. In districts where a District Machizukuri Plan has been approved, the District Machizukuri Council is understood to represent the local residents. But, under the traditional rural social structure of the town, the District Machizukuri Council is actually the District Jichikai. So, local residents, through participation in the Jichikai or Machizukuri Council within each district thus have the power to refuse land development projects over a certain size. In the area of the District Machizukuri Plan, even smaller developments will be required to pass a similar but simpler process provided by a "District Machizukuri Working Manual" (*Chiku Machizukuri Jigyo Yōkō*), but its development is still in progress.

A final interesting aspect of the Hotaka landscape protection machizukuri ordinance is its land use plan and design guidelines (*Tochi Riyō Chōsei Kihon Keikaku* which

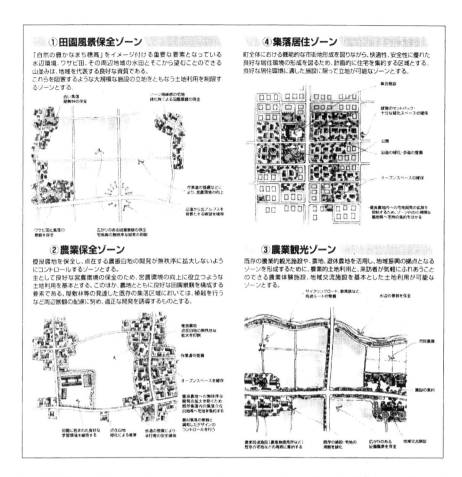

Figure 9.3 Hotaka Town zoning concept. A key aspect of the Hotaka Landscape Protection ordinance is the creation of nine new zones for areas outside the village area that was already zoned under the City Planning Law. The new zones include a "Rural Landscape Protection Zone" (#1 above), an "Agriculture Protection Zone" (#2), a "Village Residential Zone" (#4), and an "Agriculture Tourism Zone" (#3), among others.

Source: Hotaka Town (1999).

translates literally as Land Use General Management Plan). In effect the whole municipal area outside the old townsite area, which was already zoned under the City Planning Law, has been zoned into nine new kinds of zones. Each has a concept such as Rural Landscape Protection Zone, Village Residential Zone, or Cultural Facilities Zone and a design concept, shown in Figure 9.4. The machizukuri ordinance also provided a table describing suitable kinds of development within each of the zones. The idea of a new set of zones imposed on previously unzoned rural districts seems an appropriate response to the spread of development permitted by increasing motorisation, and the design concept seems to have struck a chord as it has recently been copied in other rural towns. The Hotaka approach has a number of weaknesses, however. In particular, because of landowner opposition to a strong prohibition of development in particular areas, the ordinance avoids direct confrontation with landowners over taking their land rights by avoiding the explicit prohibition of many of the more controversial land uses in specific zones, indicating instead that they must be "decided through consultation" (Yasutani 2001).

The significance of the Hotaka ordinance is that its goals are much more ambitious than the earlier land use control measures which were designed primarily to regulate the most offensive land uses. In Hotaka the goal is to propose new patterns and standards of development throughout the municipal area, and attempts to improve development patterns through persuasion and by providing an image of best practice. As with other machizukuri ordinances of the 1990s, neither the zoning nor the design guidelines are legally enforceable, and the only sanction the local government can impose on non-conforming developments is to publish the name of those contravening the ordinance. It remains to be seen how the new machizukuri approach will function in practice, and whether sufficient public and landowner support can be generated to use the new legal powers proffered by recent decentralisations to make the provisions of the ordinance legally binding in future.

Historic preservation machizukuri ordinances

The third major group of machizukuri ordinances are those for historical preservation, which share many features with District Planning and land use control ordinances, while having somewhat different origins and characteristics. The practice of historical preservation in Japan has its origins in the pre-war period, when there were limited efforts at historical preservation during the 1920s and 1930s using the Scenic Areas zoning provided by the 1919 City Planning Law. For example, Meiji Shrine in Tokyo was designated a historic site in 1920, and by 1930 34 square kilometres of Kyoto had been designated as Scenic Area (Hohn 1997: 219). The Cultural Properties Protection Law of 1950 permitted designation of specific structures, and a Cultural Properties Protection Commission was established to administer the law, carry out research and establish priorities for preservation. The main emphasis at this stage was to preserve important historical structures such as temples, shrines, and castles, and little attention was given to private buildings, town areas, or buildings built since the beginning of the Meiji period in 1868. Priorities gradually evolved, and from 1962 to 1965 the Cultural Properties Protection Commission carried out a survey of important traditional private houses, and in 1968 the Cultural Properties Protection Commission merged with the Cultural Bureau of the Ministry of Education (*Monbushō*) to become the extra-ministerial Agency for Cultural Affairs (*Bunkachō*) with expanded powers.

Public concern and pressure for more active efforts at historical preservation increased during the 1960s as economic growth speeded up and urban areas started to see rapid changes and the destruction of large numbers of traditional buildings. Growing numbers of people started to worry that traditional Japanese urban areas would be destroyed entirely and replaced with modern concrete and steel buildings. It was realised that not only individual famous buildings needed to be protected, but also whole districts of traditional buildings, even if individual buildings were not well known. Yet Japan still had no legal system for protecting historic city areas, and the city planning system has in fact been an important cause of the destruction of traditional buildings because fire protection regulations made it virtually impossible to renovate and re-use old buildings. Instead it requires them to be replaced with fireproof materials, different rooflines and a setback from narrow roads. Because of the lack of national legislation allowing the designation and protection of traditional urban areas, Kanazawa and Kurashiki cities, which had rich historic urban assets, each passed their own independent historical area protection ordinances in 1968 as municipal by-laws (Koide 1999: 74).

The protection of historic urban areas became much easier with the passage of the "Important Preservation Districts for Groups of Historic Buildings" system as a national law in 1975. That law was a great advance on earlier legislation, because it allowed the preservation of urban areas, not just individual buildings. Interestingly the passage of that national law actually greatly increased the use of local machizukuri ordinances for historical protection. This was in part because the number of Important Preservation Districts (IPDs) under national law was small with only 40 designated by 1994 (Hohn 1997: 224). It is also a result of the fact that the IPD system provides extremely strict controls over development, and not terribly generous financial support, so such designation is often opposed by local landowners. As a result, in many historical districts machizukuri ordinances have been passed instead, as it is easier to gain acceptance for their relatively weaker regulations. Also, even where IPDs have been designated, the area has usually been drawn quite tightly around a core historic district. In Kurashiki, for example, the IPD system designates the core area of the historic district, and an ordinance is used to protect a larger area surrounding the IPD. The number of such machizukuri ordinances to protect broad areas of mountains and scenery around historic areas and landmarks such as castles and temples increased markedly in the 1980s.

The old merchant town of Kurashiki is one of the best known examples of historical preservation. Kurashiki is located midway between Osaka and Hiroshima in Okayama prefecture, on the Seto Inland Sea. Kurashiki was one of the first examples of the use of a machizukuri ordinance for most of the historic preservation area, and has become a very popular tourist destination, ranking top among IPDs with 4.5 million visitors in 1991 (Hohn 1997: 227). Interestingly, although Kurashiki had passed one of the first two townscape preservation ordinances in Japan in 1968, it was only designated as an IPD in 1979, partly because it was a merchant town, not a samurai area, and samurai areas formed the bulk of early IPD designations (Hohn 1997: 222).

The Kurashiki preservation area currently has two parts, a core area which is designated as an IPD where preservation standards are strict and legally enforceable, and a surrounding larger area protected by a municipal machizukuri ordinance which is not as strict, and enforced primarily through persuasion. The machizukuri ordinance designates a Landscape Preservation District (*Keikan keisei chiku*) to which a plan and a set of development standards are applied. Standards include height limits, roof styles, building materials, etc. Two sets of standards were applied, a legally enforceable minimum standard that was backed up by a District Plan, and a set of landscape guidelines that was backed by administrative guidance through a notification and advice system. Within the Landscape Preservation District developers must notify of development plans and consult with the local government, which in turn consults with the local residents' committee. The local government can give official advice to developers, and if they do

Figure 9.4 The old merchant quarter of Kurashiki on the Seto Inland Sea. Kurashiki was one of the leaders in historical townscape preservation by municipal ordinance, designating its first preservation area in 1968, and being designated an Important Preservation District in 1979. Kurashiki topped the league of historical site tourist attractions, with 4.5 million visits in 1991.

Photo A. Sorensen 2000.

not comply, can publicise their transgression (Koide 1999: 80). A further elaboration of the Kurashiki system was seen in Hakodate, an early colonial port in southern Hokkaido. There a third ring was added to the two-ring structure adopted in Kurashiki. This covers a much wider area surrounding the historic district, and is designed to prevent large-scale high-rise developments so as to protect the visual backdrop of the IPD. Termed the "Large-scale Building Notification Area' (*Daikibo Kenchiku Todokede Chiku*), this again relies on a machizukuri ordinance and notification/consultation system.

Another of the early historical preservation movements organised by citizens to protect their urban heritage was in Imaichō in Nara prefecture, shown in Figure 1.4. Imaichō is an old temple/merchant town dating from before the Tokugawa period. Within the preservation area about 60 per cent of the buildings are very old wooden buildings of the traditional style. A local preservation movement began in the mid-1970s, and in 1983 successfully gained support for historical preservation from the local council. The local community played an essential role in stopping the building of a city planning road that would have cut through the centre of the community, and in pressing for support for preservation of the traditional buildings. Preservation efforts have been led by the local Neighbourhood Association (*Jichikai*), the Imaichō Townscape Protection Group (*Imaichō Machinami Hozonkai*), the Imaichō Townscape Protection Citizens' Consultative Committee, (*Imaichō Machinami Hozon Jūmin Shingikai*), and the Imaichō Youth Group (*Seinenkai*) (Koide 1997: 114). Three machizukuri ordinances were passed: the Traditional Building Protection Area Ordinance in 1989, the Imaichō Traditional Building Protection Area Relaxation of Building Standards Law in 1993, and the Traditional Building Protection Area Tax Reduction (and financial support for renovations) in 1993 (Koide 1999: 91). The relaxation of building standards was essential because as noted above, the Building Standards Law has been a major factor in blocking the preservation of traditional buildings.

The Imaichō machizukuri ordinance has six main articles. Article 1 defines the protection area. Article 2 establishes a notification/permit system for any changes to buildings in the area, which is administered by the town mayor and the municipal education committee. Article 3 designates an area protection plan and standards for the permit system. Article 4 establishes a consultative body to supervise the ordinance. Article 5 authorises financial support for a portion of the costs of renovations to achieve the standards of the ordinance. Article 6 authorises a system to give advice/guidance to prospective developers, and allows permit revocation, fines, etc, for projects that hinder the protection of the area. The machizukuri ordinance thus follows the now well-established machizukuri formula of defining the target area, authorising a committee, and creating an administrative guidance-based permit system to control changes within the area. In addition to these local ordinances, the area was designated an IPD by the Agency for Cultural Affairs in 1993, and a Townscape Environmental Improvement Project (*Machinami Kankyō Seibi Jigyō*) in the same year. These two designations have provided important additional funds to rebuild many of the local roads and other public facilities in traditional styles, and to subsidise earthquake-proofing and fire prevention (Koide 1997: 114).

Machizukuri and city planning

All of the machizukuri ordinances described above are characterised by three main features. First, they were passed by municipal governments in order to fill gaps and loopholes in national planning legislation that left extensive urban areas and a variety of types of development relatively weakly regulated, and severely limited the legal authority of local governments to attempt higher standards of historical preservation or development control. Second, all of the machizukuri ordinances were prepared with significant degrees of public participation. Third, they tend to have only very weak powers to compel compliance by developers, as even where the ordinance has been duly passed by a municipal council, they are not enforceable in court when developers refuse to comply. This has led to intense conflicts in a few cases, and to a remarkable amount of cooperation in the majority of cases.

The machizukuri approach seems well suited to local environmental improvement and historical preservation projects, as it provides a vehicle for mobilising the energy of local people, and ultimately without the strong support of local residents and landowners, such projects are bound to fail. It seems clear that community mobilisation will continue to be the key issue in the future. Machizukuri ordinances have finally provided a way for local people to become actively involved in protecting and improving their local environments, and residents in many communities have seized the chance with both hands and are running with it. It seems likely that in many Western countries the relatively weak regulatory power of machizukuri ordinances would be a recipe for disaster, as the social stigma of contravening community wishes is much less likely to sway decisions on property development or redevelopment. It will be interesting to see whether machizukuri continues to rely primarily on persuasion, or gradually shifts to a more strongly regulatory basis now that local governments have gained legal authority to pass binding local ordinances.

It is clear that Japan is now experiencing a "machizukuri boom". A diverse range of urban residents in cities throughout the country have become involved in an extraordinary number and variety of different machizukuri planning projects. True to tradition, savvy planners have invited some of the most prominent public participation practitioners from the West to introduce new techniques and ideas (see e.g. Sanoff 2000: 250–74). Citizen participatory machizukuri is clearly enormously important as Japan's first planning approach that is explicitly based on following the expressed wishes of local residents. The greater involvement of local residents in setting goals and priorities in their own neighbourhoods also promises to contribute to greater public support for planning and development control measures that enhance local quality of life. Decentralisation of planning powers to local government also seems likely to promote planning approaches that are more sensitive to the demands of urban residents, taxpayers and voters than in the old system which was dominated so completely by central government. As Ishida (2000: 13) has suggested, however, without improved local financial resources it may be difficult for local governments to fulfil the promise of decentralisation of the legal authority to plan. Given the long history of gradual decentralisation, it is reasonable to suggest that central government's continuing control over finances will remain an effective barrier to local autonomy.

Perhaps more decisive will be the question of how machizukuri develops from here. As suggested in Chapter 8, the key issue is not whether the process is initiated by local residents or by municipal governments, but the quality and nature of public participation that is achieved. There are many reasons why most participatory machizukuri processes will continue to be initiated primarily by municipal governments and other public bodies, not least being the statutory requirement for public participation in Master Plan formulation, and the pressing need to revitalise and renovate many older urban areas, in which intensive public participation of some sort is unavoidable. The real issues will be where machizukuri agendas and priorities are set, how the participants in Machizukuri Councils are selected, how decisions are made in the councils, and whether such decisions will have any impact on the policies of higher-level bodies.

If the old style of neighbourhood organisations, which were characterised by a general subservience to the directions of local governments and other higher authorities continues, then it is hard to imagine that the promise of machizukuri will be fulfilled. Will local Machizukuri Councils be able to set priorities that are significantly different or even in opposition to those of their municipal government? Even if they are, will they be able to make any progress in carrying them out? The process of selecting Machizukuri councils (*Machizukuri Kyōgikai*) seems certain to become a key issue. A wide variety of methods are used to select members, but it seems most are appointed by local governments or volunteer themselves out of a sense of public service or personal interest. In many cases the local Chōnaikai or Jichikai have semi-automatically assumed the roles of Machizukuri Councils. While machizukuri organisations remain marginal, the self-appointment of those who are interested may work perfectly well. If machizukuri ordinances and planning processes actually start to have significant impacts on patterns of urban change, Machizukuri Council selection processes seem likely to become an increasingly important and contested issue. At present it seems that most decision-making in Machizukuri Councils is by the time-honoured processes of consensus building. As discussed in Chapter 10, however, consensus decision-making in Japanese community organisations has often served primarily to perpetuate the dominance of a small number of locally influential men, who have in many communities been able to keep a firm hold over the Chōnaikai and Jichikai. It seems likely that one of the major challenges for machizukuri organisations in future, particularly if they become more effective and powerful players in community environmental improvement activities, will be to develop and strengthen the ways in which participants are selected as well as their internal operating and decision-making procedures.

Perhaps the biggest question for machizukuri is what its role will be in relation to city planning. So far, machizukuri has taken on a range of activities that had been virtually ignored by traditional Japanese city planning. These include the improvement of existing residential areas by widening narrow roads, providing parks, playlots and street trees, building community centres and similar local facilities, development control in loosely regulated sprawl areas on the urban fringe, and historical preservation. The question is, when will city planning itself begin to be infected by some of the more desirable aspects of the new machizukuri practices, such as the prioritisation of people's needs and quality of life? City planning seems to have continued largely unaffected by the new approaches. A good example is the city of Kobe, widely considered to be one of the leaders of machizukuri, and very supportive of the new approaches. Yet city planning in Kobe is still preoccupied with the old priorities of arterial roads and large-scale projects. City planning roads planned 40 years ago are still being pushed through existing neighbourhoods whose machizukuri groups are strongly opposed to them. The city of Kobe is also still pressing ahead with its plan to build an enormously expensive international airport on a new landfill in Osaka Bay in the face of repeated large-scale petition campaigns by Kobe taxpayers against the project. The financial viability of this airport, and its necessity, have both been questioned given the continuing lack of demand for the new Kansai airport located just across the bay, and its steeply rising debts. The more cynical observer might suggest that city planning has changed not at all, and a range of issues that city planning never prioritised – such as residential quality of life, landscape preservation, and historical preservation – have been fobbed off onto volunteer groups.

On the other hand, this is just the beginning of what is bound to be a long process of development. It may be more appropriate at this point to share the optimism of many of those involved in machizukuri organising, and hope that machizukuri processes of citizen participation in plan-making and development control continue to grow and develop, and that their impacts on the ground continue to increase.

Major urban changes in the 1990s

Continuing dual urban structure – planned and sprawl areas

It is difficult to summarise complex patterns of urban change in a few paragraphs, as a great diversity continues to characterise Japanese urban development. In the 1990s the legacy of the bubble period began to be increasingly evident, with a proliferation of the spectacular and expensive buildings started during the boom, and the spread also of vacant city lots as development companies went bankrupt and their assets were assumed by creditors. The development of new elevated urban expressways and subways continued apace. The building of high-rise condominiums resumed in downtown redevelopments as land prices dropped and new housing units become affordable again. The shift of retailing from the old model of large department stores near major railway stations and tens of thousands of small family shops in smaller retail areas to the ubiquitous convenience stores and category-killer big-box outlets on suburban highways continued. In 2001 for the first time, the largest convenience store chain edged out the largest supermarket/department store operator as the nation's biggest retailer.

Here it seems worth continuing the focus of attention on developments on the urban fringe, as it is these areas of new urban growth that will have the most important marginal impacts on long-term urban patterns and quality of life. On the urban fringe the dominant and distinctive feature of Japanese urbanisation and planning is the continuing reproduction of the dual urban structure of some planned and replanned bits, intermixed with large areas of unplanned sprawl. The proportion of all urban development that is planned and serviced with roads and main services has gradually expanded during the post-war period, but still only represents between a third and a half of all new development. A wide range of planned developments exist, including the new towns, technopolis projects, various industrial parks and goods distribution centres, numerous LR projects, and a fair number of private large-scale developments carried out under the development permission system. The most visible areas of planned development are the "New Towns", which have increased greatly in number and have improved enormously in design since the dull housing estates of the rapid growth period. Another exceptional example of large-scale planned development is the Tama Den'en Toshi (Tama Garden City) area south of Tokyo in Kanagawa prefecture, developed with dozens of LR projects over a 50-year period by the Tokyu railway, land development and department store group. These continue to be the exceptions to the rule, however, as haphazard, unserviced, incremental development still dominates development on the urban fringe.

Sprawl areas continue to spread

As shown in Chapter 7, a significant majority of new urban development continues as unplanned, haphazard sprawl. To clearly show what recent haphazard development in Japan actually looks like, it is worth examining a case study area in Urawa City, the former capital of Saitama prefecture north of Tokyo, and since 2001 a part of Saitama City, the new capital of Saitama prefecture created with the merger of Urawa, Yono and Omiya cities. It is fair to say that the case study area examined here is representative of a significant majority of metropolitan suburban areas created during the period after 1970. Figure 9.5 shows the state of completion of the arterial road network in Urawa as of 1995. It is clear that the city has had great difficulty completing its planned arterial road system. Only a small proportion of planned arterial roads have been built and improvements to roads have taken place primarily within LR areas, and secondarily of major roads leading to the town centre. Completion of the planned network will clearly be a long-term, costly business as urbanisation has proceeded well in advance of road building. Congestion is unsurprisingly severe on existing through roads which have seen dramatically increasing use resulting from the growing population and increasing car ownership.

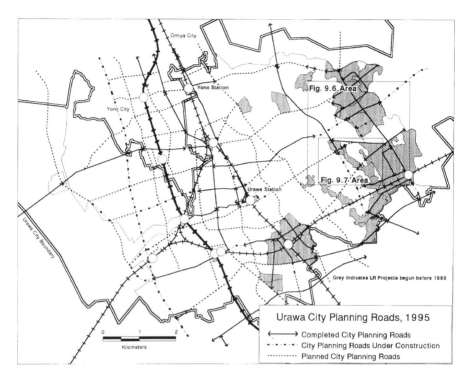

Figure 9.5 Urawa City planning roads, 1995. Although a comprehensive network of city planning roads was planned for Urawa in the 1960s, by 1995 remarkably little progress had been made in building them, even though substantial development had occurred throughout the city area. The reliance on LR is clear, as only in the LR projects and near the city centre rail stations is the road system mostly complete. Note the two boxes which indicate the area of Figures 9.6 and 9.7 which show urbanisation patterns in more detail.

Source: Sorensen (2001b).

Figure 9.6 gives a more detailed view of one part of the new urban area on the east side of Urawa, showing the road network and built up plots as of 1992. This area includes the largest concentration of LR projects in Urawa City. While inside the LR areas modified grid networks of local and arterial roads have been established, outside the LR projects the old rural road system is clearly visible. The fact that the LR areas do not always connect together means that the completed bits of the arterial road network are fragmented. Also, while the only large blocks of undeveloped land are in the non-LR areas, significant stocks of unbuilt land remain in the LR areas also, and large amounts of building have occurred outside the LR areas along the light tracery of the existing rural road network, and on short extensions to it. In 1990 32 per cent of all dwellings in Urawa fronted on a road of less than four metres in width (Saitama ken 1992). Many urban areas in Japan have become fully built up in this manner, with a gradual improvement of the road network carried out by widening here and there and retrospective provision of sewers and other services. It is a common mistake of foreign observers to see these areas as a vestige of Japan's ancient urban tradition, even though the vast majority have been built during the post-war period. This pattern of incremental build up along the narrowest of roads is of course precisely the reason why it has been so difficult to complete the planned arterials. In most cases they require substantial and expensive purchase of built up land and demolition of dwellings. It is also worth noting that in the area of Figure 9.6 the only sewer serviced areas are the LR projects. Developments outside the projects use septic tanks which must be regularly pumped out into tankers.

The only parks in the new urban area on the east side of Urawa are within LR project areas, which must have a minimum of 3 per cent of their area as park to qualify for

Figure 9.6 Roads and land development patterns, Urawa City. Starting in the late 1960s, Urawa City attempted to develop the whole east side of its new UPA by LR projects, and in the early 1980s virtually all of this area that was not already LR was designated LR promotion area using the flexible Senbiki method (see Figure 8.3, page 282). By the early 1990s only one small new LR project had been started, and most planned projects had either been abandoned or reduced in size. The result is a fragmented road system, with bits of new arterial roads scattered around the area, and with most of the greatly increased traffic using the old rural road networks.

Source: Sorensen (2001b).

central and prefectural government subsidies. The scant provision of parks is a result of the difficulties experienced in obtaining land even for roads. The paucity of public green space does not bode well for the future as the area becomes fully built up and population density increases. Particularly unfortunate is the fact that the natural environment was particularly rich, and could, given a different planning regime, have resulted in a very high quality of urban environment. As it is, the streams, the thickly wooded escarpments, and the many small wood lots are being gradually built over.

In contrast to suburban residential development in other developed countries, in Japan there is very little chance that such natural features will remain after an area is built up. New urban land developments always start with the clearance of all vegetation and the creation of absolutely level building plots by the systematic use of retaining walls, whether the land is already almost level or on a steep hillside. Very small residential plots, themselves the result of high land prices, mean that even a relatively small house will normally be built to within a metre of the lot line on three sides, leaving a small garden area on the south side of the building, whether to the side, on the street side, or behind the house. There is no space in these small plots for large trees, and only the major arterial roads are wide enough to allow roadside tree planting. Without measures to preserve green areas it thus seems inevitable that eventually a fully built up urban area lacking significant green spaces will result, even though during the decades-long process of build up there are often generous amounts of green remaining in farmers' vegetable plots and in wooded hillsides. It is often said that Japanese people move to the suburbs to achieve a better, greener environment, but as Hanayama (1986) has argued in the Japanese case, and as has long been lamented by critics of suburban residential development in the West, such a green environment is only a temporary benefit soon lost to further development. In fact it seems clear that the main reason to move to the suburbs, however distant, and however ill serviced and planned, is to be able to afford to buy a house, as land is less expensive on the urban fringe. From one point of view it seems possible that allowing relatively unrestricted development on the urban fringe may have contributed to the high levels of home ownership in Japan, which at 59.8 per cent in 1993 are comparable with those of the US and Britain (Oizumi 2002). On the other hand, by far the largest factor in high housing costs in Japan is high land costs, and many argue that this is a result of government policies, including weak land development regulations (Haley and Yamamura 1992; Noguchi 1992b; Wegener 1994).

Arriving at a simple conclusion about the net impacts of government policy on the affordability of housing in Japan is not an easy matter, but it is clear that the lack of development controls continues to create serious urban problems. Figure 9.7 illustrates the gradual process of build up in one part of the case study area, including both LR and non-LR areas, during the period 1968 to 1992. New houses and businesses are distributed rather evenly throughout the area. While new road systems have been completed only in the LR areas, a significant amount of new building has occurred along the former rural lanes in non-LR areas.

As can be imagined, road congestion is a serious problem in this area, as the only through roads are carrying a vastly increased traffic load, and former rural lanes are also increasingly heavily used, even though they will only just permit two cars to squeeze past each other. The wide road at the top left of Figure 9.7 is part of a new national highway from Omiya in the north to Tokyo in the south. The portion shown here was

East Urawa Urbanisation, 1968 - 1992

☐ Extant buildings in 1968
▨ Buildings built from 1968 - 1982
■ Buildings built from 1982 - 1992

Figure 9.7 Gradual, scattered urban development, 1968–92. This area of Urawa city is typical of many suburban areas in the metropolitan suburbs. Over 20 years after being designated as UPA, to be developed comprehensively with LR projects and by development permit within 10 years, less than half the land is built up, the new arterial road system is fragmentary, and most dwellings are serviced neither by sewer systems nor piped gas.

Source: Sorensen (2001b).

completed in the mid-1970s as part of a LR project. Virtually all of the area in this figure not yet developed by LR is "LR designated area" in the official plan, scheduled for comprehensive redevelopment if the city can only gain the consent of the landowners. As shown elsewhere, however (Sorensen 2000a), such consent is not always forthcoming, and haphazard subdivision and development in the meantime means that there are more landowners whose consent is required, and greater expense of project execution if consent can finally be obtained.

One of the most distinctive features of new residential areas in Japan such as that in Urawa is that they are characterised by constant and wholesale change. This is not merely a question of infilling new houses in the empty plots of an established road and

Figure 9.8 Heavy traffic on existing roads. One significant consequence of unplanned building on the urban fringe has been worsening traffic congestion. A strategy that was reasonably successful when everyone used bicycles and trains is now creating serious problems with increasing motorisation. Existing rural roads and lanes now carry the bulk of traffic, while the new arterial road networks are built very gradually and at great expense because of the amount of demolition required.

Photo A. Sorensen 2000.

cadastral system, but is rather a matter of the gradual transformation of the very character of the area, with major new arterial roads being pushed through existing neighbourhoods, bringing blocks of apartments and new commercial land uses associated with highway strip development. The most important changes include changes to road networks and travel patterns, increased population and built density, increases in the range and number of land uses, and the gradual, largely unplanned shift from a primarily rural and residential area to a mixed residential commercial area. Scattered plot-by-plot development, incremental completion of planned road networks, and as-of-right building within zoning limits, even where main infrastructure has not yet been built, mean that these areas are continuously under construction for many decades.

It is not a question of whether these areas might turn into slums. Land prices are far too high for that to be likely. The question is rather what kind of residential environment the new residents are getting for their investment, and whether it might not have been better, and cheaper, with a different planning regime. The fact that the minority of suburban development such as the "new towns" that is well planned and protected from unplanned change is so popular, and so much more expensive, suggests that many Japanese homebuyers prefer a more stable residential environment. So also does the recent proliferation of citizen-based efforts to protect their communities through local machizukuri ordinances during the 1990s. While the significant changes to the city planning legislation in 1992 and again in 2000 have significantly strengthened controls over development, the enormous half-built-up areas such as those examined here seem certain to absorb a disproportionate share of planning resources for many years to come.

It should not be assumed that no other alternative was open, even without a strong planning law such as that in post-war Britain. In 1968 when the new planning system was enacted the Urawa study area was almost entirely rural in land use. If different choices had been made then, whether it was enforcing slightly stricter conditions of development permission or placing strict controls on building in the route of planned arterial roads, purchase of the development rights to such land, or even outright purchase of the land, it seems likely that it would have been much cheaper in the long run.

In reviewing the incremental development of these suburban areas an impression can be gained of how narrow the conception of the eventual built urban environment must necessarily become for those charged with city planning in these circumstances. The vision of a completed arterial road network must dance in the dreams of the planners responsible, but the inability to achieve even that must stifle more ambitious ideas, such as bicycle routes, decent parks, or an urban design that uses the hills and valleys of the area to advantage or that would allow the numerous streams to flow above ground through green corridors instead of in concrete ditches beside roads.

In the end it is the continued failure to prevent haphazard unserviced sprawl that is most surprising about post-war Japanese urbanisation and planning. While the area of planned developments such as the technopolises and new towns has increased dramatically, sprawl continues be the dominant form of urban growth because of the reluctance of the government to regulate land development more strictly. And while increasingly sophisticated methods of retroactive improvement of existing urban areas are being developed, not least of which is machizukuri, it is hard not to wonder whether it might not have been easier to regulate urban development better in the first place. Certainly there is enough work to keep machizukuri activists and consultants busy for a long time to come.

The 1990s thus saw major changes to Japanese urban planning which justify considerable optimism for the future. The spread of machizukuri activism by local citizens in urban areas throughout the country, the development of Master Planning methods and the significant involvement of local people in those processes, the rapid increase in awareness of the importance of historical preservation, and the significant devolution of planning powers at the end of the decade all bode well for the future. On the other hand, the continuing weak financial independence of local governments, and the fact that they are gaining more autonomy at a time of deep fiscal crisis seems likely to limit their freedom to develop new approaches. Possibly more importantly, as illustrated by the case of Urawa discussed above, the fundamental problem of Japanese city planning remains. The power to limit the rights of landowners to develop their land remains extremely weak. Instead, the goals of planned, serviced urban development are still primarily achieved by the granting of incentives such as upzoning and FAR bonuses, and by positive methods such as infrastructure building and land development projects such as new towns and LR. These strategies have often been reasonably successful where they have been carried out. The problem is that large areas have continued to develop with almost no controls at all. This approach seems likely to become even less tenable in future, as the need for large areas of new urban land declines as discussed in the next chapter.

10 Japanese urbanisation and planning

These pages have traced the ups and downs of Japan's extraordinary twentieth century of urban industrial growth, sketched some of its numerous successes, examined some of its conspicuous problems, and puzzled over various perplexing aspects of its progress. This final chapter reviews the Japanese model of urbanisation and planning, asks what lessons might be learned from understanding the Japanese experience, and speculates briefly on what Japan's major future urban planning issues might be.

The Japanese model of urbanisation and planning

The Japanese experience has been unique on so many levels that it appears to warrant being treated as a distinctive model. In speaking of a "Japanese model" the intention is to draw attention to five distinctive features of Japanese urbanisation and planning: the consistent focus of state resources on economic development, the weak relationship of planning and civil society, the dominance of central government, the consistent preference for public building projects over regulation of private development activity, and the long tradition of self-reliance of urban neighbourhoods.

The focus of resources on economic growth

The essential feature of the Japanese model of urbanisation and planning has been that the majority of resources were consistently directed to national economic development, while the barest minimum was spent on social overhead capital. Instead the Japanese people were urged to work hard, save diligently and live frugally in support of the overarching goal of building the nation. In the pre-war period industrialisation, economic growth and military strength were desired to serve imperial ambitions, while in the post-war period economic growth became an end in itself. Priority was given to producer infrastructure, and planning and development controls were kept weak in order to allow the maximum freedom to private investment. The state invested the minimum in social overhead capital, instead putting all available resources into aiding industrial growth, while letting the private sector take care of discretionary spending on housing, sewerage, and local roads.

It is significant that the priority on economic development was not applied merely to central government spending, but also wherever possible to other actors and sectors. For example, during the rapid growth period banks were not allowed to lend money for housing mortgages so that housing would not compete with industries for scarce capital. Similarly, the ownership of private cars was discouraged through high taxes and licence fees so as to encourage savings. Local government spending also was tightly controlled through limits on allowable taxes, central government control over local bond issues, and through administrative restrictions on permissions for planning projects. Probably equally important were government policies which relieved polluting industries from responsibility for the negative externalities they generated and the strict restraints placed on the ability of local governments to independently develop more proactive approaches to regulating land development. There is little doubt that these policies contributed greatly to the "miracle" of rapid economic growth.

While rapid and sustained economic growth in the post-war period, combined with a relatively equal distribution of incomes compared to, for example, the US, did greatly increase the standards of living of virtually all Japanese, and was at least initially widely supported, there have also been considerable social and environmental costs of this strategy. The most important of these have been environmental pollution and its associated health costs, as well as environmental destruction which has had long-term impacts on both human health and natural ecosystems; regional imbalances in development which have led to decline in some areas, while others have seen unsustainable levels of development; the destruction of much of the built urban inheritance through redevelopment; and the creation of urban areas which require their inhabitants to endure poor and expensive housing, long travel times, and high taxes for a relatively low level of services.

Figure 10.1 The loss of historic townscapes. One of the biggest surprises for many foreign visitors to Japan is the scarcity of old buildings. Kyoto, shown above, is an excellent example of the rapid loss of traditional townscapes, even though, having escaped wartime bombing, it still retains probably a larger proportion of traditional buildings than any other major city in the country.

Photo A. Sorensen 2001.

It is not uncommon to present these policies as the choice of the Japanese people. Nagamine, for example, argues that in the Japanese case the country could not afford city planning and the associated social overhead investment as all economic resources were needed for catch-up industrialisation. As he puts it, "One of the major factors in accounting for the prosperity of the Japanese economy is that her people have opted to tolerate, rightly or wrongly, a meagre resource allocation for their living conditions, thereby leaving the maximum amount of resources for industrial development" (Nagamine 1986: 52). This argument raises the question whether it is really true that the Japanese people chose a meagre allocation of resources to their living conditions.

While much has been made of Japan's strong social cohesion and consensual approach, the city planning experience suggests that this is a great oversimplification. While it is true that most Japanese people were willing to go along with the government, particularly in the pre-war period and in post-war reconstruction, there has also always been much active opposition to government policy. That resulted in a wave of opposition-party-controlled local governments during the 1960s and 1970s, and again in a groundswell of grassroots movements to take charge of city planning issues in the 1990s. Until the 1970s such opposition had only very minor impacts on government policies. Since then there has only been a very gradual growth in the responsiveness of government to the wishes of the people, and the shift towards somewhat greater sensitivity to citizens' demands that has occurred has been closely related to growing conflicts over local environmental policy and urban quality of life demands.

The idea that conflict is important in Japanese society is not a new one. It arose out of a critique of the widespread characterisation of Japan prevalent among both Japanese and Western observers before the 1980s as a nation with an exceptional degree of social harmony and consensus, lacking major social divides and able to resolve many conflicts with relative ease thanks to an inclusive, consensus-based decision-making process (see e.g. Nakane 1970; Vogel 1979). That stereotype was increasingly challenged in the 1980s, however, with the greater recognition that conflict is also a part of Japanese society, although often finding expression in particularly Japanese ways (see Krauss, et al. 1984). Sugimoto in particular criticised the notion of Japan as a "consensus" society, arguing that the term "consensus" has a very different meaning in a country where the authoritarian basis of social control is so strong, and that in reality Japanese "groupism" is merely an expression of an effective system of social control. He argues that the important questions are "who defines the contents of consensus, in whose interests is consensus formed?" (1986: 67). Reich similarly suggests, "Unless precisely defined, consensus is a vague, almost meaningless word. Consensus among which groups? What are the boundaries of consensus? How much coercion is necessary to maintain consensus? Without answering or at least posing such questions, the concept helps little in explaining social processes" (Reich 1983b: 200). Pressure to achieve consensus can therefore result merely in the concealment of power relationships within groups, rather than in genuine participation in making decisions. In the case of city planning the myth of consensus served primarily to conceal the fact that there has always been considerable diversity of opinion about urban policy, and at least since the mid-1960s opposition to government plans has been the rule, not the exception. Until very recently, however, such opposition has seldom been listened to, particularly in the case of national government projects, and priorities differing from those of economic growth have been routinely ignored. Protest movements against the building of high-voltage power transmission lines, expressways, dams and garbage dumps have more often than not been steadfastly ignored. Even national government projects have been successfully opposed, however, in a few high-profile cases such as the Tokyo Outer Orbital Expressway which was first approved in 1966 and has since been blocked by vigorous opposition movements in Tokyo's western suburbs. Local governments have tended to be much more sensitive to local protest, and many projects small and large have been stalled or blocked entirely by local opposition. That is not to suggest that local governments are always responsive to their electors. Kobe, for example, often seen as a local government which is highly supportive of machizukuri and citizens' movements, has continued to press ahead with expensive landfill projects and the building of a new international airport in the face of large-scale opposition by local taxpayers.

For reasons discussed in more detail in Chapter 6, the "iron triangle" of the LDP, the bureaucracy and big business was able largely to ignore growing public concern about urban issues and continue to pursue growth-oriented public policies throughout the rapid growth period. While in the early 1970s electoral weakness prompted the government to adopt a mix of policies designed to appeal more strongly to urban voters, with the return of electoral strength in 1980 this approach was largely abandoned and the government returned to its producer-first policies. It is safe to say that the quality of life of urban residents has never been a significant priority of the Japanese government, which has steadfastly kept its primary focus on providing for the needs of industry. This single-minded determination amongst policy-makers that the standard of living of the majority of the population should be sacrificed in the interests of economic growth is a remarkable feature of Japanese society in the twentieth century, and has had profound effects on Japanese urbanisation and urban planning. As discussed at the end of this chapter, the major question for the future, given immediacy by the recent emergence of widespread activism for improved urban environmental management, is whether a new strategy that prioritises quality of life can be developed and implemented.

The weak development of civil society

A second distinctive feature that has had broad impacts on Japanese urbanisation and urban planning has been Japan's extremely weak civil society. At the risk of over-generalisation, it seems fair to say that in the other developed countries city planning originated in the activities of broad-based and shifting alliances of housing activists, sanitary reformers, professional associations, journalists, charitable housing providers, philanthropic industrialists, property developers and local governments. That is to say, the values and ideals of the international city planning movement were largely generated from within the institutions of civil society, not within the central state, which tended to follow rather than lead. Although with the professionalisation of planning and its establishment as a statutory responsibility of local government in the first half of the century much of that early pluralism was lost, the early idealism remained embedded as part of the core values of planning, and has resurfaced periodically in movements such as advocacy planning in the 1960s (Davidoff 1965), the community planning movements of the 1980s (Friedmann 1987; Marris 1982) and communicative planning in the 1990s (Healy 1996; Sanoff 2000).

To an extraordinary degree, however, early planning developments in Japan were the work of a small group of elite bureaucrats in the Home Ministry, professors at the University of Tokyo (also national public servants), and a few others. A fully developed city planning system was created based on best practice in the West, and was then operated as a national system, carried out by local governments under the direct and close supervision of the national ministry. This imposition of city planning from above has continued to shape attitudes towards city planning to the present. City planning has developed as something to be resisted, not something that communities can use to fight for better urban environments, and until the 1990s there was very little popular support for or expectations of city planning. Even today the process of citizen co-optation of planning processes for their own interests has only just begun. While it seems possible that the developing civil society of the early Taishō period might in time have generated a broader constituency in support of city planning, that avenue was effectively closed off by the nationalisation of all city planning activity by the Home Ministry in 1919, and ultimately by the elimination of civil society itself with the rise of totalitarianism during the inter-war period. After 1919 local governments had precious little independence in their planning activities, and even cities with their own city planning traditions were gradually brought under the effective control of central government. Whereas in many Western countries the establishment of city planning was the result of political pressure applied through long campaigns by a diverse grouping of planning advocates, in Japan the political space necessary for such activity

Figure 10.2 The Tokyo Metropolitan Expressway in Ikebukuro. An important feature of all the main metropolitan areas are the elevated expressway systems.

Photo A. Sorensen 2001.

disappeared during the inter-war period, and was only very gradually re-established in the post-war period. One result is that the concept that city planning and development control regulations and restrictions on private property rights are necessary to protect the public welfare has never been strongly established in Japan. Instead, city planning has been seen as an activity designed primarily to further state interests, which were often coterminous with business interests. Resistance to public infringement on private property rights is logical in such a context, and the rights associated with land ownership have remained extremely strong, posing a powerful obstacle to efforts to improve urban environments.

It seems clear that in Japan the early imposition of a fully developed planning system from above inhibited the development of significant public support for planning, as lobbying for better or different approaches to city planning was unlikely to have much influence. The lack of broader public support for planning left planning advocates in the Home Ministry and local governments weak. The elite group of Home Ministry technocrats who argued for improved city planning legislation had little outside support for their proposals, and ran into opposition both within the government, and later in implementation whenever planning proposals ran counter to local interests. Without a broad base of organisational support in local governments, or the plethora of citizens' groups and professional organisations that kept pushing environmental issues onto the public agenda in the West, it was easy for the Finance Ministry to block the financial measures that might have given substance to the 1919 city planning system. Even measures that required little direct government financial outlay, such as improved regulation of land uses, or stricter requirements for land and building developers to respect planned road networks, were difficult to implement because they encountered opposition by vested interests, but little support from potential beneficiaries.

The lack of an effective planning movement based in civil society also meant that there was little public education about the benefits of planning compared to contemporary developments in the West. One of the most important functions of planning advocates in the West was their education of the general public about the desirability and possibility of different urban futures. Such diverse interests as housing activists, sanitary reformers, settlement workers, advocates of municipal utility ownership, and bourgeois promoters of park systems or municipal expansion schemes all shared and broadcasted their belief that the solution to their preferred urban problem was more effective collective action managed by local government (Rodgers 1998). It was not necessarily the case that such collective action was directed at "progressive" ideals although there was much of that. It could just as easily be driven by local land development interests who wished to use the planning powers of local government to further their own interests as suggested by the growth coalition literature (Logan and Molotch 1987). Either way the result was local advocacy for local planning powers.

Japan saw little of the popularisation of planning ideas and values which formed such an important foundation for the development of more interventionist planning regimes in Western countries. Instead, effective government campaigns created neighbourhood associations and promoted the idea that local people should be responsible for the cleaning and maintenance of local facilities, waste sorting and removal, local policing and even the support of the poor. The idea that local governments should be responsible for a range of public goods such as the provision of sewerage, sidewalks and local roads, local parks or playlots, and facilities such as child care centres and libraries was very slow to take root in post-war Japan, and even today the idea that a quality urban living environment and minimum housing standards should be the responsibility of local government is only just beginning to take hold. Urban planning kept its early image as something imposed by central government on the people, rather than an instrument created and shaped by local action in the interest of local needs.

Finally, the lack of a viable public sphere, separate from the state, family and business worlds, in which a range of interests could exchange views on possible urban futures and formulate planning and management priorities different from those of the state, goes a long way to explaining the peculiar passivity of Japanese urban residents to often problematic urban environments. As seen in the pollution debacle of the 1960s and 1970s, it was only when local communities had no other alternative that they began to fight back. Yet even then, as shown so effectively by Broadbent (1998), real opposition and truly different priorities were often quickly suppressed and co-opted by existing structures of political articulation. And even in the often desperate cases of pollution problems and conflicts, the means of mobilisation was often through existing structures such as neighbourhood organisations, unions and or cooperatives, where a strong and determined leader was able to break with existing top-down links and resist co-optation. Many of these opposition movements were thus not really an indication of the development of civil society, but were rather breakaway segments of the older nested hierarchies, and highly prone to co-optation and collapse. On the other hand, it is also no doubt the case that the environmental movements of the 1960s and 1970s were an important precedent for the machizukuri organising that began in the 1970s, and gained strength throughout the 1980s and 1990s. Many of these groups such as in Mano in Kobe have developed much more sophisticated and independent strategies and new grassroots structures, and have been able to articulate their own goals and priorities. These have sometimes been in cooperation with and sometimes in opposition to local authorities and planners.

It is highly significant that during the 1990s the rebirth of Japanese civil society and the birth of machizukuri movements in support of local environmental improvement have been linked. While the growth of civil society goes far beyond city planning movements, and includes the growth of voluntary and advocacy organisations such as in international aid and social services, many argue that local environmental movements have played a central role in the growth of civil society (Yamamoto 1999a; Yoshida 1999). It remains to be seen whether a pluralistic civil society with a local environmental political and policy debate as one of its components will develop, or whether some other particularly Japanese arrangement will prevail. Either way, it does seem possible that the peculiar passivity of Japanese urban residents to major changes to their local environments is changing.

Strong centre – weak local government

A third essential ingredient of the Japanese model has been a strong central government and weak local governments. In the early years tight central control over local governments helped unify the new nation state, and enabled effective suppression of opponents of the new regime. The extreme centralisation of political power and planning authority established during the Meiji period has had major long-term impacts on city planning in Japan, including the top-down imposition of plans and regulations and the dominance of national over local goals and priorities. The system of government initiated during the Meiji period located power in the centre, and established the central government bureaucracy – particularly the Home Ministry – as the dominant influence in the development of the Japanese planning system. This centralisation of power furthered the rapid development of high levels of technical expertise in the central ministries and aided Japanese efforts to modernise and industrialise quickly. Central control also furthered the rapid dissemination of new policies and allowed the state to concentrate its limited resources on development of industry and of military power. In particular, central control over local governments allowed national ministries to keep a tight rein on local spending and focus available resources more effectively on key national goals. In terms of city planning the top priorities were building the roads, railways and ports which would further national integration and industrial development. Little value was placed on urban environmental quality, housing issues, or on amenities for residential areas such as local parks, local roads, or sewer systems. Strong centralisation also had the intended effect of hindering the development of democracy in Japan, while the creation of elected local assemblies with very limited powers allowed them to bear much of the burden of public dissatisfaction with government policies.

The tendency towards strong central control over city planning policy was firmly established by the nation's first City Planning Law of 1919. Ishida (2000) has argued that one of the most profound impacts of the law was precisely its centralisation of planning authority. Under the law all facilities plans and zoning plans had to be approved by the Home Minister, along with city planning budgets every year. This gave central government detailed control over every aspect of planning policy throughout the country. With the passage of the 1919 system central government bureaucrats significantly extended their powers over local city planning efforts, which having been ad hoc and unregulated, had been outside their control. Greater legal powers for city planning were accompanied by closer control by the bureaucrats in Tokyo. Further, the national legislation admitted no variation in use zones or building regulations between areas with quite different urban patterns and urban problems, and suffered from the attempt to impose a solution to Tokyo's problems on the whole country.

Centralisation of planning power during the inter-war period had wide-ranging consequences – some positive and some negative – for the development of city planning. Centralisation allowed Japan to effectively play its game of catch-up with the most advanced Western nations. In particular, the active tradition of learning from the example of foreign countries meant that very quickly a high level of technical expertise in plan-making and legislation drafting was concentrated in the central ministries. National projects such as the rebuilding of Tokyo-Yokohama after the 1923 Great Kanto Earthquake, the building of the national railway system and build up of military and industrial power, for example, were pushed forward with great speed. At the same time, however, centralisation had real drawbacks, in particular it inhibited the development of planning expertise at the local level and prevented the development of alternative approaches to planning issues. It also allowed central government to ignore the need for planning and investment in public goods that would contribute to urban quality of life. Local governments, which might have been more responsive to such needs, simply had no legal powers or finances to apply different planning standards.

The Japanese case thus supports the suggestion that the division of planning responsibilities between levels of government can have profound impacts on the nature of the planning system that develops. Because local governments are closer to the people, they also tend to be more responsive to environmental issues, which are often purely local in nature, and are more likely than central governments to respond positively to attempts to improve or maintain the local environment. This sort of responsiveness to local concerns is of course precisely why the architects of the Meiji local government system did not trust local governments to act primarily in the national interest, and was an important rationale for centralised control.

The central state grew ever stronger from the early Meiji period until the late 1960s or 1970s, and real decentralisation of planning authority only began in the 1990s. As the central government gained greater resources from economic growth and increasing bureaucratic powers, the autonomy of local governments grew ever weaker until the late 1960s, to the point where they were operated essentially as local branch offices of the central ministries. The central government bureaucracy held a deep-seated distrust of local government as concerned primarily with local, not national interests, and as a consequence deliberately kept local governments weak. The city planning system was thus highly top-down, with new planning regulations imposed entirely from the top and with little variation amongst different cities. Japan saw little of the outpouring of small-scale experimentation and local innovation seen in many Western countries, and local governments that might have been more open to demands for improved urban environments and services had few powers with which to comply.

Figure 10.3 Contemporary *nagaya*-style block in Kyoto. The building of tiny housing units for the urban poor has never really stopped in Japan, as this contemporary *nagaya*-style rental block suggests. The lack of minimum housing standards, and the enormous increase in land prices have helped to ensure that apartments such as these have continued to form an important part of the housing market. Here 16 units are squeezed onto a plot of land barely large enough to park four cars.

Photo A. Sorensen 2001.

Development projects instead of regulation

A fourth enduring characteristic of Japanese planning is that since the Meiji period the government has consistently preferred to use specific projects such as road and bridge building, port and airport construction, land development, and housing construction, rather than the development of a regulatory system that controls private development activity. To be sure, there has long been a zoning system, but that system has been relatively light in its restrictions compared to most zoning ordinances in, for example, the US. The Building Standards Law is relatively strict in its regulation of the structural aspects of buildings, and has been relatively strictly enforced, but there have been no minimum housing standards, weak restrictions on building unserviced slums, and generally weak standards on fireproofing of individual dwellings. Until the 1968 revisions to the planning system there was no system to restrict new land development or ensure that minimum services were provided, and as discussed in Chapter 7, even after the development permit system was passed the numerous and proliferating loopholes still allowed the majority of development to escape its provisions. And until the 1992 revision to the City Planning Law local governments had no legal authority to establish minimum urban plot sizes or restrict the subdivision of land. Instead of placing restrictions on the haphazard development of urban fringe land, the government has consistently promoted the use of Land Readjustment (LR) projects. Instead of enforcing minimum housing standards, the state built large-scale housing estates, and while those estates were often extensive, they never formed more than a tiny part of the housing market. Instead of imposing obligations on land developers, or restricting development in some places, government has consistently relied on ever-greater incentives and subsidies, as well as large-scale transport improvements to encourage planned development patterns.

The question of stronger regulations is not primarily one of tighter zoning to achieve more separation of land uses. The main issue is the distribution of the costs and benefits of development. In Japan, as argued above, most of the benefits of increasing land values through urbanisation flowed to landowners and developers, while the costs of providing services were borne by taxpayers, or by residents who either provided their own services or did without. During the 1980s and 1990s an increasing use of regulatory frameworks and bonuses was made to achieve public goods, such as with the Special District Plans for Redevelopment discussed in Chapter 8, which gained public plazas and roads in return for zoning bonuses. A similar use was made of Senbiki with the introduction of flexible Senbiki in the 1980s, and District Plans in the 1990s by using FAR bonuses to widen narrow roads. In all these cases the basic framework of weak regulations was retained, and public benefits were achieved in exchange for selectively weakening them. These strategies allowed considerable public gains, but also make clear the basic assumption that stronger regulation of private land use and development activity was politically impossible. Strong rights of private landowners to use their land as they see fit have been retained, and the concept that the state should limit private land development rights in the public interest has never really taken hold. While the 1989 Basic Land Law stipulates that the public interest is paramount in the use of land, in practice little has changed, and in fact the 1990s saw increasing pressure for a weakening of land regulations of all kinds in order to encourage economic activity.

The weak regulatory framework and reliance on projects has been well suited to a central government dominant system. Stronger land use and development regulations would have been unwieldy to manage from the centre because of the huge administrative burden, whereas discrete development projects lend themselves to central control. Unfortunately, the system whereby central government ministries spent increasingly large amounts of money on construction projects throughout the country was tailor-made to encourage particularism and corruption. The LDP long made effective use of its influence over spending programmes to increase its electoral strength, and to access financial support from the major land development and construction companies which have been its major financial backers. As shown in Chapter 9, systemic collusion in public works bidding (*dangō*) practices have meant that Japanese central and local government projects routinely cost an estimated 30 to 50 per cent more than they would have given a competitive bidding process, greatly inflating total costs, and providing guaranteed profits to construction firms even after a portion of the budget was allocated for the ruling party. Taxpayers have paid much more for such projects, and received much less in return than they should have. Worse, the system has taken on a life of its own, and the need to maintain the flow of construction project money has resulted in a proliferation of useless projects and the pouring of concrete for no good reason. The environmental destruction caused by the lining of rivers, retaining of mountainsides, and paving of shorelines with billions of cubic metres of concrete is only the more unfortunate when we consider the perennial lack of funds to provide badly needed investment in urban areas.

The tradition of self-reliance

One final aspect of the Japanese model must be noted; the strong tradition of neighbourhood self-reliance through participation in neighbourhood organisations (*chōnaikai* and *jichikai*). While theoretically voluntary, membership in these organisations is still almost universal in urban areas and they perform services such as information dissemination through a regularly circulated notice board (*kairanban*), organisation of local garbage collection and recycling arrangements, semi-annual neighbourhood clean-up campaigns and local park maintenance, neighbourhood watch activities, organisation of local festivals and block parties, and a range of other activities in particular areas. Self-reliance is, of course, partly an outcome of the consistent reluctance of the government to devote resources to the building or provision of services to residential areas, while it also made such a frugal approach possible. It also represents considerable historical continuity from the system of delegated responsibility for local needs of the Tokugawa period to the chōnaikai system that developed initially spontaneously during the early Taishō period and later was appropriated by the Home Ministry for wartime mobilisation, to the post-war re-establishment of the chōnaikai and jichikai after their initial abolition by the occupation. The precise role of neighbourhood organisations in Japanese urban society is a question for sociologists and anthropologists, but it seems clear that neighbourhood organisations were never only a top-down phenomenon, but also responded to real needs of Japanese urban residents, and were to a very considerable extent self-organised.

It is also clear that the neighbourhood organisations have contributed enormously to the liveability of Japanese cities, and are closely related to several very positive aspects

Figure 10.4 Urban greenery. A characteristic feature of Japanese cities that contributes greatly to their liveability is the widespread practice of growing potted plants on the roadway and sidewalks outside residences. In cities which have few large trees outside of parks and temple areas, these bits of green serve as an important visual relief.

Photo A. Sorensen 2000.

of Japanese urban life. In particular the high levels of personal safety, the cleanliness, and the general friendliness and civility of Japanese cities are widely regarded by Japanese and foreign residents alike as some of the most admirable qualities of Japanese cities. All are related to the strong sense of community responsibility that has helped to create and has in turn been reinforced by neighbourhood organisations. Japanese neighbourhoods embody Jane Jacobs' concept of "eyes on the street" or the principles of neighbourhood watch to an admirable degree. Examples of such neighbourliness abound. Neighbours are always keen to chat in passing, and quick to offer to water your plants when you are away. The foreigner who, new to a neighbourhood, puts his recyclable garbage on the curb in the wrong colour plastic bag is gently taken in hand by a bevy of neighbourhood women who explain the local regulations and then divvy up his empty plastic drink bottles and beer cans among their own correctly coloured bags.

Community solidarity is also enhanced by the almost universal enthusiasm for organised community activities, which in older districts have developed into very elaborate festivals. There are naturally many levels of involvement in such activities including organisers, participants, sponsors and spectators, and organising and participating in such activities can require significant amounts of time. There is little question that such shared activities and responsibilities go a long way towards reinforcing the sense of community that is so evident in Japanese cities. The system of neighbourhood police offices also helps to reinforce the sense that everything that goes on is noted and monitored. When you move to a new neighbourhood the genial local constable drops by uninvited in the first week to let you know that the local police office (*koban*) is entirely at your service, that there have been burglaries in the area recently, and delivers the unspoken message that the local police are aware of everything that occurs on their beat.

Given the almost universal presence of neighbourhood organisations it is somewhat surprising that a stronger civil society that could lobby for better urban services and planning standards did not develop sooner out of this strong organisational base. It seems, however, that the basic characteristic of the old chōnaikai was to function as a transmitter of information and direction from above, not to organise demands from below. This second function only started to develop from the mid-1960s in some newly formed neighbourhood organisations which lobbied for better local government services, while longer established organisations tended to support the status quo. While neighbourhood organisations have continued to function, and in some cases have adopted strategies for lobbying for neighbourhood needs, it seems that for many their basic roles have remained largely unchanged.

The recent spread of local community-based machizukuri organising efforts to improve local conditions poses important questions about the future role and structure of neighbourhood organisations such as the chōnaikai and jichikai. Will they emerge as the main players in organising machizukuri processes, as has frequently been the case so far, and if so will the old style of co-optation by local governments through locally influential men continue? Or will other styles of operation or other organisations develop with new, more democratic methods of decision-making and selection of community representatives? Similarly, it is still not clear whether such local organising will be able to move beyond a strategy of placing ever greater burdens of organising, development monitoring and negotiation on local communities, and start to have a significant influence on the way local governments do statutory city planning. Machizukuri activities have been extremely important in mobilising local activism, but have hitherto been relatively little supported by the statutory planning system. Until recent changes which devolved greater power to local planning authorities this would have been difficult in any case; but the big question for the future is whether the statutory planning system will be transformed into a stronger tool to support local urban improvement through machizukuri, or whether machizukuri will remain at the level of local voluntary activity.

The relative safety of Japanese cities, and their cleanliness and civility contribute greatly to the quality of life of their inhabitants. It seems fair to say that the real heroes of the story of Japanese urbanisation and planning, if heroes there be, are the Japanese urban residents themselves, who have managed to compensate for many of the shortcomings of urban facilities by their self-reliance and solidarity and evident flair for urban living. It is still unclear whether the recent upswing in local organising for local environmental improvement through machizukuri movements will go beyond an extension of these traditional forms of urban self-reliance towards a transformation of the planning system itself to take greater account of local needs and demands.

It seems fair to say that Japan represents a distinctive model of urbanisation and planning, although a fuller development of the Japanese model in comparison with those of other countries will have to be undertaken elsewhere. Here the focus is on how Japanese urban planning has influenced Japanese urbanisation, and on what lessons may be learned from the Japanese experience.

Japan's distinctive urban problems

Unfortunately for many Japanese urban residents, the distinctive features that have shaped Japanese urbanisation have led to great inequities in the distribution of its costs and benefits. In existing urban areas a serious problem is that large areas were allowed to build up with inadequate infrastructure and weak building regulation. Roads are less than four metres in width in many residential areas, meaning that there is no room for sidewalks and service vehicles such as garbage trucks and fire engines cannot pass. In many of these districts buildings are packed so tightly together that fires are virtually impossible to stop, as seen most recently in the Kobe earthquake of 1995. Many older urban neighbourhoods which were allowed to develop relatively free of planning regulation are quite simply death traps in the event of disaster. Parks and other emergency shelter areas are frequently inadequate. All of these deficits are expensive and time consuming to remedy, yet with the ageing of Japanese society it is particularly these older urban areas, which often house higher than average proportions of elderly residents, which most need sidewalks, quality local services, and park spaces.

A second serious problem in existing built up areas is that the weak planning system has given little protection against unwanted urban changes. Gradual change such as the intensification of residential densities is widespread because there are few restrictions against subdivision of existing lots to rebuild single family homes into two or three or four new dwellings. This means that over time, even areas that started out with good residential environments with significant amounts of green cover and open space gradually get rebuilt to dangerous building densities. Similarly, high-rise condominiums can be built anywhere except in Exclusive Residential #1 areas, meaning that redevelopment of small houses into high-rises is very common. Such "Manshon" redevelopment has been one of the main causes of the formation of residents' organisations to support machizukuri ordinances because high-rises bring sharply increased population densities, heavier traffic and a changing local environment. Unfortunately, such ordinances are a lot of work to put in place, still cover only a small proportion of urban areas, and cannot guarantee neighbourhood protection.

The other important source of unwanted change comes from major urban projects. Often led by the government, these include major redevelopment projects such as in disaster-prone high-density residential areas, major public facilities such as incinerators or garbage-processing facilities, and the building of new highways. As is true in other countries, garbage incinerators and landfills are strongly opposed by affected residents. Similarly, highway construction is often bitterly opposed by local residents who will be displaced by or live near a planned highway. In not a few cases planned highway networks have been blocked for many years by such citizen opposition, as for example in the case of the second and third loop expressways of the Tokyo Metropolitan Expressway system which were to cut through densely built up residential areas in Tokyo's western suburbs. It seems that in most cases, however, such projects have proceeded in the face of even determined opposition.

On the urban fringe a different set of problems prevails. The most serious stems from the fact that landowners on the urban fringe are able to sever and develop or sell land for urban use without the obligation of providing urban services or roads. Such developers thus gain the lion's share of the benefits of urbanisation, while avoiding responsibility for the external costs they create and impose on others while developing or selling land. As Mori argues, they receive net what buyers pay for housing sites, while leaving municipal governments to provide essential public services later (Mori 1998). Local governments and their taxpayers are thus forced to pay the high costs of retroactively providing urban services in urban areas developed in this way. New homebuyers on the fringe therefore not only pay high prices for tiny unserviced properties, but also end up paying the cost of retrofitting basic urban services such as roads and sewers through their local taxes. Other social costs of unregulated urbanisation in Japan arise from the prevalence in unplanned sprawl areas of incompatible neighbours, high travel costs and poor local services such as schools and parks. In the US, even though a relatively stricter system was in place in most municipalities, where local taxpayers felt that they were having to pay higher taxes to provide municipal services for new arrivals, active movements arose to ensure that new developments covered the full costs of new development (Porter 1986). In Japan the creation of vast new areas of unserviced urban development during the period since the passage of the New City Planning Law of 1968 seems likely to be remembered as one of the great failures of post-war public policy.

The focus on industrial growth, and the reluctance to impose obligations on developers for fear of driving up housing prices was widely seen as necessary for the pursuit of economic expansion, and higher standards of housing and public goods were to be financed later, after economic security was achieved. At the same time the strategy of encouraging the growth of land asset values to create an ever-growing capital base for industrial investment and expansion had the effect of fuelling the inflation of land prices. Land prices in Japanese urban areas were far higher than those in other developed country cities even before the speculative trading of the bubble economy drove up land prices after 1985, and have remained so even with their steady decline since 1992. These high land prices worked primarily to the benefit of a small number of net sellers of land, at the expense of net land purchasers such as new suburban residents and the suburban local governments that have to acquire public space for their growing populations.

Unfortunately the frenzied land trading and speculation of the bubble and the massive overhang of bad debt that its collapse produced effectively wiped out much of the capital base of the Japanese financial system. Japanese banks which had boasted the world's largest asset bases during the 1980s found themselves with ballooning bad loans in the mid-1990s, and had to be bailed out with tens of trillions of yen in capital infusions from the Japanese central government in 1998 and 1999. Again in 2001 there were serious fears that the banking system would collapse under the burden of bad debts that were not reported earlier. The huge asset base which provided part of the justification for hands-off urban development policies has been transformed into a mountain of public debt used to refinance the banking system.

The Japanese urban resident is thus left with the worst of all worlds. Urban development policies which encouraged the minimum of public spending, and the maximum profitability and asset growth for landowners and land developers as a part of the rapid economic growth formula have saddled urban residents and governments with huge backlogs of unbuilt infrastructure that will take generations and vast retroactive investment to remedy. Even then standards will almost inevitably be much lower than might have been the case if the public goods had been built in advance of urbanisation, either directly by local governments or as an obligation on land developers. Although there is no doubt that Japan is a much richer country for its post-war experience of rapid economic growth, the degraded urban areas, long travel times, incomplete and congested road systems, lack of public services and public space, and the cash-strapped and expensive local governments seem to have greatly undermined the possibility that such wealth will soon be translated into a higher quality of life for most Japanese urban residents. It seems clear that the unipolar focus on economic growth at the expense of other policy priorities, the overwhelming dominance of central government in virtually all decision-making, and the weakly developed civil society which effectively failed to provide any sort of base from which to challenge the priorities of central government all contributed to the creation of Japan's distinctive urban environmental quality problems.

Learning from Japan

The idea that other countries could learn from the successful Japanese experience of rapid economic growth and business management practices was highly tradable in the 1980s at the height of the Japanese economic boom. Few are peddling the Japanese model now that the boom has disappeared and economic growth has been stagnant for a decade. That does not mean that Japan has any less to teach other countries than it did a decade ago, however. On the contrary, with some of the froth of the economic bubble stripped away, perhaps now some of the deeper lessons of Japan's extraordinary century of urban economic growth can be pondered more usefully. It is not necessary to believe that any particular aspect of the Japanese experience will necessarily be replicated elsewhere to think that understanding the Japanese case may be useful.

The lessons for those concerned with urban problems and planning issues in developing countries, and those for their counterparts in the developed countries are quite different, so they are addressed separately. Probably the most important lessons are those for planners in developing countries, and particularly those in the Asian countries which have been experiencing rapid urban economic growth. While it is no doubt true that many important social, economic, political and historical factors divide these countries from Japan and from each other, at least three of the key elements identified above as characteristic of Japanese urbanisation and planning, the focus of state resources on economic development, the weak development of civil society, and the dominance of central government, are all to a greater or lesser degree seen in several Asian developing countries. This is particularly relevant as some Asian countries have deliberately followed the central government-dominant "developmental state" strategy pioneered by Japan (Cumings 1987). While it remains to be seen whether these factors will lead to similar outcomes in other countries, and there is no guarantee that they will, it is at least worth considering whether any parallels exist. Keeping those qualifications in mind, six main points stand out from the analysis of Japanese urbanisation and planning presented here. The first four are primarily of interest for those in Asian countries in the midst of rapid economic growth, while the last two are relevant primarily to those in the developed countries.

First, Japanese urbanisation shows clearly how essential is the role of effective land development controls on the urban fringe, even if these serve only to secure long-term public space needs without requiring the building of full public infrastructure such as roads, parks and sewers. Japan has shown that land for public space can become less affordable as a society gets wealthier, whereas the building of sewers, surfacing of roads, and provision of other community facilities can become increasingly affordable. In Japan vast sums have been spent since the 1980s in an attempt to fix pressing urban problems, yet while there have been many successful and innovative projects, urban conditions as a whole have improved little and new problem areas are still being created on the urban fringe. A major factor in reducing the impact of current spending on urban problems has been the shortage of public space in many urban areas, and the extremely high cost of land purchase.

Land development control systems requiring that all land development activities must allocate a certain proportion of the land developed for roads and other public needs are therefore essential to achieving good urban development in the long term. In addition some sort of system for designing future road and public space systems in advance of urbanisation is necessary. Japan had such a system in the building-line system that was abolished in 1950. That system worked reasonably effectively to structure new development in the areas where it was applied in the 1930s, although it suffered from a crucial weakness compared to its German model in that in Japan all roads above the minimum width were considered building lines, and not just those created by municipal design. That loophole allowed building on many narrow existing lanes, and the situation only got worse after 1950 when even that weak regulation of urban development on the fringe was removed.

The main method used by Japanese planners to achieve compulsory dedication of private land to public uses in the process of land development has been LR. This method was indeed a highly effective way of gaining land for public space, as landowners contributed roughly 30 per cent of their original landholding for public uses such as parks and roads, including some land for sale to pay the costs of project management and construction. Further, in the Japanese case where farmland is often highly fragmented into many small plots, such projects, by pooling many smallholdings into large blocks to be developed together, may allow more rational road layouts and better overall design than if small plots are developed individually. As clearly shown in the Japanese case, however, it is extremely difficult to achieve comprehensive development using the LR method. The result in many Japanese suburbs has been the creation of small pieces of planned development where LR projects or other large-scale development was carried out, set against a background of haphazard sprawl. In this Nagoya, which did achieve comprehensive development and redevelopment through LR, is the exception that proves the rule. Without a blanket restriction on development outside of LR projects or a universally applied building-line system on the urban fringe, and with continuing loopholes for small-scale development, haphazard sprawl development has continued in Japanese suburbs. This promises long-term urban problems and high remedial costs for future generations.

Second, it seems clear that the developmental state model of focusing public spending on producer infrastructure and postponing urban social overhead capital investments in roads, parks, and adequate public space is a high-risk strategy. There are two aspects to this point. One relates to urban planning and the achievement of high-quality urban living and working environments, while the other is the question of sustainable economic development. The Japanese case shows clearly the urban problems created by a strategy devoted exclusively to economic growth, and where urban amenity was always granted a lower priority than increasing productive capacity. Thus shoreline beaches near cities were converted to petroleum refineries and steel mills, the few broad avenues and canals in the inner metropolitan areas were covered with elevated expressways, and haphazard sprawl was allowed to continue in suburban areas. Land development regulations were kept weak in order to allow the private sector maximum freedom to develop housing in the least expensive way, while public funds were devoted elsewhere, seldom being spent on residential areas. The problem is that the best time to achieve good long-term patterns of urban development – some would argue the only time – is while cities are initially being built. Two fundamental premises of modern urban planning are that it is important to get the basic urban patterns right at the time of conversion of land from rural to urban use, and that allowing the private market to determine patterns of land use and provision of public facilities is unlikely to result in efficient or high-quality urban areas in the long run. Sadly, the Japanese case strongly supports both of these propositions.

It has often been argued that in the Japanese case there was little choice, as the country was so poor after the war and the need for economic reconstruction was great. There is clearly merit in this argument, and there is no doubt that most Japanese benefited greatly from economic growth. Japanese government policies, including the urban policies discussed here, clearly contributed to rapid economic growth, and Japan seized its chance to become the second largest economy in the world by 1972. It is impossible to say, however, whether greater attention to the various social and environmental costs of rapid growth would have significantly inhibited growth. Certainly the experience of the 1970s, when the sudden imposition of one of the strictest pollution control regimes in the world with little apparent cost in slowed economic growth suggests that the agony and death of Japan's many pollution victims was not a necessary cost of rapid growth, but merely callous disregard for human suffering.

Similarly, it is also impossible to say how a marginally stricter regime controlling land development on the urban fringe would have affected economic growth. The central government consistently argued against stronger land development controls, and against minimum housing standards in the interest of promoting investment in land and buildings, hoping that an increase in supply would keep prices low and would compensate for problems of quality in the long run. It is not clear, however, that prices would necessarily have been higher with tighter controls on development. The main factor driving rising housing prices has consistently been rapid increases in land prices, and it can be argued that these are driven primarily by the speculation allowed by weaknesses in the regulation of land development (Hebbert 1994; Yamamura 1992).

In hindsight it is clear that by far the greatest damage was wrought by the frenzy of over-investment and building of the bubble period that was encouraged by deregulation and stimulation of property development. A more tightly regulated land development system, while unlikely to prevent booms and busts in the property development industry which are a worldwide phenomenon, can act as a moderating influence. It also might have ensured that the boom in urban investment contributed to urban amenity and quality of life, instead of creating more future urban problems.

It is hard to resist wondering whether if instead of focusing exclusively on encouraging economic growth the Japanese government had pursued a more balanced approach, then economic growth might not have been similar in the long run, with less of the serious costs to individuals, communities, and the environment that accompanied the rapid growth strategy. Similarly, one cannot help but wonder whether, if the stricter development standards of the 1968 city planning system had been enforced as intended, and the various loopholes that allowed continued urban sprawl had been eliminated, then housing might not be cheaper and more spacious, and suburban environments might not be better than were achieved under the system that has been in place during the last 30 years.

Third, the Japanese experience strongly supports the proposition that delegating planning powers to democratic local governments is essential to the achievement of good city planning. One of the main obstacles to the development of a more proactive approach to city planning and land development control in Japan has been the continuing weakness of local governments. Even where local governments and their electorates clearly wanted stronger planning and better urban environments, they were legally blocked from creating stronger development control systems by central government monopoly of legal authority. The consistent refusal of central government to allow independent city planning approaches by local governments has been probably the greatest factor holding back Japanese city planning development. In part the reluctance to permit decentralisation of planning power is a manifestation of the bureaucratic imperative to constantly increase its area of jurisdiction, and the highly sectional and competitive central government bureaucracy is justly famous for this. It is also a product of distrust of local politicians, who are assumed to be prone to corruption and particularistic interests. Corruption is a risk everywhere, as changes in planning designation can create huge increases in land value. In many other countries, however, systems have been created that have allowed a degree of transparency of planning decisions and made it relatively difficult to get away with the selling of municipal planning approvals. While there is no doubt that corruption is always a danger, appropriate institutions can ensure that those involved pay the price with electoral defeat and/or criminal prosecution.

An additional factor in the reluctance of central government to allow local governments more freedom was probably the fear that they would be prone to pressure from their electors and allocate a greater share of spending to social overhead capital, thus deviating from the central government strategy of spending exclusively on producer infrastructure. That is, the fear was not only of local corruption, but that local governments might actually pursue the wishes of their electors who were pressing for better public services, as was the intent of the progressive local governments of the late 1960s and 1970s. While there were considerable achievements, particularly in social welfare provision and in creating more openness of planning processes, the decisive factor preventing real changes in land use planning was that local governments had little freedom of action. Central government proved much better able to insulate itself from public demands for better services, and could adopt a more technocratic development approach. As argued above, however, while this may have been an advantage in the early phase of rebuilding the country, in the long run the costs seem to have been very high.

In any case, the possibility that municipal politicians might behave in a corrupt manner is hardly a justification for the draconian centralisation of planning power that was carried out in the Japanese case. The argument is particularly hollow when we consider the long and sordid record of institutionalised corruption at the central government level, where the LDP in particular has been involved in an almost continuous stream of corruption scandals throughout its period in office. And while central government bureaucrats for long had a reputation as sterling and dedicated protectors of the public interest, a growing list of bribery scandals, incompetence, and sectional infighting among the bureaucracy has undermined public trust there as well. As shown in Chapter 9 these factors finally created widespread pressure for real devolution of planning authority to local governments in the 1990s. Only with the recent decentralisation of legal authority for planning have local governments begun to have any freedom to set their own planning approaches, and this has helped unleash a flood of public energy devoted to urban environmental improvement. The Japanese experience thus suggests that strong and independent local governments are a necessary counterbalance to the central government in city planning matters. Even if the central government pursues a narrow economic development strategy, local resources and energies can still be mobilised to improve local urban environments.

Fourth, the existence of strong and active civic organisations and a lively civil society seems highly important for urban governance and urban planning. In a manner similar to the way independent local governments can provide a moderating influence on central government, civil society can help to keep local governments attentive to local needs. Even where local governments have effective legal and financial powers to promote local planning solutions, they will be unlikely to be able to consistently deliver what local people want and need without the backing of and pressure from strong civic organisations. This is because city planning at the local level is inherently a political process that requires the balancing of conflicting needs and demands. Civic organisations to articulate those differing interests are thus an essential part of an effective democratic city planning process. Where civil society is weak, it is much more likely that local governments and local planning decisions will favour primarily the wishes of landowners and the property development industry, as those have the greatest financial interest in influencing planning decisions.

Civil society-based organisations are also the most likely to support an open and democratic planning process and promote a consciousness of the importance of city planning issues among local residents. Without pressure from effective civic organisations, governments are unlikely to do this on their own as it is always simpler and faster to proceed with plans and administration unilaterally and in secret than it is to do it openly as part of a democratic process. In Japan, where civil society effectively disappeared in the 1930s, only recovered extremely slowly in the post-war period, and finally regained a meaningful role in local environmental politics only in the 1990s, one consequence has been a greatly weakened voice to press either for greater social justice in the urbanisation process, or for higher environmental standards. It is significant that one of the main areas of activity of Japan's increasingly vibrant civil society in the 1990s has been in local environmental management through machizukuri organisations, and that the growth of concern about issues of urban quality of life has been an important contributor to the rebirth of civil society itself.

One final point that the Japanese case usefully demonstrates for planners in the developing countries is that good public transit systems can mitigate many other serious urban problems. Constant investment in mass transit systems, both intra- and inter-urban has created a wide range of benefits for Japanese cities and urban residents. Even though the rate of automobile ownership is as high or higher than most other developed countries, Japanese car usage and gasoline consumption are much lower (see Cervero 1998). Automobile pollution in cities is correspondingly lower than it might have been otherwise, although still a serious and growing problem. It is possible to travel virtually anywhere in Japan by public transit, a very significant benefit for all those who cannot drive or who do not own a car. This is not a small group, as it includes the young, the aged, the poor, and many disabled. Further, effective mass transit in cities improves economic competitiveness by unifying job markets and decreasing congestion for goods vehicles. Planners in the developed countries should also note that Japan has continued to improve its urban transit systems steadily, with new subway lines being opened up frequently, and new and expanded rail lines initiated. As a result mass transit has been able to maintain a large share of all travel, and even increase it in some areas, despite increasing automobilisation.

For planners and urbanists in the developed countries, there are two main general lessons that Japan offers. First, the Japanese case serves as a useful reminder of the importance of land development controls on the urban fringe. In most of the other developed countries basic planning regulations such as urban fringe development control have worked reasonably effectively in the post-war period, and have eliminated the worst problems of haphazard, unserviced sprawl. While urban sprawl is certainly still a problem, particularly in the US, there the issue is one of new development being built at very low densities and being too spread out, often leaping over considerable areas of undeveloped land. Such patterns, it is argued, create higher long-term servicing costs and increase travel needs, creating environmental and social costs. Although seen by many as a very serious problem (see e.g. Ewing 1997; Kunstler 1993), the American problem is not nearly as serious as that in Japan, where haphazard unserviced development is still permitted, as discussed above. The recently fashionable arguments for greater planning deregulation are tenable primarily because the worst aspects of haphazard urban sprawl seen in Japan have been eliminated in the other developed countries. A careful understanding of the Japanese case supports the traditional planning assumptions that land development control and regulation are necessary for the public good, and that unregulated urban development is unlikely to achieve either efficient, equitable or pleasing urban outcomes.

Perhaps the most important positive lesson that Western planners and urbanists can bring from Japan is that a high intensity of mixed use in central city areas can be a positive force in keeping urban areas vital and interesting. Certainly the problems created by mixed use seem far less than imagined by those Western advocates of a coarse-grained urban land use structure. The widely appreciated vitality, energy and urbanity of many central city areas in Japan confirm that intensive and high-density mixtures of retail, office and residential uses can help to create lively urban areas. While it is clearly still necessary to protect residential neighbourhoods, achieve historical preservation where warranted, and ensure that some noxious land uses such as polluting factories or expressways are carefully located, there still seems ample scope to encourage mixing of a wide range of uses in high density nodes close to transit facilities. In many Japanese cities the freewheeling mixed-use areas in major centres and subcentres provide some of the best that Japanese cities have to offer.

The situation in the suburbs and the urban fringe is more difficult, as the most obnoxious kinds of land uses such as heavily polluting factories, waste disposal facilities, and car-wrecking facilities tend to locate in these areas because of lower land prices. There does still seem to be good reason for restricting the location of some noxious land uses, and for tightly controlling the location and emissions of facilities such as incinerators. Encouraging mixed use does not necessarily mean the abandonment of land use planning, therefore, but merely the recognition that not all land uses need be separated.

Japanese cities in the twenty-first century

Having come this far in our examination of Japanese urbanisation and planning during the nineteenth and twentieth centuries, it is hard to resist a brief speculation about what the twenty-first century might hold in store. While it is patently impossible to accurately predict changes in systems as complex as economies and urban systems, a few major factors that will impact future changes are known, and some of the big questions can be posed.

There is no serious question that the major factor to affect Japanese urban development in the future will be demographic change. Barring foreign immigration to Japan on such a massive scale that it is quite difficult to imagine, or a sudden and huge increase in the birth rate, the Japanese population will peak in about 2007, after which it will see a steadily increasing decline, with a drop to half the current level of almost 130 million by the end of the twenty-first century. The rapid ageing of Japanese society has already begun and will continue. In 1999 15.6 per cent of the population was over 65, and that is expected to rise to 32.3 per cent by 2050, while the dependency ratio, which is currently 1 elderly for every 4.4 workers will increase to 1: 1.7 by 2050. The percentage of cities and towns with over a third of their population as elderly will rise from the current 10 per cent to 60 per cent by 2025, including virtually all cities and towns outside the metropolitan areas (Japan Ministry of Health and Welfare (*Kōseishō*) 2000). All of these factors point to a drastic slowing of urbanisation in the future, and a decline in the need for new housing and other urban investment. Even if the current recession ends and economic growth resumes, it is highly unlikely to be at a very high rate in future because of the declining population and the even more rapid decline in the workforce. New household formation, which had until the 1990s been a major factor promoting economic growth and demand for housing, will no longer provide such stimulus.

It thus seems certain that the period of greatest change in the Japanese urban system is already past. Declining population, slower economic growth, and less need for new housing or building of any kind will mean a real slowing of urban investment in future. This means that it will become more and more difficult to fix existing urban problems and improve the urban environment. This is not to suggest that urban change will suddenly end tomorrow. In fact it seems highly likely that during the next 20 years or so there will continue to be significant investment in urban areas, primarily to satisfy pent up demand for larger and better housing. In the British and Dutch cases, even with only moderate population growth, smaller household sizes mean more homes are needed to accommodate them, and rising expectations for housing as wealth increases have created huge new demands for housing land over the last decade. Japan is a wealthy country, and there is a tremendous pent up demand for better housing and a better urban environment, which may fuel significant new development even if the economy grows only slowly. As the population starts to decline more rapidly, however, it seems increasingly unlikely that major new investment in urban areas will be profitable. The big question will thus be what sort of urban development is achieved over the next twenty years or so. It seems fair to suggest that the next two or three decades will see a final major chance to shape long-term urban patterns in Japan. Will this next, and perhaps final, period of major urban investment see policies that help solve previous urban problems, or will new problem areas continue to spread? Certainly the traditional Japanese urbanisation strategy of allowing a wide range of unplanned, unserviced developments in the hope of fixing them later seems increasingly problematic in a situation of low growth.

A second major factor influencing future urban development, possibly less certain than the first but following directly from it, is that it seems unlikely that the future will see significant increases in land prices, at least not on the scale seen during the last century. Much more likely is that land prices will remain stable or continue to decline gradually, partly because of slower economic growth, but primarily because of the declining population. If such land price stability does come about in Japan it will represent a profound change to the Japanese political economy, with particularly strong impacts in urban areas. During most of the post-war period one of Japan's most enduring myths, upon which the whole structure of the land development industry and much of the rest of the economy has been built, is that land prices would always rise (Noguchi 1992b). Any investment in urban real estate, no matter how optimistic, and any investment in urban fringe land development, no matter how remote, would eventually be paid back by rising land values. This pervasive belief was, of course, self-fulfilling up to a certain point, but equally obviously could not last forever. The land myth had a number of pernicious effects on urban development that may change in future. First, it seems likely that as future expectations of enormous land price increases are accepted as less and less likely, inner urban land that was farmed or held vacant primarily for speculative purposes will have to be put to uses which yield higher returns, even if simply to pay rising taxes. Further, land development schemes in very remote locations may begin to receive more scrutiny, if only by banks and other lenders who see increased risks in such development. Both of these possibilities, if they occur, would serve to reduce the degree of new urban sprawl in the metropolitan areas, and might begin to encourage consolidation in existing built up areas.

Perhaps more importantly, it seems likely that a stable land price regime will encourage landowners of all sorts, large and small, to be much more concerned with positive and negative local environmental impacts on the value of their own property. That is, it seems likely that in the past many Japanese landowners, confident in the ever-rising value of their land, could afford to ignore nearby land uses that in North America or Europe would have neighbours howling in protest. While there are certainly a range of valid criticisms of such not-in-my-back-yard (NIMBY) movements, there is no doubt that they contribute to a heightened awareness of local environmental issues, and a greater attentiveness to local opinion by decision-makers. Stable prices thus seem likely to bring the Western discussion of negative and positive externalities to the fore in urban Japan to a degree that has not been seen in the past. It may even be that this process had already begun during the 1990s, and is one factor behind the explosion of citizen participatory machizukuri movements. More broadly, this change may contribute to raising the importance of local planning issues in local politics. Such issues have sporadically been prominent for Japanese local governments, but on nowhere near the scale seen in many of the other developed countries.

Three aspects of future urban policy seem crucial to what is achieved during the next two decades: public spending, changes to the planning system, and strategies to control patterns of growth on the urban fringe.

Public spending on infrastructure is almost certain to decline from the astronomical levels of the last ten years, as the attempts to use the construction industry to jump-start the economy were certainly unsustainable, creating massive public debts, and were not in any case successful in re-starting economic growth. There will inevitably still be considerable public spending, however, and the big question will be whether that spending will shift from large-scale projects such as expensive elevated expressways, new dams and bridges, and the new airports planned for Kobe and Nagoya, to smaller-scale interventions that would have a greater impact on people's quality of life, such as improvements in local shopping districts, the renovation of housing in older inner city areas, the building of better bicycle and pedestrian routes, or the creation of small parks. The recent MoC review of all planned project spending is a step in the right direction, but it is unclear what impact it will have on actual spending. The construction lobby is still very powerful, and it is much easier to spend money on a few huge projects, even if they are utterly unnecessary, than it is to spend money on many small projects that have a real impact on urban quality of life. Yet small-scale improvement projects in the old, high-risk areas in the inner city have been consistently denied adequate funds. For example, as noted by Evans (2001: 291), even in the rebuilding projects after the Kobe earthquake the typical cooperative reconstruction (*kyōdō tatekai*) schemes to rebuild private houses could receive only about 17 per cent of costs by combining a range of subsidies and grants. As a result many poor elderly households have simply been unable to rebuild. Evans contrasts this with the British case, where in Housing Action Areas typical subsidies were about 75 per cent, and often reached 90 per cent for the improvement of substandard housing. The steadfast reluctance of central government to allow the spending of public money to upgrade the private housing stock has been a major factor in the endurance of the high-risk wooden housing areas of the metropolitan areas (Nakamura 2001).

The important developments in city planning practice during the 1990s, including the spread of citizen-based machizukuri, the implementation of participatory Master Planning, and the moves to devolve planning authority to local governments have created considerable optimism that a new era of Japanese planning is at hand. It is still unclear, however, whether these changes will actually lead to a fundamental change in city planning practice. Most machizukuri ordinances are still defensive in nature, have little legal power to back their decisions, and require what may turn out to be unsustainably high degrees of public participation to be effective. They are also still only weakly supported by the statutory city planning system, which remains the preserve of bureaucrats. Recent efforts to link a very widespread use of machizukuri districts with Master Planning for a whole municipal area seem promising, as they seek to formally join machizukuri with statutory city planning, but such attempts are still only seen in a few places. On the whole, while there is room for real optimism, city planning practice is only changing rather slowly.

A final crucial question for the next twenty years will be whether the fundamental patterns of extensive urban fringe growth of the last twenty years will be continued, or reversed. During the 1980s and 1990s, even as much innovative work was being achieved in inner urban areas, huge areas of new urban sprawl were being created on the fringe. These areas are characterised by widely scattered development of land to urban uses, with many parcels left undeveloped, and poor road and sewer infrastructure. As new urban development slows with the decline in population, it seems likely that many of these areas will remain half developed, and the costly process of remedial improvements will have to be abandoned as inward investment dries up and the possibility of increasing the tax base through new development becomes more remote. The question then is whether the trend to population dispersal from existing built up areas will continue to fuel haphazard development on the fringe, further and further from central areas, leaving behind increasing numbers of vacated housing units and vacant properties in existing urban areas, or whether this final wave of pressure for newer and larger housing can be used to consolidate and improve existing half built up suburban areas. It is not necessary that all the land must be built up, but at least any inward investment should be used to complete essential network infrastructure, lest that become impossible in future. Given the enormous number of new large-scale land developments that have been started in recent years in locations distant from the central cities, but still dependent on them for jobs and services, the former course seems the more likely (see Sorensen 2000b). This seems certain to lead to increasingly severe problems if new building really does substantially slow in future.

Major choices still face the Japanese people about what sort of living environment future generations will enjoy. Patterns and practices of urbanisation and planning during the twentieth century provide grounds for both optimism and concern. The enormous energy and discipline of the Japanese people have allowed the building of one of the wealthiest societies the world has ever known. Public and private initiative has been mobilised towards the achievement of remarkable economic growth and enormous increases in standards of living, at the same time as ensuring a relatively equal distribution of income compared to other countries. On the other hand, the benefits of economic growth have been undermined by persistent urban problems. High land prices, low housing standards, long travel times, environmental pollution in cities and environmental destruction elsewhere have all tended to limit the improvements to Japanese quality of life that might have been expected following economic growth. It remains to be seen whether Japan will be successful in redirecting its prodigious talents and resources towards tackling these challenges, or whether it will continue to muddle along in the current direction.

Bibliography

Alden, J.D. (1984) "Metropolitan Planning in Japan", *Town Planning Review* 55(1): 55–74.

Allinson, G. (1975) *Japanese Urbanism*, Berkeley, CA: University of California Press.

—— (1979) *Suburban Tokyo: A Comparative Study in Politics and Social Change*. Berkeley, CA: University of California Press.

—— (1997) *Japan's Postwar History*, Ithaca, NY: Cornell University Press.

Amenomori, T. (1997) "Japan" in *Defining the Nonprofit Sector*, Salamon, L.M. and Anheier, H.K. (eds), Manchester: Manchester University Press.

Anchordoguy, M. (1992) "Land Policy: A Public Policy Failure" in *Land Issues in Japan: a policy failure?* Haley, J.O. and Yamamura, K. (eds), Seattle, WA: Society for Japanese Studies: 77–111.

Aoki, E. (1993) "Developing an Independent Transportation Policy (1910–1921)" in *Technological Innovation and the Development of Transportation in Japan*, H. Yamamoto (ed.), Tokyo: United Nations University Press, 72–83.

Apter, D.E. and Sawa, N. (1984) *Against the State*, Cambridge, MA: Harvard University Press.

Arisue, T. and Aoki, E. (1970) "The Development of Railway Network in the Tokyo Region from the Point of View of the Metropolitan Growth" in *Japanese Cities: A Geographical Approach*, Association of Japanese Geographers (eds), Tokyo: Association of Japanese Geographers, 191–200.

Barlow Report (1940) "Report of the Royal Commission on the Distribution of the Industrial Population", London: HMSO.

Barret, B. and Therivel, R. (1991) *Environmental Policy and Impact Assessment in Japan*, London: Routledge.

Barter, P. (1999) "An International Comparative Perspective on Urban Transport and Urban Form in Pacific Asia: The Challenge of Rapid Motorisation in Dense Cities", unpublished PhD Thesis, Murdoch University, Australia.

Beard, C. (1923) *The Administration and Politics of Tokyo: A Survey and Opinions*, New York: Macmillan.

Beasley, W.G. (1995) *The Rise of Modern Japan*, New York: St Martin's Press.

Ben-Ari, E. (1991) *Changing Japanese Suburbia: A Study of Two Present-Day Localities*, London, New York: Kegan Paul International.

Bestor, T.C. (1989) *Neighborhood Tokyo*, Stanford, CA: Stanford University Press.

Bird, I. (1880) *Unbeaten Tracks in Japan*, London: John Murray.

Breitling, P. (1980) "The Role of the Competition in the Genesis of Urban Planning: Germany and Austria in the Nineteenth Century" in *The Rise of Modern Urban Planning 1800–1914*, Sutcliffe, A. (ed.), London: Mansell, 31–54.

Broadbent, J. (1989) "Strategies and Structural Contradictions: Growth Coalition Politics in Japan", *American Sociological Review* 54(Oct): 707–21.

—— (1998) *Environmental Politics in Japan*, Cambridge: Cambridge University Press.

Calder, K.E. (1988) *Crisis and Compensation: Public Policy and Political Stability in Japan, 1949–1986*, Princeton, NJ: Princeton University Press.

Calthorpe, P. (1993) *The Next American Metropolis*, New York: Princeton Architectural Press.

Capital Region Comprehensive Planning Institute (1987) *Senbiki*, Tokyo: Capital Region Comprehensive Planning Institute.

Castells, M. and Hall, P. (1994) *Technopoles of the World: The Making of 21st Century Industrial Complexes*, London, New York: Routledge.

Cervero, R. (1989) *America's Suburban Centers: The Land Use-Transportation Link*, Boston, MA: Unwin Hyman.

——(1995) "Changing Live-Work Spatial Relationships: Implications for Metropolitan Structure and Mobility" in *Cities in Competition: Productive and Sustainable Cities for the 21st Century*, Brotchie, J. et al. (eds), Melbourne: Longman, 330–47.

——(1998) *The Transit Metropolis: A Global Inquiry*, Washington, DC: Island Press.

Champion, A. (ed.) (1989) *Counterurbanisation: The Changing Pace and Nature of Population Deconcentration*, London: Edward Arnold.

Cherry, G.E. (1988) *Cities and Plans*, London: Edward Arnold.

Cibla, D. (2000) *Decision-making processes in the light of new disaster prevention urban planning priorities: towards increasing public intervention in machi-zukuri projects?* 9th International Conference of the European Association for Japanese Studies (EAJS), Lahti, Finland.

Continental Construction Discussion Group (Tairiku Kenchiku Sodankai) (eds) (1940) "Discussion on Daido Plans", *Modern Architecture (Gendai Kenchiku)* 8: 38–49.

Craig, A.M. (1986) "The Central Government" in *Japan in Transition: From Tokugawa to Meiji*, Jansen, M.B. and Rozman, G. (eds), Princeton, NJ: Princeton University Press, 36–67.

Cullingworth, J.B. (1997) *Planning in the USA*, London: Routledge.

Cumings, B. (1987) "The Origins and Development of the Northeast Asian Political Economy: Industrial Sectors, Product Cycles, and Political Consequences" in *The Political Economy of the New Asian Industrialism*, Deyo, F.C. (ed.), Ithaca, NY: Cornell University Press, 44–83.

Cybriwsky, R. (1998) *Tokyo: The changing profile of an urban giant*, Chichester: John Wiley & Sons.

Davidoff, P. (1965) "Advocacy and Pluralism in Planning", *Journal of the American Institute of Planners* 21(4).

Dawson, A. (1985) "Land Use Policy and Control in Japan", *Land Use Policy, January 1985*: 56–60.

Doi, T. (1968) "Japan Megalopolis: Another Approach", *Ekistics* 26(156): 96–9.

Donnelly, M. (1984) "Conflict over Government Authority and Markets: Japan's Rice Economy" in *Conflict in Japan*, Krauss, E., Rohlen, T. and Steinhoff, P. (eds), Honolulu: University of Hawaii Press, 335–74.

Dore, R.P. (1958) *City Life in Japan – a Study of a Tokyo Ward*, London: Routledge and Kegan Paul.

——(1959) *Land Reform in Japan*. London: Athlone Press.

——(1968) "Urban Ward Associations in Japan – Introduction" in *Readings in Urban Sociology*, Pahl, R.E. (ed.), Oxford: Pergamon, 186–90.

Dower, J.W. (1999) *Embracing Defeat. Japan in the Wake of World War I*, New York: W.W. Norton/The New Press.

Downs, A. (1994) *New Visions for Metropolitan America*, Washington, DC: Brookings, Lincoln Institute of Land Policy.

Duus, P. (1968) *Party Rivalry and Political Change in Taisho Japan*, Cambridge, MA: Harvard University Press.

——(1999) *Modern Japan*, Boston, MA: Houghton Mifflin Company.

Duus, P. and Scheiner, I. (1998) "Socialism, Liberalism, and Marxism, 1901–1931" in *Modern Japanese Thought*, Wakabayashi, B.T. (ed.), Cambridge: Cambridge University Press, 147–206.

Edgington, D.W. (1994) "Planning for Technology Development and Information Systems in Japanese Cities and Regions" in *Planning for Cities and Regions in Japan*, Shapira, P., Masser, I. and Edgington, D.W. (eds), Liverpool: Liverpool University Press, 126–54.

Eisenstadt, S.N. (1996) *Japanese Civilization: A Comparative View*, Chicago, IL: University of Chicago Press.

Ericson, S.J. (1996) *The Sound of the Whistle: Railroads and the State in Meiji Japan*, Cambridge MA: Council on East Asian Studies Harvard University.

Evans, N. (2001) *Community Planning in Japan: The Case of Mano, and its Experience in the Hanshin Earthquake*, PhD School of East Asian Studies, Sheffield: University of Sheffield.

Ewing, R. (1997) "Is Los Angeles Style Sprawl Desirable?" *Journal of the American Planning Association* 63(1): 107–26.

Falconeri, G.R. (1976) "The Impact of Rapid Urban Change on Neighborhood Solidarity: A Case Study of a Japanese Neighborhood" in *Social Change and Community Politics in Urban Japan*, White, J.W. and Munger, F. (eds), Chapel Hill, NC: Institute for Research in Social Science, University of North Carolina at Chapel Hill, 31–60.

Fishman, R. (1987) *Bourgeois Utopias: The Rise and Fall of Suburbia*, New York: Basic Books.

Francks, P. (1984) *Technology and Agricultural Development in Pre-War Japan*, New Haven, CT: Yale University Press.

—— (1992) *Japanese Economic Development*, London: Routledge.

Fraser, A. (1986) "Local Administration: The Example of Awa-Tokushima" in *Japan in Transition: From Tokugawa to Meiji*, Jansen, M.B. and Rozman, G. (eds), Princeton, NJ: Princeton University Press.

Friedmann, J. (1987) *Planning in the Public Domain*, Princeton, NJ: Princeton University Press.

Friedmann, J. and Wolff, G. (1982) "World City Formation: An Agenda for Research and Action", *International Journal of Urban and Regional Research*, 6(3): 309–44.

Fujimori, T. (1982) *Meiji No Tokyo Keikaku (Tokyo Planning in the Meiji Period)*, Tokyo: Iwanami Shoten.

Fujioka, K. (1980) "The Changing Face of Japanese Jokamachi (Castle Towns) since the Meiji Period" in *Geography of Japan*, Association of Japanese Geographers (eds), Tokyo: Teikoku Shoin.

Fujita, K. (1992) "A World City and Flexible Specialization: Restructuring of the Tokyo Metropolis", *International Journal of Urban and Regional Research* 15: 269–84.

Fujita, K. and Hill, R.C. (1997) "Together and Equal: Place Stratification in Osaka" in *The Japanese City*, Karan, P.P. and Stapleton, K. (eds), Lexington, KY: The University Press of Kentucky, 106–33.

Fujitani, T. (1998) *Splendid Monarchy: Power and Pageantry in Modern Japan*, Berkeley, CA: University of California Press.

Fukuoka, S. (1997) "The Structure of Urban Land Administration during the Bubble Economy: Control Systems and their Operations", *Comprehensive Urban Studies (Sōgō Toshi Kenkyuu)*, 62: 165–79.

Fukutake, T. (1967) *Japanese Rural Society*, Ithaca, NY: Cornell University Press.

Garon, S. (1987) *The State and Labor in Modern Japan*, Berkeley, CA: University of California Press.

—— (1997) *Molding Japanese Minds: The State in Everyday Life*, Princeton, NJ: Princeton University Press.

Garreau, J. (1991) *Edge City: Life on the New Frontier*, New York: Doubleday.

Glickman, N. (1979) *The Growth and Management of the Japanese Urban System*, New York: Academic Press.

Gluck, C. (1987) *Japan's Modern Myths: Ideology in the Late Meiji Period*, Princeton, NJ: Princeton University Press.

Golany, G., Hanaki, K. and Koide, O. (eds) (1998) *Japanese Urban Environment*, Oxford: Elsevier Science.

Goodman, R. and Peng, I. (1996) "East Asian Welfare States" in *Welfare States in Transition*, Esping-Andersen, G. (ed.), London: Sage, 192–224.

Gordon, A. (1991) *Labor and Imperial Democracy in Prewar Japan*, Berkeley, CA: University of California Press.

Gorsky, M. (1998) "Mutual Aid and Civil Society: Friendly Societies in Nineteenth-Century Bristol", *Urban History* (25): 302–22.

Gottmann, J. (1961) *Megalopolis: The Urbanized Northeastern Seaboard of the United States*, Cambridge, MA: MIT Press.

——(1976) "Megalopolitan Systems around the World", *Ekistics* 243(Feb): 109–13.

——(1980) "Planning and Metamorphosis in Japan: A Note", *Town Planning Review* 51(2): 171–6.

Griffis, W.E. (1883) *The Mikado's Empire*, New York: Harper and Brothers.

Haley, J.O. and Yamamura, K. (eds) (1992). *Land Issues in Japan: A Policy Failure?* Seattle, WA: Society for Japanese Studies.

Hall, J.A. (ed.) (1995) *Civil Society: Theory, History, Comparison* Cambridge: Polity Press.

Hall, J.W. (1968) "The Castle Town and Japan's Modern Urbanization" in *Studies in the Institutional History of Early Modern Japan*, Hall, J.W. and Jansen, M.B. (eds), Princeton, NJ: Princeton University Press, 169–88.

Hall, P. (1988) *Cities of Tomorrow*, Oxford: Blackwell.

Hall, P. and Ward, C. (1998) *Sociable Cities: The Legacy of Ebenezer Howard*, Chichester: John Wiley & Sons.

Hama, H. (1976) "Geographical Studies of Population" in *Geography in Japan*, Kiuchi, S. (ed.), Tokyo: University of Tokyo Press.

Hanayama, Y. (1986) *Land Markets and Land Policy in a Metropolitan Area: A Case Study of Tokyo*, Boston, MA: Oelgeschlager, Gunn and Hain.

Hanes, J.E. (1993) "From Megalopolis to Megaroporisu", *Journal of Urban History* 19(2): 56–94.

——(2002) *The City as Subject: Seki Hajime and the Reinvention of Modern Osaka*, Berkeley, CA: University of California Press.

Hanley, S. (1986) "The Material Culture: Stability in Transition" in *Japan in Transition: From Tokugawa to Meiji*, Jansen, M.B. and Rozman, G. (eds), Princeton, NJ: Princeton University Press, 447–69.

——(1997) *Everyday Things in Premodern Japan: The Hidden Legacy of Material Culture*, Berkeley, CA: University of California Press.

Harada, K. (1993) "Railroads" in *Technological Innovation and the Development of Transportation in Japan*, Yamamoto, H. (ed.), Tokyo: United Nations University Press, 15–21, 49–60.

Harootunian, H.D. (1974) "Introduction: A Sense of an Ending and the Problem of Taisho" in *Japan in Crisis: Essays in Taisho Democracy*, Silberman, B.S. and Harootunian, H.D. (eds), Princeton, NJ: Princeton University Press, 3–28.

Harris, C.D. (1982) "The Urban and Industrial Transformation of Japan", *Geographical Review* 72: 50–89.

Hastings, S.A. (1995) *Neighborhood and Nation in Tokyo, 1905–1937*, Pittsburgh, PA: University of Pittsburgh Press.

Hatano, Y., Koizumi, H., Okata, J. (2000) "A Study of the Inheritance on the Structure of Space and Land Ownership in Gokenin Residents' Sites in Tokyo (Edo Kumiyashiki Atochi ni Okeru Kūkan Kōzō oyobi Tochi Shoyū Keitai no Keishōsei ni Kansuru Kenkyū)", *Collected Papers of the Japanese City Planning Association (Nihon Toshi Keikaku Gikkai Ronbun Shu)* 35: 91–96.

Hatano, J. (1994) "Edo's Water Supply" in *Edo and Paris: Urban Life and the State in the Early Modern Era*, McClain, J.L., Merriman, J.M. and Ugawa, K. (eds), Ithaca, NY: Cornell University Press, 234–50.

Hatano, N., Wakayama, T. and Ihara, M. (1984) "Some Problems of the Urban Sprawl by Named "Kizon Takuchi" in Urbanisation Control Area" *Collected Papers of the Japanese City Planning Association (Nihon Toshi Keikaku Gakkai Ronbun Shu)* 19: 121–6.

Hatta, T. and Ohkawara, T. (1994) "Housing and the Journey to Work in the Tokyo Metropolitan Area" in *Housing Markets in the United States and Japan*, Noguchi, Y. and Poterba, J.M. (eds), Chicago, IL: University of Chicago Press, 87–132.

Hatta, T. and Tabuchi, T. (1995) "Unipolar Concentration in Tokyo: Causes and Measures", *Japanese Economic Studies* 23(3): 74–104.

Hayakawa, K. and Hirayama, Y. (1991) "The Impact of the Minkatsu Policy on Japanese Housing and Land Use", *Environment and Planning D: Society and Space* 9: 151–64.

Hayami, A. (1986) "Population Changes" in *Japan in Transition: From Tokugawa to Meiji*, Jansen, M.B. and Rozman, G. (eds), Princeton, NJ: Princeton University Press, 280–317.

Hayami, Y. (1988) *Japanese Agriculture under Seige*, New York: St Martin's Press.

Hayashi, K. (1982) "Land Readjustment in Nagoya" in *Land Readjustment, a Different Approach to Financing Urbanization*, Doebele, W. (ed.), Lexington, MA: Lexington Books, 107–26.

Hayashi, R. (1994) "Provisioning Edo in the Early Eighteenth Century: The Pricing Policies of the Shogunate and the Crisis of 1733" in *Edo and Paris: Urban Life and the State in the Early Modern Era*, McClain, J.L., Merriman, J.M. and Ugawa, K. (eds), Ithaca, NY: Cornell University Press, 211–33.

Healy, P. (1996) "The Communicative Turn in Planning Theory and its Implications for Spatial Strategy Formation", *Environment and Planning B: Planning and Design* 23, 217–34

Hebbert, M. (1989) "Rural Land Use Planning in Japan" in *Rural Land Use Planning in Developed Nations*, Cloke, P.J. (ed.), London: Unwin Hyman, 130–51.

—— (1994) "Sen-Biki Amidst Desakota: Urban Sprawl and Urban Planning in Japan" in *Planning for Cities and Regions in Japan*, Shapira, P., Masser, I. and Edgington, D.W. (eds), Liverpool: Liverpool University Press, 70–91.

Hebbert, M. and Nakai, N. (1988a) "Deregulation of Japanese Planning", *Town Planning Review* 59(4): 383–95.

—— (1988b) *How Tokyo Grows*, London: STICERD.

Hein, C. (2001) "Planning Visions" in *Power, Place, and Memory: Japanese Cities in Historical Perspective*, Fieve, N. and Waley, P. (eds), London: Curzon.

Hohn, U. (1997) "Townscape Preservation in Japanese Urban Planning", *Town Planning Review* 68(2): 213–55.

—— (2000) *Stadtplanung in Japan. Geschichte – Recht – Praxis – Theorie*, Dortmund: Dortmunder Vertrieb fur Bau- und Planungsliteratur.

Honjo, M. (1978) "Trends in Development Planning in Japan" in *Growth Pole Strategy and Regional Development Policy: Asian Experience and Alternative Approaches*, Lo, F. and Salih, K. (eds), Oxford: Pergamon Press and UNCRD, 3–23.

—— (1984) "Key Issues of Urban Development and Land Management Policies in Asian Developing Countries" in *Urban Development Policies and Land Management: Japan and Asia*, Honjo, M. and Inoue, T. (eds), Nagoya: City of Nagoya, 15–35.

Hori, T. (1990) "Early City Planning" in *Yokohama Past and Present*, Kato, Y. (ed.), Yokohama: Yokohama City University, 98–9.

Hoshino, K. (1946) "Tokyo Reconstruction Area Plans (Tokyo Fukko Chiiki Keikaku ni Tsuite)", *New Architecture (Shinkenchiku)* 21(6): 3–7.

Hoshino, Y. (1992) "Japan's Post-Second World War Environmental Problems" in *Industrial Pollution in Japan*, Ui, J. (ed.), Tokyo: United Nations University Press, 64–76.

Hotaka Town (1999) "Resident Participatory Machizukuri: Outline of the Hotaka Town Machizukuri Ordinance (Shiminsanka No Machizukuri: Hotaka Machi Machizukuri Jōrei No Gaiyō)", Hotaka, Nagano Prefecture: Hotaka Machi Project Finance Department (Hotaka machi Kikaku Zaiseika).

Hough, M. (1995) *Cities and Natural Process*, London: Routledge.

Howard, E. ([1902] 1985) *Garden Cities of Tomorrow*, Rhosgoch: Attic Books.

Huddle, N., Reich, M. and Stiskin, N. (1975) *Island of Dreams*, New York: Autumn Press.

Hunter, J.E. (1989) *The Emergence of Modern Japan: An Introductory History since 1853*, London: Longman.

Iijima, N. (1992) "Social Structures of Pollution Victims" in *Industrial Pollution in Japan*, Ui, J. (ed.), Tokyo: United Nations University Press, 154–72.

Ikeda, T. (1983) "Some Facts of the Building Line System in Local Cities (Tokyo Igai Ni Okeru

Shitei Kenchikusen Unyō No Jissai)", *Comprehensive Urban Studies (Sōgō Toshi Kenkyū)* 18: 141–63.

Ikeda, Y. (1986) *The History of Japanese Social Welfare (Nihon Shakai Fukushi Shi)*, Kyoto: Horitsu Bunka Sha.

Iokibe, M. (1999) "Japan's Civil Society: An Historical Overview" in *Deciding the Public Good: Governance and Civil Society in Japan*, Yamamoto, T. (ed.), Tokyo: Japan Center for International Exchange, 51–96.

Ishi, H. (1991) "Land Tax Reform in Japan", *Hitotsubashi Journal of Economics* (32): 1–20.

Ishida, Y. (1979) "The Building Line System as a Method of Controlling Sprawl", *Comprehensive Urban Studies (Sōgō Toshi Kenkyū)* 6: 33–42.

—— (1982) "The Historical Background and Evaluation of the 1968 City Planning Law (1968 Nen Toshi Keikaku Hō No Rekishiteki Haikei to Hyōka)", *City Planning Review (Toshi Keikaku)* 119: 9–15.

—— (1986) "A Short History of Japanese Land Readjustment 1870–1980 (Nihon Ni Okeru Tochi Kukaku Seiri Seidoshi Gaisetsu 1870–1980)", *Comprehensive Urban Studies (Sōgō Toshi Kenkyū)* 28: 45–88.

—— (1987) *The Last 100 Years of Japanese Urban Planning (Nihon Kindai Toshikeikaku No Hyakunen)*, Tokyo: Jichitai Kenkyusha.

—— (1988) "Ōgai Mori and Tokyo's Building Ordinance" in *Tokyo: Urban Growth and Planning 1868–1988*, Ishizuka, H. and Ishida, Y. (eds), Tokyo: Iwanami Shoten, 83–6.

—— (1990) "Kōkyō Tōshi to Kaihatsu Rieki No Kangen", *Toshi Mondai* 81(11): 41–50.

—— (1991a) "Achievements and Problems of Japanese Urban Planning: Ever Recurring Dual Structures", *Comprehensive Urban Studies (Sōgō Toshi Kenkyū)* 43: 5–18.

—— (1991b) "Ōgai Mori's Essays on Urban Improvement: The Case of Shiku-Kaisei Ron-Ryaku (Mori Ōgai No Shiku Kaisei Ron: Shikukaisei Ronryaku O Chūshin Ni)", *Comprehensive Urban Studies (Sōgō Toshi Kenkyū)* 43: 21–35.

—— (1992) "Toward Growth Management Policy for Tokyo: Uni-Polarization Phenomena in Tokyo and Growth Management", *Comprehensive Urban Studies (Sōgō Toshi Kenkyū)* 45: 203–33.

—— (1994) "Agricultural Land Use in the Urbanised Area of Tokyo: History of Urban Agriculture in Tokyo", Paper presented at the 6th International Planning History Society, Hong Kong, 1994.

—— (1997) "Ōgai Mori's Essays on Urban Planning: Focussing on the Chapters of 'City' and 'Housing' in His Textbook of Hygiene (Mori Ōgai No Toshi Keikaku Ron: Eisei Shinpen No Toshi, Kaoku No Shō Ni Tsuite)", *Comprehensive Urban Studies (Sōgō Toshi Kenkyū)* 63: 101–26.

—— (1999) *Mori Ōgai's Urban Writings and His Period (Mori Ougai No Toshi Ron to Sono Jidai)*, Tokyo: Nihon Keizai Hyōronsha.

—— (2000) "Local Initiatives and Decentralisation of Planning Power in Japan", Paper presented at the European Association of Japanese Studies, 23–26 August, Lahti, Finland.

Ishida, Y. and Ikeda, T. (1979) "The Building Line System as a Method of Controlling Urban Sprawl #1 (Kenchikusen Seido Ni Kansuru Kenkyū – Sono 1)", *Comprehensive Urban Studies (Sōgō Toshi Kenkyū)* 6: 33–64.

—— (1981) "Some Facts Preceding the Legislation of the Building Line System in Japan (Kenchikusenseido Ni Kansuru Kenkyū, Sono 3: Meiji Shonen No Hisashichi Seigen Ni Tsuite)", *Comprehensive Urban Studies (Sōgō Toshi Kenkyū)* 12: 167–88.

Ishikawa, M. (2001) *Cities and Green Space: Moving Towards the Creation of a New Urban Environment (Toshi to Midorichi: Atarashii Toshi Kankyō No Sōzō Ni Mukete)*, Tokyo: Iwanami Shōten.

Ishikawa, Y. and Fielding, A.Y. (1998) "Explaining the Recent Migration Trends of the Tokyo Metropolitan Area", *Environment and Planning A* 30: 1797–814.

Ishizuka, H. (1988) "Amusement Quarters, Public Squares and Road Regulations of Tokyo in the Meiji Era" in *Tokyo: Urban Growth and Planning 1868–1988*, Ishizuka, H. and Ishida, Y. (eds), Tokyo: Iwanami Shōten, 71–5.

Ishizuka, H. and Ishida, Y. (1988a) "Chronology on Urban Planning in Tokyo 1868 – 1988" in

Tokyo: Urban Growth and Planning 1868–1988, Ishizuka, H. and Ishida, Y. (eds), Tokyo: Iwanami Shōten, 37–68.

—— (1988b) "Tokyo, the Metropolis of Japan and Its Urban Development" in *Tokyo: Urban Growth and Planning 1868–1988*, Ishizuka, H. and Ishida, Y. (eds), Tokyo: Center for Urban Studies, 3–35.

—— (1988c) *Tokyo: Urban Growth and Planning 1868–1988* Tokyo: Center for Urban Studies.

Iwata, K. (1994) "Overcongestion and Revisions in Urban Planning", *Japanese Economic Studies* 22(2): 39–64.

Jackson, K.T. (1985) *Crabgrass Frontier: The Suburbanization of the United States*, New York: Oxford University Press.

Jacobs, J. (1961) *The Death and Life of Great American Cities*, New York: Vintage, Random House.

Janetta, A.B. (1987) *Epidemics and Mortality in Early Modern Japan*, Princeton, NJ: Princeton University Press.

Jansen, M.B. and Rozman, G. (1986a) *Japan in Transition: From Tokugawa to Meiji*, Princeton, NJ: Princeton University Press.

—— (1986b) "Overview" in *Japan in Transition: From Tokugawa to Meiji*, Jansen, M.B. and Rozman, G. (eds), Princeton, NJ: Princeton University Press.

Japan General Housing Centre (1984). "Survey of Changes to Pre-war Housing Policy (Senzen no Jutakuseisaku no Hensen ni Kansuru Chosa)", *Nihon Jutaku Sogo Centaa*, 5.

Japan Ministry of Construction (1991) *City Planning in Japan*, Tokyo: Japan Ministry of Construction and Japan International Cooperation Agency.

—— (1975) *City Planning Yearbook (Toshi Keikaku Nenpo)*, Tokyo: Japan Ministry of Construction, City Planning Association.

—— (1992) *Construction White Paper*, Tokyo: Ministry of Construction.

—— (1996) *Urban Land Use Planning System in Japan*, Tokyo: Institute for Future Urban Development.

—— (ed.) (1957–1963) *The History of War Reconstruction Projects: 10 Volumes (Sensai Fukkō-Shi: 10 Kan)*, Tokyo: Toshi Keikaku Kyōkai (City Planning Association of Japan).

Japan Ministry of Construction City Bureau (1996) *Urban Land Use Planning System in Japan*, Tokyo: Japan Ministry of Construction (MoC) City Bureau.

Japan Ministry of Health and Welfare (Kōseishō) (2000) "White Paper on Health and Welfare (Kōsei Hakusho)", Tokyo: Japan Ministry of Health and Welfare (Kōseishō).

Japan National Land Agency (1987) *The Fourth Comprehensive National Development Plan*, Tokyo: National Land Agency (Kokudocho).

Japan Population Census (1995) *Analytical Series No.3, Population for Densely Inhabited Districts*, Tokyo: Japan Prime Minister's Office.

Jinnai, H. (1990) "The Spatial Structure of Edo" in *Tokugawa Japan: Social and Economic Antecedents of Modern Japan*, Nakane, C. and Oishi, S. (eds), Tokyo: University of Tokyo Press, 124–46.

—— (1994) "Tokyo, a Model for the 21st Century?" Paper presented to the European Association of Japanese Studies Conference, August 1994.

—— (2000) "Destruction and Revival of Waterfront Space in Tokyo" in *Destruction and Rebirth of Urban Environment*, Fukui, N. and Jinnai, H. (eds), Tokyo: Sagami Shobo Publishing, 39–49.

Jinno, N. (1999) "Public Works Projects and Japan's Public Finances", *Social Science Japan*, 17: 6–9.

Johnson, C. (1982) *Miti and the Japanese Miracle, the Growth of Industrial Policy, 1925–1975*, Stanford, CA: Stanford University Press.

—— (1995) *Japan: Who Governs? The Rise of the Developmental State*, New York: W.W. Norton.

Kamakura City Planning Department (Kamakurashi Toshibu Toshikeikakuka) (1998). *Kamakura City Master Plan Digest Book (Kamakura Shi Toshi Masutaa Puran Daijesuto Han)*. Kamakura, Kamakura City Government.

Kase, K. (1999) "Economic Aspects of Public Works Projects in Japan", *Social Science Japan*, 17: 16–19.

Katagi, A., Fujiya, Y. and Kadono, Y. (2000) *Suburban Housing Areas in Modern Japan (Kindai Nihon No Kogai Jutakuchi)*, Tokyo: Kajima Shuppansha.

Katayama, S. ([1903] 1949) *Urban Socialism, My Socialism*, Tokyo: Jitsugyō no Nihon-sha.

Kato, H. (1988) "A Historical Review of the Problems Associated with Narrow Streets in Residential Districts", Paper presented at the The Twentieth Century Planning Experience, 8th International Planning History Society Conference, Sydney, Australia, 1988.

—— (1997) "A Study on the Changes of Land Management by the Daimyo from Meiji Era to after the Second World War – the Case of the Abe Family (Meijiki Kara Showasengoki No Daitochishoyusha Ni Yoru Tochikeiei No Hensen – Kyudaimyo Abeka No Baai)", *Papers of the City Planning Association of Japan* 32: 49–54.

Kato, S. (1974) "Taisho Democracy as the Pre-Stage for Japanese Militarism" in *Japan in Crisis: Essays in Taisho Democracy*, Silberman, B.S. and Harootunian, H.D. (eds), Princeton, NJ: Princeton University Press, 217–36.

Kato, T. (1994) "Governing Edo" in *Edo and Paris: Urban Life and the State in the Early Modern Era*, McClain, J.L., Merriman, J.M. and Ugawa, K. (eds), Ithaca, NY: Cornell University Press, 41–67.

Katsumata, W. (1993) "Possibilities of Environmental Improvement Considering the Conditions of the Inhabitants in Small-Scale Residential Developments in the Suburbs of Tokyo Metropolitan Area (Shutoken Kogai Minikaihatsu Jutakuchi Ni Okeru Kyoju Jissai to Jukankyo Seibi No Hoko)", *Collected Papers of the Japanese City Planning Association (Nihon Toshi Keikaku Gakkai Ronbun Shu)* 28: 823–28.

—— (1995) "The Characteristics of the Macro-Location of Small-Scale Residential Developments in the Suburbs and Orientation of Environmental Improvement in the Areas (Kōgai Minikaihatsu Jūtakuchi No Makuro Ricchi Tokusei to Chiku Kankyō Seibi No Hōkō)", *Collected Papers of the Japanese City Planning Association (Nihon Toshi Keikaku Gakkai Ronbun Shu)* 30: 139–44.

Kawashima, N. (2001) "The Emerging Voluntary Sector in Japan: Issues and Prospects", *International Working Paper Series, Centre for Civil Society, London School of Economics*, Paper #7.

Keane, J. (1998) *Civil Society: Old Images, New Visions*, Cambridge: Polity Press.

Kelly, W.W. (1994) "Incendiary Actions: Fires and Firefighting in the Shogun's Capital and the People's City" in *Edo and Paris: Urban Life and the State in the Early Modern Era*, McClain, J.L., Merriman, J.M. and Ugawa, K. (eds), Ithaca, NY: Cornell University Press, 310–31.

Kerr, A. (1996) *Lost Japan*, Melbourne: Lonely Planet.

Kidder, R. (1997) "Disasters Chronic and Acute: Issues in the Study of Environmental Pollution in Urban Japan" in *The Japanese City*, Karan, P.P. and Stapleton, K. (eds), Lexington, KY: The University Press of Kentucky, 156–75.

Kirwan, R.M. (1987) "Fiscal Policy and the Price of Land and Housing in Japan", *Urban Studies* 24: 345–60.

Kishii, T. (1993) "On the History of Kukaku Seiri (Tochi Kukaku Seiri Jigyo no Hensen ni Kansuru Kosatsu)", *City Planning Review (Toshi Keikaku)* 42(1): 10–16.

Kobayashi, S. (ed.) (1999) *Machizukuri Ordinances in the Era of Local Rights (Chihō Bunken Jidai No Machizukuri Jōrei)*, Tokyo: Gakugei Shuppansha.

Koda, R. ([1898] 1954) "Ikkoku No Shuto" in *Rohan Zenshū*, Tokyo: Iwanami Shoten, 3–168.

Kodama, T. (1993) "The Experimentation of the Garden City in Japan", *Kikan Keizai Kenkyu* 16(1): 33–46.

Kodama, Y. (2000) "Machizukuri: Japanese Community Participatory Planning", unpublished Master of Urban Planning Dissertation, University of Washington.

Koide, K. (1997) "Arrangements and Issues of Machizukuri: Bulletin from Imaicho (Machizukuri E No Torikumi to Kadai)", *Zōkei: Community and Urban Design* 8: 114–19.

—— (1999) "Machizukuri Ordinances for Landscape Preservation (Keikankei Machizukuri Jorei)" in *Local Community Building Ordinances in the Era of Local Rights (Chihō Bunken Jidai No Machizukuri Jorei)*, Kobayashi, S. (ed.), Kyoto: Gakugei Shuppansha, 73–110.

Komiya, R. (1990) *The Japanese Economy: Trade, Industry and Government*, Tokyo: University of Tokyo Press.

Kornhauser, D. (1982) *Japan: Geographical Background to Urban-Industrial Development*, London: Longman.

Koschmann, J.V. (1978) *Authority and the Individual in Japan: Citizen Protest in Historical Perspective*, Tokyo: University of Tokyo Press.

Koshizawa, A. (1991) *City Planning of Tokyo*, Tokyo: Iwanami Shōten.

Krauss, E.S., Rohlen, T.P. and Steinhoff, P.G. (eds) (1984) *Conflict in Japan*, Honolulu: University of Hawaii Press.

Krauss, E.S. and Simcock, B. (1980) "Citizens' Movements: The Growth and Impact of Environmental Protest in Japan" in *Political Opposition and Local Politics in Japan*, Steiner, K., Kraus, E. and Flanagan, S. (eds), Princeton, NJ: Princeton University Press, 187–227.

Kudamatsu, Y. (1988) "Tokyo Olympics and Capital Improvement" in *Centenary of Modern City Planning and Its Perspective*, City Planning Institute of Japan (ed.), Tokyo: The City Planning Institute of Japan, 40–41.

Kunstler, J.H. (1993) *The Geography of Nowhere: The Rise and Decline of America's Man-Made Landscape*, New York: Simon and Schuster.

Kuroda, T. (1990) "Urbanisation and Population Distribution Policies in Japan", *Regional Development Dialogue* 11(1): 112 – 29.

Kurokawa, T., Taniguchi, M., Hashimoto, H. and Ishida, H. (1995) "Cost of Infrastructure Improvement on Sprawl Area: Costsaving Effect by Early Action (Supururu Shigaichi No Seibi Cosuto No Kansuru Ikkosatsu)", *Collected Papers of the Japanese City Planning Association (Nihon Toshi Keikaku Gakkai Ronbun Shu)* 30: 121–6.

Kurosawa, T., Teraoku, J., Youn, T. and Nakagawa, Y. (1996) "The Influence of the National Capital Region Development Plan in Saitama Prefecture (Saitama Ken Ni Okeru Shutoken Seibi Keikaku No Eikyo Ni Kansuru Kenkyu)", *Collected Papers of the Japanese City Planning Association (Nihon Toshi Keikaku Gakkai Ronbun Shu)* 31: 1–6.

Latz, G. (1989) *Agricultural Development in Japan*, Chicago, IL: University of Chicago Press.

Leupp, G.P. (1992) *Servants, Shophands, and Laborers in the Cities of Tokugawa Japan*, Princeton, NJ: Princeton University Press.

Lewis, J. (1980) "Civic Protest in Mishima: Citizens' Movements and the Politics of the Environment in Contemporary Japan" in *Political Opposition and Local Politics in Japan*, Steiner, K., Krauss, E. and Flanagan, S. (eds), Princeton, NJ: Princeton University Press, 274–314.

Local Rights Promotion Committee (Chihō Bunken Suishin Iinkai) (1997) "First Report on the Social Structure to Promote Decentralisation (Daiichikankoku: Bunken Suishinkata Shakai No Sōzō)", Tokyo: Government of Japan (Gyōsei) 226.

Logan, J.R. and Molotch, H.L. (1987) *Urban Fortunes: The Political Economy of Place*, Berkeley, CA: University of California Press.

MacDougall, T.E. (1980) "Political Opposition and Big City Elections in Japan, 1947–1975" in *Political Opposition and Local Politics in Japan*, Steiner, K., Krauss, E. and Flanagan, S. (eds), Princeton, NJ: Princeton University Press, 55–94.

Machimura, T. (1992) "The Urban Restructuring Process in Tokyo in the 1980s: Transforming Tokyo into a World City", *International Journal of Urban and Regional Research* 16: 114–28.

—— (1994) *The Structural Change of a Global City*, Tokyo: University of Tokyo.

Maejima, Y. (1989) *The History of Tokyo Parks (Tokyo Koen Shiwa)*, Tokyo: Tokyo Metropolitan Parks Association (Tokyo-to Koen Kyōkai), New York: John Wiley & Sons.

Mandlebaum, S. (1965) *Boss Tweed's New York*, New York: John Wiley & Sons.

Marris, P. (1982) *Community Planning and Conceptions of Change*, London: Routledge and Kegan Paul.

Masser, I. (1990) "Technology and Regional Development Policy: A Review of Japan's Technology Programme", *Regional Studies* 24(1): 41–53.

Matsubara, H. (1982) "A Study of Large-Scale Residential Development by Private Railway

Enterprises: The Case of Tama Den-En Toshi Tokyu Tama Den-En Toshi Ni Okeru Jutakuchi Keisei", *Geographical Review of Japan Chirigaku Hyoron* 55(3): 165–83.

Matsumoto, A. (1999) "The New Relationships of Machizukuri Ordinances and Development Manuals (Machizukuri Jōrei to Shidō Yōkō No Aratana Kankei)" in *Local Community Building Ordinances in the Era of Local Rights (Chihō Bunken Jidai No Machizukuri Jorei)*, Kobayashi, S. (ed.), Kyoto: Gakugei Shuppansha, 35–43.

Matsuzawa, T. (2000) "City Planning and Traffic Network", *Osaka and Its Technology* 36–7: 68–77.

McClain, J. (1982) *Kanazawa: A Seventeenth-Century Japanese Castle Town*, New Haven, CT: Yale University Press.

—— (1994) "Edobashi: Power, Space, and Popular Culture in Edo" in *Edo and Paris: Urban Life and the State in the Early Modern Era*, McClain, J.L., Merriman, J.M. and Ugawa, K. (eds), Ithaca, NY: Cornell University Press, 105–31.

—— (1999) "Space, Power, Wealth, and Status in Seventeenth-Century Osaka" in *Osaka: The Merchant's Capital of Early Modern Japan*, McClain, J.L. and Wakita, O. (eds), Ithaca, NY: Cornell University Press, 44–79.

McClain, J.L., Merriman, J.M. and Ugawa, K. (1994) *Edo and Paris: Urban Life and the State in the Early Modern Era*, Ithaca, NY: Cornell University Press.

McClain, J.L. and Wakita, O. (eds) (1999) *Osaka: The Merchant's Capital of Early Modern Japan*, Ithaca, NY: Cornell University Press.

McCormack, G. (1996) *The Emptiness of Japanese Affluence*, Armonk, NY: M.E. Sharpe.

McGill, P. (1998) "Paving Japan – the Construction Boondoggle", *Japan Quarterly* 45(4): 39–48.

McKean, M. (1981) *Environmental Protest and Citizen Politics in Japan*, Berkeley, CA: University of California Press.

—— (1993) "State Strength and Public Interest" in *Political Dynamics in Contemporary Japan*, Allinson, G. and Sone, Y. (eds), Ithaca, NY: Cornell University Press, 72–104.

Mera, K. (1989) "An Economic Policy Hypothesis of Metropolitan Growth Cycles", *Review of Urban and Regional Development Studies* 1: 37–46.

Mikuni, M. (1999) "The Real State and Problems of the Changes in Land Use in the Urbanisation Control Area: A Case Study in Inage-Ward, Chiba-City", *Journal of Architecture Planning and Environmental Engineering*, 34(524): 185–90.

Mimura, H., Kanki, K. and Kobayashi, F. (1998) "Urban Conservation and Landscape Management: The Kyoto Case" in *Japanese Urban Environment*, Golany, G., Hanaki, K. and Koide, O. (eds), Oxford: Elsevier Science, 39–56.

Minichiello, S. (1998) "Introduction" in *Japan's Competing Modernities*, Minichiello, S. (ed.), Honolulu: University of Hawaii Press, 1–21.

Mitani, T. (1988) "The Establishment of Party Cabinets, 1892–1932" in *The Cambridge History of Japan*, Duus, P. (ed.), Cambridge: Cambridge University Press, 55–96.

Miwa, M. (2000) "A Concise Biography of Yamaguchi Hanroku (Yamaguchi Hanroku No Ryakureki)" in *The Heart of City Building (Toshi Zukuri No Kokoro)*, Miwa, M. (ed.), Osaka: Miwa Masahisa and the Osaka City Planning History Research Group, 16–19.

Miyakawa, T. and Wada, N. (1987) "Functions of Corporate Headquarters: Concentration in Tokyo", *Japanese Economic Studies* 15(4): 3–37.

Miyakawa, Y. (1980) "The Location of Modern Industry in Japan" in *Geography of Japan*, Association of Japanese Geographers (eds), Tokyo: Teikoku Shoin, 265–97.

—— (1990) "Japan: Towards a World Megalopolis and Metamorphosis of International Relations", *Ekistics* 340–341: 48–75.

Miyake, I. (1908) *Urban Studies (Toshi No Kenkyū)*, Tokyo: Jitsugyō no Nihon-sha.

Miyamoto, K. (1993) "Japan's World Cities: Osaka and Tokyo Compared" in *Japanese Cities in the World Economy*, Fujita, K. and Hill, R.C. (eds), Philadelphia, PA: Temple University Press, 53–82.

Miyao, T. (1987) "Japan's Urban Policy", *Japanese Economic Studies* 15(4): 52–66.

—— (1991) "Japan's Urban Economy and Land Policy", *Annals of the American Academy of Political and Social Science* 513(Jan): 130–38.

Mori, H. (1998) "Land Conversion at the Urban Fringe: A Comparative Study of Japan, Britain and the Netherlands", *Urban Studies* 35(9): 1541–58.

Morimura, M. (1994) "Change in the Japanese Urban Planning Priorities and the Response of Urban Planners 1960–90" in *Contemporary Studies in Urban Environmental Management in Japan*, University of Tokyo Department of Urban Engineering (ed.), Tokyo: Kajima Institute, 8–24.

—— (1998) *Master Plan and District Improvement (Masutā Puran to Chiku Kankyō Seibi)*, Kyoto: Gakugei Shuppansha.

Morio, K., Sakamoto, I. and Saito, C. (1993) "Evaluation of Actual 'Kison Takuchi' System in Saitama Prefecture", *Collected Papers of the Japanese City Planning Association Nihon Toshi Keikaku Gakkai Ronbun Shu* 28: 253–58.

Moriya, K. (1990) "Urban Networks and Information Networks" in *Tokugawa Japan: Social and Economic Antecedents of Modern Japan*, Nakane, C. and Oishi, S. (eds), Tokyo: University of Tokyo Press, 97–123.

Morse, E.S. ([1886] 1961) *Japanese Homes and Their Surroundings*, New York: Dover.

Mosk, C. (2001) *Japanese Industrial History: Technology, Urbanization, and Economic Growth*, Armonk, NY: M.E. Sharpe.

Mumford, L. (1940) *The Culture of Cities* London: Secker and Warburg.

Muramatsu, M. and Krauss, E. (1987) "The Conservative Policy Line and the Development of Patterned Pluralism" in *The Political Economy of Japan: Vol. I, the Domestic Transformation*, Yamamura, K. and Yasukichi, Y. (eds), Stanford, CA: Stanford University Press, 516–54.

Murao, T. (1991) "Reforming Transportation in the Megalopolis: Focus on Japanese Cities", *Wheel Extended*, December: 10–17.

Murata, K. (1980) "The Formation of Industrial Areas" in *Geography of Japan*, Association of Japanese Geographers (eds), Tokyo: Teikoku Shoin, 246–64.

Murata, K. and Ota, I. (eds) (1980) *An Industrial Geography of Japan*, London: Bell and Hyman.

Murata, M. (1999) "Osaka as a Centre of Regional Governance" in *Osaka: The Merchant's Capital of Early Modern Japan*, McClain, J.L. and Wakita, O. (eds), Ithaca, NY: Cornell University Press, 241–60.

Nagamine, H. (1986) "The Land Readjustment Techniques of Japan", *Habitat International* 10(1,2): 51–58.

Nagashima, C. (1968) "Japan Megalopolis: Part 2, Analysis", *Ekistics* 26(152): 83–95.

—— (1981) "The Tokaido Megalopolis", *Ekistics* 289(July/Aug): 280–300.

Nagoya City Planning Bureau (1992) *Planning for Nagoya*, Nagoya: City of Nagoya.

Naitoh, A. (1966) *Edo to Edo-Jo*, Tokyo: Kajima Shuppankai.

Najita, T. (1974) "Some Reflections on Idealism in the Political Thought of Yoshino Sakuzō" in *Japan in Crisis: Essays in Taisho Democracy*, Silberman, B.S. and Harootunian, H.D. (eds), Princeton, NJ: Princeton University Press, 29–66.

Nakahama, T. (1889) "Housing (Kaoku)", *Eisei Shinshi (New Hygiene)* 8: 7–15.

Nakai, N. (1998) "Community Agreements: Its Theory and Practices (Machizukuri Kyōtei: Sono Riron to Jissai)", *Comprehensive Urban Studies (Sōgō Toshi Kenkyū)* 66: 69–83.

Nakamura, H. (1968) "Urban Ward Associations in Japan" in *Readings in Urban Sociology*, Pahl, R.E. (ed.), Oxford: Pergamon, 186–208.

Nakamura, M. (1997) "District Planning Forms the Foundation of Machizukuri (Chikukeikaku Wa Machizukuri No Kiban O Tsukuru)", *Zōkei: Community and Urban Design* 8: 28–37.

Nakamura, P. (1986) "A Legislative History of Land Readjustment" in *Land Readjustment: The Japanese System*, Minerbi, L., Nakamura, P., Nitz, K. and Yanai, J. (eds), Boston, MA: Oelgeschlager, Gunn and Hain, 17–32.

Nakane, C. (1970) *Japanese Society*, Berkeley, CA: University of California Press.

Narai, T., Doi, K., Mizuguchi, T. and Gojo, A. (1991) "A Study on the Flexible Operation of the

City Plans of Upa and Uca in Saitama Prefecture (Kuikikubu Seido No Unyo Ni Okeru Saitama Hoshiki No Jisseki to Koka)", *Collected Papers of the Japanese City Planning Association Nihon Toshi Keikaku Gakkai Ronbun Shu* 26: 697–702.

Newman, O. (1973) *Defensible Space: Crime Prevention through Urban Design*, New York: Macmillan.

Nish, I. (ed.) (1998) *The Iwakura Mission in America and Europe: A New Assessment*, Richmond: Japan Library.

Nishiyama, M. (1997) *Edo Culture: Daily Life and Diversions in Urban Japan, 1600–1868*, Honolulu: University of Hawaii Press.

Nishiyama, Y. (1986) "Western Influence on Urban Planning Administration in Japan: Focus on Land Management" in *Urban Development Policies and Programmes, Focus on Land Management*, Nagamine, H. (ed.), Nagoya: United Nations Centre for Regional Development, 315–55.

Noguchi, K. (1988) "Construction of Ginza Brick Street and Conditions of Landowners and House Owners" in *Tokyo: Urban Growth and Planning 1868–1988*, Ishizuka, H. and Ishida, Y. (eds), Tokyo: Center for Urban Studies, 76–82.

Noguchi, Y. (1990) "Land Problem in Japan", *Hitotsubashi Journal of Economics* 31: 73–86.

—— (1992a) *The Economics of the Bubble (Babaru No Keizaigaku)*, Tokyo: Nihon Keizaishimbunsha.

—— (1992b) "Land Problems and Policies in Japan: Structural Aspects" in *Land Issues in Japan: A Policy Failure?* Haley, J.O. and Yamamura, K. (eds), Seattle, WA: Society for Japanese Studies, 11–32.

—— (1994) "Land Prices and House Prices in Japan" in *Housing Markets in the United States and Japan*, Noguchi, Y. and Poterba, J.M. (eds), Chicago, IL: University of Chicago Press, 11–28.

Nonaka, K. (1995) "The Establishment of Modern City Planning in Provincial Castle Towns Prior to World War Two (Kinsei Jōkamachi O Kiban to Suru Chihō Toshi Ni Okeru Dai Ni Seikai Daisensō Mae No Toshi Keikaku)", unpublished PhD Thesis, Waseda University.

Obayashi, M. (1993) "Kanagawa: Japan's Brain Center" in *Japanese Cities in the World Economy*, Fujita, K. and Hill, R.C. (eds), Philadelphia, PA: Temple University Press, 120–40.

Obitsu, H. and Nagase, I. (1998) "Japan's Urban Environment: The Potential of Technology in Future City Concepts" in *Japanese Urban Environment*, Golany, G., Hanaki, K. and Koide, O. (eds), Oxford: Elsevier Science, 324–36.

OECD (1986) *Urban Policies in Japan*, Paris: Organization for Economic Cooperation and Development.

Oishi, S. (1990) "The Bakuhan System" in *Tokugawa Japan: Social and Economic Antecedents of Modern Japan*, Nakane, C. and Oishi, S. (eds), Tokyo: University of Tokyo Press, 11–36.

Oizumi, E. (1994) "Property Finance in Japan: Expansion and Collapse of the Bubble Economy", *Environment and Planning A* 26(2): 199–213.

—— (2002) "Housing Provision and Marketization in 1980s and 1990s Japan: A New Stage of Affordability Problem?" in *Seeking Shelter on the Pacific Rim: Financial Globalization, Social Change and the Housing Market*, Dymski, G. and Isenberg, D. (eds), New York: M.E. Sharpe.

Ojima, T. (1998) "Tokyo's Infrastructure, Present and Future" in *Japanese Urban Environment*, Golany, G., Hanaki, K. and Koide, O. (eds), Oxford: Elsevier Science, 197–218.

Oka, Y. (1982) "Generational Conflict after the Russo-Japanese War" in *Conflict in Modern Japanese History: The Neglected Tradition*, Najita, T. and Koschmann, V.J. (eds), Princeton, NJ: Princeton University Press, 197–225.

Okamoto, S. (2000) "Destruction and Reconstruction of Ginza Town" in *Destruction and Rebirth of Urban Environment*, Fukui, N. and Jinnai, H. (eds), Tokyo: Sagami Shobo.

Okata, J. (1980) "The Establishment of the 1919 City Planning Law, Paradigm Change in Japanese City Planning (Kyū Hō Seitei, Jisshikatei Ni Okeru Tochi Ryō Keikakuteki Hassō No Busetsu)", *Collected Papers of the Japanese City Planning Association (Nihon Toshi Keikaku Gakkai Ronbun Shu)* 15: 13–18.

—— (1986) "Paradigm Change in the Japanese Urban Planning Profession: The Formation of the Japanese Housing Policy and Its Implication to the Planning (Kyū Hō Seisakuki No

Okeru Jūtaku Seisaku to Toshi Keikaku No Kankei Ni Kansuru Ikkōsaku: Nihonteki Toshi Keikaku Paradaimu No Keisei Ni Kansuru Kenkyū)", *Collected Papers of the Japanese City Planning Association (Nihon Toshi Keikaku Gakkai Ronbun Shu)* 21: 103–8.

—— (1994) "The Genealogy of Japanese Negotiative Type Community Planning (Nihon No Kyōgikei Machizukuri No Keifu)" in *Negotiative Type Community Planning: Public, Private Enterprise, and Citizen Partnership and Negotiation (Kyōgikei Machizukuri: Kokyō, Minkan Kigyō, Shimin No Pātonāshippu to Negoshieeshon)*, Kobayashi, S. (ed.), Kyoto: Gakugei Shuppansha, 200–11.

—— (1999) "Land Use Control Type Machizukuri Ordinances (Tochi Ryō Chosei Kei Machizukuri Jōrei)" in *Local Community Building Ordinances in the Era of Local Rights (Chihō Bunken Jidai No Machizukuri Jorei)*, Kobayashi, S. (ed.), Kyoto: Gakugei Shuppansha, 111–49.

Okayama, T. (2000) "A Study on the Attributes and Historical Place of the 'Osaka Comprehensive Plan' in 1928 (Showa 3 Nen No 'Sōgō Osaka Toshi Keikaku' No Keikaku Zokusei to Rekishiteki Ishizuke Ni Kansuru Kenkyū)", *Collected Papers of the Japanese City Planning Association (Nihon Toshi Keikaku Gakkai Ronbun Shu)* 35: 73–78.

Okimoto, D. (1989) *Between Miti and the Market: Japanese Industrial Policy for High Technology*, Stanford, CA: Stanford University Press.

Okita, S. (1965) "Regional Policy in Japan" in *The State and Economic Enterprise in Japan*, Hall, J. (ed.), Princeton, NJ: Princeton University Press, 619–31.

Onishi, T. (1994) "A Capacity Approach for Sustainable Urban Development: An Empirical Study", *Regional Studies* 28 1: 39–51.

Osaka City Association (Osaka Toshi Kyōkai) (ed.) (1992) *Building Osaka: Yesterday, Today, Tomorrow (Osaka Machizukuri: Kinō, Kyō, Asu)*, Osaka: Osaka City Planning Department (Osaka Shi Keikakukyoku).

Osaka Municipal Government (2000) *Osaka and Its Technology*, Planning and Coordination Bureau, No. 36–7.

Otake, H. (1993) "The Rise and Retreat of a Neoliberal Reform: Controversies over Land Use Policy" in *Political Dynamics in Contemporary Japan*, Allinson, G. and Sone, Y. (eds), Ithaca, NY: Cornell University Press, 242–63.

Peattie, M.R. (1988) "The Japanese Colonial Empire, 1895–1945" in *The Cambridge History of Japan: The Twentieth Century*, Duus, P. (ed.), Cambridge: Cambridge University Press, 217–70.

Pempel, T.J. (1998) *Regime Shift: Comparative Dynamics of the Japanese Political Economy*, Ithaca, NY: Cornell University Press.

Porter, D. (ed.) (1986) *Growth Management: Keeping on Target?* Washington, DC: Urban Land Institute and Lincoln Institute of Land Policy.

Power, A. (1997) *Estates on the Edge: The Social Consequences of Mass Housing in Northern Europe*, New York: St Martin's Press.

Pyle, K.B. (1973) "The Technology of Japanese Nationalism: The Local Improvement Movement, 1900–1918", *Journal of Asian Studies* 33(1): 51–65.

—— (1974) "Advantage of Followership: German Economics and Japanese Bureaucrats, 1890–1925", *Journal of Japanese Studies* 1(1): 127–64.

—— (1998) "Meiji Conservativism" in *Modern Japanese Thought*, Wakabayashi, B.T. (ed.), Cambridge: Cambridge University Press, 98–146.

Regional Plan of New York and its Environs (1927–31) *Regional Survey of New York and Its Environs*, New York: The Regional Plan.

Reich, M.R. (1983a) "Environmental Policy and Japanese Society: Part I. Successes and Failures", *International Journal of Environmental Studies* 20: 191–98.

—— (1983b) "Environmental Policy and Japanese Society: Part II. Lessons About Japan and About Policy", *International Journal of Environmental Studies* 20: 199–207.

Rimmer, P. (1986) "Japan's World Cities: Tokyo, Osaka, Nagoya or Tokaido Megalopolis", *Development and Change* 17: 121–58.

Robertson, J. (1991) *Native and Newcomer: Making and Remaking a Japanese City*, Berkeley, CA: University of California Press.

Rodgers, D.T. (1998) *Atlantic Crossings: Social Politics in a Progressive Age*, Cambridge, MA: The Belknap Press of Harvard University Press.

Rozman, G. (1973) *Urban Networks in Ch'ing China and Tokugawa Japan*, Princeton, NJ: Princeton University Press.

—— (1986) "Castle Towns in Transition" in *Japan in Transition: From Tokugawa to Meiji*, Jansen, M.B. and Rozman, G. (eds), Princeton, NJ: Princeton University Press, 318–46.

Ruoff, K.J. (1993) "Mr Tomino Goes to City Hall. Grass-Roots Democracy in Zushi City, Japan", *Bulletin of Concerned Asian Scholars* 25(3): 22–32.

Saarinen, E. (1943) *The City: Its Growth, Its Decay, Its Future*, Boston, MA: MIT Press.

Saitama ken (1992) *Saitama Prefecture City Planning Basic Survey (Saitama Ken Toshi Keikaku Kisochōsa)*, Urawa, Japan: Saitama Prefecture Housing and Urban Affairs Department, City Planning Office (Saitama Ken Jutaku Toshi Bu Toshi Keikaku Ka).

—— (1994) *Urban Development Designated Promotion Areas Survey Report (Shigaichi Seibi Sokushin Shiteki Chiku Chōsho)*, Saitama Prefecture Government (Urawa: Saitama Ken).

Sakano, M. (1995) *Welfare Machizukuri and Welfare Education (Fukushi No Machizukuri to Fukushi Kyoiku)*, Tokyo: Bunka Shobō Hakubunsha.

Sakudo, Y. (1990) "The Management Practices of Family Business" in *Tokugawa Japan: Social and Economic Antecedents of Modern Japan*, Nakane, C. and Oishi, S. (eds), Tokyo: University of Tokyo Press.

Salamon, L.M. and Anheier, H.K. (eds) (1997) *Defining the Non-Profit Sector: A Cross-National Analysis*, Manchester: Manchester University Press.

Samuels, R.J. (1983) *The Politics of Regional Policy in Japan: Localities Incorporated?* Princeton, NJ: Princeton University Press.

Sanoff, H. (2000) *Community Participation Methods in Design and Planning*, New York: John Wiley & Sons.

Sapporo Education Committee (Sapporo Kyoiku Iinkai) (1978) *Sapporo Historical Maps (Sapporo Rekishi Chizu)*, Sapporo, Japan: Sapporo City.

Sassa, A. (1995) "Fault Lines in Our Emergency Management System", *Japan Echo* 22(2): 20–27.

Sassen, S. (1991) *The Global City: New York, London, Tokyo*, Princeton, NJ: Princeton University Press.

Sato, T. (1990) "Tokugawa Villages and Agriculture" in *Tokugawa Japan: Social and Economic Antecedents of Modern Japan*, Nakane, C. and Oishi, S. (eds), Tokyo: University of Tokyo Press, 37–80.

Saunders, P. (1986) "Reflections of the Dual State Thesis: The Argument, Its Origins and Its Critics" in *Urban Political Theory and the Management of Fiscal Stress*, Goldsmith, M. and Villadsen, S. (eds), Aldershot: Gower.

Schebath, A. (2000) "Fiscal Stress of Japanese Local Public Sector: Risk of Bankruptcy or Momentary Faint?" Paper presented at the European Association of Japanese Studies, 23–26 August, Lahti, Finland 2000.

Seidensticker, E. (1990) *Tokyo Rising: The City since the Great Earthquake*, Cambridge, MA: Harvard University Press.

—— (1991) *Low City, High City. Tokyo from Edo to the Earthquake: How the Shogun's Ancient Capital Became a Great Modern City 1867–1923*, Cambridge, MA: Harvard University Press.

Seko, M. (1994a) "Housing Finance in Japan" in *Housing Markets in the United States and Japan*, Noguchi, Y. and Poterba, J.M. (eds), Chicago, IL: University of Chicago Press, 49–64.

—— (1994b) "Housing in a Wealth Based Economy", *Japanese Economic Studies* 22(2): 65–92.

Setagaya Ward Branch Office Machizukuri Section (Setagaya ku Setagaya Sōgō Shisho Machizukuri Ka) (1993) "Taishidō Area Machizukuri Council's Ten Years of Activity (Taishidō Chiku Machizukuri Kyōgikai 10 Nen No Katsudō)", Setagaya Ward, Tokyo:

Setagaya Ward Branch Office Machizukuri Section (Setagaya ku Setagaya Sōgō Shisho Machizukuri Ka).

Shelton, B. (1999) *Learning from the Japanese City: West Meets East in Urban Design*, London: E.&F.N. Spon.

Shida, A. (1990) "Urban Problems and City Planning in Japan", *USJP Occasional Paper 90–09* Cambridge, MA: Harvard University, US Program on Japan Relations.

Shindo, M. (1984) "Relations between National and Local Government" in *Public Administration in Japan*, Tsuji, K. (ed.), Tokyo: University of Tokyo Press, 109–20.

Sies, M.C. (1997) "Paradise Retained: An Analysis of Persistence in Planned, Exclusive Suburbs, 1880–1980", *Planning Perspectives* 12(2): 165–91.

Silberman, B.S. (1982) "The Bureaucratic State in Japan: The Problem of Authority and Legitimacy" in *Conflict in Modern Japanese History: The Neglected Tradition*, Najita, T. and Koschmann, V.J. (eds), Princeton, NJ: Princeton University Press, 226–57.

Silberman, B.S. and Harootunian, H.D., (eds) (1974) *Japan in Crisis: Essays in Taisho Democracy*, Princeton, NJ: Princeton University Press.

Smith, H.D. (1978) "Tokyo as an Idea: An Exploration of Japanese Urban Thought until 1945", *Journal of Japanese Studies* 4(1): 66.

—— (1979) "Tokyo and London: Comparative Conceptions of the City" in *Japan: A Comparative View*, Craig, A.M. (ed.), Princeton, NJ: Princeton University Press, 49–99.

Sorensen, A. (1998) "Land Readjustment, Urban Planning and Urban Sprawl in the Tokyo Metropolitan Area", unpublished PhD Thesis, London School of Economics.

—— (1999) "Land Readjustment, Urban Planning and Urban Sprawl in the Tokyo Metropolitan Area", *Urban Studies* 36(13): 2333–60.

—— (2000a) "Conflict, Consensus or Consent: Implications of Japanese Land Readjustment Practice for Developing Countries", *Habitat International* 24(1): 51–73.

—— (2000b) "Land Readjustment and Metropolitan Growth: An Examination of Land Development and Urban Sprawl in the Tokyo Metropolitan Area", *Progress in Planning* 53(4): 1–113.

—— (2001a) "Subcentres and Satellite Cities: Tokyo's 20th Century Experience of Planned Polycentrism", *International Journal of Planning Studies* 6(1): 9–32.

—— (2001b) "Building Suburbs in Japan: Continuous Unplanned Change on the Urban Fringe", *Town Planning Review*. 72(3): 247–73.

—— (2001c) "Urban Planning and Civil Society in Japan: The Role of the 'Taisho Democracy' Period (1905–1931) Home Ministry in Japanese Urban Planning Development", *Planning Perspectives* 16(4): 383–406.

Span, E.K. (1988) "The Greatest Grid: The New York Plan of 1811" in *Two Centuries of American Planning*, Schaffer, D. (ed.), Baltimore, MD: Johns Hopkins University Press, 11–39.

Steiner, K. (1965) *Local Government in Japan*, Stanford, CA: Stanford University Press.

—— (1980) "Toward a Framework for the Study of Local Opposition" in *Political Opposition and Local Politics in Japan*, Steiner, K., Kraus, E. and Flanagan, S. (eds), Princeton, NJ: Princeton University Press, 3–34.

Stöhr, W.B. and Pönighaus, R. (1992) "Towards a Data-Based Evaluation of the Japanese Technopolis Policy: The Effect of New Technological and Organizational Infrastructure on Urban and Regional Development", *Regional Studies* 26(7): 605–18.

Sugimoto, T. (2000) "Atomic Bombing and Restoration of Hiroshima" in *Destruction and Rebirth of Urban Environment*, Fukui, N. and Jinnai, H. (eds), Tokyo: Sagami Shobo Publishing, 17–37.

Sugimoto, Y. (1986) "The Manipulative Bases of 'Consensus' in Japan" in *Democracy in Contemporary Japan*, McCormack, G. and Sugimoto, Y. (eds), Armonk, NY: M.E. Sharpe, 65–75.

Sukehiro, H. (1998) "Japan's Turn to the West" in *Modern Japanese Thought*, Wakabayashi, B.T. (ed.), Cambridge: Cambridge University Press, 30–97.

Sutcliffe, A. (1981) *Towards the Planned City: Germany, Britain, the United States and France, 1780–1914*, Oxford: Basil Blackwell.

Tachibanaki, T. (1992) "Higher Land Prices as a Cause of Increasing Inequality: Changes in Wealth Distribution and Socio-Economic Effects" in *Land Issues in Japan: A Policy Failure?* Haley, J.O. and Yamamura, K. (eds), Seattle, WA: Society for Japanese Studies, 175–94.

——— (1994) "Housing and Saving in Japan" in *Housing Markets in the United States and Japan*, Noguchi, Y. and Poterba, J.M. (eds), Chicago, IL: University of Chicago Press, 161–90.

Taira, K. (1993) "Dialectics of Economic Growth, National Power, and Distributive Struggles" in *Postwar Japan as History*, Gordon, A. (ed.), Berkeley, CA: University of California Press, 167–86.

Tajima, N. (1995) *Tokyo: A Guide to Recent Architecture*, Cologne: Konemann Verlagsgesellschaft.

Takamizawa, K., Obase, R. and Ikeda, T. (1980) "Problems Related to Narrow Roads in Urban Areas (Kiseishigaichi No Kyōai Dōro Mondai)", *Comprehensive Urban Studies (Sōgō Toshi Kenkyū)* 10: 91–117.

Takamizawa, M. (1999) "District Machizukuri Type Machizukuri Ordinances (Chiku Machizukuri Kei Machizukuri Jōrei)" in *Local Community Building Ordinances in the Era of Local Rights (Chihō Bunken Jidai No Machizukuri Jorei)*, Kobayashi, S. (ed.), Kyoto: Gakugei Shuppansha, 166–75.

Tanaka, K. (1972) *Building a New Japan; a Plan for Remodeling the Japanese Archipelago*, Tokyo: Simul Press.

Tanizaki, J. ([1946] 1993) *The Makioka Sisters*, New York: Alfred A. Knopf.

Tarn, J.N. (1980) "Housing Reform and the Emergence of Town Planning in Britain before 1914" in *The Rise of Modern Urban Planning 1800–1914*, Sutcliffe, A. (ed.), London: Mansell, 71–97.

Taut, B. ([1937] 1958) *Houses and People of Japan*, Tokyo: Sanseido.

Terauchi, M. (2000) "The Senriyama Housing Estate and the Osaka Housing Management Corporation (Senriyama Jutakuchi to Osaka Jutaku Keiei Kabushikigaisha)" in *Suburban Housing Areas in Modern Japan (Kindai Nihon No Kogai Jutakuchi)*, Katagi, A., Fujiya, Y. and Kadono, Y. (eds), Tokyo: Kajima Shuppansha, 347–66.

Teruoka, S. (1989) "Land Reform and Postwar Japanese Capitalism" in *Japanese Capitalism since 1945*, Morris-Suzuki, T. and Seiyama, T. (eds), New York: M.E. Sharpe, 74–104.

Thomas, R. (1969) *London's New Towns – a Study of Self-Contained and Balanced Communities*, London: Political and Economic Planning.

Tokyo Metropolitan Government (1989) *One Hundred Years of Tokyo City Planning (Tokyo no Toshi Keikaku Hyaku Nen)*, Tokyo: Tokyo Metropolitan Government.

Tokyo Municipal Office (1930) *Tokyo: Capital of Japan Reconstruction Work*, Tokyo: Tokyo Municipal Office.

Tokyo Prefectural Education Department, Social Bureau (1928) *Concentrated Areas of Substandard Housing (Shuudanteki Furyou Juutaku Chiku)*, Tokyo: Tokyo Fu.

Tokyo Prefecture (1930) *Imperial Capital Reconstruction Project Maps Book (Teito Fukko Jigyo Zuhyo)*, Tokyo: Tokyo Prefecture

Tokyo Reconstruction Investigation Commission (Fukkō Chōsa Kyōkai), (ed.) (1930) *History of the Reconstruction of the Imperial Capital (Teito Fukkō Shi)*, Tokyo: Reconstruction Investigation Commission (Fukkō Chōsa Kyōkai).

Tokyo Reconstruction Survey Commission (Fukkou Chousa Kyoukai), (ed.) (1930). *History of the Reconstruction of the Imperial Capital (Teito Fukkou Shi)*, Tokyo: Reconstruction Survey Commission (Fukko Chosa Kyoukai).

Tsuru, S. (1993) *Japan's Capitalism, Creative Defeat and Beyond*, Cambridge: Cambridge University Press.

Tsuya, N. and Kuroda, T. (1989) "Japan: The Slowing of Urbanization and Metropolitan Concentration" in *Counterurbanization*, Champion, A.G. (ed.), London: Edward Arnold, 207–29.

Tucker, D.V. (1999) "Building 'Our Manchukuo': Japanese City Planning, Architecture, and Nation-Building in Occupied Northeast China, 1931–1945", unpublished PhD Thesis, University of Iowa.

Uchida, I. and Nakade, B. (1997) "Study on the Actual Situation and the Primary Factor of Urbanisation Condition in Prefectural Cities and Their Surroundings", *Collected Papers of the Japanese City Planning Association (Nihon Toshi Keikaku Gakkai Ronbun Shu)* 32: 415–20.

Uchiumi, M. (1999) "The Relationship between Development Manuals and Machizukuri Ordinances (Shidō Yōkō to Machizukuri Jōrei No Jittai)" in *Local Community Building Ordinances in the Era of Local Rights (Chihō Bunken Jidai No Machizukuri Jorei)*, Kobayashi, S. (ed.), Kyoto: Gakugei Shuppansha, 22–34.

Ui, J. (1992a) "Minamata Disease" in *Industrial Pollution in Japan*, Ui, J. (ed.), Tokyo: United Nations University Press, 103–32.

—— (ed.) (1992b) *Industrial Pollution in Japan*, Tokyo: United Nations University Press.

Umesao, T., Smith, H.D., Moriya, T. and Ogawa, R. (eds) (1986) *Japanese Civilization in the Modern World: Volume 2. Cities and Urbanization* Osaka: National Museum of Ethnology.

Unwin, R. ([1909] 1994) *Town Planning in Practice: An Introduction to the Art of Designing Cities and Suburbs*, New York: Princeton Architectural Press.

Upham, F.K. (1987) *Law and Social Change in Postwar Japan*, Cambridge, MA: Harvard University Press.

Vlastos, S. (1989) "Opposition Movements in Early Meiji, 1868–1885" in *The Cambridge History of Japan: Volume 5. The Nineteenth Century*, Jansen, M.B. (ed.), Cambridge: Cambridge University Press, 367–426.

Vogel, E.F. (1979) *Japan as Number One: Lessons for America*, New York: Harper.

Vosse, W. (1999) "The Emergence of a Civil Society in Japan", *Japanstudien: Jahrbuch des Deutschen Instituts fur Japanstudien der Philippp Franz von Siebold Stiftung* 11: 31–53.

Wada, O. (1998) "Development Control in the Loose Regulation Area – the Amendment to Urban Planning Law in 1992", *Collected Papers of the Japanese City Planning Association (Nihon Toshi Keikaku Gakkai Ronbun Shu)* 33(87): 518.

—— (1999) "Guidance and Consultation of Small-scale Development Outside the City Planning Area (Toshikeikaku Kuikigai Ni Okeru Doshotori, Shokibō Kaihatsu Ni Taisuru Shidō, Kyōgi)" in *Local Community Building Ordinances in the Era of Local Rights (Chihō Bunken Jidai No Machizukuri Jorei)*, Kobayashi, S. (ed.), Kyoto: Gakugei Shuppansha, 150–53.

Wakita, O. (1999) "The Distinguishing Characteristics of Osaka's Early Modern Urbanism" in *Osaka: The Merchant's Capital of Early Modern Japan*, McClain, J.L. and Wakita, O. (eds), Ithaca, NY: Cornell University Press, 261–72.

Waley, P. (1991) *Tokyo: City of Stories*, New York: Weatherhill.

Walthall, A. (1991) *Peasant Uprisings in Japan*, Chicago, IL: University of Chicago Press.

Warner, S.B.J. ([1962] 1978) *Streetcar Suburbs, the Process of Growth in Boston (1870–1900)*, Cambridge, MA: Harvard University Press.

Waswo, A. (1977) *Japanese Landlords, the Decline of a Rural Elite*, Berkeley, CA: University of California Press.

—— (1988) "The Transformation of Rural Society, 1900–1950" in *Cambridge History of Japan Volume 6. The 20th Century*, Duus, P. (ed.), Cambridge: Cambridge University Press, 541–605.

Watanabe, S. (1980) "Garden City, Japanese Style: The Case of Den-En Toshi Company Ltd. 1918–1928" in *Shaping an Urban World*, Cherry, G.E. (ed.), London: Mansell, 129–44.

—— (1984) "Metropolitanism as a Way of Life: The Case of Tokyo, 1868–1930" in *Metropolis 1890–1940*, Sutcliffe, A. (ed.), London: Mansell, 403–29.

—— (1985) *An Introduction to Comparative City Planning (Hikaku Toshi Keikaku Josetsu)*, Tokyo: Sanseido.

—— (1993) *The Birth of "Urban Planning" – Japan's Modern Urban Planning in International Comparison ('Toshi Keikaku' No Tanjō: Kokusai Hikaku Kara Mita Nihon Kindai Toshi Keikaku)*, Tokyo: Kashiwashobo.

—— (1999) *Citizen Participation Based Machizukuri: From the Point of View of Making Master Plans*

(Shimin Sanka No Machizukuri: Masutā Puran Zukuri No Genjō Kara), Tokyo: Gakugei Shuppansha.

Watanabe, Y. (1992) "The New Phase of Japan's Land, Housing, and Pollution Problems", *Japanese Economic Studies* 20(4): 30–68.

Weber, M. (1958) *The City*, Toronto: The Free Press, Collier-Macmillan.

Wegener, M. (1994) "Tokyo's Land Market and Its Impact on Housing and Urban Life" in *Planning for Cities and Regions in Japan*, Shapira, P., Masser, I. and Edgington, D.W. (eds), Liverpool: Liverpool University Press, 92–112.

Westney, D.E. (1987) *Imitation and Innovation: The Transfer of Western Organisational Patterns to Meiji Japan*, Cambridge, MA: Harvard University Press.

White, J.W. (1976) "Social Change and Community Involvement in Metropolitan Japan" in *Social Change and Community Politics in Urban Japan*, White, J.W. and Munger, F. (eds), Chapel Hill, NC: Institute for Research in Social Science, University of North Carolina at Chapel Hill, 101–29.

Wilson, W.H. (1988) "The Seattle Park System and the Ideal of the City Beautiful" in *Two Centuries of American Planning*, Schaffer, D. (ed.), Baltimore, MD: The Johns Hopkins University Press, 113–37.

Wood, C. (1992) *The Bubble Economy*, New York: The Atlantic Monthly Press.

Woodall, B. (1996) *Japan under Construction: Corruption, Politics and Public Works*, Berkeley, CA: University of California Press.

Yamaguchi, T. (1984) "The Japanese National Settlement System" in *Urbanization and Settlement Systems*, Bourne, L. and Sinclair, R. (eds), Oxford: Oxford University Press, 261–82.

Yamamoto, H. (ed.) (1993) *Technological Innovation and the Development of Transportation in Japan*, Tokyo: United Nations University Press.

Yamamoto, T. (1999a) "Emergence of Japan's Civil Society and Its Future Challenges" in *Deciding the Public Good: Governance and Civil Society in Japan*, Yamamoto, T. (ed.), Tokyo: Japan Centre for International Exchange, 97–124.

—— (ed.) (1999b) *Deciding the Public Good: Governance and Civil Society in Japan*, Tokyo: Japan Center for International Exchange.

Yamamura, K. (1974) "The Japanese Economy, 1911–1930: Concentration, Conflicts, and Crises" in *Japan in Crisis: Essays in Taisho Democracy*, Silberman, B.S. and Harootunian, H.D. (eds), Princeton, NJ: Princeton University Press, 299–328.

—— (1986) "The Meiji Land Tax Reform and Its Effects" in *Japan in Transition: From Tokugawa to Meiji*, Jansen, M.B. and Rozman, G. (eds), Princeton, NJ: Princeton University Press, 382–99.

—— (1992) "LDP Dominance and High Land Price in Japan: A Study in Positive Political Economy" in *Land Issues in Japan: A Policy Failure?* Haley, J.O. and Yamamura, K. (eds), Seattle, WA: Society for Japanese Studies, 33–76.

Yasutani, S. (2001) *Municipal Land Use Adjustment-Type Machizukuri Ordinance in "Loose Regulated Areas": From Akasaka to Hotaka*, Tokyo: University of Tokyo, 18.

Yazaki, T. (1968) *Social Change and the City in Japan*, Tokyo: Japan Publications.

Yokoyama, G. (1899) *Japan's Lower Strata of Society (Nihon No Kasō Shakai)*: Reprinted in 1972 in *Yokoyama Gennosuke zenshū. Volume 1, Meiji Bunken*. An English translation can be found in Eiji Yutani "'Nihon no Kasō Shakai' of Gennosuke Yokoyama, Translated and with an Introduction", unpublished PhD Thesis, University of California, Berkeley, 1985.

Yoon, H. (1997) "The Origin and Decline of a Japanese Temple Town: Saidaiji Monzenmachi", *Urban Geography* 18(5): 434–50.

Yoshida, R. and Naito, Y. (2001) "Inefficient Public Works Projects Creaking under Debt Burden", *Japan Times*, February 2, 2001, 1,3.

Yoshida, S. (1999) "Rethinking the Public Interest in Japan: Civil Society in the Making" in *Deciding the Public Good: Governance and Civil Society in Japan*, Yamamoto, T. (ed.), Tokyo: Japan Center for International Exchange, 13–49.

Index

Page references in *italics* denote figures or tables.

Printed in the USA/Agawam, MA
January 2, 2013

571557.055